DUNHILL
GOLF YEARBOOK
1980

DUNHILL
GOLF YEARBOOK
1980

Edited by Mark H. McCormack

Doubleday & Company, Inc.
Garden City, New York
1980

Photo Credits

Associated Press—42, 91, 104 all, 105 below left and right, 106, 109, 110, 114, 116, 121, 125, 130, 132 both, 133, 140, 306 right, 319
Benaud—16, 328
Peter Dazeley—64, 76 both, 159 both, 169, 187, 206, 263, 280
D. Gendebien—171
Golf Photography International—9, 94, 98, 101, 102 right, 154, 159
LPGA—264 all, 265 both, 285, 291
Nene—211
Sentinel Star Photo (Bill Phillips)—105 left
Phil Sheldon—22, 39, 102 left, 147, 173, 190, 306 above, 318–19
United Press International—8, 113, 119, 135, 307

ISBN 0-385-14942-5
ISBN 0-385-14943-3 **paperback**

Contents

1   1979—The Year in Retrospect   7
2   The Masters Championship   21
3   The U.S. Open   40
4   The British Open   63
5   The PGA Championship   78
6   The World Match Play Championship   92
7   The U.S. Tour   103
8   The European Tour   158
9   The Safari/South African Tours   193
10   The Asia/Japan Tours   205
11   The Australian Tour   233
12   The New Zealand Tour   256
13   The LPGA Tour   262

APPENDIXES   301
World Money List   302
World Stroke Averages   305
The U.S. Tour   308
The European Tour   344
The Safari/South African Tours   364
The Asia/Japan Tours   371
The Australian Tour   404
The New Zealand Tour   418
The LPGA Tour   420
Miscellaneous   442

1

1979—THE YEAR IN RETROSPECT

Remember all those years through the 1960's and 1970's from the time of the emergence of the Big Three—Arnold Palmer, Jack Nicklaus and Gary Player. Remember how even early in that first decade, one of the more interesting exercises in speculation centered on who would be the next superstar, who would accomplish what those three did in tournament golf, particularly in the major championships. By the second decade, it had become pretty much—"Who will succeed Nicklaus?"—as Palmer's game tapered off with his advancing years and Player competed less frequently and with less consistency in America.

Challengers appeared during those seasons, but only Lee Trevino really compiled the kind of performance record, again especially in the big prestige events, which put him in that higher stratum. That is, until Tom Watson came along with three tremendous seasons in a row in the final years of the 1970's. In just 36 months, Watson won 15 tournaments and $1.25 million in prize money in the United States and abroad, a half-million dollars in 1979 alone. If there was a flaw in those accomplishments, it was his failure, after winning the Masters and the British Open in 1977, to embellish his record with more of those major titles that adorn the records of Nicklaus, Player, Palmer and Trevino.

Still, when he followed up his great successes in 1977 and 1978 with yet another record money-winning season and earned every available player-of-the-year award in 1979, Watson clearly solidified his reputation as a superstar. And, at the end of 1979, it wasn't a matter of being close to or of sharing the top level with Nicklaus, as it had been in the previous two years. Tom was alone at the top as the decade ended, although it may have been at least partially because Nicklaus virtually abdicated his throne in 1979. Nicklaus played in only 13 tournaments, only three or four more than he will be expected to enter until he retires completely; and for the first year of his 18 as a pro, Jack did not win a title. He had only three high finishes all year: a second-place tie in the British Open, a third-place tie at Philadelphia and a fourth in the Masters. His World Stroke Average jumped from 71.02 in 1978 to 72.44 in 1979.

Jack Nicklaus and Arnold Palmer enter a third decade as friends and rivals.

Nicklaus openly passed off the season as a slump. "I'm entitled to a slump like everybody else." However, he wasn't announcing any plans to increase his activity in tournament golf in 1980. Before the new year started, he told a press gathering in South Carolina: "The only tournaments I'm sure I'll play in are Memorial [his own event in Columbus] plus the four majors." He later indicated there would be others, but not many. His burgeoning interest in other activities in and out of golf, as well as his well-known dedication to his family, make any big increase practically impossible. It seems he will concentrate on preparing for and playing in the major championships. Most likely, Jack will win again, but a few comparative figures indicate what may lie ahead for him. The season of 1979 was the nearest full one to his 40th birthday. He won $83,059 and fell far down on the World Money List. In 1969, the season of Arnold Palmer's 40th birthday, he collected $105,128 and placed 16th in those standings. Although he remained active on the tour, Palmer had only one subsequent season, 1971, in which he improved his statistical standing among his peers. Clearly, the era of Nicklaus has ended.

Now that Watson has risen to a class by himself, he immediately becomes the target for those same questions: Who will be the next superstar? Who will take over Watson's role as number one? How soon will it happen? Since Tom is only 30, he could reign for a long time, although he still has trouble with his game on occasion, particularly with his backswing which tends to quicken in the heat of contention.

As remarkable as his record was in 1979, it did not span the entire season. The first five months were spectacular. Watson won four of his five titles, came as far as the play-off in almost capturing his second Masters, and with $353,874 in earnings, was within $9,000 of the U.S. Tour's single-season record before the first of June. Then, some peculiar things began to happen, things that used to happen to him when he was on his way up. He shot his two highest rounds of the season and missed the cut in the Open. He had two more victories in the Canadian and Western Opens, but shot 78s in the final rounds of both tournaments. It was even worse in the British Open when, after meeting the challenge for three days, he staggered in the last day with an 81, and it happened yet again in the PGA Championship in which a weak final round of 74 took him from contention to a 12th-place finish.

Tom got it all together again later, in August, and won his fifth tournament of the year—the Hall of Fame at Pinehurst—then devoted much of the rest of the year to his family. The Watsons' first child, a daughter, arrived the week of the Ryder Cup Matches in mid-September, preventing Tom's return to action there, so he played in his 21st and last U.S. event, the World Series, two weeks later and went over the half-million-dollar mark thanks to his second-place finish in the Canadian PGA Championship and his tie for second in the Taiheiyo Club Masters, one of his two November appearances in Japan. His World Money List record figure was $506,912.

Before sifting through the ranks of Watson's potential challengers, some

*Tom Watson,
golf's new king.*

attention should be paid to another golfer who, in just two years, has zoomed into that same heady superstar atmosphere. No five wins in a row, as in her sensational rookie season of 1978, but nine more titles—18 in just two seasons—and more than $200,000 were accrued by the dazzling Nancy Lopez. With what she has done by carrying the LPGA Tour to its greatest success ever, it is just as easy to acclaim Nancy Lopez a superstar as it was to use that tag on Nicklaus after the achievements of his first two seasons on the PGA Tour in the early 1960's.

Nancy can't stand still though. Nine other players among the ever-improving roster of female pros had overall winnings above $100,000. They are: Sandra Post (three wins), Amy Alcott (four), Pat Bradley (one), Donna Young (one, the LPGA), Sally Little (three), Jane Blalock (four), JoAnne Carner (three) and rookie Beth Daniel (one). The depth of real ability has grown in women's golf just as it has in the male realm. So have the purses. The LPGA plays for $5 million in 1980, compared to $1.2 million just five years earlier.

The casebook of 1979 in men's golf does not readily spotlight challengers to Watson. In fact, answer this. Don't count Watson, and who else would be deserving of golfer-of-the-year honors? Certainly none of the following who won the year's major championships could stake a legitimate claim.

Fuzzy Zoeller won the Masters championship. His early-season exploits, during which he won at San Diego, geared him up for that victory, but he did little after that, particularly in the big ones.

Hale Irwin became the U.S. Open champion for a second time. A few weeks later, Hale almost doubled with the British Open, but failed with a 78 finish in a fade similar to the 75 that evaporated all except two strokes of his big lead during the last round of the U.S. Open. He won the individual World Cup championship, that controversial event in Greece, but had only five other finishes of 10th or better in the United States and was just 16th on the World Money List.

Severiano Ballesteros became the first British Open champion from Continental Europe in 72 years. While that victory could substantiate his claim to be at the very top, Ballesteros actually had tapered off from his grand 1978 season, winning only one other tournament and yielding the European Order of Merit to up-and-coming Sandy Lyle. Seve is still not ready to take a full-time run at the U.S. Tour, having stated that, "It'll be two or three more years before I try the American circuit regularly."

David Graham became the third first-time winner of a major title in 1979 when he won the PGA Championship. He also won two other titles of consequence during the year, the Westlakes in Australia and the Air New Zealand Classic, turning around a nondescript five months of the early season for one of his typical late-season surges with an abundance of high finishes.

Trevino, who makes a habit of pairing up victories of significance, did it again in 1979 by winning the Canadian Open and the Canadian PGA Championship, much less notable events. In so doing he put together another solid season following his recovery from 1977 back surgery. He had four runner-up finishes, but did little in the major championships. Lanny Wadkins won early (Los Angeles and the TPC Championship) and late (the Bridgestone in Japan) and had a $200,000 season, a big improvement on 1978 but nothing like 1977, his PGA Championship/World Series season. Lanny continues to be too unpredictable to challenge the likes of Watson.

I would expect Watson's successor to come from one of the younger yet now rather experienced pros. Somebody like Ben Crenshaw, for whom superstardom has been predicted since his arrival on the U.S. Tour in 1973. Although he seemed to have absorbed it rather gracefully, Crenshaw has to be a tremendously frustrated golfer, for titles, particularly major ones, continuously escape him. It was another such year in 1979. After winning the Phoenix Open, he drifted along until summer. Then, starting with the Canadian Open, he finished second in five of his next six starts. Included in this remarkable string were the British Open and the PGA, in which David Graham holed two stunning, saving putts on the first two holes of a sudden-death play-off before Ben hit an errant tee shot and lost at the third extra hole. He wound up the year teaming with George Burns to win the Disney. At 28, Crenshaw is at that age when floodgates have opened for many other outstanding players.

Bill Rogers has sort of sneaked up on the golfing public. When he failed to follow up quickly on his 1978 victory in the Bob Hope Desert Classic, Rogers remained unsung among the vast number of talented players just below the star level. While he was finishing high in the standings week after week, placing seventh or better in 12 tournaments, Bill didn't really attract attention until he captured the Suntory World Match Play Championship in England, though he had the least-impressive credentials of all the foreign pros, and was runner-up in two of Japan's biggest fall tournaments.

Jerry Pate does not suffer from the same lack of recognition. The loquacious Pate, who won the U.S. Open in 1976 in Atlanta with that memorable five-iron to the final green, has had a "can't miss" tag on him ever since, but he hasn't made it yet. In fact, although his obvious skills reaped more than $200,000 in prize money in 1979, the 26-year-old Pate failed to add to his total of five tour victories. What hints at future greatness for Jerry is his affinity for the majors. He tied for second with Gary Player in the 1979 U.S. Open at Inverness, and in his four appearances in the PGA Championship he has placed fourth, fifth, second and fifth, the runner-up finish being his play-off loss to John Mahaffey at Oakmont in 1978.

Perhaps two of the players who have shown that they can win both at home and abroad, Tom Purtzer and Bob Byman, have a chance to drive themselves to the top. Purtzer, who showed fast early foot in the Open, scored his second foreign victory in the fall in the United States vs. Japan competition in the Orient; while the 24-year-old Byman, who gained international experience—and four victories—between efforts to qualify for the U.S. Tour, became the first winner of the old Florida Citrus circuit event played at Arnold

Palmer's demanding Bay Hill Club course in Orlando (henceforth to be known as the Bay Hill Classic).

Two other young players among the year's first-time winners on the U.S. Tour intrigue me with their promise, although both young men, like Byman, needed more than one try to qualify for playing privileges. One is John Fought, the 1977 U.S. Amateur champion, who broke through with back-to-back wins in the Buick Goodwrench and Anheuser-Busch tournaments in the fall. The other is Curtis Strange, another winner from Wake Forest who took the final official title of the year at Pensacola. Peter Jacobsen is a first-time winner of promise, although he's been around longer and scored his victory in the late fall in the Western Australian Open.

Jim Nelford now appears to be Canada's best player. In 1979, he was the low Canadian in his country's Open (eighth) and PGA (fourth). Of interest, too, will be the fortunes of John Cook, the 1978 U.S. Amateur champion and most prominent player starting a pro career in 1980. He will soon be followed by Bobby Clampett, Gary Hallberg, Mark O'Meara and Vance Heafner, if he manages to qualify.

A handful of other men who have done a good bit of winning on the U.S. Tour in recent seasons need to put good years together and land major titles to convince observers that they belong at even higher levels. Hubert Green heads that list and certainly has come closest to reaching the elite with his 17 pro victories, his U.S. Open win of 1977, and his near miss in the Masters in 1978. He won well over a million dollars in the 1970's. Perhaps it is his unorthodox methods or the uneven nature of his record, but it is hard to be influenced more positively about him.

Larry Nelson, Lon Hinkle, Andy Bean and Bruce Lietzke are four others who come to mind. Nelson and Hinkle, who won the expanded World Series and its $100,000 first prize, finished two and three, respectively, on the U.S. Tour money list with far over $200,000, each scoring a pair of victories. And neither had ever been in the top 10 before. It will be revealing of their talents to see how they do in 1980, whether they stay up there or fall back. That's what happened to Gil Morgan, the No. 2 money winner in 1978 who, though he scored a victory at Memphis, fell back to 29th place in 1979. Mahaffey and Bill Kratzert also faltered badly in 1979, but their tumbles can be accounted for by injuries. Bean, the No. 3 man on that 1978 list, held up much better in 1979, winning at Atlanta and topping $200,000 for the U.S. season. Although Lietzke won again in Tucson in 1979 and was among the top 10 money winners, he has not displayed the same form of his splendid 1977 campaign.

Actually, it was not much of a year in America for the older players; however, there were some exceptions. Lou Graham, who had won only three titles, including the 1975 Open, while playing the tour regularly since 1964, took three more during the last four months of 1979. Jerry McGee, another pro traveler since the mid-1960's, won twice, while Chi Chi Rodriguez and Al Geiberger scored single victories. And don't forget Trevino's Canadian double.

An almost-forgotten star became a story again during the second half of the season. Johnny Miller, winless since 1976 and counted out by some critics, came up with one of his old dazzlers, a 63 in the second round of the Hall of Fame tournament at Pinehurst. He gave Watson a severe challenge to the wire before finishing second. Inspired by that performance in late August, Miller broke through with a victory in the Lancome Trophy tournament in Paris two months later. Johnny spoke of his downfall this way in Paris: "I climbed to the top of my personal mountain and decided to sit back and relax . . . People were saying I was better than Nicklaus. I suppose I couldn't handle it. Maybe I backed off."

The international arena also was a salvation for Tom Weiskopf, another almost-great who, playing sick at least part of the time, had struggled through 20 months without a victory until he won the Argentine Open. That was, incidentally, the first stop on the newly formed South American Tour, which, in 1979, brought international circuit golf to the sixth continent of the world. (I'm afraid the seventh and last continent, Antarctica, is impervious to such an adventure.) My International Management Group, in concert with the French perfume company, Pierre Cardin, organized the five-nation swing of $40,000 national championships for the late fall. Weiskopf won at Buenos Aires after almost dropping out halfway through the final day when stomach trouble flared. Persuaded to stick it out, Weiskopf birdied the first three holes of the final round (a 36-hole tournament due to rain), and closed with a 70 and a three-stroke victory.

Ramon Munoz, Venezuela's only touring pro, landed the second title in the Chilean Open, nosing out Malcolm Gregson and Raymond Floyd by a stroke. The victory came after he was reunited with his golf clubs, which had gone astray between Greece (World Cup) and Argentina. The most sentimental victory, though, came in the Brazilian Open. Fidel de Luca, age 58, a long-time Argentinian star who was just recovering from throat cancer surgery, scored a play-off victory over his old World Cup partner and friend, Roberto de Vicenzo, 25 years after he had won the Brazilian Open. Arnold Palmer and Tommy Aaron tied for third and it should be noted that the combined ages of the top four finishers was 206, certainly evidence that golf is a game for all ages. As Palmer said afterward with considerable feeling: "It was like a walk down memory lane playing with Fidel and Roberto."

Tony Jacklin, who had ended his victory drought during the summer in the German Open, added a second 1979 title in the Venezuelan Open, breaking away from the pack with a final-round eagle. His fellow Briton, Sam Torrance, won the final event, scoring an easy victory in the Colombian Open after a pre-tournament earthquake in the vicinity had shaken everybody up. That same week, Floyd won the Costa Rica Open, a second 1979 victory to go with his win in the Greensboro Open on the U.S. Tour. Just before Christmas, the year's only unresolved tie occurred at the end of the Panama Open, when Chi Chi Rodriguez and Butch Baird deadlocked at 267. They played two extra holes in a driving rain and fading light, a tie was then declared, and everyone headed for the airport to reunite with their families for Christmas. The Costa Rica tournament was a trimmed-back version of the one-shot Central and South America Open organized by the U.S. Tour and played in 1978.

Young Bernhard Langer of Germany, a pro since he was 15, did not win on the South American Tour, but, finishes of third, fourth, fifth, third, fourth, not only made a big impression but also took first place in the South American Order of Merit, earning an exempt spot in the 1980 British Open. He is decidedly the best German golfing prospect ever. The South American Tour itself was so well-received by all involved that it was expected to go again in late 1980 with six stops this time, by adding Paraguay.

Gary Player continued to handle a world-wide schedule and continues to be an amazing golfer. He played 12 times in the United States, missed cuts five times but had good chances to win three other tournaments, including the Open, which would have given him a second set of the four major championships. And Gary has made it clear that this is his major remaining ambition in golf. He played in Europe and Australia in 1979 without winning, but back home in South Africa, he captured his country's national open for the 12th time amid a remarkable, end-of-the-year streak of four consecutive victories in South Africa (little more than a year after his Masters-launched three in a row in the United States). Remember, Gary is 44 years old.

Palmer went through his fourth winless season and celebrated his 50th birthday in 1979, and was the not-particularly-happy focal point of efforts to get a senior tour established. While Arnold was noncommittal on playing in such events, he did plan to make his first actual appearance as a senior in the TV-oriented "Legends of Golf" at Austin, Texas in the spring. That televised better-ball tournament, with its captivating play-off in 1979 in which Julius Boros and Roberto de Vicenzo defeated Tommy Bolt and Art Wall amid a flood of birdies in a six-hole play-off, actually gave senior golf more of a boost than anything else.

Whether a senior or a secondary qualifier tour develops, the main circuit, now well consolidated with a schedule which ends in mid-October, continues to flourish. The 1980 schedule carried prize money of upwards of $14 million. The only fly in the ointment seems to be TV rating problems. If they were to deepen, it would surely blunt financial growth. The world's floundering economy does not appear to be affecting golf in Europe. Perhaps the surest sign of this was the increase in the purse for the 1980 British Open at Muirfield to $420,000, a jump of $100,000 from the 1979 figure. Also the overall prize money total on the European Tour rose to $3,780,000.

In Sandy Lyle, European golf has another valid challenger for the top rank among its regular players, although Ballesteros, now that he has decided to cast his lot with that circuit, could dominate for years to come—or at least until he succumbs to the lure of the U.S. Tour's money and prestige. The main rival to Ballesteros was supposed to be Nick Faldo, like Seve and Sandy barely out of his teens. But the rangy, long-hitting Faldo struggled through a winless season in Europe and dropped far down on the money list. Instead, Lyle won the British Airways/Avis on Jersey, beat Ballesteros in a head-to-head confrontation in the Scandinavian (which fell between the wins of Seve in the Lada English Classic and the Open at Royal Lytham and St. Annes), and ran away with the second European Open, which brandishes a purse exceeded in Europe only by the British Open. In November, Sandy tied for second in the World Cup individual to cap his big season. Lyle has great strength and a solid style that should serve him in good stead over the long haul, but it will be surprising if he can hold off Ballesteros in 1980.

Brian Barnes and the controversial Mark James, surely the best technician in European golf, were double winners for Britain, but the most significant victory among the British in 1979 may have been Tony Jacklin's in the German Open. His recent career had dimmed much as Johnny Miller's had and it was ironic that his first win since 1976, like Miller's, would come in Europe. One wonders what will come from those two wins which ended dry spells for those two outstanding players of the recent past. Peter Oosterhuis again campaigned primarily in the United States with only moderate success, remaining winless in America for a fifth year after piling up 19 victories in Europe and elsewhere.

Australians and South Africans picked off an unusually large number of titles on the European Tour in 1979. Graham Marsh, who it seemed was again everywhere in the world at some time during the year, scored two of his three 1979 victories in Europe, the Dunlop Masters and the Dutch Open, to go with his win in the ANA Sapporo in Japan. This was all after a season of slim pickings in the United States. Greg Norman, the latest, youngest (24) and perhaps strongest of the Australians to move into the international arena, captured the Martini for a second time. It seems safe to say that he and Jack Newton, who won the Australian Open and another tour event there, rank with Marsh and David Graham as the leading Australian internationals in the game today, with Rodger Davis a possibility to catch up to them. Norman won in Australia and placed fifth in the British Open. He also won at Hong Kong and the early-season Traralgon Classic at home and now has eight victories in his four-year pro career, while Newton's record now boasts 20 victories. Marsh has 33 titles to his credit, but still has not landed a major championship.

Player's remarkable showing at the season's end in South Africa tended to overshadow what his countrymen had done earlier in the year in Europe. Dale Hayes had another splendid season, winning the Spanish Open, losing a play-off to Barnes in the Italian Open, scoring two other second-place finishes, and placing fourth on the Order of Merit behind Lyle, Ballesteros and James. Gavin Levenson (a Belgian), Mark McNulty (from Manchester), and Hugh Baiocchi (Swiss) also won in Europe, as did Rhodesia's Simon Hobday, a regular on the South African and European Tours. Hobday, who took the Madrid Open, launched the 1979 South African Tour in the fall with a victory in the Rhodesian Open. Faldo got a boost for 1980 the following week when he avoided a shutout year with his triumph in the ICL International before Player took command.

The story in Asia in 1979 was, once again, centered around Isao Aoki and the Taiwanese. Although all of his four wins occurred in Japan in 1979, Aoki had another outstanding season. However, with three fewer victories and without the massive first place purse he collected at the World Match Play Championship in England in 1978, Aoki slipped a few notches on the World Money List in 1979. Still, with his ventures outside his country, Aoki is bringing the caliber of Japanese golf to the world's attention. He played in six U.S. tournaments and, although never a serious contender, he did well enough to indicate that he could probably win if he gave it a full-time shot, something he has given no indication of wanting to do. Another indication of Aoki's ability is a comparison of his earnings from World Match Play 1978 through World Match Play 1979 against the record breaking winnings of Watson over the same months. Playing in different arenas, both won five times during that period and Isao's $330,000 stacks up quite favorably against the $472,000 compiled by Watson mostly on the richer U.S. Tour. However, the extensive Japanese Tour spans nine months and carries prize money of $5 million, so Aoki and the other leading Japanese golfers really don't have much incentive to play very often in other parts of the world.

The Taiwanese, in general, again dominated the Asia Circuit and fared well in Japan. They had a new man out front, Lu Hsi Chuen, a rookie at age 26 and the nephew of Taiwan's best-known international player, Lu Liang Huan. Lu Hsi Chuen burst on the Asia Circuit with three victories and overall honors

Peter Thomson played his last major tournament in the Dunhill Open. He will still enter some small events and do television commentary.

for the 10-tournament 1979 season. Although he missed the 36-hole cut in his first British Open, and he won no other titles, Lu the Younger was still impressive in other parts of the world. He earned a half dozen high finishes in Japan, shot a strong three rounds in the World Cup in Greece and had a final-round 69 at Firestone in the World Series. He seems to be cut from the same personality mold as his uncle—pleasant, smiling, able to cope with conversations in English—and could become an international star in the years to come.

The year 1979 also saw politics mar the World Cup and threaten its future . . . saw the shocking death of Salvador Balbuena, 29, one of Spain's leading pros, on the eve of the French Open . . . the passing, too, of Kim Hall, the director of the Asia Circuit and long-time leading figure in Asian golf . . . the formal retirement of Peter Thomson from tournament golf.

World Cup officials, who have run into political problems in the past, were forced to play in Greece without the South African team of Hayes and Baiocchi. The Greek government barred them at the last minute after a U.N. subcommittee applied political pressure. The sponsoring International Golf Association, facing this and other problems involving the acceptance of nationals of certain countries in other countries, appears to be at a crossroads. It must decide whether to proceed with the matches in whatever countries it chooses, disregarding political considerations which might rule out some players, or to be careful and selective and to choose politically-free sites, or to abandon the 27-year-old series on the premise that "everybody plays or we don't play at all."

Final verification of Watson's predominant No. 1 position in the world of men's professional golf comes from the latest mathematical computations involved in the Mark H. McCormack Proficiency Rating System, which I devised 12 years ago and which I contend gives the most accurate measurement of the rankings of the leading players in the game. First an explanation of its principles and how it works. It deals with four factors: (1) a span of three seasons instead of the usual one; (2) the theory that money winnings and stroke averages alone do not fully compare player against player; (3) stature of tournaments and caliber of fields considered; (4) victories merit extra credit. Taking these factors into consideration, a point scale was created to apply to all tournaments carried in summary form in the appendix of this *Annual* and those covering the 1977 and 1978 seasons. The point values vary with four categories and are decreased each year from 1979 back to 1977. The categories are:

Class 1: The U.S. and British Opens, the Masters and the PGA championship.

Class 2: U.S. Tour events in which at least 13 of the 15 leading money winners of that particular year competed.

Class 3: U.S. Tour events in which from 10 to 12 of the leading money winners competed.

Class 4: All other U.S. Tour events.

Certain events carrying particular status or with especially strong fields are placed in higher categories or assigned special point scales. Here are the specific point assignments for each of the three years covered by the 1979 ratings:

1979

Class 1: Top 10 finishers—30 points for winner, 24 for second, down to 16 for 10th.

Class 2: Top 8 finishers—25 points for winner, 19 for second, down to 13 for eighth.

Class 3: Top 6 finishers—20 points for winner, 14 for second, down to 10 for sixth.

Class 4: Top three finishers—12 points for winner, six for second, five for third.

1978

Class 1: Top 10 finishers—25, 19 to 11 points.

Class 2: Top eight finishers—20, 14 to eight points.

Class 3: Top six finishers—15, nine to five points.

Class 4: Top three finishers—10, four, three points.

1977

Class 1: Top 10 finishers—20, 14 to six points.

Class 2: Top eight finishers—12, nine to three points.

Class 3: Top six finishers—11, five points to one point.

Class 4: Top three finishers—Eight points, two points, one point.

And thus we have at the end of 1979:

The Top 25 Golfers in The World

POS.	PLAYER	1977	1978	1979	TOTAL
1	Tom Watson, *U.S.A*	130.5	134.5	250	515
2	Jack Nicklaus, *U.S.A*	103	150	63.5	316.5
3	Hale Irwin, *U.S.A*	57.5	118.5	117	293
4	Lee Trevino, *U.S.A*	32.5	97.5	134.5	264.5
5	Gary Player, *South Africa*	61	90.5	101	252.5
6	Isao Aoki, *Japan*	30	112.5	104.5	247.5
7	Hubert Green, *U.S.A*	70	103.5	53	226.5
8	Ben Crenshaw, *U.S.A.*	41.5	75	99.5	216
9	Severiano Ballesteros, *Spain*	63	79.5	57	199.5
10	Lanny Wadkins, *U.S.A.*	44.5	39	110.5	194
11	Bill Rogers, *U.S.A.*	20.5	19	154	193.5
12	Jerry Pate, *U.S.A*	30	65	98	193

13	Graham Marsh, *Australia*	61.5	60.5	64	186
14	Andy Bean, *U.S.A.*	21.5	82	70.5	174
15	Tom Kite, *U.S.A.*	20	54.5	97	171.5
16	Larry Nelson, *U.S.A.*	16	18	118.5	152.5
17	David Graham, *Australia*	23.5	22	102	147.5
18	Bruce Lietzke, *U.S.A.*	36	32.5	75.5	144
T19	Tom Weiskopf, *U.S.A.*	44	55.5	39	138.5
	Fuzzy Zoeller, *U.S.A*	14	31	93.5	138.5
21	Greg Norman, *Australia*	22	47.5	51	120.5
T22	Bill Kratzert, *U.S.A.*	15	66.5	38.5	120
	Raymond Floyd, *U.S.A.*	54	28.5	37.5	120
24	Gil Morgan, *U.S.A.*	18	82.5	12	112.5
25	Lou Graham, *U.S.A.*	39.5	25.5	44	109

Watson's superiority in the 1977–79 period covered by these McCormack ratings is reflected most definitively by his margin over runner-up Nicklaus—198.5 points—the biggest advantage since the system was introduced. When Tom ended Jack's 10-year domination of first place in 1978, it was by a mere 18 points. Although Watson's 515 points represented the highest first place total in four years, it was far off the 627 points Nicklaus compiled in the 1971–72–73 period.

Hale Irwin's consistency shows again. He was No. 3 man for the third straight year, and ranked No. 2 and No. 4 the two preceding years. Lee Trevino's second excellent season in a row jumped him to fourth, his highest position since 1973. Gary Player, who has never been lower than seventh in 12 years, held his fifth spot, thanks to his four straight wins at the end of 1979. Nicklaus, Trevino and Player have never missed the rankings since their inception. Neither has Tom Weiskopf, but he tumbled to 19th place this time. Poor seasons pulled down Raymond Floyd and Gil Morgan and knocked Andy North, Bob Shearer, Don January and Jumbo Ozaki from the top 25. They were replaced by three American pros—Bill Rogers, Larry Nelson and Fuzzy Zoeller—and Aussie Greg Norman. Rogers' arrival was particularly impressive. He had only 39.5 points the first two years, but compiled 154 in 1979, more than anybody else except Watson, in joining the list at 11th place. Nelson did almost as well in placing 16th.

Besides Trevino, Isao Aoki and Lanny Wadkins made notable gains on the 1979 list. Aoki, one of the six non-Americans among the 25, moved up from 10th to sixth and Wadkins from 20th to 10th. The other non-American finishers were Severiano Ballesteros (ninth), Graham Marsh (13th), David Graham (17th) and Norman (21st). The other top 10 placers were Hubert Green (No. 7) never worse than ninth in his six years in the ratings, and Ben Crenshaw (No. 8) who joined the group at ninth place in 1976 and has been fifth, sixth and eighth since then.

The ratings give one other indication about what's happening on the tours of the world. With only eight men finishing with more than 200 points, as compared to 11 at the end of 1978, it appears that more players are winning tournaments and making high finishes these days.

As usual, the year 1979 produced an abundance of new records and those performances are detailed in subsequent chapters. One in particular intrigues me. I wonder how much boasting Sam Trahan does about his 18-putt round and eight-putt back nine in the IVB Philadelphia Classic? He broke longstanding U.S. Tour records, but must have mixed feelings about it, at best, considering that he missed 14 greens and chipped in three times. It all resulted in a 70, not exactly a classic round, though certainly unique. If nothing else, Trahan would qualify as a nominee for "Scrambler of the Year" if such an award existed.

2

THE MASTERS CHAMPIONSHIP

The Masters, for all its glory and tradition, has never been noted for its strong starting fields, not in the last 25 years at least. For one thing, the number of players who tee off Thursday morning is usually somewhere in the 80's, roughly half that of a normal PGA event, or even the U.S. Open. Of those 80-odd, there are various categories of golfers who "cannot win." Foremost in these would be former champions of advanced age or faded ability.

On Wednesday morning of this years's tournament, I was strolling the lovely old course, enjoying the dogwood and azalea in full bloom, when I chanced to see Doug Ford tee off at 14 in a practice round. His drive caught a tree on the left from where he chipped out on the fairway. His third shot left him still short and his pitch ran over the green. Four strokes, par for the hole, and he was still not ready to putt.

Ford won the 1957 Masters and thus is entitled to a lifetime entry in the tournament, but, of course, he will never win again. Sam Snead, at 67, has a better chance, but he cannot win either. From this year's field you could add Bob Goalby, Art Wall, Gay Brewer, almost assuredly Charles Coody, Tommy Aaron and, alas, Arnold Palmer. Arnold is still Augusta's favorite; he always will be, but a fifth green jacket seems out of the question.

Another category of player who "cannot win" is the amateur, simply because no amateur ever has . Billy Joe Patton gave it a whirl in 1954 and Ken Venturi led for three rounds two years later before shooting an 80 on Sunday to lose by one stroke. Charlie Coe finished second by a stroke to Gary Player in 1961, and that was even closer than it looks on paper, since Palmer led Player by a shot at 18 and then double bogeyed to give the title to Player. But other than these few, no amateur has posed a threat; and these days only a handful, three or four at best, make the 36-hole cut.

Then there are the foreigners. Player, a South African, has won three times, but that's it . Spain's Severiano Ballesteros won in 1950 but, for the most part, foreigners have been no serious threat. I do feel that this is a changing situation. As golf flourishes on an international scale, players from overseas will pose more of a challenge to American supremacy. I am simply speaking of the past 25 years.

Until this past Masters, there was always a fourth (and final) category of golfer who "could not win." That was the first-timer. With the obvious exception of Horton Smith, winner of the first Masters in 1934, and of Gene Sarazen, who won the following year, no first-time visitor to Augusta had ever won. The most obvious reason is the deceptiveness of the course, with its undulating fairways which demand accurate placement of tee shots, and its roller coaster greens,certain sections of which you do not want to be on when the pins are cut elsewhere. The first thing most first-timers do when they arrive at Augusta National is to seek out some old hand with whom to play a practice round. If you stroll the course on the three days of practice leading up to the start of play, you will see such a familiar tableau: the experienced Masters player, say Raymond Floyd, standing on a tee, gesturing right and left with his arm, while someone like Larry Nelson watches and listens. The same sort of schooling takes place on the greens, the veteran pointing out where the pin placements will be during the week.

Such instruction has undoubtedly helped, but never enough. Invariably, it seems, the brash young pro, who so recently looked like a world beater on national television as he won the Doral or the Greensboro Open posts a 75–76—151 and misses the cut. First-timers sometimes have been a factor in the tournament: Bert Yancey was tied for the lead as late as the 66th hole in 1967.

Well, now you can scratch that category and say hello to Fuzzy Zoeller, tradition-breaker. Frank Urban Zoeller, Jr. The FUZ, his initials, is where the name Fuzzy comes from; but certainly there is nothing fuzzy about his personality or his game. With the exception of Lee Trevino, no player on the tour yaks it up more with the galleries. Fuzzy Zoeller came to Augusta by way of the San Diego Open, which he had won, and which was his first victory in a four-year career which has been steadily on the rise. He turned pro in 1973 when he was 21, won his player's card and $7,318 in 1975, by 1978 had moved up to 20th on the money list with $109,055, posting second place finishes at Greensboro and New Orleans. The San Diego Open earned him his invitation to the Masters, and at the time of the tournament, he was the third money winner behind Tom Watson and Lanny Wadkins.

Who would have guessed that Fuzzy Zoeller's name was in the proper position?

While it is true that Zoeller won the 1979 Masters, it must also be said that someone else lost it, that person being Ed Sneed, a good-looking man in his mid-30's with a smooth swing. Sneed has spent much of his career explaining that, no, he is not related to old Sam or J. C., that they are *Sneads* and he is Sneed. As we shall see, he carried the burden of the lead in this tournament for most of the third round and all of the last; and, had he not given way to the enormous pressure of that two-day period, Zoeller would have been just another second place finisher. And, by Fuzzy's own admission, he would have been happy to take it. He was, after all, four strokes behind when he teed off on the 71st hole.

But that was Sunday. Let us drop back three days to Thursday, a grey, hot, humid morning with the threat of rain in the air. For the first time since 1966, Jack Nicklaus was not the favorite. Nicklaus, off to his worst start since he became golf's dominant player, had won up to the Masters only $11,309. Everywhere he went, he was asked, "what's wrong?" And Jack could only shrug. In Jack's place as favorite was Watson, winner of the Heritage Classic two weeks earlier and on his way to a second consecutive record money year.

The excellent condition of the course plus the muggy stillness of the day were indications that the scoring would be low, and, indeed, before 11 A.M. Lanny Wadkins was looking as if he intended to set a course record. After eight holes he was four under par, having birdied the second and the eighth holes, which were the two par-fives, as well as the fifth and seventh. "I was hitting irons right at the flag," Wadkins said.

Lanny turned in 32, but the 10th, 11th and 12th, unquestionably the toughest three-hole stretch on the course, turned him inside out. His approach at 10 caught the bunker to the right of the green. He came out short of the pin, putted boldly past it, and missed coming back. Double bogey six. At 11, he hit wide of the green to the right and avoided the pond on the left. But then he chipped weakly and two-putted for a bogey. He used a seven-iron at the short par-three 12th and landed in Rae's Creek. By the time he was in the cup, he had another double bogey and had sailed from four under to one over. Down from the scoreboards around the course came Lanny Wadkins and his red four. He finished the nine with a 41, and 73 for the day. Sometimes 73 is not a bad score, but this was not one of those times.

"It was an interesting day," he said later. "No question about it. There's a lot of tournament left. I've just got to hang in there and hope I have a hot round." As it turned out, Lanny did hang in there, playing the rest of the tournament in four under par to tie for seventh, five strokes back. Five strokes. Give Wadkins three pars on Thursday on the 10th through the 12th holes, and . . . well, everyone has a story like that.

While Wadkins was self-destructing at the start of the back nine, Leonard Thompson, playing with Gene Littler in the day's first pairing, was several holes ahead, in the process of putting the first sub 70 score on the leaderboard. A long hitter, Thompson missed only one green, the par-three 16th on the way to a 68, making birdies on the fifth, seventh and eighth on the front side and the predictable birdies at 13 and 15 coming home. "My putting was only adequate," Thompson said later. "It might have been a really low round." Thompson missed a three-footer at the second hole and a two-footer at No. 10. His only bogey came at nine, where he three-putted.

Thompson was not the only player to have putting problems at the ninth. Gary Player, the defending champion, was sailing along at three under par for eight holes, when he hit an approach at nine which appeared to stop about four feet short of the hole. Alas, the ninth green slopes severely back toward the fairway and the ball trickled back, gathered speed, and came to rest just off the front edge of the green. Player putted from there and when the ball appeared to come to rest just short of the cup he hustled up to mark it; but the ball came back again, not as far this time, but enough so that he missed again and took a bogey. "I had a good chance to be four under and suddenly I'm only two under," he said. Gary then played the back nine in 37 for a 71. "I'm in good position for a first round," he said. "I'm hitting the ball very well."

One group ahead of player, Bruce Lietzke was posting the day's low score, a 67. "It was an easy stroll in the park," he said. Lietzke birdied all four par-fives as well as 14 and 16. At 17, having made four birdies in a row, he missed a five-foot putt and as so often happens, that seemed to snap the spell. Using a three-wood off the 18th tee, he drove left and his approach was short and to the left of the green. He chipped to five feet but, "it was a scary putt," and he missed for his only bogey of the day. "I was in a trance until the 17th," Lietzke said. "For five weeks in 1977, I was in an absolute trance. I didn't think about the swing at all. I had no negative thoughts. I'd just stand over the ball and pull the trigger."

It seems this is a running joke among Lietzke's pals on the tour. "They catch me when I'm thinking about something else and ask me who I played with. Sometimes I have to think for a few minutes. They think that's ridiculous and maybe it is, but my concentration is so good I can block everything else out."

Lietzke is the prototype of the modern golfer—big, strong, long-hitting, young (he's 27) but experienced. He won twice in 1977 and again at Tucson in '79. Sometimes there are first-round leaders you know cannot last. That was not true of Lietzke. On Thursday evening most of the knowledgeable folk on the veranda in front of the clubhouse were of the opinion that Lietzke, combining youth, experience and strength, might easily come back the next day with another 67. But perhaps they were under the impression that this was the Tucson Open.

Of course, there were four players only a shot behind and one of these was the new king of golf, Mr. Watson. Tom had a round which might have been anything, a 63, or even lower. He jumped right off with birdies at two and three, bogeyed five and seven to go back to even par, and then birdied eight and nine to turn at two under. "That's the mark of a champion," said Vinnie Giles, the veteran amateur player, as he eyed the leaderboard. "He shrugged off the bogeys and got back where he was."

It could be reasonably argued that Watson might have birdied the last 11 holes. Having gotten two at eight and nine, he hit close at 10 and dropped the putt, had a 25-footer stop inches short at 11 and sank a 10-footer at 12. "Playing 10–11–12 in two under par is like stealing," Watson said later. At 13 he hit a gorgeous three-iron eight feet from the pin, missed the eagle putt, but made an easy birdie. He was now five under and leading the tournament, since Lietzke was three holes behind him and had not yet made his string of four birdies in a row.

At 15, Watson's drive was huge, leaving him only 188 yards from the front of the green. It was here that he and his caddie had a mild disagreement. "Leon never says anything until I ask him," Watson said later. "He always wants me to hit too much club on 15. Today he was right. I asked him for a six-iron. Nothing but silence. Then I asked, 'Do I have to hit it good?' Leon replied, 'Oh yes, you have to hit it good.' "

Watson went with the six-iron anyway, but during the swing, the slight breeze which had been blowing with him died and the ball fell into the pond in front of the green. A chip and two putts gave him his third bogey of the day, a two-stroke swing on the hole. He then parred in for his 68.

While the round could have been much better, Watson was pleased. In his role as the favorite, he was anxious to get off to a good start and 68 was certainly that. A few moments after he finished, as he was describing his round to the press, Joe Inman dropped a 3½-foot putt at 18 for a birdie to bring home his own 68. Inman had no bogeys and he birdied the third, eighth and 13th, as well as the final hole. Those birdies at the par-five eighth and 13th uncovered a remarkable statistic. The year before Inman had finished ninth, six shots behind Gary Player, which was a highly creditable performance. He had made 16 birdies during the tournament and not one had come at a par-five. That's virtually impossible. Inman also finished well in the U.S. Open (11th) and the PGA (12th).

"My game seems suited to the majors," he said. "I like to think of myself as a thinking man's player. It's more likely that I'd win the Open or PGA than here because of the par-fives. I have to give away too many shots here to the longer players."

The fourth 68 belonged to Ed Sneed, the tragic hero of the 1979 Masters. Sneed came to Augusta in the midst of his best season, having earned some $52,000, much of it for finishing second to Watson at Hilton Head two weeks before. Like Inman, Sneed made no bogeys, although he executed a few hair-raising putts and nearly tossed away the whole round at 15. He got there at four under with birdies at previous three par-fives as well as the difficult 10th, where his five-iron approach stopped a foot from the pin.

But 15 nearly ruined it all. Sneed hit a good drive, then got caught up in the same wind confusion which had plagued Watson an hour and a half earlier. Thinking that there was a breeze blowing in his face, he selected a four-wood. The ball carried over the green and a weak chip back left him still short. Now came the delicate shot. A chip too strong might have carried across the green and into the pond, which could have resulted in as much as an eight, a triple bogey, a 71 instead of a 68. But Sneed put the ball two feet from the pin and made his par. "I saved the round there," he said. "It could have been a disaster."

Ed Sneed is an articulate Virginian out of Ohio State, but not the same caliber of player as two other Buckeyes, Jack Nicklaus and Tom Weiskopf. His success has been limited to three victorles, one of them the Tallahassee Open in 1977, when the big boys were at the Tournament of Champions, and he had not yet challenged to win a major. Why he has not been more successful is a mystery. His swing is among the more fluid in the game and he is extremely bright. He is the best backgammon player on the tour as well as a dabbler at bridge, chess and billiards. He is a funny man, a deft needler with a dry sense of humor, and his imitations of Gary Player, Miller Barber and Arnold Palmer's swing (backwards) have kept many a golf party laughing.

In a group of five at 69 was Nicklaus who, bad year and all, seems to be able to play Augusta National on memory. Jack birdied both par fives on the front nine, but bogeys at nine and 11 put him back to even. Then he birdied the other two par-fives and added another at 17 to finish three under. Perhaps the key shot in his round was a one-iron at 13 when he was even. Nicklaus hit the ball thin and it went on a line toward the creek in front of the green. Luckily for Jack, the ball hit just over it, the momentum carried it onto the green and he was able to make a birdie.

The other four 69s belonged to former champion Bill Casper; Andy Bean, a genuine threat to win a big one soon; Lou Graham, 1975 U.S. Open champion; and Craig Stadler, a former amateur champion, whose career as a pro has been undistinguished and whose two first-round scores in previous Masters had been 79 and 80. Oddly, of these four players, it was Stadler who was to have the greatest impact on the tournament. But of course, as we know with the wisdom of hindsight, none of the aforementioned first-round leaders were to win.

Fuzzy Zoeller teed off at 12:37 with Lee Trevino, the two of them talking and waving their arms as they walked up the hill on the first fairway. Zoeller picked up some Masters Steuben glass when he eagled the eighth hole, getting home in two and dropping a 25 footer. He was then three under, but he lost two of those strokes when he was introduced to the perils of the par-three 12th. Zoeller hit into the famed Rae's Creek and took a double bogey. A birdie at 15 got him in with a 70, a nice opening round for a first timer at Augusta, and just far enough off the pace to draw no attention in the press. In short, a pleasant position.

On Friday there was no doubt that the bad weather would be a factor. The air was heavy and damp; a huge dark cloud hovered over the valley as the first players teed off; and the word tornado appeared on the leaderboards around the course as the day wore on. TORNADO WATCH IN EFFECT was the first message. Later it was amended to TORNADO WARNING and, finally, TORNADO ALERT. As it turned out, a tornado did hit 22 miles from the Augusta

National, close enough to keep everyone nervous during the early afternoon and to suspend play for roughly an hour and forty-five minutes.

Ed Sneed was an early starter, off at 10:03 when the day was merely dark and damp and still. In the early going, he was hitting everything close and failing to make putts. He did hole a four-footer for a birdie at No. 4 to go five under, but through 12 he missed many putts in the 10-foot range. Birdie putts, that is. Sneed was not to have anything like a bogey all day, completing 36 holes without a serious mistake.

At 13, Sneed reached the green with a four-wood and two-putted for a birdie that put him six under par. He also reached 15 in two for another birdie, hit his tee shot at 16 some 10 feet from the pin and made that, and then pulled one out of the darkening sky at 17, sinking a 45-footer. Par at 18 gave him a 67 and a two-day 135, nine under for the tournament.

Sneed then retired to the upstairs grill in the clubhouse to watch the weather. At a little after 2 P.M the black skies opened up, and the rainfall which had been only a sprinkle for hours, increased into a full-fledged deluge, accompanied by high winds. Play was suspended, and it seemed likely that it would remain suspended for the rest of the day. If so, would Sneed's 67 count? No one seemed certain of the rule. If half the field could get in, perhaps the round would count, but at the time of the suspension, only a third of the players were in. Some thought that if Saturday were to be a continuation of play, rather than a new round, everyone had to have completed nine holes. Alas, Doug Ford and David Graham had teed off the first hole just minutes before the rain began. Everyone had a different theory, and a state of chaos existed in and around the clubhouse and the press tent.

Sneed was not the only player who hoped the round would count. Craig Stadler had played only seven holes but he had birdied four of them: the first three holes and the fifth. On Thursday, he had birdied five of the last seven on the way to a 37–32—69, so that he had a string of nine birdies in 14 holes. Ray Floyd, who shot 70 the first day, had completed the front nine in 33 and was most anxious to continue. First-day leader Lietzke was about to complete the front nine in 35 to put him six under; it was only later that he probably wished play had ceased then and there.

And there were others who probably wished the storm would continue forever, or at least until dark. Jack Nicklaus had bogeyed three holes on the front nine, a 39, and when play was suspended, he was only one under par on the 13th tee, eight shots behind Sneed. Ben Crenshaw was on his way to an 80 and out of the tournament.

However the worst of the storm passed by 3:45 and shortly after that play was resumed. Stadler immediately birdied the eighth, his 10th birdie in 15 holes, and finished the front nine in 31. Nicklaus birdied 13, 15 and 18 to finish with a 71 and 140, four under par. "Any time you're around 140 at Augusta you're in good shape," Nicklaus said. "If I hadn't shot 32-39 I'd be a lot less happy."

Floyd, who had won at Greensboro the week before, birdied the 13th and 17th on the back nine to complete a 68–138. "Obviously my chances are excellent," he said. "My game is at its peak." Just before the storm, Seve Ballesteros chipped into the cup at No. 8 for an eagle three, then birdied 10, 13 and 14 on the backside to finish in 68–140. After 36 holes, Ballesteros had played the par-fives in eight under par. Joe Inman added a quiet 71 to his 68 of the day before, while Leonard Thompson did him one better, a 70, giving him a six under par 138, which put him just three strokes behind Sneed. Watson, two under for the day when the storm caught him at 11, looked as if he might challenge for the lead when he birdied 13 to go seven under. But a bogey at 14, a second-straight visit to the pond at 15 (he got his par but, of course, no birdie), and a final bogey at 17 when he hit over the green, brought him home in 71 and 139. So he was tied with Inman.

Lietzke came undone after the rain, having completed the front nine in 35. He hit into the rear trap at 11 for a bogey, and after hitting over the 12th green, chipped only three feet, and had to sink an eight foot putt for another bogey. Shook up, he drove into the left woods at 13 and failed to make a birdie. On his two-iron second shot at 14 he hit a tree and had the ball bounce back to nearly the same spot from which he hit it. It took a 15-foot putt to give him only a bogey. A final bogey at 17 got him home in 40 with an unhappy 75. "I lost something during the delay," Lietzke said later. "But I still feel good about my position." At 142, he was seven strokes away from the lead.

While Lietzke suffered because of the rain, two other players were challenging the course record. We left Craig Stadler just as he completed the front nine in 31, with most of the birdies coming before the rain. On the back nine, everything he hit seemed to be right at the flag, but none of his putts would drop. "It started raining again after we went back out," he said. "The greens were slow." Stadler did get one final birdie at 15 to post a 66 for the day which tied him with Sneed at nine under.

Stadler is a burly young man of 215 pounds or so whose career has not been helped by his temper. Once his caddie, unable to accept any more abuse, walked off in the middle of a round. A spectator ducked under the ropes and carried on for Stadler. "My temperament is a lot better than when I was a junior," he said after his round. "I'd throw clubs, slam them to the ground—the whole bit. I still get hot now and then, but it doesn't stay."

The best round of the day was not completed until early the following morning. Miller Barber was three over par after an opening 75, and had played only one hole, which he birdied from 10 feet, when play was halted. When it resumed, he birdied the second, third, fifth and ninth holes to turn in 31. Still, at two under for the tournament, he was not among the leaders, so his name was not on the leaderboards around the course. It was some time before word started filtering back to the clubhouse that a potentially record-breaking round was in progress. Barber birdied the 10th as the light began to fail, then parred the difficult 11th and 12th. But at 13, where anyone bent on breaking a record would certainly expect a birdie, or perhaps an eagle, Barber chipped over the green and wound up with a destructive bogey, his only of the day. Barber could no longer see well. He wears sunglasses when he plays and as the late afternoon darkened, there was no time to replace them with normal glasses, which presumably were not in his bag. "I was ready to stop playing," Barber said. "If they hadn't stopped it, I would have. When you can't see, you can't see."

Barber missed a nine-footer for a birdie at 14. At 15, he was over the green in two. Barely able to see the hole, he chipped and was surprised and delighted when the gallery—"most of them my house guests"—exploded in cheers. Barber had knocked the ball into the cup on the fly for an eagle. He now needed only one birdie on the final three holes to tie the course record of 64, or two to break it.

He did not get a chance until early Saturday morning. Play was halted by darkness with six pairings still out on the course. Sneed and Stadler would be the 36-hole leaders, no doubt about that; but no 36-hole cut could be determined, no Saturday's pairing sheet could be drawn up, until those 12 players finished.

Saturday dawned, and was as beautiful and still as Friday had been dark and windy. At 8 A.M. Barber and the others wandered down into the valley. Barber parred 16, and dropped a birdie putt at 17 to give himself a chance at a record 63 and a $50,000 bonus which *Golf Magazine* was offering to anyone who set a course record in a major championship.

Alas, Miller did himself in with his drive, which was too far to the right. He cut a six-iron to the left fringe about 40 feet away with a tough break to figure out. "It wasn't a makable putt," he said minutes later, "but I decided to make it." He did not, but the ensuing tap in gave him his 64 and put him at five under for the tournament, just four shots behind the leaders.

And what, you may ask, about Fuzzy Zoeller? Where had he been during that hectic, stormy Friday and how did he do? Well, Fuzzy had a ringside seat for Sneed's fine 67 since he played alongside him. Zoeller shot a respectable 71, to tie for 11th with Bill Kratzert, which was very nice for a first-timer. Still, there was absolutely no reason for anyone to notice him and, indeed, no one did.

As so often happens at any golf tournament, the cold statistics at the end of the day do not reflect the internal, hidden battle. This year many names bobbed up for a few minutes only to disappear. Few knew how close it was for several hours until Sneed took charge and moved off by himself, while his pursuers spun their wheels, unable to chase him.

Trevino will go unremembered at the 1979 Masters except for a few moments on this gorgeous Saturday when his name crept onto the leaderboards. He birdied three of the first five holes to go three under, six strokes off the lead. Still a long way off, you may say, but at that point he was tied with Zoeller, the eventual winner. Gary Player was that far behind on Sunday morning the year before and we all know what he did. So after five holes Trevino was in the chase, but he played the last 13 in one over par and by dusk quietly disappeared, 10 strokes off the lead.

Several players, unnoticed so far, suddenly appeared. Tom Kite, no stranger to Augusta or its leaderboards, after a 71–72 start, came home in 68, low round of the day. Australian Jack Newton was tied with him after a 69. The key to Newton's round was what he called a miracle birdie at 15, when he apparently hit his second shot into the pond. Seeing that the ball had barely rolled in and that he could still hit it, he did so; and the ball squirted out onto the green. From there, he sank a 20-footer.

But unquestionably the most meaningful emergence, especially in the light of the next day's events was that of Fuzzy Zoeller. Fuzzy got off to a fast start, with birdies on the first, fifth, seventh and eighth holes, to go seven under midway through the afternoon. At that moment, Sneed was in the lead at nine under; Stadler, eight; Watson, Barber and Zoeller, seven. Nicklaus and Floyd were five under, so that there were six players within four strokes of the lead. Zoeller cooled slightly the rest of the way, but his 69 put him at 210, six back of Sneed at the end of the day and only two strokes behind Watson and Stadler in second. If Sneed should have a bad round on Sunday, the old hands said, Zoeller had a chance.

But Fuzzy disagreed. "I played with Ed yesterday," he said, "and I've never seen anything like it. He hit right at the flag all day." Zoeller seemed content to be playing well on his first appearance. "It's a privilege to play here, easy to get into the mood. Golf to me is a pleasure and I enjoy being out on the course whether I'm shooting 69 or 79." Zoeller is noted as one of the longest hitters on the tour, a tremendous asset at Augusta, but he used to be wild. "I didn't know where the ball was going sometimes," he said. "Now I try to swing within myself. Sometimes when I'm downwind, I'll let it out." He did so at the ninth Saturday, driving the ball nearly 300 yards and leaving himself only a nine-iron to the green.

Tied with Zoeller at 210 was Lietzke, who rebounded from his dismal, rainy-day, back-nine 40 to shoot 68. Surprisingly, Lietzke managed only one of his four birdies on the par-fives, and that was the second. He made no bogeys. He was especially proud of a pitch at the fourth which saved a par. "There was a mound between me and the green. I bounced it up; it hit the top, and trickled down a foot from the hole." Lietzke was also proud of his round. "A lot of people expected me to fold after yesterday," he said. "I had something to prove to myself and I did. Today makes up for yesterday."

Well, not quite. He was six strokes back. Only a stroke ahead were Stadler and Watson. Stadler hung reasonably close to the lead for the first hour, then slipped well into the pack, and finally rallied at the end of the day to tie Watson for second. The first sign that this would not be Craig's day came at the second hole, when he failed to make the almost obligatory birdie. He bogeyed the fifth when his approach was to the left of the green, and then disastrously bogeyed the par-five eighth hole, giving him a 38 going out. When he hit into the pond at 11 and took six, he had fallen to only five under par and was barely in the top 10. But birdies at 13, 15 and 17 got him back to only two over for the day, a 74.

"I drove poorly," said Stadler. "And I missed three or four makable putts on the front nine. My chances are not nearly as good as they were this morning. He [Sneed] is not making any mistakes and that's the key."

Watson, good as he is, was making mistakes which were costing him dearly, and Saturday was no exception. Tom set himself up for an excellent round when he played the front nine in 34 for the third straight day, but his experience at 10 shook him up. His approach to the green sailed left and his ball hit a woman in the face. Although the ball landed on the fringe of the green, instead of somewhere remote, and Watson was able to get his par, he couldn't keep his calm.

Holes 13 and 15 continued to plague Watson. At 13, Watson's approach went into the ditch guarding the green. After taking a drop, he made an excellent pitch, getting his par; but he had missed his birdie. He cleared the pond at 15 for the first time in the tournament, but three-putted for par. When he parred in, he had a discouraging 70. "No birdies at 13 and 15 [he had, in fact, made one] is the difference between last year and this. I've been in the water three times. Last year I wasn't in once."

While Watson wasn't giving up, he felt Sneed was the strong favorite. "There is no reason why a player of his caliber should not win," he said. "He is swinging well and has confidence. George Fazio really helped him. The only way I can win is for Ed to play poorly and me play well." The next morning the local Augusta paper translated this last statement into this headline: WATSON HAS HOPES SNEED WILL COLLAPSE.

Certainly on Saturday there was no hint that Sneed would "collapse." He finally made a bogey, his first in 58 holes, dating back to the last round of the Heritage Classic. His approach at the fifth was a bit too strong and after a good pitch to five feet, he missed the putt. But birdies at the two par-fives gave him 35 for the front, a score any leader will take.

On the back side, a six-iron at 12 left him four feet from the pin and he made the putt to go 11 under. At 13 his drive settled perilously close to a small pine cone, so Sneed elected to play safe short of the ditch, then pitched close and dropped the putt. That put him 12 under. He also played safe at 15 and had to settle for par. Three more pars gave him a 69, his third straight sub–70 round. At 204, he had a five-stroke lead.

He was immediately asked about his plans for the final round. "I don't think I'll be too conservative," he replied. "At the beginning of the round, I'll do just what I've been doing all week. If I have a big lead on the back nine, I wouldn't want to do anything foolish on the water holes. If my lead was only two or three strokes, I'd have to be more aggressive."

Ed didn't think the hours until Sunday's tee off time would be difficult. "We've rented a house. I have my family and we've invited some friends here. My kids will give me enough diversion tonight. With them around it's not hard to find something to do."

With that, Sneed went out to practice his putting stroke. "I want to get my rhythm back," he said. "My putting wasn't particularly good in spots today. I just didn't get the ball to the hole." Indeed, it was this very facet of the game which would betray Ed Sneed the following day. But the trouble certainly seemed remote in the lingering sunlight of that Saturday evening. Sneed spoke confidently. "I think from this position I should be able to win. I have five shots. But I still have to go out there tomorrow and do it."

Sunday was clear but windy, one of the breeziest days in recent years. Nicklaus, eight strokes back, had felt he needed a 67 to have a chance, but when he observed the wind, amended the score to 68. Jack teed off at l:04, seven pairings and nearly an hour ahead of Ed Sneed, who was paired with Craig Stadler. Immediately in front of Sneed and Stadler were Watson and Zoeller. Nicklaus birdied two and eight, but a bogey at four, where he missed "an easy putt," gave him a 35 for the front nine, not the kind of score you want when you're eight strokes back.

Meanwhile, several holes back, Watson was applying some pressure. Two big shots at the second put him on the back fringe and he got down in two for a birdie. On the next hole, he drove too far right to approach the green by air, being blocked by pine limbs, but a little pitch and run stopped 10 feet from the flagstick and he made the birdie putt. That cut Sneed's margin to three, for Ed, having reached the second hole in two, three-putted for par.

After parring three, Sneed hit what he described as a "pretty good four-iron" at the fourth, but a gust of wind seemed to catch the ball and it fell short into a bunker. Bogey. Two holes later, at the par-three sixth, Sneed also caught a bunker with his tee shot and he failed to come out the first time. His second attempt got him close enough for a bogey, but he was two over after six and showing signs of the strain.

His lead had not diminished entirely but it was partly due to bogeys in front of him (or in Stadler's case, beside him). Watson's charge aborted when he hit over the fourth green and bogeyed, but even so he was only two strokes back as he played the seventh. And what of Zoeller? He was still merely one of the minor characters, Watson's playing partner, just as Stadler was Sneed's. Fuzzy failed to birdie the second, and like Watson and Sneed, he bogeyed the fourth. Having started the day a stroke behind Watson, he was now three back. ("Don't worry about the man behind us," Zoeller's caddie, Jariah Beard, had said. "The man next to you is the one to beat.")

Craig Stadler was still a factor. Having bogeyed the first, he birdied the next two, and when he parred the next three, he had gained three strokes on Sneed and was only two back, tied with Watson. But then he faded, plummeted really, bogeying holes No. 7, 9 and 11 over and out. Even an eagle at 13 didn't help that much, as he shot a 76 to tie for seventh.

Sneed and Watson both parred the last three holes of the front nine, so that Zoeller, with his first birdie of the day at eight, gained a shot on both. This, then, is how the leaderboard looked as the last two groups moved through the turn.

Sneed	−10
Watson	−8
Zoeller	−6

Up ahead, Nicklaus had started to move. Having turned at five under for the tournament, he birdied the difficult 10th, sinking a 25-foot putt. "After that, I sort of got excited," he said later. He parred 11 and 12, then reached the 13th in two with a gorgeous one-iron. His putt for an eagle failed by an inch, but the birdie put him at seven under, three off the lead.

And, seconds later, he was two off the lead as Sneed missed a five-footer at 10 and bogeyed the hole. Nicklaus had been short in two and chipped six feet from the cup, but the putt did not drop. So he was only nine under and Watson, who had parred the 10th, was only a stroke back. Zoeller, also with a par at 10, was still six under, tied with Tom Kite.

Tom Kite? Did you know he was in the tournament? Kite is what Dan Jenkins of *Sports Illustrated* calls a lurker, a player who always seems to be just off stage, rarely, if ever, in the spotlight. At Augusta he finished third in 1977, fifth the year before that, and 10th in 1975. This year a third-round 68 after a 71–72 start put him at five under, seven strokes behind Sneed. A birdie at the fourth hole put him at six under and straight pars through 12 kept him there. Thus Kite was technically very much in the tournament. As a matter of fact, he would move ahead of the eventual winner; but then, as we shall see, he quickly took himself out of it, a guest at the party.

Up ahead at 15, Nicklaus hooked his tee shot so much that he could not try for the green in two, a personal disaster. A birdie at this point had seemed an absolute necessity, and an eagle was always a possibility. Now the latter was out of the question as he laid up short of the pond. A good chip and putt would get him his birdie, but Jack has never been noted for his short game.

Behind him, Sneed had reached the 11th green in two, but was a long way from the cup. Watson, at the same moment, hit over the 12th green, but the ball rolled back down the bank and stopped in the fringe. Zoeller, too, was over the green, but he was in a bunker. The 11th and 12th greens are less than 75 yards from one another, so the huge gallery at the hairpin turn known as Amen Corner could watch the struggle of all three players. Indeed, the players traditionally watch each other at the turn not so much to find out what the other has done as to alternate strokes. A roar from the crowd could easily unravel someone in mid-swing.

Sneed's approach putt on No. 11 left him with an ugly six-footer. Zoeller, at the 12th, came out of the bunker but was 15 feet away. Watson chipped from the fringe and saw his ball roll right at the hole and lip it, stopping inches away. A par and still eight under. Zoeller missed and dropped to five under. Sneed, now threatened by Watson for the lead, dropped his testing putt, and was still one stroke ahead.

Such are the vagaries of golf that Nicklaus, thinking that he needed a birdie at 15 and probably one more if he had any chance of catching the leader, was, at that point, actually two strokes ahead of the eventual winner. Jack's chip over the pond was delicate. The pin was cut in the front portion of the green, and as it floated in the air a gust of wind seemed to grab it. The ball landed short, on the bank in front, and trickled slowly down into the water, causing little ripples.

33

Now the birdie was gone and probably the par, too. But, while the gallery in the grandstand was giving him an ovation, Nicklaus circled the pond, and surveyed the problem. The ball was barely in the water, so he had a shot. On went his rain jacket, up went his right pant leg, and into the water he stepped. There is, of course, no way you can practice such a shot, no way of knowing how the ball will come out. Nicklaus swung and, when the splash had subsided, there was his ball no more than 10 feet from the pin. Perhaps no one in the game is tougher on putts of this nature than Nicklaus and it proved true once again. Jack rammed the ball right into the heart of the cup and came away from 15 with a miracle par. Still seven under, still two strokes behind Sneed.

Moments after Nicklaus made his putt, Sneed put his tee shot in the back bunker at 12 and, as he crossed the bridge over Rae's Creek to the green, it seemed certain that he would not win. He had played the front nine in two over par, making no birdies, had bogeyed the 10th, and saved himself from another at 11 with that six-footer. Now he was looking at another potential disaster.

The important shots of the Masters can come in rapid-fire sequence. Nicklaus hit his tee shot at No. 16 no more than 15 feet from the pin, giving him a chance for a birdie, and earning him a roar from the crowd. And back at 13, another roar as Tom Kite's bid for an eagle missed by an inch. The birdie put him seven under, tied with Nicklaus, two back of Sneed. Still another roar, this one at 12. From the bunker, Sneed came close to a birdie, practically holing out. The par kept him in the lead. Watson, meanwhile, had driven way right on 13. No chance to get home in two. Zoeller had driven well.

Now back to Nicklaus, over the ball at 16. Still over it. Motionless. The putt, too far to the uphill side, broke fast and went into the cup. Shades of 1975, when Nicklaus sank his classic 40-footer to beat Tom Weiskopf and Johnny Miller. Nicklaus was then only one stroke behind Sneed. He was tied with Watson and, if he only knew, three shots ahead of Zoeller.

At this moment in the last round, Sneed, hounded by his pursuers, began to pull away and look like a clear-cut winner. Everything that happened in the next half hour or so seemed to work in his favor. Watson's second shot at 13 was to the right-hand side of the fairway, giving him a downhill approach to the pin; while Kite, with a birdie putt of perhaps 17 feet at the 14, missed. Then Nicklaus drove far right at 17: not a real problem in itself, but it forced him to hit to a green he could no longer see because of a huge mound in front of him. Nicklaus' approach at 17 was long, hitting well past the pin and bounding down an embankment, giving him an almost impossible third shot. Watson chipped 15 feet from the pin at 13, not as easy a birdie as such a player expects at that hole. Apparently needing an eagle to get back into the chase (remember, he was only five under, four strokes back), Zoeller was on in two at 13, and two-putted for a birdie. Six under.

That probably wouldn't have concerned Sneed, even if he had been aware of it. What did register on him, I'm sure, and what he undoubtedly saw, was Watson missing his birdie putt. That birdie would have given Watson a share of the lead. On the other hand, Sneed could not see Nicklaus, as he chipped back at 17, to get the ball no closer than 20 feet. When he missed the putt, he had negated his birdie at 16 and was only seven under. Sneed certainly would have been interested in watching that.

Sneed contributed to his run of good fortune by chipping three feet from the pin at 13. Two holes ahead Kite was struggling, failing to reach the par-five in two and having to settle for par. Still seven under, two back. And now three back as Sneed dropped his putt for a birdie at No. 13 to go 10 under. Should you ever see a rerun on television of that putt at 13, observe it closely as a harbinger of things to come. It was not hit well. It rolled up to the cup, hesitated as if making up its mind, and only then dropped.

Still the good things continued for Sneed. Watson's approach at 14 was short, rolling back down the slope to the fringe. Nicklaus, hitting his second at 18 and desperately needing a birdie, hit far from the pin. Sneed himself drove far right at 14, but anyone who has been to Augusta National knows that when you drive into the pines, there is almost always an escape route, so scattered are the trees. Indeed, Ed found one and bumped his approach almost to the front edge of the green.

But this was after a discouraged Watson had tapped in a bogey putt at 14. Watson's approach putt had left him six feet short and he had missed his par; it was the second straight year he had three-putted 14 on Sunday and again it was to cost him dearly. At about the same time, Nicklaus was finishing his attempt at a sixth title, two-putting at 18 for a 281 total, seven under. And Tom Kite, still ahead of Zoeller as he teed off at 16, fell behind him with that stroke, the ball falling into the pond. The ensuing double bogey knocked him out forever. He finished fifth at 283.

There were several times during the last hour and a half of the 1979 Masters when it seemed as if Sneed had made the decisive stroke, the winner, and one such stroke was at 14. His approach putt left him six feet from the cup, almost exactly on the spot from which Watson had missed. But Sneed did not miss. The par kept him at 10 under, three ahead.

At 15, needing an eagle, Watson gave it a try with a grand second shot which carried the pond and left him no more than 15 feet away. Zoeller was also on in two, although television coverage did not show a single shot he played on the hole. Nor was there any comment when he two-putted for a birdie to go seven under. Watson's eagle attempt was shown, but he missed. He made the birdie, however, and was eight under.

Both Watson and Zoeller hit nicely to the 16th green, about as far away as Nicklaus had been, then stopped in their tracks to watch Sneed hit his third shot to 15. It was a beauty, another one of those shots that "sealed the victory." The ball stopped three feet from the pin. In sequence, Watson and Zoeller continued their walk to the green; each putted for a birdie, Zoeller first, Watson next; and each missed. As they walked to the 17th tee, Sneed tapped in his three-footer for the birdie at 15, again a tentative stroke; but it did go in. With three holes left, he was three ahead of Watson, four ahead of Zoeller and Nicklaus, who, of course, was finished.

At 16, Sneed hit an intelligent drive for a man with a three-stroke lead on Sunday. The pin was left, as always, tucked behind the long pond. You will remember that shortly before, Tom Kite, needing a birdie, had gone into that hazard. Sneed, needing par, hit to the safe side of the green, perhaps a shade too safe. He left himself a monster putt which, when he struck it, pulled up short and broke sharply left, stopping five or six feet from the cup. It was not surprising that he missed, nor was it particularly alarming. "I still had a two-stroke lead," he said later. "I had control of the tournament. I didn't feel tight."

While Sneed was putting at 16, a significant event was taking place at 17. From 14 feet away, Zoeller rolled in a birdie putt to go eight under and at that point, for the first time really, it dawned on everyone that Zoeller had a chance. Slim, but a chance. A birdie at 18 and one more bogey by Sneed. Something like that .Then Watson missed a 10-foot birdie putt at 17, which would have put him one behind Sneed, and he marched off to 18 tied with Zoeller.

Sneed's drive at 17 was good, but his second shot was slightly long, rolling to the back fringe. His approach putt was apparently close enough, close enough on a Thursday, maybe, but not on this Sunday. From less than four feet away, with the shadows gathering across the green, Sneed missed. Now he was in trouble.

So were Watson and Zoeller on 18. Tom drove into the woods on the right, but had an escape road if he played a slice. Taking his time, he walked all the way up to the green to check the pin placement.

Zoeller, meanwhile, had driven perfectly, but his approach and first putt were undistinguished and he was still eight feet away, faced with a bogey that would take him out of the chase at the very instant he had entered it. Watson hit his second shot well enough under the conditions, but his ball wound up on the back of the green, leaving an impossible downhiller. He got the ball close enough for his par, but it didn't look like that would do it. And just as Zoeller was stepping up to his testy eight-footer, the giant leaderboard near the 18th green flashed the word that Sneed had dropped another stroke at 17. Coolly, Fuzzy rolled in his putt to stay even with Watson, and now he was only one away from the lead.

Using a three-wood, Sneed drove safely at 18, but his seven-iron approach was hit a little thinly. It sailed right and came to rest on the brink of the right-hand bunker, mere inches away from being in. As he walked up to the green, Sneed received the ovation he deserved, but he was hardly in a position to enjoy it. His face reflected the pressure he was under. He bent over his ball and studied it. Then he asked an official if he could remove a cigarette butt nearby. Finally, using a wedge, he chipped the ball toward the hole. When it stopped rolling, it was perhaps five feet below the hole, the best he could have hoped for considering the delicacy of the shot. It gave him an uphill putt, no breaks right or left.

It was the kind of putt golfers dream about, a situation they fantasize about as they practice. "I need this putt to win the Masters." Sneed inspected the line. "I read it to break right," he said later. "My caddy agreed. I aimed for the lip."

The ball, not well struck, moved up to the front left edge of the cup and hung there. For a second, it seemed it might topple in. Sneed, in agony, walked up to it, leaned over and took a careful look to see if it was moving. It was not. He tapped the ball in and the Masters had its first sudden-death play-off.

It was in 1976 that the Masters broke tradition and announced that the 18-hole play-off was a thing of the past, but in the three years following, there had been no ties. It appeared that there would have been one the previous year. Tom Watson needed only a par to tie Gary Player but he bogeyed. And a few minutes later, Hubert Green, needing a birdie, hit his approach three feet from the hole. When he did, hundreds of fans began the trek out toward the first green, while others, perhaps more knowing, headed toward the second, a birdie hole. They were all wrong; Green missed his three-footer, and Player won the Masters.

Over the ensuing months, the Masters announced a further change, stating that any play-off would begin at the 10th hole, explaining that the viewing was better on this and the next few holes. Also, of course, television was better prepared to show those holes.

Some 10 minutes after Sneed's putt failed to drop, the three combatants gathered on the 10th tee. Three coins were produced and everyone turned up a tail. The three flipped again; two more tails, but Sneed got a head. His honor. Watson won a private flip with Zoeller and went second. All three drove well down the left side. Zoeller's ball was slightly ahead of Watson's which was ahead of Sneed's.

The 10th hole is perhaps the most difficult one on the course, a 485-yard par-four. It slopes down from the clubhouse, bends slightly to the left, though not enough to be called a dogleg, and continues to an elevated green watched over by elegant pines at the rear. It is a beautiful golf hole but a tough par, as are the next two holes. The three of them are by far the toughest three-hole stretch on the course.

All three players had driven down the left side of 10, which was the place to be. Sneed, away, hit first, using a six-iron, and put his ball no more than 11 feet from the pin. Watson, about 170 yards from the pin, which cut toward the left center, used a seven-iron and wound up the same distance away as Sneed.

Now it was Zoeller's turn. "I couldn't find a place for my ball," he was to say later. He used an eight-iron and wound up 15 feet away. You couldn't ask for three better approaches. Zoeller played his 15-footer to break left and it did, but not until it had passed the cup on the high side. "I thought I'd made it. I figured the first one in had it. When I missed I had to hope that the others would miss, too."

Watson and Sneed were so close to being equidistant from the cup that officials had to measure (using the flagstick and then an envelope) to determine who was away. It was Sneed. By this time the light was beginning to fail at the 10th green, which is always shaded by the tall pines, so the line was hard to read, but it appeared to be straight. Sneed stroked the ball well, but it slid by an inch to the left.

Now the tournament belonged to Tom Watson, the favorite four days before. One putt and it was his. He had been missing similar putts all day, but it seemed likely that he would make this one. But unlike the other two players, Watson did not stroke the ball well, and it went to the right of the hole. "It was a very simple putt," he said. "I thought I was going to win right there, but I hit it poorly."

On to No. 11, another par-four, this one 445 yards long. The approach is downhill to a green with huge mounds in front and a pond tucked in at the front left side. The pin, of course, was in that direction and to the back, which was the Sunday placement. Hogan used to say that any time he was on the 11th in two he had made a bad shot, preferring to avoid the pond even if it meant being just off the green to the right and taking his chances with a chip and putt. (I'm sure Ben was exaggerating slightly and surely in a play-off he would have been bolder.)

Again, all three players hit splendid tee shots and again it was Sneed who hit the first approach. Using a five-iron, he hit the ball solidly, but it was a bit too strong, hitting on the back portion of the green and bounding into a bunker. Watson lofted a high shot which hit short of the pin and rolled up to a distance of some 15 feet. Zoeller, able to use an eight-iron after a huge drive, drew his shot in from right to left, a beauty that left him only eight feet away.

Sneed's position now seemed hopeless. Even if the others missed it looked as if he would bogey. But from an ugly downhill lie in the bunker, he hit a shot which rolled gently toward the pin, looked for an instant as if it would drop, but missed by an inch. It was such a remarkable shot, especially given the circumstances, that even Zoeller and Watson applauded. Still, he had missed; and now Sneed had to pray that the others would, too.

Watson did. His 15-footer was straight at the cup, but it died an   inch or two short. Watson looked to heaven in disbelief. Now it was Zoeller's turn and he went about it quickly. The line seemed straight and that is how Fuzzy played it. There was never a doubt as the ball went straight at the center of the cup and disappeared. Up in the air went Zoeller's putter, followed by Fuzzy, arms extended high overhead. He hugged his caddy, Jeriah Beard, who after 23 years had picked himself a winner.

Of course, one has to feel sympathy for Ed Sneed and, indeed, in the moments following Zoeller's putt, Watson walked over to Sneed to console him. Sneed had been forced to shoulder the burden of the lead for 36 holes and he had held up well until the last three of regulation. Zoeller, as he teed off on the 71st hole, was four strokes back and playing for second place. "When I finish second or third it's like winning," he said.

There was no real pressure on him until the play-off. Perhaps that is an argument in favor of the 18-hole play-off. "I would have preferred 18 holes," said Watson later, an understandable wish since his chances would have been better at the longer distance. But beyond that, perhaps Zoeller should have had to experience the pressure of going home Sunday night and wrestling with the reality that the next day he could win the Masters. It would have been interesting to see how he would have borne the pressure. We'll never know.

Gary Player slips Masters jacket over Fuzzy Zoeller's shoulders,
as Arnold Palmer looks on.

3

THE U.S. OPEN

I would be enormously surprised if any of you have ever heard of a golfer named Podge Ferguson. He has never won a tournament of consequence, nor is he famous for teaching one of the great players, as with Jack Grout and Jack Nicklaus. Yet, he has had a significant impact on golf in recent years. Podge Ferguson is the reason Hale Irwin plays golf.

Irwin grew up in Baxter Springs, Kansas, in the extreme southeast corner of the state, where Kansas, Oklahoma and Missouri meet. It is quite a bit removed from the major population centers; the closest cities are Tulsa, Oklahoma, Wichita, Kansas and Springfield, Missouri. It is not surprising that anyone living in this little town saw very little of the great golfers of the time. Even a visit from Podge Ferguson, therefore, was an occasion, and Irwin's father took young Hale out to see the exhibition matches.

"I don't know where Podge lived," Irwin tells people, "but he would come to our little town and put on exhibitions. He hit what looked like prodigious drives to me. I got the golf bug right there."

In the years since Irwin first became addicted to golf, he has developed into one of the best players of the 1970's. In June 1979, he became the 14th player to win the United States Open Championship at least twice. That put him in rather elite company, with, among others, Walter Hagen, Gene Sarazen, Bob Jones, Ben Hogan, Cary Middlecoff, Julius Boros, Ralph Guldahl, Bill Casper, Lee Trevino and Jack Nicklaus. The fact that only 14 players have been able to win more than once in the 79 times the Open has been played is a fairly good indication that those who do are something special. Consider the great players who haven't: for example, Byron Nelson, Lawson Little, Arnold Palmer, Lloyd Mangrum and Craig Wood.

The qualities essential to winning major competitions are fairly obvious. First of all, a player must have length, the ability to play finesse golf and be able to putt. Second, he must know what shots should be played. Third, he must be able to play the great courses, the kind which demand variety in shots and intelligence in planning. The fourth is perhaps the most important of the principal ingredients. Above all, the player must be a competitor. Look at the men who have won the Open championship—Hogan, Jones, Trevino, Nicklaus. Losing simply has been unacceptable to them. This doesn't mean that they never lost. Certainly they did, and they lost with an outward grace. Yet, losing was nearly unendurable.

That final quality is perhaps Irwin's greatest strength. He is a fierce competitor. (Some other tour players call him downright nasty.) When he is on the golf course, he is grim; he is intense and totally absorbed in the job at hand. Perhaps his competitive spirit has been nurtured by playing other sports, because, unlike most other tour players, Irwin is not exactly a one-game man. He played defensive back for the University of Colorado's football team, and as a kid he played everything. Baseball was his favorite game, and he says he could play all nine positions.

By the time he was in eighth grade, Irwin knew his mission. When asked to write an essay on what he wanted to do when he grew up, Irwin wrote that he wanted to be a professional golfer. And at that stage, Hale had not even seen a pro tournament, though he soon did. When he was 13, his family moved to Boulder, Colorado, and when he was 15, he went to the U.S. Open at the Cherry Hills Country Club in Denver. It was the Open that Arnold Palmer won.

"I went for a practice round," he recalls. "The tickets for the actual tournament cost too much. The thing I remember most is seeing Ben Hogan go to the practice tee and unload an entire shag bag full of brand new golf balls. I didn't know anybody practiced with new balls." He also remembers Sam Snead walking gruffly by him after Sam had played the first hole badly, and he remembers the tee shots of Dutch Harrison. "Where my tee shots began to drop, his were just beginning to take off."

By then, though, he already had decided on his future, he kept up his other athletic interests—particularly football. Any pro-football thoughts Irwin might have had vanished in one moment during the opening game of the 1966 college season: Colorado kicked off to the University of Miami, and all 10 of Irwin's teammates were blocked out of the runback. "The ballcarrier ran right over me," Irwin laughs. "I still have his cleat marks on my chest. I knew then that pro football wasn't for me."

Two years later, late in 1968, Irwin became a regular on the pro golf tour. Most of Irwin's victories, including his two Open Championships, have been won over classic and difficult courses. Through 1979, he had won the Heritage Open twice over the Harbour Town Golf Links in Hilton Head, South Carolina; the Los Angeles Open at the Riviera Country Club, site of the 1948 U.S. Open; and the Western Open at Butler National Golf Club, near Chicago. (Butler is not by any means a classic course, but it is certainly very difficult.) He also won the Hall of Fame Classic in 1977 over the No. 2 Course of the Pinehurst Country Club. Irwin was devastating at Pinehurst, scoring 264 for 72 holes, 20 under par. (Some people at Pinehurst claim that the old course was not particularly difficult as it was set up, but Irwin's score is impressive, nonetheless.)

*Hale Irwin and two of his prizes—
wife Sally and the U.S. Open trophy.*

Irwin is also an extraordinarily consistent player. Until the Crosby Pro-Amateur, which opened the 1979 season, Irwin had not missed the 36-hole cut since the Tucson Open of January 1975. He has played through 86 consecutive tournaments, the third longest string in the history of the tour. Byron Nelson played through 113 tournaments in the 1940's, and Jack Nicklaus played through 105 in the early 1970's. Irwin also has been among the 10 leading money winners every year since 1973.

It is surprising that he has not won more often. Until the 1979 Open, Irwin had not won in the United States since 1977. During that year he had won three times—the Atlanta Classic in the spring, the Hall of Fame in August, and the San Antonio Texas Open in September. He did win both the Australian and South African PGA Championships in 1978, and he received the low individual trophy in the World Cup in Greece late in the year. He, however, has yet to win the biggest foreign tournament of them all—the British Open. Nor has he ever won the championship of the PGA of America or the Masters.

Neither Irwin nor anyone else has an explanation for this surprising scarcity of first place finishes by a player of such quality. Significantly, he was not among the players looked upon as a potential winner when the 1979 Open began, even though he had won at Winged Foot, a course which has many qualities in common with Inverness, particularly the exceedingly fast and contoured greens. Also overlooked was the fact that, of the 13 tournaments he had entered earlier in 1979, Irwin finished in the money in 11 and in the top 10 in four. He was third in the Jackie Gleason tournament in Florida, tied for third in both the Houston Open and the Bay Hill Classic in Orlando, Florida, and for ninth in the Hawaiian Open. Yet going into the Open, he had a strokes-per-round average of 71.33, quite a bit above his 70.65 of 1978.

Most of the attention prior to the Open was focused on Jack Nicklaus, Tom Watson and Andy Bean. On Nicklaus simply because he is Nicklaus, on Watson because he has been the leading player in the game for three years, and on Bean because he had been having a very hot hand at that time. Nicklaus, however, was having a rather disappointing season. (It turned out to be the worst in his career.) He had not won a tournament since the British Open the previous July, a period of 11 months. This was the longest he had gone without a victory since he joined the tour in 1962, and many people close to the game blamed it on his playing in so few tournaments. At the time of the Open, he had played in only eight and for the entire year he played in only 12 in the United States. Of those eight, he had finished among the top 15 in three of them, including the Masters, in which he was a stroke behind Fuzzy Zoeller, Ed Sneed and Tom Watson, all tied for the lead. Nicklaus defended his schedule, pointing out that he had, indeed, won the British Open and that he had missed winning the Masters by two strokes.

Despite the denials, the men who have won consistently while they played sparingly in competition have been rare. Only two men, in fact, can truly be said to have won on a lean diet of competitive golf. They are Bob Jones and Ben Hogan. Jones, for example, seldom played in more than three or four tournaments a year. In 1923, he played in only the Open and the Amateur, and he won the Open and lost in the second round of the Amateur. The following year he played in those two again, winning the Amateur and finishing second to Cyril Walker in the Open. Even in 1930, his greatest year, he played in only seven tournaments, and won six of them including the Open and Amateur championships of both the United States and Great Britain, along with the Southeastern Open and the Golf Illustrated Golf Vase, in Britain.

In 1953, Hogan's greatest year, he played in six tournaments and won five, including the Open, Masters and British Open. (This is without question the best year that anyone has had since 1930.) Hogan and Jones were, of course, rare individuals. They had the capacity to perform at their very best almost on call. On the other hand, despite his magnificent skills, Nicklaus is not able to do this on the same scale as Jones and Hogan.

Tom Watson came into the Open as the bona fide favorite. He had already won four tournaments (Lanny Wadkins and Fuzzy Zoeller had won two), he had won $353,874, and it was only June. He had won both the Masters and the British Open in 1977; he was in contention in all four of the major championships in 1978; and he was among the three men in the play-off at the Masters in the spring when Fuzzy Zoeller won on the second extra hole. From the beginning of 1977 through the Atlanta Classic which was a week before the Open, Watson had won $1 million in prize money and 14 tournaments. As a matter of fact, he was leading the money winning list and ahead in the Vardon Trophy race (for the lowest scoring average) for a third consecutive year. No one had ever done that—not Nicklaus, not Hogan, nor even Byron Nelson during the war years. In addition to the four tournaments he won, Watson had been second in four others and hadn't finished lower than fourth since the middle of March.

Normally cool-headed and largely unpretentious, Watson sometimes even looks at himself in awe. "There are times," he said a day or so before the

Open began, "when I think that when I'm playing well, I can beat anybody." In his last five U.S. Opens, he had finished ninth or better, and he claimed, "I could have won twice. Maybe this is the year."

After Watson won the Memorial Tournament, even Nicklaus marveled at his game. "It's obvious," he said, "that Tom is playing the best of anyone in the game today." Miller Barber concurred. "I've been around a long time. I've seen the Palmers and the Nicklauses. I saw Hogan's last tournament. You could tell that each of them had that drive, that something extra. I think Tom has that desire, too. That temperament. He wants to be a great player. Maybe God gives some people something he doesn't give the rest of us."

Winning the Open might not have been an obsession with Watson, but it was surely on his mind. "With the exception of Sam Snead," Watson said, "no one has been a great player without winning the Open. It's the national championship. You must win consistently and you must win the Open to be considered a great player. It's the one I've been looking forward to; it's the one I want to win. But no one can say he's going to win a specific tournament. All you can do is try to have your game at a peak when the big one comes along and then go out and try as hard as you can."

Despite this, Watson came into the Open far from his peak. He was not driving very well, and he didn't try to hide it. In a meeting with the press, he was all gloom. "The best driver has the best chance of winning here, and I'll have to drive the ball better than I am. And I'm not too happy with my irons either, and long-iron approaches are imperative here." He did concede that he was chipping and putting well, thank heavens, and so there was some hope. "Sometimes being a little defensive about an Open can be good, too," he said, philosophically. "It could keep you out of a lot of trouble."

While Watson may have been off his game, Andy Bean certainly wasn't. For the second straight year he came into the Open fresh from winning a tournament. The week before the Open, Bean had shot 265 at the Atlanta Country Club and won the Atlanta Classic by eight strokes, the largest winning margin since Raymond Floyd won the Masters by eight strokes over Ben Crenshaw in 1976. His score was 23 under par, the lowest in relation to par for the year.

"I think," Bean said, grinning as he arrived in Toledo, "that if I make 25 birdies this week like I did last week, I definitely will have a good chance to win." True, but he would have to avoid bogeys, too, something he had not done in his previous few Opens. Both his 1977 and 1978 Opens were spoiled by either a bad round or a bad hole. At Southern Hills in 1977, he went into the final round only one stroke behind Hubert Green. Bean shot 79 and didn't even threaten.

In 1978 at Cherry Hills, he simply couldn't play the 18th, admittedly a very difficult hole, but not so difficult that Bean can be excused for making two double bogeys and a bogey to lose five strokes on that hole alone. Five over par on the last hole and he lost by four to Andy North. "I never knocked it in the water," Bean said with a shrug, "but I couldn't get it in the hole. Last year I made a lot of birdies, but I made a lot of bogeys, too. Hopefully, this year I'm smarter."

Bean's plan was to shoot for the center of the greens all week, because the greens at Inverness are so small that if a ball lay anywhere on one, it couldn't be too far from the hole. It was an interesting strategy. Somehow, however, it worked only sporadically. He shot 70 in the first round to share the lead, but in two of the last three he had scores of 76 and 80.

While players such as Nicklaus, Watson, Zoeller, Bean and some others were attracting a major share of the attention, Andy North, winner of the 1978 Open (practically by default), was being ignored. It wasn't so much a case of his winning but of everyone else losing, and almost right away he dropped back into obscurity. His reaction to the lack of attention was, if anything, mature. "That's the way it should be," he said as he looked at a knot of reporters clustered around Nicklaus. "I haven't done anything since then to get excited about. Somebody told me today that I was an unknown before the Open. I told him I still am." North doesn't want to be obscure; he'd certainly like to have been more of a factor in 1979 than he had been. In 17 tournaments, his best finish was seventh at Inverrary. He missed the 36-hole cut four times, and in his previous four tournaments he'd finished 41st, 67th, and missed the cut twice. He had won only $35,000 and stood 62nd on the money winning list.

"I've had a terrible year, professionally," North admitted. "Nothing has gone right with my game; I've missed cuts and haven't made much money. But I try to keep things in perspective. Just look around at the rest of the world. I have a friend, a very close friend, who has cancer. Compared to what he's going through, my problems are nothing."

North is essentially a low-key person who has enjoyed his life since he became a golf pro in 1972. "I've planned it that way," he said. "I think I've gained something from winning the Open, both personally and financially. I'm not looking for the fast buck from some quick deal. No, I don't feel cheated; I want to build a career that means something to me."

He's continued to play in exhibitions for charities, to give clinics for kids, and to spend as much time as he can with his wife, Susan, and his two daughters. "Every year I go down to the PGA Academy of Golf for the junior program. It's fun to watch kids 13, 14 and 15 do whatever you tell them to do. They go from hitting awful shots to good ones and they feel you've done something for them. I'd rather do things like that that make me feel good and help someone at the same time. I had someone to help me along at that age and I want to give some of it back."

As North saw it, the 1979 Open would be pretty much the same as the 1978 Open: the man who kept his drives on the fairway and putted well figured to win. "I'm not discouraged," he said when someone brought up his record. "I have confidence in my game. I'll give it my best shot; that's all I can ask of myself."

When the Open began, the possibility that North might win again was not altogether unthinkable, considering the course where the 1979 championship was being played. The Inverness Club is not unlike Cherry Hills Country Club, where North had won the previous year. At 6,982 yards, it measured just shorter than Cherry Hills (7,083), but played longer because the high altitude in Denver allowed the ball to carry greater distances. At Inverness, five of the 13 par-four holes are under 400 yards, which is much like Cherry Hills. The strength of the similarity, however, is not distance, it is in the character of the two courses. Both courses were built in the 1920's. They have had time to mature, time for the trees to grow and to develop charm and familiarity. The greens on both are small, much smaller than the greens built in the 1950's and 1960's; they are very fast and they are contoured—not severely but enough to make any downhill putt an adventure.

Inverness is one of the best maintained courses in North America. Its greens are legendary, on an equal footing with those at Oakmont and Merion in their speed and trueness of roll. For the Open, they are normally cut to a height of 5/32 of an inch, about the thickness of 12 playing cards. Once a ball begins to roll downhill on those slick putting surfaces, it shows a remarkable disinclination to stop. Its fairways are narrow, although (with a few exceptions) they are not closed in by trees, so there is considerable maneuvering room overhead. The course has 110 bunkers; though one of its strongest holes, the seventh, a 452-yard par-four, has none at all. Inverness can be stretched to nearly 7,000 yards for the big occasion, but normally it plays much shorter, around 6,500 yards, about the same as Merion. As a matter of fact, it has some of the feel of Merion, with greens which demand approaches from the one best angle.

Inverness was conceived in 1903 near Toledo, Ohio, an industrial city on the western shore of Lake Erie. In those days, it was fashionable for Americans to name golf courses for either Indian tribes, such as Shinnecock, or for Scottish clubs, such as St. Andrews. The name Inverness was chosen for the Scottish club which took its name from Inverness Castle, where Macbeth murdered Duncan. The Scots not only generously gave permission to use the name, but suggested that the Americans use their crest as well.

Inverness was redesigned by Donald Ross, a Scotsman whose volume of work was astounding. Ross is given credit for either designing or re-designing 600 courses in the United States, among them some of our finest: such as, Pinehurst No. 2, Seminole, Plainfield, Oakland Hills. The original course, designed by a man named Bernard Nichols, was supposed to be nine holes. When Nichols finished, however, he was one short, and there were only eight. The oversight was corrected by adding a 167-yard par-three. That hole eventually became the 13th, a very strong hole where the 1973 United States Amateur ended. Nichols' course served nicely for a while, but in 1919 Inverness brought in Donald Ross and he gave the club the course it basically still enjoys.

Inverness today bears the imprint of three of the best architects who have practiced the art. For the 1957 Open, Dick Wilson strengthened Ross's design, mainly by tightening the bunkering around the greens and relocating some fairway bunkers which were no longer in play.

Then in 1976, George Fazio stopped by Inverness to do what started out to be a relatively small piece of work. The USGA had requested that he raise the front of the 17th green, which had tilted severely over the years, in preparation for the 1979 Open. Before Fazio left, the Inverness directors, to their astonishment, had agreed to the construction of four new holes, the elimination of four others and the installation of two new tees. Repair of the 17th green was included in this package.

Fazio said he was horrified to see a clutter of three tees and two greens all within pitching distance of the 18th tee. He had envisioned the ultimate golf traffic jam. With the revisions, the critical area would become open and airy. One of the eliminated holes was the historic par-four seventh. It was combined with what had been the par-four sixth and the par-three eighth to create a par-five hole which became the most controversial in many an Open.

It is always a little sad to lose so historic a hole, but in reality the seventh was no longer like it was in 1920, when Ted Ray reached the green with his tee shot four times. In those days, the hole played to 334 yards, a dogleg left across a deep chasm. Four times Ray cut across the dogleg, a spectacular accomplishment requiring a carry of at least 275 yards; and all four times he scored birdies. He won by one stroke over Harry Vardon, the greatest player of his time.

Every Open played at Inverness seems to have been memorable. Eleven years later Billy Burke and George Von Elm tied at 292 after 72 holes. The play-off for the Open in those days was 36 holes. They tied again and had to play a second 36 holes. At the end of the second play-off, Burke was one stroke ahead.

The Open returned in 1957 and when Jimmy Demaret finished with 283, it looked as if he would win. However, Dick Mayer came to the 18th needing a par-four to tie, a birdie three to beat Demaret. His approach settled perhaps 18 feet behind the hole, and Mayer rolled it in for the birdie which gave him 282. When Mayer's putt dropped into the hole, Demaret, watching from a window in the clubhouse said only, "the boy holed a wonderful, wonderful putt."

It was not over just yet. Out on the course Cary Middlecoff, the defending champion, needed a second 68 for the day to tie Mayer. He came to the 18th needing one more birdie to do it. His approach settled about 10 feet to the right of the hole. Middlecoff played it just right; he tapped the ball lightly, it broke severely left and dropped into the cup. He had played the last 36 holes in 136 strokes, a truly remarkable performance. It was all he had to offer, however. The next day he shot 79 and Mayer won the play-off.

The changes brought about by Fazio led to a great deal of criticism by the players, who simply do not believe that changes to a course, especially changes such as those at Inverness, are the work of the club and not of the USGA. They see such changes as a determined effort by the USGA to keep Open scores high and to "protect the integrity of par."

"The USGA doesn't want to recognize that today's players are better than ever before," Hale Irwin said on the eve of the Open. "They seem willing to do anything to prevent us from shooting scores that would make us appear better than the great names of the past.'' Watson agreed. ''Why can't the USGA leave the great courses alone and stop worrying about what we shoot?''

Criticism of another topic emerged as well. Players questioned the composition of the 153-man field itself. The USGA had adopted a policy of inviting the leaders of some foreign orders of merit into the Open without requiring them to qualify. Among the beneficiaries of this policy were Severiano Ballesteros, who led the 1978 Continental Order of Merit; Hugh Baiocchi, leader of the 1978 South African Order of Merit; Greg Norman, who led the 1978–79 Australian Order of Merit; Isao Aoki, leader of the 1978 Japan Order of Merit; and Hsu Sheng San, leader of the 1978 Asian Golf Circuit.

They are all good players, no question of that; but should they have been invited into the field without qualifying? I don't think so. Consider this. Only the 30 leading money winners from the previous year's PGA Tour are exempt from qualifying for the Open. The 31st was Jay Haas, the 32nd was Grier Jones, the 33rd was Jack Renner, the 34th was Bob Murphy, and the 35th was Gibby Gilbert. Look at those names, compare them to the foreign players who were extended exemptions, and ask which group accomplished more during 1978. Was leading the Asian Golf Circuit more difficult than finishing 31st on the PGA's money winning list? Did Hsu Sheng San show himself to be a better player than Jay Haas?

Of the five foreign players invited to compete, only two made the cut and only Aoki broke 300, with a 299. Greg Norman shot 302. Baiocchi shot 87 in the first round and withdrew. Hsu shot 79–84—163, Ballesteros 79–81—160 and both missed the cut. In defense of Ballesteros, he was ill at the time. Over the last few years he has shown himself capable of playing in this company. In my view, however, that is not sufficient reason to be given a free pass into the most important golf tournament in the world.

Others agree. Arnold Palmer, who has meant more to the Open over the years than all the foreign players together, was upset when he learned that those players were exempt. Arnold had to qualify, but he might not try again. ''I did not say I would never play in another USGA event,'' Palmer told one reporter. ''I did say I may never qualify for another USGA event. Not playing in our major championship would take something away from me,'' Palmer went on, ''but I will give it serious thought before I will try to qualify again.''

In spite of the controversy, Fazio's plans for Inverness were completed at the time of the Open. He had combined the sixth, seventh and eighth holes. Thus, two short par-four holes and a par-three became the eighth hole, a par-five of 528 yards. It is, indeed, a very good hole. It requires a tee shot of fairly good length placed to the right of a nest of bunkers which once guarded the sixth green. The ball must not go too far or else it will catch a downslope and leave the player with a hanging lie. If the shot is long enough, however, the green can be reached in two by the very daring. It is well protected by bunkers and by a rough which pinches the fairway close to the green.

The normal method of playing the eighth is to place the second shot short of the bunkers and then pitch on to the smallish, shallow green. The green is protected on the left by three bunkers and a stand of tall fir trees. The green is on two levels, and thick pine trees to the rear await all but the most accurate of second shots. The fairway bends severely to the left in the drive zone, and therein lies its flaw.

The eighth hole runs parallel and to the right of the 17th, a par-four which also bends slightly to the left. Certain members of Inverness have found that a hooked tee shot from the eighth, which carries over a line of maple, pine, spruce, ash and assorted other trees onto the 17th fairway, is not necessarily a disaster. Rather, it can cut as much as 70 yards off the length of the eighth and bring the green within range of an iron shot approach. If a mere club member can learn this, does one think for a moment that players on the PGA Tour will not discover this short cut? In fact, they learned very quickly that they did not even have to hook the shot over the trees. Standing on the eighth tee, the 17th fairway opens invitingly to the left. All that's needed is a relatively straight tee ball and the second shot might need only a club as short as a six-iron.

Nothing happened during the practice rounds. Probably none of the players wanted to alert the USGA to the possibilities and so they played the hole conventionally. Peace ended early on the morning of the first round. Lon Hinkle was in the sixth group to leave the first tee. He reached the eighth tee at about 10 o'clock. At that time he was one under par. Being the first man off the tee, he drew a one-iron from his bag and drilled it through the opening in the trees to the left of the eighth tee and onto the 17th fairway.

"I think I'm going that way, too," said Chi Chi Rodriguez, who was paired with Hinkle and Greg Norman. Rodriguez used a driver, however. Norman played the hole as it was designed. Hinkle next played a three-iron. He shot over the pines which protect the eighth onto the green and two putts later he had his birdie four. Rodriguez played a four-wood over the trees, but made only a par-five.

As Hinkle and Rodriguez played their tee shots down the 17th fairway, two marshals were having a conversation.

"Hey," said one. "They can't do that. I mean, they can't. Or can they?"

"I'm afraid they can, and have," the other marshal replied.

Next on the tee were Bob Shearer, the Australian, Forrest Fezler and Dave Eichelberger. Shearer and Fezler played conventionally, but Eichelberger needed help. He was five over par, so he told the marshals to lower the rope, he was taking the short cut.

"I'll bet Donald Ross is laughing in his grave," a spectator said to Eichelberger. "You can bet on that," Dave answered. "I'll bet the USGA will do something."

Officials were alerted to the situation and they came speeding to the site. For the next hour everything went normally. Nicklaus didn't try it, nor did the notorious gambler Severiano Ballesteros. Then came Jerry Heard. He played down the 17th with a three-wood and a six-wood into a green-side bunker. He made a birdie. By then spectators were searching the skies for golf balls which seemed to be coming at them from all directions. Jim Simons came along later to birdie the hole and John Schroeder made par. At the end of the day, six players had taken the short cut. Three scored birdies and three made pars.

"I felt kind of ornery," Hinkle said later, "like I had been caught with my hands in the cookie jar. Now I feel sort of special because I did it first. This may be my only claim to fame in this Open." Hinkle had done something similar in the New Orleans Open in 1978. "I got three straight birdies going down the wrong fairway. I didn't try the fourth day, but I won the tournament by one stroke."

"I don't feel badly about what we did," Rodriguez said later. "I mean, I'd rather feel guilty and win than not feel guilty and lose."

Meanwhile, the USGA was trying to determine what should be done. Jim Hand, chairman of the championship committee, the man responsible for setting up the course for the Open, blamed himself for not seeing the opening when he inspected the course a month earlier. But now, what could be done to prevent players from going down the 17th? The USGA had two choices. One block the opening somehow. (Rodriguez speculated that we'd see the biggest hot dog stand in the world in that opening by the next day.) Two, move the tee markers forward, so that the tee shot would be played from a spot past the opening.

After some consideration, the USGA decided against moving the tee markers ahead because the integrity of the hole would be sacrificed by doing this. Instead, it decided to plant a tree in the opening. There was some precedence for this. Back in 1965, when the PGA Championship was played at the Laurel Valley Golf Club, in Ligonier, Pennsylvania, players were taking a short cut on the third hole during practice rounds. During the night before the tournament began, a 40-foot fir tree was planted in the path of the short cut and from then on nobody could take advantage of this defect in the design of the course.

Two things were different from the way the PGA and the USGA went about their problem. When the PGA did it, the deed was done before the tournament actually began. And they planted a real tree, an honest-to-gosh obstacle, which is still there and which was impossible to play around. When the USGA attempted it at Inverness, however, the tree was planted between rounds, after the tournament already had begun. And the tree was hardly an obstacle at all. It was a 24-foot, Black Hills spruce, 16 feet across at the base; and when it was set into the ground at 5 o'clock or so in the morning, it turned out to be a minor inconvenience, not an obstacle at all.

Players continued to hit down the 17th fairway, even though they did no better in relation to par than those who played the hole conventionally and even though there was a high risk of failure or miscalculation in choosing this route. It was as if the USGA had challenged them, and they had risen to the challenge. There is a breed of players, believe me, who like to do nothing so much as to tweak the mustache of the USGA. Of course, the drive to outwit the architect enters into the challenge, too, and there is nothing new in this. Bernard Darwin wrote of it in his classic book of essays, *Golf Between Two Wars:*

There is another difficulty in the way of the architects. The attitude of the general body of golfers towards them sometimes strikes me as like that of the public towards the police. Men know that they cannot get on without police and are in theory full of gratitude and admiration for them, but at the same time they are always on the watch to catch them out, and become on very slight provocation decidedly hostile. So the golfers are always ready to catch the architect tripping. They will not stand at his hands ingenuity that they think goes beyond a certain point. If he designs a hole with, as they think, too small a margin of safety; if the hole has too indistinct and baffling a skyline; if it calls for too exact an achievement; if it debars them from doing what they want to do and makes them do something that they don't want, they shout in chorus, "Away with it," and that hole, sometimes rightly no doubt but sometimes wrongly, has to go. The average golfer does not appreciate subtlety and if he thinks he is being "got at," he raises the flag of revolution.

I recall one hole which I saw essayed by the players of all four countries in international matches. The architect meant them to play it one way and they were resolved to play it another. This was a one-shot hole across something of a dip, of the length, for such good players, of a full spoon shot. The green was small; it was guarded in front, and behind it was a wilderness of really appalling trouble. To stop a full bang on that green was very nearly impossible, and its creator did not intend it to be possible. He had carefully designed a little place of safety, short and rather to the right, and he meant people to play an iron shot to this plateau and thence a run-up to the green, with a more or less certain four and the hope of a three. Would these lusty young internationals stoop to such a method? They would not. I only saw one, a very strong man, stop a big high spoon shot on that green. The rest were like the little man in *Pickwick* who killed himself in defense of his great principle that crumpets were wholesome. They killed themselves to prove that a hole that is within their reach must be reached in one shot. It may be that the hole was not entirely satisfactory and I am not saying whether those young gentlemen were right or wrong, intelligent or rather stupid. They were at least quite determined to revolt; they sacrificed themselves for a cause and I believe the hole has since been altered.

After the Open, the eighth at Inverness was not changed; but, instead, an entire grove of trees has been planted near the tee, and should the Open return there in some future year, no one will take that short cut again.

The birdie Hinkle made that day helped him shoot par 70 and he shared the first-round lead with Keith Fergus, Lou Graham, Andy Bean and Tom Purtzer. Another seven players were a stroke behind at 71. In this group were Jerry Pate, the 1976 champion, Tom Weiskopf, Jim Colbert, Bill Rogers, Larry Nelson, Dana Quigley and John Cook, the Amateur champion.

Inverness, which at first sight didn't look particularly terrifying, turned out to be a sterner test of golf than most of us imagined. For the first time since 1974, not one player shot in the 60s in the opening round, and for the entire day no one was able to dip more than two strokes under par at any time. The five players with the lowest scorers were: Bruce Lietzke, Bob Murphy, Hinkle, Fergus and Nelson. Hinkle and Fergus, of course, finished at 70, even par. Nelson shot 71, Murphy 72 and Lietzke 74. The wind and blazing sun baked the fairways and greens. "It was like trying to stop shots on pavements," Weiskopf said. "You could hit a great shot and get nothing for it." Dave Eichelberger five-putted the 12th, a par-three; and Don Iverson, a club professional and former tour player from LaCrosse, Wisconsin, took two consecutive sevens on par-four holes.

It was also a very long day. It took 14 hours for the 153-man field to complete play, and two men were penalized two strokes for slow play. The first penalty went to Thomas Innskeep, an amateur from Fort Wayne, Indiana, who was in a group which took an hour and 15 minutes to play five holes. The second was given to Brad Sherfy, from Los Angeles.

Even some of the good rounds were weird. Purtzer, for example, began with a bogey, a double bogey and a triple bogey within the first five holes. After a beginning like that, you're left wondering if you'll finish at all. But Purtzer did better than just finish. He made eight birdies during the day, though he played the first nine in 39 in spite of making three birdies.

His fifth hole (one of the new ones created by Fazio) was quite an adventure. It is a par-four of 401 yards which doglegs left at the drive zone. A stream borders the right side and a young oak tree stands sentinel at the left side of the bend. Unless the tee shot reaches past the tree, the fairway is made quite narrow by the overhanging branches. Purtzer pushed his tee shot too much to the right and into the stream. He took off his shoes and socks and hit the ball into the fairway. From there he played a seven iron over the green and under a bush. He had to play out left handed. Lying four. He chipped on and took two putts from 12 feet. "An easy seven."

Bad as he was on that nine, Purtzer was devastating coming back. He began by saving par on the 10th with a nice chip to a foot. After pars on the 11th and 12th, Purtzer birdied five of the last six holes. He rolled in a 12-footer on the 13th, struck a marvelous three-iron six inches from the hole on the 14th for a second birdie, dropped a 15-foot putt on the 15th, and a 12-footer on the 16th. He needed two putts to get down from 30 feet on the 17th, a 431-yard par-four which he reached with a nine-iron second. He closed out his round with another birdie at the 18th, holing a 10-foot putt, having played the second nine in 31 strokes.

Graham also had to do a lot of scrambling to save his round. He was out in 36 with two bogeys and a birdie and back in 34 with two birdies. The key to his round, though, was the way he saved five pars on the last 11 holes. He came out of a bunker to within six feet of the cup to save a five on the eighth hole. He chipped to within a foot of the cup on the 10th, pitched to four feet from the rough on the 14th, hit a seven-iron into a bunker on the 15th and came out four feet away, and hit into another bunker on the 16th and saved his third straight par.

Bean was two over after 10 holes, but he made three birdies in the last six holes and saved pars on two others, once from a bunker, and once from behind the green after he over clubbed on his approach. "The last six holes changed my round," Bean said. "The wind changed my strategy. I had to go to the driver and the three-wood where I had been using irons in practice. The wind was blowing in the other direction."

Of the co-leaders, only Keith Fergus made his move early. He was out in 33 with three birdies and a bogey. He came back in 37, one over par.

Nicklaus and Watson were disappointments. Nicklaus was in good shape coming to the 18th, only a stroke over par; but the last hole proved his undoing. The 18th at Inverness is perhaps the shortest finishing hole in modern Open history. It is only 357 yards long, but the green is set on a plateau and the ground falls off sharply all around. The green is small, and very slick. The right bank is very steep, and Nicklaus missed the green to the right. The hole was cut close to the right side, so Jack tried to play a soft little flip that would barely reach the green and trickle to the hole, but his shot didn't reach the green. Next, he deliberately bladed a wedge, a shot he uses often in situations such as this, but the ball ran well past the hole. He took two putts and staggered off the 18th with a double bogey six. He was now three over par.

"I think 72 would have been a good round today," Nicklaus said when it was over, "but 74 isn't a bad round, and a 69 or 70 tomorrow would put me back in there." Well, it didn't happen. He shot 77 the next day, and that was the end of him. A 72 followed in the third round and a 68 in the final round, but Nicklaus never really figured in the Open.

Watson made no excuse for his 75, but watching him, it was obvious that he was not on his game. His driving was erratic and nothing else was much better. Still, he tried to make a brave show, holding his hands out, palms up, as if to say, "What can you do?"

"I'm guiding the ball like a weekend golfer who's going bad," he admitted. "I'm not making very many free swings at it." That was pretty much of an understatement; he hit only 11 greens and only saved par once when he missed a green. Still, like the ant and the rubber tree, he had high hopes. "I don't feel like I'm out of the tournament yet," he claimed. "Nobody really made a move today, but I've got to relax and come out tomorrow with a fresh attitude."

The leaders after 18 holes:

Andy Bean	70	Bill Rogers	71
Keith Fergus	70	Jerry Pate	71
Lou Graham	70	Jim Colbert	71
Lon Hinkle	70	Larry Nelson	71
Tom Purtzer	70	Joe Inman	72
John Cook	71	Calvin Peete	72
Tom Weiskopf	71	Ed Sneed	72
Dana Quigley	71	Dale Douglass	72

Other scores of interest:

Isao Aoki	73	Arnold Palmer	76
Gary Player	73	Lee Trevino	77
Hale Irwin	74	Fuzzy Zoeller	77
Jack Nicklaus	74	Andy North	77
Tom Watson	75	Severiano Ballesteros	77

When the second round began, 12 players were within one stroke of one another. When it ended, two men—Tom Purtzer and Larry Nelson—were tied for the lead at 139 and only Hale Irwin was within three strokes of them. The field was stringing out, which was to be expected. Irwin was at 142, Bill Rogers was at 143 and six others were at 145, six strokes behind. Some players at least were beginning to get the hang of Inverness. Irwin and Nelson had both shot 68s and Purtzer shot a 69.

The temperature had hovered around 90 most of the day, and a gusty wind played games with the golfers. The 36-hole cut fell at 151, the highest it had been in five years. Andy Bean, one of the leaders at 18 holes, shot 76; John Cook, the Amateur champion, went from 71 to 80; Keith Fergus went from 70 to 77; Lou Graham went from 70 to 75; Lon Hinkle went from 70 to 77; Dana Quigley from 71 to 78 and Bob Murphy from 72 to 79. Some of the leaders hung on. Tom Weiskopf and Jerry Pate shot 74 after their opening 71s; Rogers went from 71 to 72.

Despite the newly transplanted spruce tree, some players continued to play down the 17th fairway. Even before he putted out on the seventh, Hinkle climbed to a slight knoll behind the green, looked at the eighth tee and grinned broadly. When it was his turn to play the eighth, he hesitated for a moment and then spoke to the marshal on duty.

"Take down the rope over there," he said. "And the stakes, too." The crowd cheered. He looked over at the 17th, saw George Burns and John Schroeder and signaled to them that he intended to play down the 17th fairway. He hit the ball left and heard it nick some branches as it narrowly missed the spruce.

"I don't see it," he said.

"Perfect," someone called to him. Then Schroeder waved his hands back and forth, palms downward, like an umpire signaling "safe." It was, as it turned out, a good shot.

Chi Chi Rodriguez teed his ball on the butt end of a scoring pencil (he had hollowed out the end in the shape of a shallow cup with the metal instrument normally used to repair ball pits on greens) and sent a shot flying over the top of the tree. "That's nothing but a Christmas tree," he said scornfully. Perhaps, but his tee shot rolled into the rough, he hit a tree with his second shot, and made a bogey six.

Hinkle under clubbed his second, using a seven-iron. His ball dropped short of the green into a bunker, but he came out and holed an eight-foot putt for his second birdie on the hole in two days. It was, however, the last bright moment of his day; he shot 38 on the first nine and 39 on the second for 77. The next day he shot 76 and finished with 81. On his next two tries at the eighth, he made a par and a bogey.

No one paid attention to Norman during those first two days because he played the hole conventionally both times. On the second day he played a driver from the tee, a two-iron onto the green and holed his putt for an eagle three.

Meanwhile, Watson, who had talked bravely about turning his game around, was having no luck at all. His driving was completely undependable: He would drive into the right rough on one hole, into the left on another. As he walked toward his ball, he'd occasionally stop and take a mock practice swing, trying to pin down the cause of his problems. He began the round terribly. His tee shot went into the right rough, he took three more to reach the green and three-putted for a seven, three over par. He made another seven on the eighth, where once again he drove into the rough and put his second shot in a hazard.

Watson was out in 42, but as he began his homeward nine, birdies on the 10th and 11th gave him a brief glimpse of hope. Soon, however, the hope evaporated. He drove into a bunker on the 13th hole, a 523-yard par-five, played a seven-iron out, hit his third shot over the green and struggled to a bogey six. His round became truly hopeless on the 14th. He hooked his tee shot into the bank of a horseshoe-shaped bunker, walked into it very quickly and, instead of accepting the loss of that stroke, he tried to reach the green with his second, using a fairway wood. The shot he played was pitiful; he pulled it far left behind a row of trees which separate the 14th and 15th fairways. He was blocked from the green completely, though somehow he managed to make a bogey five. He picked up two more birdies coming in, but it was clear that Watson was finished. In the second nine, he shot a very respectable 35, but he had a total of 152, a stroke above the cut. "I was embarrassed," he said later. "I can't describe it in any one word. It was sloppy, careless. It was a day when I didn't have much control. It was disappointing. There is no excuse for the way I played. I had a lack of feel and a lack of confidence."

Purtzer seemed to be playing equally erratically, but with much better results. Purtzer, at that time, was 27 years old. A graduate of Arizona State University, he had been on the pro tour since 1975 and had already won the 1977 Los Angeles Open. He wasn't quite as unstable as he had been in the first round, but he was bad enough. He was two over par for the first 10 holes and he birdied four of the last eight. The previous day he birdied five of the last six.

In spite of his success, he was downright embarrassed by his tee shot on the 18th. He played a three-wood and hit the ball wildly, into the crowd to the right of the hole. The ball rolled onto a shirt lying on the grass. "If you can shank a wood," Purtzer said sheepishly, "that's what I did. I looked up and saw someone running for cover. It was the worst shot off the tee I can remember. I can't believe anyone on the pro tour could hit the ball that badly, but I did."

Because the ball was lying on the shirt, Purtzer could lift the ball and drop it without penalty. He was about 135 yards from the hole, and he hit a wedge about as well as it can be played, dropping the ball a foot from the hole, and ran in the putt for a birdie three. He overshot the second green, under clubbed on the fifth and went into a bunker, hit a three-wood tee shot into deep rough on the 10th, and bogeyed all three holes. Then his luck changed. He birdied the 11th with a 10-foot putt, holed a 25-footer on the 13th after driving into the rough, drove into the rough at 16, played a wedge short of the green and chipped in from 40 feet. "I easily could have shot 75 or 76 today," he admitted when it was over.

Nelson's position at the head of the field was possibly more surprising to him than to anyone else. He had been playing so poorly in the practice rounds on Monday and Tuesday that he telephoned his wife and told her he'd probably see her on Saturday. He changed his mind after he shot 70 on Thursday, but was still amazed that he had tied for the lead on Friday, at 139, three under par. First of all, nature was working against him. When he awoke on Friday morning, the wind was blowing at 15 to 20 miles an hour and Nelson had a late starting time. By the time he teed off, the greens would be dried out which, indeed, they were by the time he got to them.

"I just didn't think there would be any low scores today," he said. "Then, I got to the course and saw that Purtzer had 69 and Irwin 68."

He began his round with a bogey on the first hole, having missed a putt of about six feet. But he kept plugging away, trying to keep his approaches below the hole. He finally made up that stroke with a birdie on the fifth, placing his five-iron approach within four feet of the hole. He made another birdie at the ninth, again from inside four feet; went two under on the 11th, where he holed a 25-footer, his only sizeable putt of the day; at the 13th, he dropped another four-footer to go three under; hit a seven-iron within three feet of the hole on the 16th to go four under; and then lost that stroke with a bogey five on the 17th.

"I'm where I am," Nelson said, "because I haven't had too many putts from above the hole. I think I've three-putted only twice."

The leaders after two rounds:

Tom Purtzer	70–69—139	Lou Graham	70–75—145
Larry Nelson	71–68—139	Jim Colbert	71–74—145
Hale Irwin	74–68—142	Ed Sneed	72–73—145
Tom Weiskopf	71–74—145	Dave Stockton	75–70—145
Jerry Pate	71–74—145		

Other scores of interest:

Andy Bean	70–76—146	Chi Chi Rodriguez	73–76—149
David Graham	73–73—146	Lee Trevino	77–73—150
Gary Player	73–73—146	Andy North	77–74—151
Arnold Palmer	76–73—149	Jack Nicklaus	74–77—151

Some who missed the 36-hole cut:

Tom Watson	75–77—152	Severiano	
Raymond Floyd	76–76—152	Ballesteros	79–81—160
Johnny Miller	74–78—152	Hsu Sheng San	79–84—163

The outcome of the 1979 United States Open championship was actually determined on the third day. When it began, Hale Irwin was three strokes behind Tom Purtzer and Larry Nelson. When it ended, he was five strokes ahead of Purtzer and six ahead of Nelson.

It was also the best-scoring day of the championship. The wind was light, the pin placements were not very severe and more of the players were on their games. No one had broken 70 in the first round and only three shot under 70 in the second; but in the third round, nine players were under 70. Irwin and Weiskopf both shot 67; Andy North had a slight revival and shot 68 and six players shot 69.

Sometimes it seems as if one good round feeds another. Weiskopf was paired with Jerry Pate, third from the last group off the tee, and Irwin was with Bill Rogers just behind them. They could see how well the others were doing and they seemed to respond. When the round ended, Irwin had 209, Weiskopf was next at 212, and Pate was at 214, tied with Purtzer, whose misdeeds finally caught up with him. He shot 75. Nelson shot 76 and was another stroke behind at 215.

Weiskopf, Irwin and Pate played inspired golf, hitting one glorious shot after another. The day reached its climax on No. 13, where Weiskopf made an eagle three and Irwin rolled one in right after it.

It was somehow fitting that Weiskopf should threaten to win the Open at Inverness. "My Dad brought me to the 1957 Open here," he said one afternoon. "I was 15. I watched Sam Snead and Cary Middlecoff as if they were gods. I knew right then that this was the life for me."

Weiskopf had been close in the Open before. In 1976, it looked as if he, Al Geiberger and Jerry Pate might tie, but then Pate hit that memorable five-iron three feet from the cup on the final hole and won. The following year Weiskopf was third and he was fourth in 1978. But he has never won, and the prospects that he would win in 1979 were not very good; for he was in the midst of a rotten year.

"It wasn't until three weeks ago that my health was worth a damn," he told a friend. "My stomach was in terrible shape. I finally went into the hospital in March and they found an ulcer." He lost 18 pounds and his golf suffered. He had other problems, too. Two weeks after he learned of his ulcer, his house in Arizona burned to the ground. "I wasn't in a very good frame of mind when the Masters came around. I was really messed up. The doctors put me on a stricter diet, and the weight began to return." At the time of the Open, he was up to 186 pounds, not a bad weight for a man 6-foot-4, and his attitude seemed better.

"Don't make it sound as if I came out of my deathbed to come here," he said. "It's been a bad six months, worse than any I've ever gone through, but I've learned from it. I'll be okay now. When it comes to golf," he went on, "I'm a traditionalist. I think winning the British Open, the U.S. Open, the Masters and the PGA is where the real proof of your accomplishments lie. I've had a lot of good chances to win these four tournaments, but I've only won the British Open. But every time I come close, like I am now with 18 holes to go, I get a great thrill from it." Then he reflected a little. "There are some young kids watching us in 1979; maybe some even think of us as something special. Maybe one of them will be in a U.S. Open in 10 or 15 years, telling his story like I'm telling mine. That, for me, is a thrilling thought."

Weiskopf played a very fine 33 on the front nine, nine holes which were a bit more rocky than one might think. Five times, for example, he got down in one putt, twice for birdies. He holed putts from 12 feet on the first and from seven feet on the third and three times he one-putted for pars.

Irwin was out in 34, playing erratically. He had four pars, three birdies and two bogeys. He birdied both the second and third, and canceled those two strokes with bogeys on the sixth and seventh. Then he birdied the eighth, dropping a sand wedge third within eight feet of the hole.

By then, Nelson was dropping out of the fight. He was four over par after six holes and had made a six on the fourth, at 466 yards the hardest par on the course. As we know, he ended with 76 for the day. Purtzer was hanging on with 36 out, but he was about to shoot 39 on the second nine to finish with his 75.

Irwin went three under par for the day with successive birdies on the 11th and 12th, then showed just how tough he can be in a tight situation. As I said, he was playing immediately behind Weiskopf, who began the day three strokes behind him and had picked up one on the first nine. Irwin was watching every stroke Weiskopf played and he was giving him a very close look on the 13th. Weiskopf had played a fine drive on this hole, a 523-yard par-five, if you remember.

There was a time when a hole such as this was as fine a par-five as you can imagine. The drive zone rolls and tumbles downhill toward a flat area which leads to a creek cutting squarely across the fairway. From the far bank of the creek, the ground rises to a slick green protected on the left by a long, narrow bunker, and on the right by a smaller bunker. Twenty-two years earlier the rise was allowed to grow into rough, but it was clipped fairway in 1979. Also, 22 years earlier players weren't hitting the ball so far. In 1957, some of the Open field lay up off the tee so that the second shot could be played from a level lie.

By 1979, however, the way to play the hole was to hit the tee shot as far as you could and go beyond that area of rolling ground. Weiskopf, a man who can hit the ball enormous distances, did just that. He had only a four-iron shot to the green, hit it crisply, and the ball rolled to a stop just eight feet from the hole. He holed the putt for the eagle and was only a stroke behind Irwin.

Irwin had seen Weiskopf's shot and he knew he had to do something. He played his tee shot down the left side, where there is also a level spot to the side of a finger of high ground. When Weiskopf holed his putt, Irwin pressed his lips together, said something to his caddie about making an eagle of his own, and drew out his two-iron. The shot he played was absolutely classic. Irwin, however, has always been a superb long-iron player. When he won his first Open in 1974, he hit a glorious two-iron onto the 18th at Winged Foot. This shot was every bit as good. It soared toward the pin and came down just three feet from the hole. The shot had traveled 225 yards. He made the putt, of course, and with that, won the Open. That eagle put him five under par for the day, and four strokes ahead of Weiskopf.

"It was inspiring to see Tom make his eagle," Irwin said at the end of the day. "Seeing him do something like that made me feel more aggressive. It's a great feeling to know you are capable of getting two strokes back on someone like him. I hit that two-iron as good as I can hit it."

Both men had problems on the 14th. Weiskopf drove into a stand of trees and to recover had to play his ball out to the other side of the fairway. He hit the ball too hard and it landed close to another tree, still not on the green. He chipped on and holed a short putt for a bogey.

While this was going on, Irwin had to wait and there was little doubt that the delay had an effect. Hale pushed his tee shot into the right rough, played his second shot left of the green, pitched on and two-putted, also for a bogey. He followed with another bogey on the 15th, where he was short of the green with his second.

In the meantime, Weiskopf had birdied the 15th and cut the deficit to two strokes. Irwin, however, increased his lead to three strokes once again before finishing at the end of the day.

The third round leaders were:

Hale Irwin	209	Tom Purtzer	214
Tom Weiskopf	212	Larry Nelson	215
Jerry Pate	214	Lee Elder	215

Irwin was last off the tee on Sunday, the final day, paired with Weiskopf, just behind Pate and Purtzer. It was a strange day. It began with both Pate and Purtzer making strong runs at the lead, then dropping back; and it ended with Irwin almost throwing away the championship.

If anyone was going to challenge Irwin that last day, it looked as if it would be Purtzer. He birdied the first hole with a lovely pitch within a few feet of the hole, added another birdie on the second, parred the third, and then ran in a very long putt for his third birdie on the fourth. He had played the first four holes in threes.

Pate wasn't far behind. He began with a par-four on the first and followed with birdies on both the second and third and another par on the fourth. At that stage, Purtzer was one under par and Pate was one over. Irwin, playing a hole behind, had birdied the second but lost a stroke on the third, and so he was still four under par, pulling away from Weiskopf. Tom bogeyed the first two holes, but then parred the third.

At that stage, with Irwin and Weiskopf on the fourth tee and Purtzer and Pate on the fifth, they stood like this in relation to par:

Irwin	−4	Pate	+ 1
Purtzer	−1	Weiskopf	+ 3

This, however, was the end of the road for Purtzer and Pate, because at that point they began to play some very sloppy golf. On the fifth hole, Pate carried his approach over the green and into a bunker. He hit his sand shot a bit thin and sailed it back over the green. Then he stubbed a chip shot and when he finished he had a six. Pate was not out of it quite yet, but he soon would be. Purtzer had his troubles with No. 5 as well, and made five.

Purtzer's bid died on the eighth, that controversial par-five. Both he and Pate tried the short cut. Pate's ball landed just off the fairway, but Purtzer's shot went very wild. After clearing the spruce, the ball began to curl right and carried nearly to the bottom of a ravine. I don't know how it threaded its way through those trees, but when Purtzer found it, he had absolutely no shot. He could do nothing more than pop the ball out of the trees and into a clearing of high grass. From there he pitched over the trees blocking the green, but onto the edge of a bunker. When he tried to play from the sand to the green, his ball knicked the limb of a tree and fell into another bunker. He was on in five, down in two, for seven. He didn't figure again. Pate, meanwhile, had to struggle, but he still made par-five. He died on the next hole, however, when he drove into some trees and made six, losing two strokes to par. Pate and Purtzer both played the first nine in 37.

The pressure on Irwin, meanwhile, was intense. Not that anyone was closing in, but it is only natural that breathing becomes difficult if you are leading the final round of the United States Open championship. Irwin had felt the pressure the night before and had very little sleep. "The last time I looked at a clock," said Hale's wife, Sally, "it was 3 A.M. and Hale was still awake. When I woke up at 6 A.M., he was awake, too."

"I was so pumped up I didn't want to eat," Irwin tried to explain, "and I was hungry. In the middle of the night, my stomach was growling."

Irwin began the last round well enough, holing a six-foot putt for the birdie on the second, but he hit over the green on the third onto a spectator's blanket. He was given a free drop, but still bogeyed the hole. He lost another stroke on the fifth, where he three-putted from 30 feet, and he seemed in trouble again on the seventh, a 452-yard par-four (perhaps the finest hole on the course, even though it hasn't a single bunker). Irwin's tee shot made him shake his head as it headed into the heavy rough and among the little chocolate drop mounds lining the left side. When he found it, Irwin first drew an iron club from his bag. Then he studied the lie for a moment, changed his mind, drew a five-wood from his bag, slashed the ball from the grass and sent it to the back of the green. He made his par.

Irwin then got perhaps the best break of anyone in that Open. His tee shot on the eighth went astray, soaring far to the right into the trees. As you stood there and saw the ball disappear, and heard its sound clattering back among those trees, you had to think that Irwin was about to throw the Open away. Miraculously, the ball careened back out of the trees and dropped onto the fairway. Irwin had a clear shot.

From there, he played his second to within 80 yards of the green. It left him a simple pitch, but he hit the ball badly. It came off the club a little low and obviously was about to skip over the green into the crowd. But, no! It hit a yard short of the flagstick, banged into the pin and stopped eight feet away. He holed it for a birdie. Therefore, when Irwin parred the ninth, he seemed to be coasting home. He was six strokes ahead of Weiskopf and seven ahead of Purtzer and Pate.

While this was going on, Gary Player was making a move. He had gone into the last round trailing Irwin by nine strokes at 218. When he went out, he believed he could win if he shot 66, although it hadn't been done yet. But when he began with a bogey five, it certainly didn't look possible, and actually, it wasn't. Player birdied both the 17th and 18th and finished with 68 and 286, two over par.

As Irwin turned for home, he was still four under par and six ahead of Player. Tee shots, however, were still causing him trouble. At the 10th, he played a three-wood from the tee and hit it to the right, into a fairway bunker. From there he played a nine-iron onto the green 10 feet from the hole. Par. On the 11th, he played his three-wood behind a tree. Bogey. At the 12th, a 167-yard par-three, his eight-iron settled seven feet from the hole and he ran it in for a birdie.

It was his last birdie of the Open. From then on, it became not so much a matter of coasting in, but of surviving. Everything he hit seemed to go off line. He drove into the left rough on the 13th, had to lay up short of the creek with his second, pitched on and two-putted for par. He continued to have trouble driving into a bunker on the 14th and losing a stroke, not only to par but also to Weiskopf, who parred.

Irwin was then four strokes ahead. He saved par on the 15th after placing his second in a greenside bunker. He came out within two feet of the hole and made the putt. Irwin seemed to seal his championship with a fine straight drive down the 16th, an eight-iron onto the green and two putts for another par. Weiskopf bogeyed and Irwin once again had five strokes in hand with two holes to play.

Now came the dramatic part of the last day. From the 17th tee Irwin played another three-wood and again lost it into the right rough. His five-iron came down short and left of the green in a bunker. When he played out, it seemed as if there was not much sand in the bunker; consequently, the ball sailed over the green. He chipped back, but the ball took the downhill roll and ran perhaps 12 feet past. He two-putted for six.

Here was an opportunity for Weiskopf to pick up a couple of strokes and put added pressure on Irwin. Instead, Weiskopf ended out of second place, a stroke behind Pate and Player, both in with 286, two over par. Weiskopf was three over.

Irwin was one under par, three ahead of Pate and Player, and only a tragedy could keep him from winning. Still, he played shakily. His tee shot drifted into the right rough. The hole was cut just about where it had been in 1957—in the lower left corner, tight behind the two frontal bunkers and close against the single bunker on the left. Irwin played a nine-iron and pulled it a little. The ball dropped into the left bunker. Judging from the way he hit his explosion shot on the previous hole, anything might happen here. Certainly the Open wasn't over yet.

Then he played as good a shot as one can ask for under those circumstances. The ball settled about six feet from the hole and that was it. He missed the first putt, but it didn't matter. The second putt dropped; Irwin had the Open by two strokes with 284, matching par for 72 holes. Pate and Player had finished with 286.

Later, when he had time to reflect on what had happened, Irwin talked about his second Open. "Finishing with a double bogey and a bogey is not my idea of championship golf, but it's two strokes better than the next guy and that's all that counts. It was the hardest day of work—I can't call it golf—that I've ever had. At no time did I feel I was safe. It was especially hard because this is a tournament I wanted to win very badly. I sure didn't want to throw it away, but this was not your casual round of Sunday golf. I built up a sizable lead and I didn't know what to do with it. I wanted to play perfect golf, but I also hoped they would get into trouble. If you want to say the whole field choked, they did, but this is the U.S. Open, not the USGA better ball or interclub championship."

Irwin couldn't explain his lack of control. "My woods were terrible," he said. "I couldn't hit the fairway with a three-wood—or anything. I didn't play around the driver, I played the club I thought I should use, but I couldn't hit any of them straight."

Still, he was extraordinarily pleased with the victory, as he should have been. "This is fantastic," he beamed. "This means so much to me. I think my star will shine a little brighter. Very few men have won two Opens. You'd have to be sitting here to know how proud of myself I feel."

4

THE BRITISH OPEN

Lawson Little once delared that the man who wins championships is the man who plays his bad shots best. He was entitled to pontificate. In his day, he was the nonpareil among amateurs, winning the championships of both the United States and Britain in successive years: 1934 and 1935. One of those victories was achieved at Royal Lytham and St. Annes, where the 1979 British Open Championship was played and won by the man who undoubtedly played his bad shots best. Severiano Ballesteros hit and held only a handful of fairways in his last two rounds and yet beat Jack Nicklaus and Ben Crenshaw by three strokes.

Oddly enough, when Little won at Lytham, he played just about as badly as he had played well the year before, but he played his bad shots better than his opponents and won the tag, "The Man Who Could Play Matches."

In Little's day, Lytham measured only about 150 yards shorter than it did a generation and a half later; but in the years between, the shrubs and brushwood, rare hazards on a seaside course in Britain, have grown formidably and have added to the perils of the course. There is heather, too, and broom, imported from a member's Scottish grouse moor when the course was laid out nearly a century ago. Usually seaside links in Britain are as nature created them, but at Lytham the hand of man has been unusually active. Here and there mounds have been created to add variety and, incidentally, vantage points for spectators. The result is one of the most demanding examinations in golf to be found anywhere. True, the examination paper is rather ill-balanced. Three of the four one-shot holes are in the first nine along with two of the three par-fives.

And yet, in the conditions prevailing throughout the 1979 championship, even the long sixth and seventh were pushover birdies for anyone who could keep his drive in play. For four days the wind blew hard and cold out of the northwest, just as it had done five years earlier when Gary Player produced some of the best golf of his distinguished career and won easily with 282, the only total below par. (He had three rounds of 69, 68, and 70, and faltered only in his third round of 75.)

Severiano Ballesteros has the British Open trophy to himself.

So distance downwind was no object, but it was a different story coming home, where there was one par-five, the 11th, and one par-three, the 12th. The rest were nominally par-fours, but in the conditions on each of the four days of the championship, two of these holes, the 468-yard 15th and the 453-yard 17th, were par-fives for all but a few of the longest and straightest hitters. Even Nicklaus once had to go with wood at the 15th after a perfect drive, and even then he just made the front edge of the green. Twice he had to fire one-irons for his second to the 17th to finish pin high.

In 1974, the fairways were iron and the rough thin and accommodating except in patches. This time the fairways were firm but better grassed and the rough long and tenacious, almost up to the fringe of some greens. It was therefore a sterner test, made the more searching because the wind was bitterly cold, driving sharp showers of rain, and the sun shone only fleetingly.

No American or other overseas entrant who had played in 1974 and again in 1979 can be blamed if he thinks twice about entering the next Open at Lytham. When you have to wear three or four sweaters and rain pants to keep warm in mid-summer, and furry mitts like Bob Charles and a wind-proof jacket like Ballesteros between shots, the problem of keeping the ball in play and your heart high is almost more than the human spirit can endure. It is then that, in order to survive, resolution and stamina, to say nothing of technique, must be generously spiced with patience.

Great players like Tom Watson were blown to oblivion on the final day. Even so meticulous a technician as Hale Irwin, the laurels of his recent Open triumph at Inverness still fresh on his intellectual brow, looked exhausted as he soared to a final 78. A par round would have earned him the rare achievement of winning both championships in the same year and thus setting himself alongside Bob Jones, Sarazen, Hogan and Trevino.

Although the conditions were slightly worse in 1979 than five years earlier, scoring was on the whole slightly better. In 1974, only six scores below 70 were returned over the four days; in 1979, there were twice as many. The cut-off after two rounds in 1974 was 156 (14 over par); in 1979, it was four strokes fewer. After three rounds, the cut-off was 231 in 1974; five years later it was 227.

Some of the improvement was due to the fact that in 1974 the 1.68 ball was used for the first time in the Open Championship. Players were, therefore, not as ready to handle the big ball in a big wind on British links as they are now. Player, it is true, insisted in 1974 that it had made no difference to him, but he was sailing along on Cloud 9 all that year and could have won playing with a doughnut and an umbrella.

One measure of the severity of the conditions in 1979 was given on the first day by Nicklaus, as experienced and knowledgeable a golfer as there is in the entire world. When he heard that an unknown British golfer, Bill Longmuir, from an obscure course in Essex, had returned a first-round score of 65, he expressed vigorous disbelief. It must be a fiction, he insisted, "and the player's name's fictitious, too." But it was true, and reminds one of the famous quotation by an old Scotsman informed of a similar improbability, "It's no' possible, but it's a fact!"

Admittedly, Longmuir, whose only previous achievements had been to win a tournament on the Safari circuit in Africa and one in New Zealand (to say nothing of a personality contest he had entered some years earlier when he was strapped for cash), had rather the better of the weather. Starting early, he also had the best of the greens, although they were as near perfect as human skill and loving care could produce for the whole week.

In brief, he went out in 29 against a nominal par of 35, although the sixth and seventh were easily within reach of two shots and thus par was, in fact, 33. Still, his score equaled the lowest outward nine ever accomplished in the Open and that put his name into the record books. He had five successive birdies from the third through the seventh, parred the eighth and shot his second two at the ninth. He birdied the 10th and had another two at the 12th, consisting of a fiendishly difficult and long one-shotter, played into a wind which swept loose shots out of bounds. He was then eight under par.

Of course, he could not keep it up. Under the prevailing conditions, the last five holes were so difficult that one expert, Peter Alliss, the former British Ryder Cup player, reckoned that any good golfer would be content with dropping only two strokes to par over that stretch. That is precisely what Longmuir did. He took fives at the 445-yard 14th and the 468-yard 15th, but then finished like a lion with three par-fours. He had to hole uncomfortably long putts for his fours at the last two, but hole them he did, and shot 36 coming home for a round of 65.

Just how good a score it was became more clear as the day wore on. Nobody got within three strokes of Longmuir. Hale Irwin came closest with 68. That was a remarkable round because he took 35 to the turn, which was virtually two over par that day, and then came home in 33, which was unbelievably good. Not only was the back nine desperately difficult in the wind, but the holes were cut in awkward positions, notably at the 13th and 16th, where the flags were placed close to the windward edge of the green. The drive had to be placed at the exact spot on the left of the fairway to allow a pitch to the flag. Irwin managed to do this.

Jerry Pate, the former U.S. Open champion, was able to control his long, slow swing in the high wind and his score of 69 put him in third place. The only other score under par was a 70 by Isao Aoki of Japan, who had played admirably and had putted miraculously the previous year at St. Andrews. His swing is the worst-looking of anyone in the top class, but he does obey one categorical imperative enunciated a century ago by Sir Walter Simpson: "The ball must be hit." It is his putting, however, that sets him apart from other players. He cocks up the toe of the club, addresses the ball off the heel, grips and stands as though he were playing a chip shot rather than a putt, and then knocks the ball into the hole from any distance. He does everything wrong and yet gets the right result.

Jack Nicklaus played the sort of round we have come to expect from him at the start of the Open Championship—a 72. It could have been several strokes fewer; and it could also have been at least two strokes more, for he had the rare bonus of a hole-in-one at the fifth, which helped him to go out in 32, three under par. The long, difficult inward half proved more difficult even with his great power and his cerebral control of both himself and his strokes. Well, he did reach the 15th in two shots and only a handful of players had done that all day. And he also reached the 17th in two, but he took rather feeble fives at the drive-and-pitch 16th and at the last hole, where the second shot was no more than a medium iron for him. That added up to 40 home. Not bad, but nothing close to what he or his legion of admirers would have liked.

Tom Watson, most people thought, had the sort of method which would hold together well in the wind; but he began rather tentatively and took 37 to the turn, five strokes more than Nicklaus, eight more than the unlikely Longmuir. However, he birdied the long 11th into the teeth of the wind and that seemed to settle him. He played the last seven holes each in par and there he was, also at 72.

Ben Crenshaw, who putts like an angel, played a very odd round. He began horribly, dropping a stroke at each of the first three holes, which were, of course, downwind. But, as most did, he birdied the sixth and seventh, and got out in 37. He still had his anxious moments, notably at the 15th, where he had to come out of sand and hole the putt to escape a two over par six. But he drove beautifully the whole way home, missing only one fairway, and he thoroughly deserved his inward 35. He ended with a round of 72 to join Nicklaus and Watson.

Gary Player, who had won so handsomely on the same course five years earlier, never got his game together and took 77. His disappointment may have been eased a little because his son, Wayne, playing a couple of holes in front of him, finished two strokes ahead of him. Johnny Miller and Hubert Green also took 77, Miller having destroyed himself at the 17th, where he took a seven. Lots of players, indeed, were literally at sixes and sevens, many of them collected at, of all places, a short hole—the 12th—where nearly a dozen players sliced out of bounds.

Like Player, Tony Jacklin was revisiting the scene of a great personal triumph, in his case 10 years earlier. He was paired with Fuzzy Zoeller, the Masters champion, and Masashi (Jumbo) Ozaki, the Japanese siege gun. Zoeller, who had allowed himself little time to adjust to British conditions of course and climate, or to recover from jet lag, played cheerfully but indifferently for nine holes and, like Jacklin, reached the turn in 37. When he started back with a brace of birdies, it looked as though Augusta had bred a possible challenger. But his tee shot to the 12th was swept out of bounds and he never recovered from the triple bogey six he suffered there. He limped home in 41 for a 78, and clearly his chance was gone.

Jacklin fared better. He had to struggle, possibly because his tempo is now swifter than it was in his great days, but he had recaptured his putting touch and also his talent for bunker play. It was almost like old times when he holed a good putt at the last hole for a three and ended with a 73, to the great delight of the loyal masses in the bleachers.

Ballesteros, who was to stand the golfing world on its ear three days later, was a very late starter, paired with Trevino and the pencil-slim Ken Brown, a young British Ryder Cup player, who is one of the slowest players on the circuit but also one of the world's great putters. Trevino and Ballesteros like to get on with it and, although both started steadily enough, for a time it looked as though Brown's painstaking play might affect them. But all three performed handsomely, considering that they finished in the chill of the evening long after the dinner gongs had rung through the hotels of St. Annes. Trevino came in with par 71, Brown with 72, and El Cid from Spain with 73.

Trevino's 71 was matched by three other players: the little known but appropriately-named Terry Gale from Australia; the old warrior Orville Moody from America; and Britain's own Peter McEvoy, Amateur champion in 1977 and 1978 and leading amateur at St. Andrews the year before. McEvoy is a strong golfer who is used to playing in the best company (he has played in the Masters), and he finished Wednesday with a fine flourish, a bunker shot to within a couple of inches at the last hole.

Thursday's weather was a carbon copy of Wednesday's. Again, the wind was out of the northwest and blowing strongly, not a cruel wind, but a good deal more than a stiff breeze. Again, it was bitterly cold and waterproof trousers were almost standard dress. Yet, miraculously, scoring was better than on the first day. Maybe the players had come to terms with the conditions. Maybe they had learned something from that first round. Whatever the reason, there were three times as many scores below par on the second day as the first.

One of these came from an early starter, at the uncharitable hour of 8:30 A.M. Mark James, a former British Walker Cup player who was fifth in the Open Championship at Birkdale in 1976, played some wonderful iron shots on the road home to come back in 35 for a round of 69. He has a swing so short it could be accommodated in a telephone booth, rather like the style of Doug Sanders; and, like Sanders, he has wonderful hands and can maneuver the ball with uncommon skill. Unlike Sanders, he is no laughing cavalier of the links, as he played four days straight before he was seen smiling. On Thursday he attacked the course as though he hated it, which he probably did, having had three sixes on the back nine in his previous round of 76. At the very least, he showed on the second day that the course could be tamed if one had the nerve and talent to do it.

One of his playing partners, Tom Kite, showed just such nerve and talent, at least for the first nine holes. He began with two birdies, had two more birdies at the sixth and seventh, and was out in 32. He is such a methodical, neat player, with no extravagances of style or demeanor, that he seemed headed for a good score to add to his first-round 73. But the inward nine destroyed him. He took 42 to stagger home for 74 and 147.

Kite's story was not uncommon. Jerry Pate went out in 34 with twos at the first and ninth, but took 40 back for an aggregate score of 143 for the two days. Mark Hayes fared even worse. He went out in 31 and, alas, took 44 on the return.

Longmuir, the first-day hero, carried a terrific burden because no one expected him to survive. After dropping a couple of strokes in the first four holes he played with admirable composure, and, although he took a terrible six at the 15th and dropped two strokes to par there, he finished like a Scottish lion with a birdie at 16, a five at No. 17 (which was virtually par for the hole that day), and a three at the last hole, where he holed a long putt to his own and the gallery's manifest delight. A 74 under those playing conditions was eminently respectable. A 74 by a man unknown to fame 24 hours earlier was a triumph of character.

Zoeller pulled himself together and shot a 72, which might have been even better if more of his putts had dropped. Jacklin, too, missed enough putts to drop some strokes and his 74 put him too far behind to offer much of a chance to repeat his 1969 triumph.

Tom Watson was the first of the great men to make a genuine challenge. He is such a compact player, with such sure and strong hands, that he looks capable of anything. Mainly because he was driving uncertainly, he was not at his best Thursday, and he had to work uncommonly hard for his figures; but he played one shot that was the admiration of all. At the formidable short 12th, he let his tee shot get away from him and he was rather lucky that the ball did not bounce out of bounds. It came to rest on sand at the edge of a road, with a bunker and a steep bank between him and the flag. He nipped the ball off the hard surface and pulled it up four feet short of the hole. Fortified by that brave three, he came home in 36 for a splendid 68 and a halfway 140, two under par.

Then came the round of the day, in fact, the round of the championship, possibly the greatest round ever played in the Open in all its long history since young Tom Morris played the 12 holes of Prestwick in 47 strokes in 1870. Severiano Ballesteros went around in 65.

It can be argued that this merely equaled Longmuir's score of the previous day, but the rebuttal is: It is one thing for an unknown to have his day of days and produce the round of his life, but it is an entirely different matter for an established player, one of the favorites for the title, to produce such a score. His first round of 73 had left him little leeway. Another 73 would have put Ballesteros out of contention, but his 65 put him right in the middle of it, though not, as it turned out, in the lead.

But even more remarkable than his score was the way he did it. He went out in 33, which was just what a player of his caliber should do. Then he slipped a little and, after 13 holes, was over par for the tournament, and two under for the round, with the fearsome five finish to come. Trevino, one of his playing partners, was even after 13 and his other partner, Ken Brown, was one under.

Then Ballesteros rose to his might—and what might it was. He was reported to have been given a tip by the ever-helpful Trevino which improved his long shots, something about releasing his left side. Tip or no tip, Ballesteros proceeded to go crazy. He got a three at the difficult 14th with a good putt, another three at the diabolic 15th, where, short in two, he holed a short pitch. He missed from about eight feet for his birdie at the relatively easy 16th, but pounded onto the 17th green with two stupendous shots and holed from 20 feet for another birdie. Then at the 18th, where he hooked his drive onto the downslope of the back of a bunker, he manufactured some sort of push shot of about 160 yards into the cross wind which landed a few feet from the hole and so he got still another three.

He had played the fearsome final five holes in 3 3 4 3 3 —four under par on a day when many players reckoned par was 4 5 4 5 4. So he came back in 32, making up no fewer than seven strokes on Trevino, who finished with 73 for 144, and six strokes on Brown, who finished with 71 for 143.

When Hale Irwin, who started two hours after Ballesteros, was told what the Spaniard had done he was dumbfounded. "He did what?" he exclaimed. "He must have cut out some holes!" His reaction was like Nicklaus' on the first day, when he learned of Longmuir's feat. Neither of these experienced players thought that it was possible for anyone to shoot 65 at Lytham in the prevailing conditions.

Irwin, however, did not let the news throw him off stride. He played what was, in its own way, almost as remarkable a round. Sure, it was 68, three strokes more than the Spaniard's score, but he did not drop one stroke to par during the round and no one else in the championship could say as much. In fact, Irwin had only one hole over par in his first round and to go 36 holes on a championship course such as Lytham in that kind of weather with that score was truly sensational, if not quite as spectacular as the performance of Ballesteros.

In his second 68, Irwin had twos at all three of the short holes on the front nine, but he failed to get his birdies at the par-fives, otherwise he, too, might have been knocking at a 65. He finished with six straight fours, for which his sound putting was more responsible than his somewhat wayward driving. Yet he dropped four strokes to Spain's golden boy.

Nicklaus had the best chance of chasing Ballesteros. His round began very well. He birdied the second, got a two where he had his ace the day before at the fifth, birdied the sixth and the eighth, and got another two at the ninth. So he was out in 30 and anything was possible. When he got another birdie at the 10th, he seemed in full charge. And then came disaster.

Like so many others, but so unlike him, he let his iron shot get away in the cross wind at the one-shot 12th and the ball came to rest, unluckily, so near the back of a greenside bunker that he had to make a very steep back swing. He just got out, onto the bank of the bunker, and he failed to chip close enough to get even a bogey four. That cost two strokes and he dropped three more in a row from holes 14 through 16, mainly because he left his second shots too far from the flag.

Having taken 40 coming home the previous day, he seemed likely to do even worse this time; but then, as he has done so often in the past, he rose to the challenge. He hit a perfect drive into the wind at 17, a perfect one-iron shot over all the bunkers and the bushes and the rough, and, of course, he holed his putt for a three. He got his four at the last hole, but that was 39 home for 69 and a total of 141, where he was joined by a little known New Zealand professional, Dennis Clark, who had shot two identical rounds.

Crenshaw, starting in the last round, seemed as if he might threaten the leaders. He made an excellent start with a two, had another birdie at the sixth and was one under for the championship with only four holes to play. If he could have finished like Ballesteros, he would have tied him, but lightning didn't strike twice.

Crenshaw was brought back to earth at the now infamous 15th, where a splendid drive went just too far and into a bunker. Crenshaw went from that bunker to another and finished with a six, but he kept his head and squeezed home in 71 to tie at 143 with Jerry Pate, Ken Brown and the bright American, Bob Byman, who added a fine 70 to his earlier 73.

There was one other score of real note on this second remarkable day—a 68 for the day's only 142 by Graham Marsh, the methodical, unspectacular Australian. At 144 were two of the Japanese, Aoki and Ozaki; Orville Moody and amateur Peter McEvoy shared 74s and a total of 145; Hubert Green was virtually dead at 148 despite a gallant 71; Ray Floyd was at 149; Johnny Miller and Zoeller were at 150, along with young Wayne Player. Gary shot 74 for 151. Andy North and Tom Weiskopf, who played as though his heart wasn't in it, failed to qualify for the third round, along with the top quality British players Bernard Gallacher and Sam Torrance.

The third day of the championship began with some welcome sunshine which took the edge off the northwest wind. It was a day for two sweaters rather than three or four, but the forecast was ominous. The rain which was predicted for late afternoon arrived on schedule to increase the rigors of play.

So long as the weather remained superficially kind, scoring was not at all bad. One of the five Japanese who survived the cut, Toru Nakamura, brought in a 67 before lunch, but he had just made the cut and so his 219 was clearly not an indication of what was really possible. Gary Player pulled himself up into respectability with a 69, but the first real thrust came from Mark James. Scowling through his Zapata moustache, he also scored 69, his second in a row. His total of 214, only one over par, represented a real challenge to the favorites. Christy O'Connor, the veteran Irishman famed for his talents as a wind player, scored a par 71, a splendid flourish for one in his mid-50s; but he, too, had just made the cut and was too far behind to be more than a survivor.

Pate and Ozaki, who had been handily placed after two rounds, were soon in trouble and finished with 76 and 75. Crenshaw, who has been a persistent threat in the British Open in recent years, began splendidly with a birdie two; but he mixed birdies and bogeys, five of one and six of the other, and could do no better than 72 for the day, though by late afternoon it was a score to be envied and many of the players would gladly have accepted it.

Tom Watson, for example, hung a millstone around his neck at the second hole, where, playing an iron from the tee to thread the narrow fairway, he sliced out of bounds despite the strong right-hand wind. He never really recovered from the two over par six that error cost him. He did fight back for a time, but, in the driving wind and rain at the end of his round, he finished with three fives against the par of three fours. He was lucky at the 18th to get his five after fading into an unplayable lie in the bushes. So Tom took 76 for 216 and seemed unlikely to repeat his great success at Carnoustie in 1975 and his even greater achievement in the famous head-to-head duel with Nicklaus in 1977.

Longmuir, with whom he was partnered, had an even worse start than Watson and at one time looked as though he were going to disappear into the obscurity from which he had sprung the first day. But he hung on bravely, and was rewarded for his resolution by once again holing a longish putt on the last green for a three. But he was at 77 for the day, and at 216 along with Watson.

In the meantime, other players who hadn't been considered too much were making their own modest charges. Bob Byman did 72 for 215, where he was joined by quite the most picturesque player in the tournament, the sturdy Australian Rodger Davis, who is rated highly in his own country and who sports a nice line in plus-twos and brilliantly colored sweaters. He is much more than a coat hanger, however, as his round of 70 proclaimed, for it was compiled mostly after the weather had turned nasty.

Fellow Australian Greg Norman, a flaxen-haired giant who hits the ball like a kicking kangaroo, did 72 for 216, as did Japan's Aoki, and also McEvoy. The amateur's three-round total of 217 was a great performance by any standard and it put him one stroke ahead of Brown and Trevino, who had slipped a little with rounds of 75 and 74.

It was once again the sort of day when Nicklaus, if he was on top of his game, could put his stamp on the tournament. But, of all times, he played a miserable tee shot at the first, was bunkered and dropped a stroke. He looked likely to drop another, or maybe more, at the next hole when he was wide of the green in two; but he manufactured some sort of pitch shot which finished in the hole. Now, surely, he would be off and running. When he got a birdie at the fourth, the first of the holes played into the wind, he looked ready for another good front nine, but he took six at the sixth, which was virtually a loss of two strokes on the par-five and he was 34 at the turn.

He took another six at the long 11th, again failed to get his three at the short 12th, where he had taken five in his second round, took three timid putts on the shortish 13th, and was in dire trouble with the terrifying last five holes coming up. However, like the marvelous player he is, he met the challenge with his usual massive composure, played each of the holes in par and finished in 73 for 214, alongside James.

This gave the second-day leaders—Irwin (68-68—136) and Ballesteros (73-65—138)—a wonderful opportunity. Each had a special incentive to do well. Irwin wanted to win both the U.S. and British Open titles in the same year, and Ballesteros wanted to become the youngest winner of the Open Championship in more than a century. He would also be only the second Continental player ever to win, the other being Arnuad Massy, a Frenchman, in 1907.

Ballesteros found himself in a position similar to the one he had created three years earlier at Birkdale, located a few miles south of Lytham. At that time, he led the field after two rounds, again after three, and was paired for the last 36 holes with Johnny Miller, then at the peak of his powers. Ballesteros was a boy of 19—exuberant, cheerful and gloriously uninhibited. He hit the ball with abandon; at times to remote parts of the course, but he had tremendous powers of recovery and a silken putting touch.

Now he was three years older, and although plagued with nagging back trouble, he was bigger and stronger and still as uninhibited as ever, hammering the ball with fury. He still had his deftness on and around the green and, although he did not smile as often as he had three years earlier, at least he was not petulant as he had been at Turnberry and St. Andrews. Rather, he was composed and aware of his opportunity. He was also fortified, of course, by many victories in different parts of the world, including the United States; and only a week or so before the Lytham championship he had easily won a major tournament at the Belfry course, headquarters of the British PGA.

Now he was paired with Irwin, one of the really formidable competitors in the world of golf. Irwin is a beautiful striker with a swing which seems foolproof. He's the master of the long and medium irons and a sound, if not spectacular, putter. It would clearly be a fascinating duel, the chief danger being that each would be concerned with what the other was doing and forget their pursuers.

Ballesteros put himself in jeopardy at the second hole, where he played almost as bad a tee shot as Watson had immediately in front of him. He found his ball unplayable in bushes beside the railway and had to trudge back and play three off the tee. That gave him a six against Irwin's four, and he was four strokes behind. Irwin lost a stroke at the next hole, but the Spaniard misjudged his second shot and lost one as well. They played rather up-and-down golf to the turn, which Irwin reached in 35 and Ballesteros in 36.

Then Irwin, not happy with his driving into the wind, dropped strokes at the 10th and 11th. Ballesteros got his pars and was only one stroke behind. But

Hale got hold of himself and played the next five holes in par while his partner, driving all over the course, dropped strokes at the 14th and 15th. Seve dropped another stroke at the 17th with a wayward tee-shot, but even at that picked up a stroke on Irwin, who took a six. Irwin seemed to have destroyed his chances when he drove into a terrible place in the bushes at the last hole, but, miraculously, he had both a lie and a line to the flag. He played a splendid recovery just through the green, chipped up and holed from eight feet for his par. It was the sort of hole that, if things had worked out differently, one would have tagged as "the hole that won the Open," for Irwin could easily have taken six or worse. Ballesteros just missed his three at the 18th, and so both finished in 75, which put Irwin at 211 and his young challenger at 213 (the exact reverse of the totals which Ballesteros and Miller took into their final round at Birkdale three years earlier). Now Irwin had to protect his lead with the young pretender poised to snatch the crown. Nicklaus was treading on their heels, along with James, who had shown at Birkdale that he could make a final-round flourish. Crenshaw, Byman and Davis were only a stroke behind Nicklaus and James.

The final day was again proof that wind is the ultimate hazard in golf. Once again it came out of the northwest, not so hard as to make golf a torture, but hard enough to put a premium on both power and accuracy. The players might not have liked it, but it wasn't as bad as St. Andrews had been the year before when three days of east wind were followed by a final day when the wind came out of the west and imposed a radical modification of clubbing.

At Lytham a player knew that if he used, say, a five-iron at No. 1 on Friday, he could use the same club on Saturday or, at worst, the club on either side of that. Whereas if the wind had turned around and had come from the southeast with equal strength he might have needed his biggest iron or even a wood.

When play began, there were about a dozen players left who had a realistic chance—Irwin, and those within six strokes of him. On the first two days, Longmuir and Ballesteros had shown what could be done with a little luck and a lot of resolution, as had Nakamura on Friday. The leaders had also demonstrated that even the best were vulnerable in severe conditions.

Though he had been singularly frail on Friday, Watson was only five strokes behind and, if he could get off to a good start, there was no saying what might happen. But Watson missed his chance. He took a sloppy six at the third, three-putting from nowhere, and then dropped another stroke at the next hole. He took a seven at the seventh, 40 to the turn, and disappeared with a final round of 81. So, too, did Longmuir, the first-day hero, who finished a stroke worse. That was rather sad because it squeezed him out of the first 25, and lost him an exemption from qualifying at Muirfield in 1980.

But if Watson succumbed, his partner, Aoki, for a time looked as though he might take the ancient trophy back to the Far East. Starting five strokes behind Irwin, he birdied three of the first six holes to come back to even par. If he could have got the birdie four at the seventh, instead of a six, there is no telling what might have happened. Even so, he was out in 33 and when he started back with two birdies, he was actually leading the tournament. But he could not keep it up over the final punishing stretch and he faded to a 75 for 291.

Trevino went out in 34 and, like Aoki, collapsed coming home; but Davis, a sartorial rhapsody in blue after his scarlet and cream of the day before, played with wonderful composure in partnership with Crenshaw. Both got their threes at the first hole despite being bunkered and Davis went on with three pars and three birdies to get within sight of a wonderful outgoing nine. He dropped a stroke at the eighth but got it back with his second two of the round at the ninth, so he was 32 at the turn and one under par for the tournament. At that stage he, too, was leading the field, but again he could not keep control in the long trip home and visited bunker after bunker. He shot 41 back for an aggregate of 228, a praiseworthy score, but, for Davis, only a chastening what-might-have-been.

His regrets could have been no sharper than Crenshaw's. He again mixed birdies and bogeys but he had more of the birdies and reached the turn in 33, which made him even par for the tournament. He was still even with two holes left to play. If he could hold on to the finish, he would set a challenging target. Alas, the 17th was his downfall. He drove into the right rough, played an ambitious wood second which finished in deep rough, from which he could only hack out into a greenside bunker. He played his usual competent recovery to five feet, but for once his putting failed him. With that six, his total was 286.

Would anyone provide a final round challenge? Nicklaus could not, nor could James, with whom he was playing. Jack began ominously with a bogey after a hooked tee shot; and, when he dropped another stroke at the fourth, he was three over par and only one among many. But the fifth yielded two, he got his birdie at the sixth and was back in the game, only one over. Then he stumbled again and took 36 to the turn. He was two over at the point where Davis had been one under. Once again Nicklaus displayed his enormous resolution by coming back with a four at the 542-yard 11th. Playing into the eye of the wind, he survived his bogey hole, the 12th, with a par three for once; then he played a weak pitch to the 13th and took three fatal putts. He took three putts again at the 15th after reaching the fringe with two great shots into the wind; and, improbably, but characteristically, he holed a 25-footer on the 16th for a birdie.

He was not done yet. When, to the roar of the crowd, he hit a perfect drive at the 17th and an immaculate one-iron to 25 feet, Nicklaus must have had high hopes. But his putt stopped an inch short, dead in line. He did get his four at the last hole, but only a three might have put pressure on Ballesteros. In fact, Jack did well to get his four because, after an enormous drive right up the middle, he hit his six-iron heavy into a bunker shot, and had to make a fine explosion shot and hole out from four feet. The crowd acclaimed it as though it were the winning stroke. So he and Crenshaw were at 286, right among the leaders in a championship which Nicklaus has won three times and in which he has finished second or tied for second seven times. Who will dare say he is over the hill? Certainly none of the vast number of admirers in Britain to whom he is a demi-god.

So at that point it all boiled down to whether Severiano Ballesteros could become the youngest player to win the Open championship since young Tom Morris in 1872. Gary Player was 22 years and eight months old when he won his first Open at Muirfield exactly 20 years earlier, but Seve's birthday was in April and he was therefore 22 years and just over three months old.

He fired his six-iron shot onto the first green and holed his putt for a two, a great beginning to his round. It was as if to show Irwin that he was determined that the quiet American with the immaculate swing would have to work hard to place himself in the ranks of Jones, Sarazen, Hogan and Trevino. On the other hand, Irwin's trouble developed early. He had a stroke of luck at the second hole when his ill-hit tee shot finished in a good lie between two bunkers; but he failed to make the most of the break, left his second shot short, and then took three putts for a double bogey.

That put the young caballero ahead and it remained that way to the turn, Ballesteros out in 34 to Irwin's 37. Seve was driving to all points of the compass, but he seemed to contrive a way to put those crooked shots into places where the rough had been trampled flat by the crowds. His iron shots from unlikely spots were gems, though sometimes rather uncut gems as when, at the sixth, he hooked to kingdom come and then fired a nine-iron recovery 40 yards too far.

He could not recover from another crooked drive at the 10th and dropped a stroke to par, but so did Irwin, who was now beginning to look weary. When the American took three putts at the 11th, he was two strokes behind Ballesteros and the fireworks were just about to start. Both got threes from just off the 12th green and then Ballesteros made his first real knife thrust.

The dogleg 13th was nearly reachable downwind and Ballesteros unleashed a huge drive, but he bit off too much and the ball was trapped 40 yards from the flag. He made a heroic recovery but the ball had so much spin that it squirmed off the green onto the fringe, pin high. Irwin, meanwhile, had played an immaculate tee shot and a pitch to 20 feet. Ballesteros played a run-up shot and, when the ball was 10 feet from the hole, he began to pursue it, hands and club raised, first in expectation, then in ecstasy as the ball toppled in. Irwin had to settle for a conventional four and the loss of another stroke.

Ballesteros was now in full stride; clearly he had the scent of victory. But the sweet smell of success was soured a little at the next hole when he took three putts after a fine recovery from the rough. Irwin, who watched his ball scamper over the green into a difficult place after a good drive and what looked to be a fine iron shot tucked under the wind, also dropped a stroke.

Ballesteros hit his drive at the awesome 15th into the wind, seemingly harder than a ball can be hit. He almost decapitated himself with his follow-through and made one wonder not why he has a bad back but that he has any

Ben Crenshaw was second again in the British Open. His day will come.

Severiano Ballesteros captured the British Open from out of the rough.

back left at all. He then thumped his iron shot from the rough into light grass short of the green, played an exquisite pitch over a bunker to the hole and he was virtually home free, provided he did nothing outrageous.

But that is what he proceeded to do. The 16th is like the 13th, a drive-and-pitch dogleg to the right. Ballesteros went with the driver again when common prudence should have made him take an iron and play safe. He again hit a tremendous shot but again he bit off too much and his ball finished in a small official car park about 50 yards from the green. But he was lucky once again. The ground was beaten flat, the cars were locked and therefore immovable obstructions and he was allowed a free drop. He then celebrated his good fortune by playing a fine pitch over a nest of bunkers to 20 feet, and proceeded to hole the putt. Irwin got an orthodox par and dropped a stroke to his rival's unconventional birdie.

Now Ballesteros could afford to play quietly over the last two holes, but that is not his way. Once again, he went for the big hit at the 17th and finished in the rough, again in a reasonable lie. Maybe it is just his strength that makes the lie reasonable, but whatever its nature he thumped a long iron recovery which finished in a greenside bunker. He came out none too well, but he holed the putt with that air of inevitability which had settled over his play almost from the starter's, "Play away, please."

Now all he had to do was avoid disaster at the last hole. Two three-iron shots would have taken him to the green, but once again he took his driver for the tee shot. However, there's a sane head on the young shoulders; although he drove into the rough, Seve made sure it was the left rough, not the right where there are bushes and a flagpole and all manner of obstructions. He deserved to get a good lie and he did. Then he quite casually knocked the ball in the general direction of the green with a five-iron and was actually striding after the ball when it was still in flight. The ball finished 10 feet from the front edge of the green and, wisely again, he took the safest of all clubs, the putter, and eased the ball 35 yards nearly dead to the cup. He holed the putt and walked into history.

There was no extravagant gesture, no punching of the air, no throwing of the ball into the crowd—just a rather shy smile as Irwin, with wonderful grace and generosity, put his arm around the young man's shoulders in congratulation before he was engulfed in Latin embraces by his three golfing brothers.

Irwin himself had slipped to a final round of 78, which left him six strokes behind the winner. Ballesteros was the only man to break par for 72 holes and at that by a single stroke. Nicklaus and Crenshaw shared second place three strokes behind the winner. Mark James, who had played Nicklaus almost shot for shot, was fourth and the top British player, as he had been at Birkdale when he finished fifth. He and Ballesteros seem to flower in Lancashire just as Nicklaus blooms in Scotland.

For the rest, McEvoy finished first amateur again; indeed, he was the only amateur, because Wayne Player failed to survive the 54-hole cut. And there must be a valedictory word of praise for Peter Thomson, the great Australian, who shares with Braid and Taylor the distinction of having won the Open five times. He was a month short of 50 when he completed this, his last appearance in the championship, and his four rounds of 76, 75, 72 and 74 were an eloquent tribute to his true and simple methods and to his thoughtful appraisal of this perplexing game.

The victory of Ballesteros was immensely popular, for all the world admires courage and gaiety and youthful audacity. It may be, indeed, that Irwin's play suffered a little, especially on the final day, due to the crowd's obvious attachment to his companion, though they did not withhold praise from Irwin when he produced a capital shot or holed a difficult putt. Irwin inspires respect for his play and demeanor; Ballesteros, like Palmer, inspires both respect and affection in equally generous measure.

Possibly only one person in the vast crowd who had witnessed the finish could have had any reservations about the winner, apart, of course, from those players who might have won, "if only. . . ." He was the engraver, whom the Royal and Ancient have on hand to put the winner's name on the trophy in the 10 minutes or so between the last putt and the start of the presentation ceremony. He might have wished that, say, Kite or Aoki had won instead of the man with the longest surname, bar one, in the final field.

5

THE PGA CHAMPIONSHIP

It was back to Oakland Hills Country Club for the Professional Golfers Association Championship for the second time in eight years. Back to where Gary Player scored his second PGA title triumph in 1972. Back to the scene of four U.S. Opens—1924, won by Cyril Walker; 1937, won by Ralph Guldahl over Sam Snead in a heart breaker; 1951, when Ben Hogan conquered what he called "The Monster"; and 1961, won by Gene Littler.

The suburban Detroit course had changed quite a bit since Walker's time, thanks to golf architect Robert Trent Jones. But the only change since Player's triumph was at the par-four seventh hole, and most of the players didn't like the newly designed green, saying it was out of character with the rest of the course. Be that as it may, No. 7 proved not to be the vital hole in the 1979 championship, but just one of a string of tough holes.

Perhaps the only thing that hadn't changed over the years was the difficulty of the course. The members play it as a par 72, but for championship play the No. 8 and No. 18 holes are played as par-fours, making par 35–35—70. And it had been the proud boast of Oakland Hills members that par for 72 holes had never been broken in a major tournament.

That boast was shattered, due somewhat to wet weather, but primarily to the ability of the modern professional player. In this case the principal attackers were David Graham, Ben Crenshaw and Rex Caldwell, and they didn't shave an inch off the course's competitive record—it was more like feet.

Graham and Crenshaw tied at 272 and Caldwell was two back at 274. And in another dramatic finish, Graham had to win the tournament not once, but twice, thus escaping a morale-shattering defeat that could have affected his career. For in the tension-packed final minutes of the tournament, Graham blew a two-stroke lead at the 72nd hole. Then he went out and defeated Crenshaw on the third hole of a sudden-death play-off with some marvelous—nay, unbelievable—putting.

The victory climaxed a fine six-week showing for Graham. He had had such a streak once before on the American tour, in 1976, when he won the Westchester Classic and the American Golf Classic in a space of a few weeks.

But before the hot streak began, the 33-year-old Australian seriously contemplated looking for another line of work, aside from playing golf for a living.

"I thought about maybe going into club design work full time, or maybe some other golf-related work," said Graham, perhaps the most knowledgeable man in club design on the circuit. And if he were to turn to another job, it had to be connected with golf. When he was 14, Graham wanted to quit school and go into golf, but his father said if he did, he'd never speak to him again. Graham did and his father kept his word.

"But I don't want to talk about my problems," said Graham after his big victory. He had a much more interesting topic for discussion: his flirt with the PGA title records of 63 and 271 as he carved out a 65 in the final round at Oakland Hills. Then the capper, his comeback from deep despair after he had double-bogeyed the final hole and slipped into a tie with Crenshaw.

"I felt like I played the first 16 holes as good as I possibly could play," he said. "I knew starting today it would be a long day. I knew I had to make a lot of birdies. When I birdied the first two holes, I was in the thick of things, and after that I just concentrated on getting the ball on the greens.

"I had only one three-putt green in the tournament, and on these greens, that's something. I think the turning point came when I birdied No. 7 and 8. I made a long putt [30 feet] for a birdie at 10 and a good putt [eight feet] at 11. I knew I had the situation under control.

"I don't think it hit me what was going on until the middle of my backswing on the 18th tee. I woke up then to what was going on out there. The whole situation hit me. I started to think 'PGA Championship,' and I hit a dreadful tee shot."

The pushed drive went far beyond the huge gallery, but it left him with a relatively easy shot to the green. However, he and his caddie were so far off the beaten path, Graham didn't know what club to use. He ultimately chose the wrong one and it led to a double-bogey six. Instead of winning by a shot or two, Graham was in a deadlock with Crenshaw, who only two weeks earlier had placed second in the British Open, after making an improper club selection at the 71st hole.

The play-off, the third in a row since the PGA went to a sudden-death system, produced a demonstration of sheer intestinal fortitude by Graham, who rolled in nerve-wracking putts at the first two holes to tie Crenshaw, then won the tournament for the second time that day by sinking an eight-foot birdie putt at the par-three third hole.

Graham had won three previous tournaments on the U.S. Tour and seven other international tournaments, but he didn't agree the PGA was his first major triumph. The 1977 Australian Open, he noted, had a strong field.

The field at Oakland Hills was even stronger and it included a Jack Nicklaus still looking for his first victory of the year. It was to be his final tournament of 1979, marking the first time since Nicklaus joined the tour in 1962 that he would go through a year without winning at least one American tournament.

As mentioned, the 7,014-yard Oakland course was little changed since 1972. But this time the "Monster" never got off its knees. Rain, the great equalizer for difficult golf courses, took all the punch out of the course and the rough was not nearly as high or as tenacious as it customarily is for a major championship. The only complaints were directed at the No. 7 green, which was redesigned for the tournament by Trent Jones.

No. 7 is a 409-yarder that doglegs right uphill to a green invisible to the players. After a good drive, it's a short-iron shot, but the problem was that Jones left little green to hit and few places to put the pins. Most pros said there are no places to cut a hole. It is a long, narrow, undulating green surrounded by bunkers. If it hadn't rained and the green had been hard, the players would have worn out their sand wedges there.

If it hadn't rained . . . but it did. Frequently. And the muggy conditions never gave the course a chance to dry. It was almost a repeat of the year before, when Oakmont had been humbled by the pros after rainy weather had made it helpless. Oakland Hills' greens were soft and not very fast, and it seemed everybody got a boost from low practice-round scores.

"I played a round with Raymond Floyd today," said Nicklaus the day before the tournament began, "and when we were finished he asked me if I knew what he had shot. I said, 'I wouldn't have a clue.' He said, 'I had seven birdies.' He had just shot 63 very quietly."

John Mahaffey was the defending champion, but nobody gave him a chance to repeat. Mahaffey had hurt his wrist at Pebble Beach in January and he was just starting to get his form back after a three-month layoff. The central figures were Tom Watson, who had won four tournaments and nearly $400,000, and Nicklaus, who could tie Walter Hagen for the most PGA championships with a fifth win.

"I feel I'm ready. I've been hitting the ball well; I just haven't been putting," said the optimistic Nicklaus. "I'm never happy when I haven't won, but I've been getting myself in the position where I haven't been able to win. This is the last major and the last tournament of the year for me.

"I've prepared myself to play in four tournaments [the four majors]. We've played three and I haven't won. Now there's one left. Everywhere I go I get the same questions about when I am going to win, I get tired of the questions. I've been out here 18 years and I plan to be out here a few more. But I won't be out here for many more if I try to beat my brains out just to win another tournament."

Nicklaus opened with a 73, shot a 78 the third day, and finished far back at 294.

Watson was less optimistic. His swing had gone sour and on the practice tee he consulted with Byron Nelson, trying to get the kinks out. Watson had won $387,386, all but $33,512 of that before the end of May.

"I'm not striking the ball well at all," Watson confessed. "If I could just concentrate on one thing, I think I'd be all right, but I'm thinking of too many things and I'm kind of confused. My thinking on the course is disorganized. I don't feel right when I get over the ball. It's a matter of being confident. The consistency isn't there and you get frustrated. So you have to go back to the fundamentals. But it'll come back. It always has and it always will."

It came back only briefly for Watson. He opened with a four-under-par 33-33—66 as Oakland Hills took a terrible beating. A total of 15 players broke par and 11 others tied it.

"I hit a lot of good shots with every facet of my game, and I got away with a couple of bad shots," said Watson. "Except at the last hole, where I buried my ball under the lip of the bunker in front of the green. I had to hit it sideways; I couldn't go for the flag."

Watson had six birdies on the windy day, sinking putts of 12, 25, 6 and 2 feet at holes No. 7, 8, 14 and 15 and two-putting the two par-fives, the 521-yard No. 2 and the 567-yard No. 12.

"I'm taking my club straighter away and this allows me to extend my radius," said Watson, explaining a change he had made in his swing. "I'm excited again about playing. It's difficult to play golf if you don't have confidence in your swing."

Watson held the lead with nine holes to go the previous year at Oakmont and eventually he and Jerry Pate lost to Mahaffey in a play-off. It had no bearing on his first round at Oakland Hills, he said. "I'm not any more or less determined as a result of last year," he added.

Arnold Palmer, Billy Casper, Isao Aoki and Severiano Ballesteros received special invitations to play, but none were around at the end. Ballesteros, the British Open champion, declined because of an ailing back and the others missed the cut. Palmer virtually bowed out when he shot an 81 in the first round, leading to only the third time he failed to make the cut in 22 PGA championships. The only other time he failed to break 80 was when he opened with an 82 in 1969, then withdrew because of a hip injury.

Rex Caldwell, one of those "who's-he?" players who always crop up in a major tournament, was in second place with a 33-34—67; a stroke behind him were other little-known players, Ron Streck and Jay Haas. Then came a gang at 69, including Graham, Crenshaw and Pate.

Caldwell, a blithe spirit, is a story in himself. The 29-year-old Washington State native joined the tour in 1975, and in the last tournament of the year, the Texas Open, he made a 10-foot putt on the last hole of the last round and won $500, just $94 more than he needed to keep his tour card.

"I was one of those guys who came out here in 1975 and people bet I wouldn't be here in 1976. And I almost wasn't," laughed Caldwell.

Caldwell made his PGA championship debut at Oakmont the year before, and even though he made the cut he exited before it was over. He signed for an 80 in the third round although he shot an 81, an error he discovered just before the final round. But in his second visit he played as if he were an old hand. He birdied Nos. 1, 2 and 5, then played even par the rest of the way on the first round, offsetting a bogey at No. 9 with a 10-foot birdie putt at No. 15.

"I drove it extremely well. I missed only two fairways," said Caldwell. "That was the key to the whole thing. And I didn't take chances on the tucked pin positions; I just tried to hit the greens."

Streck had five birdies, four on the back nine, on which he shot 32. Haas played Oakland Hills' version of Augusta National's "Amen corner"—the ninth through 11th holes—in three over par, taking a double bogey at the 225-yard No. 9 and a bogey at the 413-yard No. 11, after hitting the sand at both holes. But he played the other 15 holes in five under par.

Frank Conner, another spear-carrier, made a hole-in-one at the ninth hole with a three-wood. Incidentally, Streck made the second ace of the tournament in the second round, sinking a two-iron shot at the 201-yard No. 17.

Friday dawned warm and sunny, but by mid-afternoon ominous gray clouds scurried overhead, constantly threatening to open up. They never did, but the course remained soft and the players picked on it again. The most successful was Alan Tapie, who turned in a five-under-par 65 and vaulted to within two shots of the lead at 138.

This also was the day that Crenshaw and Graham showed they were going to make determined efforts to win. Crenshaw shot a three-under 67 and moved into first place at 136. Graham scored a 68 that moved him into a tie for second place at 137 with Caldwell and Haas. Watson slipped to a 72 and into a four-man tie at 138.

"Each time I play a course, I learn a little bit more about it," said Crenshaw, who had never played Oakland Hills before. "I'm just learning by my mistakes. I'm a firm believer that you got to knock on the door first before you can get in there. I just want to get in position on the last nine holes so I can just use my head and win it. I'd love to win it, I'd give my eyeteeth to.

"But any golfer in his twenties [Crenshaw was 27] doesn't use his head all the time. If I had a year's more experience, I might have won the British Open this year. You just learn more each day you play."

Crenshaw missed the green at the 444-yard opening hole and bogeyed. But he made five birdies before he bogeyed again, at the par-three 17th. Graham looked as if he would tie Crenshaw for the lead, but at the 18th hole he hit what he called "a not indifferent drive, then put a bad swing on a six-iron" and the result was a bogey. Prior to that he had made six birdies, putting them together in pairs, at the second and third holes, seventh and eighth and 12th and 13th, the longest putt from 20 feet.

"I played well the last six or eight weeks and I feel confident from the way I'm playing," said Graham. "I'm kinda disappointed in my performances in the majors. I'm a straight hitter and a good long-iron player, and that's what you have to be in the majors. But I've never done well in them."

Hardly anybody took Haas seriously, even though he was only a shot off the lead. He made five birdies, including a 30-footer at the 18th green; four bogeys and nine pars. "I had a lapse in the middle of the round [at the eighth and ninth holes, which he bogied] when I hit bad long irons," the quiet Wake Forest graduate said.

Caldwell had a 2:30 P.M. starting time and said, "I felt like I wouldn't tee off until Saturday." It was a long morning, although it didn't seem to affect his game. At the ninth hole he nearly holed a 100-foot chip shot, and at the 11th he hit a chip shot off a cart path to within four feet of the cup to save par.

"I did a lot of work out there. I never had any relief. It seemed like I had to do something on every hole," he said.

It seemed as if Tapie was doing something on every hole — something good. He birdied the first hole from 12 feet, No. 2 from four feet, No. 7 from 18, No. 8 from 25, No. 15 from 12 and No. 18 with a 50-foot chip-in as he tied Oakland Hills' competitive record. Except for a triple bogey at the first hole and a double bogey at the 14th, he played almost as well in the first round, on which he shot a 73.

"I was going to play conservative. I was going to play for the wide side of the greens. But I was probably too critical of myself; I'm probably hitting the ball better than I think," said Tapie. "After the birdie at 15 I was just trying to make some other birdies, and I did. I've set other course records—but this is the PGA, and this is Oakland Hills."

Pate, after his second straight 69, felt he was in a good position. "Two or three under will win the tournament. Most scores in the Open and PGA come back down. Pressure tends to back everybody up to par," he said.

Watson's driving problems returned. He hit his tee shot in four fairway bunkers and took bogeys at two of the holes as he shot a 72. "Obviously, it [the swing change] wasn't perfected. I let it get away to the right four times and once to the left," he said. "Some days you have it and some days you don't."

Bruce Lietzke, with 69–69, also was at 138 and, like Watson, was having trouble with his swing before the tournament began. He had taken three weeks off prior to the tournament and had played little golf during that time.

"I'm new at major championships. I don't gear my game around them," said Lietzke, explaining why he didn't have his game sharp as he came to Oakland Hills. To Lietzke, the PGA championship is just another tournament.

"The layoff showed in practice," he added. "As of Wednesday I had not found it [his swing]. But concentration brought back memories of three good weeks of golf I had before my vacation. Through concentration and imagination I concocted a golf swing that held up the last two days. When you're not playing well, you have to improvise and find a swing you can work with. It isn't a swing I like, but I am getting results."

Others had swing problems, too, but were unable to iron them out. Sam Snead, 67, made the cut with 73–71; nephew J.C., 37, didn't with 72–76. Palmer, Casper, Tom Weiskopf and U.S. Open champion Hale Irwin also failed to qualify for the last two rounds. It took 146, an abnormally low score for Oakland Hills, to make the cut.

After 36 holes, here's how they stood:

Crenshaw	69–67—136	Tapie	73–65—138
Haas	68–69—137	Watson	66–72—138
D. Graham	69–68—137	Pate	69–69—138
Caldwell	67–70—137	Lietzke	69–69—138

Until the third round on Saturday, rain had been merely a constant threat during play, thick gray clouds floating by like the Goodyear blimp. Most of the moisture fell during the night. The threat finally became reality in the third round, turning what had been a hot, sunny day at the beginning into a wet, windy and, for some, terror-filled time late in the afternoon.

Detroit is a fine sports area and the crowds had been building every day. An announced crowd of 20,264 turned out for the first round; the figure was 25,526 for the second. On Saturday, it was said 34,368 were on the course. So you can imagine the bedlam as that many people frantically scurried for cover when a rainstorm hit at 6:30 P.M., with nine players still on the course.

"All those who are not working are advised to leave the press tent," said a sepulchral voice over the loudspeaker as winds of 50 miles per hour buffeted the press tent. Then a hard rain plunged out of the yellow sky, causing play to be suspended for 45 minutes. Pate, Hubert Green, Leonard Thompson, Haas, Caldwell, Watson, Crenshaw, Graham and Tapie were the only players who hadn't completed their rounds before the delay.

Until the rain came, it had been quite a day. Poor Oakland Hills had been subjected to another beating—19 rounds under par, making it 52 for the first 54 holes. Caldwell and Jack Renner had 66s and George Burns, Peter Jacobsen and Gene Littler had 67s. Caldwell's round moved him into a two-stroke lead over Crenshaw, 203 to 205. And the margin could have been wider.

"I hit all my shots well except for the shot at 18." said Caldwell. "I almost missed my tee time there. I was in the ABC trailer during the rain and I didn't know play had started again. I had to run over, put my tee in the ground and swing. I wanted to take a couple warm-up swings, but I didn't have time for that. I had to burn a four-iron to the green; I probably should have hit a three-iron. I just hit a bad shot. When you're drawing out steel to a long green, you tend to get tight a little bit."

Caldwell bogeyed, and instead of leading by three, he was ahead by two. Still, it had been a most amazing day for a man many of the other pros refer to as a "space cadet," a free-spirited person who speaks his mind.

"I hit it a little harder because I knew I was hitting it well, and so I was hitting it farther," said Caldwell. And for a while he put a lot of distance between him and second place.

Crenshaw birdied the par-five second hole by two-putting from 40 feet, but he bogeyed the par-three third after missing the green. Haas birdied Nos. 2 and 3 and temporarily went in front at five under par for the tournament. It was very temporary. Haas's game slid downhill after that as he took a 73 for 210.

Meanwhile, Caldwell saved par with a 10-footer at the first hole and Crenshaw got it up and down at the fourth and fifth for pars as the round gave promise of being an old-fashioned dog fight. Like Haas's lead, that also was temporary.

Caldwell rolled in a 30-foot snake for a birdie at the fifth hole, then dropped putts of 10, 12, and 12 feet at holes Nos. 7, 8 and 9 as he made the turn in 31, four under par. He knocked in an eight-footer after hitting a wedge to the 413-yard No. 11, putting him eight under for the tournament. And suddenly he had a four-stroke lead on the field.

"I was enjoying myself out there. I went 28 holes without a bogey on this course. I just put the club in the slot and fired away," said Caldwell, with a big grin. However, he ran out of birdies after missing a four-footer at the 12th hole. Crenshaw narrowed the gap.

Crenshaw played erratically, five birdies and four bogeys, and he attributed at least one bogey to the weather. "We were on the 15th tee when we caught the bad weather," he said, "and we went ahead and played the hole. We had a 40-mph wind in our faces and I hit a low five-iron to the green—and the wind never touched it. It went over the green." Every bogey he got was a result of missing a green.

One over par after eight holes, Crenshaw came back with a 20-foot putt for a birdie at the ninth hole, a 15-footer at the 10th and two putts from 50 feet at the par-five 12th after a bogey at the 11th. When play resumed after the rain delay, he hit the flag with his second shot at the 405-yard No. 16 and dropped a 12-foot putt for birdie.

"I didn't play too well," Crenshaw admitted. "In a 72-hole tournament you can have a bad stretch of golf. I hope mine is behind me and I got away with a 69. I feel confident. I didn't play well and shot 69. You have to be happy with that."

Graham birdied the fifth, sixth and eighth holes, but played two-over-par golf the last 10 holes and was almost overlooked with his 70. "I thought four 69s would win, but now I'm not so sure," said Pate after he turned in his third consecutive 69.

"I had just hit my best drive at 18 when play was halted. I had 225 yards to the pin. I hit a one-iron to within eight feet—it was the best shot I hit all week—and I didn't make the putt. I haven't been aggressive enough with my putter.

"We were going off the 10th tee when Caldwell hit his shot to the ninth green and Hubert shouted, 'Rex, if you keep playing that way, you're going to have to change your image.' But Rex is a good player. The only thing that might prevent him from winning is pressure. He's got the game and he can putt. He's going to have to shoot about 70 or 71 in the final round, but with Watson and Crenshaw chasing him . . . well, they can make anything, anytime from anywhere. My chances are good, too."

Watson found the groove again, recovering from a slow start to notch birdies at the ninth (three feet), 12th (two putts), 13th (six feet) and 15th (30 feet), his only mistake coming at the 14th, which he bogeyed.

"I had a good round of golf. I drove very well. But I hit three bad irons and they cost me bogeys," noted Watson. "I'm looking forward to tomorrow. I played with Rex today and he played an excellent round of golf. I feel my chances are good. If I get out of the box quick tomorrow, I'll have a chance to put pressure on the leaders." Watson chipped to within two feet to save par at 17, but he missed a six-foot birdie putt at 18 after a great four-iron to the green.

"If you asked me three days ago whether I'd be leading this tournament after three rounds, I'd have said you were crazy," said Caldwell. "I've never led a tournament going into the last round. I led the Buick Open last year going to the 16th hole, but I didn't lead at the beginning of the round. I'm still going to hit for the center of the greens. Those holes can getcha—you can bogey 'em all. But if the swing feels good, I'll try to squeeze it in there. Hell, I'll be nervous. You can make book on that."

Nicklaus, caught in a bogey groove, stumbled to a 78. It was his worst round of the year, a score he exceeded in the PGA Championship only twice before, when he shot 79s in 1968 and 1978 and missed the cut.

Here's the way they stood with 18 holes remaining:

Caldwell	67–70–66—203	Streck	68–71–69—208
Crenshaw	69–67–69—205	Lietzke	69–69–71—209
D. Graham	69–68–70—207	Littler	71–71–67—209
Watson	66–72–69—207	Gilbert	69–72–68—209
Pate	69–69–69—207		

Caldwell had vaulted from 137th place on the money list to 42nd with $68,451 in 1978, crediting most of his gain to improved putting. Going into the PGA at Oakland Hills, he was in 60th place on the money list with $47,675 and had made the cut in 18 of 25 tournaments, his best finishes a fourth at Tallahassee and a fifth at Greensboro. He was not exactly an untested pro, although he had seldom felt the pressure that accompanies being in contention for first place in the final, frantic holes of a major tournament. Now here he was in just that position. Few thought he would hold up. Of course, Caldwell disagreed. And to his credit, he was correct. He held up very well. The problem was, Graham and Crenshaw also played extremely well.

A crowd of 35,569 streamed onto Oakland Hills for the final round, looking for a shootout. The fans got that and much more.

Crenshaw stirred up the crowd by sinking putts of 20, 10 and 20 feet for birdies at the first three holes to put him at eight under par for the tournament. Caldwell dropped a 15-footer for birdie at the short third, putting him and Crenshaw in a deadlock for the lead.

Graham also was busy early. He rammed in a 30-footer for a birdie at hole No. 1, then followed with an eight-footer at No. 2 after a fine shot from a bunker to go five under. He trailed by three strokes with 15 holes left and he was optimistic. "When I made those birdies at the first two holes I was in the thick of things. After that I concentrated on getting the ball on the greens," he said.

Meanwhile, the only other one among the contenders who started fast was Lou Graham, who began his round birdie-birdie-birdie. But Graham was eight strokes behind when the round began and virtually out of the chase. Watson bogeyed the second hole and eventually succumbed when he bogeyed No. 10 and followed with a triple bogey at No. 11, taking three shots to escape from a fairway bunker. Pate also bogeyed No. 2, and another bogey at No. 10 put him hopelessly behind with nine holes to go. Ron Streck got to four under for the tournament with birdies at the first and fourth holes, but bogeys at Nos. 6 and 7 wiped him out, relegating him to a fourth-place finish.

So it was left to Crenshaw, Caldwell and David Graham to battle it out. And Caldwell could do nothing but watch the other two pull away.

Graham hit an eight-iron to eight feet at the seventh and dropped the putt for birdie. He followed by sinking a 15-footer at the difficult eight after rapping a five-iron to the green. A par at No. 9 gave him a four-under 31 on the front nine. Crenshaw three-putted the sixth green—his first three-putt of the tournament—and seemed to use radar on a birdie putt at No. 9, the 45-foot snake giving him a 32 on the front nine. Caldwell three-putted No. 7 for a bogey and saved par with an 18-footer at No. 9 as he went out in 35.

With nine holes remaining, here's how it looked:

Crenshaw	-8	Streck	-2
Caldwell	-7	Haas	-2
D. Graham	-7	January	-2
Watson	-4		

Don January bogeyed the 10th hole and played even-par golf the rest of the way. Streck got to four-under with birdies at the 11th and 13th holes, but he couldn't keep up the pace. In fact, the way Graham was going, nobody could match his action.

Graham's 30-footer dove into the cup for a birdie at No. 10, and he had the lead all to himself. Crenshaw, playing in the threesome ahead of him, bogeyed the hole after twice playing shots out of sand. Graham made it four birdies in five holes by sinking an eight-footer at No. 11.

In the testing five-hole stretch of No. 7 through No. 11, Graham had gone from five under par to nine under, three ahead of Crenshaw. Caldwell, with a four-footer for a birdie at No. 11, trailed by a stroke.

"I thought when I made the birds at seven and eight and when I made that long putt for bird at 10 and a good bird at 11, I was in control," said Graham. "I was in control of my game; I was in control of my emotions. I felt calm. I knew the situation I was in and I felt I had control."

Caldwell hit a bunker at the 14th green and bogeyed, which dropped him to seven under. Crenshaw made a four-footer at No. 12 and a 30-footer at No. 13 to move to eight under, within one stroke of Graham.

At the 388-yard No. 15, with the wind in his face, Graham knifed a four-iron shot 188 yards to within three inches of the hole, putting him 10 under for the tournament and two ahead of Crenshaw.

And now a few more things than just winning the PGA championship entered the picture. *Golf* magazine had offered $50,000 to anybody who broke the 18-hole or 72-hole records in any of the four majors—the Masters, U.S. and British Opens, and the PGA championship. The PGA records were 63 and 271.

Graham was seven under for the day; if he played the final three holes in one under, he had a 62 and the record. If he played the final three in only even par, he had a 270 for the route. "The bonus money never occurred to me," said Graham. "Winning the PGA would just be most rewarding to me."

Graham's drive at the par-three 17th hit the green, but went off the back edge. He chipped 12 feet short from a difficult lie . . . then made the putt for par. Crenshaw finished with pars for a 67 and 272. Caldwell bogeyed No. 18. All Graham had to do to win was make no worse than bogey.

Graham's journey from the 17th green to the 18th tee was a nightmare. What security existed was inadequate to control the huge crowd and Graham was pushed, elbowed, stepped on and nearly knocked off his feet on the way to what everybody believed would be the final hole of the tournament. One of those who believed it was over was Caldwell, who also found the route to the 18th tee a struggle.

"After he made the putt at 17, I thought there was no way he could lose the golf tournament," stated Caldwell. "The way he was striking the ball, you had to believe there was no way he could lose it."

Two strokes up with perhaps the most difficult hole left to play—you bet there was a way Graham could lose it. A poor drive . . . a bad bunker shot . . . a terrible pitch. There were a number of ways. And Graham seemed to find one when he pushed his drive far right, out even beyond where the crowd milled.

"I had no idea where the ball ended up because of the sun. But Bob Rosburg [doing course commentary for ABC-TV] said, 'It's perfect. You've got a good lie.' And I breathed a sigh of relief. The only problem was I couldn't get any yardage. There was sprinkler at 154 yards and one at 184 yards, but because of the people, neither my caddie nor I could get to them. I was really guessing with my second shot. I thought I had somewhere in the neighborhood of 160 yards to the front of the green, so I decided to hit a six-iron . . . and as it turned out, it should have been a seven.

"Somebody told me later Watson had hit a seven-iron from the same place. I should have deliberated playing short. I was so pumped up, I almost hit the clubhouse. I hit the six-iron 205 yards."

The ball took off like a rocket and scattered the people sitting on the hillside behind the green. It came to rest on the side of the hill, where the grass had been flattened by the fans. Graham had a downhill shot to a green that sloped away from him. Only a superb chip would get him close enough for a par; but Graham didn't need a par—all he needed was a bogey to win.

Graham chipped, the ball popped in the air, took a few bounces, then stopped in the untrampled grass short of the green. "Gary Player asked me in the clubhouse afterward why I didn't just chip the ball on the green. I told him I was afraid I might chip it into the bunker on the other side of the green," noted Graham.

So now he had to get down in two for victory. The nervy Australian hit what looked like an excellent chip, the ball rolling tantalizingly close to the hole, then stopping five feet below it.

"I had a putt that went right to left and I was confident. I was making them all day," said Graham. "I was just scared of hitting it too softly. It was not a difficult putt, but I hit it 12 inches by and I thought, 'My God, what the hell's going on out here? Everybody's excited.' I had to regroup."

Graham holed the putt for a double-bogey six. The $50,000 for an 18-hole record had gone long before, and now the $50,000 for the 72-hole record had disappeared with it. And, for the moment at least, so had the PGA Championship. Graham had just shot a five-under-par 65, a magnificent round, for a total of 272, one off Nichols' PGA title tournament record. And he was in a play-off with Crenshaw.

Caldwell could have joined them had he birdied the 18th hole, but Rex bogeyed it for a 71 and 274. "It was a consolation bogey. I had nothing to lose and I was just trying to chip in to get in the play-off," Caldwell said.

"I didn't strike the ball as well today as I did yesterday, but I kept it in play. The only reason I didn't win was because I was not hitting it close enough to the hole. I was always 25 and 30 feet away, and that's not close enough on a day like today. I just had a bad day at Black Rock with my putter.

"I was never nervous. I was very confident. It didn't bother me that the other guys were making pars and birdies. I thought I had to shoot one or two under to win. And I was proved correct.

"Until 14, I was only one back. I felt no pressure. His [Graham's] shot at 15 was an unbelievable golf shot. I was upset with myself at 17. I thought I had a chance to birdie, but I didn't hit the putt solid. But I'm not unhappy. My showing got me in the Masters and I won a lot of money."

The big money—$60,000 for first place—was still to be decided. "David and I are good friends," said Crenshaw. "It seemed a little strange that we were going out in a play-off."

Here's the way it went:

No. 1, 444 yards—Both failed to reach the green with their second hoist, but Crenshaw was just off the front edge. Graham's pitch went 25 feet past the hole; Crenshaw ran his 50-foot approach to within two feet of the cup.

"Jerry Pate had the same putt from the same place in the morning. I knew the putt broke to the left," said Graham, who hit the hole dead center to maintain the deadlock. "When I made that putt, I thought, 'It was meant to be.' I was very down when I went to the scorer's tent [after the 18th hole]. I had never experienced that before [blowing a lead on the final hole of a tournament]. When I had a chance to win golf tournaments with a lead, I won. I think when I made that putt, people said, 'There's a guy with guts.' "

No. 2, 521 yards—Both went for the green with their second shots at the par-five hole and once again Crenshaw looked as if he was in position to win. Graham's ball wound up off the back right edge and from there he chipped to within 10 feet of the hole—10 long feet. Crenshaw, on the back fringe, missed his bid for an eagle by two inches. Graham dropped his birdie putt on top of Crenshaw's birdie.

"I thought I had him those first two holes, but he kept making those putts," sighed Crenshaw. "The four-wood I hit at the second hole was one of the best four-woods I ever hit in my life, only 14 feet from the hole.

"At the first hole I felt I had it. Obviously he putted well all day and he still had the feel of the putter in the play-off. He had to make the putts and he did."

No. 3, 202 yards—Crenshaw had played the par-threes in three under par, birdieing all but the 17th hole, in the final round. Graham was one over, parring all but the 14th.

However, time had run out on Crenshaw. He had his chances to win and Graham fought him off. Now it was Graham's turn. Crenshaw blocked himself out on a four-iron and his tee shot sailed to the right, coming down in a bunker above the hole, which was cut into the right side of the green. Graham also rapped a four-iron and it was a beauty—"My second-best shot of the day," he acknowledged—stopping eight feet from the hole. It was a cinch par, a likely birdie, considering the way the Australian was putting. Crenshaw's blast left him with a 15-footer and his par putt lipped out. Bogey. Graham needed only two putts to win, and this time there was no doubt he would do it. His birdie putt went in and Graham raised his arms in triumph as his caddie put a bear hug on him.

"I've finished in second place four out of the last six weeks," said Crenshaw. "I don't like second place worth a damn. I've got to work like hell. I've got a lot of work to do on my game.

"I was fortunate to get in the play-off. My hat's off to David. To play a round like that in a major championship and double bogey the last hole for a 65—that's playing."

Indeed, it was playing. But Graham has played well in many places during his pro career without drawing accolades. "The 69 I shot in the 1969 American Golf Classic on Firestone Country Club's north course, because of the wind—that was the only thing I can compare with it," said Graham.

"I think people failed to recognize my ability as a long-iron player. I always score well on the one-, two- and three-iron courses."

The PGA Championship was Graham's fourth on the American tour. His first came in the 1972 Cleveland Open in a playoff with Bruce Devlin and his other two came in 1976, in the Westchester and American Golf Classics. But he's won numerous tournaments around the world, including the Australian Open and South African PGA in 1977.

"I felt like I've put a lot into the game. I've won tournaments around the world. When I won the Australian Open, it had its strongest field ever," said Graham. "I feel I haven't got the recognition or the benefits out of winning my own national championship I should have gotten."

Graham entered the PGA Championship on a hot streak. He finished in the top 10 five times in the six tournaments preceding it, pushing his winnings for the year to $73,209. He nearly doubled his earnings with the $60,000 he picked up with his PGA triumph.

And poor Oakland Hills, it was left a shambles. "They didn't play the real Oakland Hills," said one disgruntled club member. "The rough wasn't bad and the greens weren't fast." And, of course, he was correct. Nobody could do anything about the weather, which set up the course for low scoring, no matter where the pins were placed. It was similar to 1978, when wet weather had left Oakmont unprotected and Mahaffey, Watson and Pate tied with eight-under-par 276s. A total of 66 rounds under par were turned in over Oakland Hills' hallowed grounds, four by Crenshaw (69, 67, 69, 67). Graham had 69, 68, 70, 65.

Caldwell's 274 (67, 70, 66, 71) was good enough to win every PGA Championship except 1964, when Nichols blasted out his 271 at Columbus Country Club, and 1979, when Oakland Hills was torn asunder.

Graham's victory also had its rewards for another player, one who challenged only briefly early in the tournament. Had Crenshaw won, he would have qualified for the U.S. Ryder Cup team. Graham is not a member of the PGA, so his victory put the No. 12 man, Lee Elder, on the team for the first time.

Graham left his mark on the fans and on Crenshaw, and a couple of hours afterward he made a big impression on the assembled press, too. As the questioning wound down, a representative of the Ramada Inn at which Graham stayed during the tournament arrived with a jeroboam of champagne.

"My good friend, the late Tony Lema, used to celebrate his victories by treating you fellows to champagne," said Graham. "I'm new at this. Here's the champagne. Enough of this talk. It's time to do some serious drinking."

Skol!

David Graham at the PGA Championship.

6

THE WORLD MATCH PLAY CHAMPIONSHIP

The Suntory World Match Play Championship, built upon the traditions of 15 years and enhanced by the contributions of its new sponsor, Suntory Limited, the Japanese distiller, was an overwhelming success in every respect. For the third time in four years, there was a change in sponsorship. This might seem to indicate instability, but, as a founder of the championship, I can verify that has not been the case. Also, to quote Dan Jenkins of *Sports Illustrated,* "The Piccadilly World Match Play which later became the Colgate World Match Play and is now the Suntory World Match Play Championship, has, in a sense, become a sort of "London Open," taking its place in sporting and social circles alongside Wimbledon, the Henley Regatta and Royal Ascot. . . . Now after 15 years, it is firmly established as one of the finest tournaments played outside the U.S.A."

When Carreras Rothmans withdrew after 13 years, Colgate-Palmolive carried the banner for the next two autumns under David Foster, who had a tremendously beneficial impact on professional golf during his tenure as chief executive of that corporation. Mr. Foster's illness and his subsequent retirement were followed by the decision to curtail Colgate's sports activities. This decision in no way reflected poorly on the World Match Play Championship, but was rather a redefinition of corporate policy. Colgate continued to support the championship and, I am pleased to say, Mr. Foster has remained a member of our International Advisory Committee.

At the time of Colgate's withdrawal, I immediately approached Suntory Limited and Keizo Saji, a gentleman in whom I had complete confidence to entrust the World Match Play Championship. Suntory has for many years regarded the sponsorship of sports events as a means of contributing to international good will. The first Suntory Open in Japan was held in 1973. In a short time the tournament became one of Japan's major national sports events. Suntory has also been among the sponsors of two U.S. Tour events, the Hawaiian Open and the Glen Campbell Los Angeles Open. The company's sports interests extend to the Suntory World Tennis Cup, played in Tokyo, and corporate volleyball and badminton teams that have acquired international reputations. In addition, Suntory's support has been extended to a range of activities including music, fine arts and environmental protection.

Through Suntory's television sponsorship, Japanese viewers have watched previous World Match Play Championships, the British Open, the Masters, and Wimbledon. Suntory is a major corporation with interests that led to a natural bond with the World Match Play Championship. Founded in 1899 by Shinjiro Torii, father of Keizo Saji, the present chairman of the board and president, Suntory is the oldest distiller in Japan and one of the largest in the world, with 1978 sales of £1,200 million. The product line consists of over 200 beverages, and Suntory products are distributed around the world. Suntory also represents many of the leading British labels in Japan, and London is included in its chain of Suntory restaurants.

With Suntory as the sponsor, the championship, I am certain, will continue to prosper as a fifth major event. The first Suntory World Match Play was the first in which all four winners of the world's major golf titles competed. There were 12 contestants in all, four fewer than in the Colgate years. In reducing the field, the Salver or consolation tournament was eliminated and only the losing semifinalists were scheduled to return for another day. Even though the number of contestants was reduced by a fourth, the prize fund was cut only slightly, from £130,000 to £110,000. On the average, the players were earning more than ever. First prize was £30,000 and second prize £18,000. There was £12,500 for third place, £9,500 for fourth, £6,000 for each of the second-round losers, and £4,000 for each of the first-round losers. And that was in addition to the use of chauffered automobiles and elegant homes in the Surrey countryside for each of the players.

The line-up at Wentworth consisted of:

● Isao Aoki, the defending champion, leader of the Japan PGA Order of Merit and, most certainly, one of the best golfers in the world today.

● Severiano Ballesteros, the winner of the British Open.

● Hale Irwin, the winner of his second United States Open and twice (1974 and 1975) the World Match Play champion.

● Fuzzy Zoeller, the winner of the Masters.

● David Graham, the winner of the U.S. PGA Championship and the 1976 World Match Play.

● Gary Player, the greatest match golfer of his era and five times (1965, 1966, 1968, 1971 and 1973) the World Match Play champion.

● Lanny Wadkins, the winner of the U.S. Tournament Players Championship.

● Vicente Fernandez, the winner of the Colgate PGA Championship.

● Sandy Lyle, the leader of the European TPD Order of Merit.

● Mark James, the No. 2 golfer on the European TPD Order of Merit.

● Toru Nakamura, the No. 2 golfer on the Japan PGA Order of Merit.

● Bill Rogers, a promising young American player.

I mention Rogers last because, almost invariably, that is how he was noted until he became the Suntory World Match Play champion. In a sense,

Rogers had to "prove himself" to a doubting press and public, even though he held sixth place on the U.S. money list entering the tournament and was second in his last two tournaments, the Texas Open and the World Series of Golf. One magazine carried the heading: *Who Is He? And What's He Doing Here?* Bill was there in keeping with one of the finest World Match Play traditions—that of introducing the best young American golfers to British followers. He could have been there as the U.S. Open champion, having played superbly in that tournament before placing fourth. He was second in four other tournaments, third once, fifth once, sixth once and seventh twice.

Rogers had no reason to apologize for his presence. He did say, "I know a lot of people could have been invited before me. I only hope that perhaps foreign soil will be good to me and I can become a winner." Four days later, this was his comment: "I've never had so much fun in my life. I came here playing good and driving straight. Wentworth is like a tough, tight American course. And I had the underdog incentive. I love match play. This is a great tournament."

The first-round pairings were determined in a public drawing several weeks before the tournament, at the time the 12 contestants were announced. Aoki, Ballesteros, Irwin and Zoeller received byes into the second round. James was selected to go against Graham, with the winner to play Aoki. Fernandez was placed against Wadkins (the winner to play Ballesteros); Rogers and Lyle were paired (the winner to play Irwin); and that left Nakamura with the unenviable task of meeting Player for the chance to oppose Zoeller in the second round.

Once again, huge galleries came to Wentworth's West Course and, for the first time in the tournament's history, none of the matches ended before the 16th hole, a commentary on the high standard of play of all 12 golfers. From the first round when Player overcame a huge deficit and won, to the second when Aoki scored an extremely rewarding hole-in-one, to the third when Aoki

Bill Rogers was on the prowl to victory in the Suntory World Match Play Championship.

out-battled Ballesteros over 40 holes and Rogers out-birdied Zoeller in an explosive duel, to the fourth when Rogers went to the final green to oust the defending champion, this was a World Match Play Championship that will be remembered as one of the best.

When Japanese writers asked Player to explain his remarkable recovery and defeat of Nakamura on the last green, Gary replied, "I'll give you a Japanese word for it: *nintai.*" Knowing Player's staying power, English journalists were not surprised to learn that *nintai* meant endurance. With 11 holes left, Player was four down. But Gary, with that fighting spirit for which he is known, wore down the gallant Nakamura as he has beaten so many opponents over the years.

Nakamura is occasionally referred to in his country as the Japanese Gary Player. The Japanese version, on this day, was almost as tough a competitor as his more famous opponent. They were not more than one stroke apart through the morning round, then Nakamura won the fifth, sixth and seventh holes to be four up in the afternoon.

That might have been the end for most golfers, but not Gary Player. Nakamura assisted him by bogeying the eighth hole, then Gary drilled a three-iron to the 12th green for a two-putt birdie. The margin was reduced to two. Sensing a revival, the crowd began cheering for Player. This possibly unnerved Nakamura. He hit into a bunker and lost the 14th to Player's par-three. One down with four to play, Gary received a break at the 15th. He buried his drive in the trees on the left, but got line-of-sight relief because of a television tower. Instead of having no shot at all, he had a view of the green and halved the hole.

Player drew even at the 16th on Nakamura's bogey. Nakamura was down for the first time of the afternoon on the 17th. Following his best drive, Player reached the green with a three-wood and eight-iron, scoring birdie from five feet. Nakamura hooked his drive into the trees and took par. The 18th was sheer agony for Nakamura. He pushed his second shot into the trees. Player was also dangerously close on the right but hit safely to the green. Although Nakamura made a fine recovery shot, he was left to concede the hole and the match. In defeat Nakamura said simply and gracefully, "I learn much about this great man."

Other first-day matches were not so spectacular, but they were very interesting, nevertheless. If James had holed a 12-foot putt on the eighth green in the afternoon, it is likely that Britain would have had a player in the second round. A win there would have left Graham three down at a stage when the match seemed to be slipping away. But James failed to hole the putt and, as so often happens, the match completely turned around within the space of a few holes. The U.S. PGA champion had a blistering run of birdie, birdie, eagle, and birdie after the turn and won, 3 and 2.

James could not hole the shorter putts with regularity, although he made several long ones and he also hooked a couple of drives into the trees. As a result, James let slip several opportunities when he might have taken a comfortable lead in the morning. He won the last three holes of the first 18 and was one up. He was ahead to the turn in the afternoon, then Graham put on the burst that finished him off. James had placed his tee shot at the par-three 10th just 12 inches from the hole in the morning. He hit another great six-iron in the afternoon, within 18 inches of the cup. But Graham birdied from 15 feet to half the hole. David won the 11th with another birdie from eight feet and won the 12th with an eagle, hitting a two-iron to 15 feet. The Australian went ahead at the 13th with a birdie from 12 feet after James hit into a bunker. Five under par for those four holes, and also five under for the afternoon, Graham won with a par at the 16th.

Making his first appearance in the World Match Play Championship, Lyle let his chances (and Britain's) fall by the wayside against Rogers, another newcomer to this classic whose last real match-play experience was back in the 1973 Walker Cup matches at Brookline. Rogers, who really seemed to enjoy this form of golf from the outset, had a few uneasy moments after being four up with four holes to play. He took two more holes to clinch the match, 4 and 2.

Rogers quickly took the lead in the afternoon, winning three holes in a row from the second. Lyle was four down after the seventh and still four down after the 14th. He remained in the match with a par at the 15th because Rogers three-putted, then bowed out when his second shot from the rough at the 16th flew into the trees. Rogers' 4-and-2 margin was the largest in the opening-round matches, but Lyle by no means had a poor performance. He was one over par and, on those figures alone, might have won any of the other three matches.

Little Fernandez put up a stubborn fight against Wadkins, and only a late burst by the American tipped the scales, 3 and 1. Wadkins seemed to have the measure of Fernandez early on, going two up at the sixth, but they were even after the morning round. Fernandez went ahead for the first time with a par at the fifth in the afternoon, but Wadkins squared the match again at the ninth, despite a bogey, because Fernandez took six. They swapped birdies, Wadkins at the 10th and Fernandez at the 12th. A par at the 15th was enough to put Lanny in front to stay, and he finally got the better of Fernandez with a par birdie at the 16th. In a final, desperate attempt, Fernandez drove into the trees at the 17th and shortly thereafter conceded the hole to Wadkins' safe par.

In the second round, the four seeded players—Aoki, Ballesteros, Irwin and Zoeller—were introduced. The morning mist had not yet cleared before the defending champion set off one of the most dramatic days in the history of the championship. Aoki won for himself a piece of Scotland with a seven-iron shot that hit a foot right of the hole and bounced into the cup. The hole-in-one entitled Aoki to a £45,000 home (and furnishings worth another £10,000) alongside the new Glendevon course at Gleneagles. The prize was provided by The Bovis Group, a patron of the championship and owner of the £7 million development. With that stroke alone, Aoki was assured of winning more that week than any golfer ever had in one tournament.

And Bovis was not entirely out of pocket, having "insured" against the loss by placing a £1,000 bet with Ladbroke's at 40-to-1. While Bovis benefited from what was, most certainly, the most publicized shot of the year, the bookies were less than delighted. A spokesman for Ladbroke's was quoted in the next morning's papers as saying, "It was a great start to the day. We were £40,000 down by the time I reached the office." The odds might have been less, had Ladbroke's realized that Aoki had twice before scored aces in competitions sponsored by Suntory in Japan!

When the ball fell into the hole, Aoki and his opponent, Graham, threw their arms around each other and danced about the tee. Then they settled back for a tough match, while Aoki won, 3 and 1. Graham had won the first hole and was seven feet from the pin before Aoki scored his ace; they were level after two holes. Aoki birdied the sixth to go ahead. They halved all the holes until Graham won the 13th with par. Graham won two more holes and lost one, completing the first 18 one up. Aoki squared the match on the first hole of the afternoon and went one up at the third, but Graham again went ahead with his birdies at the sixth and ninth holes. Three consecutive wins by Aoki to start the last nine, two with birdies, put him in a commanding position, and the final blow came at the 17th, where he holed an eight-footer for birdie.

In defeating Wadkins, 3 and 1, Ballesteros plotted a different route to the greens from that which had led to the Open Championship. Grimly determined to win the World Match Play, and with his brother Manuel advising him, Ballesteros was using a new, custom-made driver from (appropriately enough) Japan, with a very stiff shaft and a slightly more lofted face. "No more photos of Seve in the trees," he had said before setting out against Wadkins, to whom he lost three matches (along with Antonio Garrido) in Ryder Cup competition. Ballesteros, who previously had experienced disaster in the trees at Wentworth, never hit a drive with his customary abandon, instead controlling his swing and his strength to keep the ball in play. Even so, he and Wadkins matched distances off the trees. But Seve's determination to play within himself resulted in several approach shots being short of the green.

He won the 18th hole to go one up for the morning round, kept that margin after 27 holes, and went two up at the 10th after Wadkins missed the green and took bogey. They matched scores over the next six holes, then Ballesteros clinched the decision with a birdie at 17. Wadkins chipped-in three times during the match, but generally paid the price for inconsistency, while Ballesteros never missed a fairway with his driver. "I think I lose patience soon," Ballesteros said in that humorous and innocent manner of his. "The fairway, the green and two putts. It's all too boring. I have nothing to think about. When I am in the bunkers, the trees and the water, then I have something to think about."

The surprise of the Irwin–Rogers match was not so much that Rogers won, but that Irwin's play hardly suggested that the outcome might be otherwise. Irwin was never ahead over the 34 holes. He won only two holes, and those were in the morning round, before being eliminated, 3 and 2. Rogers was

Gary Player

two up after nine. Irwin won the short 10th with a par and the long 12th with a birdie. They were all square after 18. In the afternoon, Rogers made steady progress toward victory. He moved into the lead at the third when Irwin drove in the rough, then holed a 40-foot birdie at the fourth to go two up. Irwin was never able to put any pressure on Rogers because of his lackluster putting.

Rogers also was in luck at the 10th hole, where he flew the green with a three-iron shot. The ball struck a spectator and dropped to the side of the green. Rogers was able to make his par three for a half. Rogers followed that with a birdie from seven feet at the 11th to go three up. "That really got me going," he said, "and from then on, I was in the driver's seat."

The second round ended as it began, with high drama, this time supplied by—who else?—Gary Player. But Gary couldn't perform another miracle against Zoeller, who said afterward that, while winning the Masters was a great thrill, it was even more exciting to hole a 15-foot putt on the 18th green to defeat one of golf's all-time greats. "To me, at 27, that is tremendous," Zoeller said.

In the morning Zoeller was two up at the turn, but Player drew even after 12 holes. They swapped holes for a while, with Zoeller winning the 14th, losing the 15th, winning the 16th, losing the 17th, and winning the 18th to be one ahead.

Again, it was cut and thrust in the afternoon, as Zoeller went two up with a par at the second, then Player hit back with a birdie at the fourth and a par at the fifth to square the match. Zoeller won the seventh and Player the eighth, and the next four holes were halved. Zoeller birdied the 13th to regain the lead, but lost the 15th with a bogey.

Twice toward the end Zoeller made critical putts for halves, from 10 feet for par at the 14th and again from 10 feet for birdie at the 17th. Determined to get close to the green at the 18th, Player took his driver for his second shot and smashed the ball deep into the trees on the right. He was given line-of-sight relief because of a television tower, but was still buried in the woods. Gary managed to gain the green, then failed to hole his 20-foot putt for birdie, and Zoeller sank his climactic 15-footer.

The semifinal match between Aoki and Ballesteros, which Aoki won on the fourth extra hole, equaled the longest in the history of the championship, the 1973 final when Player defeated Graham Marsh. Aoki's victory was in the classic Player tradition for, like Player on the first day, Aoki came back from four down with 11 holes to play. The tragedy for Ballesteros, who desperately wanted to win the title, was that he missed the simplest of chances at the 38th hole, the par-three No. 2, Aoki's lucky hole. Ballesteros was on the green, 20 feet from the cup, while Aoki was in a bunker. Both took bogeys, as Seve missed his par from four feet.

Ballesteros had his stamp of authority on the match in the morning, being two up at the eighth after Aoki missed the green. He was three up at the 10th, with Isao again missing the green. Aoki had to one-putt three of the last four holes to avoid falling farther behind. Ballesteros extended his lead to four with a birdie from one foot at the first. Still four down after the seventh, Aoki won the eighth with a birdie and the ninth with a par. Ballesteros drove into the trees at the 15th, narrowing the margin to one.

The turning point came at the 17th, where the caution that Ballesteros had shown all week possibly led to his undoing. After a good drive, he selected a wood for his second shot; then, after a brief pause, he reached into his bag for an iron. In the morning round, Seve had hit a glorious three-wood a few feet short of the green on this 571-yard par-five. This time he was well away. Aoki, also short in two, played a magnificent pitch to five feet and holed the putt once Ballesteros had missed from seven feet. The match was all square. Ballesteros missed from 10 feet on the 18th, sending them to extra holes.

He failed to hole a 12-footer at the first and followed with that stunning lapse at the second. Both scored pars at the third, this time as Ballesteros missed from 15 feet. His patience running out, Ballesteros drove into the trees at the par-five fourth, reached the green with his third shot, and was left with a putt from 20 feet. Aoki played a masterful pitch to four feet for his third. After Seve missed the putt, Aoki was clear to the final once again. Isao said it was the toughest match he had ever played, and "I was fortunate because Seve could have won all three of the first extra holes." Ballesteros, in turn, had no second thoughts about having returned the three-wood to his bag at the 17th. "I was short because I didn't hit my iron very well," he said.

Although Zoeller outdrove his former teammate at the University of Houston, Rogers set the pace in their friendly semifinal encounter. Twice Rogers was three up on Zoeller. Each time, the Masters champion squared the match. Not until the 34th hole did Rogers have an advantage to keep, then he increased it at the last, winning two up. Their match must rank, for sheer thrills, among the all-time outstanding performances in the World Match Play Championship. Both went around in 67, five under par, in the morning. Rogers returned with 67 in the afternoon to Zoeller's 69. They provided a feast of wonderful golf for the spectators, scoring 23 birdies and two eagles. Zoeller eagled the 18th in the morning and Rogers the fourth in the afternoon.

Bill started in merciless fashion, having birdies at the second and fourth, and was three up after those four holes. Then came Zoeller's turn. He won the next three holes, two with birdies. Fuzzy was ahead for the first time at the ninth, scoring a birdie, and was two up after the 10th, where his six-iron shot was a fraction from being a hole-in-one. Again, it was Rogers' time to produce the fireworks. He won the 11th, 12th and 13th holes, twice scoring birdies, to go one up. The margin did not change until the 18th. Zoeller, on the fringe with two massive wood shots, holed a monster putt of 60 feet for eagle.

The low scoring came just as fast and furious in the afternoon, although neither player had any combative feelings. As Rogers told the press later, "That Zoeller is really an amazing fellow. He was walking along, whistling and singing like it was a walk in the park. Me? Heck, I was busting my butt off just to keep up with him." Rogers birdied the second from five feet and Zoeller birdied the fourth, only to have Rogers top him with an eagle from 12 feet. Bill was three up again after his birdie at the sixth. In the space of four holes, Zoeller drew even, producing birdies at the 11th, 12th and 14th.

Then Zoeller severely jeopardized his chances by hooking his drive on the 16th into the trees and losing a hole at that critical stage to Rogers' par. Zoeller made a valiant try at the 17th and was pin high, just off the green in two. There, Rogers sank a 25-footer for a matching birdie. At the 18th hole, Zoeller hit another wayward drive and could only score a par. He conceded a birdie to Rogers as he was preparing to place his ball for a nine-foot putt. Zoeller asked, "Can you make that?" Said Rogers, "I don't have to. I've got two putts for it." Fuzzy inquired again, with a smile, "Can you two-putt?" Rogers nodded and Zoeller said, "Well, pick it up. Congratulations."

If Rogers had been competing in a 72-hole stroke tournament on the final two days at Wentworth, he undoubtedly would have won. Over four matches of 18 holes, Bill finished 19 under par with rounds of 67, 67, 67 and 68. Aoki was 11 under for his last four rounds with 72, 67, 69 and 69. Those statistics give a clear indication of the merit of Rogers' narrow one-up victory over the defending champion. The winning putt came on the 18th green, a pressure-filled attempt of seven feet, with which Rogers made no mistake.

Having started as a 33-to-1 outsider, Rogers gained a thoroughly deserved victory, although there was little, if anything, to choose between his play and that of Aoki. He praised Aoki not only for his fine golf but also for his courtesy, and said it was a great thrill to have beaten Aoki, whom he ranked as one of the top three in the world. "He was an unbelievable competitor," Rogers said, "and I always knew it was going to be a fight from the word 'go.' "

Rogers struck the first blow, hitting a six-iron to four feet at the par-three

Isao Aoki

second and, for a moment, it seemed he might emulate Aoki's by-now-historic hole-in-one. Aoki responded immediately with a birdie of his own, nailing a three-wood to three feet at the third hole. Aoki also birdied the fourth to take the lead. Rogers squared the match with a par at the seventh, where Aoki pushed his drive, then incurred a penalty as the ball moved, eventually taking six on the hole. Rogers was bunkered by the green at the ninth and Aoki went one up with a par. Both were out in even-par 35.

At the 12th, Rogers was again bunkered by the green, came out to eight feet and holed the putt to avoid going two down. A birdie at the 14th from three feet enabled Rogers to draw even. Aoki birdied the 15th from 12 feet, with Rogers missing from seven feet. At the next hole, Rogers squared the match once more, almost holing a nine-iron shot for eagle and settling for a winning birdie. He won the 17th with another birdie as Aoki missed the green. Both scored birdies at the 18th and Rogers was holding a one-up advantage to begin the final round.

Back at his favorite, the second hole, Aoki won with a 20-foot birdie. Rogers took the fourth, however, with a two-putt birdie while Aoki hit into deep rough with his second shot. Two holes later, Aoki won by pitching to five feet. Isao's first mistake of the afternoon occurred at the par-three 10th, where he pushed a three-iron shot which finished down a steep bank. Although Aoki pitched to 10 feet, Rogers was 20 feet away with his tee shot and made a par to Aoki's four. From there to the 15th, no holes were won. Each golfer scored three pars and one birdie. Rogers hit his drive at the 15th into a bunker and took three strokes to reach the green. Aoki's approach was five feet from the cup. He made that putt for a birdie to square the match.

101

Rogers had the chance to be one up at the 17th, sitting in superb position 20 feet short of the green in two. He elected to putt, but struck the ball too firmly and it went 12 feet past the hole. Aoki, safely on the green in three, took two putts for a par and a half. At the 18th, both had good drives and second shots. Rogers was 75 yards short and Aoki, only a few yards from the green. Rogers expected Aoki to birdie the hole and felt the relentless pressure to match it. He did so with a gloriously high pitch with his sand wedge, allowing the ball to hit past the hole and spin back to seven feet.

Then the tension shifted to Aoki's shoulders. Isao, who had been so consistent with his pitches and chips, left this one 12 feet short. His putt grazed the hole, but remained outside. Rogers took his time in sizing up the winning seven-footer, then sank it for the victory. What more can be added about the championship match than what Rogers said afterward: "Gosh, that was just about as good a match as could be played."

The agony (above) *before the victory* (left).

7

THE U.S. TOUR

So accustomed have we become to inflation that Tom Watson's money winning accomplishments on the 1979 PGA Tour were not given the acclaim they might have received in an era when the economy was less heated. Watson won only five tournaments, but he had so many high finishes that he accumulated a record $462,636. That's more than $100,000 over what he earned in 1978, when he set a PGA record with $362,429. That's also about four percent of the total $12.6 million handed out, and considering the number of players capable of winning, it's quite a feat.

After all, it's only money; but that makes it no less amazing. In one year, Watson won more on the tour than most men have won in a career. He won the Heritage Classic, Tournament of Champions, Nelson Classic, the Memorial and the Hall of Fame. The first four paid $54,000 each to the winner, the last $45,000, for a total of $261,000. To compare Watson's performance, let's take a look at some of the past money winners:

	Year	Wins	Winnings
Sam Snead	1938	7	$ 19,534
Byron Nelson	1945	18	$ 63,335
Ben Hogan	1946	13	$ 42,556
Ben Hogan	1948	11	$ 32,112
Arnold Palmer	1960	8	$ 75,262
Lee Trevino	1971	5	$ 231,202
Johnny Miller	1974	8	$ 353,021
Tom Watson	1978	5	$ 362,429

Watson won the money title for the third straight year, tying a record set by Jack Nicklaus from 1971 to 1973. His two-year total of $825,065 broke a tour record and he moved into sixth place among the career leaders with $1,671,433. It figures that he also had the best tour scoring average—70.27 for 82 tournament rounds, up .11 from the previous year. Truly, it was again Tom Watson's year.

Winnings for a single season weren't the only tour record which fell, nor was Watson the only record setter. A total of 35 players won $100,000 or more, bettering by 10 the previous high reached in 1977. Seven players picked up $200,000 or more, one higher than the old record set in 1978. It took $67,886 to make the top 60, some $12,000 above the previous cut-off point.

A total of 12 players won a tournament for the first time, led by Larry Nelson, who took the Inverrary and the Western Open and was a runner-up among the money winners with $281,022. The other first-time winners were Bob Byman (Bay Hill Citrus), Mark McCumber (Doral-Eastern), Bobby Walzel (Magnolia), Wayne Levi (Houston), Calvin Peete (Milwaukee), D.A. Weibring (Quad Cities), Jack Renner (Westchester), Howard Twitty (B.C.), John Fought (Buick-Goodwrench, Anheuser-Busch), Ed Fiori (Southern) and Curtis Strange (Pensacola).

Two other records were set, and one of them may last forever. When 67-year-old Sam Snead shot a 66 in the Quad Cities Open, he became the first touring pro ever to shoot a score under his age. A man would have to be about 67 to set that record, and Snead may be the last of a kind.

Above: *Mark McCumber at the Doral-Eastern Open.*
Above right: *Jack Renner at the Westchester Classic.*
Right: *Bob Byman at the Bay Hill Citrus Classic.*

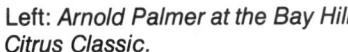

Left: *Arnold Palmer at the Bay Hill
Citrus Classic.*
Below left: *Gary Player at the Sun City
Classic.*
Below: *Jack Nicklaus at the Memorial.
All three golf greats hosted their
own events in 1979.*

Sam Trahan, a little known 24-year-old pro from Cocoa, Florida, set an all-time record by using only 18 putts while scoring a 70 in the final round of the IVB-Philadelphia Classic. At the same time, he also tied a record for the fewest putts used for nine holes, with eight on the back nine at Whitemarsh Country Club. Trahan missed 14 greens and chipped in three times.

Meanwhile, an era—the Palmer-Nicklaus era—ended. Palmer, who turned 50 in September, won only $9,276; but much more surprising was Nicklaus, who placed 71st with $59,434. The 39-year-old veteran went through a trimmed-down season without a single victory. In 17 previous years on the tour, only once before had Nicklaus won less than $l00,000, and that was in 1962. He had never been lower than fourth on the money list. Gary Player, the other member of the one-time Big Three, continued to play solidly, placing 53rd with $74,482; but, like Nicklaus, Player reduced his American appearances.

A new generation has taken over, and its leader is Tom Watson.

John Mahaffey at the Bob Hope Desert Classic

Bob Hope Desert Classic—$300,000
Winner: John Mahaffey

This year the tour began with perhaps the most grueling test on the schedule—the Bob Hope Desert Classic—a five-day, 90-hole, pro-amateur which is played over four courses. It's a heckuva way to begin the season after a two-month layoff.

Yet the players turned out as if it were a designated event, as if they were obligated to be there. Even Jack Nicklaus, who usually doesn't make his yearly debut so early in the season, entered the contest. All 128 pro berths were taken, which didn't make everybody happy. Those with holdover spots from the final tournament of 1978 and the "rabbits" hoping to win a place had to take the week off.

Appropriately, the winner was John Mahaffey. Appropriate because Mahaffey had won the PGA Championship the year before and then climaxed what had been a great comeback year with the individual title in the World Cup. The runner-up in the classic was Lee Trevino, a fellow Texan and another guy just off a fine comeback year.

For the first four rounds, each pro is paired with a different trio of amateurs each day and takes turns playing LaQuinta, Bermuda Dunes, Indian Wells and Tamarisk. Sometimes it becomes very confusing, something like playing golf by telegram. But the amateurs all depart after the fourth round, leaving the surviving pros to fight it out at Indian Wells.

Bob Murphy, who said he has adjusted to wearing glasses after struggling with them for six months, turned in a seven-under-par 65 at Indian Wells and tied a pessimistic Charles Coody for the first-round lead. Mahaffey started with a 66 at Tamarisk. But the big attention-getter was 55-year-old Art Wall, who opened with a 67 and came back the next day with another 67. Wall, unfortunately, couldn't sustain that pace and didn't break 70 in the last three rounds.

In the second round, Mahaffey hit his drive out of bounds at hole No. 2 at LaQuinta, then reeled off seven consecutive birdies—one short of the PGA record—for another 66 which put him into first place, 12 under par and two strokes ahead of Wall. Of Mahaffey's seven birdies, two came from 30 feet and two from about 10 feet.

Meanwhile, at the end of the second round Trevino was seven back at 139 and Nicklaus was at 140, with 54 holes remaining. Trevino revealed that he was suffering from a heavy virus, but he had been preparing diligently for the new season since the end of the year and his work started to pay off.

He shot a 66 at LaQuinta in the third round and pulled to within two shots of Mahaffey, who had shot a 71. Leonard Thompson and Keith Fergus were tied for second, one shot behind Mahaffey.

While television centered its attention on the celebrity foursomes at Indian Wells in the fourth round, Mahaffey, playing in comparable seclusion at Bermuda Dunes, shot another 71. Trevino pulled to within one stroke of him with a 70 at Indian Wells.

The fifth and final round was a struggle among Mahaffey, Trevino, Mark Hayes, Wally Armstrong, Grier Jones and Leonard Thompson; but in the stretch it was only Mahaffey and Trevino. Trevino caught up to Mahaffey twice, the second time with a downhill birdie putt at the final green.

Now it was up to Mahaffey. Birdie the final hole and win, or par it and go into a play-off. Mahaffey's drive left him with an awkward lie; the ball was above his feet on the edge of a trap. Somehow Mahaffey got the ball down the left side, pitched to within 12 feet, then sank the putt to win.

The tour was off and running and the PGA champion had the reins.

Phoenix Open—$250,000

Winner: Ben Crenshaw

Going into the Phoenix Open at the rain-soaked Phoenix Country Club, Ben Crenshaw hadn't won in some 18 months. A bad shot here, a missed putt there, some just plain bad luck had all contributed to his misfortunes. But so had the abilities of the other players.

"Tour players are getting better and better," he said. "They're shooting lower scores. It's unbelievable what you have to do to win a tournament."

This was said after Crenshaw, himself, had turned in one of those unbelievable rounds, a 10-under-par 61 in the second round. Without it, he might not have won. As it was, he edged Jay Haas by just one stroke, to win 199 to 200, in a tournament which, because of torrential rains, was reduced to

54 holes and was in jeopardy of not being played at all. The money-making pro-am was washed out entirely; and the first round, scheduled first for Thursday and then for Friday, was wiped out both days and wasn't played until Saturday. Lift-and-clean rules were put into effect on some fairways; the tournament was reduced to 54 holes; and the purse was cut to $187,500.

When the tournament finally got started on a cold, sunny day, Haas moved into the lead with a six-under 65, putting him one ahead of Lon Hinkle, Jerry Pate, Jim Colbert, Andy Bean, Andy North, Butch Baird and Bruce Lietzke, and two ahead of Crenshaw. It seemed as if the whole field was on his heels.

Haas wasn't able to hold onto his lead in the second round, even though he had a 67 for 132. After three pars, Crenshaw dropped a 25-foot birdie putt at the fourth (actually No. 13, since he started on the back nine). "That putt told me something. If I would move the ball back an inch in my stance, my putter would go through straighter. I adjusted on the 15th hole," Crenshaw said.

At 15, he made an eight-footer for a birdie, then followed with birdie putts of 15, 12, one and three feet on the next four holes. After a par, he reeled off three more birdies on putts of one, eight and four feet, giving him nine birdies in 11 holes. A 10-footer gave him a birdie at the final green, as he captured his 61 for the day and moved into a four-shot lead over Bean and Pate.

Tom Kite carved out a 63 in the third round, which was to give him third place at 202. But the final round was primarily between Crenshaw and Haas, although Haas got no closer than within two strokes of Crenshaw, and that was with a 12-footer for a birdie at the final green. After some worrisome moments in the rough, Crenshaw got a par at No. 18 for a 71, two-putting from 30 feet.

Andy Williams San Diego Open—$250,000
Winner: Fuzzy Zoeller

Ever since he had led the 1974 tour qualifier, good things had been predicted for Fuzzy Zoeller. His nickname derives from the initials of his whole name—Frank Urban Zoeller—and the name itself draws attention to somebody who is obviously clean-shaven. But even more deserving of attention is the fact that Fuzzy could hit the ball long distances and that he was a product of that well-known golf factory, the University of Houston.

However, Fuzzy likes to have a good time as much as he likes playing golf, maybe even more. In his rookie year in the tour he won $7,318, "and spent $40,000," he noted. Then he "reformed." But he still didn't regard winning tournaments as his primary concern, and he wasn't upset that after four years he hadn't gone home with the winner's check.

"I'm not really frustrated about not winning," he said. "How can you complain about making $22,000 to $25,000 for four days of work? So I haven't won; winning isn't everything. My theory is that winning is just a happening."

And when it finally did happen for Zoeller, by five strokes in the San Diego Open, the most memorable thing for everybody was not so much that

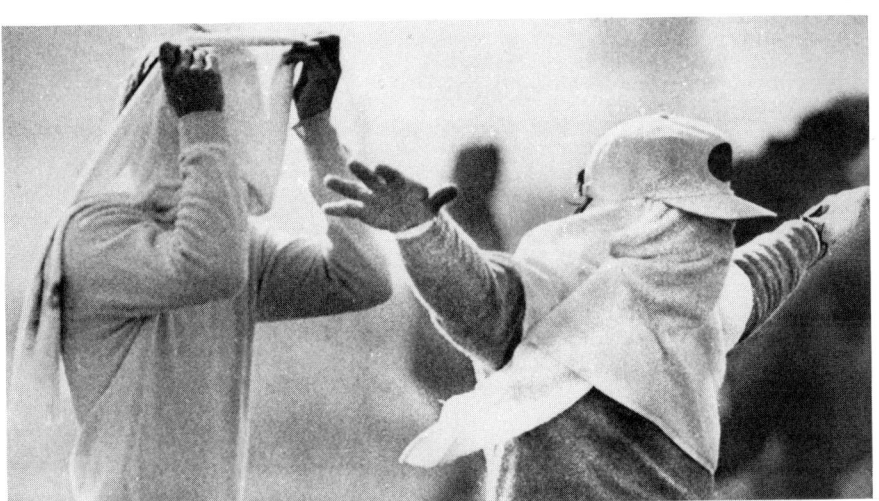

Bill Rogers (left) *and Lee Trevino never expected so much trouble in the sand at Torrey Pines.*

Fuzzy won, but that the weather was so peculiar—peculiar for San Diego, that is.

Wherever they go early in the season, the pros have to be prepared for all kinds of weather. That's why they pack rain gear, tassel caps and hand warmers along with their double knits and sun shields. The rain gear and the tassel caps were out in abundance in the first and fourth rounds. The first day, the wind blew up to 50 mph and the wind-chill factor made it 15 degrees. The last day, there was wind again, plus rain which turned to hail and caused play to be suspended for 12 minutes. (It's difficult to putt over hailstones.)

As a result, Zoeller's 76 in the first round wasn't all that bad. Tommy Aaron, the former Masters champion who was forced to qualify for tournaments for the first time in 15 years, shot a three-under-par 69 at Torrey Pines' North course for the first-round lead. At the South course, even though the tees were set up, only Jim Simons was able to match the par of 72.

The middle rounds were played in San Diego-like weather, sunny and warm. Jerry McGee, with a 67 for 138, took the halfway lead; but a 74 the third day ruined him. Meanwhile, Zoeller shot a 67 in the second round and another 67 in the third and suddenly he was in a position to score his first victory.

"All I was trying to do in the final round was play for pars," said Zoeller, who reeled off 17 pars and a 15-foot birdie putt at the final green on a day when the weather conditions made even par a good round. Wayne Levi was the only player to break 70; and his 68 earned him a tie for second place with Tom Watson, Bill Kratzert and Artie McNickle.

"It's the second most exciting event of my life," said Zoeller, whose wife was expecting their first child about the time Zoeller would be playing in and winning his first Masters.

Lon Hinkle at the Bing Crosby National Pro-Am.

Bing Crosby National Pro-Amateur—$300,000
Winner: Lon Hinkle

The Crosby. Now there's a tournament which is synonymous with bad weather. And once again it ran true to form. There was so much water on Wednesday, the day before the tournament began, that it looked as if Carmel Bay had overflowed its beaches. But, except for the second round when a bone-chilling wind swept the course, the tournament itself was played in reasonable weather.

Nobody who throws victory away has a good excuse, although at the Crosby, Lon Hinkle and Mark Hayes seemed to have been looking for them. Hinkle rallied to win with a 12-foot birdie putt at the third hole of sudden death. But Hayes will probably always look back to the 15th hole of the final round, where he four-putted for the first time in his life and quickly lost a three-stroke lead.

There were some changes in the tournament this year: CBS replaced ABC as the telecaster and decided that only 25 pro-am teams should make the cut for the final round. The network also decided not to telecast the play-off to the East and Midwest. Nathaniel Crosby, a one-handicapper who took over direction of the tournament after the death of his father in October 1977, wanted more skilled amateur players in the field. This cut out a lot of the Hollywood celebrities and some of the fun.

Jay Haas, playing at Pebble Beach, and Graham Marsh and Mike McCullough, opening at Cypress Point, shot four-under-par 68s to take the first-round lead. Hinkle started on the back nine at Spyglass Hill and turned in a 32–38—70. Typically bad Crosby weather took over in the second round and as most scores went up, Hinkle took over the lead with an almost incredible 68 shot at Pebble Beach. Pat McGowan had a startling 36–30—67 at Cypress Point, but he trailed by four.

Television coverage of the third day was at Pebble Beach and while the nation watched non-contenders and celebrities struggle, Hinkle fashioned a 69 almost in seclusion at Cypress Point. That put him five shots in front of Hayes, who had a 66 at Pebble Beach. It looked as if in the final round, the battle would only be for second place; but it wasn't.

On the final day, Hinkle hit his second shot out of bounds at the first hole at Pebble Beach and after eight holes he was four over. After 11 holes, Hayes was two under, putting him two shots in the lead. A three-putter at No. 14 by Hinkle made the margin three.

But Hayes, usually so cool and collected, came apart at the 15th hole. He hit his approach into a greenside bunker and blasted out seven feet above the hole from where he four-putted. Goodbye: lead. At the 16th, he three-putted. Goodbye, victory. Well, almost.

At the 18th, Hayes corkscrewed in a six-foot birdie putt for a 72 which deadlocked him at 284 with Hinkle, who had a 77, and Andy Bean, who had thundered in with a 69. Bean dropped out of the play-off with a bogey at the second hole, and Hinkle won it with his 12-footer at the third, his only birdie in 21 holes.

"This was probably the toughest day I ever had," said the relieved Hinkle.

Hawaiian Open—$300,000
Winner: Hubert Green

Ever since the first ball was hit at the first tournament of the year, the PGA tour players had battled bad weather. Rain, wind, cold, sleet, even snow had made life miserable.

But here they were in Hawaii at the Waialae Country Club in Honolulu. Things had to get better. Doesn't Hawaii always have perfect weather? Well, no. At least it didn't for the Hawaiian Open. It rained. And it rained some more. It was warm, even muggy, but there was so much water that it was a wonder the tournament went the 72-hole distance. It also was surprising that Hubert Green could shoot a 21-under-par 267, which was more strokes than a winner has been under par since Johnny Miller won at Tucson in 1975. Not surprisingly, Green won by three strokes.

After the first day, however, 21 under par looked like a good possibility. The first round was played in typical Hawaiian weather; and Jay Haas, Lanny Wadkins and Lindy Miller took advantage of it to turn in 65s. Haas, missed only one green and birdied it with a chip-in. Miller one-putted 11 times and Wadkins eagled the final hole with a 20-foot putt for a 30 on the back nine.

Came the rain. The second round was stopped twice in the morning, and the rain came and went for the rest of the day. Nevertheless, three of the morning players—Fuzzy Zoeller, George Burns and Dan Halldorson—took the lead after 36 holes with 134. Burns turned in a 63, which he said "was probably the best I've ever played." Green, with 68-67, trailed by a stroke.

The start of play in the third round was delayed for three hours by more than an inch of rain, leaving puddles all over the course. However, Green put together a nine-under-par 63, which gave him a four-stroke lead at 198. The key to his success was six birdies in eight holes, starting at the eighth.

The final day: drizzle, heavy rain and wind gusting to 40 mph. "I don't know how hard it was blowing, but the last time I played in conditions comparable to this was in England," said Green.

You wouldn't have known it by his score. He birdied the first, sixth, seventh and eighth holes to go six strokes ahead, and coasted in, leaving only the battle for second place, worth $32,400, to be decided. Zoeller won that with a fine 65; and Larry Nelson, with a 67, pushed into third place.

Joe Garagiola Tucson Open—$250,000
Winner: Bruce Lietzke

Several changes had taken place when the tour got back to the mainland for the Tucson Open. One was in the weather, which was perfect: warm and dry. Another was in the course. The Tucson National Golf Club, customary site of the Tucson Open, had not fully recovered from some extensive work done on it, so the tournament was played at Randolph Park's North course, a municipal layout which at 6,708 yards is more than 400 yards shorter than Tucson National.

"It's a bump-and-run course and I like Tom Watson's chances," said Lee Trevino, speaking of the defending champion and two-time British Open winner. "He plays those British courses real well with their small greens where you land it short and let it run up to the pin. . . . Of course, I play 'em pretty well, too."

So does Bruce Lietzke. "Marty [Fleckman, who tied for fifth place] and I grew up in the Beaumont-Port Arthur area of Texas and we played the municipal courses there. They were a lot like these—hard fairways and greens."

Lietzke proved that he hadn't forgotten how to play that type of course when he started off with a 63 in the first round. That gave him only a one-stroke lead over Tommy Aaron, Mike Brannan, Jim Nelford and Curtis Strange; but he never gave that lead up for the rest of the tournament.

He had his moments of anxiety, however. A 66, followed by a 68, gave him a two-stroke lead over Watson, Fleckman and Jim Thorpe, a lead that had shrunk from five shots with eight holes to go in the third round. Then there was some doubt that Lietzke would be able to complete the tournament. He aggravated an old injury during the third round, pulling a muscle in his right side on his drive at the 18th hole. But he cut down his swing in the final round and, aided by a birdie at the first hole and an eagle at the third, he won by two strokes over Watson, Thorpe and Buddy Gardner with 265.

It was the highest finish ever for Thorpe, one of the few black players on the tour; but he was no happier than Frank Beard, who tied for 21st place. Now a nonexempt player, Beard finally cracked the $1 million mark in career winnings with his check for $2,600.

Lanny Wadkins blasted two early-season wins in Los Angeles and Jacksonville, then won in Japan.

Glen Campbell Los Angeles Open—$250,000

Winner: Lanny Wadkins

The Riviera Country Club in Los Angeles "is my favorite course in the West," says Lanny Wadkins. "The key is keeping the ball in play with these tight fairways."

For three years in a row Wadkins had come close to winning the Los Angeles Open. And if he hadn't won the tournament in 1979 nobody would have blamed him if he'd dug a hole on the 18th green and stepped into it. In fact, the 18th nearly cost him the tournament. But in his final bout with it he got a standoff, and that was enough for a one-stroke victory, his first on the tour in 18 months, since he had won the World Series of Golf in 1977. (He did earn himself the PGA Championship that same year.)

No. 18 at the Riviera is a 458-yard dogleg right which plays like a par-five when the wind blows. Even when it isn't blowing, the 18th is an extremely difficult hole. Trees on the right side force one to drive down the left side, and a grassy slope to the left of the green makes any shot from there a heart-stopper.

Wadkins faced such a situation in the final round. Moments before, Lon Hinkle had chipped from the downhill lie and dropped a 12-foot putt for par, leaving Wadkins with the necessity of making par to win. In his three previous jousts with the hole, Wadkins had gone bogey-bogey-bogey. This time, however, he chipped from almost the same place as Hinkle, then rolled in a 10-footer for the par, winning with a 72-hole total of 276, eight under par.

In the first round, Wadkins, one of the early starters on the back nine, opened with a 66 which tied him for the lead with Charles Coody, Japanese star Masashi Ozaki and Rod Curl. Hinkle took the lead away on the second day with a 69-136, and after 54 holes, Hinkle, Wadkins and Kermit Zarley shared the lead at 207. Fuzzy Zoeller might have made it a four-man deadlock except for a four-putt green (from six feet!) at the 17th hole.

Zarley had a special reason for wanting to win. Stan Anderson, a friend who had been his host during the tournament for the past eight years, had died of a heart attack on the morning of the first round. And, in fact, Zarley did lead the final round until he hit a drive out of bounds at the seventh hole; and he stayed in contention until he bogeyed the 15th from a bunker.

Now it was Hinkle vs. Wadkins. Lanny took the lead when he hit a sand wedge eight inches from the cup for a cinch birdie at the 613-yard No. 17. Then came the breath-stopping 18th. In the first round, Wadkins had hit the trees and bogeyed; in the second, he three-putted; in the third, his drive landed in a fairway divot and he failed to reach the green. Now he faced a delicate downhill chip from a grassy hillside to a fast green. But this time he was equal to the task.

"I had a good attitude when I teed off at 18. I figured the hole owed me something," he said.

Bay Hill Citrus Classic—$250,000
Winner: Bob Byman

Of the late winter tournaments, the Bay Hill Citrus Classic was being looked forward to with the most interest. The former Florida Citrus Open had been moved from Rio Pinar Country Club in Orlando, Florida, to the nearby Bay Hill Club. And it was the first PGA tour event scheduled for Arnold Palmer's course.

Bay Hill, 7,102 yards with a par of 36–35—71, is about 125 yards longer than the par-72 Rio Pinar. And with overseeded rough and numerous water hazards, it was expected to produce higher scores than Rio Pinar. That it did and, if Palmer had had his way, the winner would have been over par.

As it was, much to Palmer's chagrin, the PGA field staff moved up the tees on some holes and shied away from difficult pin positions on others. The result was a seven-under-par 64 by Andy Bean in the first round, and six-

Andy Bean jokes with his father, Tommy, after finishing the second day of the Bay Hill Citrus Classic.

under-par 72-hole lows of 278 by Bob Byman and John Schroeder. This led to a sudden-death play-off which was won by Byman at the second hole. The year before at Rio Pinar, the winning score had been 274, 14 under par.

"I asked the PGA to let 'em play the whole course, but they put the pin positions in the easiest positions and moved up several tees," said Palmer after Bean had turned in his 64 in the first round. "I wouldn't mind people shooting 64s if they shot the whole golf course. I built some pin placements in this course and they didn't even use them. It wasn't even a challenge."

It turned out Bay Hill is very much a challenge, especially when the wind blows, as it did for the final two rounds. Lee Trevino hit three balls into the lake at No. 6 in the third round and withdrew after scoring a 78. Jack Nicklaus twice caught the water with drives at No. 8 in the last two rounds and staggered in with a 78 in the final round. Lon Hinkle took an 11 at the par-five No. 6 and missed the cut. Tom Watson's charge fizzled when he hit a ball in the water at No. 8 on Sunday; and Palmer, with a four-over-par 9 at the 18th hole on Sunday, closed with an embarrassing 80 on his own home course.

And so it went. Bean began bogeying the second round, his one-time six-shot lead dwindling to two over Ed Sneed after 36 holes. Byman, who had made it into the tournament with a 72 in the Monday qualifier, shot a one-under 70 in the third round for a total of 207, which put him one stroke ahead of Schroeder, Sneed and Rex Caldwell. Bean backed up with a 76 for 209.

Byman birdied three of the first five holes in the final round, then held on as all of his challengers but Schroeder fell back. The par-four No. 18 proved costly for Bean, Bill Rogers and Hale Irwin. Bean and Rogers bogeyed it; and Irwin's rush was stalled by a par. So the three of them finished in a tie at 279, one stroke behind Byman and Schroeder.

Schroeder, who chipped in for a birdie at the fifth hole, played the back nine in two over par, and that was enough to catch Byman, who had played the last eight holes three over. The tying hole was the par-three 17th, a 223-yarder which Schroeder birdied.

Byman muffed a chance to end the play-off at the first hole when he missed a 10-foot birdie putt, but Schroeder handed him the victory at the second hole when he hit a poor approach and failed on a six-footer for par.

It would have been high drama had Palmer won, but he could take a vicarious delight in the way the first tournament at his course wound up. Byman, age 23, went to Wake Forest on a scholarship fostered by Arnold Palmer. It took Byman three tries to earn his PGA Tour card, and in between his second and third attempts he made a name for himself elsewhere in the world. He won the 1977 Dutch, Scandinavian and New Zealand Opens and repeated in the Dutch Open in 1978. Under PGA terms, he was a rookie when he won at Bay Hill, but actually he was a world-wise young man.

Jackie Gleason Inverrary Classic—$300,000
Winner: Larry Nelson

By the time the Inverrary Classic came on television for the final round, the tournament was over. And as everybody could plainly see, Jack Nicklaus had won again. At least, that's the way it looked.

What greeted the at-home viewers was film of Nicklaus' win in the 1978 tournament, his sensational five birdies on the last five holes which nipped Grier Jones by a stroke. When the cameras swung back to reality, it was Larry Nelson who was putting an unchallenged end to Nicklaus' rule at the Ft. Lauderdale area course.

Nicklaus won the Tournament Players Championship at Inverrary in 1976 and the Gleason there in 1977 and 1978. But this time he barely made the cut with 74–72 and finished 20 strokes behind the winner: 294 to Nelson's 274.

Nelson, age 31, started playing golf when he was 21 and four years later had earned his tour card. A steady player—"I had to learn how to hit hooks and slices"—his improvement has been rapid. And it was his steady play which earned him his first victory.

Tommy Aaron, the former Masters champion who was back again with the Monday qualifiers, tied with Wayne Levi at 66 for the first-day lead. In the second round, Hale Irwin scorched Inverrary with a 62, two under the course record, to tie Aaron for the 36-hole lead at 135.

Irwin was nothing less than sensational in his 10-under-par 62. Starting on the back nine, he birdied No. 10 from eight feet and dropped a gimme for an eagle three at No. 11. He birdied from seven feet at No. 15 and 25 feet at No. 16. His birdies coming in were at No. 2 (eight feet), No. 3 (15 feet), No. 4 (25), No. 6 (30), and No. 8 (seven). "My putts were all in the middle of the hole," the happy Irwin noted.

Larry Nelson at the Jackie Gleason Inverrary Classic.

But Irwin came back with 72-73 and placed third, six strokes behind, as the steady Nelson strode to his first triumph. Nelson fought the wind for a 67 and a four-shot lead over Irwin and Jones after 54 holes. "This is the largest lead I've ever had after three rounds. . . . I'd like to finish tomorrow with a six-shot lead instead of a four-shot lead," said Nelson.

Heading into the final nine holes, Nelson had his six-shot lead and then carved out nine straight pars to protect it. Jones, who was runner-up the year before, came in second again with 277, the same score he had shot the year before.

"Larry deserved to win. I can't play much better than I did," said Jones.

Doral-Eastern Open—$250,000
Winner: Mark McCumber

As the winter segment of the PGA Tour ended, the most noteworthy aspect of it was the "who he?" players who won. Fuzzy Zoeller (San Diego), Bob Byman (Bay Hill Citrus) and Larry Nelson (Inverrary) all had won for the first time. Now along came Mark McCumber to make it four first-time winners, and the third in a row. Like Byman, he had to earn a spot in the Monday qualifier.

McCumber turned out to be the biggest surprise of them all. A stocky, 5'8" 170-pound Floridian with the ability to hit a ball a long distance, McCumber finally won his tour card in the spring of 1978 after five failures. He had won four mini tournaments and was the National Pee Wee champion in 1967; but there was little to indicate the 27-year-old pro would win in his first full year on the tour.

In the beginning, it did look as if one of the tour's lesser lights would shine. Alan Tapie, still looking for his first triumph after five years on the tour, led the first round with 66 and, following a 69 on Saturday, was in front again after three rounds. In between, Bill Kratzert had held the lead with 67–69—136.

Meanwhile, the tournament's big names were having their troubles. Tom Weiskopf, the tournament's defending champion, just made the cut with 147, then took a 79 in the third round, which included four penalty strokes for having too many clubs in his bag. Jack Nicklaus, still struggling, also survived with 147, and finished with the same score for the final 36 holes.

McCumber trailed Tapie by a shot and led Rogers by the same margin going into the final round. Tapie slipped to a 37 going out and McCumber went one stroke in front of him with a 35. Rogers also went out in 35 and they were tied as they headed into the stretch.

McCumber never lost his lead. He won by one shot and figured it was a birdie at the 528-yard No. 8 hole which provided the margin. He had missed five putts of 15 feet or less on the first seven holes, a performance which can certainly stretch one's nerves. "I had 237 yards into the wind on my second shot, so I decided to cut a 3-wood and hit it over the green," he recalled. "I hit a safe chip shot 20 feet from the pin and that's where my patience paid off."

That birdie gave him his edge and when Tapie went bogey, double bogey, bogey at the 11th, 12th and 13th holes and when Rogers bogeyed 12 and 13, McCumber had daylight. It wasn't a safe position, however, even after he birdied the 419-yard No. 14. Rogers also birdied 14 and when McCumber bogeyed 15, the distance between them was only two strokes.

It remained two strokes when McCumber teed off at the Blue Monster's No. 18, rated as one of the greatest finishing holes in golf. Playing it safe, away from the water on the left, McCumber hit his second shot toward the grandstands on the right and the ball went over them, landing near a hot dog stand. McCumber was permitted an unobstructed drop and hearts jumped into throats as his pitch failed to make the green. His chip shot came up eight feet short, but he dropped the putt for bogey. "I felt I had a good chance to win if I bogeyed and got in the house at nine under," said McCumber after he had calmed down and wiped the tears from his eyes.

Now it was up to Rogers to birdie and force a play-off, a tremendous task. Rogers' four-wood second shot missed the green to the right and he did well to get down in two from there, relegating Rod Curl to third place.

Tournament Players Championship—$437,292
Winner: Lanny Wadkins

After the third Tournament Players Championship at Sawgrass, the only happy thought for everybody but Lanny Wadkins was that they'd only have to return once more to the hated Jacksonville, Florida, seaside course. The Players Club, under construction nearby, will host the TPC starting in 1981.

Whatever bitterness Wadkins might have had toward Sawgrass was assuaged by the $72,000 he earned for his five-stroke victory. It was further softened by the fact that he shot 67, 68, 76 and 72 for a 283 total, five under par. At Sawgrass, that's bringing the monster to its knees.

"I just had a fortunate week, I guess," said Wadkins after his remarkable performance. "Nobody in his right mind likes to play in conditions like this and I've never considered myself a really good wind player. But I hit some of the best shots I've ever hit in my life and I made some key putts."

Sawgrass is so difficult because it's an inland type course situated along the ocean. Most of the greens are elevated and guarded front and back by bunkers, eliminating the possibility of playing run-up shots, which are normally played on seaside courses. And to compound the problem, the TPC is played in March, when the wind blows and blows and blows.

When there's no wind, the course can be a pussycat, which was demonstrated in the practice rounds and in the first round of the tournament. Kermit Zarley took the first-round lead with a record-tying 66 and 52; others broke par. There were 20 scores under 70, an amazing fact since in the two previous TPCs at Sawgrass a total of only 11 scores under 70 were turned in.

Things began returning to normal (for Sawgrass) on the second day, as the wind came in warm and sometimes wet out of the southwest, steadily increasing in velocity. And players scattered before it. Zarley ballooned to a 70. Gary Player missed the cut with a 70. Tom Weiskopf, Severiano Ballesteros and Lon Hinkle failed to break 80 and also departed. Lanny Wadkins somehow

*Lanny Wadkins at
the Tournament Players
Championship.*

shot a 68, performing a small miracle by not taking a bogey. George Burns also stunned the field with a 66 which included nine threes. That put him in second place, three shots behind Wadkins'135.

"That may be one of the finest rounds I've ever played. The second day was the key to the whole week," Wadkins said afterward.

Defending champion Jack Nicklaus, in contention with 67-73 after 36 holes, was the biggest victim as the winds howled even more fiercely on the third day. Nicklaus staggered in with an 82, matching his highest round as a pro. Skinny Jack Renner, with a 71, was the only player who broke par, his 214 total moving him into a tie for second place with Burns, Bill Kratzert and Lee Trevino, three shots behind Wadkins, who maintained his edge with a 76.

Trevino, a fine wind player, was expected to give Wadkins his biggest challenge the final day; but the wind, even stronger than it was the day before, stymied him. Trevino took a 79, which was not all that bad considering that 25 of the 71 starters failed to break 80. The field as a whole averaged 78.46. Bob Murphy, a native of Florida, struggled to an embarrassing 46–46—92.

Wadkins' only threat came from Tom Watson, whose 71 was the only under-par round of the day. But Wadkins, scrambling for pars and birdies, never let Watson get closer than three strokes. That came when Wadkins bogeyed No. 10 after hitting a sand trap and two holes later three-putted from 35 feet. However, Watson three-putted No. 15 after Wadkins one-putted 13 and 14, for pars and Lanny ended his worries with pars at 15 and 16.

The clincher was a 12-footer for birdie at the final green, giving him a final edge of five strokes on Watson, who grabbed second place with his 71, easing past Renner by a stroke. Watson's hopes died on his three-putt green; but for most of the players all hope ended when the first wind was felt. Their only hope was that it would blow away Sawgrass.

Sea Pines Heritage Golf Classic—$300,000

Winner: Tom Watson

When Tom Watson is good, he can be very good, and when he's bad, he's not that bad. That's the way it was in the Sea Pines Heritage Classic. Watson was good, very good, in the first two rounds, and though he was comparatively bad in the third round he virtually had stashed away his 12th victory on the U.S. Tour.

The result was a 65–65–69–71—270 which broke Jack Nicklaus' tournament record by one stroke and netted him a five-stroke victory over fast-closing Ed Sneed.

"It feels great to win on a golf course you really like. Winning is nice any time, any place, but it doubles the pleasure to win on a great course," said Watson. "And Harbour Town is a great golf course. There is not a weak hole out there."

Maybe not, but under the ideal weather conditions, Watson made Harbour Town look like child's play. And it was the way he played Harbour Town's version of Augusta National's "Amen Corner"—the 10th through 12th holes—which earned him his easy triumph. Those three holes measure, respectively, 416, 422 and 402 yards.

"They comprise one of the hardest stretches on the course at any time and today we had to play them into the wind," said Watson after his opening 65 gave him a one-stroke lead on Lanny Wadkins, still hot after his win in the TPC the week before. "If you can get through that stretch even par, you ought to wind up with a pretty good score, and I played them two under."

Wadkins, aided by a hole-in-one at the 17th hole in the second round, stayed in the early chase with 66–67, but then he later tailed off with 74–75. Watson also had a spectacular shot in his bag, a nine-iron across the huge trap which borders the 367-yard No. 16 fairway which went into the cup for an eagle two. That was the big shot as he played the last four holes of the second round in four under par, pulling away from Wadkins, who had finished hours earlier.

Watson's 130 after 36 holes gave him a three-stroke edge on Wadkins and he spread the difference to eight strokes after 54 holes, again primarily on the way he played 10, 11 and 12. Watson's two-iron shots at 10 and 11 set up easy birdie putts, while Wadkins bogeyed both holes, for a four-stroke loss.

After three rounds, it was a one-man race, and Watson was almost assured of his first victory of the year. Sneed made the run for second place a one-man affair, too, as he came in with a 66 for 275, four ahead of the third-placers, Mike Morley and Tom Kite.

Greater Greensboro Open—$250,000

Winner: Raymond Floyd

It's funny how golf reputations grow. Jack Nicklaus and Gary Player always peak in the majors; Arnold Palmer always used to come from behind; Tommy

Ray Floyd at the Greater Greensboro Open.

Aaron always finished second; and Raymond Floyd is a great front-runner who never charges to a win.

But sometimes the script is changed. Floyd, at one time six strokes out of the lead, finished birdie-birdie at Forest Oaks Country Club for a final-round 67 and a 72-hole 282 which earned him a one-stroke decision over Player and George Burns in the Greensboro Open.

It was not a victory Floyd had expected. He sent his wife and two children on to Augusta for the Masters in the morning of the final round and admitted he didn't feel his chances of winning were good. "I was six down to the leader and I don't have a reputation for making such runs," he said. "I'm one of those guys who gets in front and nobody can catch him. In my 17 years on the tour, I've never come from behind more than a couple of shots."

For a change, the GGO, always well attended, had a strong field. Usually many of the big names pass it by as they ready for the Masters which comes the following week. But this time it included Player, Floyd, Tom Weiskopf, Lanny Wadkins and Hale Irwin. In the end, however, it was a total collapse by Jack Renner in the final round which opened the door for Floyd to win and for Player and Burns to make bids to tie him.

There was a five-man deadlock for the lead after 18 holes, which Renner broke with a 71 in the second round. This gave him a 139 total at the halfway point, which put him in front all by himself. A two-under-par 70 in the third round gave him a 209 total, putting him one shot ahead of Bobby Wadkins, whose third-round 67 was the best score for the first three days.

Renner felt that, "Anybody will have to shoot a very, very good round to beat Bob or me. They'd have to shoot in the 60s because I don't believe both of us will have bad rounds." But Renner, following that statement, went out and shot an embarrassing 80 the final day. As Renner fell away, Wadkins took over with a birdie at the ninth hole. But a bogey at No. 11 dropped him back to a tie for the lead with Burns at five under par. Floyd and Player were a shot behind.

"I looked at the leaderboard and figured I'd have to birdie the last two holes. I figured that six-under was the number that had to be shot," noted Floyd.

Floyd trailed Wadkins by four strokes at the turn and began his charge by sinking a 20-foot birdie putt at No. 12 and getting another birdie at No. 13 from three feet. At the 184-yard No. 17 Floyd hit a four-iron into the wind to within 18 feet of the hole and dropped the putt for birdie, putting him in a tie for the lead with Wadkins, Burns and Player. At 18, Floyd used a three-wood off the tee to get the necessary hook, then knocked a seven-iron 25 feet from the cup, against the collar of the green, and poked the putt square into the middle of the hole. "When that putt went in, all of a sudden my knees went weak," Floyd said.

Floyd was six under and now his challengers had a target. Only Player almost hit it. Player's seven-iron to the 18th green left him with a five-foot birdie putt to force a play-off. But Player's attempt slipped past on the left.

Floyd had played the final nine in a four-under 32 and on this day the non-charger was the only one with a charge left at the end.

Magnolia Classic—$50,000
Winner: Bobby Walzel

He needed a vacation, so Bobby Walzel thought he would pass up the Magnolia Classic, which is played in Hattiesburg, Mississippi, while the Masters is being run off at Augusta. Then Walzel thought about the friends he had in Hattiesburg and figured that playing in the Magnolia really would be like a vacation.

Walzel didn't get to enjoy it, however, until the final day when he shot a 65 and bested Buddy Gardner on the second hole of a sudden-death play-off. They had tied at 272, eight under par.

For a while it had looked as if Walzel wouldn't even be around for the final two rounds. He opened with a two-over 72 on the wet Hattiesburg Country Club course. That put him seven strokes behind Dave Lundstrom's leading 65. Lundstrom's 68 kept him a shot ahead after 36 holes and Walzel's 68 was just good enough to make the cut by a stroke.

Lundstrom retreated with a 72 the third day as Scott Simpson took the lead at 202 with a 66. Walzel, with a 67, was at 207. That gave him a much earlier tee-off time than the leaders on the final day. Several times he thought he had blown his chances, especially after he missed birdie putts at 13 and 15 and failed to birdie the par-five 17th. But Walzel hit an eight-iron six feet from the hole at 18 and dropped the putt for an eight-under 272.

Wren Lum and Ed Byman were both eight under with two holes to play, but Lum bogeyed and Byman double-bogeyed at 18. Gardner birdied 17 to go eight under, but he failed on a 25-foot birdie putt at 18, and ended tied with Walzel for first.

In the play-off, only the second in the 12-year history of the Magnolia, Walzel drove behind a tree but saved par at the first hole. On the second, a

215-yarder, Gardner missed the green and failed to get it up and down. Walzel won by two-putting from 20 feet.

Tournament of Champions—$300,000
Winner: Tom Watson

It's called the Tournament of Champions, but the 1979 edition was really the "tournament of champion"—Tom Watson. Watson's victory in the T of C at LaCosta was almost routine, a job which left him with a six-stroke margin over runners-up Jerry Pate and Bruce Lietzke. That gave him two firsts and two seconds and $181,000 for the month of April, a phenomenal performance.

"It feels good to win again," grinned Watson, who had gone two whole weeks without a win. "Go home, Tom. Stay home. Have more babies," teased Lietzke, referring to the fact that Watson's wife was due to give birth to their first child in September.

Watson had just come from a play-off loss to Fuzzy Zoeller in the Masters and might have been expected to be mentally down. He wasn't. Analyzing his Masters performance, he said he had putted "somewhat tentatively" and that, "I'm still on a high." Then he went out and putted more aggressively at LaCosta and left everybody in his dust.

Ron Streck opened the tournament with three straight birdies, the third a 40-foot chip-in. But, by the ninth hole, Watson was in command with a three-under-par 33, and he never lost the lead the rest of the way. Watson had a 69 at the end of the day, the only player in the select field to break 70. Streck trailed by a shot with a 70, but didn't break the par of 72 in the other three rounds.

Watson hit all the greens in the second round for a six-under 66 and the charge was on. Lietzke also had a 66, but his first-round 72 left him trailing by three strokes.

Watson maintained his margin with a 70 in the third round, even though he missed eight fairways while trying to change to a fade after playing a hook at Augusta National. Pate blasted out a 65, one shot off the tournament record. That moved him into second place, but he was still three back of Watson. Lietzke also had a 70, putting him in a deadlock with Pate. Lietzke stayed close due to two man-sized putts, a 50-footer at the 12th hole and a 40-footer at the 17th.

The final round nearly turned into a joke. After five holes, Watson had extended his lead to seven strokes, but a double-bogey six at the 366-yard sixth hole hurt, and the first thing he knew his lead was down to only two strokes over Lietzke. But that was only temporary. Lietzke broke his seven-iron trying to get his ball away from a tree trunk at the 10th hole; then Watson broke his spirit with birdies at the 11th, 12th and 13th holes.

Watson's final score was 275, which is 13 under par and was the second lowest score in the 11 years the T of C has been played at LaCosta. The $54,000 he won raised his earnings for the year to $229,966. Until 1971, nobody on the PGA tour had ever won that much money in a single year, let alone in the first four months.

Tallahassee Open—$100,000

Winner: Chi Chi Rodriguez

Everybody who plays in the Tallahassee Open would rather be playing somewhere else. The Tournament of Champions at LaCosta is only for winners, while the Tallahassee is for the others, those who hadn't won in the previous 12 months.

Juan (Chi Chi) Rodriguez, the outgoing 43-year-old Puerto Rican who powders the ball despite weighing only 135 pounds, has known the best and the worst on the tour. He has played in the Masters; he was on the 1973 Ryder Cup team; he won seven PGA tournaments; and in 1972, he was No. 12 on the money-winning list. But Chi Chi hadn't won since he captured the Greensboro Open in 1973. If he was going to play in a tournament this week, it had to be at Tallahassee. So Chi Chi played at Tallahassee, and oh, how he played! He shot 66, 69, 67, 67 over the 7,124-yard Killearn Golf and Country Club course for a 72-hole score of 269, a 19-under-par total which broke the tournament record by four strokes. He won by three strokes over Lindy Miller, who also beat the record originally set by Lee Trevino in 1971.

"I'm back, fellows," said Rodriguez. "I think I am just coming into the prime of my life and I am going to play well now for years." He hadn't played well in the pro-am, and that might have been the key to his victory. After shooting a 78, Rodriguez bought a used set of clubs, and they seemed to come equipped with magic.

Bob Mann led the first round with a 64, but Rodriguez trailed by only two. He tied for the lead after 36 holes, and going into the final round he was deadlocked with Bobby Wadkins for first place. Wadkins picked up two early birdies to pull ahead, but he plunged into trouble on the back nine and ultimately finished with a 72, which placed him third at 274.

Rodriguez birdied the first hole and bogeyed the fourth before picking up steam. After the bogey, he birdied five of the next six holes and was in front to stay. Rex Caldwell's chances were diminished when he hit a wood out of bounds at the ninth hole. He placed fourth with 71-275. Miller shot 34–34—68, but all that gave him was second place. "If somebody had been closer to him, I think he would simply have made more birdies," said Miller.

"After I got that last birdie at 10, I started playing for the greens and not the flag. I was using my head on a golf course for the first time in a long time," said Rodriguez, who had 20 birdies in the four rounds, 13 with putts of 10 feet or under.

Funny thing about the Tallahassee: the winner never returns. It's an "official" tournament and the champion qualifies for the Tournament of Champions the following year.

First NBC New Orleans Open—$250,000

Winner: Hubert Green

Considering the talent of the players on the tour, it's unusual that more tournaments aren't decided by play-offs. And not just with two players, but three, four or five. Perhaps it's because in the tense final holes of a tournament one or two players are able to handle a decisive situation while others, for whatever reason, aren't.

A case in point is the New Orleans Open. Had Lee Trevino or Curtis Strange been able to take advantage of their birdie opportunities; had Steve Melnyk been able to play the 16th hole properly; had Frank Conner and Bruce Lietzke been able to hole one more birdie putt, the outcome might have been different. It also might have been different if Hubert Green had not been able to make pars after two shots he called "terrible" at the final two holes. When the moment of truth came, Green was up to the challenge and he won by one stroke with a 15-under-par 273 at the 7,080-yard Lakewood Country Club course. Lietzke, Melnyk, Conner and Trevino finished in a deadlock at 274. Green, who earlier had won the Hawaiian Open, complained that his putting was not good; but somehow he strung together 69, 67, 69, 68, and when he needed it in the tension-packed final moments of the tournament, his putting stroke didn't fail him.

Conner, a nonwinner since joining the tour in 1974, grabbed the first-round lead with a 65 and he hung in the rest of the way. He trailed by only a stroke going into the final round and even after a poor start recovered for a 70 which earned him $16,500, his best paycheck ever. But he missed birdie putts of 11 and 20 feet on the final two holes and admitted, "I got too cautious."

Trevino started 68-67, which put him in front after 36 holes. He played an amazing tournament—no bogeys. "I could have been 25 under if I'd made a few putts. It wasn't to be my day. I hit all my putts well. They went through the break or I played too much or I didn't play enough break. I wasn't reading the greens too well,"said Trevino, after he missed seven birdie chances in the final round on his way to a 70.

Hubert Green, usually the straight man, tumbles in laughter at the New Orleans Open.

Strange, with a 67, moved ahead after 54 holes, but the sensation of the third round was Bob Gilder, who broke the course record with a 10-under-par 62 which included a three-putter for bogey. "It'll come down to making a few putts," said Strange, who couldn't make them the final day.

Meanwhile, despite his protestations, Green was making a few putts and missing a few as well. In the second round, he birdied six of the first seven holes, but had to settle for a 67 after three-putting two greens. The final round was a tight scramble. Usually, there were three players tied for the lead, but not always the same three. Green jumped in front with a 10-foot birdie putt at the 16th hole, then had to work hard to get pars at the final two holes. At the 210-yard No. 17, he hit a "terrible" two-iron to the fringe and two-putted from 100 feet for par. At the 18th, he hit another "terrible" shot out of the rough to the front edge of the green, 70 feet from the hole. His first putt went six feet past. If he had missed the second one, five players would have been in a play-off. "I gave it a good stroke," he smiled after the winning putt dropped.

Melnyk was the most disappointed of the also-rans. "It was my tournament. I lost it," he said. The hole which hurt the most was the 380-yard No. 16, a dogleg right with water on both sides of the fairway. In the first round, Melnyk bogeyed after getting an unplayable lie and, in the third round, he hit a ball in the water. In the final round, he needed only pars on the last holes to tie with Green, and he hooked his drive into the water. He would have had one more chance if he had made a birdie putt from 10 feet at the final hole. But the ball just touched the cup on the low side.

"I was lucky to win," said Green.

Houston Open—$300,000
Winner: Wayne Levi

Every year a few players emerge who look as if they have the tools to take a prominent place among the tour's stars. One such is Wayne Levi, a 26-year-old blond, who qualified for the tour in the spring of 1977 after two failures. Levi teamed with Bob Mann in the Disney World National Team Championship in 1978, and accounted for 15 of his team's 19 birdies in their winning effort. He didn't stop there. Going into the Houston Open at rain-soaked Woodlands Country Club, Levi had already earned $63,033 for the year with five finishes in the top 10.

Levi opened with 69–65, putting him in a tie with Mike Brannan (68–66), and one stroke behind Hale Irwin (69–64 and Sammy Rachels (68–65). Rachels and Brannan had earned tickets to the tournament in the Monday qualifier. Rachels was medalist with a 65 and Brannan got in as the fifth alternate.

The second round was played on Saturday after an all-night thunderstorm had prevented play on Friday, and that set up a 36-hole final on Sunday. The rain softened the course and the one who took the most advantage of the conditions was Levi, who fired a course record 63 in the third round, one shot better than the former mark, tied by Orville Moody, Hale Irwin and Bob Gilder in the second round. That gave him a 54-hole total of 197, the best for that distance at that point on the 1979 tour, and a three-stroke lead. "That was the best round I've ever played. I didn't hit the ball very close, but I'm putting well and I have a lot of confidence on the greens," said Levi between rounds. He couldn't have gotten much closer to the cup. One birdie putt was 20 feet, but the other seven ranged from 18 inches to 15 feet.

Levi concentrated on keeping his drives out of the wet rough in the final round and he succeeded, missing only two fairways. But he still made three bogeys and was forced to make two sensational pars. At the 10th hole, his only smart escape from the deep rough was a seven-iron pitch to the fairway and he followed that with a 200-yard two-iron shot to within two feet of the cup for a par. At the final hole, his approach to the green went into a greenside bunker and he came out poorly. But he thrilled the crowd by sinking the 25-footer for par. Brannan was deadlocked with Levi with 10 holes remaining, but he bogeyed holes No. 9, 10 and 11 and fell four behind when Levi birdied the 12th. "Tiredness just set in," said Brannan, who took a 70 and placed second at 270.

Levi's 268, capped with a final-round 71, tied the tournament record set by Bob Charles in 1963 at the Memorial Park municipal course. And back in Oswego, New York, Levi's friends were only surprised that he had taken so long to win a tournament on his own. Levi had been a star at Oswego State College and in two years there had lost only one match. When he failed to win his tour card twice, he went to Florida to compete on the mini-tours and won so much money he didn't need a sponsor when he finally got his tour card.

Byron Nelson Classic—$300,000
Winner: Tom Watson

Most touring golfers adopt a *que será, será* attitude toward tournaments. Their fate is predestined; what will be, will be, they figure. It soothes the pain of losing. That is why Bill Rogers, Larry Nelson, Jerry Pate and Lanny Wadkins didn't weep and wail after Tom Watson scored his third victory of the year in the Byron Nelson Classic. Although well they might have, especially Rogers.

The skinny Rogers tore into a marvelous three-iron shot at the 422-yard finishing hole and the ball hit the pin and caromed a foot away. Had it gone in, Watson, playing in the final group behind him, would have needed a birdie to tie. As it was, Rogers' birdie still forced a play-off after he and Watson tied at 275, five under par at Preston Trail.

Watson won the toss and let Rogers drive first at the 15th hole, the opener for the play-off. Both hit fine drives, but Watson's was longer at the par-five hole. Both then hit three-woods. Rogers came up 30 yards short of the green, and Watson's ball nestled into an uphill lie in a bunker about 70 feet from the hole. Rogers hit his pitch thin, but once again it hit the flagstick, this time leaving him with a breaking putt of three feet. Victory appeared in his grasp.

However, Watson hasn't emerged as the dominant player on the tour by luck. He knows a little bit about how to play. Faced with the necessity of getting has ball close to the cup, Watson popped it out and the ball rolled to within 10 inches of the hole. He tapped in the putt and, like the spectators, prepared to go to the next tee. However, Rogers missed his putt and Watson had his third Nelson Classic triumph in five years. "I think it's the best round of golf that I have ever played," said Rogers of his final 66. "Every shot I got over I felt great. If there is one consoling factor, it's that I lost to the greatest player in the world."

The circumstances which led to Watson's triumph all happened during the third round. Watson took the first-round lead with a 64 and Nelson—Larry, that is—pulled three strokes ahead of him at 133 with a 68 in the second round. Rain, wind and humid 85-degree weather made play interesting and also helped contribute to the demise of Wadkins, who opened with a 67, 67 and was three under par when he reached the par-three No. 11 hole. After a nightmare which included a plugged ball in the mud of a hazard and a two-stroke penalty when his ball hit the lip of a bunker and clipped him on the leg, Wadkins had an eight and eventually carded a disastrous 78. Pate was the leader when he reached the 18th green; then he four-putted from 40 feet. But the most tragic figure besides Rogers was Nelson. At the 15th fairway, Nelson took a drop from a ground-under-repair area. After he addressed his ball, it moved during the backswing and he informed the scorer he had incurred a one-stroke penalty. Only he had seen it, and it was enough to keep him out of the play-off.

Que será, será.

Colonial National Invitational—$300,000
Winner: Al Geiberger

The Colonial Invitational at the Colonial Country Club in Fort Worth, Texas, was like a reunion at the old folks' home. At the finish, the contenders were Al Geiberger, age 41; Gene Littler, age 48; and Don January, age 49. The only older player in the tournament was Julius Boros, who, at age 59, was still good enough to make the cut and win $754. Ultimately, Geiberger won by a stroke with a six-under-par 274 on the plush 7,151-yard Colonial course, but not without a mighty struggle. Going into the final three holes, Geiberger, Littler and January were in a deadlock for the lead. The shootout was decided by a couple of fine shots by Geiberger and a couple of unfortunate ones by the others. It also was another comeback for Geiberger, the man of many comebacks. This time it was from a poor start in this, his 20th year on the tour. Prior to picking up $54,000 in the Colonial Invitational, he had won only $5,321 in 1979.

It seemed as if everybody took a shot at the course record of 63 set by Dale Douglass in 1970. Four 64s were shot; but the one which counted most was by Geiberger in the third round. It came after rounds of 68, 69 and gave him a four-shot edge on Barry Jaeckel and five on Leonard Thompson, who had led after both the first and second rounds with 65-68.

Jaeckel and Thompson didn't threaten in the final round, but others did.

Littler, who had trailed Geiberger by six shots at the start of the day, birdied the second, third and fourth holes and got within two shots of him when the skinny Californian bogeyed the fourth. Geiberger also bogeyed from the sand at the 10th; three-putted the 13th; and suddenly he and Littler were tied for the lead. Meanwhile, January, playing four groups in front of them, had birdied the first, second, fifth, ninth, 11th and 12th holes, changing a nine-stroke deficit into a deadlock for the lead. That's the way they stood until the climactic final three holes. January got his only bogey of the day when he flubbed a chip shot at the par-three 16th. He finished with a magnificent 65, but that one mistake was fatal.

At the 183-yard 16th, Geiberger swung a five-iron and it was almost perfect. The ball backed up to within an inch of a hole-in-one. If Orville Moody hadn't shot an ace earlier in the day, he would have won a car offered for the closest shot to the pin. "My caddie got in the way and I didn't even see it," said Moody. The birdie put Geiberger two up on January and when Littler came up with a double bogey after a poor tee shot at 17, Geiberger had a two-shot lead on January and three on Littler. Geiberger dropped an eight-footer for par at the 17th hole and as it turned out, that was a vital putt. January missed an eight-foot birdie putt at the final green; so Geiberger had the luxury of needing only a bogey for a win, and that's exactly what he got, after a wayward drive which showed his anxiety. Littler made a 12-footer for birdie at 18 to tie January for second place at 275.

Memorial Tournament—$329,885
Winner: Tom Watson

Gene Sarazen was the honoree for the fourth annual Memorial Tournament at Jack Nicklaus' Muirfield Village course in Dublin, Ohio. Tom Watson won it, but the most prominent of the cast of characters was Jupiter Pluvius, or whichever god it is who controls the weather. At any rate, after the pro-am on Tuesday until the final hour or so on Sunday, the weather could be described in only one word: rotten. How rotten was it? Well, had the tournament been scheduled on any other course, it might have been cancelled. But Muirfield Village drains so well that each time after the greens were squeegeed, the show was able to go on. And the play of Watson, who won by three strokes with 73–69–72–71—285, was nothing less than astounding.

At the Memorial, the pro-am is played on Tuesday, with former President Gerald Ford and Bob Hope as the featured contestants. Tuesday was a good day. The course was soft from weekend rains, the weather sunny and warm. It gave no indication of what was to come. Craig Stadler eagled three of the par-five holes and broke the course record with an eight-under-par 30–34—64; but Stadler didn't find the touch again until the third round of the tournament when he shot a 67, and that left him nine strokes behind Watson.

Rain, wind and falling temperatures comprised the setting for the first round. (And the weather got no better for the next three rounds.) Lanny Wadkins took the first-round lead with a three-under 69, making five birdies on

Tom Watson accepts the Memorial trophy from Jack Nicklaus.

the front nine for a four-under 32. Only three others broke par—Mike McCullough, Mac McLendon and Ed Sneed—as the field averaged 76.3 strokes a man. Tim Simpson scored a hole-in-one at the 214-yard No. 4, but still went out in 41. Jim Simons, the defending champion, had an 80; and Bill Kratzert, runner-up the year before, had an 81. So it went, and so it was to go the rest of the week.

The temperature was 43, but a 30 mph wind made the chill factor 13 degrees in the second round. "It was a typical British day, but the 4½-hour round seemed like eight hours," said Watson, who turned in perhaps the finest round of the year. Watson shot a bogey-free 69, the only under-par round of the frigid day, and took a four-stroke lead at 142. Play was so difficult that day, in what some people call the fifth major, that Arnold Palmer made the cut with 75–81; six players didn't break 80 over the first two rounds; and Roger Maltbie, the 1976 Memorial winner, struggled to a 92. Miller Barber turned his second round around with a 32 on the back nine, staying in contention at 147. "It's fun to have a different kind of day, but today was beyond the extreme," said Watson.

Stadler made eight birdies and took only 24 putts as he shot a fine 67 in the third round, but that only put him in a tie for ninth place. Watson shot an even-par 72 and maintained his four-stroke lead, as Barber moved into second place at 218 with a 71. Watson completed 26 holes without a bogey, before he double-bogeyed the short eighth hole, his only mistake of the day. He got those shots back by sinking a 30-footer at the ninth hole, then hitting a four-iron 192 yards to within 18 inches of the cup for a cinch birdie at the 430-yard No. 17.

Barber, with birdies at the 11th, 13th, 15th and 17th holes, got to within two strokes of Watson, but went from the mountain top to the pits on the final hole. At 17, he had clouted a five-iron shot 175 yards to within five inches of the hole; however, at 18, he shanked a six-iron into the crowd and wound up with a double-bogey six. "I was going to be cute. I was going to hit a soft drop shot—and I almost hit my foot," said the 48-year-old Barber. "But that's golf. It's the first time I've been in contention in six or seven months and I got a little excited."

In the final round, Jack Nicklaus birdied three of the first five holes, then bogeyed his way to a 74 which tied him for third place at 220 with Lon Hinkle and Tom Kite, who had 72 and 74, respectively. However, Nicklaus took bogeys at the first and sixth holes; Kite couldn't get anything started; and Hinkle strung together bogeys as they all slipped out of the chase. That left the race to Watson and Barber, but it really wasn't a race at all. Barber birdied the first hole, putting him three strokes behind, and that's the closest he got. Watson two-putted the par-five fifth hole for birdie and tapped in a 20-footer for another birdie at the sixth. That put him six ahead and even though Barber got his birdie machine working again on the back nine (he had four birdies for a 33 and a 70), the Memorial Tournament was Watson's.

Barber had 19 birdies in the tournament, 11 in the last two rounds. Watson had only nine birds and an eagle, but he also had fewer bogeys. And considering the conditions, that was most remarkable. "Tom just stayed right in there. He didn't make any mistakes. He didn't give anybody any air. He played outstanding golf," said Barber admiringly.

Kemper Open—$350,000
Winner: Jerry McGee

After Jerry McGee had sunk the final, clinching putt and was thinking about how nice the $63,000 check would be as a birthday present for his wife, Jill, the huge crowd around the 18th green burst into "Auld Lang Syne." McGee understood. This was the last Kemper Open to be held in Charlotte, North Carolina, ending an association which had begun in 1968, and it was a sentimental time. The tournament was to move to Washington, D.C., in 1980, and there were a number of good reasons for the shift, as well as a number of bad ones. Three PGA Tour tournaments already were played in North Carolina, the Washington area would be more beneficial for the sponsoring Kemper Insurance Co., and more money would be raised for charity.

However, the reasons behind the move, advocated by Commissioner Deane Beman, seemed weak in light of the history of the tournament at Charlotte. The crowds turned out, charity benefited and Quail Hollow Country Club provided a fine venue. Instead of sulking at the loss of the tournament, Charlotte area residents turned out to give it a big farewell. More than 30,000 showed up on each of the last two days, even though a threat of rain hung heavy on the final day and an overnight rain had threatened to make the course unplayable. But with the field starting on both nines, the tournament climaxed

Jerry McGee at the Kemper Open.

without a hitch. Although Jerry Pate may not agree with that. Nor Craig Stadler.

Stadler, who had set a course record at Muirfield Village in the pro-am a week earlier, got the Charlotte finale off winging, rewriting the Quail Hollow record with a 10-under-par 62 in the first round. But he had to settle for second place. McGee birdied the first five holes and missed a few opportunities along the way, but at the end he had a 61 and the lead.

The exhilaration of the round lasted one day. In the second round, McGee turned in a 74; Stadler carved out a 69, and the heavy-set Californian rumbled into a four-shot lead. J.C. Snead moved into third place with a 65, five strokes behind, as heat and humidity took their toll on the field. After 54 holes, it was still Stadler and McGee, only now they were deadlocked for the lead after a 73 and 69, respectively; and Pate, with a 64, trailed their 204 total by one stroke. Stadler stumbled to a 41 on the final nine and an eventual 76 which dropped him into a tie for seventh place, as the final moments boiled down to a showdown between the two Jerrys.

Pate moved in front at the 10th hole, but McGee dropped an 18-footer at the 16th, putting them all even with two holes to go. Then came the climactic 17th, a 202-yarder over water. After an interminable wait on the tee, McGee hit a two-iron which came up 20 feet from the hole. Pate struck the same club, but, figuring it was too much, he let up on the shot and the ball wound up in a wet sand trap behind the green. Pate's blast barely got out, leaving him with a chip. He hit it well, almost holing it. McGee, who had blown birdie chances at every

Jerry Pate had his best year financially, but he did not win.

hole from the 13th through 16th, hit the cup with his 20-footer and it disappeared into the bottom. Birdie! It was a two-stroke swing and McGee wasn't about to let his third victory on the tour slip away on the final hole. McGee putted from off the green from a grassy lie at the 18th hole and put it inches away, and though Pate's eight-footer for birdie merely cut the margin from two holes to one, McGee was the winner.

And after he had outlasted Pate on Sunday, McGee admitted that his initial 61 had had an effect on him. "When I shot the 61 on opening day, I was supposed to win the tournament—you're a dog if you don't—so I put more pressure on myself," he said.

"Should old acquaintance be forgot . . ." sang the crowd, and now, on every New Year's Eve, McGee will probably think back to the final Kemper Open at Charlotte.

Atlanta Classic—$300,000
Winner: Andy Bean

Joe Inman is one of the most loquacious men on the tour and he had plenty to talk about at the Atlanta Golf Classic at the Atlanta Country Club. Every sentence out of his mouth seemed to be punctuated with "golly," or "gee whiz," or "gosh." But what else could he say after he totaled 15 under par on a very good golf course and still finished eight strokes behind? Inman's comments were about the performance of big Andy Bean, who blasted out a nearly unbelievable 11-under-par 61 in the third round, then followed with a fine 67 for a 72-hole 265. It was like two tournaments in one. The first one consisted of the first 36 holes, when it seemed as if everybody was shooting scores under 70. Then came the second 36 holes, and they all belonged to Bean.

An indication of what was to come was given in the first round when Mark Lye jumped off with an elegant 63 for a four-stroke lead. In the second round, Inman moved in front by one stroke over Grier Jones, with a 64 for 135. Bean tacked a 67 onto an opening 70 and trailed by two. Then came the third round, and here came Bean!

He started innocently enough, matching Inman's 32 on the front nine. Then Bean went birdie-birdie-birdie-birdie-par-par-birdie-birdie-birdie for a 29, five strokes ahead of everybody, and Inman was wondering what had happened. "This is unreal," said Inman in awe. "I thought if I shot a 68, I might not be in the lead because there were so many so close . . . but I didn't think I'd be five shots behind. At the turn I saw I hadn't lost my lead, but the next time I saw a leaderboard I was two shots behind. Then I was another. I thought they must be putting birdies up for Andy before he made them."

Bean's 61, the third such score on the tour at that point in the season (Ben Crenshaw had one at Phoenix and Jerry McGee had opened with a 61 in the Kemper at Charlotte the week before), shattered six Atlanta Classic records: Dave Eichelberger's course record of 62, Inman's mark of 30 on the back nine and the nine-hole record, the best third-round score, the 54-hole mark (Bean had 198), and the middle-two-rounds record (Bean was 67–61—128).

"What was Andy doing out there—skipping some holes?" remarked Fuzzy Zoeller, who had a fine round of his own, a 64, yet lost ground. "This is the best round of golf I ever played," admitted Bean. "Oh, I had a 59 and 60 in college, but never have I played this well. I was hitting the ball close to the hole all day and making putts."

The tournament wasn't over, of course. But it virtually ended at the first hole of the final round when Bean knocked in a 20-footer for a birdie after Inman had dropped one from 30 feet. "That just killed me," said Inman. "It was almost like he was saying, 'Don't even think about winning, boy. You're playing for second and don't forget it.'" Inman did forget it, until he hit a shot into a bunker at the 12th hole and suddenly noticed Zoeller was only a shot behind him. "That's when I decided second was better than third and tried to protect what I had and let Andy have what he had," said Inman, who finished with a 70 and 273, leaving him three ahead of David Graham and Jones, who tied for third.

Despite difficult pin placements, Bean shot a five-under 67 the last day and when they totaled up his accomplishment and handed him the $54,000 check, everybody knew why Inman was so effusive in his praise of Bean. The big Georgian had missed only two greens in 72 holes, had made 25 birdies and had taken only two bogeys, both by three-putting. It was a one-man show.

Lee Trevino at the Canadian Open.

Canadian Open—$350,000

Winner: Lee Trevino

Granted, Tom Watson had a fantastic year in 1979. But just imagine how good it would have been if his game had not inexplicably gone awry at the most inopportune times. Such as at the U.S. Open at Inverness, when he missed the cut. And then in the Canadian Open the following week, he let victory slip through his fingers with a 79 in the final round. But that goes with being in contention so often. Nerves and a delicate putting touch can hold up only so long. In the Canadian, it seemed to be Watson's swing which broke down as he tried to charge a course which just won't be charged.

So the winner was Lee Trevino for the second time in three years, ending a 14-month drought for him. "This means a lot to me, beating Watson by coming from behind. But everything is inevitable. There are times you just don't play well," Trevino said.

Watson played well for three rounds over the difficult, Jack Nicklaus-designed Glen Abbey course in Oakville, Ontario, and site of the Canadian Open for the third time. Trevino seems to find the course suited to his game. He won by four strokes there in 1977, finished two strokes behind in 1978, and this time won by three.

Unseasonable weather combined with the difficulty of the course made playing conditions a struggle. The weather was only good the first day and Australian Jack Newton took advantage of the perfect conditions to carve out a course record of 64—three strokes under the former low.

High winds and low temperatures sent the scores soaring in the second and third rounds. Trevino passed Newton in the middle of the second round; then a couple of double bogeys forced him to step aside for Watson, who took a three-stroke lead with a 69. A 72 in the third round maintained Watson's margin and set the stage for the turnaround in the final round. "Watson's the best out here right now and he's playing really well," said Trevino after the third round. "He can be caught, but it's gonna be awful tough, especially on a golf course like this." It figured that Watson could shoot even par and win, which was a correct assumption. But he didn't.

The weather had warmed, but the wind continued to blow on the final day. At the 157-yard third hole, Watson hit his tee shot into the water, barely got his chip across the lake, got on in four, then two-putted for a triple-bogey six. That made it a new race, although Watson stayed in it until he bogeyed the 11th, 12th and 13th holes. Now Watson had to catch Trevino, and he gave it a try. After bogeying 17, Trevino led by only a stroke. So he went for a birdie at the 517-yard finishing hole and got it, almost chipping in for an eagle. That put pressure on Watson to go for the green in two. He tried, but once again his ball went into a lake. Watson stumbled in with a 78 and Ben Crenshaw, with a 71, beat him out for second place by a shot with 284, three strokes behind Trevino.

"You can't charge on this course," said Crenshaw. "I think Tom tried too much [after the triple bogey]."

"I was confident and I was a lot more confident after I heard he'd triple-bogeyed the third," said Trevino. "It's tough to come back from something like that, especially on a course like this. There just aren't many birdie chances, so you start pressing."

It was a disappointment for Watson. But the $23,800 he earned gave him $377,674 for the year. With the season a little more than halfway completed, he had toppled the one-year money record of $362,428, which he had set a year earlier.

Danny Thomas Memphis Classic—$300,000

Winner: Gil Morgan

Just when it appeared as if Larry Nelson had the Memphis Classic championship in his pocket, Gil Morgan pulled his "Willie the Dip" act. It was a neat bit of pickpocketing, and it brought Morgan his first tournament victory since the World Series of Golf the year before. It was a satisfying triumph for other reasons as well. Memphis was a second home for Morgan. He attended the Southern College of Optometry there, getting his doctor's degree in 1972, the year before he joined the PGA school. So, when he sank a 60-foot birdie putt from the fringe at the second hole of the play-off with Nelson, the cheer which went up was as much for the man as it was for what he had done.

Both Morgan and Nelson were just faces in the crowd for the first 54 holes. Morgan took the lead for the first time in the final round, with a birdie at the 15th hole. Then Nelson caught him with a five-footer at the final green, setting up the sixth play-off of the year.

Mark McCumber and Pat McGowan, who dropped a 55-footer at the 15th green, had tied for the first-round lead with 67s. Australian Jack Newton, with a 68-138, took over after 36 holes. Overnight rain and a swirling wind inflated the scores at the Colonial Country Club on the third day as Brad Bryant, a second-year pro, moved in front of the field with a four-under-par 68 for a 209 and a one-shot lead over Tom Kite. Bryant faded with a 76, while Kite and Bean battled for the lead through much of the final round. But both eventually gave way to Morgan and Nelson. Morgan finished with a 66 and Nelson a 65, deadlocking them at 278. Kite placed third at 280 with a 70.

Play-off time. At the first hole, No. 15 on the card, both went to four-irons on their approaches. Nelson hit the green and Morgan got to the fringe, but both took two from there. At No. 16, a par-five, Nelson's second went into a bunker in front of the green. Morgan came off his long iron and it went right, into the crowd. Morgan came up with a fluffy lie and his pitch didn't quite make the green. He was still away and hitting four while Nelson was in the sand, waiting to hit his third shot. Morgan, who said, "I began to get bolder with my putter last year and it made a difference," putted from the fringe and the ball rolled unerringly toward the hole, hitting the flagstick and dropping in. The reaction of the crowd and the sudden turn of events seemed to unnerve Nelson. At any rate, his blast didn't make the green and, faced with a 15-foot chip shot to tie, he missed.

Western Open—$300,000

Winner: Larry Nelson

There is a common assumption in golf that if a man loses a play-off he will go into a blue funk which may last for weeks. If it's a major championship, it could have a profound effect on his career. But it's an incorrect assumption. Case in point: Larry Nelson. The week before the Western open, Nelson lost a sudden-death play-off to Gil Morgan in the Memphis Classic, and he could have been deeply wounded by the defeat. The prematurely balding pro picked up his first golf club when he was 21 years old; and now, 10 years later, he was on the PGA Tour, and just learning how to win (which he had done for the first time at Inverrary). But Nelson has the attitude that winning isn't the end-all; second place is not bad, and it pays pretty well, too. If Nelson had his way, he'd play in obscurity, just as long as his scores counted. That outlook helped carry him to his second victory, in the Western Open at the Butler National Golf Club, a course which penalizes anybody who puts a smidgen of doubt in his swing.

Butler is so difficult that a number of top names pass the Western for various reasons: the arduous course, because the tournament falls between the U.S. and British Opens, and because the pros aren't permitted to use their regular caddies. Nevertheless, there were enough outstanding players and enough action to keep everybody happy. Tom Watson and Ben Crenshaw were there and both figured in the outcome. Crenshaw, in fact, lost to Nelson on the first hole of a sudden-death play-off (making it two play-offs in two weeks for Nelson), after they had tied with two-under-par 286s. Watson, still struggling after missing the cut in the Open, once again collapsed in the final round of a tournament he was in a position to win.

Bobby Clampett, an amateur from Brigham Young, stirred up the most interest in the first two rounds. He opened with a three-under 69 which tied him for the lead with Jim Simons and Bruce Devlin. Clampett was the reigning Western Junior and Western Amateur champion. Therefore, his early lead raised the interesting possibility that he could win all three championships of the Western Golf Association in one year. He stayed in the chase with a scrambling 72 the second day, leaving him one shot off the pace set by Devlin (71–140) and Nelson (69–140). But Clampett had shot his wad. He finished 78–77; but his 296 was still outstanding for somebody so young.

Nelson's 70 in the third round put him on top by a shot over Watson and four over Dan Pohl, who went birdie, birdie, ace at the third, fourth and fifth holes enroute to a 71. Crenshaw trailed by five. Watson had 18 birdies in the first three rounds, but he didn't get his 19th until the 12th hole of the final round, and by that time it was too late. Nelson picked up a stroke on him on the front nine, then birdied the 11th hole. But here came Pohl. He birdied No. 12, and then got another at No. 14, moving him into a deadlock for the lead with Nelson. But Nelson birdied No. 15 and Pohl bogeyed the last three holes, and slipped back to a third-place tie with Devlin.

Meanwhile, Nelson double-bogeyed No. 17 and Crenshaw caught him by going birdie-par-par over the difficult three final holes. That set up another play-off, but it didn't last long. Nelson struck a nine-iron three feet from the hole at the 16th, the opening hole for the play-off, and the best Crenshaw could do was a par. The $54,000 check moved Nelson into second place among the money winners with $235,097 and clinched a spot for him on the Ryder Cup team.

Greater Milwaukee Open—$200,000
Winner: Calvin Peete

If you liked the Larry Nelson story, you'll love the Calvin Peete tale. Remember that Nelson didn't start playing golf until he was 21, and that, in 1979, he became a winner for the first time. Well, step aside, Larry Nelson, here's Calvin Peete. One of the few blacks on the tour, Peete was 23 and selling clothing and jewelry to migrant farmers when he had his introduction to golf in 1966. He played the game at a party the farmers threw at the end of the season, and all Peete remembers about the round he struggled through is that he made one par.

But his interest was piqued and when he heard shortly afterward that people were making more than $200,000 a year playing the game, well, Calvin Peete decided maybe he ought to change his business. He worked hard and, in 1975, on his third attempt, he got his tour card. Peete was born in Detroit, Michigan, one of 19 children raised by his father, who married twice; and he knows what it is to scratch out a living. He had to quit school after the eighth grade to work. A memento of his days as a jewelry salesman are two tiny diamonds implanted in his front teeth, which he used to advertise his business.

Peete still has the diamonds and they sparkled when he smiled after scoring his first tour victory in the Milwaukee Open, and picking up a check for $36,000 with a final-round 65 which left him five strokes in front of the field. Peete had been playing well before Milwaukee. He tied for sixth at New Orleans, finished seventh at Houston and fifth at Dallas. But when he opened with a 69 at Tuckaway Country Club, nobody took notice. It looked as if somebody who hadn't won for some time, or somebody who had never won, might finally break through, but Peete wasn't even given a nod.

The most likely prospects appeared to be Andy North, who hadn't won since the U.S. Open the year before, or Ed Dougherty, who had drawn some attention when he led the PGA briefly at Firestone in 1975. North shared the first-round lead with Victor Regalado, Mike Reid and David Eger at 66. Dougherty tacked a 66 onto his opening 67 and grabbed the lead by a stroke over Regalado after 36 holes. Peete, three strokes behind, moved into position with a 68 in the third round, which tied him with Reid and Lee Trevino for second place, one stroke behind Dougherty, who had a 70. The betting was on Trevino, who improved two strokes each day (70, 68, 66).

But Peete birdied the second, third, fifth and ninth holes in the final round and with nine holes to go he led the chase, one stroke in front of Regalado. ''I felt like I could win,'' said Peete, and he went out and did it, getting birdies on the 11th and 12th and ending the day with a birdie from 25 feet at the 18th hole. Jim Simons, with a 67, came from out of the pack to tie Regalado and Trevino for second place at 274. Peete already had qualified for the Western by placing in the top 16 in the U.S. Open and now he also had a place in the Tournament of Champions. ''I never thought I'd get there. I've never had so much money. I'm very happy,'' he said.

Ed McMahon Quad Cities Open—$200,000
Winner: D. A. Weibring

Before D.A. Weibring was born, Sam Snead had already scored 65 of his 84 victories on the PGA tour, including three in the PGA championship and two in the Masters. That was in 1953, and time has done little to tarnish the skills of the Hall of Famer. Although Weibring scored his first victory on the tour in the Quad Cities, it was Snead who made everybody sit up and take notice. And had the British Open not been played at the same time, perhaps his accomplishment would have been greeted with even louder acclaim. What the 67-year-old Snead did was match his age in one round and two days later best it. That's the first time anybody ever did that on the tour—and it may be the last time.

The Quad Cities is played at Oakwood Country Club in Coal Valley,

Sam Snead, who entered only eight U.S. Tour events, shot 66, one stroke below his age, in the Quad Cities Open.

Illinois, which is not one of the Quad Cities. (They are Davenport and Rock Island, Iowa, and Moline and East Moline, Illinois.) At 6,514 yards, Oakwood is a short course which produces many low scores. Weibring won with a 14-under-par 266, a record for the seven-year-old tournament, and 51 others finished under par. One of these was Snead, whose 67 and 66 helped him finish at 277. At Oakwood, 66s and 67s were common, but coming from a 67-year-old man, they were extraordinary.

Still, the title chase was elsewhere, and even lower scores were shot to earn it. George Cadle opened with a 63 for the first-round lead, but gave way in the second round to Weibring and Rod Curl, who both started 67-65. Weibring then shot a 69 (at Oakwood, that's "skying"), and after three rounds, he trailed Dan Halldorson, who was a 200, by one stroke.

Halldorson staggered to a 73 in the final round and watched a horde of people go past him. The ones who went by the fastest were Weibring and Calvin Peete, who still retained the touch which won the Milwaukee Open the week before. Weibring, whose given name is Donald Albert (he uses the initials so people won't call him Junior), toured the front nine in a three-under 32 in the final day and seemed to be in command. But up ahead, Peete had put on a terrific finishing kick, with birdies on the final three holes for a 63. One of the toughest things in golf is to have to shoot for a score and now Peete had put the target on the board: 268. But Weibring was up to the challenge. He dropped a 15-foot putt for an eagle three at the 514-yard 15th hole and followed that with a five-footer for birdie at the 16th, zipping in with a 65 for 266.

At the finish, there were a lot of happy people. Weibring, a 26-year-old, third-year tourist from Quincy, Illinois, scored his first victory; Peete passed the

$100,000 mark for the year with his $21,600 check; Ken Still placed third and won $13,600, more than he had won the previous two years combined; and Snead, who proved that age is no great deterrent in golf.

IVB Philadelphia Classic—$250,000
Winner: Lou Graham

When he won the Philadelphia Classic at suburban Whitemarsh Valley Country Club, Lou Graham became the 21st man on the PGA tour to pass $1 million in winnings. He seems to have done it by nickels and dimes. Graham joined the tour in 1964, and for the last decade he has placed among the top 60 money winners. But his decision over Bobby Wadkins in a play-off for the Philadelphia Classic title was only his fourth win. His third, also in a play-off, came in the 1975 U.S. Open. And afterward Graham admitted that he had questioned whether his career was on the decline.

"I was wondering if I could still play, if I was wasting my time. I had lost my confidence and it was becoming a very trying thing," said Graham. "I had a stretch of hardly winning any money. It's a strange feeling, since in years past I had opportunities to win and I was always near the top. This year I've been shooting two, three shots higher and the best finish I've had was an 11th place."

It seemed as if he was going to be relegated to another one of those finishes after three rounds of the Philadelphia Classic. Then he burst out of the pack with a 64 to tie the tournament record. That put him seven under par, for 273. Wadkins had a chance to beat him out, but he bogeyed the 18th hole after his drive landed smack behind a tree. And Graham quickly ended the play-off with a 30-inch birdie putt.

"I feel terrible," groaned Wadkins. "I came to win and I was in position to win. . . . I felt good enough to make pars on the final two holes, but it didn't happen. Maybe if I wasn't so pumped up, I wouldn't have hit the ball far enough to get to the tree. I was dead up against it—and I didn't have a chain saw."

To recap the play of the tournament, the first round was on again, off again as rain stopped play for two hours and eventually suspended it for the day, forcing a number of players to complete their rounds the following morning. Bill Rogers and David Graham, who played 18 holes on Thursday, shared the lead with 65s. After 36 holes, J.C. Snead matched the tournament record with a 64 for 132 and the lead; but Wadkins came in with a 67 the third day and went into the final round with a one-stroke lead at 203.

However, on the final day, there were so many people on his heels with nine holes to go that it seemed as if he were running in front of a stampede. Jack Nicklaus came in with a 65, but that still left him one stroke shy at 274. Graham went Nicklaus one better, and that got him into a play-off with Wadkins, who had shot a creditable 70. "This is my most satisfying tournament since the Open. It's been a long year and I hope the slump is over," said Graham after he pocketed the $45,000 winner's check, bringing his lifetime winnings to $1,027,397.

Sammy Davis, Jr. Greater Hartford Open—$300,000
Winner: Jerry McGee

It seemed as if the Hartford Open would never end. And if it did, the climax would be played with scuba gear before an audience made up of fish and mermaids. In other words, it rained in Hartford. So much that the tournament didn't end until just two days before the start of the Westchester Classic, and even then it was a 36-hole windup.

Nevertheless, or maybe because of the conditions, Jerry McGee back-stroked his way to rounds of 68, 67, 67, 65 for a 72-hole 267 and a one-stroke decision over Jack Renner. It was the fourth victory of his 12-year career for McGee, his second of the year and it came amid the mental pressure of an upcoming court suit with his former sponsors. Early in the tournament, it became apparent that the winning score would be low. (McGee's 267 was 17 under par for Wethersfield Country Club.) The expectation was set up when George Cadle began with a birdie-eagle-birdie enroute to a 62 and a three-shot lead after the first round. But few expected the turn the weather would take.

The beginning of a Nor' easter greeted the early starters on Friday and the winds began to build. At 4:30 P.M., the storm broke in all its fury, the low-hanging black clouds unleashing heavy rain and winds which reached 65 mph. There were still 69 players on the course when the storm hit and along with everybody else, they went scurrying for cover under permanent structures, rather than tents, which quickly proved unsafe. Two support poles in the press tent snapped, and everybody and everything got drenched by the wind-driven rain. After the storm, the 14th green had to be cleared of broken glass.

Before the deluge, J.C. Snead had finished with a 66 for a 36-hole 131 and the lead, a lead he was to hold for four days. The rain continued Saturday, but 55 of the 69 on the course were able to complete their second round. One of those was Mark Hayes, who somehow birdied two of the last five holes for a 66 and 132, ending one stroke behind Snead.

A 36-hole windup was planned for Sunday, but an overnight rain didn't let up and it was rescheduled for Monday. More rain, bringing the total to 3½ inches. Two rounds on Tuesday. With the assistance of squeegees, the local fire department, which pumped water out of the bunkers, and hay, to give spectators some footing, the show finally went on under clearing skies on Tuesday. Cadle, who had backed up with a 73 in the second round, came back with a 66 and shared the 54-hole lead at 201 with Renner, who also had a 66. McGee trailed by a stroke. Renner appeared to be on his way to his first pro victory in the final round, leading with two holes to go. But McGee birdied three of the last five holes for a 65, snatching victory away from Renner, who had a 67. Cadle had a 69 for 270 and a share of third place with Curtis Strange, who came flying in with a 65.

Manufacturers Hanover Westchester Classic—$400,000

Winner: Jack Renner

When last we saw Jack Renner, he was drying out his clothes, drowning his sorrows and hoping the rain at the Hartford Open hadn't shrunk the smoothness out of his swing before the Westchester Classic. It hadn't. Renner wears a white cap like Ben Hogan and he played like Hogan as he won the second richest tournament of the year with a nervy final round which netted him a one-stroke edge on Howard Twitty and David Graham, the newly minted PGA champion. (Only the Tournament Players Championship, with a $440,000 purse, offered more money than the Westchester. The World Series of Golf paid $100,000 to the winner, but that was a limited tournament.)

Renner had done well just prior to Westchester. He tied for 12th in the PGA with a 66–70 finish two weeks before and just two days before had taken second in the Hartford Open. But when he went into the final round trailing Graham by three shots, he said, "Realistically, I have no expectations of winning."

Neither did Graham at the start of the week as he returned after taking a week off following his victory in the PGA in a thrilling play-off with Ben Crenshaw. Nevertheless, Graham opened with a six-under-par 34–31—65 for a three-stroke lead which made some of the players concede an early victory to him. "This would be an important, personal thing to me, to win," said Graham. "I'm only trying to prove something to myself, not to the press, nor the world, that I can win a major and come back and win again."

Westchester Country Club in Harrison, New York, is only 6,603 yards long, but the greens make up for what it lacks in length. They are small, hard and uneven and after he had forged into the lead with a 67 for a 36-hole 136, Tom Kite said, "The putting is atrocious. The greens are hard, fast and bumpy and there's not much grass on them. The scores are much higher because of this."

Tom Watson, heading toward $400,000 in winnings, opened with a 69, but the water-lined 16th hole kept jumping up and biting him after that. However, Watson tied for tenth at 282 and the $10,000 he won made him the first player to reach the $400,000 plateau.

Graham, who said he had a mental letdown which contributed to a 73 the second day, regrouped for a 69 in the third round, giving him the lead again, this time by a stroke over Scott Simpson. But it was still anybody's golf tournament, as big Peter Oosterhuis proved by tacking up a 63 early in the fourth round. That gave him a 279 and everybody else a target. Only three beat it: Renner, Howard Twitty and Graham; and one tied it: Simpson.

Renner did it first, with birdies on Nos. 16 and 18 for a 67 and 277. Twitty caught a bunker at the 18th green and could manage only a par for 67 and 278. Graham missed a 12-foot birdie attempt at the 17th green and just missed on a long eagle putt at the 18th to tie Twitty with a 71. Renner might have been a stranger to most, but he has a solid golf background. He took his first tentative chips and putts at age two, played competitively at age six and won the Junior World and U.S. Junior championships before ultimately turning pro and joining the tour in 1977. He has a sister, Jane, who is a member of the Ladies PGA tour. He'll no doubt be heard from again.

Colgate Hall of Fame Classic—$250,000
Winner: Tom Watson

It was the last Colgate-sponsored Hall of Fame Classic at Pinehurst No. 2. Colgate, under new leadership, pulled out as sponsor of the tournament as part of its reduction in sports backing. If there was something good attached to the move, it was that the PGA was looking for a late-August date for the World Series of Golf, which now gets lost amid the football season.

Well, it may have been the last, but it was a dandy. In the climactic moments it matched the golden boy of the recent past against the tour's present superstar on one of the world's premier golf courses.

Johnny Miller, who had plummeted from his super years of 1973–75, virtually rose from the dead to come close to his first victory since the Bob Hope Desert Classic in 1976, only to be picked off by awesome Tom Watson on the second hole of a sudden-death play-off. Watson's $45,000 check pushed his earnings for the year to a record $447,636 and gave him more than $1 million in winnings since the beginning of the 1977 season.

So many exempt players had passed up the Hall of Fame that 62 Monday morning qualifiers made the field, even those with scores up to 76. Pinehurst is a great course; but the greens, which had been transplanted from bentgrass to Bermuda, were still soft and the course still was not in the condition of years past. The low scoring proved that.

Dana Quigley, who qualified on Monday with a 75, jumped out to the first-round lead with an eight-under-par 31–32—63. Quigley was a story in himself. Less than two weeks earlier, his small boat had capsized in high seas off Narragansett Bay in Rhode Island, and he had helped his companion, a less skilled swimmer, to shore in a struggle which took half an hour. Quigley was cut and bruised and the ordeal was still affecting his swing when he got to Pinehurst. To compensate, he tried putting cross-handed, and it worked—for one round. However, Quigley didn't break par in the final three rounds.

Miller charged up the galleries in the second round as he blasted out a 63 which gave him a three-stroke lead at 132. Starting on the back nine, Miller had birdied three of the first six holes; then he birdied five in a row, holes No. 18, 1, 2, 3 and 4. Another birdie at No. 7 put him 10 under for the tournament, but a bogey at No. 8, a par-four reduced from par-five, kept him from tying the course record.

"I felt a tingle all over; I felt I couldn't do anything wrong," said Miller, a new Miller who seemed more mature. "The difference between a 63 and 73 out here is so little, it is scary. It probably is between the ears. What the difference is, is thinking you can make a shot and knowing you can. . . ."

Miller fell off to a 70 the third day. He still was in the lead, but by only one shot over Watson, who had a 65, and Keith Fergus, who had a 67. Watson made seven birdies that day, including a two-putter at the 531-yard No. 16, a hole which was a key one for him the next day as well.

Miller, Watson, Fergus and Danny Edwards fought it out in the final round, but Fergus and Edwards surrendered with bogeys at the last two holes. Watson caught up to Miller by hitting a three-wood to the 16th green, then dropping a long putt for an eagle three. Miller matched that with a magnificent shot of his own, a three-iron which set up an easy birdie at the 17th green. However, Miller hooked his drive under the trees at 18, pitched poorly and bogeyed for a 70 which deadlocked him with Watson at 272, two strokes in front of Fergus.

Both parred the first play-off hole. At the second, Watson hit a seven-iron shot 175 yards, the ball going over the green and onto the downslope. Watson won by two-putting. It had been a long time since Miller had been in that situation, but at least he had a taste of what victory used to be like.

B.C. Open—$275,000
Winner: Howard Twitty

Howard Twitty had been one of those fringe players who from time to time pops up as a contender for a round or two, then settles back for a good payday. That kind usually plays so well so often that you know they'll eventually win one. Howard Twitty's time came in the B.C. Open at the En Joie Golf Club in Endicott, New York.

Twitty had come out of the amateur ranks with a fine reputation, including two runner-up finishes in the NCAA tournament and two All-America notices while at Arizona State. Before trying for the tour, he played in Asia and won in Thailand. At 6'5" and 220 pounds, he figures his growth stunted his development as a golfer. But now he's full grown and he showed that his golf game is, too, by shooting 69–70–64–67—270, winning by a stroke over Tom Purtzer.

Purtzer bogeyed the 72nd hole and it proved fatal. That gave both Twitty and Doug Tewell a chance to win with pars at the final hole. Tewell blew it, collapsing with a double bogey. Twitty raised Purtzer's hopes by hitting a hook off the tee, then failing to reach the green. But a chip from the fringe and a successful putt brought the necessary par.

The B.C. has a lot going for it, primarily the enthusiasm of the tournament volunteers, but it has some obstacles, too. It's played on the first weekend of professional football; many of the big stars compete in the Canadian PGA championship; and usually the weather is atrocious. This time the weatherman cooperated and there were enough name players to go around. There also were a number of fringe players the likes of Twitty to make it an interesting tournament.

Curtis Strange, a former NCAA champion enjoying a fine, although still winless, year, opened with a seven-under-par 64, giving him a one-stroke lead over another promising non-winner, Alan Tapie. A 67 gave Tapie the 36-hole lead by one over Gil Morgan (67) and 263-pound Larry Webb. All three began to fade in the third round. After 54 holes two more non-winners, Tewell and Brad Bryant, were in the lead at 202 and Twitty trailed by only a shot after a sizzling 64. Tewell had a 66 and Bryant a 68.

Then came the final round and Purtzer's mistake at the 18th green, followed by a big sigh of relief from Twitty. The $49,500 check lifted his earnings to $167,391 for the year and proved that, yes, there is a place for a big man on the PGA Tour.

American Optical Pleasant Valley Classic—$250,000
Winner: Lou Graham

Like the Kemper Open and the Hall of Fame Classic, the Pleasant Valley Classic, officially called the American Optical Classic, was a tournament whose future was in jeopardy. Cuz Mingolla, who founded the tournament in Sutton, Massachusetts, had died in May, and his son, Ted, indicated that the tournament would no longer accept a September date after its contract ran out in 1980. In September, many of the big-name players are winding down their season, knowing that most of the money they earn will go to the federal government in income taxes.

John Mahaffey, the 1978 PGA champion, pulled out before the tournament began; and two former PGA champions, Ray Floyd and Lanny Wadkins, were among 11 who withdrew after the first round, further diluting the field of talent.

It also didn't help that this year the first round was postponed because of heavy rain brought on by Hurricane David, which necessitated a 36-hole final on Sunday, always a disheartening turn. But a record crowd of 44,300 showed up the final day, so maybe there's still hope for Pleasant Valley.

But enough of this negative business. Enough very good players remained and two of the best, Lou Graham and Ben Crenshaw, made it an exciting final day. As far as the crowd was concerned, the only thing better would have been if Crenshaw had won, for Gentle Ben seemed to have many fans in Sutton, Massachusetts. But Graham beat him out by a shot and earned a spot in the World Series of Golf with his second victory of the year.

Crenshaw and Graham went into the final round deadlocked for second place, a stroke behind David Edwards' 205. But in the closing moments, it was Graham vs. Crenshaw and the fans let Graham know who they were rooting for. As Graham walked onto the 17th green to size up an 80-foot chip shot, somebody in the large crowd on the hillside shouted: "A lot of green. Don't choke!"

"It made me more determined. I wanted to show that guy something," said Graham, who chipped to within a foot and tapped in the putt as Crenshaw's birdie at the 18th hole was posted on the scoreboard. Graham parred No. 18 for a 69–275 to Crenshaw's 70–276.

It was the fifth second-place finish for Crenshaw in six tournaments, including a play-off with another Graham, David, in the PGA title tournament. "When you finish second that many times, you've got to be playing very well. I'm trying to look at the positive side," said Crenshaw. "My game's more consistent. I'm building confidence and my attitude's better. I'm maturing."

Crenshaw, with a 67, was a stroke out of the opening lead, shared by Terry Diehl, David Thore and Ed Sabo, and at that time was a stroke ahead of Graham. Graham took the 36-hole lead with a 67–135, gave way briefly to Edwards after 54 holes, then took charge in the final round as Edwards collapsed with a 77.

After he birdied the 12th hole from two inches, Graham led Crenshaw by three strokes, a lead which was reduced to two when Graham bogeyed No. 14. But the best Crenshaw could do on the finishing holes was to save par two times and to birdie the 18th hole, as Graham, Mr. Consistent, held on.

"I should have won more," said Graham, 41, looking back on a career in which he had won only five tournaments. "In one stretch in 1973, I was one shot back three weeks in a row. I thought to myself, 'What can I do? Why am I consistent?' I don't really know. I'm a good driver, not a great driver. I'm a good iron player, not a great iron player. I'm a good chipper. At times, I'm a steady putter. When you put those together week after week, I guess that's why."

Ryder Cup Matches
Winner: United States
This was supposed to be the year that the 11-year domination of the Ryder Cup Matches by the United States would be broken. Instead of just Great Britain

Ken Brown (left) *and Mark James were the "odd couple" of the Ryder Cup matches.*

and Ireland teaming up against the Americans, members of the British PGA and European TPD were permitted to play, making the European team much stronger. Only two players who were not from the British Isles were added: Severiano Ballesteros and Antonio Garrido, both from Spain. But they were enough. Ballesteros was the reigning British Open champion and the two Spaniards had teamed to win the World Cup two years earlier.

The venue was the Greenbrier course in White Sulphur Springs, West Virginia, a 6,710-yard layout which had been refinished by Jack Nicklaus into quite a test, including greens which broke a thousand ways and fairways lined by deep rough. Nicklaus, who had missed qualifying for the matches for the first time since he became eligible, was called away when his father-in-law died two days before the start of play and missed the opening ceremonies. Tom Watson, the record-setting money winner, also had to make a hurried departure to join his wife, Linda, who gave birth to their first child, a daughter, the day before the first matches.

So things looked good for the European side. But the result was still the same. The United States won, 17–11, giving the Americans a 19–3–1 record in the biennial event.

But forget the score. The matches actually were closer than they had been in recent years. And if it hadn't been for some heroics by Larry Nelson and Lanny Wadkins, the outcome might have been very different. The absence of Watson forced U.S. captain Bill Casper to make a line-up change and he came up with a gem, deciding to have Nelson replace Watson as Wadkins' partner. Mark Hayes, who hadn't played in a week because of the birth of his first child, took Watson's spot on the squad for singles play and accounted for one of the American victories the final day.

Nelson and Wadkins swayed the outcome in favor of the Americans. And they did it largely by attacking the strength of the European team: Ballesteros and Garrido. The Americans defeated the Spaniards, 2 and 1, in the opening four-ball match; then whipped Bernard Gallacher and Brian Barnes, 4 and 3, in foursomes play in the afternoon as the United States took a 5½–2½ lead after the first day.

In the Saturday morning foursomes, Nelson and Wadkins made it two straight over Ballesteros and Garrido, 3 and 2; then won their four-ball match in the afternoon, 5 and 4. Sunday is devoted to singles and Nelson triumphed over Ballesteros, 3 and 2; but Wadkins had his Ryder Cup winning string ended at seven, including three in 1977, by Gallacher, 3 and 2.

"I don't think I'm a hero. If there was a hero, it was Lanny," said Nelson, who got into the matches with finishes of fourth, second and first in the final three qualifying tournaments. "He spent the first two days teaching me match play and his aggressive nature got me going."

Victories by Gallacher and Barnes over Hale Irwin and John Mahaffey and by Ballesteros and Garrido over Fuzzy Zoeller and Hubert Green were the only points the visitors earned the first day. The second day was a turn-around, the Europeans winning five of the eight matches, cutting the Americans' lead

148

to 8½–7½. The U.S. wins were scored by Nelson-Wadkins, who defeated Ballesteros-Garrido twice, and Irwin-Tom Kite, who edged Tony Jacklin-Sandy Lyle, 1 up.

So the final day of singles was pivotal and Casper went into them with only four players experienced in Ryder Cup competition: Wadkins, Irwin, Lee Trevino and Hubert Green. And he almost lost Trevino. The night before the matches, each captain had to choose a player he would withdraw in case somebody on the other team had to pull out (everybody on the 12-man teams was to play in the singles), and to place that name in an envelope. Misunderstanding, Casper placed Trevino's name in it. Mark James of Great Britain and Gil Morgan of the United States both had shoulder injuries, but Morgan said he could play. An hour before the first tee-off time, James pulled out. When Casper discovered his mistake, John Jacobs, the European captain, graciously permitted him to correct it and Morgan was benched in favor of Trevino.

Nelson birdied the first three holes against Ballesteros, and he was the only American player with a clear-cut lead as the matches went into the final holes. Nelson made three more birdies on the back nine; then watched along with Wadkins, who had already lost to Gallacher, as the other matches came in. Kite birdied from two feet at the 16th hole and held off Jacklin; Hayes dropped a 12-foot birdie putt at the 18th green to beat Garrido; and Mahaffey defeated Barnes, all by one-up scores. Green applied the clincher, with birdies on the final two holes for a two-up decision over Peter Oosterhuis.

Gallacher was the leading point-getter for the Europeans with four victories and Barnes was next with three points. Lee Elder, the first black to play for the United States, teamed with Andy Bean for a 2-and-1 verdict over Oosterhuis and Nick Faldo in the opening four-ball matches and went 0-for-3 the rest of the way, but it didn't dampen his enthusiasm.

"This far exceeds the Masters. If far exceeds my first tournament victory. It far exceeds anything I've done, personally, in my life," Elder said.

Buick-Goodwrench Open—$150,000

Winner: John Fought

After he won the U.S. Amateur in 1977, John Fought thought he could lick the golf world. Then came the rude awakening, with two failures at winning his tour card, and then a seemingly endless number of Monday morning qualifiers after he got it in the fall of 1978. "The competition is so much better here. The mini-tours, amateur golf, none of it is even close to this," he said. "When I got through qualifying school, I thought maybe I could win a tournament, but saying you'd like to do it and doing it are so different."

Prior to the Buick-Goodwrench Open at Warwick Hills in Grand Blanc, Michigan, Fought (pronouned Foat) had made his best showing as a pro in the Western Open, in which he tied for 13th. Then, suddenly, he was a winner, beating Jim Simons on the second hole of a sudden-death play-off after he had finished 68–69 for 280.

Simons, seeking his third victory in three years, closed with a nifty five-under-par 67, but Fought caught him by sinking a six-foot birdie putt at the 72nd green. Both missed birdie putts at the first play-off hole, then Fought won at the second with a par after Simons missed the green at the 185-yard hole, and pitched over it on a shot from hardpan.

The Buick is played opposite the Ryder Cup Matches and a dozen of the big name players were at the Greenbrier. David Graham, who had won the PGA championship at nearby Birmingham, Michigan, and struggling Tom Weiskopf were in the field, but the tournament was made up primarily of those seeking a first win or enough money to make the exempt top 60 list. And it seemed as if everybody was in contention.

Cesar Sanudo and Ed Dougherty shared the first-round lead with 67s, but Dave Eichelberger held it for the next 36 holes with 70–72 for 210. A total of 15 players were within two shots of the lead with 18 holes to go, and with nine holes left only three of them had abandoned the chase. But then came Simons, followed by Fought, and the only one who had a chance to catch them was Eichelberger. He needed a birdie to win, a par to tie at the 18th hole, but the dogleg 461-yarder plays tough. Eichelberger's drive caught a fairway bunker and he ultimately bogeyed for a 71 and 281.

Fought became the 10th first-time winner of the year!

Anheuser-Busch Golf Classic—$300,000
Winner: John Fought

When you're hot, you're hot, and obviously even a 1,500-mile journey won't cool you off. John Fought made the trip from Grand Blanc, Michigan, to Napa Valley, California, 50 miles north of San Francisco, and his game didn't drop a degree.

The first-year pro, who had just won his first victory as a pro at the Buick-Goodwrench Open, came back the following week to score another startler in the Anheuser-Busch Classic. It's the first time since 1975, when Roger Maltbie won two in a row, that a rookie scored consecutive victories on the tour.

The shot that did it for Fought was a 10-foot birdie putt at the 18th green at Silverado Country Club's North course on the final day. That, and the confidence gained in his surprise win at Grand Blanc. "That's what happens when you win one. You believe you can win another," said Fought. "I stood up there over the final putt and told myself, 'John, you can win this.' And then I won it."

Fought won it by a stroke over Alan Tapie, Bobby Wadkins and Buddy Gardner with 69–68–71–69—277. The $54,000 check gave him $81,000 for the two weeks' work, moved him to 32nd place on the money list with $103,227 and gained him a place in the World Series of Golf as a multiple winner. The 1977 U.S. Amateur winner, who had twice failed to get his PGA Tour card, had suddenly blossomed into a winner.

The 25-year-old from Portland, Oregon, hung close all the way before breaking a four-man deadlock with his climactic birdie putt at the 72nd hole. The tournament is held on Silverado's two courses the first two days, half of the field playing the 6,870-yard, par-72 North course, while the other half plays the 6,619-yard, par-72 course. Then they switch courses the second day. The final 36 holes are played on the longer North.

Fought played the North and took a position three strokes out of the lead as Mark Lye and Wadkins opened with 66s at the South. Lye calls Silverado home. He played there from the time he was 13 and the 26-year-old pro caddied in Kaiser Opens there as a youngster. So he had a built-in cheering gallery.

Lye's gallery was silenced in the second round when he shot a 72 and fell four strokes behind Lou Graham, whose 66 gave him the 36-hole lead at 134. But Lye rebounded for a 67 which deadlocked him for the 54-hole lead with Lon Hinkle, who had 69–66–70. At this point Fought trailed by three strokes.

Lye moved ahead by two strokes as the leaders made the turn in the final round and champagne glasses were already being raised in tribute in the homes which border the course. However, the cheering quickly died as Lye bogeyed the 10th hole, then took a double bogey at the 387-yard No. 11 after hitting his drive into the rough. He struggled in with a 75 and a tie for sixth place. Hinkle, meanwhile, had his troubles early and also shot a 75.

So it was Fought, Wadkins, Gardner and Tapie in the charge to the wire, and Fought won. Of the four, Fought was the only one who had ever won as a pro and the memory of how to do it was still fresh in his mind.

World Series of Golf—$400,000
Winner: Lon Hinkle

For some reason, the World Series of Golf doesn't have the aura of a major tournament, but it should have. All season long, players try to qualify for the 36-man field at Firestone's difficult South course; but, when the time comes to play, there are always a few who find reasons not to be there. Maybe in 1980, when the tournament is moved up a month, its status will change.

The 1979 tournament was played the final weekend in September, right smack in the middle of the football season and at the climax of the major league baseball races. It's a great time to play golf in the North, but by this time some pros are ready to call it a season, figuring the tax man's going to take most of what they win anyway. Not everybody feels that way, of course, for many can get motivated by the World Series' top prize of $100,000, the biggest pay-off of the year.

Because of withdrawals, including British Open champ Severiano Ballesteros, the PGA had to reach down to the 25th man on the money list to fill the field, which was increased to 36 men, primarily to make it seem more like a tournament than a club invitational. Lon Hinkle won by a shot over Bill Rogers, Larry Nelson and Lee Trevino; and if Hinkle didn't seem to be taking it seriously, well, that's the way Hinkle is.

The 30-year-old pro from Dallas, by way of Flint, Michigan, had scored his second victory in little more than seven years on the tour in the Bing Crosby Pro-Am in February. By the end of April, he had won more than $100,000 and, despite his protests, he seemed to be satisfied. His attitude in the past had been to set a goal, reach it, then have a good time.

He had a good time at Firestone. He had won $146,275, a high for him, prior to the World Series and it seemed as if he had his mind more on his wife, Edith, and their one-year-old daughter, Monique, than the task at hand. Apparently, it had no ill effect on his concentration. Hinkle shot 67–67–71–67—272; that's eight under par over one of the world's most difficult par-70 courses.

Rain, six inches of it, soaked the Akron, Ohio, area the week before the tournament. Andy Bean took advantage of the soft conditions to scrape out a six-under 64 for the first-round lead, then sat on his two-stroke edge over J.C. Snead and Graham Marsh as the rain paid a return visit and wiped out play on Friday.

That set up a double round on Sunday. (That's routine for regular tour events, but should it be used for something as prestigious as the World Series?) The delay presented problems for some and helped others. Lee Trevino, for instance, figured his aching back wouldn't stand up through a double round. As it turned out, it held up very well and Trevino finished with a 66.

Nelson, on the other hand, welcomed the day of rest. He had come into the tournament with a stomach virus and the Friday rest helped cure it. Nelson nearly won the tournament; in fact, he might have, if he hadn't stumbled badly at the 17th hole on the final round.

Tom Watson, taking aim at a $500,000-plus season, turned in a 65 on Saturday despite missing an easy birdie putt at the final hole and his 133 put him one up on Hinkle after 36 holes. Bean, meanwhile, went from 64 to 75 and was out of the chase. One of Hinkle's shots that day was a beauty. Blocked by trees on his approach to the 16th green, he deliberately skipped his ball across the water in front of the green and parred.

The start of the Sunday rounds was delayed for an hour and a half by fog, creating possible problems for both television and for people with reservations out of Akron. When the fog lifted, Jerry Pate went out and shot a magnificent 65 in the morning to take the 54-hole lead at 205. But Pate played the first three holes in the afternoon in four over par and eventually straggled in with a disheartening 76.

With the brakes on Pate, the final round turned into a struggle among Nelson, Watson, Trevino, Bill Rogers and Hinkle, although Hinkle didn't really get into it until the last few holes. At the 221-yard No. 15, Nelson bogeyed after hitting his drive into a bunker and missing a six-foot putt. Even so, when he teed off at No. 17, he had a two-shot lead and looked as if he were in command. But at the 17th he used an eight-iron on a 143-yard shot and the ball plopped on the downslope of the little bunker in front of the green. The pin was down front; Nelson would have to pull off an outstanding shot just to have a chance for par. He didn't, and the ball went 65 feet above the hole. His first putt on the slick green went 15 feet past the hole to the fringe. He missed coming back for a double-bogey six and suddenly he was the leader no more. "Out of 100 or so eight-iron shots I hit, I figure I may hit one fat," said Nelson of his approach at 17. "That was the 100th."

Meanwhile, Hinkle holed a lengthy putt at 17 and even though he missed a birdie chance at 18, he had made up four strokes on the final four holes and was in the lead by one stroke as his pursuers came down the 18th fairway. Nelson drove into a fairway bunker, erasing his chances. Watson hit his tee shot behind a pine, ending his hopes. Rogers was eliminated when he found the sand at 17. Trevino, aching back and all, was the final threat and he just missed a good-sized birdie putt at the 18th as the crowd in the renovated viewing area behind the green groaned.

Much to his surprise, Hinkle, the man who had gained some fame by taking a shortcut in the U.S. Open at Inverness, had scored his third victory and had pushed his earnings for the year to $246,275, making him No. 3 on the money list. Indeed, Hinkle did have a good time at Firestone.

San Antonio Texas Open—$250,000
Winner: Lou Graham

When Lou Graham joined the tour in 1964, many people predicted eventual stardom for him. He has a smooth swing with a big arc and a composure that doesn't ruffle. The predictions looked as if they were about to come true when the balding Tennessean won the Minnesota Classic in 1967. However, his only other victories in the intervening years came in the 1972 L&M Open and the 1975 U.S. Open. When Graham turned 41 in January of 1979 and got off to a poor start, many figured the veteran pro's career was on the decline, its promise unfulfilled. Even Graham admitted he had negative thoughts.

But it's always darkest before the dawn and for Graham the sun was about to rise. He beat Bobby Wadkins in a play-off for the Philadelphia Classic title, won the American Optical Classic at Pleasant Valley six weeks later, and lo and behold, here he was picking up another victory, his third in 11 weeks. This one was in the San Antonio Texas Open and he scorched the Oak Hills Country Club course with 69–64–69–66—268, winning by one stroke over Eddie Pearce, Bill Rogers and Doug Tewell, a non-winner who folded on the final round.

Peter Oosterhuis grabbed the first-round lead with a 65, then quietly disappeared as Graham and Lee Trevino pulled in front after 36 holes at 133. Tewell, who had opened with a 66, carved out a neat 63 on the third round and suddenly found himself in an unfamiliar position, leading a tournament going into the final round. Graham, who trailed by five strokes after 54 holes, birdied two of the last four holes for a 66, then watched as Rogers and Tewell made valiant bids to catch him. But Rogers missed a 35-foot birdie putt at the par-three 18th and Tewell failed on a 12-footer for a 72.

"I was trying to get my mind prepared for a play-off. I could hardly watch,'' said Graham, who earned $45,000 for his victory. That gave him more than $190,000 for the year, a personal high. Not bad for a guy who only a few months earlier thought his career might have ended at 41.

Southern Open—$200,000
Winner: Ed Fiori

The Southern Open at Green Island Country Club in Columbus, Georgia, was the second tournament on the 1980 Winter Tour, but for 1980 exemption purposes, for many it was the next-to-last chance to avoid the dreaded Monday qualifiers. It was the second-to-last chance for people such as Ed Fiori, Mike Reid and Artie McNickle. Fiori and McNickle needed a win in the last two tournaments to make it; Reid could do it with a win or two high finishes.

Fiori made it, defeating Tom Weiskopf on the second hole of a sudden-death play-off. Reid and McNickle merely came close, increasing their earnings by tying with Calvin Peete, one stroke behind Fiori and Weiskopf.

Weiskopf. Now there's a name that, for the most part, had been absent from the headlines during the season. Weiskopf hadn't won since the Doral-Eastern Open in 1978. He had won little more than $52,000 in 1979 and was back there among the crowd pushing for the top 60. But Weiskopf didn't have to worry about gaining an exemption; as one of the leading all-time money winners, his place was assured. Fiori, McNickle and Reid had to worry.

So did Mike McCullough, No. 57 in 1978, but way back going into the Southern. McCullough looked as if he had a charge under way when he opened with 65–69 at Green Island, giving him a one-stroke edge on Gibby Gilbert and Jerry Pate and two strokes on four others, including Weiskopf.

From August on, Tom Weiskopf played steadily and he almost won the Southern Open.

Fiori, with 69–72, trailed by seven strokes. But McCullough retreated with 73–74 in the last two rounds and watched the parade go by.

First came Peete, who took the third-round lead with a 67 for 203. However, Peete fell off to a 72 in the final round, and that was one stroke too many. Then came Reid, but Reid bogeyed three of the last four holes and took a 71. McNickle made a bid, but his closing 69 wasn't good enough.

Finally, here came Fiori and Weiskopf. Fiori birdied the 17th hole for a 68 and 274 and Weiskopf caught him with a birdie at the 18th hole for a 70. Weiskopf missed his chance to win on the first sudden-death hole. Fiori caught a trap, then missed a nine-footer. "I just made a bad putt," said Weiskopf after missing a three-footer. He didn't get another chance. After Weiskopf missed a 25-foot birdie putt at the par-three 16th hole, Fiori dropped a 13-footer for the victory, $36,000 and a year devoid of qualifiers.

Pensacola Open—$200,000
Winner: Curtis Strange

Of the 34 players who had won more than $100,000 going into the last official tournament of the year, 14 had not won a tour event. But even in these days of $300,000 purses and $50,000 pay-offs, money is still a pretty accurate indication of how well a man has played. And for most, they believe that the next time out could be their week for victory. Curtis Strange's time came at the Pensacola Open.

The Pensacola is a critical tournament for those battling for places on the top 60 exempt list. Strange was already assured a place with more than $100,00 in his pocket, but only a win would remove whatever doubts remained in his mind. "I've always heard the first win was the hardest, and it certainly was for me," he said after a tense struggle with Bill Kratzert, which he won by one stroke with 69–71–62–69–271. Kratzert earned $21,600 for second place, making him the 35th hundred-grand winner with $101,623.

Strange, who had an outstanding amateur career at Wake Forest, joined the tour in 1977; but he admits that, like so many others, he found it difficult to handle its demands. In 1979, he learned how to deal with them better and he had some promising outings prior to Pensacola. So he didn't panic when Kratzert and Morris Hatalsky opened with 64s at watery Perdido Bay Country Club, leaving him five shots in arrears. Nor did he when Hatalsky added a 69 the second day for the lead at 133, putting Strange seven behind. Patience, that's the word.

Strange made his move in the third round with a 10-under-par 62, a course record which put him in the driver's seat, one stroke in front of Orville Moody. "I hate to say this, but I think the course owed it to me," said Strange. "I played exactly the same way the first two days and was four under. The difference this round was that the putts fell."

They didn't fall as frequently in the final round, but a six-foot putt at the 15th hole following a five-iron second shot provided Strange with an eagle and gave him the luxury of a bogey at the final hole to win. Kratzert had suffered with tendinitis of the wrists most of the season, and it had caused him to alter his swing. "I just bunt the ball down the fairway," he said. However, he made it close with three birdies on the last four holes for a 68 and 272.

Strange became the 12th first-time winner of the year, tying a record set in 1968 and tied in 1969. But he wasn't much happier than Mark McCumber. With a tie for 47th place, McCumber earned $513.71, giving him 60th place on the exempt list with $67,886, just $48 more than Miller Barber, who missed the cut. (McCumber had been on the exempt list as a result of winning the Doral-Eastern Open, but that exemption was due to run out at the time of that tournament the following March.)

Mike Reid had a chance to beat out McCumber for No. 60, but as he had done in the Southern Open a week earlier, he bogeyed three of the last four holes, tying for the 26th place and picking up $1,420. He finished the year in 66th place with $64,046.

Walt Disney World National Team Championship—$250,000
Winners: Ben Crenshaw and George Burns

Ever since the National Team Championship has settled down in Walt Disney World in Orlando, Florida, in 1974, it has become a tournament which has pumped new life into ailing carees. Because it is an unofficial event, the money doesn't count toward exemption status, although the winners earn exemptions for the next year, if they need them.

Sammy Rachels and Jeff Hewes certainly did. Rachels had ended the regular season with only $17,305 and Hewes was in even worse shape with $3,180. So it was that when Rachels and Hewes came to the 15th tee in the final round of the Team Championship, their hearts were beating a little fast. They had overcome a four-stroke lead by Ben Crenshaw and George Burns to forge into a deadlock and they were rolling. The customary Disney World tale looked as if it was about to unfold.

This time the ending was different. Burns chipped in for a birdie at the 15th hole and then followed with a 35-footer at the 16th and Crenshaw-Burns won by three strokes with a best-ball 255, while Rachels-Hewes tied for second place with Peter Jacobsen-D.A. Weibring and Scott Bess-Dan Halldorson.

The ending was not without its dramatic highlights, however. It was the first victory for Crenshaw since the Phoenix Open the second week of the season, ending many months of near misses. And it was the initial tour triumph for Burns, though he had been in the top 60 every year since 1976, his first full year.

"It was his time. George was the backbone of our team and I can't be happier for him," said Crenshaw. "This week proves to him that he can win and we're going to see a different person next year. He was letting it get to him that he hadn't won. The enjoyment this week was getting to see George win."

Forrest Fezler and Larry Ziegler, with 61, took the first-round lead, but Crenshaw-Burns was one of the teams only a stroke behind them. A 66 in the second round left Crenshaw-Burns one in arrears of Jim Colbert-Mike Sullivan (62-65) and Tom Purtzer-Howard Twitty (63-64). But they took command with another sixty-two in the third round, leading by four strokes over Rachels-Hewes, Bruce Fleisher-Tom Jenkins, Gibby Gilbert-Grier Jones and Gary Koch-Curtis Strange.

Crenshaw-Burns found their most serious threat in Rachels-Hewes, playing right alongside them in the final round, in the last group of the day. Crenshaw-Burns held onto their four-stroke lead and even when Rachels chipped in for an eagle three at the 10th hole their margin was reduced only a stroke as Crenshaw countered with a five-foot birdie putt.

But Rachels-Hewes had opened a crack and they wiped out the deficit as Hewes dropped a nine-footer at the 12th hole and Rachels made 10 and seven-footers at the next two holes. But despite the pleadings of the crowd, Rachels and Hewes were done as Burns made his key birdies at 15 and 16. Hewes and Rachels picked up $10,500 each; but it wouldn't buy them happiness, which in their case was a year's exemption from qualifying.

8

THE EUROPEAN TOUR

There were 17 different winners in the 22 events that comprised the 1979 European Tour. That statistic provides an accurate reflection of the year. It was quite remarkable simply because of its diversity. Severiano Ballesteros won the Open Championship, but he did not dominate the tour as he had for the three previous seasons. Surprisingly, Ballesteros had but one tour victory. His chief rival, Nick Faldo, did not win at all.

At long last, Tony Jacklin did win. The South Africans had a superb year, including victories by Dale Hayes, Hugh Baiocchi, Gavin Levinson and Mark McNulty. Just four players won more than once, led by young Sandy Lyle, who claimed first place on the Order of Merit with three triumphs. Mark James, Brian Barnes and Graham Marsh, the latter playing while on brief leaves from America, were the double winners.

In the early weeks, Barnes and Hayes were the golfers to watch. Barnes scored birdies on three of the final five holes, coming from five strokes behind in the last round to win the Portuguese Open. Brian led at the start of the fourth round in the Spanish Open, but took a triple bogey in the early going, and Hayes won by two strokes with a fine chip at the 18th hole. After Simon Hobday won the Madrid Open, Hayes and Barnes resumed their duel in the Italian Open. It was not settled until the fourth play-off hole, with Barnes the winner.

Still, they were looking over their shoulders, as the tour leaders did throughout the year. "I think it is impossible to finish ahead of Seve Ballesteros in the Order of Merit," Barnes said. "He plays too well in too many events." The following week in France, Ballesteros gave his first strong performance, tying for third place behind Bernard Gallacher. The lingering memories of that tournament, however, were not of Gallacher or Ballesteros, but of the untimely death of Salvador Balbuena on the eve of the first round. Balbuena, 29 years old, left a wife and two children.

The tour entered Britain with the Colgate PGA Championship at St. Andrews, the last time, as it turned out, that the tournament was sponsored by Colgate-Palmolive, because of a change in corporate policy with the retirement of David Foster. Nick Faldo equaled Neil Coles's record for the Old

Above left: *Britain's Nick Faldo.*
Above: *Tony Jacklin's revival was complete with his victory in the Braun Trophy/ German Open.*
Left: *Lee Trevino congratulates Sandy Lyle, No. 1 on the European Order of Merit.*

Course with 65 in the first round, then stumbled to a 10th-place finish. Strong, cold winds created nightmarish conditions, and the winner, Vicente Fernandez, scored 39 on the last nine. The average for the fourth round was 77.3 and Fernandez' total was par 288. That was also the winning total the next week at Wentworth as Greg Norman won the Martini International in soggy, dismal weather. Attention at Wentworth centered on John Morgan, who had won twice on the 1979 Safari Tour but was trying for his first major European title. Morgan led entering the 36-hole finale and placed second with Antonio Garrido.

Sandy Lyle achieved his first victory in the British Airways/Avis Open at La Moye in Jersey. Lyle, 21 years old, the son of Hawkstone Park professional Alex Lyle, gave credit to his father and to Tony Jacklin, his playing partner. "Tony encouraged me all the way and gave me a piece of sound advice at the last," he said. "As I prepared to hit my second shot, he told me, 'Just take your time and knock it on the green.' I tried it like a practice shot and knocked it

159

within five yards for a birdie." His winning margin was three strokes over Howard Clark, four strokes over Jacklin and three others.

Jacklin made another of his frequent challenger challenges in the Belgian Open, tying for ninth, six strokes in back of Levinson, another first-time champion. The Welsh Classic was determined in a three-hole play-off with James defeating Eddie Polland and Mike Miller. McNulty took a five-stroke victory in the Greater Manchester Open. Ballesteros' one triumph was the Lada English Classic at The Belfry, which came at an ideal time before his ultimate goal, the Open Championship. "I needed this for my confidence," he admitted. Press coverage of the Lada Classic was focused on an early duel between Ballesteros and Faldo. The next week, Lyle took Ballesteros to the wire and defeated him in the Scandinavian Open. They matched stroke for stroke, both scoring three-under-par 69s, and Lyle won by the three-stroke margin, which he set by scoring 65 in the third round.

Graham Marsh remained in Europe for an extra week after the Open Championship, a fortunate decision, for he won for the first time in 21 months, claiming the 32nd victory of his illustrious career in the Dutch Open. Pressure was mounting in the following weeks among the contenders for positions on the Ryder Cup team. Des Smyth and Maurice Bembridge intensified the race by winning the Sun Alliance European Match Play Championship and the Benson & Hedges International, respectively. Then came the Braun Trophy/German Open, with Tony Jacklin regaining some of his past glory. He withstood a terrific 66 by Lanny Wadkins to record that first triumph since 1976. "Lanny came at me with both barrels," Tony said, "and that was just what I needed. It kept me going for birdies."

Jacklin was again the dominant figure in the Carrolls Irish Open, but James won after Jacklin and Howard Clark fell back in the last round. Baiocchi then took the Swiss Open title by five strokes over fellow South African Hayes. Lyle won the European Open at Turnberry, with outstanding first and fourth rounds, and established his grip on the Order of Merit lead. Ballesteros played two more tournaments in an effort to catch him, but the winners were Michael King in the SOS Talisman Tournament Players Championship and Marsh in the Dunlop Masters.

Portuguese Open— £ 28,810.69

Winner: Brian Barnes

Doug Sanders once remarked, "If you don't get an invitation to the Masters, it's like being out of the world for a week." Amusing, but not entirely true.

Though the world may hardly have noticed, professional golf was played that week outside of Augusta, Georgia. In fact, more golfers were playing outside than within the well-secured bounds of the Augusta National Golf Club. In Hattiesburg, Mississippi, 125 players were entered for the Magnolia Classic, while in Vilamoura, Portugal, another 155 players were beginning the European tour in the absence of Severiano Ballesteros and Nick Faldo, both among the 72 Masters invitees.

The field for the Portuguese Open included Wayne Player, who had been an Augusta spectator the year before, when his father won the Masters for the third time. His mother and four sisters had returned for Gary's Masters defense. Wayne was starting out on his own, playing as an amateur in five continental championships. He was two strokes above the 36-hole cut-off score. We shall hear more of this 17-year-old lad.

Several contestants in the 1979 Portuguese Open had instead been in earlier Masters—Harold Henning, Tony Jacklin, Dale Hayes. And the winner, Brian Barnes, was following the advice of the 1951 British Open champion, Max Faulkner, his father-in-law.

Early in the last round, Barnes was five strokes behind Francisco Abreu of Spain. Abreu began with a birdie and an eagle, while Barnes had bogeys on two of the first four holes. "I reckoned it was all over," Barnes said. "I was playing poorly and he had his tail up." Abreu took a double bogey at the fifth hole and bogeys at the sixth and ninth holes, but still was three strokes ahead after his birdie at the 11th. Barnes drove into the trees off the 12th tee and had to hack his way out. At that unlikely moment, Barnes found the inspiration he needed. "Max has helped me to rebuild a new swing—turning on the backswing rather than tilting," he said. "And suddenly it came back when I hit a three-iron onto the putting surface."

The Scot made birdies on three of the last five holes and won by two strokes, his 35-foot birdie putt on the 17th providing the decisive blow. Abreu followed that putt by jabbing his 15-inch putt past the hole, taking a bogey for a two-shot swing. Barnes won by that margin with his 72 and 287 total, five under par. Hayes was third, four strokes behind. Hayes's 69 in the third round was only the sixth sub-par score in Vilamoura's 10-year history.

Barnes also shot 69 in the first round, when Irishman Des Smyth took a stroke off the course record with his 67. Smyth had led the Irish Order of Merit, but had never finished higher than 14th in a European tour event. He led for two rounds, then faded with 79 and 80, tying for 12th place as the heavyweights took over.

Abreu, 35, a former wrestling champion and German and Madrid Open golf champion, had rounds of 71, 70 and 73 before his 75 on the final day, enabling the six-foot-two Barnes to slip past. Barnes, 33, a Ryder Cup player, won the Zambian Open in his last appearance. "It's a great way to start the season," he said. Even better than playing in the Masters? Perhaps.

Spanish Open— £ 34,750
Winner: Dale Hayes

As an 18-year-old prodigy, Dale Hayes won the 1971 Spanish Open. Four years later, he was Europe's leading money winner. Hayes then spent two years in the United States, failing to make his mark. The South African was "very excited" to win the Spanish Open for a second time.

In America Hayes almost forgot how it felt to win. His confidence was shattered. He expected *not* to win and perhaps that was his undoing. He returned to Europe in 1978 and started winning again—perhaps because he expected to. He won the Italian and French Opens and the Ram Salver, the consolation tournament of the Colgate World Match Play Championship, finishing the year with $112,821.

Third in the Portuguese Open, Hayes won the second event of the 1979 European tour, shooting 66 to overtake Brian Barnes in a finish similar to that which gave Barnes a victory the week before. Barnes's clash with Francisco Abreu was all but forgotten amid the controversy in Torrequebrada over the next several days. Forgotten, too, was the fact that Dale Hayes was Europe's No. 1 before most people ever heard of Severiano Ballesteros.

Ballesteros would not play for his national championship until the sponsors, Benson & Hedges, agreed to pay an appearance fee of £ 3,000. Though two years ago Ballesteros was made a Master of Sport by King Juan Carlos, there is no love lost between Ballesteros and the Spanish Federation. Golf is not yet a popular sport among the Spanish masses and, as Ballesteros said, "People would only take note if I won the British Open." Indeed, the sponsors were in a foul mood when Ballesteros failed to qualify for the last 36 holes. He shot 81 in the first round and could not redeem himself, even with 70 in the second.

It was the third time in five tournaments that Ballesteros failed to qualify, having already missed 36-hole cuts in two of his four American appearances. His 12th-place finish in the Masters indicated a return to form, but Ballesteros promptly met his doom on the eighth hole at Torrequebrada. Ever willing to take a chance, Ballesteros gambled too often. The eighth hole covers 396 yards, with a sharp dogleg left. Most golfers played a long iron or three-wood from the tee, then a short iron to the green. Instead, Ballesteros went for the green with his driver, needing a carry of 300 yards to a narrow opening, the entire route out of bounds. He had done it before, four times, while winning the 1978 Spanish under-25 championship. On his fifth try, Ballesteros failed. He also failed on his next, finally scoring nine against par-four. He also took double bogey six on the 16th hole, exchanging angry words there with Maurice Bembridge over a ruling, and had to par the last two holes for his 81.

Torrequebrada, a new course outside Torremolinos on the Costa del Sol, was built by Pepe Gancedo on rocky hills above the Mediterranean. Designed with power and delicacy in mind, Torrequebrado includes ravines, waterfalls, lakes and twisting fairways that rise and fall toward big, rolling greens, making it wonderfully attractive to the eye against the backdrop of the foothills of the Sierra Morena Mountains.

Though the course was opened in 1976, the record until this tournament was 70. Martin Poxon, Jose-Maria Canizares and Hugh Baiocchi were the first-round leaders with 67s, then Poxon and Canizares tied with 137s after 36 holes. In that second round, Canizares flew a seven-iron shot into the cup for an eagle on the eighth hole, the scene of Ballesteros' downfall. Barnes struck for 66 in the third round, while Hayes had 67, improving from his 70–75 start. He was tied for seventh place, four strokes behind Barnes.

Early in the last round, Barnes was in trouble, taking a triple-bogey eight on the sixth hole. Hayes heard the news and "it really lifted me. I realized Brian wasn't the man to worry about anymore. I concentrated on my playing partner, Nicky Price, because he was ahead of me." When Price hit into the water off the 12th tee, Hayes switched his attention back to Barnes, who had rallied with three birdies. Hayes made a brilliant chip to the final green and sank the short putt for a two-stroke margin, later saying, "I thought if I could make one more birdie in the last four holes to go nine under par, I would win. As it was, I was fortunate enough to play them in two under."

Madrid Open— £33,100
Winner: Simon Hobday

There were two popular explanations of why Simon Hobday won the Madrid Open. One, Hobday needed the money. Accepting his £5,514 check, the Rhodesian golfer said, "The great thing is that I can keep it. There's £15,000 of my UK earnings frozen under Bank of England sanctions in Jersey."

The other theory, possibly related, was that Hobday won because he had an urge to take his game more seriously. He usually is a gregarious individual who enjoys a few beers, maybe more than a few, each evening. "Most times I drink as much as I can," Hobday jokingly said. "But this week I had a feeling I was playing well."

Although Hobday was content to sip orange juice, the weather alone was reason enough for one to seek stronger drink. Snow was lingering on the mountains and there was a strong, cool wind during the tournament week at Real Club de la Puerta de Hierro. Hobday shared the lead for two days with 67 and 73, then sprang two strokes clear with 71 in the third round.

Severiano Ballesteros was then gaining attention, moving within four strokes with his 68. He gambled with his driver, as he did unsuccessfully in the Spanish Open. Again, Ballesteros was tempted by a short par-four hole, the downhill, 310-yard 13th. Most others hit safely short. Ballesteros went with a full-blooded driver to the small target below and was rewarded with a two-putt birdie. Hobday later went for the same green, but hooked his tee shot into impenetrable scrub. He made three with his second ball for a disappointing, but not disastrous, bogey.

Hobday also dealt with a potential crisis on the second hole in the last round. His wayward drive came to rest behind a tree. "Golf is all about going forward," he said. He chose a seven-iron—on the assumption that was the club he needed least—then snapped it in two on his follow-through. "It was a dreadful decision," he said later, "and a pity, really, because I needed it twice after that." Hobday expected a challenge from Ballesteros, but it never materialized. He heard cheers for the Spaniard and once thought he had lost the lead. Only at the 17th hole, while standing in a bunker, did Hobday ask a spectator what was happening. He was well ahead and won by two strokes over Gordon Brand with his 74 and 285 total, three under par.

A former South African Open champion, the 38-year-old Hobday was once a farmer in Zambia, playing golf for fun. When the political climate changed there, he was given 48 hours to leave the country, loaded two furniture vans and headed for Salisbury, where he sold cars for a time.

That was hardly enough action for him, so he tried his luck as a professional golfer, starting in South Africa, then coming to the European circuit in 1970. He won over £15,000 and the German Open in 1976. The Madrid Open was his second European victory and the third of his career.

Even when the winner's check was his, secure against any sanctions, Hobday refused the offer of a beer. That prompted Mark Wilson to write in the *Daily Express:* "I do wish he had kept the secret of his success to himself. There are those members of my club who have long held the splendid tippler as a shining example to our wives. . . . You blithering idiot, Simon. . . . We shall all now be expected to get home in time for Sunday lunch!"

Italian Open— £33,520

Winner: Brian Barnes

Europe's two leading players were locked in a play-off to determine who, after only four tournaments, would win his second title. They went four holes before the decisive strokes were made. But this ballooning rivalry was deflated quickly. The winner, Brian Barnes, had what he wanted. It wasn't the Italian Open trophy that Barnes wanted, but the opportunity to tell the press that he and Dale Hayes had agreed beforehand to split the prize money. "I have wanted to do it for years," Barnes said, "but I have never been in a situation where I could, where I won the play-off."

His motivation was simple. "I hope," Barnes said, "that the system will change." His reasoning was that "pros are contracted to play 72 holes. If at the end two, three or four are tied, they are all winners as far as I'm concerned. They should split the money and split the Order of Merit points. . . . A play-off is a lottery and there is only one reason for a play-off—the public." He contended that, for most professionals, titles were meaningless except in the four major championships. Barnes would have play-offs for those titles—18-hole play-offs, not the sudden-death variety now authorized by the Masters and American PGA.

As much as everyone wants closely contested tournaments, no one likes play-offs. A sudden-death play-off is, indeed, a lottery. The practice of the 18-hole play-off has increasingly been criticized as an expensive anachronism. Barnes was correct in disclosing the deal. He should have done it on the first tee. If the players are splitting the money, the public should know before going out to watch, as Barnes would agree. (Incidentally, purse-splitting is ruled out in America.)

It is unfortunate that apparently few championships in Europe are highly valued. Sports need touches of drama and romanticism. Those elements were clearly present at Monticello in the adventures of amateur Wayne Player, Gary's son, and Michael King. Wayne shot 81 in the first round. He battled back and was five under par after 13 holes. He took a triple bogey on the 14th, but finished admirably with 71, only to miss the 36-hole cut by one stroke.

A former Walker Cup player, King was making his first inroad to success as a professional. He was in second place in the Madrid Open with one round remaining, that being his highest standing in five years on the tour. As you might expect, he shot 76 and finished sixth. In the Italian Open, King either led or shared the lead through three rounds, starting the final day tied with Ben Crenshaw. Hayes and Vicente Fernandez were one stroke behind and Barnes was in the group two strokes back.

The 29-year-old King made three birdies over the first five holes, dropped a stroke at the seventh but regained it on the ninth. He made the turn in 33 strokes and was three ahead of Hayes, his closest challenger. Then King crashed to 74 and a 286 total, tying for ninth place. He made no excuse, other than that he lost his composure. "Every time I'm up there, I learn some more," he said. "I'm coming closer."

Barnes and Hayes were tied at 281, three strokes ahead of Fernandez and Sam Torrance. Barnes had 67, with three birdies and an eagle over the last seven holes. Hayes made two birdies and an eagle early on the last nine, but three-putted the par-three 17th hole and finished with 68. They halved the first three playoff holes with pars, then Barnes made a 12-foot birdie putt after Hayes hit into a bunker. For a few minutes, it seemed to be an exciting finish.

French Open— £37,500
Winner: Bernard Gallacher

Any recollection of a golf tournament usually features the champion—in this instance, Bernard Gallacher. The French Open, held near Lyon, offered far more lasting impressions than that. One could not forget the poignant time when Severiano Ballesteros left in tears; or when Gary Player, finding comfort in his family, stopped to see the wild flowers his six-year-old daughter had picked along the course.

Early on the morning of the first round, Angel Gallardo entered the clubhouse and, seeing a familiar face, asked, "Have you heard about Salvador?"

"No, I haven't seen him today."

"*Morte,*" Gallardo said.

There was disbelief and shock over the death of Salvador Balbuena the previous evening. Tones were hushed as players took to the course and reporters rushed to meet mid-morning deadlines with the sad news. Balbuena, 29 years old and with a wife and two children, fell dead after having dinner with Antonio Garrido, Manuel Pinero and Jose-Maria Canizares. The Spaniards had talked into the night, consoling each other and Balbuena's widow by telephone and trying to decide whether to play. Garrido, Pinero and Canizares were too disturbed and withdrew from the tournament. It was suggested that the others contribute a portion of their winnings to the family. "No," Ballesteros said firmly, "we will play and we will give it all."

Ballesteros kept saying to his caddie, "There's nothing I can do. I might as well play." Balbuena's widow came to Lyon to wait until the body could be sent home, and Ballesteros sat with her each evening. A requiem was held

Saturday in the church of Villette d'Anthon. Under the circumstances, Ballesteros' play was remarkable. He was seven strokes behind leader Hugh Baiocchi beginning the final round and dropped two more strokes in five holes. Ballesteros then birdied six of eight holes, starting at the ninth, and tied for third with Baiocchi. He contributed more than half of the £3,964 won by the six remaining Spaniards.

Player's week began with a reunion with his son, Wayne, whose five-week tour was deemed valuable experience, even though he didn't go past the second round of any tournament. The rest of the family was there, providing a restful atmosphere despite the protests from an anti-apartheid group over his presence. Player responded to them on French television, "No, I am not an ambassador of apartheid. Anyone who says that is just starting propaganda. I try to be an ambassador of good will and love. I am a sportsman, not a politician at all. I do not believe in apartheid in sports, and I have done many things trying to show that."

Only three years earlier, the French Open champion was a black South African, Vicent Tshabalala, and Player was instrumental in bringing Tshabalala there. While protests were being directed at Player, he and other white South Africans were dominating the tournament. There were five among the top 18.

Baiocchi began the final round three strokes ahead and went four strokes clear with his 60-foot birdie putt on the third hole. He went from one extreme to the other in the windy conditions and took four putts on the 14th green. Ballesteros and Nick Faldo, among others, also had chances to win. Gallacher's last challenge came from an unlikely contender and a fellow Scot, Willie Milne, who had won just £937 the previous year. Milne had three eagles in the earlier rounds and, after dropping four strokes on the first nine, charged back with three birdies and a hole-in-one. They were in the same group and Gallacher was a stroke in front as they played the 18th hole. Both had chances for birdies but settled for pars, as Gallacher finished with 68, five under par, for a 284 total.

As a final note to this bizarre week, Milne, who shot 72, was confronted with a squabble over whether he would receive a car for the hole-in-one, as advertised by error in the tournament program. Golf Europeen Tournaments bought Milne a 1980 Mercedes 200, even though the program offer was not binding, according to French law. Golf Europeen recognized that the issue was one of sport rather than law, and set out to rectify the situation. This, of course, could not be done in a few days and, unfortunately, was magnified in the press.

Colgate PGA Championship— £50,000
Winner: Vicente Fernandez

The Colgate PGA Championship followed the British Open at St. Andrews by just 10 months and many people were saying that had only Jack Nicklaus returned, we might have re-created that memorable week. Two runners-up to Nicklaus—Raymond Floyd and Simon Owen—were back along with sixth-place-finisher Peter Oosterhuis, who was at home for several tournaments after a miserable spring in America. Gary Player was seeking his first victory at St. Andrews, and U.S. Open Champion Andy North was trying to win on his first trip to Great Britain. The defending Colgate PGA champion was Nick Faldo, and everyone remembered his stirring performance the previous summer, when he was seventh in his introduction to the Old Course. There were great expectations.

By Sunday afternoon, St. Andrews had the flavor of a major championship, but not the one we had in mind. It was more like the 1975 U.S. Open than the 1978 British Open. At Medinah, you will recall, young Tom Watson played so well for two rounds that some were conceding that victory was his, that Watson had secured his seemingly inevitable stardom. But as the weather took a turn for the worse, so did Watson's fortunes. There was Tom Watson, and here Nick Faldo. At the 1975 Open, a golfer thought to be a mere journeyman survived to become the U.S. Open champion. There was Lou Graham, and here Vicente Fernandez.

Before the Colgate PGA, Faldo played four tournaments, two in America and two in Europe, and was a contender in only the French Open. Newspapers were saying he was complacent. That was far from the truth. He could not remember ever practicing more. The basic problem was his putting stroke. He was raising the blade on the backswing. At home between tournaments, Faldo came across a Bullseye putter he used as an amateur. He made a few strokes on the carpet, liked the feel, and tossed the putter in his car. He used it in the pro-am, but debated until the last hour whether to switch from his Ray Cook model for the tournament. Once that decision was made, the agony was over, at least for two days. His shot placement was remarkable and his putting touch simply brilliant. He went four strokes ahead.

Faldo equalled Neil Coles's record for the Old Course with 65 in the first round, and his total for 36 holes was 135. Watson also shot 135 in matching the 36-hole record for the U.S. Open. Watson tied for ninth with 290 and Faldo 10th with 292. Graham won in a playoff after shooting 287 and Fernandez narrowly avoided a play-off with 288. So much for similarities. Medinah was par 71 and St. Andrews par 72. The rain created havoc in one tournament and the wind in the other.

Strong, cold winds had a definite influence, starting on the second afternoon, after Faldo returned with his 70. The conditions became increasingly difficult. Birdies were rare on the homeward holes into the wind. Faldo's nines in the last two rounds were 37–41 for 78 and 35–44 for 79. Of the last six players, only Fernandez broke 40 on the final nine Sunday and his score was 39. The average for the last day was 77.3. Those figures lend perspective to Faldo's play. He was first sensational, then slightly worse than average.

Player came within a stroke of a play-off just by scoring pars on the last 10 holes. To do that, Gary needed a driver and two three-wood shots on the 567-yard 14th hole and two drivers on the 461-yard 17th hole. "The toughest conditions I've ever seen," he said. "That's the best I can play." Player had finished long before his name appeared on any leaderboard. His 71 and another by Floyd, who placed three strokes behind, were the best scores of the day. But Player's 289 total, one under par, became a formidable target only when the 12 golfers behind him were on the closing holes. There were six pace-setters during the round, including Faldo and the 554-hole leaders, that disparate trio of North, Gordon Brand (not to be confused with John Bland) and Des Smyth (pronounced Smith). North was the major champion, guided by the legendary caddie Tip Anderson; Brand was after his first victory, and Smyth was after his first four-figure check. As success is relative, only Smyth succeeded. He earned £1,405.

The £8,330 winner's check was lost by Baldovino Dassu, then won by Fernandez on the notorious 17th or Road Hole. A par-four, the 17th was played in an average of 5.1 strokes for the last round and 4.6 strokes for the tournament. There were six birdies in the first round, two in the second, one in the third and none in the fourth. Dassu took the lead with a long birdie putt at the 16th hole and dropped it just as suddenly. He went onto the road behind the 17th green with his third shot and took four strokes from there for a triple bogey. Fernandez, just behind Dassu, was 40 yards short of the Road bunker in two strokes. He had two alternatives, as the flag was placed just beyond that steep bunker. He could try to clear the bunker and hold the narrow green, a difficult shot under any circumstances, or he could play cautiously to the right and probably score a bogey. Fernandez was willing to take the risk because "I knew I was trying for the lead." He stopped the shot 15 feet beyond the hole and made par. With another tough par at the 18th, Fernandez posted 75 and stood a stroke clear for the biggest victory of his life.

Fernandez, 33 years old and from Buenos Aires, most recently played two seasons on the American tour before losing his card. Over the previous winter, he entered 11 South American tournaments, won seven, and was second three times. He is a likable, determined little fellow who has walked with a limp all his life. He had to overcome a prenatal accident and nongolfing background to become an international champion. Earlier in the year, he was third in the Madrid Open, 12th in the Italian Open, and 14th in the French Open after leading for two rounds.

A victory on the Old Course was to be treasured, even though Fernandez had to admit, "I didn't know of St. Andrews until after I went on the tour." He came to know St. Andrews during the week and quite unexpectedly became part of its lore.

Martini International— £42,000
Winner: Greg Norman

Greg Norman ended the Martini International on a respectable note after a soggy, dismal week in which the scores were horrendous. He faded a three-wood shot perfectly around the trees on Wentworth's 18th hole and made a birdie from seven feet to win the championship by one stroke. The newspaper headlines were much richer than the scores, with several references to double

*Australia's
Greg Norman.*

Martinis for Norman, who also won that title two years ago. It was the young Australian's 10th career victory and his fifth in six months.

No one broke par for 72 holes, and Norman matched it with 288. Norman's 67 in the second round was the lowest score of the tournament. He entered the 36-hole finale one stroke behind John Morgan and won with rounds of 72 and 74, beating Morgan and Antonio Garrido. Severiano Ballesteros needed birdies at the last two holes to clear the 36-hole cut off, then tied for seventh place merely by finishing with 70 and 72. Other under-par scores were by Tienie Britz (who went from 76 to 69), Manuel Pinero (who went from 70 to 83) and Brian Barnes, whose scores (79 and 71) were less interesting than his antics. Barnes was six minutes late to tee off and, according to a notice in the press tent, was "seen to react unfavorably" when later informed of the two-stroke penalty. Barnes was told as he stood on the fourth tee and reportedly hurled the tee marker into an adjacent garden.

It was that kind of week.

New Colgate PGA champion Vicente Fernandez came within a stroke of the lead twice, in the second and fourth rounds, and immediately hit out of bounds each time; Nick Faldo and Bernard Gallacher missed the cut; Tony Jacklin got into contention, then shot two 77s; Neil Coles missed a one-inch putt, stubbing his putter in the ground behind the ball; Francisco Abreu took either four or five putts, his marker wasn't sure which. Abreu fluffed his chip and was upset when his next shot hit the hole and spun out three feet. Four or five putts later, Abreu's ball was still two inches from the cup. As one observer noted, Abreu exhausted his patience, then exhausted his knowledge of the English language. He said, "Thank you," retrieved the ball, and left. Enough was enough.

Despite all that, Morgan received most of the attention before Norman holed out as the winner. They were in the final pairing. Morgan, 35, was 11 years older than Norman, but a tournament novice in comparison to the blond youngster. The Royal Liverpool professional, Morgan had been on tour for only two full years of nine because of his club duties. He had never before led a European tournament at the halfway stage, although he won two Safari Tour events early in the spring.

Two weeks earlier, Gary Player had given Morgan some advice to the effect that his stroke was better than his temper. Gary would have been pleased at the result. Morgan awoke before the second round with a headache, pulled a thigh muscle stepping off the first tee, badly topped a three-wood on the 18th hole, but still scored a birdie to retain the lead, saying "I could see the funny side of what I had done."

But Norman was striding toward his inevitable test on the American circuit. He got the lead with his birdie on the 17th hole during his par-72 round in the morning, and was never behind while shooting 74 in the afternoon. Ahead of that pairing, Garrido posted the 289 total, which they played against on the final hole. Norman needed a birdie to win and Morgan a birdie for the possibility of a play-off. Morgan made his three-foot birdie, but never had the chance to try the putt under championship pressure, because Norman had already won the tournament with his seven-footer. It was just as well for Garrido, who seemed to have no heart for the game, much less a championship play-off. Still mourning the death of Salvador Balbuena, Garrido said he didn't know when he would play again.

British Airways/Avis Open— £30,000
Winner: Sandy Lyle

It was difficult to believe that Tony Jacklin had gone three years, since the 1976 Kerrygold International, without winning a tournament. He had chances to win five of the first eight tournaments of 1979 and made his strongest challenge in the British Airways/Avis Open at La Moye in Jersey, his home island. He tied for third, four strokes behind, despite his 75 in the second round. The winner was Sandy Lyle, who, at the age of 11, had watched on television as Jacklin, then at the peak of his glory, won the 1969 British Open Championship.

The son of Alex Lyle, the Hawkestone Park professional, Sandy was Rookie of the Year in 1978 and won £5,233. He matched those earnings in nine weeks in Africa and carried over the momentum to the start of the 1979 European Tour. He tied for seventh in the Portuguese Open and tied for sixth in the Spanish Open. In a dozen tournaments, Lyle was not once over par. Then came a skid that, after winning, Lyle attributed to the pressure of trying to gain a berth on the Ryder Cup team. Realizing this, Lyle redirected himself and decided to concentrate only on a top-20 place in the Order of Merit.

Lyle could also credit his first big European victory to encouragement from his father from the time he was three years old, and from Jacklin in the last round. "Tony encouraged me all the way and gave me a piece of sound advice at the last," he said. "As I prepared to hit my second shot, he told me, 'Just take your time and knock it on the green.' I treated it like a practice shot and knocked it within five yards for a birdie." He finished three strokes ahead of

Howard Clark and four ahead of the third-place group of Jacklin, Bernard Gallacher, Sam Torrance and Michael King.

Jacklin and Gallacher broke away with seven-under-par 64s in the first round, including Jacklin's masterpiece of an eagle on the 18th hole, a two-iron shot from 215 yards to within inches of the hole. Tony was also putting solidly, but that touch deserted him in the second round. He hit one costly iron shot as well, for double bogey, and scored 75 to Gallacher's 69. Lyle had 66s in the first and third rounds and 71 in the second, while Gallacher tacked on 69 to lead by one stroke entering the last day. To no avail, Jacklin finished with two 68s. Lyle also posted a closing 68, and described it as "a rather boring round with no frightening bits." Pars were enough to sweep Lyle into the lead, as Gallacher dropped four strokes in the first four holes, eventually taking 73. Clark, winner of the 1978 Portuguese and Madrid Opens, once came within a stroke of Lyle, but bogeyed the 16th and 17th, finishing with 69. There was no real suspense after that because Lyle, under Jacklin's calming influence, hit safely to the final green for a two-putt birdie he did not need.

Belgian Open—£ 32,300
Winner: Gavin Levenson

The Belgian Open started with a familiar note, which was expressed well by Peter Dobereiner: "At the risk of appearing like one of those sad figures who has to keep repainting the words 'The End of the World is Nigh' on his sandwich board because the colors fade with the passing years, I must insist that Tony Jacklin's revival is at hand."

But again, Jacklin did not win. He tied for ninth, six strokes behind Gavin Levenson, with whom he shared the opening-round lead. Tony was not distressed, but rather pleased to remain a front-runner week after week. Having a 68 start, Jacklin said, "If it doesn't come this week, I won't worry. I'll be patient." He suffered a four-putt green in the second round and fell off the pace, while Levenson continued against such challengers as Mark James, Baldovino Dassu, Nick Faldo, Michael King and Bobby Cole.

The Belgian Open drew an impressive crowd.

The victory was Levenson's first since turning professional seven months earlier. He became a pro at age 25 because he felt that South Africa's exclusion from such events as the Eisenhower Trophy would prevent further improvement as an amateur. He is in the mold of Gary Player—five feet and seven inches tall, 140 pounds and a fanatic for physical fitness. His nickname is "Legs" because of his impressive power, his prodigious length off the tees resulting from an exaggerated leg action.

Levenson was accustomed to championship pressures, having won 11 of his last 16 tournaments as an amateur. He either held or shared the lead through all four rounds over the Royal Waterloo course near Brussels. The course is unusual in that it ends with three par-five holes, assuring flurries of birdies and possibly eagles. Levenson finished with three birdies, just what he needed for a comfortable three-stroke margin over King, Cole and Faldo. His total was 279, with all four rounds under par 73.

James and Dassu held the lead with Levenson after the second round, which was most notable for Dassu's course-record 66 and Peter Barber's hole-in-one. Barber, who did not win any money last year, was rewarded with a BMW car worth £14,000, nearly three times the first prize of £5,382. Levenson shot 68 in the third round and went three strokes clear of Dassu and four ahead of Jacklin, Faldo and club pro Robin Fyfe.

He was seriously challenged only once in the last round, after dropping two strokes in the first seven holes. That enabled Dassu to tie, but Levenson pulled away with a 25-foot birdie on the 10th hole, followed by his final string of three more birdies. Faldo came forward to share second place with a similar finish, having eagle, par and birdie on the last three holes. He joined King and Cole, who was taking a week off the American circuit, at 282.

Faldo was left in a predicament like that of Jacklin in what was rapidly becoming an unusual season in European golf. With such winners as Gavin Levenson, nine tournaments had been completed without a victory by either Faldo or his rival for European supremacy, Severiano Ballesteros.

Welsh Classic— £30,000

Winner: Mark James

An Englishman (Mark James) defeated an Irishman (Eddie Polland) and a Scot (Mike Miller) to win the Welsh Classic. While Britain was assured of a champion, England could not count on James until his par-four on the third play-off hole. He was the first English winner of the year on the European Tour, but not without a struggle. He had to contend with his own temper, with interference from spectators and, finally, with Miller and Polland.

Polland finished in 31, scoring birdies on the last two holes to join the play-off with his 67, four under par. Both James (70) and Miller (67) had birdies on the 17th hole of regulation play for their 278 totals. Those three golfers were one stroke ahead of Sandy Lyle and Bob Charles, who closed with 66 and 68, respectively.

At the first play-off hole, James needed a 15-foot putt for par to remain in

Mark James at the
Welsh Classic.

the match. Polland dropped out after the second hole, scoring par against the birdies by James and Miller. Then James won with a par when Miller bunkered his approach shot.

James first gained notice in the second round. Having started at the 10th hole, he gouged a chunk out of the 17th green when he threw away his putter in disgust. That outburst resulted in a £20 fine. But James had no reason to complain further. He needed just nine putts and completed the other nine in 29 strokes. With his 68 and 138 total, James was tied with Miller and Tony Jacklin for third place, two strokes behind Pip Elson and one behind Polland.

The 25-year-old cousin of the tennis Mottrams Elson took only 24 putts in the first round and scored eight birdies for his 64, seven under par and the course record at Wenvoe Castle, Cardiff. He did it with a putter that he borrowed from Bill Longmuir, having lost his own putter in Jersey. "Losing the putter seemed like a major catastrophe at the time, and I was a bit worried over what would happen this week," Elson said. "Fortunately, Bill, a good friend of mine, had a new Ping putter just like my old one and he let me use it." Elson took 10 strokes more in the second round for 74, while Polland advanced to second place with his 66.

James continued his putting streak into the third round, playing the first nine superbly in 32 and another 68. He jokingly said, "If I could put those two halves together, I would have a nice round." It was good enough to lead the field, as Elson shot 75 and Miller needed a lucky bounce to stay within a stroke of first place. Miller's 69 might have been 71 had his approach shot to the 18th hole not struck a spectator on the ankle. He hit a "flier" eight-iron from the rough through the green. The ball hit a spectator's ankle and bounded back so close to the hole that Miller had only a tap-in putt for his birdie. "The ball would have gone fifteen yards through the green if it hadn't been stopped," Miller admitted.

A spectator also interfered with James' shot on the second hole of the final round—and it cost him a stroke, rather than saving two strokes, as had happened to Miller. The spectator stepped from behind a tree just as James hit,

173

stopping what appeared to be a skillful recovery shot. James made another bogey at the next hole, but birdied the following two holes. He lost his lead with bogey on the 15th, then made the vital birdie from eight feet on the 17th.

Greater Manchester Open— £ 30,000
Winner: Mark McNulty

What a year for the South Africans! With one exception they were in contention for every European championship and produced three winners in Dale Hayes, Gavin Levenson and, in the Greater Manchester Open, Mark McNulty. South Africans were out of the first 10 only in the Welsh Classic, the same week, incidentally, that Gary Player tied for second in the U.S. Open. Before McNulty's victory at Wilmslow, the best finishes by South Africans were:

Portuguese Open Dale Hayes (third)
Spanish Open Dale Hayes (first)
Madrid Open Tienie Britz (second)
Italian Open Dale Hayes (second)
French Open Hugh Baiocchi (third)
Colgate PGA Gary Player (second)
Martini International Tienie Britz (fourth)
British Airways/Avis Hugh Baiocchi (seventh)
Belgian Open Gavin Levenson (first)
Welsh Classic Jeff Hawkes (twenty-seventh)

McNulty was a five-stroke winner in the Greater Manchester Open, recording a 13 under-par 267 total. He led from start to finish, equalling the course record in the rainy first round with 64, six under par. He had few challengers and only one anxious moment. That came at the 11th hole in the third round. McNulty had expanded his lead from four to six strokes through nine holes. He then bogeyed the 10th and sent his pitch over the 11th green into a parking lot and in bounds by only five yards.

A Rolls Royce had to be moved before McNulty could inspect his lie. There was another delay as McNulty sought a ruling about playing the ball from the flintstone surface. Tournament official George O'Grady decided Mark was entitled to a free drop, since the surface was man-made, but the drama was not over. A Ferrari was then in his way. McNulty, who had been munching on chips from a nearby concessions booth, took a second drop and calmly pitched to seven feet and holed his putt for par four. O'Grady remarked, to no one in particular, "You've probably seen the shot that will win the tournament." McNulty completed the round in 71, one under par and his worst score of the week.

Twenty-five years old, McNulty is in his second season on the European circuit. He earned a pre-qualifying exemption in 1978, winning £ 5,987 for 43rd place on the Order of Merit. His top finish was fourth in the Cacharel under 25's, but the highlight of his season was a 3-and-2 victory over Severiano Ballesteros in a duel of birdies in the Sun Alliance Match Play tournament. He took sixth place there.

He kept his composure through the week at Wilmslow, having his caddie remind him on every tee to swing slowly. He admitted to being nervous at the start of the second round, after that 64, which included eight birdies and two bogeys. "I felt no pressure except on the first tee, where I was a bit shaky," he said, "but I hit a good one and that settled me completely."

Vicente Fernandez was one stroke behind after his 65 in the first round. Fernandez bogeyed the first four holes of the second round and recovered for 70, while McNulty posted 66 and moved four strokes in front of Neil Coles. Manuel Pinero played the second nine in 29 strokes for a 66 in the third round and was three shots behind after McNulty's 71. There was no threat for the title, as McNulty shot another 66 in the final round to Pinero's 68.

Lada English Classic— £50,000
Winner: Severiano Ballesteros

When Severiano Ballesteros finally won, he won by the largest margin thus far in the year—six strokes in the Lada English Classic at the Belfry, Sutton Coldfield. He had all the freedom he needed on the controversial Brabazon course for his powerful but erratic game in this new tournament sponsored by Lada, the Russian car company.

His best previous 1979 finish had been third in the French Open and this victory, the 16th of his career, came at an ideal time before he faced his ultimate goal, the British Open. "I needed this for my confidence," he said. He had convinced himself that his problems had all been in his head. Earlier, Ballesteros was thoroughly mystified. "I don't understand it," he said. "Before this season, I worked harder than ever. Every day I hit shots and played golf. I ran. I trained and trained. And then nothing happened. I lost my feel. I can only wait for it to come back."

Ballesteros did not lead the Lada until the third round. Rodger Davis was the only one below 70 in the first round, having three-under-par 69. He was four strokes ahead of Ballesteros and two in front of the second-place group. The colorful Davis, who unfailingly wears plus-twos—a narrow version of plus-fours—shot 73 in the second round but remained in the lead while Ballesteros and Nick Faldo advanced, both with 71s. Davis' hopes for his first European victory were crushed by his 83 in the third round. Faldo also stumbled to 77 as Ballesteros again shot 71 and went two strokes clear of Simon Hobday. With another 71 Ballesteros finished at 286, two under par and six ahead of Hobday and Neil Coles.

This massive and maligned Midlands course seems to bring out the best in Ballesteros while frustrating most others. Brian Barnes was most critical of the Brabazon, built in 1977 by Peter Alliss and Dave Thomas, saying "This course will not be fit for tournaments for 30 years." The players were allowed to clean and place their golf balls on the fairways. Barnes said, "It's embarrassing for us professionals to be seen on television in the middle of the summer playing winter rules."

In the Hennessey Cognac Cup matches in the autumn of 1978, Ballesteros made the newspaper headlines with one swing on the Brabazon's 10th hole, driving the green on that short par-four in winning his match against Faldo. He had at least one spectacular shot in each of the last three rounds of the English Classic. For example, there was his drive on the 18th hole in the second round. The 18th is one of the best holes on the Brabazon, a splendid and dramatic finishing hole, having water in front of the tee and another lake to be crossed before the green. The hole measures 474 yards, nearly enough to be a par-five. Ballesteros had such a mammoth hit with just the right amount of draw that he needed only a nine-iron for his second shot. He was merely 139 yards from the flag, meaning that his drive had traveled 335 yards through a cross wind. He finished off the hole properly, with a birdie from five feet. In the third round, again with his new Japanese driver, Ballesteros not only drove the 16th green from 346 yards but also hit through the green and had to chip back on with his second shot. He nearly holed the chip for an eagle.

In the final round Ballesteros was nursing a hook and his most memorable shot traveled no great distance. Rather, it was saved by a dinghy, a small, overturned boat in the water alongside the eighth hole. Ballesteros, for once, let the hook get out of control. It seemed certain that the ball would go in the lake, but instead it hit the boat on the water's edge and bounced back onto land. He made the most of his good fortune, hitting on eight-iron to the green and holing a twelve-foot putt. Just when Ballesteros was facing the prospect of a double-bogey, he instead made a birdie. It takes some luck to win by six strokes.

Scandinavian Open— £ 31,800
Winner: Sandy Lyle

The British were particularly optimistic after the Scandinavian Enterprise Open because it appeared that another young star had emerged and that Sandy Lyle had joined Nick Faldo to bolster the nation's long-term golf prospects. While many thought Lyle was capable of winning on the European circuit, the general view might have been that he was one year away from that success. He surprised us by his maturity on the course, not only in being a frequent contender and winning twice in the span of six tournaments but also in withstanding the toughest challenge that European golf can offer. That challenge, naturally, was Severiano Ballesteros on his best days.

The Scandinavian championship was one of the year's best tournaments. The crowds added immeasurably to that feeling. Some of the largest galleries ever on the Continent were at the Vasatorps course in Helsingborg, Sweden, while Lyle matched Ballesteros stroke-for-stroke in the final round. Both had three-under-par 69s, as Lyle maintained the three-shot lead he established with his 65 on the third day. His final total was 276, 12 under par. An American player, Mike Krantz, was in the battle for a while. Krantz, who also had 65 in the third round, started one stroke behind and tied Lyle with two birdies in three holes starting out. He eventually slipped to 73 and took third place alone, five strokes behind Lyle but three ahead of the fourth-place finishers, Ken Brown and Dale Hayes.

Having won the British Airways/Avis Open, Lyle was fourth in both the Welsh Classic and Greater Manchester Open and seventh in the Lada English Golf Classic before taking his second championship in the Scandinavian Open. His performances were due as much to his remarkably even temperament as to his great length from the tees. "I do have the odd bit of fiery temper when things aren't going right, but not when anybody is looking," said Lyle, 21 years old and in his second professional season.

While Lyle shot 73 in the first round, Faldo gave an indication that this might instead be his week to win, having 69 to share the lead with one of the lesser-known Australian players, Mike Ferguson. Faldo one-putted five greens in a row, three for birdies, while playing the last nine in 32.

A swirling wind toughened the conditions for the second round, and both Faldo and Ferguson were blown from contention. Faldo had 78 and Ferguson 75. The new leader was Brown with a conservative 70 for a 141 total. The duel that was to decide the tournament, Lyle versus Ballesteros, was developing. They were tied for second place, one stroke behind, along with Hayes.

In the third and fourth rounds, Lyle and Ballesteros were in the same grouping. Lyle quickly took the advantage. He came home in 30, including six birdies, in the third round and sprinted in front by three strokes. Midway in the final round Ballesteros was two strokes behind and in second place, once Krantz fell away. Far from being unnerved, Lyle produced three shots that secured the victory. Ballesteros played a marvelous pitch-and-run shot to the ninth green within a yard of the hole and certainly a birdie to close the gap. But Lyle played within six inches and restored his margin. He followed with birdies on the 10th and 11th holes and left Ballesteros to settle for second place.

Dutch Open— £ 30,100

Winner: Graham Marsh

Graham Marsh and Hale Irwin are alike in so many ways, as Marsh has often said, "It's really unusual for us to be friends. Sometimes it's hard for people like that to be friends." They are similar in style and temperament. It would be difficult to say who has been the more successful golfer, since Irwin has spent most of his career in the United States and Marsh in the Far East. They had the distinction in 1978, along with Bill Kratzert, of earning the most money in the history of the game without winning a tournament. Irwin was ninth on the world list with $232,417, Marsh was 13th with $189,555 and Kratzert 14th with $189,389.

Irwin cracked that jinx in 1979 by winning his second U.S. Open title and, a few weeks later, Marsh followed suit by winning the Dutch Open. There is really no comparison between those championships but, nevertheless, Marsh's victory served as a reminder that he is an international star of the highest standard and deserves to be mentioned in the same fashion as his best friend.

The victory was the 32nd of Marsh's career, while Irwin has won 11 U.S.

tournaments plus two World Match Play Championships. Marsh has always felt that a top-10 finish in America was the same as a victory anywhere else. Before the Dutch Open, Marsh had two such finishes—fourth place in the Danny Thomas Memphis Classic and seventh in the Western Open. He also was seventh in the British Open. But Marsh had been close so many times, he needed the victory to erase the doubts in his mind.

He last won 21 months earlier in the Lancome Trophy, completing a two-week spree in which he also won the World Match Play Championship. Those were his fourth and fifth victories of 1977, and he was third on the world list with $275,130, trailing only Tom Watson and Jack Nicklaus. That, of course, was the year Irwin convinced Marsh that he must play in America. He played in 17 U.S. tournaments, was a top-10 finisher in seven, and won the Sea Pines Heritage Classic. His other victories were in Japan, his golfing home, in the Chunichi Crowns and Wizard tournaments. It has been said many times that only one golfer, Gary Player, has been able to maintain an international schedule with notable success. Marsh, admittedly, was exhausted when he returned to Australia in the autumn. He was tired physically and, for the moment, had fulfilled his ambitions by proving that he could win in the United States. "After that," he said, "I didn't want to come out and start the grind again immediately."

The year truly became a grind once Marsh discovered that he was not holing those crucial putts that determine first or some lower place. "What a difference a putter makes," he said. "This has been the most frustrating year I've ever had." His putting and troublesome hip injury plagued Marsh on into the spring of 1979 until his fortunes began to improve in Memphis.

As always, the British Open was on his schedule, but the inclusion of the Dutch Open was "an 11th-hour decision." What luck, after so long a drought! He did not lead until the final day. He shot 71 in the first round and was four strokes behind Jeff Hall, a 22-year-old struggler on the European circuit. John Bland shared first place with Hall after 36 holes following his course-record 66, then added 72 for a two-stroke cushion. Marsh had rounds of 70 and 74 and started the last round with a five-stroke deficit.

Seven different players were atop the leaderboard during the round—Bland, Marsh, Malcolm Gregson, Nick Job, Tommy Horton, Manuel Pinero and Geoff Parslow. Marsh had three birdies in his 70 for a 285 total to finish one stroke ahead of Gregson and Antonio Garrido. Marsh's most important putt, the sort he had been missing for 21 months, was for par on the ninth. He came out of a bunker and sank a 20-footer while Bland fell from the lead with a double-bogey there.

Sun Alliance European Match Play Championship— £ 40,000
Winner: Des Smyth

It was typical in a week of upheaval, in which so many notable heads rolled from the start, that the winner should come from among the pre-qualifiers in the Sun Alliance European Match Play Championship. Irishman Des Smyth played his way from obscurity into the Ryder Cup, and with the Sun Alliance victory and the £6,660 first-prize check lifted his earnings to more than £11,000 for the year. Smyth, 26 years old, had previously distinguished himself largely in the Colgate PGA Championship, where he tied for sixth place after sharing the 54-hole lead. That was the first time he had ever won a four-figure check.

In the final, Smyth defeated another little-known golfer, Nicky Price of South Africa, winning with a 10-foot putt for eagle on the 18th hole. The preliminary rounds had pointed strongly to a final between Antonio Garrido and Brian Barnes. Barnes played solidly, but in the quarter-finals ran into Smyth, who seemingly could do no wrong on the greens. Garrido's play was superb until the semifinals, when he visibly ran out of steam in losing to Price. Smyth defeated Carl Mason by one hole in the other semifinal, setting up a championship clash that gained the large crowd's excited attention despite the fact that neither of the finalists was previously regarded as having any spectator appeal.

Smyth went round in 69, two under par at Fulford, and Price shot 70. After Smyth captured three holes in a row from the third, he was in front all the way to the 17th. The match really began to take shape after the turn, at which point Smyth was two up, having shot par 35 to Price's 37. Price took the 11th with a birdie and, at the 15th, Smyth hit a fine four-iron to eight feet to go two up again. Price responded with a birdie on the 16th and squared the match at the 17th, where Smyth slightly pushed his approach shot and the ball hit a spectator. And so they went to the last hole, a par five of 488 yards, where they both drove well and got up easily with irons. Price was on the fringe, and Smyth was 10 feet from the cup. The 22-year-old South African's putt eased to a halt at the edge of the hole and Smyth, who produced devastating putts all week, holed out to top Price's birdie with an eagle.

Tony Jacklin, Nick Faldo and the fourth-seeded player, Colgate PGA Champion Vicente Fernandez, all were knocked out in the first round. Jacklin lost to Stephen Rolley, a Yorkshireman who now lives, like Jacklin, in the Channel Islands. Faldo fell to Mike Steadman from Cleve Hill Municipal Club, who had "not won a penny piece" all year until he had collected £1,500 the previous week as runner-up in the Club Professionals Championship. In another match indicative of what was to follow, Fernandez lost to Price. Defending Champion Mark James, Sandy Lyle, Howard Clark and Eddie Polland lost in the second round, and the march was on toward an inglorious but thrilling final.

Benson & Hedges International Open— £60,000
Winner: Maurice Bembridge

The competition for berths on Europe's Ryder Cup side was intense as the deadline drew near. After the Benson & Hedges International Open, yet another name was on the list of potential qualifiers—Maurice Bembridge. By winning that tournament with its impressive £10,000 first prize, Bembridge rose to the coveted 10th place on the Order of Merit. The first 10 players on the list after the Carrolls Irish Open, merely two weeks later, would qualify to play against the Americans in September at White Sulphur Springs, West Virginia. The remaining two players on the 12-man team would be chosen by a committee consisting of Team Captain John Jacobs, ETPD Committee Chairman Neil Coles and Severiano Ballesteros, the leader of the Order of Merit for the previous year.

Americans, who pay little heed to either the selections or, indeed, the Ryder Cup matches, can scarcely appreciate the attention that is focused on the procedure by the British press and the pressures that are brought to bear on the golfers, with a countdown similar to that in the final weeks of the U.S. baseball season. Entering the Benson & Hedges International, the Ryder Cup Points Table (published every week in all the newspapers) was as follows: Severiano Ballesteros (32,934), Brian Barnes (23,083), Bernard Gallacher (20,655), Sandy Lyle (20,429), Mark James (18,829), Antonio Garrido (14,540), Nick Faldo (13, 534), Ken Brown (12,231), Michael King (12,173), Des Smyth (11,211), Neil Coles (9,764), Baldovino Dassu (9,446), Malcolm Gregson (8,824), Manuel Pinero (8,796), Eddie Polland (8,563), Howard Clark (8,159), Tony Jacklin (7,847), Gordon Brand (7,798), John Morgan (7,772), Francisco Abreu (7,645).

While the first five players seemed secure in their Ryder Cup positions, the others anxiously watched the day-to-day scores and the tensions multiplied with the victories by Bembridge and by Smyth the week before in the Sun Alliance European Match Play Championship. Smyth had only just settled in 10th place when Bembridge replaced him. The Benson & Hedges International was also notable, from a Ryder Cup perspective, in the performances of Brown, Sam Torrance, Jacklin and King. Brown took second place, two strokes behind Bembridge, and moved from eighth to sixth place on the list. Torrance tied for third with Brazilian Jaime Gonzalez, ineligible for Ryder Cup consideration, and took over 12th place. Jacklin advanced from 17th to 13th on the Ryder Cup list with his fifth-place finish and King, who tied for sixth in the Benson & Hedges, held onto the ninth spot.

Bembridge's scores over the par-71 St. Mellion course near Plymouth were 67, 67, 69 and 69 for a 272 total, 12 under par. The victory was his first on the European tour since 1975, although he was a winner in Kenya earlier in the spring. The key to Bembridge's triumph was his short game. He had only one three-putt green all week, and he saved par from off the green five times in the final round alone. Brown's birdies on the 14th and 17th holes, the latter from 30 feet, put Bembridge under the gun on the final hole. Then Brown risked all by playing boldly for an eagle on the par-five 18th but instead took a par to Bembridge's birdie.

Braun Trophy/German Open— £37,150
Winner: Tony Jacklin
The most heartwarming victory on the European circuit must have been Tony

Jacklin's triumph in the Braun Trophy/German Open. British followers, in particular, had suffered with Tony as he struggled in recent seasons. As I remarked after the British Airways/Avis Open, those close to Jacklin felt this would be the year for his breakthrough. He did so with a thoroughly determined performance, having to hold off one of golf's real competitors, American star Lanny Wadkins. You could even give Wadkins some of the credit for Jacklin's victory in a week when it appeared that Tony was destined to come close but again to fail.

Jacklin started the final round with a margin of four strokes over Howard Clark and seven strokes over Wadkins. He won by two strokes, shooting 71 while Wadkins fired 66 in the same threesome. Antonio Garrido, with 67, shared second place. "Lanny came at me with both barrels," Tony later remarked, "and that was just what I needed. It kept me going for birdies, which was just as well, with Antonio also charging at me."

The triumph was Jacklin's first on the European tour since 1974, when he won the Scandinavian Open, although he did win the Kerrygold International in 1976. He did not mince any words about how he felt about being back in the winner's circle, saying, "Just now I feel better than when I won the [British] Open. I've been through so much. I have read books on psychiatry, dieting—everything—to try and find a cure. Two years ago I was so depressed that I was on the verge of quitting, but I struggled on." He added, "In my heart, I knew I would never win again until I started putting well, and that's what I've done with a putter loaned to me by Ben Crenshaw [at the Italian Open earlier in the year]. I'm also using a new stroke. I've worked endless hours perfecting it."

Jacklin shot 68 in the first round and was one stroke behind the surprise leader, Patrice Bagnoud of Switzerland. He took the lead with another 68 in the second round, but there were shudders over his horrendous eight on the par-five 17th hole. There, Jacklin was distracted at the top of his backswing by a sudden burst of applause from a nearby green. He hooked his tee shot into woods and, on his first recovery attempt, the ball ricocheted 40 yards deeper into the trees. He hacked out, hit to within 25 yards of the green and there found a tight lie. He fluffed his pitch shot into a bunker and finished with the triple bogey.

Clark was four strokes behind after the second round and remained in that position after 54 holes, as Jacklin had 70 for 216. When Jacklin dropped a stroke on the par-three fourth hole in the last round and Clark got a birdie there, the margin was only two strokes. Clark, however, faded badly and Jacklin gained six strokes on him in six holes. With his birdie from 15 on the 10th hole, Jacklin was five strokes clear of the field and it seemed that the remainder of the round might be a mere stroll in the park.

Then came Wadkins, who nearly made a hole-in-one at the 11th while Jacklin took a bogey. There was a three-stroke swing after Jacklin drove into the trees on the 12th hole. But Jacklin was equal to the pressure, made birdies on the 13th and 17th holes and said afterwards, having finished with his 71 for 277, "I have restored my faith in myself." He also restored his position on the

Ryder Cup team, advancing from 13th place to eighth on the Points List with one tournament remaining.

Carrolls Irish Open— £60,000

Winner: Mark James

For the better part of the week, it appeared that Howard Clark's name might be on the list when the final points were tabulated for the Ryder Cup team following the Carrolls Irish Open. That did not occur, as so often was the case in this topsy-turvy European season. The surprise of the Ryder Cup selections, to the delight of the many Irish golf followers, was 26-year-old Des Smyth. His nomination by the three-man committee came after Clark, the leader after both the second and third rounds, fell to a seventh-place tie during the final day's play. The winner of the Irish Open, Mark James, was previously qualified and Clark's showing left him in 13th place in the Ryder Cup points table.

The first 10 automatically qualified: Severiano Ballesteros (34,372), James (29,529), Brian Barnes (26, 419), Bernard Gallacher (22,340), Sandy Lyle (21,550), Ken Brown (19, 241), Antonio Garrido (17,897), Tony Jacklin (17,702), Michael King (15,369) and Nick Faldo (15,334). The selectors by-passed the 11th man, Maurice Bembridge (13,621) while choosing Smyth (12,057) and U.S. PGA Tour regular Peter Oosterhuis. Smyth's initial reaction was a delighted "I can't believe it." Ryder Cup Captain John Jacobs explained, "Awkward decisions have to be made at times and, although Bembridge finished a place above Smyth, we decided that the Irishman should go into the team along with Peter Oosterhuis. Smyth has a great match-play record, as he proved when taking the European title. The only thing we doubted about him was his fitness, but Neil Coles played with him and he is more than satisfied that his wrist trouble is now over."

Had fitness been most important among the criteria, Smyth might not have been chosen and James certainly would not have won. After the second round, James later admitted, "I had a lot of pain at the top of my right thigh and thought about withdrawing. But I decided to wait and see how I felt on Saturday morning." He felt well enough to shoot 69, a significant improvement on his earlier scores of 73 and 75, and closed within four strokes of Clark, who needed either first or second place to be assured of a Ryder Cup berth. Clark earlier had rounds of 71, 69 and 73 before stumbling to his fourth-round 75. He trailed John Bland by two strokes after the first day, then sprang two strokes clear of Jacklin after 36 holes. The third-round summary had Clark leading Jacklin and Simon Hobday by one stroke with many golfers clustered closely behind. Three strokes separated the first six players, four strokes the first 11 (including James) and five strokes the first 17. The battle everyone anticipated on the last day at Portmarnock developed curiously without the two most likely contenders, Clark and Jacklin, who also finished in that seventh-place tie.

Jacklin was perhaps the dominant figure of the tournament, nevertheless. The warmth of the Irish galleries, estimated at 50,000 for the fourth round, was unmistakable with shouts of "Go get 'em, Tony!" Jacklin, having just won the Braun Trophy/German Open was truly revitalized, playing with immense freedom and purpose. "I now feel I am in control of my destiny again," he said. "My victory in the German Open after five years could turn out to be the most significant thing in my life!"

It was probably asking too much for Jacklin to record back-to-back victories, but what a finish that would have been. It was highly dramatic as it was, with James shooting 65 and finding that score to be barely enough to hold off American import Ed Sneed, who also had 65. Sneed was playing in the groups ahead and waited as James played the last two holes. Then James had to wait as yet another American, Mark McCumber, finished. McCumber needed an eagle-two to tie and, in flamboyant fashion, sent his caddie 127 yards to tend the flagstick. "Trouble was, the wind changed as soon as he reached the green and I had the wrong club," McCumber said ruefully. "I didn't dare call him back." McCumber was short of the green, took three strokes from there and placed third, two behind James.

Only then could James breathe easily. "I could not believe this guy Sneed," he said. "I thought four under par would win it. But when I got to four under, so did he. I went to five; so did he. I wasn't sure I was safe at six."

Swiss Open— £ 53,000
Winner: Hugh Baiocchi

With the pressures of qualifying for the Ryder Cup side so fresh in their memories, it shouldn't have been surprising to find that many of the European team members took the week off, literally or figuratively, during the Swiss Open. Michael King did not enter, missing his first tournament of the year. Severiano Ballesteros and Nick Faldo, to name two prominent Ryder Cup players, failed to qualify for the final 36 holes and only two of that elite dozen were among the first 10 finishers—Antonio Garrido and Ken Brown. In their place among the leaders were a number of South Africans, two drop-outs from the American tour and one highly underrated Italian. Hugh Baiocchi, continuing the excellent showings by South Africans on this circuit, was the winner by five strokes over countryman Dale Hayes, Garrido and that previously mentioned Italian player, Delio Lovato.

Americans Mitch Adcock and Rafe Botts took the headlines in the first two rounds. Adcock, who led the opening day with 66, lost his U.S. PGA Tour player's card in 1978 and was trying the European tour for a second time. He eventually tied for fifth, six strokes behind Baiocchi, and earned a much-needed £1,731. While Adcock is a youngster, Botts is well into his 40's and his appearance on the European tour this spring was unexpected but warmly received. Anyone who has ever met Botts, however briefly, will understand. He is extremely pleasant and likable and might have become quite an attraction in golf had he been able to consistently produce low scores in America. It was nice to see him share the second-round lead with Baiocchi and finish in the top 10 as well.

Baiocchi is another of the real gentlemen of the game. Hugh had not won in Europe since taking the 1977 Sun Alliance Match Play Championship and, late though victory came in 1979, I am sure that he would have been highly disappointed to have gone through another season without winning. He had played well for most of the year and could have had several victories. The winner's check of £8,064 boosted Baiocchi to eighth place on the Order of Merit, an indication that his play has been to Ryder Cup caliber, even though he was not eligible for the matches.

Baiocchi and Botts were tied at 135 after identical rounds of 68 and 67. With 68 in the third round, Lovato took the lead by a stroke over Hayes, while Baiocchi was two behind, along with Ewen Murray. For those who would wonder about him, Lovato's name could not be found even in the small print of the Tournament Player's Guide, for the simple reason that he plays in hardly any tournaments. Indeed, this was only his second year. Still, Lovato is the reigning Italian professional champion and placed 11th as the lowest Italian in his country's open championship. The few players who have been his partners have been very impressed. Lovato kept the pace for 10 holes of the fourth round, then dropped four strokes over the next three holes. Meanwhile, Baiocchi was surging, having started with two birdies and played the first nine in 31 on the way to his winning 67.

European Open— £105,000
Winner: Sandy Lyle

Occasionally, the most crucial moments of a golf tournament will pass virtually unnoticed. This was most certainly true about Sandy Lyle's victory in the European Open at Turnberry. Mention that tournament and most people will recall that Lyle shot 65 in the final round. While the score was praiseworthy, Turnberry's vulnerability in the absence of protective winds is an established fact, at least since the Open Championship was played there in 1977. More important than his 65 was Lyle's play over the last seven holes in the first round, when he salvaged 71 after being out in 37. Otherwise, Lyle might have placed little better than Tommy Horton, who tied for fourth and was eight strokes off the winning score with his first-round 74 and final-round 66.

Credit for an astute bit of reporting must go to Michael Williams of the *Daily Telegraph,* who took note of the whippery conditions in the first round by saying: "With the wind again in the south, players had to make their score in the first 11 holes and then do their best to hang on to it." Then Williams went a step beyond his rivals in the press with a commentary beginning, "An exception was Sandy Lyle . . ."

The first-round leader was little-known Tony Charnley, from Woodlands in Northants, who stood 87th on the Order of Merit. Charnley made three birdies over the first six holes, was out in 32 and dropped one stroke to par to close at 68. Severiano Ballesteros drew most of the attention with his 69, sharing second place with Vince Baker. It was only the second time since winning the Open Championship that Ballesteros had broken 70. "It's nice to be back," he said. "It's not that I have been playing that badly, but the ball has not been running for me." This day, luck was on his side. He dumped a three-iron shot into the large bunker in the bottom right-hand corner of the sixth green. He could scarcely see the flag and appeared destined to score bogey four. Instead, he holed the shot for birdie. He was bunkered again at the seventh hole and sank a 10-foot putt for birdie.

American Bobby Wadkins, the defending champion, took 75 in the opening round and was not a factor; nor was Larry Nelson, who started with 77. Both were among the top-20 finishers, while the championship was left to the European and British stars: Ballesteros, Lyle, Horton, Ken Brown, Neil Coles, Mark James, Peter Townsend, Sam Torrance and Jose-Maria Canizares. In the second round Lyle shot 67 and Ballesteros 69. They shared the lead, one stroke ahead of Ken Brown. Reports from that day centered on speculation of a repeat of their Scandinavian duel, but it developed differently. James was off to 64 and Coles 66 on Saturday and they went a stroke ahead of Lyle (72) and four ahead of Ballesteros (74). The fourth round was notable for two reasons, Lyle's burst at the start, scoring threes on the first seven holes, six for birdies, and his replacement of Ballesteros atop the Order of Merit with the victory, his third of the year on the European Tour. Lyle played most of the final round with an almost insurmountable margin, winning by seven strokes over Hayes.

The week did more to improve young Lyle's reputation than that of the European Open. To quote his father pro Alex Lyle, "This puts him ahead of our plans. Last year we aimed for the top 60 so we were happy with 49th. This year the objective was a Ryder Cup place to go with his Walker Cup honor." As for the second European Open, I heartily agree with Peter Dobereiner of the *Guardian,* who called it "A disappointingly downbeat and poorly attempted promotion." It was hardly an event of international stature and, at best, marginally justified its name as a championship involving the European players.

SOS Talisman Tournament Players Championship— £ 50,000
Winner: Michael King

One of the frequent themes of the 1979 European Tour was the progress of Michael King, whose name first appeared among the leaders during the Madrid and Italian Opens and who played so steadily throughout the year that he earned a berth on the Ryder Cup team without winning a tournament. Always cheerful and courteous, even in moments of disappointment as he learned to cope with the pressures of top-level competition, the 29-year-old King was a sentimental choice to win before the year was out.

His victory in the SOS Talisman Tournament Players Championship was rightfully hailed as a respite during a gloomy period for European golf, a time that often was marked "by controversy, fines, downright bad manners and total disregard for public image," Michael McDonnell wrote in the *Daily Mail.* King "restored some style to his profession" while winning at Moor Park against an international field that included Gary Player and the recently crowned U.S. PGA champion David Graham.

It was fitting that King should win, if only because his disposition matched that of Ivor Freedman, the bubbly Managing Director of SOS Talisman Co., Limited, sponsor of the championship.

"SOS Talisman?" you may ask. That is a story in itself.

The Tournament Players Championship was begun in 1977, underwritten by my International Management Group as part of the rescue operation after Carreras Rothmans withdrew from sponsoring the World Match Play Championship. The TPC was the 72-hole stroke-play event necessary to meet the requirements for the continuation of the World Match Play, sponsored for two years by Colgate-Palmolive and now by Suntory Limited.

While moderately successful, the TPC was in the shadow of the World Match Play. In order to assure that it would become a truly great event on the European calendar, a tournament with an identity of its own, my company set out to find an appropriate sponsor.

Our initial contact with Ivor Freedman was not related to golf but, rather, Muhammad Ali, who had agreed to endorse the SOS Talisman range of medical identification jewelry. Mr. Freedman was very interested in associating his product with sportsmen, so that it would not become stigmatized as simply a medical tag. His marketing approach made a great deal of sense and provided for an easy extension into the arena of professional golf which proved to be beneficial to both SOS Talisman and the tournament.

With SOS Talisman as the sponsor, there also was a change in venue from Foxhills to Moor Park, which has been the setting for many important tournaments over the years. It was at Moor Park, for instance, that Gary Player first competed in Britain. That was 1955, Gary having left South Africa with £ 100 in his pocket, a loan from his father which he later learned was acquired through an overdraft. Gary added to his nest egg enroute by winning the Egyptian Match Play, but was nowhere among the leaders in that Spalding tournament at Moor Park. The following year, however, Player finished third, thanks to a hole-in-one at the 10th, which, he still recalls, was made with a nine-iron.

Player was part of this year's exciting finish as well, after the opening rounds in which the attention was, regrettably, focused on Ken Brown, who was left out of the pro-am because of his ill manners in an earlier event, and who was fined £ 100 for his slow play in this tournament. The leader for those first two rounds was Ewen Murray. The Scot had two 68s to lead King by two strokes and Player by four. Severiano Ballesteros' scores should also be noted, although he was never a contender. Ballesteros, playing for the sole purpose of catching Order of Merit leader Sandy Lyle, did not even survive the 36-hole cut with rounds of 78 and 75.

The third day, Murray slipped to 74 and was tied by King, who had 72, while Brown remained in the news by scoring an ace at the 10th, the hole on which Player had made an ace 23 years earlier. Gary, meanwhile, matched King's 72 and was two strokes behind. The three players who would decide the championship—King, Player and defending champion Brian Waites—were in

*Graham Marsh at the
Dunlop Masters.*

the same group for the last round. Waites shot 68, but King held off the challenge by firing 71 for a 281 total and a one-stroke victory. Player could not maintain his game and fell to fourth place with 74, five strokes behind King and two behind third-place finisher Murray, who also had 74.

Dunlop Masters— £60,000
Winner: Graham Marsh

As Graham Marsh stood in the 18th fairway on the final day, tied for the lead with Isao Aoki and Neil Coles, he was not playing with the utmost confidence. He recognized that the only club for his next shot was his three-wood and, he thought, if not for that club he would not be in this predicament.

He reached into the bag, thinking, "This thing owes me one."

Sure enough, Marsh got the shot he needed to win after having had such mediocre results with his fairway woods all week. He drilled the ball low into the wind, gaining the front edge of the green, from where he took two putts for his second European victory of the year and the 33rd of his career.

The Dunlop Masters was also notable for Severiano Ballesteros' final-gasp attempt to remain atop the European Order of Merit for the fourth consecutive year. The Spaniard did not finish high enough, however, to overtake Sandy Lyle, who won the title with £39,808 to Ballesteros' £37,206. Thus, Peter Oosterhuis' record of four successive Order of Merit titles remained untouched.

This showcase event for Dunlop, again won by a Dunlop staff player, was held on the new course at Woburn, north of London. The property is part of the estate of the Marquis of Tavistock, whose father, the Duke of Bedford, was among the first to open stately homes to public view. Included in the property is a safari park and a golf course set in a magnificent forest. The course came under criticism from several golfers, including Tony Jacklin, who said the greens were too hard. Jacklin used the occasion to remind the British of the differences between their course conditions and those in America:

"We can forget about beating Americans in the Ryder Cup until we get our greens right," Jacklin said, after sharing the first-round lead with Tienie Britz, Pip Elson and Michael King. "We have some good young players but they must be able to rely on the greens when they face three-footers and four-footers. Look at the greens at the Greenbrier for the match. They were superb. The American pro can rely on such greens and know he's going to get them most weeks. It's an exception if we get them. I would like to see a meeting between all the greenskeepers on courses we are due to play during the season so that some advice could be given and some consistency found."

Nevertheless, Marsh restated his intention of playing less on the American circuit and more in Europe during 1980 after having been the U.S. tour for three years and gained only one victory. Marsh, whose 283 total included rounds of 70, 68, 72 and 73, apparently was willing to sacrifice course conditioning for less competition than he found in America, where the margin between winning and losing was so very narrow.

Lancome Trophy— £ 23,670

Winner: Johnny Miller

First, a flashback to the 1976 Masters. Johnny Miller had completed a practice round and 20 reporters were waiting for him, as they always seemed to be in those days. They were talking about Johnny's blazing scores in the previous Masters, when he had escaped the 36-hole cutoff by one stroke and, by that same one-stroke margin, came short of beating Jack Nicklaus for the championship. "My game," Johnny said, "is like a phantom." Three months later, Miller struck again with 65 in the final round to topple Severiano Ballesteros in the British Open.

The description "phantom" has proved particularly appropriate for Miller because, in a sense, he has had a phantom-like career from his out-of-the-blue 63 to win the 1973 U.S. Open onwards. Who would have thought, in July of 1976, that Johnny Miller would not win again for over three years? Who could adequately explain the elusive nature of golf, especially when played with such flashes of brilliance?

Johnny Miller's win in the Lancome Trophy was his first in over three years.

After Miller finally did win again, by three strokes in the Lancome Trophy, he tried to explain it this way: "I climbed to the top of my personal mountain and decided to relax. Other guys have to climb every mountain, but I'm not like that. In 1975 people were saying I was better than Nicklaus. It was an unprecedented state and, I suppose, I couldn't handle it. Maybe I backed off. I don't know. But I went away and worked on my ranch and ruined my golf muscles. I went three months and only played one round of golf."

That statement may not be totally convincing, but Miller had given indication of a revival a few weeks earlier at Pinehurst, going to a play-off before losing to Tom Watson in the Colgate Hall of Fame Classic. When he turned up outside of Paris at St. Nom-la-Bretche for the Lancome, Johnny declared, "I'm hitting the ball well enough to win, certainly as good as any of the other guys here. That is a judgement, not a boast."

His competition in this 12-man invitational was formidable, consisting of Lee Trevino, the defending champion; Suntory World Match Play champion Bill Rogers; European Order of Merit leaders Sandy Lyle, Mark James, Tony Jacklin, Brian Barnes and Dale Hayes; U.S. Tour stars Raymond Floyd and Arnold Palmer; American amateur Bobby Clampett and the respected Frenchman, Jean Garaialde.

James began with 69 and led by one stroke over Miller, who said, "The way I hit the ball, I shot 66 today, but it only came out as 70." In the second round, Floyd had a superb 65 in heavy rains for a two-stroke lead over Jacklin, who had 67. Miller was four shots behind after his 71. Floyd's margin was nothing that Miller could not overcome with three consecutive birdies early in the third round on his way to a 69 while Floyd took 74. No one could pressure Miller on the last day. Floyd's threat was halted by a couple of early bogeys and he he shot another 74. Lyle and Trevino advanced to share second place with 284 to Miller's 281, wrapped up with a final 71.

"What pleases me about this victory is that it repaid all my friends who didn't desert a sinking ship like rats," he said. "A lot of people said Johnny Miller was through. Well, they were wrong. This doesn't compare to my wins in the majors, but it is one of the most important in my life. Maybe THE most important."

World Cup

Winners: Team - United States (Hale Irwin and John Mahaffey); Individual - Irwin

The message of the 27th World Cup, in the words of champions John Mahaffey and Hale Irwin, was this: "It would seem that a common ground can always be found in sport if governments would allow it."

The government of Greece, under pressure from a United Nations subcommittee, would not allow the South African team of Dale Hayes and Hugh Baiocchi to play and, for a time, it was questionable whether the tournament would be held. Irwin and Mahaffey, the United States team, considered withdrawing but decided there was "little to be gained" by doing so. They played, along with golfers from 45 nations, but not before issuing a statement which

Take-off over the 17th green at Glyfada during the World Cup.

noted that ''we find it deplorable that politics and governments must concern themselves so deeply about the participation of South African athletes in world events. We entertained the thought of withdrawing from this tournament in protest. But we found little to be gained by this action. We instead chose this means to express our regrets and hope that our fellow players will agree with us. Our sincerest best wishes to the players from South Africa because they are indeed gentlemen. We hope that these kinds of situations will cease to appear in the future.''

The situation upset everyone there. Even though the tournament continued, a deep sense of frustration and anger lingered at Glyfada Golf Club, near Athens. The same United Nations subcommittee, which concerns itself with anti-apartheid, made a similar attempt in 1978 without success when the World Cup was held in Hawaii. A less powerful country than the United States, the Greeks felt they were in an impossible bind. There were unconfirmed reports of various sanctions that might be imposed against Greece, if the South Africans were allowed to play. The Greek foreign minister, George Rallis, asked John Ross, executive director of the International Golf Association, to expel Hayes and Baiocchi. Ross refused, leaving that task to Rallis himself. At the official dinner that evening, the South Africans were greeted warmly, then Rallis made a speech which, in effect, was the official ouster. He concluded, ''If I had not been in the position I am, I too would have stood and applauded.''

The absurdity of the whole matter has been pointed out many times, in this and previous years: The South African PGA Tour is nonracial and the black golfers, numbering nearly 50, have an equal chance of qualifying for the team. But so much for the follies of governments.

The United States was in control of the tournament from start to finish, although Taiwan and Scotland both threatened the Americans. Mahaffey began with 67 and Irwin had 74 for a three-stroke margin over Taiwan's rookie team of Lu Hsi Chuen and Chen Tze Ming. Mahaffey's 71 and Irwin's 70 in the second round boosted their lead to eight strokes over second-place Scotland. The Scots, Sandy Lyle and Ken Brown, picked up six strokes in the first four holes and actually went ahead of the United States midway through the third round. Then, at the par-five 12th, Lyle took double-bogey and Brown bogey, while the Americans played through in one over par. That was the final team challenge and attention was then focused on individual honors.

Mahaffey, who struggled to an 80, eliminated himself in the third round. Spain's Antonio Garrido was, at the same time, advancing near the top with a course-record 66 and World Cup-record 30 for nine holes. Aside from Garrido, the individual contenders as the fourth round began were Irwin, Lyle, Germany's Bernhard Langer and Brazil's Jaime Gonzalez. Irwin, the U.S. Open champion, birdied three of the first six holes and turned in 33 to Langer's 35 and the championship became a two-man duel. They were even with four holes to play after Irwin's bogey on the 14th. Langer bogeyed the 17th, allowing Irwin to ease to a two-stroke victory. Hale shot a closing final-round 69 for his 285 total, while Langer had 72 and 287 to share second place with the fast finishing Lyle, who also shot 69.

In the team standings, the United States held a five-stroke margin over Scotland, 575 to 580. Spain was third with 290, Brazil was fourth with 594 and Taiwan fifth with 595. It was also interesting to note that there were no scores in the 100s, a common occurrence in World Cup competitions that include so many teams not expecting to win, but merely to share in international goodwill. It was a fine commentary on the improvement of golfing skills in those countries, such as Yugoslavia, which featured 15-year-old amateur Marko Vovk, the youngest player ever to compete in the World Cup. Vovk shot 99 in the first round but achieved his goal—not to finish last—when Italy's Baldovino Dassu had to withdraw after two rounds.

All the golfers, from Irwin to Vovk and Dassu, shared the same spirit for, as Irwin said, "This is the one time we can all join hands and be one." And he continued, "I would just as soon the World Cup would disband before succumbing to political pressures."

Moroccan Grand Prix—US $71,500

Winner: Mike Brannan

In addition to the dozen first-time winners on the American PGA Tour in 1979, there were many outstanding young golfers about whom we shall be hearing more in future years. This latter group includes Mike Brannan, formerly an All-America player at Brigham Young University, who earned a top-60 exemption in his first year on the circuit and was second to another youngster, Wayne Levi, in the Houston Open. Although Brannan did not win in the United States, he managed to close out his first season with a win in the Moroccan

Grand Prix, finishing two strokes ahead of fellow Americans Alan Tapie and Ed Fiori.

Before joining the tour, Brannan was highly regarded in the amateur ranks, if not one of the handful considered as "can't miss" prospects for professional success. Most of his victories were in California, his home state, but he played well enough on national excursions to be included on the 1977 Walker Cup team. And you can be sure that he wasn't a total stranger to the organizers of this lavish invitational tournament over the rugged par-73, 7,478-yard Red Course at Dar-es-Salam. The reason is that Brannan, a Mormon, is a special friend of Bill Casper, who, in turn, is a special friend of the tournament host, King Hassan II.

Brannan was in command for most of the tournament, although he shot 77 on the last day and won by two after starting the round with a seven-stroke cushion. Barry Vivian of New Zealand was the first-round leader with six-under-par 67, five strokes ahead of Brannan, Fiori and Irishman Eddie Polland. Brannan took charge with 70 in the next round while Vivian shot 76, falling to second place. He expanded the lead from one to seven strokes in the third round with a 69 to Vivian's 75. Fiori, Tapie and Antonio Garrido were then nine strokes behind at 220, but they proved to be stronger challengers than Vivian. Brannan's closing 77 provided for a four-under-par 288 total. Fiori and Tapie both had 70s for 290 totals and Garrido finished with 72 for third place with a 292 total. Vivian posted a 77 and was seventh with 277.

9

THE SAFARI / SOUTH AFRICAN TOURS

How many times have we heard Gary Player say that, barring unforeseen injury or illness, he would be winning championships well into the 1980's? His prediction was untarnished as the 1970's came to a close with Gary winning the last four tournaments on the six-event South African circuit. Now 44 years old, Player is proving to be the most durable of the Big Three that began dominating golf in the 1960's. This year was the first in which Player kept on winning, while Arnold Palmer and Jack Nicklaus did not. I believe it will not be the last. In fact, I think Gary may break Sam Snead's record for career victories before he's finished. Snead is credited by independent researchers with 135 victories. Gary's total is now 118, with his wins in the Lexington PGA, Kronenbrau "1308," South African Open and Sun City Classic. He was winless earlier in the year, although he placed second in the Greater Greensboro Open, Colgate PGA Championship in Britain and the United States Open, each time after starting the fourth round with a tremendous deficit.

In addition to the South African Tour, this chapter also includes the rapidly improving Safari Tour, which is frequented in the spring by many of the same British and European golfers who come to South Africa later in the year. All four of the Safari tournaments, in fact, were won by British players. John Morgan won the Nigerian Open and the Lusaka Open as a prelude to a highly respectable year on his home circuit. A former school teacher, Morgan had never won, but he must now be considered as a better-than-outside shot for any European titles. Maurice Bembridge ended a four-year drought by winning the Kenya Open, the showcase of the Safari Tour, and later took the Benson & Hedges International Open in Britain. Brian Barnes and Sandy Lyle closed out the tour in the Zambian Open, with Barnes winning a duel which would be resumed at home.

Simon Hobday, newly crowned as Rhodesian Sportsman of the Year, began the South African Tour with a triumph in the Zimbabwe Rhodesian Open, winning over Dennis Watson in a play-off. It was Hobday's second victory of the year, following the Madrid Open. Then young Nick Faldo, one of Britain's best prospects, overcame the disappointments of his winless European season to claim the ICL International championship, beating Denis Watson.

Player began his four-tournament romp in the Lexington PGA, after arriving weary from Australia. He came from behind there, again in the Kronenbrau "1308," and again in the South African Open. He extended his own record by winning the South African Open for the 12th time, shooting 66 in the last round to make up six strokes on third-round leader Ian Mosey. To cap things off, Gary won on his own course, taking the Sun City Classic title at the Gary Player Country Club in Pilansberg.

Nigerian Open— £ 25,740
Winner: John Morgan

John Morgan had never won a tournament in nine years split between the tours and his club duties. From the start of the Safari Tour he erased that stigma, winning twice by five-stroke margins. The 35-year-old Englishman took first place in both the Benin Open, a 36-hole preliminary tournament, and the Nigerian Open.

"The hardest thing is having in your mind that you are going to win," said Morgan, who had seldom before been a contender. "You can't just hope you'll win. You must knuckle down and make sure you win. Overcoming the mental problem, setting your resolve is the hardest part."

Although Morgan won easily, he had to struggle well into the last round. Malcolm Gregson, Pip Elson, Ewen Murray and Tommy Horton were much in contention. Gregson was the first-day leader with 66. Elson posted 64 in the second round to lead Murray by one and Morgan by two strokes. Horton had 65 in the third round, sharing first place with Morgan. The closing holes were easier and Morgan seemed to find extra momentum on those while posting rounds of 67, 67, 68 and 67 for his 269 total, 15 under par at the Ikoyl Club in Lagos. He birdied three of the last five holes in the opening round, five of the last seven in the next two rounds, and fought back Elson and Horton with five consecutive birdies in the final round, starting on the 12th hole.

Physical strength and a cool head were among the keys for Morgan, a former math instructor who struggled with several club jobs when he started in golf and who supplemented his income for two years by doing construction work. He believed that running 100 miles a week during his school days played a vital role in his victory under the tropical heat. He said, "I can honestly say I never really tired. In fact, I seemed to get stronger."

The pattern of his scoring reflected that. And in the fourth round, Morgan kept his composure when a downpour suddenly quickened the pace of the sand-and-oil putting "browns." Horton, at that point, made two bogeys and never caught up.

Kenya Open— £ 40,000
Winner: Maurice Bembridge

A strong organization and a worthwhile charity can be basic ingredients of a successful tournament, whether that tournament is held in Akron or Nairobi. In the American mold, the Kenya Open has emerged as Africa's most promising championship. Behind the Kenya Open is an imaginative director, London-born John Spurling, who recognized its possibilities in the early 1970's. The beneficiaries are Kenya's handicapped children, with over £ 30,000 raised each year in a celebrity pro-am linked to the first two rounds of the tournament.

The celebrities and international stars are treated to a weekend before the tournament at the exclusive Mount Kenya Safari Club. Their presence, in turn, has enabled Spurling and the Variety Club, which oversees the charity, to build a broad base among Kenyan businessmen to support the charity and a first-rate tournament. On-course operations meet British and American standards. There are efficient up-to-the-minute scoreboards and excellent catering services. The purse of £40,000, Africa's largest, is in line with those on offer by British and European organizers.

The 12th Kenya Open was won by Maurice Bembridge, who also won the first two Kenya titles in 1968 and 1969. Bembridge, a Briton who now lives in Iowa with his American wife, had not won since the 1975 German Open. That was a year after his most memorable feat, a 64 that tied the course record at Augusta National. Bembridge needed a play-off birdie to defeat Bernard Gallacher, who came from five strokes behind with his 65 in the last round.

Bob Charles, Simon Owen and Gary Cullen were the first-day leaders with 66s; then Bembridge, setting the Muthaiga course record which Gallacher tied, went two strokes clear of Owen with 65 for a 132 total. With his 69 in the third round, Bembridge was comfortably in front, leading Owen and Cullen by four strokes. He was under par again in the final round with 70 for a 271 total, but needed a six-foot birdie in the play-off to win.

Lusaka Open— £ 18,696.10
Winner: John Morgan

In case anyone thought his Nigerian Open victory was a fluke, John Morgan produced an encore in the Lusaka Open that was even more convincing. "What is so pleasing about the Lusaka Open," Morgan noted, "is that it is on a real golf course with proper greens, not browns."

He did not win by five strokes this time, only two strokes. He had a five-stroke lead to start the last round, but Trevor Powell wiped away the entire margin with five birdies in the first nine. Morgan then swung the tournament his way again with two crucial birdies. The first was with two putts after a three-wood shot to the front of the 13th green. After Powell failed to clear the water on the par-three 16th, Morgan put his five-iron shot ten feet from the flag and birdied again for a three-shot swing. He was four strokes ahead with two holes remaining. Powell couldn't make enough birdies to catch him. Morgan's winning total was 282, two under par.

With the victory, Morgan had virtually dominated the four-tournament Safari Tour, had convinced any skeptics and had been forced to reshape his goals for the forthcoming European season. "I started the year thinking I would try to win a tournament," he said. "Then, crash-bang, I had won three. Now I don't want just any title. I want a major European title."

Zambian Open— £ 30,000
Winner: Brian Barnes

In retrospect, the Zambian Open, final event of the Safari Tour, was an apt prelude to the European circuit, which began a few weeks later in Portugal. Brian Barnes and Sandy Lyle, whose names were continually posted on leaderboards throughout Continental Europe and Britain during 1979, were also the dominant figures of this championship.

Barnes, winner of two of the first three European TPD tournaments, achieved his first victory of 1979 on the strength of one spectacular score, a nine-under-par 64 in the second round. With that, Brian had a three-stroke margin, which he maintained over the last two days.

Lyle gave indications that he might become more of a threat in Europe, though it was still too early to even dream he might be No. 1. He shot three 69s but his 76 in the third round prevented him from taking a run at Barnes's lead. Lyle closed with a 283 total, while Barnes's winning figure was 280, 12 under on the par-73 Ndola Golf Club course. David Jones and Brian Waites were third with 284, and Gordon Brand completed the first five with 285.

Lyle, Jones, Bernhard Langer, Bob Wynn and Martin Poxon led the first day with 69s. Neither Wynn nor Poxon managed to break the top 10, however, as Wynn shot 77 and Poxon 78 in the third round. Barnes stormed to the front with his 64 in the second round. With another 69, Lyle was in second place and Langer shared third place with Dennis Dornian. Sandy took that 76 in the third and dropped seven strokes behind as Barnes posted 72 for a 207 total. Behind him at 210 was Jones, then came Waites at 211. Barnes's 73 on the final day was his worst score of the week, yet the best any of his challengers could muster was the 69 by Lyle.

Zimbabwe Rhodesian Open—R30,000
Winner: Simon Hobday

If anyone could stumble out of bed and win a tournament, that person must be Simon Hobday, who is probably as well known for his after-hours exploits as for his golfing ability. The evening before the third round of the Zimbabwe Rhodesian Open, Hobday was honored as the Rhodesian Sportsman of the Year with a banquet at the posh Monomatapa Hotel in Salisbury. The festivities continued for Hobday until the wee hours, well past three in the morning, and he went to the golf course after four hours of sleep, admittedly "feeling like a zombie." It came as a surprise, but it shouldn't have, that Hobday then shot a seven-under-par 65 to break the course record at Chapman Golf Club. Unshaven but grinning broadly as he stepped from the course, Hobday said, "It can't be all bad, can it? I played in a dream."

The round, which included nine birdies, put Hobday one stroke ahead of Denis Watson. A play-off for the title was required the next day after Hobday shot 70 and Watson 69, both finishing with totals of 275, 13 under par. Simon won with a par on the second hole, when Watson drove into the trees left of the fairway and later fluffed a chip, taking a double-bogey seven. It was the third home championship in two years for Hobday, and followed his victories in the 1978 Rhodesian Dunlop Masters and Victoria Falls Classic. And the 65 was his third course-record score in three weeks. He prepared for the championship by shooting 66 in the Victoria Falls pro-am (although he lost the 54-hole event by a stroke to Phil Simmons) and by posting a 64 in the Springmaster at Wingate (he won that title by four strokes).

Watson, Bobby Verwey and Cobie Legrange shared the opening-round lead with 67s, one stroke ahead of Hobday, Harold Henning, Mark McNulty and Vince Baker. Verwey sprained his left wrist on Wednesday before the tournament but was putting well nevertheless and had seven birdies. He and Legrange took 73s in the second round, while the up-and-coming Watson claimed first place with a 68 for 135. McNulty was second at 137 and Hobday was third at 140, along with Verwey and Legrange. After that second round, Watson was disappointed for having not scored better. "I was a bit lucky," he said, "but I also did some bad thinking in places."

The halfway lead was about as close as Watson had come to winning such an important tournament as this. "I don't know what it's like to be ahead," he said, half-jokingly. "I've never done it before." He obviously was on edge as the third round began, three-putted twice in the first 11 holes and came home with 71 to Hobday's sparkling 65. "I must say I was a bit jumpy early on," said Watson, "but, still, I'm well in the picture and I'll be charged up tomorrow."

While Hobday, winner of the Madrid Open, was seeking to add another 1979 title, others in contention after three rounds included the group at 209, four strokes behind, consisting of Verwey, Henning, John Bland and Nicky Price. Verwey continued his struggle with the injured wrist, but he did think of quitting after jarring it at the ninth hole. A doctor there gave him a pain-killing injection and several pills. He had a 69, Bland shot 67, and Henning and Price had 68s. McNulty also was still in the running, despite his 73 for 210. He was two strokes clear of John Fourie and Legrange, who faded badly to 72 and 212 after picking up three birdies in four holes to go seven under par for the tournament.

Henning and McNulty made the biggest advances in the final round, although they finished some distance from the play-off score. Henning's closing score was 66 and he took fourth place, four strokes behind. McNulty was third, two strokes back after his 67 for 277.

ICL International—R40,000

Winner: Nick Faldo

After his play-off defeat in the Zimbabwe Rhodesian Open, Denis Watson felt that he was prepared to win and perhaps even deserved to win. But Watson was due to find greater disappointment in the ICL International at Kensington. He led by four strokes with 11 holes to play, then, in his words, "everything just went wrong." Watson shot 76 and the winner with a record-equaling 65 was Nick Faldo.

He, too, felt deserving of a victory. Faldo had begun the year with hopes of becoming Europe's No. 1 player, but was winless while another young Englishman, Sandy Lyle, took that position away from Severiano Ballesteros. "To win this tournament means as much as any tournament I could possibly hope to win," said Faldo at the prize-giving ceremony, finding new resolve for 1980. "I haven't won for more than a year and the pressure seems to wear you down."

Arriving for the ICL, Watson said he regarded the Rhodesian tournament as a victory. "I don't care much for a play-off unless it is over 18 holes," said the 24-year-old former Rhodesian, with reference to the mistake that cost him the title. "I am now ready to win," he said. "Golf is a learning game. First you learn how to make the cut, then you learn about running in the top 10, then you learn about leading and winning. I'm ready to win now."

Meanwhile, a controversy was brewing over the recently landed British group that included Faldo. They were promised exemptions from pre-qualifying. Unexpectedly, there were 190 entrants and, with 150 places under PGA rules, pre-qualifying would be necessary for some. The PGA granted the British exemptions for the ICL, but advised that they would pre-qualify for future tournaments. There were complaints about that and grumbles from South Africans who felt they were more entitled to any exemptions than the visitors. Other than that and pouring rain that threatened the first round, the tournament went without a hitch until Faldo sank his concluding putt, at which time, to the dismay of officials, two young boys scuffled on the green for a souvenir.

Bobby Cole was involved in a three-way tie after the opening round, joining Nick Job and John Fourie with 66s. Watson was among those with 67s and Faldo was in the group of 68 shooters. Cole's putting was fantastic and he birdied five of the first seven holes. "I've had such a rotten year in the U.S., and my putting was so uncertain that today's great putting round is almost too good to be true," he said. It was indeed too good to be true, and Cole did not break 70 again. "I played terrible," he said afterward. Fourie remained in contention until midway of the fourth round, when he dropped three strokes in a row. "But I am enjoying my golf now for the first time in a long while," he said.

Watson, who had an eight o'clock tee time for the second round, awoke with a terrible belly ache and was frantic before setting out to tie the course record with 65 and take the lead by two strokes over Fourie and Faldo, who had 66. Watson said, "At one stage I thought I was going to black out, but a couple of Cokes settled my stomach enough for me to see out the round." He returned with yet another 65 in the third round for a 197 total and Fourie, his closest challenger, was four strokes behind. At that stage, Faldo was six strokes behind and pleased to be there. "I started badly but held it together," he said. "It was a bad round, but whereas I have been shooting 76 in Europe, I made 69 here." Left-hander Phil Simmons equaled Watson's course record with 65 but was 10 strokes down, while the most significant move seemed to be on Nicky Price's 66. Despite five bogeys, Price climbed to third place along with Faldo and two others. Allan Henning also shot 66 and was seven strokes behind, while Harold Henning was eight back following his 69.

Price fell away with an eight on the par-five eighth hole, leaving five prime contenders in the final round: Watson, Fourie, Faldo, Allan and Harold Henning. Fourie dropped out with three consecutive bogeys starting at the seventh hole, then Watson stumbled, losing four strokes in three holes starting from the ninth. Faldo and Harold Henning both turned in 32, Allan in 34. The Englishman was aware of little of the above, not seeing a leaderboard until the 15th. To his own amazement, Faldo was leading the tournament. He recalled, "Walking to the 15th green I thought I was three behind and I was thinking, 'What the hell do I do now?' Then I saw I was in the lead." What Faldo did was to birdie two of the last three holes for his 65 and 268, defeating Allan Henning by three strokes. Allan was pleased to be second with his 67—"It was my best performance in a couple of years," he said—but Harold was disgruntled for having "choked" a six-foot putt on the 16th. "I knew that if I holed the putt I would win," said the 45-year-old Henning, who was third with Watson and Fourie. "It would have put me at 14 under. But I choked. It has taken me 25 years of golf to learn how to choke. What happened after that didn't matter. I knew I had blown it there. I made two fives on the last two holes, but it wasn't because I was tired. It didn't matter anymore." It is likely, at that moment, young Dennis Watson, though half Harold's age, would have agreed with the sentiment.

Lexington PGA—R83,000
Winner: Gary Player

Who has experienced jet lag more often than any other athlete in history? Gary Player, of course. There is no close second. The wonder of it is that Player continues to win under the most testing of circumstances. But even Gary, as fit as he is, was exhausted after a nine-hour trip home from Australia for the Lexington PGA at the Wanderers in Johannesburg. "My whole metabolism is upside down," he was saying, "and the only way I can sleep at the moment is by taking a strong sleeping tablet."

Seldom one to discount his chances, Player took a dim view of his prospects in this tournament. You can guess who won the Lexington PGA. With 66s in the second and third rounds and with a rainout of the fourth, Player had his first victory on home soil in nearly two years, since he won the 1977 South African Open and ICL International on consecutive weeks.

It was a come-from-behind victory, Dale Hayes having started with a brilliant 65 while Player was well behind with 71. Hayes was spraying his tee shots in the second round, but finished with 70 for a one-stroke lead over a little-known American, 22-year-old Jimmy Johnson. Nicky Price, Bobby Cole and Nick Job were third at that stage, having 136 totals, while Player was in the group at 137 with Allan Henning, Denis Watson, Mark McNulty and Hugh Baiocchi, among others. Player and Henning both followed 71s with 66s, and Watson took the opposite route to his total. Gary had a bogeyless round that could have been sensational, if a few more putts had fallen, but he said "The fact I'm in contention is a bonus. I don't feel strong at all. My hands are even shaking, and I hate doing anything I can't do well.

"I don't feel good enough," Player concluded, "and I think it will take a miracle for me to win here. But being close to the lead is more than I expected."

He then went out and took the lead, and the victory as it happened, with another 66 in the third round. Hayes had an uninspiring 71 and seven golfers went past him. Harold Henning shot a 65 for 204 and was one stroke behind Player, along with Watson, Price and Cole. Job and Hayes were at 205, then came Baiocchi and the American, Johnson. Gary was attacking the hole relentlessly for his 66, and nearly holed out twice with his second shots. His approaches to both the fifth and 10th holes were only a couple of feet from the cup. Yet, he was still very defensive about his position. "You can hardly call one shot a lead," he warned. "I won three tournaments coming from seven behind last year, so this is still anybody's tournament."

As I mentioned, there was no fourth round because of the rainout, which led to three days and nights of nonstop rain. It was as if Gary's stamina needed no further tests before he was rewarded with his 115th career victory. The three-round results also left Johnson, who had been a professional for only six weeks, the leader of a strong American contingent in the tournament. With his tie for 10th place, Johnson finished ahead of such better-known countrymen as Calvin Peete (tied for 14th), Rod Funseth (tied for 21st), John Mahaffey (tied for 28th), Andy North (tied for 43rd) and Don Bies (tied for 51st).

Kronenbrau 1308—R83,000

Winner: Gary Player

Credit Calvin Peete with the best quote of the entire South African tour. Taking note of Gary Player's scores for the last 36 holes of the Kronenbrau 1308, the black American remarked, "They say this southeaster of yours separates the men from the boys. Well, I reckon that Gary is the only man out here!" Player's rounds of 70 and 68 provided for a six-stroke victory at Milnerton, whereas Peete had shot 64 on that same course under calm first-day conditions. "I was satisfied," Peete said then, "but I do realize that somebody took the day off—your southeaster."

During the first round there was, at worst, a gentle breeze. "It was," said Gary, "a day when somebody could break 60." Peete came closest with his 64 but there were many low scores, including 65s by four British players, ICL International winner Nick Faldo, David Russell, Michael King and Bill Longmuir. Former American PGA Champion John Mahaffey and John Bland posted 66s, Player had 67 and there were 44 others who scored under Milnerton's par of 72. Peete was a hit in South Africa, having made a name for himself at home earlier by winning the Milwaukee Open, finishing second at Quad Cities the following week and eventually placing 27th on the U.S. PGA Tour money list with over $127,000. The "Man With The Diamond Teeth"—as the newspapers called him—had two eagles in that opening round, shared the lead through 36 holes and eventually placed fourth, scoring 74 and 72 when the winds reached their strength.

Player, advancing towards his second triumph in two weeks, shot 65 in the second round, with the weather again on the mild side. He and Peete were tied at 132. Within three strokes of them were Mahaffey, Irishmen Des Smyth and John O'Leary and Britishers Faldo, King and Longmuir. When Peete tumbled with 74 in the third round, O'Leary came to the front with 68, tying Player at 202 after Gary's 70. Smyth was third with 70 and 203, then came Hugh Baiocchi with 68 and 205 and Faldo with 70 and 205.

At last, the southeaster was blowing, if not at its full force. At the par-five 18th hole, Faldo had needed a seven for his second shot in the second round. He instead needed two drivers in the third round. Smyth also hit two drivers and still was short of the green. And Player was rapidly gaining confidence. He said of his 70, "I feel that I really played well, but the putts would not drop." Baiocchi, preparing for a defense of his South African Open title, shared honors for the day's low round (68) with Scotsman Brian Marchbank and Americans Jay Haas and Keith Fergus. Peete, on the other hand, bogeyed four consecutive holes starting at the eighth for his 74.

Player was the only one to truly tame the southeaster in the fourth round, steadily gaining strokes on the field with his 68. It was a vintage round, Player at his most devastating. O'Leary's game fell apart, although he did place second with a 74. The Irishman did not receive a favorable ruling at the 10th hole, when his ball rested close to a mole run, and dropped shots there and at the 11th, 14th and 18th. Smyth, who also shot 74 and was third, seven strokes behind, saw his chances vanish at the 14th when his tee shot was caught in a sudden gust of wind and finished in an unplayable lie behind some bushes.

Yellow Pages British Airways South African Open—R65,000
Winner: Gary Player

Thinking of Gary Player's victory in the South African Open, I am reminded of that Saturday evening of 1978 in Augusta, Georgia, when I wished Gary good luck before the final round of the Masters. Then seven strokes behind, Gary said, "Mark, I can shoot 65 tomorrow and still win this thing." He did win, not with 65 but with a magnificent 64, and he followed that with two more victories in the Tournament of Champions and the Houston Open.

On the eve of the South African Open, Player standing six strokes behind the leader, said virtually the same thing to his dear friend, George Blumberg. Again, Gary's only mistake was in forecasting the score. Rather than with 65, Player won with 66 in another rush reminiscent of his great Masters triumph. It was his third consecutive victory and his 12th win in the South African Open, surpassing by three the previous record held by Bobby Locke. "A dirty dozen," Gary said, smiling, during his press interview. "It meant so much to me to win out there today, because I really believed I could do it."

The championship at Houghton, sponsored by Yellow Pages and British Airways, ended much as did the 1978 Masters. Ian Mosey, who had led from the second round, missed a short but tricky putt, taking a bogey with three strokes at the final green to lose by a shot. Though under tremendous pressure all day, Mosey handled his emotions well. He came to the prize-giving and earned even more respect from the South African spectators. "Ten minutes ago, I didn't think I had the guts to come up here and say a few words," said Mosey. "But I know now I have guts and I'm here . . . I can't explain how I felt over that putt (18 inches), for I can't remember it. All I know, having now thought about it, is that once I knew I hadn't won, I seemed to go into a dream."

The 28-year-old Englishman had rounds of 68, 70, 69 and 73 for his 280 total, while Player finished at nine-under-par 279 with scores of 67, 75, 71 and 66. Gary sounded the warning in the fourth round with four consecutive birdies from the start. When he nailed birdies at the 15th and 16th, Player was bearing down unmercifully and came to the 18th seeking another birdie which he believed, correctly, would clinch the title. "I was so keyed up going up 18 that I simply didn't know," Gary said. "I had struck the best drive I had hit all week, and all I was concerned about was winning. I knew I could do it, even with Mosey still in front." But Player's approach was wide of the 18th green and he had to settle for a par after chipping so close to the hole that it brought gasps from the crowd. Just as in the Masters, Gary then had an agonizing wait until the tournament was decided.

Mosey was in trouble from start to finish at the 18th. His tee shot drifted into trees on the left. "I could have kicked myself," he said. "Instead of pulling away when a butterfly settled on the ball, I carried on . . . But I don't want to moan. Gary beat me and that's the story. Yes, I'm disappointed, but that's what sport is all about and I am sure I'll win one day—maybe soon."

Player was the first-round leader with five-under-par 67, one stroke in front of Mosey and Robbie Stewart. There were few low scores on the demanding Houghton course, even in mild conditions. Returning with 71, Allan Henning said, "No unknown will get to the top this week. All I can say is that this course is really long and difficult. I'll take level par 288 for 72 holes and laugh." Player's round included five birdies and an eagle, but he lost strokes on two of the less testing holes. After bogeying the second, he birdied the fourth from 25 feet and had only a tap-in for another birdie at the fifth after a six-iron approach. He eagled the seventh from 60 feet. "I was grateful for that start," Gary said. "I can't really explain it, but I was very nervous at the start of the round. It didn't improve but, despite slightly shaky hands, I managed to putt well."

Mosey birdied the seventh, where Gary got the eagle, and was out in 36. He returned in 32, with birdies at the 10th, 11th, 14th, 16th and 18th. In the second round, Mosey went in front with 70 for a 138 total, while a disgruntled Player fell into the pack with 75 for 142. Gary was at first disturbed by the slow play, then left the course because of lightning. Under these unsettling circumstances, he had an up-and-down performance, dropping shots at the third and eighth holes, bouncing back with birdies on the 12th and 13th, then losing strokes again with three putts on the 16th and 17th. Mosey chipped in for birdie on the 18th to go one stroke in front of Henning and two ahead of Simon

Hobday and Mark McNulty. "It's the first time I have ever led a major tournament," Mosey said, "and I think it's marvelous. I like hard courses because I'm a straight hitter, and being in contention doesn't worry me."

People were considering Mosey more seriously after 54 holes, when it appeared he might actually become the third foreigner to win this championship, following Tommy Horton in 1970 and Bob Charles in 1973. Mosey shot 69 in the third round and was two strokes ahead of the second-place golfer, Simon Hobday, who also had 69. Henning and McNulty were four strokes behind and Player six. Mosey and Hobday jostled throughout the round, and Simon even took the lead before Mosey stroked in a 35-foot birdie at the 13th, starting a four-birdie run. "And let me tell you, they were all good putts. No short ones," said the elated Mosey. His other birdies were from 20 feet at the 14th, 18 feet at the 15th and 24 feet at the 18th. Player's 71, meanwhile, did not represent what his round could have been. He was frustrated whenever he began to make a move, particularly so at the 13th. He birdied the third, then bogeyed the par-five seventh. He drew within a stroke of the leaders with birdies at the eighth, 11th and 12th, then hooked his one-iron tee shot at the 13th into the woods. An almost unbelievable recovery with a six-wood left Gary with another opportunity, but he chipped weakly. He was left further behind than he cared to be, but he was not out of it, as he would prove the next day.

Sun City Classic—R100,000
Winner: Gary Player

It can be said without exaggeration that reaching Pilansberg was more of a strain on Gary Player's nerves than winning the Sun City Classic there for his fourth consecutive victory. In all seriousness, Player's group, which included Arnold Palmer and several of his American pals, took off for the tournament in a small, apparently overloaded airplane. The pilot could scarcely get the aircraft above the 500-foot level and everyone on board was grateful when they landed safely.

You would have had to search to find anyone willing to bet against Player winning the tournament, as ridiculous as that may seem. If there was a sure wager in professional golf for 1979, this may have been it. Player had won three times in a row and this, the final event of the South African circuit, was being held on his course, a layout which Gary knew well and which few others knew at all. Palmer was on hand to help with the christening of this inaugural event at the Gary Player Country Club, and the remaining entrants were basically the same golfers who had taken part in the previous five tournaments. The golf course, less than a year old and not yet in championship condition, was unfortunately the subject of some harsh criticism from Bobby Verwey, Gary's brother-in-law. Verwey took exception to the fact that preferred lies were granted and also objected to Gary's choice of grasses. To which Gary responded, "I am not interested in what Bobby Verwey said at all. It's my golf course. They can either come and play if they want to or, if they don't want to, nobody is holding a gun at their heads."

Verwey was the second-place finisher, after leading through 36 holes.

Player took charge in the third round with 67 and expanded his margin from two to four strokes with 70 in the final round for a 278 total. Nicky Price, Des Smyth and Denis Watson were under 70 for the fourth round to crack the top five, along with Tertius Claassens, while Palmer was 11th. Arnold started with 69, placing two strokes behind leader John O'Leary and one behind Verwey. Gary then was three off the pace with a 70.

O'Leary and Palmer sagged in the second round, taking 79 and 76 respectively, and Verwey advanced to first place with his 71 for a 139 total. Then Gary burst through with his 67 and was on his way to his fourth consecutive win, also his fourth of the year, and the 118th of his career.

10

THE ASIA/JAPAN TOURS

Isao Aoki dominated pro golf in Japan in 1979. Nothing surprising about that. Taiwanese pros monopolized titles and money on the Asia Circuit in 1979. Nothing new there, either. Well, yes, there was. While most of the established Chinese stars enjoyed good campaigns on the 10-tournament tour, three rookies in their mid-20's, fresh from long stints in the amateur ranks, emerged to strengthen measurably their country's already existent and long-standing domination of golf in that part of the world.

Most impressive of the three is Lu Hsi Chuen, the 26-year-old nephew of the famous Lu Liang Huan, China's best-known international performer. The younger Lu, at five-foot five, 140 pounds, made the most brilliant professional debut the Asia Circuit has ever seen. He won three times (Singapore, Malaysia and Indonesia), a feat accomplished only twice before in tour history—by veteran countryman Kuo Chi Hsiung in 1975 and by his uncle in 1974. He was second at Hong Kong, third at two other stops, was out of the top 10 only twice in his 10 starts and ran away with the circuit championship and Order of Merit money list. Shen Chung Shyan, another of the first-year pros, who was seasoned by eight years of amateur golf, won the Korean Open and had several other impressive tournaments, while the third newcomer, Chen Tze Ming, missed the winner's circle but had two late-season seconds and enough strong showings to finish fifth on the money list and sixth in the overall circuit championship. In the fall, he and young Lu were dispatched to Greece to represent Taiwan in the World Cup Matches and responded with a fifth-place finish in the team competition.

Not that the older Chinese pros are ready to step out of the picture. Mr. Lu, in fact, was the other winner for Taiwan on the 1979 Asia Circuit and two other Chinese veterans had outstanding seasons in Japan. Kuo captured the prestigious Japan Open and two other titles in a five-week period in the fall, while Hsieh Min Nan nailed the Japan PGA Championship and a 36-hole event and lost to Aoki in the finals of the Japan Match Play Championship. Hsu Chi San had two seconds, a third and seven top-10 finishes on the Asia Circuit. Kuo, Hsu, Hsu Sheng San and young Lu qualified for the British Open from their top four finishes in the circuit standings.

That reflected further the domination of the Chinese and at the same time

Twenty-six-year-old Lu Hsi Chuen of Taiwan, holding the trophy presented to him at the Singapore Open by SGA president Chief Justice Wee Chong Jin of Singapore.

a problem that is creating unfortunate situations in international golf, illustrated most openly and vividly at the 1979 World Cup in Greece—certain countries barring players from certain other countries on political grounds. In the Asia circumstance, Mya Aye, who finished less than five points out of the fourth-place position that would have put him in the British Open, had to skip Taiwan, where Burmese nationals cannot obtain visas. What's more, Aye won the nontour Philippine Masters against a potent field gathered for the Philippine Open the following week.

The Asia season began and ended with victories by veterans. Ben Arda won the Philippine Open for a third time with that championship in a temporary limbo because of a dispute over the Philippines' noncontribution to the 1978 circuit prize purse. A new administration in the country's golf association in 1979 agreed to settle the debt, harmony was restored, and the Philippine Open was restored to the circuit retroactively. The veteran at the other end of the season, Hiroshi Ishii, saved the Japanese from a 1979 whitewash on the circuit, taking the Dunlop International when the tour reached his country for its final event. Once again, the Japanese troupe that played most of the Asia Circuit lacked virtually all of the nation's better players—and it showed. Until Ishii won at Ibaraki, a Japanese pro had not won on that tour since Yurio Akitomi scored in the 1977 Thailand Open. For the first time ever, Americans won two different circuit events in the same season as Mike Krantz scored a play-off victory in the Thailand Open and Gaylord Burrows landed his second Asia win in the Indian Open. Greg Norman, the powerful, blonde Australian, added another peg to his fast-growing international reputation when he won the Hong Kong Open in his first ever and only 1979 appearance on the circuit.

Administratively, the Asia Confederation took steps in concert with recommendations from a panel of the leading players to improve and standardize the tournament operations, to try to assist through scheduling and other means tournaments that have weather and other problems, particularly India and Indonesia, and to attempt to attract more of the better players from other parts of the world. However, Asia golf went into its 1980 season with a huge void following the death of Kim Hall in late 1979 after major cancer surgery. Hall had been a leading figure in the game in Hong Kong and throughout Asia for many years and had proved an able administrator when he succeeded Skip Guinto as the Asia Circuit coordinator in 1978.

While Aoki didn't quite come up to his dazzling 1978 season, in which he won six tournaments in Japan, the Colgate World Match Play and $361,904 on the World Money List, he was heads and shoulders in front of everybody else on the 58-event, $5.6-million Japan Tour that spans the better part of nine months and includes 33 full-fledged tournaments. The lanky Isao, now 37, scored four victories during the season, running his 15-year record to 30 victories, 26 of them since 1972. Aoki wins important titles. He repeated victories in the Chunichi Crowns and Japan Match Play and won the Kanto PGA and Japan Series later in the year. His major goals now must be initial victories in the Japan Open, the Dunlop Phoenix and the Taiheiyo Club Masters, the only big ones in Japan that have thus far escaped him.

Besides Aoki and the aforementioned Kuo and Hsieh, who captured Japan's Open and PGA, respectively, only three other players scored multiple triumphs in Japan in 1979. Toru Nakamura took the Mitsubishi Gallant, Tohoku and Kansai PGA, while Masaji Kusakabe won the KBC Augusta and Suntory tournaments and Yasuhiro Miyamoto the Sapporo Tokyu and Kansai Open.

Norio Suzuki essayed a rare Japanese victory in the rich Taiheiyo Masters, but several other important titles went out of the country with foreign players as non-Japanese pros won 10 tournaments in all. The Wadkins brothers each bagged a big one—Lanny the Bridgestone and Bobby the Dunlop Phoenix—and Tom Purtzer captured the individual competition in the U.S. vs Japan Matches to give three crowns to Americans. Graham Marsh added another Japanese title, his 17th, in the ANA Sapporo and Mya Aye took the Pepsi Wilson tournament. Time and again, it appeared that Lu Liang Huan would add a Japan victory to his China Open win in 1979, but one of the year's most bizarre penalties in the April Dunlop International seemed to set the tone of disappointment for his season in Japan. He was knocked out of a second-place finish there when he was penalized two strokes for playfully rolling his ball into a cup from short range after he had missed a putt there and decided to amuse the crowd. Subsequently during the season, he had a finish in each position in the top nine—except first place.

The season, though, was probably even more crushing for Masashi (Jumbo) Ozaki, who went without a victory for the first season since he came to the fore in Japanese golf almost a decade ago. In fact, Ozaki missed his best chance to prevent that happenstance when he lost a play-off to Teruo Sugihara in the Yomiuri (formerly the Wizard) Open. Also shut out at the victory window in 1979 was another big winner of the past, Takashi Murakami, and the highly promising young star, Tsuneyuki Nakajima.

Japanese galleries got their first look at the new Chinese star, Lu Hsi Chuen. Lu added to his bankroll off his half-dozen appearances, but his first venture on the Japanese Tour was far from explosive. His further achievements would be one of the many things to watch in the 1980 season.

As mentioned before, the 1979 season began with the—

Philippine Open—US $100,000
Winner: Ben Arda

Even though not a part of the official Asia Circuit, the Philippine Open did not suffer for a field in its usual lead-off position in the Far East season. Nobody even hinted at a boycott and most of the players intending to play the full tour showed up at Wack Wack Golf and Country Club, the tournament's usual first-class site. After all, a $100,000 purse in that part of the world is nothing to be passed up over a questionable matter of principles. The only real disappointment from the standpoint of the field was the last-minute scratch of what would have been the appearance of the biggest American star in many years in the Philippine Open. Jerry Pate, the No. 10 money winner in the world in 1978, wired a withdrawal notice the day before the start of the tournament, pleading flu attack.

Whether Pate's presence in the tournament would have made any difference in the outcome is doubtful. Ben Arda, the aging Toy Tiger who has played so many rounds over the tough 7,134 yards of Wack Wack's East course that he has lost count, staked himself to a four-stroke lead over the first 54 holes and eased home the winner with a closing 75 for 286. Despite the weak finish, the 50-year-old Arda (49 at the time) had three strokes on the field at the finish in winning his national championship for a third time, 16 years after the second. The first was in 1961. Since 1963, Ben was runner-up at Wack Wack three times, won seven other Asia Circuit events, one in India in its pre-tour period and three titles in Japan. The victory was particularly lucrative for Arda since, as a native-born Filipino, he collected a $7,000 cigarette company bonus to go with the $25,000 first prize.

Never before in the 64-year history of the venerable tournament had a player led from start to finish, so it was appropriate that the country's No. 1 golfer of all time would be the one to do it. Arda, who hadn't won since the concluding Dunlop International event of the 1977 season, had only a piece of the lead after Thursday's first round. With a three-under-par 69 he shared first place with Japan's Tsutomu Irie, who had barely qualified for the tournament Tuesday with a 78.

In a way Arda may have won the tournament in that first round. After going three under par on the first 10 holes, he squandered all the strokes with a triple bogey via woods and water at No. 11. With the poise of a veteran, though, he recovered with three more birdies on the last five holes for the 69 to catch Irie, who teed off at daybreak with the first group. Only six others, all with 71s, broke par the first day among the 149 starters from 16 countries. Among those six were two-time Philippine Open champion Hsieh Yung Yo, the circuit's top career title-winner, and two Americans—Gaylord Burrows and Bruce Douglass.

Arda moved ahead alone for keeps the second day, relying on effective chipping with "play-it-short" strategy. He one-putted eight of the last 12 greens on his way to 71 and 140. Irie faded with a 74, the challenge taken up by Kuo Chi Hsiung, the 1975 winner at Valley and one of the bases for pre-tournament favoritism of the Taiwanese delegation. Kuo, a contender and high finisher in the Philippines every year since his victory and the holder of the tournament record of 64 (1978), moved in a shot behind Arda with a 67 for 141, birdieing the last two holes. Hsu Sheng San, another former champion, was tied for third at 142 with Yoshikazu Yokoshima.

Another 71, the product of three birdies and two bogeys, enabled Arda to open his four-stroke lead Saturday at 211 as his chipping again was his forte. Kuo caught Ben twice on the front nine but fell back badly with an incoming 41. At the three-quarter mark, Irie (72), Hsu Chi San (69) and Lu Hsi Chuen (69) were next at 215, Lu giving his first indication of things to come in future weeks although he was to sink Sunday with an 80. While it didn't seem to bother Arda, strong complaints were voiced about the five-to-six-hour rounds that were common that day even though the reduced field only numbered 75 and the weather was good.

Rarely will 75 even save a leader in the final round of a tournament, particularly in sunny, hot weather. But the nature of his 75 and the absence of a really good round by anybody in a position to challenge made Arda's victory easy. By the 11th hole, where he made his second and last birdie of the day, Ben was seven strokes clear of all competition. He then bogeyed five of the last six holes, not an auspicious finish by any means, but the 75—286 put him comfortably ahead of Hsu Sheng San and Hung Fa, who had 73s for 289 and tied for second place.

Cathay Pacific Hong Kong Open—US $100,000

Winner: Greg Norman

It was more like the older days at Hong Kong in 1979, more like the 1960's and early 1970's when the Australians would pop in and win the Hong Kong Open—Peter Thomson, Frank Phillips, Kel Nagle and others. The country's newest young star—24-year-old Greg Norman—restored Australia's hold on the championship at Royal Hong Kong in 1979 with a strong, three-stroke victory on rounds of 70, 66, 69 and 68. His 273 total was, oddly, six under par because of the intermixed use of the club's two 18-hole courses.

The powerful, blond Aussie, whom some journalists, perhaps a bit prematurely, describe as looking and playing like Nicklaus, considered his victory at Hong Kong another step in his preparations for an eventual shot at the U.S. Tour—"I reckon in 1981"—after further grooming on the European circuit. He already had won in Australia, Japan and Europe before the Hong Kong triumph, which came in his first appearance (and only one of 1979) on the Asia Circuit. The check—$20,000—was his biggest ever.

The finish turned into a David and Goliath duel between Norman and Chinese rookie Lu Shi Chuen, somewhat surprisingly because Graham Marsh got off to such a fast start. Marsh, another Aussie who won on the Asia Circuit early in what was to become a great career, does not normally blow leads as badly as he did at Hong Kong, but his putting, which had been ineffective earlier in the year in America, let him down badly over the final 36 holes at Royal Hong Kong.

Beefed up by the presence not only of Norman, Marsh and several other Australians, but also by other one-shot appearances of such British stars as Tony Jacklin and Nick Faldo and several of Japan's better players, a huge field of 203 from 20 countries teed off the first day on the Eden (par 69) and New (par 70) courses. Marsh had the best start—a 66 on the New course that included an eagle deuce at the seventh hole. Actually, he had to share the lead with Hsu Chi San, who had six birdies and three bogeys for his 66 on the par-69 Eden course. Most of the better players got in between 67 and 70, although Jacklin disappointed with a 74 and never got into serious contention. An 80 in the third round eventually kayoed Faldo after a 68–70 start.

Marsh was four under again the second day with a 65 on the Eden and had first place to himself at 131. Young Lu popped into the picture there with a 65 of his own to go with 68 and tie him at 133 with Hsu Chi San, who added a 67. Both played Eden Friday. Hisashi Suzumura of Japan was at 135 and six others, including Norman with a 66 at Eden, rested at 136. Marsh, playing confidently from "the moment I stepped on the first tee," didn't have a bogey in his solid round.

On Saturday the surviving 95 players faced a Composite course comprised of holes from both of the 18s with a par of 70 and the Taiwanese players fared best over the "new" layout. Trying to extend Taiwan's Hong Kong victory streak to six years in a row, the junior Lu and Hsu forged in front with 69s for 202. Marsh drove behind a tree on the first hole and he spent the rest of the day in trouble, taking six bogeys enroute a 74, which dropped him three strokes off the lead and into a tie with Norman, whose tremendous length helped him to an eagle at the par-five 12th enroute his 69.

Norman and Lu were paired as the final group Sunday and it became apparent early that one or the other would be the winner as both Hsu and Marsh started poorly and faded from contention. Lu also had early trouble and quickly yielded the lead to the powerful Australian, who was outdriving him by as much as 30–40 yards at times. Greg went in front at the fourth hole on a birdie-bogey swing with Lu and held it until he bogeyed the ninth hole. Lu jumped ahead with a birdie at the 10th, but the lead swung the other way again as Lu bogeyed the 11th and Norman birdied the 12th and 13th. Bogeys by Norman at the 14th, Lu at the 15th and Norman at the 16th and pars by both at the 17th kept it tight right to the finish, but Norman wrapped up the victory by holing a 14-foot birdie putt on the final green, while the Chinese newcomer bogeyed for 74 and dropped into a three-way tie for second with Hsu (also 74) and fellow pro rookie Chen Tze Ming (70) at 276. Marsh absorbed a 76 and tied for seventh.

Singapore Open—US $50,000

Winner: Lu Hsi Chuen

Though it is not always valid, most professional golfers will concur that "the first win is the hardest.'' Lu Hsi Chuen surely agreed after putting his sensational rookie year on the Asia Circuit into high gear with his first pro victory in the Singapore Open. He was just one of a dozen or more potential winners after 54 holes and had to be haunted a bit by weak finishes the two previous weeks when he also had shots at victory.

Lu overcame that specter with a sturdy 69 in the final round at Singapore Island, but even that wasn't enough. It merely tied him at 280 with one of Asia's best players—Hsu Sheng San, the circuit champion twice in the previous three years. It took Lu two overtime holes to put the title on his record as the Singapore Open decision came through a play-off for the fifth time in the 18-year history of the tour. It was the fourth time in five years that the tournament produced a new winner on the circuit. However, unlike the other three—Yutaka Suzuki and Kesahiko Uchida of Japan and Terry Gale of Australia, the newest Taiwanese star was not to fade decisively back among the also-rans in the events that followed.

The first three rounds at Singapore Island's 6,645-yard Bukit course set up the exciting finish this way:

First Round—Hsieh Min Nan and Walter Godfrey, with 69s, headed a massive logjam that included nine men at 70 and seven more, including Lu, at par 71.

Second Round—Hsieh shot 70 to take a two-stroke lead as the contenders thinned out a bit. With 70—141, Lu was tied for second place with a real international group—Australia's George Serhan, Britain's Kevin Jones and Maurice Bembridge, Thailand's Sukree Onsham and Taiwan's Wu Chin Fa. Hsu Sheng San was four back after 72-71—143.

Third Round—Little-known Fritz Gambetta fired the week's best round Saturday—a six-under-par 65 that included an incoming 29—to surge into first

A true international star, Isao Aoki continued his brilliant pace.

place, a new spot for him. At 209, the 32-year-old American led the quintet of players who were to finish in the top five positions Sunday—Lu and Hsu along with Kazunari Takahashi, Godfrey and Min Nan, who slipped to 72 for his 211 Saturday.

Gambetta plunged from sight quickly in the last round as heavy rain once delayed play for 45 minutes and drizzles plagued the tournament all afternoon. Gambetta went out in 39 as Lu seized the lead with a solid front nine of 33 on seven pars and birdies at the fourth and fifth holes. Although he three-putted twice for bogeys coming in, the junior Mr. Lu had first place to himself until Hsu finished the par-five 18th spectacularly by hitting the pin with his 50-yard wedge pitch and tapping in a one-footer for a birdie. Lu followed in the last group and missed a 12-footer for the victory.

The two halved the first extra hole after hitting approaches so equally close to the cup that a coin toss was needed to decide who was to putt first. Lu won the flip but both missed the putts. Lu then wrapped up the win with a brilliant two-iron tee shot on the 205-yard second hole that stopped only three feet from the cup. He never holed out as his veteran opponent trapped his tee shot, blasted long, missed the par putt and conceded the $10,000 victory.

Malaysian Open—US $60,000
Winner: Lu Hsi Chuen

Things were as easy for Lu Hsi Chuen in the Malaysian Open as they were difficult for him the week before in grinding out his initial pro victory at Singapore. Just a week after he bested the extremely able veteran Hsu Sheng San in a play-off at Singapore, Lu followed up with his second pro victory in a runaway at Royal Selangor in Kuala Lumpur. He won by seven, embellishing his final round with a hole-in-one for 70 and 277, an almost predictable winning score. (Since 1972, the victor in the Malaysian Open has shot within the remarkably narrow gap of 276 and 279.) His victory itself, though, was much less predictable. Back-to-back wins by a single player are rare on the Asia Circuit; in fact, in the entire world of professional golf. Furthermore, Royal Selangor had been just about the only port of call on the tour in recent years that had not been dominated by the irrepressible Taiwanese. Only in 1976, when Hsu Sheng San defeated Mya Aye in a play-off, had a Nationalist China player left Kuala Lumpur with the championship before Lu's overwhelming victory in 1979.

Although the victory went elsewhere, it was a good week for the Americans, as five of them finished among the leading 12, an unprecedented feat for the relatively inexperienced Yanks in Asia. Ron Milanovich, a 25-year-old Pennsylvanian who had failed in his first shot at the U.S. Tour in 1977 and was making his first venture through the Far East, signaled the good week for the Americans with his opening 68. Milanovich, who hadn't won a cent in the first three tournaments, produced five birdies and a bogey as he tied Rudy Lavares of the Philippines for the first-round lead. They were a stroke in front of an interesting group of four—Lu, who had an eagle and three birdies; Hal Underwood, the most globe-trotting of all American pros; Ben Arda, who has never missed a Malaysian Open; and Mayalayan Ramayah, off to a start that would lead him to a seventh-place tie and the best performance ever in the tournament by a native-born Malaysian.

When Milanovich faltered the second day with 75, Mike Soli, another American, took over as a co-leader with Lavares, the 33-year-old Philippines World Cupper who added a 71 for 139. Soli's scores were reversed. With 71, Lu remained one stroke off the pace, tied at 140 with Japan's Tsutomu Irie, who had seven birdies, and produced a 67 over a course softened by a heavy overnight rain. Kuo Chi Hsiung also shot 67 to move into contention at 142.

Lu charged to the front Saturday with a near-flawless 67. The brilliant round, fashioned with six birdies and a bogey, put the young Chinese star at 207, five in front of his closest pursuer, Walter Godfrey, who made three early birdies in succession and shot 69 for 212. Soli (74) dropped back into a deadlock at 213 with Irie (73), Mya Aye (68) and Chen Chien Chin (72). Lavares came acropper with a 75, dropping back to 214 with Ramayah, Milanovich, Chang Chung Fa, George Serhan and Yurio Akitoma, the 1977 Thailand Open winner who made the week's second hole-in-one but only shot 73.

A steady front nine virtually sewed up the title for Lu. After his outgoing par 36, he made pairs of birdies and bogeys on the next seven holes before sinking his seven-iron tee shot at the 147-yard 17th for the tournament's third ace, the icing on the cake for the smiling young Mr. Lu. Milanovich, with 70, and Irie and Chen with 71s, tied for second at 284.

Thailand Open—US $40,000
Winner: Mike Krantz

Mike Krantz had been hoping that his increasing experience might pay off with a victory on the Asia Circuit some day, but when it came—in the 1979 Thailand Open—it literally floored him. The slender six-footer from Long Beach, California wound up flat on his back in the clubhouse minutes after holing the 20-foot birdie putt that gave him that triumph, the victim not of the excitement of the moment but of the heat. Instead of being escorted to the awards presentation, Krantz was transported by ambulance to the nearby hospital for treatment of the dehydration he had suffered in the 95-degree heat at Bangkok.

The victory came in a play-off and, ironically, his losing opponent also had been a medical patient just three weeks earlier. Jaime Gonzalez, a 24-year-old Brazilian of promise who was playing the Asia Circuit for the first time preparatory to taking a shot at qualifying for the U.S. Tour, suffered cracked ribs in a freak accident when a ferry he was riding after the Hong Kong Open docked with a violent jolt that also injured quite a few other passengers.

Thailand was Jaime's first start since the accident and he acquitted himself very well. After three rounds he was in second place, tied with Bruce Douglass of the U.S. and George Serhan of Australia at 211 a stroke behind leader Ireneo Legaspi of the Philippines, who won the Malaysian Open a decade ago. Krantz, 27, in his fourth year on the Asia Circuit, appeared too far back at 215. A 74 that day had damaged his strong bid of the earlier rounds, when he opened with 18 straight pars for 71 and followed with a six birdie-five bogey 70. Hsu Chi San, the 43-year-old Taiwan veteran, led the first day on the strength of his four-under-par 67, then yielded first place by a stroke to Legaspi in the second round as the Filipino put a pair of 70s on the board for 140. Krantz was tied with Hsu at 141 and Gonzalez at that point was at 143 after rounds of 74 and 69.

The American, who won twice during 1978 in the Otago Charity Classic in New Zealand and the Dunhill Match Play in Indonesia while earning more than $34,000 outside the U.S., had one advantage going for him Sunday. Off in the fifth-from-last group, Krantz was able to post his final 67 on the board and let the others try to catch him. He wired together an eagle chip-in at the par-five 12th and five birdies with three bogeys for the 67 and a two-under total of 282.

Legaspi fell out of the chase early. After nearly breaking to a big lead Saturday with a four-birdie front nine, the Filipino veteran lost all but a stroke of his lead on the back nine and the slide continued Sunday as he bogeyed four of the first five holes. For awhile Sunday, it appeared another American, Bruce Douglass, would nail the title. Douglass, who shot 66 Saturday, parred the front nine the last day and led by a shot before crashing under four bogeys coming home. Serhan never challenged as he shot 74, so only Gonzalez, who perfected his game enroute All-American status at Oklahoma State and now lives in Tulsa, had a chance on the final holes against Krantz. Jaime was two over on the front nine, then birdied the 11th and 12th holes to get back to even par for the day and two under for the tournament. Six steady pars after that produced the tie, his 12-foot birdie putt on the final green lipping out.

Krantz, who experienced early signs of his illness during the nervous wait, shook it off in the play-off. He matched good drives with Gonzalez, was outside him as both hit the green with their approaches, then holed the winning 20-footer. Jaime's putt from 15 feet stopped on the lip and the Thailand Open had its second American champion (Howard Twitty had won in Thailand in 1975 before establishing himself as one of the better young players on the U.S. Tour).

Incidentally, it was the swan song of the Thailand Open at the world's most distracting tournament course, because expansion has become necessary at the country's most important airport, which literally surrounds the 18 holes.

Indian Open—US $30,000

Winner: Gaylord Burrows

Others on the Asia Circuit find reasons to skip the Indian Open—its remoteness from the other locales, the minimum prize money, the desire to take a brief mid-season break from the arduous travel, and the wilting weather of that tour. Not American Gaylord Burrows, though. How, during the six years he had played in the Far East, could the Louisiana resident pass up returning to the country of his birth and visiting his parents, who have lived in India since the senior Burrows retired from government there? However, although cherishing that title so highly because of the family ties, Gaylord had experienced nothing but frustration in the five previous starts he had made in India prior to the 1979 tournament. His 18th-place finish in 1978, worth $522, was his best ever in the only Asia Circuit championship that was dominated by Australians and Americans in the 1970's.

The 35-year-old Burrows had little hope of anything better when he arrived at the Delhi Golf Club in its picturesque setting in the heart of New Delhi in late March of 1979. Although he had enjoyed good seasons in Asia in 1977 and 1978 and had scored his first victory in the 1977 Indonesian Open, Burrows had floundered through the first five tournaments on the 1979 circuit "playing my worst golf in six years."

The first round provided no hint of anything different as Mike Krantz, quickly shaking off the heat exhaustion that had felled him after he won the Thailand Open a few days earlier, began as if he would duplicate Lu Hsi Chuen's two-in-a-row feat earlier in the season. Krantz opened with 67 for a two-stroke lead over Australian Brian Jones, a two-time Indian open winner; Tom Ducey of the U.S. and Shen Chung Shyan, one of only three Taiwanese in the depleted field that had just 53 starters from overseas. Krantz was still on top after 36 holes as he added a 69 for 136 and drew five shots ahead of his nearest competitor, the veteran Peter Thomson, who won his first of three Indian Opens in 1964, has been a strong booster from abroad of golf in the country and recently redesigned the 6,925-yard Delhi course. At that point, Burrows (73–70) and Hsu Chi San (75–68), who was to be Gaylord's strongest challenger in the stretch, trailed by seven.

His game deserted Krantz the third day. He bogeyed the last three holes for 76, yielding first place to Hsu, who shot the day's best round—67—for 210. Burrows had another 70 and was right in the midst of the fight at 213. The bogeys continued to plague Krantz Sunday. He fell out of contention with bogeys on the first three holes on top of the three at the end of Saturday's round, but held to par the rest of the way for 75 and third place. That left things in the hands of Burrows and the 41-year-old Hsu, a phlegmatic player with three circuit victories on his record.

In his six years in Asia, Burrows gained a reputation as a hot-and-cold player and he showed traces of that in the exciting run for the Indian Open title that Sunday. He went birdie-eagle-birdie at the close of the front nine to take a two-stroke lead with an outgoing 33. Then, he backed up with four bogeys on the next six holes. With par golf over that stretch, Hsu went ahead by two. Just as abruptly, the pendulum swung back to the American. Gaylord holed a 20-footer at No. 16 and a four-footer off a brilliant tee shot at the 153-yard 17th for birdies while Hsu was taking bogeys at both holes. Burrows' conservative par-five at the 533-yard 18th secured a one-shot victory on 71—284 as Hsu gamely birdied that last hole for 75 and 285, his second runner-up finish of the season.

The victory, worth $5,225 to Burrows, marked the first time in circuit history that any American had won twice and only in the Indian Open have two different U.S. pros reached the winners' circle. Burrows succeeded Bill Brask, who did not return to defend his 1978 victory. Since the Indian Open became a part of the circuit in 1970, Australians have won six times, with Taiwanese players scoring in 1970 and 1974. Because of his birthplace, it could be argued that Burrows was the first Indian winner since P. G. Sethi triumphed in the second Indian Open in 1965.

Indonesian Open—US $45,000
Winner: Lu Hsi Chuen

Lu Hsi Chuen set aside any thoughts there might have been that he could be a mere flash in the pan when he scored the third victory of his rookie season on the Asia Circuit in Indonesia, following a different route to that title than those he traveled on his play-off win at Singapore and his runaway in Malaysia. Some doubts may have arisen when the younger Mr. Lu tailed off the next two weeks, although he finished in the top 10 the second week at New Delhi thanks to a closing 70.

Actually, that strong finish was a tip-off of what was coming later that March weekend at Jakarta Golf Club. Playing deftly over the short (6,400 yards) Rawamangun course, Lu produced a string of rounds that resulted in the best 72-hole score in the six-year history of the tournament—272—and should have brought the 26-year-old Taiwanese newcomer an easy victory. It would have, had it not been for Mya Aye, the experienced pro from Burma who has had remarkable success in Indonesia—victory in 1976; play-off loss in 1977; second in 1979; sixth, eighth and 22nd in the other years. Lu cruised along behind Aye for three rounds, then nosed him out by a stroke with a final-round 68 for the eight-under-par 272. It was six strokes back to the next finishers—Don Klenk of the U.S. and Sukree Onsham of Thailand at 279.

Aye displayed his affinity for Indonesia at the start with the season's lowest round—63—taking a two-shot lead over Shen Chung Shyan, opening strongly for a second week in a row. Japan's Kazunari Takahashi was at 66, Lu and Jaime Gonzalez, the U.S.-residing Brazilian, at 67 and 11 others at 68 and 69 as the 70 par took a beating. Lu pulled within a stroke the second day with another 67 as Aye slipped to 70. Six others remained in contention within five strokes of Aye. The thinning-out came in the third round. After Mya shot 69 for 202 and Lu 70 for 204, only American Bob Henderson 69—206 was even close—and he collapsed with 77 Sunday.

The duel between the veteran and the rookie carried throughout the last round. Lu, with three birdies and a bogey, went out in 33 to tie for the lead as Aye shot a par 35. Mya slipped only one over par on the back nine, but it was fatal as Lu's 35 coming home scored the 68—272. Klenk also fired a 68 for the third-place deadlock with Onsham.

As it turned out, the victory not only put $6,800 more in Lu's bank account but also clinched the Asia Circuit championship for him, although nobody knew it at the time. As it turned out, he had enough points then to finish first, even if he didn't make another point the remainder of the year.

China Open—US $50,000
Winner: Lu Liang Huan

He made them cry "Uncle!" After noting with considerable pride the great accomplishments of nephew Lu Hsi Chuen during the first seven weeks of the Asia Circuit, the veteran Lu Liang Huan called attention to himself and kept it in the family with a resounding victory in the China Open, which he had won for the first time in its debut on the Asia Circuit 13 years earlier.

This time it was the eighth tour victory for the world-renowned Taiwan star and it came amid unusually moderate weather. The scoring was generally high, though, a circumstance attributed mainly to rather crusty greens and the difficult set-up of the course—Kuo Hua Golf and Country Club in the mountains of Peitou between Taipei and the northern coast. Kuo Hua was being used for the China Open for the first time but had been the scene of Mr. Lu's victory in the 1978 China PGA Championship. Only 13 sub-par rounds were scored in the tournament, seven in the final round when early-morning fog and rain delayed the start of play for 90 minutes.

Lu led the event from start to finish, surviving an aching back and a final-round 74 to win with a one-under-par 287. His margin was two strokes over rookie Chen Tze Ming, of whom many had expected more in his first pro season than of nephew Lu after both ended outstanding amateur careers in 1978. The senior Lu's triumph marked the sixth consecutive China Open victory by a native son and the 11th win in the tournament by a Taiwanese player in the 14 seasons the event has been a part of the Asia Circuit.

The tournament's biggest purse ever—$50,000—attracted a 170-man field to the 6,866-yard course, when ill-timed pre-tournament work resulted in the treacherous greens when anticipated rains did not materialize. The 44-year-old Mr. Lu launched his victory sweep with a 70, as two-time China champion Kuo Chi Hsiung was the only other man under par at 71. Five players matched par, but young Lu saw his hopes for an unprecedented fourth win in a single Asia Circuit season dim with an opening 76. He followed with 75 before rallying to a seventh-place finish—perfectly respectable.

It took only a par round Friday for Lu Liang Huan to double his lead to two strokes over Hsu Chi San (72–72). Chen Tze Ming made his move, shooting the tournament's only round in the 60s—68—for 145 after his opening 77. The picture up front didn't change Saturday as both Lu and Hsu fashioned 71s, Lu missing a chance to widen the gap after going out in 34. Chen tossed away his challenge with a 74 in light of the closing 70 that jumped him into the second-place finish.

His chronic back trouble kicking up so badly that he had some doubts that he could finish, Lu faltered early in the final round. He bogeyed three of the first seven holes and lost the lead to Hsu, who held it for four holes before three-putting the 12th green and wound up with a 75. Lu gamely strung pars together, then capped the victory before the big 18th-hole gallery. He nailed his eight-iron approach just six feet from the cup and holed his only birdie putt of the day for the 74 and two-shot victory.

If there is any doubt about the Taiwanese monopoly at home, consider that the next five finishers behind Lu and eight of the first nine were Nationalist Chinese pros, even though half the starters hailed from other countries.

Korean Open—US $60,000
Winner: Shen Chung Shyan

So often when youngish pro golfers win their first tournaments, they are labeled surprise champs, unknowns, no-names. Most often these tags are really accurate at that particular time in that particular tournament. Yet, when their records and performances are traced back a few tournaments, it usually turns out that those appellations actually don't fit. Such certainly was the case when Shen Chung Shyan joined the long list of Taiwanese champions on the Asia Circuit with his victory in the Korean Open.

The 27-year-old Shen, a pro for only five months at the time, had not exactly wallowed in obscurity during the previous two months of his initial pro trip on the Asia Circuit. In India he started fast, blew to an 82, and still finished 13th. In Indonesia he opened with 65 and placed sixth. In China just the week before Korea he tied for 11th. Shen was ready and surely not an unknown to his fellow competitors when they teed off at Seoul Country Club, the scene of the country's golf championship for the first time since 1972 when the Koreans still dominated the tournament. (Koreans won the Korean Open its first five years on the Asia Circuit.)

Just as almost everywhere else, the Korean Open remained solidly in the hands of the men from Taiwan in 1979. Although Shen's two-stroke victory with the season's highest score—289, one over par—was only the third Nationalist Chinese win in Korea, it was the third straight victory for Taiwan on the 1979 tour and the fifth of the season. And, along with Taiwan, Korea remains one of only two circuit events in which Caucasians have not yet broken through, disregarding Sergeant Orville Moody's conquests when he was in the Army there during Korea's pre-tour days.

Not to grate against the "unknown" premise just expounded, but two unlikely names appeared at the front after the first 18 holes of the 1979 tournament, played for a record $60,000 purse. Lim Kian Tiong of Singapore, who had tied for fifth in Thailand, matched 68s with Kuo Chi Hsiung, the 1975 Korean winner, while American Mike Soli came in at 69 with Chen Tze Ming and Hsu Sheng San. Shen, Lu Hsi Chuen and two Koreans started with 70s.

By the end of the second round, the Taiwanese had taken charge. Chen led with 71—140, followed by Shen at 72–142, Kuo and Lu at 143 and the two Hsu's, Chi San and Sheng San, at one-over-par 145s. Soli skied to 79 and Lim orbited to 84. Eighteen holes later, Shen and Chen had a duel on their hands. Both were at 213 and the next man was Hsu Sheng San at 220 after a 75. Both Kuo and Lu took 78s.

The two rookies proved that last day that they were not immune to high scores. In fact, you could say that Shen "under-staggered" Chen to the title on a relatively calm day when scores around par were common. The others were just too far back to take advantage of the leaders' foibles, which were mostly on the greens. Playing in separate threesomes, both men went out in 39, then bogeyed the par-five 11th and the 13th. Shen also bogeyed the 14th, but actually won the tournament and the $11,000 first prize with an eagle on the par-five 15th and pars on the last three holes for 76. Chen kept his hopes alive until the last hole, but took a final bogey there for 78 and the runner-up spot for the second week in a row.

In another similarity to the preceding Sunday, Taiwan players occupied the first five and seven of the first nine places in the final standings. Lu Hsi Chuen tied for third, actually clinching the circuit title that had been virtually conceded to him for several weeks.

Dunlop International—US $100,000
Winner: Hiroshi Ishii

It took a homebody veteran to save his country from an embarrassing, second straight shutout on the Asia Circuit. Winless in 1978, Japan again had an admittedly weak traveling team go through the first nine events of the 1979 season without a victory and with few high finishes before reaching home for the wind-up of that season and the start of the richer Japan Tour. Hiroshi Ishii changed things at Ibaraki Country Club near Tokyo, where all of the "name" Japanese stars swung into action in the $100,000 Dunlop International. The 37-year-old Ishii, scoring the eighth victory of his 19-year pro career, played an extremely steady tournament with rounds of 70–68–70–70, the 10-under-par 278 giving him a three-stroke victory and the $20,000 first prize.

The triumph of Japan's 1969 PGA champion not only saved face for the Japanese on the Asia Circuit but also ended a string of three victories by foreigners in the Dunlop and its predecessor event, the Sobu. Over the years since Japan joined the Asia Circuit in 1962 with the Yomiuir, pros from six different countries have won the season-ending event in Japan. Only five Japanese players have won during that time.

The presence of Japan's best players at Ibaraki was immediately evident. Fujio Kobayashi, the reigning Japanese PGA champion, took the lead with a four-under-par 68. Jumbo Ozaki had 69 and among the nine who shot 70 were Ishii, who had won the Bridgestone against a strong field in late-season 1978; Isao Aoki; and two other Japanese players who did not make the tour and were to wind up sharing second place at week's end—Tateo Ozaki and Seiji Ebihara.

Cold, rainy weather that dampened the first round continued Friday, but it didn't seem to bother Ozaki. The veteran Japanese star and national hero added a 67 to his opening round, taking a two-stroke lead over Ishii with his 136. Ishii had his best round, the 68, to take second position, a shot in front of American Mike Soli, who had made a few small splashes and earned more than $5,000 earlier in the season; and two ahead of Kobayashi, Lu Liang Huan, the 1974 winner, and Burma's Mya Aye. Ishii completed his move to the top Saturday with his two-under-par 70 for 208. That put him a stroke in front of Mr. Lu (69) and two ahead of Ozaki (74) and Kazunari Takahashi (68), who had made the best showing, as it was, of the Japanese who played the full circuit.

The record shows correctly that Ishii won easily Sunday by three strokes, but for all those on hand (except a couple of tournament officials) the finish was quite exciting and seemingly closer than it actually was. Ishii, Lu and Takahashi were playing together in the final group and, as they came to the last holes, Ebihara had already broken the course record by two shots with 64 and Tateo Ozaki (68) was tied with him at seven-under-par 281. When Ishii bogeyed the par-three 17th, the scoring system showed him dropping to 10 under with Lu supposedly at eight under and Takahashi at seven under.

Hiroshi hooked his drive at the 18th and overshot the green slightly from a tough lie in the rough. With Lu on in two, the potential for a tie was there, it seemed. However, Ishii chipped expertly to three feet, Lu missed his birdie try, both holed out, and the Japanese pro appeared to have won by two over Lu. No, said the officials, by three over Takahashi, Ozaki and Ebihara as they informed a stunned Lu that he must take a two-stroke penalty for "practicing" on the fifth green after he had tapped in a short putt. Innocently for the amusement of the gallery, the popular Mr. Lu had picked the ball out of the cup and rolled it by hand back into the hole. As a result of the bizarre penalty, Lu was dropped into a tie for fifth at 282 with Aye and Aoki.

For the second year in a row, the circuit champion did it without benefit of points in Japan. Lu Hsi Chuen never got it going at Ibaraki and tied for 40th, missing the points as Hsu Sheng San did in 1978 when he inadvertently signed an incorrect scorecard and was disqualified.

Technically, the official Japanese Tour season was already in progress before the Dunlop International was played. A handful of 18- and 36-hole events launched the season in Japan in the weeks just before the Dunlop. The only scheduled full-length tournament with a big purse during that period—the Shizuoka Open—produced a slightly tainted victory for Akira Yabe when heavy rains washed out the Friday round and it could not be rescheduled. Yabe captured the abbreviated event, making up a three-shot deficit Sunday in the $125,000 tournament with a one-under-par 71, winning by two strokes over Kikuo Arai and Shigeru Noguchi with his 217.

For the record, the other early-season winners in the shorter events were: Hsieh Min Nan with a 134 in the $60,000 Kuzuha International in Osaka, the 18th title for the 39-year-old Taiwan veteran, and Kosaku Shimada with a 70 in the Asahi Toy/Kyosen Invitational, along with three play-off winners—Hiroshi Ishii out of 68 in the Tobu Pro-Am a month before his victory in the Dunlop, Takahashi Kurihara from a 149 in the Aso National Park Open and Shichiroh Enomoto out of a 142 in the Yamanashi Pro-Am.

As it had three times in the past, including 1978, the Chunichi Crowns, richest of the early-season tournament at $300,000, went to Japan's No. 1 pro, Isao Aoki, in a tight finish at Nagoya. Coming off the greatest year ever recorded by a Japanese golfer, Aoki nosed out Haruo Yasuda and Toru Nakamura by a stroke with his 70—279 finish. Isao never trailed enroute his 27th victory in a prime field of 116 that included virtually all of the top stars of

Asia and Australia and five U.S. pros, in for the week from America. He was tied with Kenji Mori at 67· the first day, with Lu Liang Huan, Graham Marsh and Yasuda at 140 the second day and with Lu at 209 the third day before nipping Yasuda and Nakamura.

Toru closed with a 67 and missed a short birdie putt on the final green that would have put additional pressure on Aoki, who was behind him on the course. Aoki was breezing with a four-stroke lead after 14 holes until bogeys at the last two holes cut the margin. Still, he was the first pro in the 20-year history of the Chunichi Crowns to win it two years in a row. His earlier victories were in 1973 and 1975. Lu Hsi Chuen gave the Japanese galleries their first good look at his competency, finishing fourth at 283 in his first appearance in Nagoya.

The two-round Kanagawa Open at Yokohama Country Club bridged a week's gap to the established Fuji Sankei, and Kenji Mori picked up the crown by a one-stroke margin with his 68 the second day after starting with 75. The 68 was the best score of the tournament.

The Fuji Sankei then produced the initial first-time winner of the season. Shoichi Sato, who had toured without a win for nine years, became the first player ever to get into a Japanese Tour event through a qualifier and wind up in the winners' circle. Sato advanced from a four-way tie the first day at 68 into a two-way deadlock with Aoki the second day at 139, then fell four strokes behind with a third-round 75. Aoki, sighting his second win of the year, went three shots ahead with his 71 for 210 as Jumbo Ozaki took second place with 69—213. This put the 31-year-old Sato into the final threesome with Aoki and Ozaki, potentially a very intimidating circumstance for a nonwinner. It didn't cow Sato, though. In fact, he fired back-to-back birdies at the start of the back nine to take the lead and he never relinquished it, although he had to hole a six-foot par putt on the 18th green after Aoki missed from eight feet for a potential-tying birdie.

Aoki didn't miss any crucial putts the following week at Totsuka Country Club in Yokohama, where he proved that, in addition to everything else, he is a master of defense. Just as he had in the Chunichi Crowns three weeks earlier, Aoki repeated a 1978 victory, edging Hsieh Min Nan, the Japan-based Chinese player, in the finals of the Japan PGA Match Play Championship. It was a one-up triumph for the survivor of the 32-player field, in which Hsieh was the only foreigner.

Aoki, off to a fast start in the 1979 season, reached the finals through four stiff matches the first three days. All of the matches—against Masaru Amano and Yasuhiro Miyamoto the first day, Toru Nakamura the second day and Kosaku Shimada the third day—went to the final hole. Other than his quarter-final match with Naomichi Ozaki, Hsieh had the same kind of finishes in ousting Takaaki Uehara and Jumbo Ozaki the first day and Yoshitaka Yamamoto in the semifinals. Hsieh led early in the final match and was two up until he missed a short par putt at the 15th hole. Aoki parred there, birdied the par-three 17th and played the final hole perfectly, getting a victory concession after Hsieh hooked his drive and ultimately missed his par putt.

For 1979 they added a fourth round to the Wizard, a limited-field invitational, and changed its locale and, hence, its name to the Yomiuri Open, no relation to the former Asia Circuit event, which was played at Tokyo's Yomiuri Country Club. This one, with its field of just 35 pros and seven amateurs, was played for $150,000 at Osaka's Yomiuri and produced an exciting finish in which two of Japan's winningest pros nosed two of Taiwan's finest veterans out of a play-off. Then Teruo Sugihara nabbed his 36th victory on the second extra hole.

The 41-year-old Sugihara took the Yomiuri lead in the third round with a 72–71–71—214 after the 1978 Wizard winner, Toru Nakamura, opened in front with 69 and Kosaku Shimada and Tsuneyuki Nakajima went to the fore the second day with 141s. Jumbo Ozaki had victory within his grasp Sunday until he knocked his second shot out of bounds at the par-five 16th and took a double-bogey. He parred the last two holes for 72—287 and waited as Sugihara, Lu Liang Huan and Hsieh Yung Yo, who comprised the final group, tried to beat him on the final hole. Sugihara missed an eight-foot birdie putt but tied Ozaki with his 73. The Taiwan stars both needed birdies to join them, but Lu two-putted and Hsieh dropped to fourth place when he three-putted. The play-off went two holes, Sugihara sinking a 24-footer on the 18th green and Ozaki missing from only seven feet. Teruo, still winning in his 22nd pro season, collected $30,000 and a new car.

Nakamura, the 28-year-old former World Cupper, had played well in the early tournaments, a hint of things to come at the end of May when he won the Mitsubishi Gallant and Tohoku Classic on consecutive weekends. On the highly competitive Japanese circuit, this hadn't happened since Ozaki took two in a row in 1974, one of them, ironically, being the Tohoku.

The sweep developed slowly as Nakamura, the Mitsubishi defender, started with a two-over-par 74 at Oharai and trailed Kazuo Hashimoto by six strokes when he followed with 72 the second day. He was still four back of Yasuhiro Miyamoto (213) after his third-round 71—217 as Miller Barber, the consistent veteran from the U.S., moved into second place at 215. Toru then jumped over four players Sunday to take the $30,000 first prize with a four-under 68 for 285 despite a bogey on the last hole. He edged Yoshio Kusanagi (70) by a shot and Barber (72), Ozaki (68) and Masaji Kusakabe (70) by two in the tight finish. Barber, who shot a course-record 67 the second day, had three back-nine bogeys after eagling the 10th hole.

Nakamura's 12th career win came in an even more difficult manner the following Sunday in the Tohoku at Nishi Sendai in Sendai. Again after 54 holes, he found himself four shots off the lead, this time trailing the Dunlop winner, Hiroshi Ishii, who had wrested the lead from Yoshio Kusayanagi with a second-round 67 and added 69 for 205. Hsieh Min Nan, another hot player in the early going of 1979 in Japan, was in between at 206. The three battled through the stretch, Nakamura falling a stroke behind when he three-putted the 16th. But he fought on and gained a tie with 69—278 when he holed a 27-foot birdie putt and Hsieh missed from closer range. A hooked drive cost

Ishii a bogey and a spot in the play-off. As at the Yomiuri two weeks earlier, the overtime went two holes and was decided by a long birdie putt on a par-five hole, as Nakamura sank a 27-footer after playing a tough third shot over a bunker. When Hsieh couldn't top Toru's birdie, Nakamura had the victory.

The pupil defeated the teacher in mid-June when the circuit moved to Hokkaido for the Sapporo Tokyu Open at Kokusai Country Club. Yasuhiro Miyamoto caddied for and learned much of his golf from Teruo Sugihara at Ibaraki in Osaka and it was Sugihara who gave him his strongest run for the first-place money of $25,000 in the Tokyu, which in 1977 was one of the six previous victories of the 30-year-old pro. Actually, Miyamoto was pretty much in command after storming into a four-shot lead the second day with a five-under-par 67 for 136. He was still four in front of Lu Liang Huan and Masaji Kusakabe after his third-round 71. Sugihara cut the lead to two with an outgoing 33 Sunday, but couldn't get closer as Yasuhiro scrambled for pars on the last two holes.

Mya Aye, who has been Burma's solitary performer in the world of professional golf for nearly two decades, joined a distinguished roster of champions of the Pepsi-Wilson tournament in 1979. When he scored his wire-to-wire victory at Hachinohe Country Club at Aomori in Northern Japan, Aye followed in the heels of Jumbo Ozaki, Peter Thomson, Graham Marsh, Isao Aoki and Hsieh Yung Yo as a Pepsi winner. It was a particularly heartening victory for the small Burma pro, who has done well in Asia but in 19 years had put only two previous titles on his record—the 1976 Indonesia Open on the Asia Circuit and the 1975 Shizuoka Open.

Even though he had taken a four-stroke lead at 201 (64–70–67) after 54 holes, Aye was not considered a shoo-in entering Sunday's finale. He had broken that far on top after leading by just one despite the 64 and falling into a tie at 134 with Ben Arda at the halfway point. In the four-man group at 205 were double 1979 winners Aoki and Nakamura, along with Sugihara, and the 206 bunch included Hiroshi Ishii, another multiple winner of the year, Lu Liang Huan and Kuo Chi Hsiung. The final day came up windy, evaporating the low scoring of the earlier rounds so that Aye's 73 eased him home with a three-stroke triumph at 274. Mya opened the door slightly with an outgoing 37 to lose half of his lead but, after trading birdies and bogeys on the next four holes, he parred in for the three-shot edge over Ishii.

Aoki and Nakamura scored their third victories of the season simultaneously on the first of July when, as usual, the Kanto and Kansai PGA Championships were held over the same four-day period. The two wins abounded with similarities as the two stars of Japanese golf took the lead in the second round of each tournament, widened the gap the third day and finished well in front of the field.

Aoki's five-stroke victory, the 29th of his career, came in the Kanto, a tournament in which he was defending champion and in which he has enjoyed great success during the 1970s. Isao moved four shots into the lead the second day, when he put together a 66 for 134 to supplant Ozaki and Minoru

Nakamura. A par 72 on a rainy day at Higashi Tsukuba Country Club in Ibaraki Prefecture was good enough to widen Aoki's margin to six the third day and, even with 73, he breezed to the triumph Sunday with his 279.

After Hiroshi Ishii and Shigeru Uchida shot course-record 65s in the opening round of the Kansai PGA at Tokinodai Country Club in Ishikawa Prefecture, Nakamura took charge. A 69–66–135 gave him the second-round lead by a stroke over Yasuhiro Miyamoto. He widened the gap on Miyamoto to three with a third-day 68 and won by four over Miyamoto and Uchida with a closing 70 for 273, scoring the 13th victory of his career. Aoki collected $15,000 and Nakamura $10,000 for the No. 1 finishes.

Unlike mid-summer on the U.S. Tour, the Japanese circuit schedules a group of relatively small, often sectional tournaments at a time when several of its top players head for Europe, the British Open and, in some cases, one or two other European events. As a result, the tournaments in Japan are usually shorter, the winners are lesser known and their rewards are relatively small.

This wasn't true, though, of the first of the shorter events—the Nagano Open at Suwako Country Club. Fujio Kobayashi shot 74–66—140 and the 1978 Japan PGA champion edged four others for the $10,000 first prize. In the following weeks, Takemitsu Uranishi collected $5,000 for his 69–71—140 win in the Wakayama Open; Akio Toyoda picked up $7,500 for his play-off victory over Koichi Inoue in the 54-hole Toyama Open after both shot 211s; Mitsuhiro Kitta received $5,000 in another play-off off the same score in the Hyogo Open, beating Ichiro Teramoto and Tsutomu Irie; Katsuji Hasegawa ran away with the Chiba Open, his 69–66—135 giving him an eight-stroke victory and $7,500; Koichi Uehara won the same amount in the 27-hole Nigata Open with the unusual final score of 106, and in yet another overtime event Kazunari Takahashi went two extra holes to beat Takashi Kurihara in the Gunma Open after both finished with 140s.

The second staging of the Australia-Japan Goodwill matches also came in this period. This unique event, conceived by Peter Thomson, pits eight pros and eight amateurs (four men and four women each) of the two countries in a series of four-ball and singles matches over three days. As with such events as the Ryder and Walker Cup Matches, no prize money was up. Japan avenged its loss in Australia in 1978 by routing the Aussies, 53 points to 27, at the exclusive 300 Club course near Yokohama. The Japanese women pros were undefeated in their 12 matches.

The 72-hole tournaments returned in August, first with the awkwardly titled Kokudo Keikaku Summers tournament at the Shirasagi Country Club in Utsunomiya. Its winner had no greater a reputation than many of the other summer victors just mentioned. Norio Mikami, 32, duplicated the feat of Shoichi Sato in the Fuji Sankei by winning the Kokudo Keikaku after making the starting field via the Monday qualifier. Mikami and another nonwinner, Minoru Hiyoshi, moved past Lu Liang Huan to share the third-round lead at 209, Mikami doing it with a 66. Lu, the second-round leader at 139, slipped two strokes behind with 211, but figured to overtake the leaders Sunday. It didn't work out that way as the eight-year pro, Mikami, advanced to a two-stroke lead on the front nine, gave signs of cracking when he bogeyed the 14th and 16th holes, but birdied the 17th and parred the last hole for 70—279 and a three-shot victory over Kenji Mori and Kazuo Yoshikawa.

Another surprise occurred the following week when the Mizuno tournament was played at Tokinodai Country Club, scene of the Kansai PGA just six weeks earlier. Mitsuhiro Kitta, a 37-year-old pro with an undistinguished playing record, spurted from behind in the final round of the Mizuno with a 67, defeating Teruo Sugihara and third-round-leader Ichiro Teramoto by two strokes with his 272. He shot the 67 despite a double-bogey, carding an eagle and five birdies in his fast final round. Sugihara led the first two days with 66–67 and Teramoto shot 70–65–67—202 for the lead after 54 holes. But Kitta wound up with the $20,000 first prize.

Kansai defeated Kanto—the West beat the East—in the 30th annual duel that is another specialty on the Japan circuit. Led by Kosaku Shimada (65–68), the 12-man Kansai team rolled to a 1,373-to-1,415 victory, only the seventh victory in the long series for a West team. Shimada collected $25,000 as medalist in the two-day tournament at Sanbongi Country Club in Sendai.

Kuo Chi Hsiung's strong bid for his first victory on the Japanese Tour was gone with the wind in the KBC Augusta tournament in Kyushu in late August. The Chinese veteran from Taiwan, whose only victory in Japan had been in the 1978 Dunlop International, the finale of the Asia Circuit, shot 67, 66 and 71 in the first three rounds of the KBC Augusta at Fukuoka Country Club, holding first place at the end of each day. However, the strong winds in advance of an approaching typhoon seriously affected the high fades that are the staple of Kuo's game. Even though the tournament was shortened to nine holes (the back nine) on the last day to escape the full brunt of the oncoming storm, Kuo yielded his lead and the tournament to Masaji Kusakabe, 33, a 13-year pro veteran with nine previous victories. Kusakabe, who had trailed by two after 54 holes, shot a 34 on Sunday for the winning 240, three strokes better than Kuo posted for the unusual distance. The win paid $30,000 to Kusakabe.

A lesser cast of Japanese pros saw action at the same time in the Hokkaido Open at Mitsui Kanko Tomakomai Country Club. Masaichi Sato, with rounds of 71–72–69–67, scored a five-stroke victory with 279, nine under par. Only Hiroshi Yamada, the runner-up, had a chance to catch Sato and he shot 73 the last day.

Graham Marsh returned to his favorite golfing grounds at the end of August and promptly scored his 17th victory in Japan with a come-from-behind win in the All Nippon Airline Sapporo Open. The Australian star, who had spent most of the year on the U.S. and European Tours and had captured the Dutch Open, actually needed only a par 72 at Sapporo Golf Club to stage the rally of sorts, as the combatants in the ANA Sapporo encountered strong winds and rain in the final round on Japan's northern island of Hokkaido.

What a final nine the weather produced! After 11 holes, the lead was in the hands of this august group—Aoki and Ozaki, Japan's greatest players; Lu Liang Huan, who led Marsh by a shot after 54 holes; Kikuo Arai, one of Japan's better players; and Marsh himself. None of the others could cope with Marsh's charge from that point. Having just salvaged a par at the short 11th from between two trees, Graham birdied the next two holes to go a shot in front of Arai and his third birdie of the finishing surge at the 17th hole wrapped up the 72 for 71–73–68–72—284 and two-stroke victory over Arai. Aoki and Lu finished at 287, Ozaki at 288 and Teruo Sugihara, who had won the ANA Sapporo the previous two years, wound up at 289.

A similar "gang" finish developed the following Sunday in the $200,000 Suntory Open at Narashino Country Club near Tokyo. Halfway through the final round, another five-man deadlock for the lead had developed, this time including Masaji Kusakabe, Kosaku Shimada, Haruo Yasuda, Yoshihisa Iwashita and, again, Mr. Lu. Hubert Green, in from America for the week and the first-round leader with 65, also would have been in that group at nine under par, had he not just double-bogeyed the ninth hole by leaving a bunker shot in the sand.

Kusakabe, just two weeks beyond his first 1979 victory in the KBC Augusta and the Suntory champion in 1977, eventually forged a stroke ahead of Lu when he holed a 23-foot birdie putt at the 17th, parred the 18th for 69 and 277 (earlier rounds of 66–73–69) and watched as Lu, needing a birdie to tie, came up short of the green and missed the chip for birdie at the par-five finishing hole.

In 1953, Taiwan's Chen Ching Shui captured the Japan PGA Championship. For the next quarter century, even though more and more foreign pros contested for the title, it remained in the hands of the home pros. Then, Chen's son-in-law—the able Hsieh Min Nan—ended that domination at Asami Country Club in Ibaraki in mid-September. The 39-year-old Hsieh, who has accumulated 19 titles in his fine 15-year career, held off the late charge of Teruo Sugihara to score a one-stroke victory, his 19th.

The Chinese star, who has lived and played in Japan for seven years, closed with a hard par and 71 for 272, 18 under par, just enough to edge gallery favorite Sugihara, who birdied two holes coming in and just missed a tying putt on the last green, settling for 67—273. The win made up for disappointments Hsieh had suffered in the spring when, after winning the 36-hole Kuzuhu International, he lost to Isao Aoki in the finals of the Japan Match Play and to Toru Nakamura in a play-off in the Tohoku Classic.

Yasuhiro Miyamoto and Masaru Amano were the biggest achievers in pro golf's busiest week in Japan in late September when five 72-hole tournaments are played over the same four days in different parts of the nation. Amano landed first money of $20,000 on the strength of his sizzling 65 finish in the Kanto Open at Ikaho Country Club in Gunma. It enabled the 1978 Golf Digest champion to overtake Jumbo Ozaki, who finished at 280 with Kenji Mori and Kikuo Arai, two strokes behind the winner. It was another disappointment for Ozaki as another strong bid for his 39th pro win and first of 1979 failed.

Amano eagled the first hole Sunday, tied for the lead with a front-nine 31 and went ahead to stay when Arai bogeyed the 10th and he birdied the 11th hole.

Miyamoto, who took the Sapporo Tokyu in mid-June, also came from behind the last day in posting 70–74–72–67—283 and a one-stroke victory over Toru Nakamura in the Kansai Open at Rokko Kokusai Golf Club in Kobe. It blighted the surprise performance of 28-year-old amateur Fuminori Sano, who was never out of the lead the first three days and took a three-shot advantage into the final round. Miyamoto also collected $20,000 for his victory. The rewards were smaller in the other three events. Kinichi Matsuoka defeated Takeshi Shibata in a play-off for the Chubu Open title after both shot 290s; Hideto Shigenobu scored a two-stroke victory in the Chugoku-Shikoku Open and Yurio Akitomi, the 1977 Thailand Open victor, won by eight in the Kyushu Open.

Yoshitaka Yamamoto was equally decisive in registering his ninth tournament victory and first of the 1979 season over the Happonmatsu course of Hiroshima Country Club in the Hiroshima Open. He, too, was eight in front when the shooting ended, turning what was expected to be a real fight in the final round into a rout. Yamamoto had overtaken the hot-shooting Mya Aye the third day, moving a stroke in front with 67 for 204, 12 under par. But Yoshitaka went out in 32 Sunday to open his lead to five strokes and breezed home with 66 for 270 and the eight-shot triumph over Yoshikazu Yokoshima and Haruo Yasuda, as Aye and Taiwan's Chen Tze Ming, the third-round runners-up, both took 74s for 279.

It was almost poetic justice that Kuo Chi Hsiung should win the Gene Sarazen Jun Classic, the season's second tournament cut short to 63 holes by bad weather. Kuo, launching the hottest golfing stretch of his fine career, battled to an overtime victory at the Jun Classic Golf Course in Tochigi, stopping 24-year-old Ikuhiro Funatogawa with a scrambling par on the fifth hole of sudden death, the longest play-off of the season. In the earlier 63-hole tournament—the KBC Augusta—Kuo had carried the lead into the final round and lost it over the nine-hole stretch that last day to Masaji Kusakabe.

In the Jun Classic, the Taiwanese star was in a three-way tie for first at 210 as he and 65 others waited out a morning rain postponement that caused the officials to decide on a nine-hole finish on the back nine. Funatogawa, playing ahead of co-leaders Kuo, Kobayashi and Nakajima, bogeyed the last hole for 35 and watched as the Chinese pro, the only man with a chance, also bogeyed the 18th for 38 and a matching 248. The tense, five-hole play-off ended on a sad note for the younger player, as Kuo made a great par from far off the green at the par-three 17th and Ikuhiro, on the putting surface with his tee shot, three-putted from 35 feet.

The Tokai Classic, which had seven different winners in the previous eight years, added yet another new name to its roster of champions in 1979 when Tsutomu Irie scored his first victory in five years of professional playing. Irie, 31, one of the few Japanese to have played well at all on the Asia Circuit earlier in the year, had done little back home until the tour reached the Miyoshi

Country Club at Nagoya in mid-October. Opening rounds of 70–69—139 put Irie just a stroke behind American strongman Andy Bean, the leader, who had come across the Pacific with Andy North for the tournament. When Bean, who won the rich Dunlop Phoenix the year before, managed only a par 72 Saturday, Irie and Ben Arda took over the lead at 207, Arda with 67 and Irie with 68.

The race was a tight one in the early going Sunday. In fact, after an Arda bogey at the 10th hole, the Filipino was even par for the day and tied for the lead at nine under par with Irie and Masaji Kusakabe. It was virtually all Irie after that as he birdied four holes in a row from the 14th and wound up with a 68 and a five-stroke victory over Hsieh Min Nan and Kusakabe. In a companion Tokai women's 36-hole event Saturday and Sunday, Ayako Okamoto finished with 140 and the title, two strokes ahead of the country's No. 1 woman pro, Hisako (Chako) Higuchi.

Kuo Chi Hsiung had to be wondering when he was going to be a contender in a normal tournament after he had captured his second victory in three weeks in the Golf Digest tournament at Tomei Country Club, Shizuoka. Twice before when he was running at titles, he was involved in nine-hole final rounds, winning one and losing one, as recounted earlier. He won again in the Golf Digest and this time the weather knocked out a full round—the Friday.

Fujio Kobayashi might have been the biggest loser to the rain-out. The Friday weather seemed to put a damper on his fast start—an opening-round 64 that gave him a three-stroke lead over Isao Aoki, who apparently was so exhausted from the European tournament competition from which he had just returned that, despite the 67, he withdrew when the postponement occurred. Kobayashi still led by three when the second round was played, but he had "only" a 70 and Kuo was moving up—69–68. Another 69, a solid round of three birdies and 15 pars, carried Kuo to an easy triumph as Kobayashi could manage only a 75 for 209, three behind the winner and just a shot ahead of Namio Takasu.

Lanny Wadkins completed a unique double in the Bridgestone at Sodegaura Country Club, Chiba. Wadkins, surely one of the world's leading players at the present time, made the long trip to Japan at the end of October mainly for one reason—the sister-tournament arrangement the Bridgestone has with the Glen Campbell-Los Angeles Open that takes the winner of each of these two events to the other every season. Lanny won at Los Angeles and so went to Japan with Hale Irwin and Lon Hinkle for the tournament. The 1979 Bridgestone turned into virtually a two-man battle from start to finish between Wadkins and Japan's Yoshihazu Yokoshima, a 27-year-old whose only previous victory came on the same course, but in the Chiba Open of 1977. It went like this:

Wadkins began with a flawless, one eagle-four birdie 66, the same score with which he opened at Los Angeles in February, and led Yokoshima by a stroke. Yoshikazu did not have a bogey either. He did the next day, but came up with a back-nine 32 for 68 to move two shots ahead of the American, who had three birdies and two bogeys for 71 and 137. On Saturday, the duel came head to head as the two played in the same final threesome. Lanny outplayed Yoshikazu, 69 to 71, and the two finished 54 holes tied at 206 and three strokes in front of their nearest competitors, Ikuhiro Funatogawa and Fumio Tanaka.

Wadkins' experience and savvy paid off Sunday. The 29-year-old American stuck to his guns after falling four shots behind Yokoshima when the Japanese pro birdied the sixth and seventh holes. Lanny came right back with birdies of his own at the eighth, ninth, 12th and 13th to catch up and went ahead to stay when his younger opponent bogeyed the 15th hole. They both birdied the 16th and parred in, Wadkins for 71, 277 and the $20,000 first prize, Yokoshima for 72, 278 and the $10,000 runner-up cash. It was Lanny's first win ever in the Orient.

Kuo Chi Hsiung found yet another out-of-the-ordinary way to win a tournament in the most important of his three victories on the 1979 Japanese Tour—the Japan Open. After his weather-shrunken wins in the Jun Classic and the Golf Digest tournament, the hot-running Chinese veteran wound up in a rare four-man deadlock in the Japan Open after the regulation 72 holes over the King Course of Hino Golf Club. It took four extra holes before he eliminated Yoshitaka Yamamoto, the last other play-off survivor, and claimed the prestigious championship. It marked the third straight year that the national championship went to a foreigner and the first time in the expansion 1970's that it was captured by one of Taiwan's powerful battery of stars. Severiano Ballesteros, who won it in 1977 and 1978, finished only two strokes behind the four-way tie.

As so often happens, some unexpected players rode the top shelf for two days, while several of the big-name pros struggled. Five lesser lights—Shigeru Kubota, Masami Kawamura, Tadami Ueno, Noribumi Mizuno and Yoshinori Kaneko, an 18-year-old college student—led with 70s over the 7,043-yard course in Shiga, while Ballesteros shot 74, Isao Aoki 75 and Jumbo Ozaki 79 on his way out of the tournament via the 36-hole cut. Two of the first day's leading quintet were still on top Friday as Kubota and Ueno shot 69s for 139s. They were two better than Kenichi Yamada and Kuo, who had 71–70 for his 141.

Kubota clung to his lead Saturday with a one-under-par 71 for 210, but the wolves had gathered menacingly at his heels. Yamamoto and Kuo were at 211, American Lon Hinkle was at 213 and Aoki, Teruo Sugihara and Shigeru Uchida were just another stroke behind, Aoki rallying from 148 with a 66. As also so often happens, the 28-year-old Kubota, unaccustomed to the pressure of leading a major tournament for three days, succumbed to it Sunday, tumbling all the way to 13th place when he shot 79. When Kuo and Yamamoto could do no better than 74, the door was open to others. Aoki, whose gaudy record does not yet bear the Japan Open title, took advantage and, in fact, led the tournament when he birdied the 16th. But he missed a three-footer, bogeyed the 17th and parred the 18th for 71.

Roichi Uehara joined the play-off with 65, the best round of the tournament, but immediately bogeyed the first extra hole and dropped out along with Aoki, who parred, as Kuo and Yamamoto birdied the par-five 16th. The two survivors then parred the 17th and 18th and returned to the 16th. Kuo birdied it again for the triumph, dropping a seven-foot putt as Yoshitaka failed from the same distance. The $40,000 prize gave the Taiwan ace earnings of more than $100,000 in five weeks.

Japan continued its string of victories in the ABC U.S. vs Japan tournament, even though Tom Purtzer of the U.S. ended Aoki's individual mastery at two in a row. The tournament, played at Sports Shinko Country Club in Hyogo, pits nine-man teams from each country in a 72-hole competition. The best eight of the nine scores on each team are compiled each day toward the final team result. The U.S. fielded one of its stronger teams for the event in 1979 and gave the best of the Japanese pros a real run for the team title before bowing by just five strokes (compared to 53 in 1978). Japan is now 6–3 in the tournament and has won the last five years.

The Americans started impressively with a seven-stroke lead as Ray Floyd shot 66, Purtzer 69 and Ed Sneed 70 for the first three places. Purtzer, with 67—136, and Floyd, with 74—140, exchanged positions the second day and the Japanese closed the gap to a single stroke. Purtzer continued his brilliant play Saturday with his third straight round in the 60s, the 68 running him nine strokes ahead of Floyd and helping the team to widen its margin to four. A par round and 276 gave Purtzer a monstrous 10-stroke victory; Bill Rogers, the World Match Play champion, moved into second place with 71 for 286, but Japan pulled out the team victory with its depth bringing a nine-stroke swing.

While the team event was being played, many of the other Japanese pros competed in the 54-hole Omote Zao International Tohoku Open at Yamagata. Hideo Ishii, with rounds of 69, 73, 73 for 215 edged three other players by a stroke to win the $10,000 first prize. Among the three runners-up was Koichi Uehara, who had been one of the play-off losers in the Japan Open the week before.

The Japanese finally found the formula to draw the American stars en masse—play two of their richest tournaments back to back in the late fall after the U.S. Tour has ended and immediately after the ABC U.S. vs Japan to keep those Americans around for the next two weeks. With no releases needed from U.S. tournaments, some restful time off, the big money up for grabs and the clustering of the tournaments to eliminate the old one-week round trips, virtually all of the 1979 leaders on the U.S. Tour arrived for the $300,000 Taiheiyo Club Masters, which had been moved back into mid-November from its usual October dates to fall between the U.S. vs Japan and the $244,800 Dunlop Phoenix.

Six of the top 12 money winners on the 1979 U.S. Tour, led by Tom Watson and Bill Rogers, played in the Masters at the Gotemba course of the Taiheiyo Club and were joined by two others from the top 10—Andy Bean and Fuzzy Zoeller—in the Phoenix. Yet, with all of that American strength, the Japanese in the person of Norio Suzuki cracked the five-tournament streak of victories by U.S. pros in the Taiheiyo Masters.

The Americans may have gotten a hint of what was coming in the first round when Masaru Amano, 37, who had won the Kanto Open in October, opened on top with a 66 and Kosaku Shimada and Lu Liang Huan joined former winner (1976) Jerry Pate in second place at 68 as Watson started with a 73. Amano remained in front after 36 holes with a par 72 for 138, but the Americans were close by in large numbers. Watson moved up with 69 and, in fact, Suzuki, at 73–69, was one of only three other non-Yankees among the top 11 at that point.

Norio, 28, who had 11 victories on his record but none yet in 1979, made his move Saturday with a five-under-par 67 (six birdies and a bogey), jumping into a first-place tie with Rogers at 209. Amano dropped to 211 with his 73 as Watson, with a 68, and Rod Curl, who had a 67, moved ahead of him, too, into the 210 slot. With three others at 211, the challenge for the title Sunday came from many directions. But Suzuki outfought the pack with a one-under-par 71 and finished two strokes in front of Watson and Curl, who had 72s, and Rogers, who slipped to a 73. The weather ruled out anything sensational. It rained heavily off and on early in the day and the leaders had to sit out a fog suspension before settling matters. Suzuki built his lead with birdies on the 10th and 12th holes and hung on to score the biggest victory of his career.

Bobby Wadkins followed on the heels of his older brother in the Phoenix, as that title left the country for the sixth year in a row, four times in the hands of Americans. Wadkins, 28, whose brother Lanny captured the Bridgestone a month earlier at Sodegaura, succeeded Andy Bean, who defended unsuccessfully, missing the cut. Bobby won the rich Phoenix in somewhat unusual circumstances. He led by one stroke after three rounds, shot 73 the last day at Phoenix Country Club, Miyazaki, and won by three strokes against the potent field that included not only Watson, the World and U.S. Tour leading money winner, but also Sandy Lyle, Europe's No. 1 man in that department.

The Japanese had the upper hand early. Though Yasuhiro Miyamoto was the last home winner of the tournament in 1973, hopes were high in the galleries as Takahiro Takeyasu, Shigeru Uchida and Namio Takasu shared the first-round lead with Yank John Fought at 69 and several others were also well placed. Takasu had first place to himself Friday with a 70 for 139 as Wadkins moved from 20th into second place with 67 for 140. Bobby took the lead Saturday with a one under par 71–211 as Takasu slipped to 73 and into a tie at 212 with Lyle. After two poor rounds, Watson fired a 67 to generate a chance for himself by getting within four shots of the top. However, Tom managed only a 74 Sunday for 288 as Wadkins, with two birdies and three bogeys, shot the 73 for 284 to beat Takasu and Lu Liang Huan at 287. Bobby then had two victories—the Phoenix and the 1978 European Open in England—on his record, although he had yet to win on the U.S. Tour.

Aoki, who finished 76–77 in the Phoenix and had gone since July 1st without a victory, bounced back so strongly in the novel Japan Series at the end of November that he scored one of the most decisive wins ever in Japan. Aoki built a three-stroke lead the first two days when the tournaments started at Osaka's Yomiuri Country Club and ran it to a 13-stroke triumph when it concluded the last 36 holes at Tokyo's Yomiuri. It was a suitable climax to another excellent year for Japan's ace, as he accomplished the rout against a select field that included 18 of the year's top Japanese and Taiwanese performers.

At Osaka, where the two-site event always begins on a Wednesday, Isao carded a 68 for the opening-day lead as only Masaji Kusakabe, with 69, joined him in the 60s. At that, Aoki almost was a "birdie" victim at the fifth hole, where he hit a good approach to the blind green and didn't see a crow swoop in and steal the ball. Spectators did, though, and that evidence saved him from a two-stroke penalty. Ozaki's last hope for a 1979 victory died that day as he took an 81. Aoki shot an erratic 71 Thursday—an eagle, four birdies and four bogeys—and built the three-stroke lead (over Taiheiyo Masters winner Suzuki) to carry to Tokyo on the travel day.

He ended the competition for all practical purposes Saturday when the tournament resumed, producing a near-flawless, six-birdie 66 for 205 and a nine-stroke margin over the ever-present Sugihara, who had a 67 himself. Isao widened his final edge to 13 with a closing 71 for 276, believing the fact that he was not in top health during the week and proving the golf adage that you can't beat an ailing player. He had two birdies and a bogey as he repeated as the Series champion and picked up his fourth victory at the end of the regular Japanese season in early December.

11

THE AUSTRALIAN TOUR

The 1979 season in Australia fostered a large amount of national pride, even though seven titles fell to visiting pros during the long campaign. However, when the big chips were down in the major events, the leading Australians came through more than they have been doing in other recent years (especially in 1978, when the Australians took a backseat to the Americans in the main tournaments).

Jack Newton took the Australian and New South Wales Opens, David Graham the Westlakes Classic, Stewart Ginn the PGA Championship and Rodger Davis the early season Victoria Open. Furthermore, Newton, Ginn and Bob Shearer topped the Order of Merit. Only at the year's end were Americans able to make inroads, as young Peter Jacobsen beat a potent international field, recruited for the 15th Anniversary Western Australian Open at Perth, and as an obscure Californian, Rick Mallicoat, landed the South Seas Classic in Fiji.

Newton has the reputation of a man who enjoys a night out almost as much as he enjoys sinking nasty, 60-foot sidehill putts. The image has been well earned and Newton is honest enough to admit it. He is also one of the toughest competitors ever produced by Australian golf and, in his own way, one of the most dedicated. He has the additional talent of being a magnificent front-runner. That's not to say he cannot win from behind, but he is the man his fellow Australian professionals least like to see in the lead in the early rounds of a tournament.

In 1976, he won the New South Wales Open at Royal Sydney by 10 shots, leading all the way and finishing 19 under par. He did it again in 1979 when the event was at the Lakes, finishing 11 under par and winning by nine shots. His fierce, attacking policy and great temperament were well demonstrated that day and even more so a few weeks later when he scrambled his way to a win in the Australian Open, the Dunhill-sponsored championship at the Metropolitan course in Melbourne.

David Graham has never been quite satisfied with his form in Australia, although he won the Westlakes Classic, had only 17 ahead of him in the PGA, eight in the Australian Open, and ran second in the Western Australian Open.

Of course, his biggest achievement of the year had been his capture of the U.S. PGA Championship and he capped the season in fierce winds by winning the Air New Zealand Classic in Wellington.

Graham must be bracketed with the great sportsmen Australia has produced in the past 30 years. There are many stories about his determination as a competitor and most of them probably are true. He's not afraid to make a point, and once or twice in Australia he has evoked anguished mutterings from officials whose feelings had been slightly injured. The thing about Graham, though, is that he thinks before he talks and his comments on the game are constructive. He has become a figure of stature on the Australian scene and his thoughts should be welcomed by those in charge of the game at both amateur and professional levels.

The hard luck tag of the year hung on Greg Norman. He won the first tournament at Traralgon, was well placed in several other events, but three-putted the final green at Metropolitan to miss a play-off with Newton in the Australian Open. He did win the Martini event at Wentworth in England and, when his full record for the year is closely perused, one can see that he actually did extremely well. He is still the most promising young golfer in Australia and it is not a question of whether or not he will reach the top, but just when it will happen.

Bob Shearer was again plagued by illness, but played some fine golf nonetheless. His charge of five successive birdies in the final round of the Australian Open was responsible for much of the excitement that day.

A milestone in Australian golf was reached when Australian great, Peter Thomson, sank his final putt on the second day of that same Open. It was the last major championship for Thomson, the PGA president. Although he will play an occasional small event in the future, he retired at age 50 to devote most of his time to work in the media, in golf course construction and to work with Odyssey, an organization dealing with the treatment and rehabilitation of drug addicts.

The Tournament Players' Section of the Australian PGA was formed with Graham Marsh as president. That group will have a considerable and beneficial effect on golf in Australia in future years.

Now, let's turn a detailed report on the 1979 season.

Traralgon Loy Yang Classic—A.$15,000

Winner: Greg Norman

Greg Norman successfully defended his Traralgon Classic title with an 11 under par score of 277, winning by three shots from Ian Stanley and Glenn McCully. It was Stanley's 20th "bridesmaid" finish since turning professional. Norman, four shots off the lead after the opening round, in which Bob Shaw shot a brilliant 65, steadily drew away from the field, despite Stanley's two 68s in the final rounds.

Glenn McCully was making a comeback to the tour. He had won a tournament in New Zealand in 1970, but in 1971 dropped off the circuit. Later in the year he was to lead the Westlakes Classic field into the final round only to fall away under strong pressure from the eventual winner, David Graham.

Norman decided to play in the tournament in order to win just $100, which would move him into the lead in the Australian Order of Merit. He was in second place behind Graham Marsh at the time and was seeking automatic exemptions for the British Open and the World Series of Golf. Although the Traralgon course is only 6,342 yards long, it provides a stiff test even for the long hitters and only half the field bettered par in this event.

Tattersall's Tasmanian Open—A.$20,000
Winner: Marty Bohen

Marty Bohen cruised away with the Tasmanian Open at Woodrising, winning by four strokes from Terry Kendall. The American was never headed, not even on the second day when Rob McNaughton shot an astonishing 63 which included chipping into the hole on the 18th for a par. McNaughton's round included seven birdies and eleven pars and broke the record previously held by New Zealander Walter Godfrey by one shot. It also bettered McNaughton's own first round by 10 shots which was quite a turnabout.

Though in the lead after two rounds, Bohen was pessimistic about his chances. "My driving is so bad I'm afraid I have no real chance of winning this golf tournament," he lamented. However he must have got it all together very quickly because the third day brought a 67; then the final-round 70 for 271 enabled him to beat off all his challengers.

Greg Norman boosted his Order of Merit standing by finishing third along with McNaughton, who was unable to reproduce his 26 putts of the second day but hung on well for the lesser placing.

Victorian Open Championship—A.$60,000
Winner: Rodger Davis

It is not much fun finding yourself in a sudden-death situation with one of the greats of golf, but Roger Davis came of age when he defeated Gary Player at the second play-off hole of the Victorian Open. For Player, it was yet another disappointment in a sudden-death play-off situation. (His play-off record now stands at 20 losses and only four wins.) For Davis' it was a more pleasant golfing milestone. He is a most talented young player and in the British Open later in the year finished a creditable fifth. One of Davis' greatest advocates is Keith Miller, a former Australian Test cricket great. Miller, himself a talented amateur, has often caddied for the young professional.

Under the promotional skills of Tony Charlton, the Victorian Open has come a long way. The more staid of the golfing world flinch when Charlton moves in with his fashion models, parachutists, tented villages, lady golfers and a yearly overseas guest star; but the ordinary golfing public does not flinch at all. They applaud. This year, the standard of the field, the publicity, the promotion, the quality to the play and Charlton's expertise drew 16,000 people to the final round when Davis and Player staged their battle.

There was also plenty of excitement on opening day when 21-year-old Richard Lee badly jarred his right leg as he leaped high into the air on the 15th tee. Still, he didn't feel a great deal of pain for the remainder of the round, or for the rest of the night. He had just hit his five-iron into the hole at the 155-yard par-three 15th, and Tony Charlton had insured a hole-in-one for $20,00 prize money with the National Mutual Building Society. First prize in the tournament was only $8,000 and Lee said later, "I don't care what happens from now on at Kingston Heath—I just know I am going to try to qualify for the British Open." The $20,000 was slightly more than ten times the value of the prize money he had earned since turning pro nine months before.

Two of the stars of the tournament, Graham Marsh and Greg Norman, shot 77 and 81, respectively, in the wet, windy conditions on the second day. (In their duel for leadership of the Order of Merit, Marsh was then $3,800 in arrears.) That day belonged very much to Marsh's friend, Terry Gale, who, despite a savage bout of tendonitis in his right wrist, shot a fine 69. Tied with him at 143 was Geoff Parslow; but Player, with some indifferent putting, could manage only 76 for 148, alongside Richard Lee.

Player fought back well the next day, holing a 50-foot putt at the 17th and then a 25-footer at the final hole for a 70. With several other players falling away, he was now just one shot behind former champion Guy Wolstenholme, who was at 217. Both Parslow and Davis were also at 218 with Player and a head-to-head confrontation was looming.

In the final round, Wolstenholme was the first to fall off the leaderboard and eventually he shot 77. The big challenge came from Tony Gresham, one of the finest golfers to come from the amateur ranks since the war. His 68 was a model of consistency and was equaled only by Greg Norman, who incredibly finished only two strokes off the lead after his second-round 81. Norman had to be called back by the officials that day who reminded him to sign his scorecard. No such problem on the final day when, for a while, he was leader in the clubhouse.

At one point, five players shared the top of the leaderboard at two under par: Davis, Player, Parslow, McDonald and Wolstenholme. Davis, Player and Parslow got home with 73s for 291 and went to the play-off holes, No. 7 and No. 18. The South African had the tournament for the taking on the first hole. His six-foot putt was in all the way, but suddenly darted right and lipped the hole. Given his chance, Davis put in a 16-footer at the next hole for a birdie and won the biggest prize of his life.

Side benefits were an automatic exemption for the European circuit and the British Open and partial exemption on the Asian and Japanese circuits. Rodger had every right to say, as he opened a cold beer, "This means a hell of a lot to me."

Dunhill South Australian Open Championship—A.$25,000

Winner: Peter Senior

Increased competition seems to be bringing out the best in Australia's amateur golfers. Tony Gresham has for many years been a fine player, Jeff Senior won the Queensland Open at mid-season and Graham Stevens only faltered at the final hurdle to go down in a play-off to Peter Senior in the South Australian Open at Adelaide.

Stevens had a three-stroke advantage over the field with only 16, 17 and 18 to play, but he bogeyed all of them for 73 and the tie at 282. He missed a putt of only one foot on No. 16, and used the wrong clubs on his approaches on the final two holes. Then Stevens hooked his tee shot behind a bush on the first hole of the sudden-death, and Senior made no mistake with a birdie three. It was Senior's first tournament victory after 12 months as a professional and the win was all the more meritorious because of the consistency of his golf.

Gresham, who, in the Victorian Open, had been only one stroke behind winner Rodger Davis, and Parslow and Player, again played solid golf to finish four shots away from the winner. These two performances foreshadowed his excellent play throughout the year.

Davis finished with Gresham at 286, but the first-round leader, George Bell, slipped back after carding 67 with some prodigious hitting off the tee.That first day he had broken his own driver while practicing, and borrowed one from his girl friend, Julie Bretherton. Bell is one of the country's biggest hitters around, but the rest of his game is rather wayward, as evidenced by his $1,000 winning in 12 months. This was the first time in his career that he had led the field in a major event. But from that point on Senior, Bob Shaw and the two amateurs, Stevens and Gresham, surged past him, with Stevens giving way to the pressure over those last three holes.

Hard luck note: Glenn McCully holed-in-one at the seventh instead of the 12th, where the prize was a car.

Australian Masters— A.$30,000
Winner: Barry Vivian
There are easier ways of making a living than running a golf tournament, as Ian Stanley found out in the inaugural year of the Australian Masters at Huntingdale. "Stan the Man," one of Australia's top players, acted as an adviser to the organizers and gained a few grey hairs as he wrestled with the problem of getting the field together.

Lee Trevino was to be a starter, then declined. Then there was a scramble for top Australian players and the prize money dropped from $50,000 to $30,000. Appearance money disappeared altogether. Bob Shearer and Jack Newton, close friends of Stanley, played, returning from the States where the Bay Hill Citrus Classic was being played at the same time. Greg Norman made a rush return from Hong Kong, where he had just won the Hong Kong Open and a first prize of $17,500. Stanley appreciated the support of his long-time friends and, in the end, it all turned out well.

If the organizers were a trifle nervous, that was nothing compared with the way the winner felt on the 72nd hole. Barry Vivian of New Zealand was shaking, and little wonder, as he shot a final 80, which is one of the highest rounds ever to win a tournament anywhere in the world. Certainly it is the highest in Australian professional golf history.

The New Zealander led all the way with 67–69–73, but then, with Shearer breathing down his neck on the 6,955-yard course, his nerves began to get the better of him. "At the back of my mind all day was that Shearer was there." Finally, on the 18th hole on the fourth day, Vivian, who needed only a bogey five to win, hit his second shot into the left trap and his third into the crowd behind the green. His approach left him with a 30-inch putt and he said later that it looked like 30 feet until it fell into the hole for the winning 289.

Shearer's second prize was $3,600. Ironically, the day before, his horse, Bold Diplomat, had won $1,400 more than that by finishing fourth in the prestigious Blue Diamond Stakes in Melbourne.

Western Australian PGA Championship—A.$15,000
Winner: Richard Coombes

"Anyone who shoots seven bogeys in the final round of a golf tournament just doesn't deserve to win," said Roger Davis after the Western Australian PGA, in which he had shared the lead with Richard Coombes four shots ahead of the field, and then let it all slip. In fact, it was only his brilliant putting which earned him second prize ahead of charging Mike Ferguson.

Only one player, Terry Gale, bettered 70 the first day when showers and a very strong southwesterly breeze posed major problems for everyone. Then Mike Ferguson staged a welcome return to form with a fine 69 to follow his par round of 72, but a 76 on the third day cost him any real chance of winning, provided Coombes held up to the pressure. In the 1978 Queensland Open, Coombes led for the first three rounds, but finished sixth. However, the New Zealander made no such mistake at Melville Glades, in 1979. He produced the same, steady iron play which had been a feature of his golf all week, and even though he said, "That was the longest 18-hole round of my career," he handled it well. He finished with a par 72 for 285, beating Davis by two strokes.

Royal Fremantle Open—A.$15,000
Winner: Terry Gale

Terry Gale spent the four days before the Royal Fremantle Open hard at work on the practice tee trying to iron out a kink which had appeared in his swing. He obviously got it right, since he won the Royal Fremantle, finished second the following week, and bobbed up with another win seven days later in the Nedlands Masters. Collecting $8,000, in three weeks at the quiet time of the circuit, was quite useful.

Also rounding into form was Queenslander Mike Ferguson, who had been very much upset with his game, until fellow professionals Alan Murray and Len Thomas sorted out his bunker play and driving problems, while they were on tour in Malaysia. The benefits were immediate. He had a third-place finish at Melville Glades; then at Fremantle an eagle-three at the 18th gave him a share of the tournament lead after 36 holes.

Ray Hore, winner of the event three years earlier, was tied with him at this stage, but Hore followed up with par 72 and a 69 and Ferguson fell back. Hore played a wonderful nine holes on the last day in a desperate effort to catch Gale. He picked up birdies on 11, 15 and 18 and barely missed forcing a play-off with Gale, who needed a par to win at the 18th, and made it with a final three-foot putt for 71 and 280.

Once again, Rodger Davis had a mixed round. Out in a superb 33, he took 42 to come home and, after having been in the lead at the 10th, finished back in the ninth spot.

The W.A.Y. Celebration Open—A.$20,000
Winner: Terry Kendall

New Zealand's golfers had a good year in Australia, and Terry Kendall added to their enjoyment with a runaway victory at Mount Lawley, beating Western Australia's Terry Gale by five shots in the W.A.Y. Celebration Open. Kendall, an unflappable character, finished eight under par and led from the first hole of the second round, when he sank a 12-foot putt for birdie. The first-round leader from Queensland, 25-year-old John Victorsen, slumped in the third round, but fought back well with 69 on the final day to tie for 11th place.

Kendall did not win a tournament in 1978 in Australia, but his overall consistency allowed him to finish in the top 10 of the Order of Merit. Often he gives the impression of taking too little time with his game, but a solid swing and sound putting stroke have enabled him to remain one of the outstanding players in Australasia over the years. Once he carded his second-day 69, no one could pull him back and a third-day 70 eased him five shots ahead of Gale, with Rodger Davis the only other top player poised for a serious challenge.

Kendall coasted home with his one under par 71 on the fourth day despite very strong southwesterly winds which blew from the time he teed off. "No worries," he said later. "Where I come from in New Zealand, the trees grow sideways because of the wind."

Nedlands Masters—A.$15,000
Winner: Terry Gale

Terry Gale again. No worries for the local boy here as he defeated his fellow Western Australian professional, Ross Metherell, by five shots in conditions perfect for golf. Gale was never headed from the moment he teed off, even though he had returned from Europe only a few days before the event and had not fully shaken off the effects of the journey. His opening 69 came after he was out in par-36 and then had birdies at 10, 13, 14 and 15. He began in similar fashion in the second round with birdies at the first, second and fourth and then at nine, 10 and 11, enroute a 68.

Metherell could be well satisfied with his performance, for he was most consistent other than in the third round, in which he was two over par. He had been having problems in the past 12 months as he tried to shake off a neck injury sustained in a car accident. However, his golf remained consistent throughout the circuit after this second-place finish and he later played in the World Cup in Greece with Col Bishop.

Gale's 71 on the final day was sound, and his 279 total set a new record for the event, which he has now won five times.

Joe Jansen New South Wales PGA Championship— A. $15,000

Winner: Stewart Ginn

Stewart Ginn announced during the pro-am event at Penrith that he would be a strong contender in the New South Wales PGA, and he followed that statement up with one of the easiest victories of the year. With 275, he finished with an eight-stroke margin over runner-up Richard Coombes. Strong westerly winds blowing off the mountains had no effect on his immaculate iron play and he finished 13 under the card. It was Ginn's first tournament after a long lay off, during which he had been trying to eliminate the hook shot which had plagued him for two years.

After ordinary rounds of 73-74, Bob Shaw broke the course record with a third-round 66, but then fell away again with 75 to tie for eighth position at the end. Richard Lee, the young player who won $20,000 for a hole-in-one at the Victorian Open, did it again on the last day. Strangely, his close friend, Greg Hohnen, also had a hole-in-one two days earlier, though not at the same hole. Neither received a cent for the performance this time.

Ginn's final-round 67 was a pointer to his success later in the year and, almost prophetically at the prize-giving, he said, "I feel very relaxed at the moment and I'm hitting the ball with a great deal of confidence. I'm hoping now that I can win one of the big ones later this year—the Open or the PGA."

Win TV Illawarra Open—A.$20,000

Winner: Mike Ferguson

Chill southerly winds and rain are not the ideal ingredients for a golfer from Queensland's sunny Gold Coast, but Mike Ferguson battled through in great style to win by a shot from Chris Tickner in the Win TV Illawarra Open. Despite the conditions, Billy Dunk set a course record of 66 on the second day after Tom Linskey had already broken the existing record with 68 in the opening round. However, Linskey's performance on the first two days was uneven.

For Ferguson it was the beginning of a very good run, though he said later that his putting was letting him down. "I'm hitting the ball well but I'm really struggling with the putter." Ominous words perhaps for his fellow professionals, as he was still able to win with a one over par round of 73 on the final day and a par 288 score for the distance. In doing so, he passed Stewart Ginn and Billy Dunk, both of whom had been two shots ahead of him at the end of his third round.

Tooth's Gold Coast–Tweed Classic—A.$20,000

Winner: Mike Ferguson

Earlier in the year the living legend, Sam Snead, had scored a stroke lower than his 67 years in the final round of the Quad Cities Open, an official U.S. tournament. On the first day at Tweed Heads, he just missed doing it again, and his 69 was good enough to put him in second place only one shot behind Lyndsay Stephen. This happened after Snead and two other seniors in the event, Tommy Bolt and George Bayer, had been awakened at 3 A.M. by a telephone prankster. Snead said, "That was about as well as I can play these days. I'm having trouble with a pinched nerve in the neck and back trouble, and I reckon once I've played in my 40th Masters next year I'll be calling it a day."

Snead, in fact, finished tied for ninth place, eight shots behind Mike Ferguson and Stewart Ginn, who returned seven under par totals of 281. On successive days, Ginn hit the high and low performance of the field, following a record-breaking seven under par 65 on the second day, with a horrendous 78 on the third. While he was shooting his 65, he shaved the cup with long putts on several occasions and his playing partner, Jimmy Martin of Ireland, said, "It was a round that could have been anything from 65 to 60." But the next day, with a strong wind blowing from the north, it was a different story, and, although Ginn fought back with fine 69 on the fourth day, the best he could do was a tie with Ferguson. The latter played steady golf on the third day, didn't panic when he bogeyed three holes on the front nine, and came back with four birdies.

In the final round, Ferguson had gone five up on Ginn at the half-way mark before a turnabout occurred. Ginn holed his second shot from 100 yards at the 11th for an eagle, Ferguson bogeyed 13, 14 and 15, and the two players were even. Ferguson had a chance to win at the 18th but his five-foot putt slid past the hole. He won the play-off on the third extra hole, the par-five 520-yard 18th, by hitting a three-wood second into the center of the green. "It was just about the best shot I have ever hit in my life," he said, and it won him his second tournament in two weeks.

Dunhill Queensland Open—A.$30,000
Winner: Jeff Senior

Amateurs rarely win professional golf tournaments. It is certainly not a comforting situation for the pros, when an amateur does step in for a victory. But, when it happens on a score of nine under par, there is little anyone can do about it other than smile and offer congratulations.

Jeff Senior of Queensland became the first amateur in 12 years to win the Queensland Open, carding an impressive 279 for the 72 holes and adding more luster to the family name. His brother, Peter, a professional, had won the Dunhill South Australian Open earlier in the season. Second in the Queensland event was Jack Newton, who was seven under par and revving up for a big success in the New South Wales and Australian Open championships later in the year.

Senior is a 23-year-old electrical engineering student who, as an amateur this year, represented Queensland in the national series in Perth and represented Australia in Great Britain and Japan. He and the rest of the field had to play 36 holes on the final day because the first round had been completely washed out by a torrential morning downpour.

Newton's 66 on the delayed opening day was one shot ahead of Ian Stanley. Senior, with 68, was even with Billy Dunk and just ahead of a number of other players. A second-day 68 put Newton two strokes ahead, but another amateur, Glenn Cogill, astonished spectators with an eight under par 64 which took him within four shots of the lead. He faded a little from there to finish at 286.

Senior shot a 71 the second day, a 73 in the morning third round, and then in the afternoon a magnificent final 67. Newton, penalized a shot for grounding his club in a hazard, simply couldn't catch him. Senior holed a 50-yard wedge shot at the seventh hole and never looked back from that moment. Vaughan Somers finished a creditable third, Billy Dunk was a stroke behind at 284. For Newton, the only comfort to balance the mediocre, third-round 75 which ruined his title bid was that Senior was unable to accept the winner's check of $6,000. Even finishing second as a professional can have its advantages.

Citizen Watches Seniors' Open Championship —A.$25,000
Winner: Tommy Bolt

Tommy Bolt again! That tempestuous character of senior golf! He started off by shooting a great 68 on the opening day of the event and then fought off challenges from Jack Fleck on the second and third days to win by a shot, with 214 to Fleck's 215. It was a great performance, but it took a tricky little four-foot downhill putt at the last hole for him to pocket the $5,000 winner's check. It was another splendid senior tournament, well-publicized and superbly run by consultant Tom Ramsey. Sam Snead, George Bayer, Art Wall, Dow Finsterwald and Christy O'Connor were the other star overseas attractions, while Kel Nagle led the home challenge.

In the pro-am preceding the event, Bolt was so fed up with his putter that he bent it carefully around a branch after a succession of missed putts. The new one, bought at Ted Stirling's pro shop, certainly did the trick. Although Finsterwald kept pace with him on the opening day, Bolt moved smoothly to a three-shot lead at 140 after the second round in cool conditions.

Bolt played very well on that second day from tee to green, hitting fifteen greens in regulation. But, after opening with a birdie at the relatively short, par-four first hole, he managed to sink only two more putts to beat par.

Fleck had his chance throughout the last nine holes on the final day but he three-putted the 10th from only 12 feet, a miss which was to be the difference between a play-off and second place.

When the pair came to the 18th, they both hit their tee shots through the back of the green. Then, in a last-ditch effort, Fleck played a glorious little chip to within a foot of the pin. Bolt had a four-foot putt for the win, and after taking his time, put it straight into the back of the hole. Then he whipped around to the crowd and said, "I'll bet you're sorry to see that go in."

He was convinced that the majority of the crowd was cheering for Fleck, who had staged a comeback on the par-five 16th, where he had an eagle. It was an enthralling final day, other than for overlong speeches at the presentation ceremony. Bolt said he would be back to defend his title next year, providing two conditions are met. First, his photograph must appear on the front cover of the tournament program—in color. Second, if he wins the title for the third successive year, he keeps the trophy. Worth it, too. There's about $10,000 of silver in that cup!

Victorian Garden State PGA Championship—A. $50,000
Winner: Ian Stanley

Controversy has never been far away from the Woodlands Garden State PGA Championship in Melbourne, which Doug Mason organizes. In 1978, it was a telephone call to complain about Lanny Wadkins' performance in the first round. This year Jackie Newton, Jack's attractive wife, was the one under fire; for she supposedly called Mason to complain about his treatment of Newton. Newton vacationed in Newcastle rather than play in the tournament this year. According to Jackie, he pulled out because his air fare and accommodations were not being paid for by the tournament organizers. At least, that's what Mason said.

Newton flatly denied it and classed it as, "a load of garbage. . . . I've supported the Australian circuit as much as any other player who competes in the United States or Europe, probably more so, and it really hacks me off to hear this junk from Mason."

It provided an unpleasant start to the tournament, made even more unsettled by the fact that the pro-am the day before had to be called off because a severe thunderstorm hit the course around three in the afternoon. Bobby Wadkins was the American representative in 1979, Lanny being otherwise engaged, and Bobby had his own problems because two pieces of baggage and his golf clubs had been mislaid on the flight from San Francisco.

Bob Shearer had arrived back from America, luggage intact, but despondent about his form and his health. He had lost almost 30 pounds following another illness involving low blood-sugar early in the year. He had to follow a special diet which excluded alcohol and sugar and called for big, between-meal snacks of boiled eggs, apples, oranges, biscuits and high-protein chocolate bars. "I'm like a walking green grocery shop when I'm out on the golf course," he said. "Worse still, it's taken 30 yards off my drives and has forced me to change my swing pattern."

In the end, all the dramas and traumas were overcome and Ian Stanley, the bridesmaid of Australian golf, came out on top, winning a dramatic play-off against Stewart Ginn at the second extra hole after both had shot 286s.

The Woodlands course is very tight. You must drive straight and accurately to win. To add to the players' problems, the first day was played in rain and winds of near gale force. In light of that, the scoring was nothing short of astonishing. Greg Norman, Shearer and young Queenslander, Gerry Taylor, headed the field with 69s and two New Zealanders, Terry Kendall and Craig Owen, were at 70, along with Canadian, Bob Beauchemin, and Queenslander, Bryan Smith. At 71, were Wadkins, Terry Gale and Stanley. Norman, an early starter, had the best of the conditions with only the strong winds to contend with that first day. Once it began to rain, the course became nearly impossible. After eight inches of rain in 14 days, the course superintendent had been unable to use mowers on some of the fairways. Shearer appealed to the Match Committee at the end of the first day to implement a rule allowing the players to clean and place their ball after lifting it from the "heavy" fairways.

The most remarkable round of the second day was played by young David Armstrong, who shot 70 after taking 40 strokes on the front nine. He had birdies from 10 through 14, notched another one at 17 and completed the back nine in 30. At the end of that second day, Stanley was in the lead with 70 added to his first-round 71, and Shearer was two strokes behind at 143.

Shearer came close to a disaster on the third day. He received news on the 10th fairway that his horse, Bold Diplomat, had won the $52,000 first prize in the Caulfield Guineas and he immediately birdied the 10th, 11th and 13th. Then came the bad news. The jockey of the second-place horse had lodged a protest. Shearer later denied that news of the successful protest had been responsible for his bogeys at 14 and 18. "It was the damned slow play that upset me," Shearer said. "That's got to be one of the slowest rounds of golf I've ever known."

Shearer and Stanley are great friends and, though things weren't going right for Bob, certainly the last day went wonderfully for Ian. No one broke 70 in the final round (Bobby Wadkins was the only player to shoot 70, in fact); but Stanley and Ginn, tied at the start of the final day, both had par 72s to finish in a play-off. Stanley knew that this was his chance. In recent years, he had been having a frustrating time of it, winning only three tournaments, but finishing second 19 times. "If only the sequence could be reversed," he said, "my record would be fabulous, but these days I seem to make the game very nerve-wracking for myself."

That was exactly what he did late in the fourth round. After 14 holes he was leading Ginn by one stroke, but he threw away shots at the next two holes with weak approaches. He fought back, finished two under the card for the tournament at 286. Ginn, in the last group, was two holes back, but it looked odds-on that Stanley would again finish second. He was a downcast figure alongside the 18th green as Ginn strode onto the 17th, having hit the green in regulation figures. But he three-putted. Now Ginn needed a par-four at the final hole to tie Stanley and produce a sudden-death play-off.

There is nothing easy about the 18th. And Stanley, now with a spring in his step, left the back of the green to prepare for the play-off, in case it should happen. Sure enough, Ginn hit his drive a little bit too close to the corner and pushed his second shot into an area alongside a gum tree far to the right side of the green. He was lucky that the ball landed clear of any obstruction, and he played a superb chip to three feet from the cup and holed the putt to tie with

Stanley. Both had pars on the first play-off hole, then Stanley rolled in a six-footer for victory and $10,000.

It was one of the most popular victories in recent years in Australian golf. Stanley, Ginn and Shearer are all good friends and Shearer said, "I feel as happy as if I'd won the golf tournament. I'm hoping now that Ian's win will do a lot of good and be the start of a very good run."

CBA Westlakes Classic—A.$65,000
Winner: David Graham

The major part of the Australian golf circuit begins toward the end of October, about the time the U.S. Tour is winding down. The Australian tournaments of note are the CBA Westlakes Classic, followed by the New South Wales Open, the Mayne Nickless PGA at the Royal Melbourne Composite Course and the Australian Open, which normally signals the end of intensive tournament activity. This year the golfing officials added the $150,000 Western Australian Centenary Open and all five tournaments attracted strong fields of local and overseas players.

David Graham, the U.S. PGA winner, came back. Bob Shearer, Greg Norman, Graham Marsh, Bob Charles, Jack Newton, Simon Owen, Gary Player, Seve Ballesteros, Hubert Green, Bruce Delvin, John Lister, Jerry Pate, Johnny Miller, Barry Jaeckel, Jim Nelford, Curtis Strange, John Schroeder, Mark James, Stewart Ginn, Fuzzy Zoeller, Ed Sneed, Maurice Bembridge, Victor Regalado, Bill Casper and Billy Dunk headed the fields for these tournaments and promoted intense interest in golf throughout the country.

When David Graham flew in for the Westlakes, he was confident enough to say that he wouldn't have bothered coming if he didn't think he could win the tournament. Asked which player he thought should start as the tournament favorite, he half-smiled and said, "Well, I think possibly you could put me in that bracket." Five days later he had confirmed his statement by winning the event by two shots over slim American, Gary Vanier, and Bob Shearer. Vanier had a sizzling 67 in the last round to threaten Graham's lead over the back nine holes. Before the tournament began, Graham predicted that something around a six under par 282 would win the event and, as it turned out, he was three strokes astray at 285 in picking up the $13,000 winner's check.

Many were backing Bob Shearer as the potential victor after his practice and pro-am round. In fact, Shearer's 69 on opening day was only one off the first-round 68 of Peter Senior who, earlier in the year, had won the South Australian Open Championship. (Senior is only 20 years of age but already has a problem with putting "yips." "At the moment I'm terrified of anything under three feet," he said. "In fact, I have to change my grip on the putter to have any chance of holing a putt of that distance.") Terry Kendall also had 69 and Christy O'Connor and young Charles Henderson, playing in his first season, were at 70. So, too, Glenn McCully, who shot a brilliant 66 the next day to go into a five-stroke lead in the tournament.

Those problems were minor compared to the ones faced by Shearer, whose history of illness this year has been one of the major reasons for his lacklustre performances. He was so ill on opening day that concerned organizers were told he might have to pull out during the round because of food poisoning. "I have never felt as sick. It was far worse than having a terrible hangover," Shearer muttered at the end of his 69. No one had a really happy-go-lucky story to tell. Terry Kendall's was the cheeriest press room quote. "I played a load of garbage," he said after his 69.

McCully was about the most unlikely second-round leader imaginable with an aggregate of 136 and a five-stroke cushion on the next group of players. He is 30 years old and the professional at the Ringwood Public Course in a Melbourne suburb. On that day, it was his putting which made all the difference. He holed putts of 15 feet, 30 feet, 15 feet, 20 feet, three feet, 60 feet and three feet for birdies at holes No. 4, 8, 9, 11, 12, 13 and 14. Earlier in the year he had finished second to Greg Norman in the Traralgon Classic, and although he had been working at his public course professional job for several years, he had also won tournaments in New Zealand and Adelaide in 1971 and won the PGA in 1976 in Victoria.

It all fell apart for McCully on Saturday. At 6:30 in the morning he injured vertebrae in his neck while bottle-feeding his 14-month-old son and had to rush to a chiropractor to get himself in shape to take the first tee.

From that moment on nothing went right. Glenn shot 76, which left Shearer, Graham and Vines poised just two shots behind him and Mike Ferguson, who had a splendid 70 in the third round for his 212. McCully went straight to the practice area after signing his card for the third round to try to eliminate a dangerous push with his irons. "Blocking cost me three shots at the 13th and 17th holes," he said. "What I have to do tomorrow is go out and attack all the time, otherwise I'll be swamped by all these top-line players." Swamped he was, as he took an 82 to finish at 294, tied for 15th place, but he had some fine competitors alongside: Graham Marsh, Bob Shaw, Simon Owen and Maurice Berbridge, among others.

It was a day when Shearer should have won his first tournament of the year in Australia. By the time he had played seven holes, he was three strokes in the lead after birdies on five, six and seven, but he bogeyed the ninth and dropped three more shots on the homeward run. Worse still, two of those bogeys came on the last two holes, just before Graham played the decisive shot of the tournament at the 17th.

Attacking the flag on the short par-three, Graham finished just over the bunker on the right side and 18 inches off the green in a very ordinary lie. He was 25 feet from the pin, and although he didn't have the best of stances, he put the ball in the back of the hole. When David stood on the tee at the 18th, he didn't know that he now could win with a bogey, because Shearer had bogeyed the final hole a few minutes before.

He made no mistakes though. He hit a beautiful drive off the last tee and an accurate second into the heart of the green, then took the regulation two putts for his two-stroke victory over Shearer and Vanier. Graham said afterward, "That's only around 70 per cent as well as I can play. I just kept on struggling along. My main problem was with my irons. I wasn't nearly as sharp as I'd like to be."

Vanier, who picked up a check of $6,000, had shot 80 on Monday to qualify for the event. He said, "If you shoot 71 or over in America, you probably don't qualify—that's the difference out here." This was Vanier's first Australian tournament and, although physically not very big, he made a favorable impression with his driving and long-iron play.

New South Wales Open Championship—A.$60,000
Winner: Jack Newton

"I don't want to blame anyone, but I'm going to kill my wife when I get home tonight."

An unusual quote from an international golfer, but that's what Jack Newton said after playing in the first round of the New South Wales Open and shooting a superb 69. It seems that his wife, Jackie, who has the job of setting the alarm, making sure it goes off and making sure that husband Jack wakes up, forgot to press the button. Jack was 120 miles away from the Lakes Golf Club in Sydney, and had intended to catch a small plane from Newcastle which would have given him plenty of time to be on the first tee at his scheduled 8 A.M. starting time.

No alarm. No taxi. No plane. He managed to snap up the last seat on the next flight leaving 30 minutes later. When he arrived at the Sydney airport, he had to beat on the window to alert the pilot that he had to get off the plane before everyone else's luggage was unloaded. Then there was a dash across the airport to the taxi terminal and a promise of a $20 tip to the driver for the one-mile trip if he could get him to the tee on time. Jack's father, who often caddies for him, was packing up the clubs and untying his caddy number when his son burst around the corner of the clubhouse just as his name was being called for he last time.

What a way to start a tournament! And what a tremendous will it shows if you can go from that kind of beginning to share the lead on the first day, move into a two-stroke lead on the second day, three on the third day and finish up with a nine-shot margin. Jack Newton is an incredible man. Weather conditions were absolutely perfect for the tournament. For the first three days, there was hardly a cloud in the sky and only a light nor'easterly wind blowing. The wind became strong and gusty on Sunday , though Newton's great strength served him well in spite of it.

Gary Vanier hung on with a 72 on Friday to add to his first-round 69. Bob Charles made a momentary charge, as did Wayne Grady, who shot a fine 68 to go with his first-round 74. Grady played some spendid golf on Saturday to fire 70 and stand only three shots behind Newton. His was the local challenge which most threatened Newton on Sunday, although the further along they went, the further Newton forged ahead. It was interesting to watch Jack in the strong wind that final afternoon as, instead of hitting harder and harder, he seemed to become more and more relaxed.

"There was a very good reason for that," Newton said later. "I had the good fortune to be paired with Jack Nicklaus in the Tournament Players Championship last year and found I was hitting two clubs less than Nicklaus on a number of my approach shots. I knew this couldn't be right and there must be some reason for it, and it was probably because I was thinking the wrong way. After we talked about it, I realized I'd been trying to belt the cover off the ball instead of swinging easily and lowering my percentage of errors, which I'm now trying to do. I reckon if I can continue to play like this, I could win one of the big tournaments in Melbourne, the PGA or even perhaps the Australian Open.''

One of the strong features of Newton's game at the Lakes was his driving. It was a timely performance as he was using for the first time in a tournament a new driver called ''The Master,'' made by an American company, of which Jack is a director. ''It's made all the difference to my game,'' he said at the press conference after the event in which he was so very nearly a disqualified non-starter.

Mayne Nickless PGA Championship of Australia—A.\$125,000
Winner: Stewart Ginn

In 1976, Australian golfer Stewart Ginn ''blew'' a major golf tournament, the Chrysler Classic at the Royal Melbourne Composite course; but he made amends in this year's PGA championship with a courageous victory on the same layout. In conditions which were ideal the first three days, no one was able to break par of 284. The course was at its usual best with lightning fast greens producing many problems for all players.

Ginn knows the Composite Course very well and, like Bob Shearer, has a deep affection for it. As a boy he would occasionally take a day off school to sneak in a game. Later, when playing top class golf as an amateur, he became assistant secretary at the course, then later turned professional. Twice earlier in the year he had lost play-offs, the first to Mike Ferguson and then to Ian Stanley. He made no mistakes this time, and his local knowledge of the trouble spots on the course and of the play on the greens must have been of vital importance to him.

Hubert Green set the pace the first day with 68. The only other player to break 70 was Australian Chris Tickner, at 69. Green was under no illusions about the task in front of him. Heavy rains in recent weeks had left the Royal Melbourne fairways lush and they provided little run. The greens had a glassy look about them, indicating that they would provide a supreme test, even for a former U.S. Open winner. ''I think they're breaking us in gently,'' Green said of the greens and pin placements on the opening day. ''Maybe they don't want too many guys slashing their wrists on the first night.''

That's probably just how he felt Friday evening after shooting a horrid 79. At one point, it seemed as if it could well have been 83 or 84, but he fought back well. He four-putted the fourth green and took three putts at holes No. 6, 7 and 13. The greens were tinder dry and very fast. One player, David Galloway, even saw his ball slide back downhill into the hole after he'd hit his first putt 12 inches past.

Green wasn't the only golfer to have conflicting opinions about the course. Johnny Miller, fresh from victory in the Lancome Trophy in France, was quoted: "I'm happy with my game for the first time in years."That was pro-am day. But after the first round of the tournament, with 77 against his name, he was wondering aloud if it would be possible to play as badly again so he could miss the cut. Wayne Grady solved the problem another way. He missed his wake-up call, his tee time, and was disqualified.

Shearer slipped in quietly to take the second-round lead with a second 70. He was lucky that he had an early start and had passed most of the problem holes before the wind started to blow. Even luckier than that was his birdie four at the 17th, where his badly sliced second shot had to be declared unplayable. He dropped with a one-shot penalty and hit a nine-iron 125 yards into the hole. That was balanced immediately by what he termed "dumb thinking" on the 18th. In trying to attack for another birdie, he declined to go for the 100 feet of green to the left of the pin. Instead he plugged the ball in the right-hand bunker and took a double-bogey six.

As so often happens, the third day sorts out the tournament and it was then that the eventual winner, Ginn, made his charge. There was nothing amusing about the pin placements. The strong, hot north wind continued to blow and the greens were even faster and more terrifying than the previous day. None of this seemed to matter to Ginn. When he started the day, he was tied at 143 with New Zealand star Simon Owen, three shots behind Shearer. Owen held on well with a 73 Saturday, but Shearer fell back with a disastrous 77. Ginn fired the only sub-par round of the day—a 69—and suddenly had a four-stroke lead in the tournament. Shearer and Bob Charles, who was a stroke further back at 217, were still in it on the Royal Melbourne Composite Course which has the ability to turn a tournament around in the space of nine holes. Green was struggling, having added a 77 to the previous day's 79, but Miller had come back strongly with 72–74 after his first-day 77.

Ginn's round was one of complete confidence. "I'm very pleased with the way I'm playing at the moment," he said. "In fact, I have played very well all year and could have won four tournaments leading up to this event." Part of his confidence stemmed from the fact that he had not gone to Europe earlier in the year, but had remained in Australia to sort out his swing problems. This had been so successful that, after the third round, he was able to say, "I'm four shots in front and the way I'm hitting the ball I could win by another four."

Well, it didn't quite work out like that, though with a one over par 72 for 284 he had a comfortable enough victory. He had to combat the normal Melbourne weather pattern of four seasons in a single day. Play was even suspended at one stage for 70 minutes while storm water drained from the greens. However his worrying moments were few, though at the 18th there was a slight chance for Bob Charles to put pressure on him. Ginn had hit his second shot well past the pin and had a nasty downhill putt. Charles decided to go for the flag, which was tucked behind part of the large bunker on the right-hand side of the green.

"I reasoned if I could make birdie, it would then put a lot of pressure on

Stewart,'' the New Zealand left-hander said. But his second shot from 150 yards out failed to clear the bunker by 12 inches and the gamble cost Charles $2,800. In bogeying, he finished tied for second with Shearer. Scott Simpson and Green played superb final rounds of 69, and Simpson finished in a most creditable tie for fourth with Owen.

It was a complete triumph for Ginn. It was his biggest win since turning professional in 1971, and it followed a victory in the New South Wales PGA and his second place showings on the Gold Coast and in the Victorian PGA.

Dunhill Australian Open Championship—A.$150,000
Winner: Jack Newton

For Jack Newton it was ectasy and recompense for that agonizing day at Carnoustie in 1975 when he three-putted the 72nd hole and eventually lost the British Open to Tom Watson. For Greg Norman it was agony. He three-putted the 72nd hole at Metropolitan and missed his chance for a play-off with Newton for the Australian Open title.

It was a magnificent tournament, full of emotion at the end, packed with exciting golf for the big crowds who attended. The Dunhill Company, in its first year of sponsorship, provided excellent organization. The course was in very good condition once the Committee eased the rough a little just off the fairways. It had been allowed to grow to such an extent that often players were better off being five yards off the fairway rather than five inches. The final day's play was one of the most fluctuating and fascinating seen in Australian golf in many years. By his own admission, Newton played "a load of rubbish" but still managed 72. He said later, "A few years ago I'd have shot 80 playing that way, now my concentration is so much better if things aren't going well."

There was little hint of the excitement to come on opening day. None of the really big names were at the top of the board and no one was able to break 70. Newton shot 74, Norman and Graham Marsh 73 and 76, respectively, Hubert Green 76, Fuzzy Zoeller 75, Gary Player 74, Seve Ballesteros 79 and Ed Sneed 80. The north wind blew fiercely from mid-day on, making it difficult for the players. It was one of those days which leaves a championship as wide open at the end as at the beginning. Strangely, Paul Hart, one of the leaders of the first day, was the player who hit the opening shot of the tournament. His 70 and the 70s of Trevor Johnson and Deray Simon owed a great deal to their skill with the putter.

David Graham, who had fired a 62 in the pro-am the previous day, had a 74, and followed that with a similar effort on Friday when conditions were quite different. The wind blew from the opposite direction and steady rain made things difficult, but Norman with a 69 and Marsh with a 68 surged to the top of the leaderboard. Both played excellent golf, with Norman, the blond, strapping Queenslander, showing immense length off the tee and carding five birdies in taking the lead at 142. He also had a little side contest with Fuzzy Zoeller to see which one of them could hit the longest drives. At $100 a crack. Norman was an easy winner, which provides some indication of his power; for Zoeller, when he lets out shaft, is a very big hitter indeed. Marsh putted well as he took second place at 144 and Jack Newton played a solid par round which left him just four shots off the lead at 146.

Some famous names barely survived the 152 cut, and one who missed it by 10 shots was Queensland pro Vaughan Somers. At the third hole in the second round he nine-putted in one of those bizarre incidents which sometimes afflicts golfers. "Just say I went off my head," he said later. "Tell them I missed a tricky four-inch downhill putt for an 11." It all happened when Somers charged his putt for par and went four feet past the hole and missed the return. He miscalculated trying to backhand the next, and suddenly started hitting the ball from either side of the hole, twice when it was still moving.

The third round brought the start of the Newton surge. Backed by a big gallery, the popular New South Welshman played some marvelous golf, marred only by a desperate triple-bogey at the third hole, where his six-iron approach was too strong. He had to chip out sideways, went too far, duffed his next shot and three-putted. It would have numbed a lot of golfers, but Newton bounced back with a great eagle at the par-five eighth and a birdie at the 14th.

Meanwhile, Marsh and Norman were engaged in a tremendous tussle, Marsh driving accurately and hitting his approaches to the heart of the green, Norman holding his lead intact although a little wayward off the tee. He was in eight bunkers during the round, so he was quite satisfied with his 73. When the leaderboards were completed at the end of a day in which conditions had been ideal, Norman at 215 was one stroke ahead of Newton and Scott Tuttle of the United States, with Marsh another stroke back. Lurking just behind them and still very much in contention at 218 were Player and Bob Shearer.

The final day was one to remember for Australian golf. Veteran golf watchers could not recall a more emotional and pressured finish to a tournament. First, Norman held the lead, playing in the last group with Tuttle and Shearer. Just in front of them on the course were Newton, Marsh and Player, and those six virtually had the tournament to themselves after the first few holes. When Tuttle and Player fell back, it became an all-Australian challenge with Newton slipping into the lead at the ninth. He had birdied the second and the fourth, bogeyed the fifth, but was still out in 36. Then came the change in the leaderboard when Norman double bogeyed the 10th.

Shearer had gone out in 39, two over the card. Suddenly he birdied holes 11 through 15, producing some of the magic so well-known to his Melbourne fans. With that dazzling spurt, he went a shot ahead of Newton with three holes left to play. It caused tremendous excitement. And just a little earlier, Newton had caused some excitement of his own, as he evoked a terrific roar from the crowd at the 15th when he chipped in from 50 feet to save his par. The previous hole he had double bogeyed and someone of lesser heart may have faded at that point.

Now Norman's putting was under pressure, though his driving and approach play were still holding together. He didn't miss a fairway in the 18 holes and only missed two greens in regulation. But twice, at 15 and 17, he missed vital putts and, when he came to the 18th tee, he knew he needed a par-four to tie with Newton, who had already finished at 288, with Marsh one shot higher. Marsh had birdied the last hole with a 20-foot putt.

Norman's drive on the 441-yard final hole was good, his approach left him 15 feet from the hole for his birdie and victory. But he charged the putt, finishing three feet past and the return putt spun out from what seemed to be the middle of the hole. "I just hit it a touch too hard," he said later. "It wasn't a bad putt." It was a costly one for Norman, however, for it meant a difference of $16,000 as well as the prized title for the rising young star.

Newton was generous in victory. He said, with obvious reference to Carnoustie, that he knew how Norman felt three-putting to lose the event. He added, "This is the greatest thrill of my life. When I began as a professional, I had two ambitions—to win the Australian Open and then the British Open. It almost worked in reverse but that's history now."

Western Australian 150th Anniversary Open—A.$150,000
Winner: Peter Jacobsen

Having an overseas player win an Australian anniversary tournament seemed almost indecent, but no one could begrudge Peter Jacobsen his success at Lake .Karrinyup in Perth, Western Australia. It must have been particularly pleasing for the 25-year-old Jacobsen, who hails from Portland, Oregon, because the field he beat included other American players such as Jerry Pate, Curtis Strange, John Schroeder, Bill Casper and Barry Jaeckel; the strong Australian contingent of Graham, Newton, Marsh, Ginn, Shearer, and Devlin; and overseas stars like Owen, Charles, Lister, Ballesteros, Nelford and Regalado.

His victory in the 150th Anniversary Western Australian Open was no fluke. He began by shooting 71, two shots behind the leaders Pate and Terry Gale, and went on with 70–70–68. Before the tournament began, Marsh had predicted that 12 under par 276 would win, but the course tamed all but Jacobsen.

The pre-tournament happenings tended to raise one or two eyebrows, since no one was certain if the event was being run by the Western Australian 150th Anniversary Committee, the Western Australia Golf Union or the PGA. Neither were they certain when the course was to be available for practice, or what the qualifying conditions were to be, or whether the small or the big ball was to be used. Fortunately, it was all sorted out before the start and PGA President, Peter Thomson, celebrated by winning the pro-am at Bunbury with a five under par 67.

Local bookmakers installed Graham Marsh as the favorite at 3–1 on the morning of the event. But the talented Australian was playing in the tournament under some duress. He should have been in Japan defending his Dunlop Phoenix title in a $300,000 event; and Japanese officials and Dunlop executives were not amused by Western Australia's insistence that Marsh play in Perth or by the fact that they exerted pressure on him to stay. It says a great deal for Marsh's hometown loyalty that he played in the Anniversary Open at all.

The week got off to a slightly wacky start when 70 players teed off at Mount Lawley to quality for the 72 spots still available in the tournament. It wasn't until the last trio had hit off that the imbalance in the numbers was noted. One or two faces turned a pale pink, and not from the hot sun either.

By the time the second day's play had been completed, the local golf fans were enthralled by the exciting playing of John Lister and Simon Owen of New Zealand, and by Seve Ballesteros, Jerry Pate, Barry Jaeckel and Jacobsen. The latter, although well-known in the States, had many scurrying for their record books to check his past performances. At the top of the leaderboard at 139, along with Lister, was Vaughan Somers, who shot a blistering 68.

Jacobsen strengthened his chances Saturday by slipping past Somers with his second 70, for 211. He drove the ball magnificently, putted very well, and no one looked more confident on the greens. His main problem was that locked in the lead with him was Bob Shearer, a non-winner on the Australian circuit for the year and hungry for success. His brilliant 67 was a typical Shearer effort, complete with straight driving, low raking irons into the greens and superb putting. And it began right on the first hole where he slotted a 15-footer. An eagle at the third really got him rolling. So, going into the final round, Shearer was the favorite, although Jacobsen was tied with him and Jerry Pate was just a stroke behind.

No one really gave Peter a chance against that pair of experienced campaigners, though everyone hoped he would play well enough to boost the spirits of his wife, who was under medical care in their Perth hotel. Play well enough? He killed off the rest of the field as though they were in second gear and he had moved into overdrive. At one stage Jacobsen came close to breaking the course record of 63 set by Gary Player back in 1974. He holed a good putt for a birdie on the first hole and, followed by the biggest golfing gallery ever seen in Perth, he proceeded to stride away from the field.

The further he went, the more solidly he struck the ball off the tee. He was seven under and had a three-stroke lead at the turn. Would he falter if real challengers appeared? He never made it possible to find out, as he pulled off successive birdies at 10, 11, 12 and 13. The latter one, with a 50-foot curling putt, brought a tremendous ovation from what was now a thoroughly pro-Jacobsen crowd.

He had one or two shaky moments at the 15th and 16th holes when he pushed his drives to the base of banksia trees, but he had such a cushion of strokes that it was simply a matter of hanging in. Finally, he won by five shots over David Graham, whose 284 edged out Charles, Marsh, Jaeckel and Ballesteros for second place by a stroke. Graham, Charles and Marshall had 70s in the last round and played well, the more credit to Jacobsen for his superb 68. Shearer and Pate ended with 75 and 74, respectively.

The local hero, Marsh, was in contention throughout, but his putting occasionally let him down. Graham was a bit wild off the tee; but Charles, with

69-70 on the final two days, was a possible threat to all of them. He was running in form at the right time, with the New Zealand circuit about to begin.

For Jacobsen, it was the biggest check of his career. Not even the Australian taxman's insistence on "borrowing" $10,000 of the $30,000 could dim the pleasure. It could mark the start of improved times for Jacobsen, as it has for other overseas players who have won their first tournaments in Australia. Ed Sneed, Bob Byman and Tom Kite are among those who have done well in Australia and been able to follow up with success in the United States.

South Seas Classic—F.$40,000
Winner: Rick Mallicoat

First Jacobsen, then Mallicoat. Just when Rick Mallicoat was in the depths of golfing despair, he produced a final-round 68 to beat Wayne Grady and Mike Ferguson by a stroke in the South Seas Classic in Fiji, and to make the hearts of his sponsors beat a little faster. Those sponsers, 10 in all from the Bel Air Club in Los Angeles, had indicated they would like to see some results from 26-year-old Mallicoat. Understandable. On the 1979 Australian circuit, his tournament earnings had totaled just $2,000. On the 6,908-yard Pacific Harbour Golf Club layout, he stormed home to snatch another $8,000 after starting the final round six shots behind Grady. He was assisted to a degree by the runners-up and Maurice Bembridge, all of whom let victory chances slip away over the finishing holes.

Grady had started the tournament with a magnificent 66, as well as with such a severe bout of sunburn that there were grave doubts if he would be able to conclude the event. It wasn't that he had been lazing by the pool at the delightful holiday resort. Rather, his right hand and face, exposed for the first time to the the Fiji sun, were badly swollen at the end of the day. Even with Grady on opening day was Ted Ball, inspired by a recent tip on his grip from Graham Marsh. Greg Norman was two strokes further back and California-born Mallicoat was with a large group at 71.

Mallicoat had plenty of problems. His wife Marsha, pregnant and ill, had flown home to America from New Zealand and money was running out. This was his fifth tournament on the circuit and his placings had been 42nd, 38th, 22nd and 11th the previous week in Dunedin. Although he shot 73 the second day, he still moved within four shots of Ball. All the leading players fell back that day, with Greg Norman filing a written complaint to the tournament committee over the pin placements. "This is not the U.S. Open," he said. "The layout is tough enough without sadistic pin placements."

Tempers were close to the surface in the 100-degree weather. In the past three years, the popular tournament, founded by Tom Ramsey, had been played in September, when the climate is more sultry than hot at the idyllic Pacific Harbour resort. Twice it has been sponsored by Gilbeys, this time it was by the Southern Pacific Hotel Corporation. (It seems Dunhill is interested for next year, following the success of their Australian golf sponsorships and a special exhibition involving Singapore cabinet ministers and Senior players Tommy Bolt, Art Wall, George Bayer and Jack Fleck.)

The event is the last chance for players to advance in the Order of Merit and gain exemption into some important international tournaments. It was particularly important for Stewart Ginn and Bob Shearer, who were within $4,000 of one another in the prize money list when the tournament began.

After the third round, Shearer was seven shots from the lead, which had reverted to Grady, who fired 70. It was made possible by some great work around the greens and some superb putting which brought him five birdies. He was only one shot ahead of Norman going into the last day. The latter came home in 32 and declared himself confident for the final round. "But I won't be playing defensively. If I win it will move me into fourth place in the Order of Merit and give me an exemption from qualifying for the British Open." With Mike Ferguson third at 213, the leaderboard looked a little like an advertisement for Queensland.

Ferguson looked to have the tournament in his grasp late in the final round. Norman's chances went with a double bogey seven at the 11th. Then Bembridge, two shots in the lead standing on the 12th tee, frittered away strokes with some indifferent putting. By the time the last group of Grady, Ferguson and Ball reached the 16th tee, Ferguson was two strokes ahead. But he missed a tiny putt at that hole and bogeyed the 17th, which Mallicoat had just birdied. Even so, with Mallicoat getting his par at the 399-yard 18th, Ferguson could still have forced a play-off with a par. His drive was good, but his nine-iron approach found the bunker and he took three more to get down. To make matters worse for Ferguson, Grady sank a long putt for a birdie at the 18th to tie him for second place. Those final three holes cost Ferguson thousands of dollars.

It was a wonderful victory for Mallicoat. He has been trying to acquire his player's card for four years in the States. "This win may have opened the door for me," he said, pocketing the $8,000 winner's check. This, and the previous victory by Peter Jacobsen in Perth, certainly opened the door for the young U.S. pair and put a damper on the Order of Merit aspirations of several Australian golfers.

12

THE NEW ZEALAND TOUR

The New Zealand Tour, a victim of Australia's growing program, shrunk to only two pre-Christmas tournaments in 1979: the Air New Zealand-Shell Open at Heretaunga in Wellington and the New Zealand Open at St. Clair in Dunedin. The Open at St. Clair replaced the usual Otago Charity Classic. It was not just the shrinking tournament list which depressed New Zealand enthusiasts. The weather at both tournaments was foul and extremely demanding on the players and the Heretaunga event was played in the sad aftermath of a major air crash in the Antartic.

David Graham, the lean Australian, brought to Heretaunga the fine form which had made 1979 such a good year for him. He played majestic golf to win New Zealand's richest event by the startling margin of eight strokes with a five under par total. Graham did not play at Dunedin and the popular Rodger Davis placed third there. With that and his second at Heretaunga, he just topped Graham as the top money winner. Behind them came New Zealand's Simon Owen, Australian Stewart Ginn, who won the Open, and Bob Charles, the veteran New Zealander.

Because the New Zealand PGA Championship, which is the final event each season in New Zealand, started in 1978 and finished on January 2, 1979, it was not reported in the previous edition of this book. Therefore, it should be noted that Charles capped his best season in recent years by capturing that event. Accounts of that championship and the two November-December events which took place later in 1979 follow in chronological order.

New Zealand PGA Championship—N.Z. $30,000
Winner: Bob Charles
Bob Charles looked like anything but a tournament winner as he putted out on the 18th green in the first round of the $30,000 New Zealand PGA Championship at Mt. Mauganui. He tapped a downhill 25-footer and then stalked the ball as it rolled toward the cup. Although the birdie putt dropped, it brought no joy to Charles. He couldn't get interested in the round which he took in 72 strokes, one over par. He just wanted to get off the course.

Three days later Charles walked off that same green, smiling widely after scoring his second victory in the PGA Championship. His first had come 17 years earlier when the championship was decided by match play.

Charles won by three strokes over Guy Wolstenholme, though in the early days of the tournament, it seemed as if the finish would be much closer. In the opening round, the lead was shared by two Australians, Paul Firmstone and Bill Dunk; and two New Zealanders, Richard Coombes and Barry Vivian. All had shot three under par 68s. It was disappointing scoring on the scorching hot day. As Dunk said, "I don't think 68 is a good score around here."

Lurking ominously with a 70 was a three-time winner of the event, John Lister. He had a typical Lister round: one eagle, five birdies, three bogeys and a triple bogey. But he was playing better than in any other of his New Zealand appearances that season and his putting had been sharpened when he adopted a more upright stance.

On day two, Lister broke through with 66, a score which wasn't bettered during the week. He had five birdies and said afterwards, "I played as well yesterday—the bad breaks cost me. Today I hit some bad shots but managed to recover. At crucial times I made the right putts." His two-round total of 136 was a stroke behind that of defending champion Simon Owen. Firmstone was the only survivor of the first-round leaders, shooting a 71 for a tie at 139 with Terry Kendall and with Charles, who had shot a 67.

New Year's Eve followed the second round and it was to have an effect on the tournament. Lister danced in the New Year and, when he left for home, he felt a twitch in his back. He had a rub before he teed off, but the muscle injury grew worse, and the round deteriorated. He had a disappointing 80.

By the day's end, the tournament was down to five men. Owen and Charles had the third-round lead at 206, seven under. Owen had a 69 and Charles another 67. Two strokes back were Guy Wolstenholme, who should have won the previous year, and Kendall. At 209 was Bob Beauchemin, a young Canadian left-hander who had shot a record 30 (six under) on the back nine in the second round.

Owen had complained that he had not had one decent putting round in the tournament and hoped that the final day would produce it. It didn't and he fell back to 75 and third. Wolstenholme chased Charles home. After nine holes, Charles led by three. However, two bogeys followed and by the 13th he led Wolstenholme by only one stroke. The par-five 15th was to be decisive. Wolstenholme missed his birdie, Charles didn't and the margin was then two shots.

The 17th, a demanding par-three, was even more decisive. Charles, feeling the pressure, fell off his tee shot and put it in an impossible position. Wolstenholme was three feet from a two. Charles chipped up to within 12 feet and made the putt for his par. Wolstenholme missed. "It was an impossible three," said Charles. "When my putt snuck in on the edge, I think it must have shattered Guy." Wolstenholme bogeyed the last hole, but he still held second by a stroke. Charles had a 71 and it was typical of the last-day scoring that only Dunk with 70, Ross Morpeth with 69 and Harry Berwick and Murrary Young with 68s could better par. Charles' four-round total of 277 was seven under.

Air New Zealand-Shell Open—N.Z.$75,000
Winner: David Graham

Before the Air New Zealand-Shell Open even started, David Graham, the hottest player in the field, indicated that he wished to withdraw. Fellow Australians Bob Shearer and Rodger Davis went along with him. But it wasn't a walkout. As the three were playing the pro-am before the tournament with top New Zealand officials such as former Prime Minister Sir John Marshall and Governor-General Designate Justice David Beattie, Air New Zealand, the major sponsor, suffered a tragic loss. A fully laden DC10 on a sightseeing flight to the Antarctic slammed into the slopes of Mount Erebus, killing all 257 on board. Abruptly, golf seemed unimportant.

There was no excitement when the players teed off in the first round, as workmen scurried around taking down the Air New Zealand advertising signs. The flags were lowered to half mast. The organizers met in hurried session. Morrie Davis, Air New Zealand chief executive, had been told of the tragedy while still at the course during the pro-am and was whisked back to his Auckland headquarters late Wednesday night. The next morning he pleaded with the golfers, as a personal favor, to go on with the tournament. Graham and the others agreed to his request, which came after the PGA had released both Air New Zealand and Shell from any contractual obligations for the tournament. As in showbiz, the show had to go on.

The air crash was not the only thing to mar the tournament. In 1976, when Simon Owen won the New Zealand Open at Heretaunga, then with a vastly different layout, the wind had not played much of a part in the fortunes of the players. Instead, it was the rough which was the downfall of players who strayed from the narrow fairways. By 1979, however, the sponsors had exerted influence on the club. The rough was nicely under control, the greens speedy, if a little bobbly, and the fairways offered a good cushion for a sweetly hit ball.

Rain had been scarce before tournament week. Far from being spongy as many players had expected, the greens required overnight watering before they would hold a ball. But the officials at Wellington Golf Club, which has a proud history stretching back to the beginnings of the area, were unable to do anything about the wind. At least, it didn't rain. At least, it was warm. But after the tournament the players said that they had never encountered such wind.

On Tuesday, the practice day, the winds were gusting up to 60 knots from the northwest. There was a lull during the pro-am, but the wind resumed in the first round and built up during the rest of the week, maintaining a steady westerly blast of up to 58 knots. Good, consistent golf was impossible.

"How do you live in this wind?" asked Graham. "How does a golfer hang on to a swing?" The locals answered the first question as they swayed backwards into the breeze to maintain balance. He, himself, answered the second question. Before the tournament started, Bob Charles had predicted Graham would win the tournament. Charles, who had finished close behind Graham in Perth the previous week, was not playing badly himself, but the first-round eyes were definitely on Tom Kite, who eagled the par-five 18th on the first day to go from two under into a two-stroke lead over Rodger Davis, Barry Vivian, Rick Barker and Brian Jones with his 67. But after the first day, Kite was never again a real force.

In the second round, it was Graham who fired the four under 67 for 137. One of the others around was a 27-year-old pro from Jackson Hole, Wyoming, named John Godwin, who shot 72-67. Godwin, who had tried the U.S. Tour in 1975, admitted that if he were to win he would be the most surprised man on the course. Davis was up there. So was Simon Owen. When Owen added a third-round 72 to his first two par-71s, he looked to be the real challenger. But the gutsiest performance came from Davis.

One of the most popular players in Australasia, Davis rushed away from the course Friday to shower and change in his hotel before attending an official function. Getting into his bath, he slipped and fell. When he regained consciousness, the bathroom was rolling around his head and blood was everywhere from a gash in his chin. The cut took 11 stitches to close. His jaw sore and aching, Davis went to the practice fairway the next morning to try to find a swing that would give him a chance to continue. That he found one—he was never sure where—was a miracle in itself. He punched his irons with virtually no follow-through, twirling away to avoid touching his tender jaw. He managed a one over 72 to hold second place going into the last round.

Out in front and looking really good was Graham. There was no hassle to his step on the course. He was totally in control. After all, he had a five-shot cushion over Davis with just 18 holes to play. For the first time, New Zealand television got behind a golf tournament, showing almost every shot played on the last five holes in the final two days. The coverage was exhaustively advertised, so it was not surprising that on the final day, when the winds were reaching their most miserable heights, the galleries had a distinct absence of spectators. Graham kept on smiling. After his 70–76–69 start, produced with the aid of a new putter bought the previous week, David played it cool during the front nine.

Nobody made a move. Of all the players close, not one was able to muster a charge. Some of the best golf of the tournament had come in the third round from Mexican Victor Regalado, whose 68 in the conditions was superb golf. Although he managed a 73 in the final round, he could do no better than tie for third with Charles. The New Zealander was one of the only three players, the others being John Lister and Terry Kendall, to match par in the final round. Lister had blown his chances with a third-round 81, while a starting 78 hadn't helped Kendall. But he still climbed to ninth with subsequent rounds of 73, 71 and 71.

They had all started too far back. The start to the week naturally had not helped and it was not until the 67th hole, when Graham double bogeyed to drop back to three under for the tournament, that the tournament really came alive. At that stage, Davis, a hole in front, was only two shots from the lead. Trying to steer his drive across the wind, Graham had ended up in a grove of trees. He played up an adjacent fairway, then over clubbed his third. He flew the green and only the gallery prevented him from disappearing into the bushes. "If I had gone in there, I was looking at an eight," he afterwards admitted. But a little chip and two putts got him down with a double bogey six. Davis missed his big chance there for the $12,500 first prize. Three consecutive bogeys on the closing stretch took him away from the lead and he eventually finished with a 76, eight shots back.

There were no other traumas for Graham. Playing No. 18, he produced one of the best shots of the tournament on the 555-yard par-five. His one-iron flew 280 yards pin high to shut out the field—73 and 279, winner by eight strokes.

Although he managed a two-putt birdie to close, he still retired the new putter in dissatisfaction. "You want it?" he asked Aussie golf writer Tom Ramsay during the interviews later. "You got it!"

New Zealand Open—N.Z.$50,000
Winner: Stewart Ginn

The 63rd New Zealand Open brought the dapper Stewart Ginn his first major success in New Zealand, and Ginn deserved his victory. In wildly fluctuating weather, he performed steadily while nearly all the others had scores to match the vagaries of the playing conditions. Although only 29, Ginn has been on the New Zealand circuit for seven years. His was a popular victory. He attributed it to concentrated practice with his putter after a disappointing performance in the Airlines Classic at Heretaunga. He had seemed quite unable to find the hole there, but at St. Clair, his putting was a marvel of consistency.

He was only one of the crowd after a spectacular first day when, in excellent conditions, 20 players broke par, 12 of them in the 60s. Ted Ball, the chain-smoking, 40-year-old Australian, whose swing approaches the speed of light, shot clear with an astonishing 63, eight under. It was a record for the new St. Clair layout. He made a modest opening with five pars. Then, with authoritative irons and superb putting, he had a run of six birdies. He went seven under with another at No. 13 and at the 14th, a 528-yard par-five, he sank a 35-foot putt for an eagle. The magic, however, left him then and did not return. He was bunkered at 17 and dropped a shot. Still, his brilliant display left him two ahead of Simon Owen, who played an almost-faultless round. He, too, started quietly but eagled nine, and birdied 10, 11, 14 and 15. Ball had only 23 putts, Owen almost as few. Rodger Davis, still wearing stitches in the side of his jaw after his mishap at Heretaunga, turned five under, but then the putts started slipping away and he finished at 67 with Britain's Martin Foster and Bob Charles.

The knowing ones, in discussing Ball's great score, recalled the previous New Zealand Open at Wanganui. There Ball led the field by six shots going into the final round, but in appalling weather blew it with a 78 and finished fourth, three shots behind Bob Shearer. The popular Ball suffered a somewhat similar fate at St. Clair. The weather on the second day was bitterly cold; only five broke par this time and only one player shot in the 60s, and that was Ginn with a 68. Among the failures was Ball with, yes, a 78. It was a struggle for everyone in the Antartic temperatures, but Ginn's persistence and competence gave him a par on the first nine and birdies at 17 and 18 put him three under for the round.

But Owen, wearing a pair of especially warm gloves, was still there with his 71. Another who finished with a par round was Brian Barnes of Britain, who had the foresight to put on a pair of long johns. At that stage, Owen looked like a winner. He not only led with 136, two in front of Ginn and Charles, but also was playing particularly well. However, on the back nine he lipped out six times. In the rain, hail and strong winds, Foster's driver went sour and he was not sighted again.

Owen held Ginn at bay on Saturday and kept his two-stroke lead going into the final 18 holes. Charles fell well back, so Ginn's nearest challenger for second place was Barnes, at 211 two behind Ginn. In the final round, Ginn continued on his methodical way, parring the first eight holes and surging into the lead with birdies at holes No. 9, 10 and 14. He finished two under at 69. But it was heartbreak all the way for Owen. He dropped a shot after being bunkered at the first hole, then played steadily enough until the sixth. If a single shot cost Owen the title, it was his eight-iron there. It put him in an almost impossible position in a flax bush and he took a double bogey. Then he three-putted No. 12 to go four over for the day. Owen made a brave effort the rest of the way, but could get only one shot back. He was feeling that the holes "seemed to have lids on them today." And Ginn was closing the door firmly with precise putting as he finished a comfortable three shots in front. Australian Brian Jones shot a spectacular 64 to jump into sixth place and Terry Gale climbed into fourth with a 67.

13

THE LPGA TOUR

Nancy Lopez did not win five consecutive tournaments in 1979. Aside from that, however, her second year on the Ladies Professional Golf Association Tour was virtually identical to her first. Lopez was again, without question, the dominant LPGA golfer and her personal magnetism was the most obvious factor in the circuit's continued popularity growth. Although Melton reaffirmed her individual role, and did so despite some healthy and formidable challengers, the LPGA and commissioner Ray Volpe were not without headaches.

Of all professional sports tours, the LPGA benefited the most from the sponsorship of Colgate-Palmolive. Now, it is entering the 1980's with that support drastically reduced following the retirement of David Foster as Colgate's chief executive officer. As Volpe said, "David Foster and his emphasis on sports promotion . . . was the initial catalyst to make the LPGA go." After Colgate's budget trimming, the LPGA retained the highly successful Colgate-Dinah Shore Winners Circle but lost the sponsorships of the Colgate Triple Crown, Colgate European Open and Colgate Far East Open. The times ahead may be rockier than expected for the LPGA but, thankfully, there is Nancy Lopez Melton.

In her first complete season, Lopez won those five tournaments in a row and, in the process, lifted the LPGA from the back sports pages into the headlines across America and the world. She meant more to her sport than any performer since Arnold Palmer and millions waited to see what she would do for an encore, some perhaps wishing, in twisted logic, that she would fail. She did not. In fact, she gained even more respect for ability to handle with extraordinary grace the pressures of life in a fishbowl. For 1979 she had a partner in this venture. On January 6 she married Tim Melton, a television sports announcer whom she met at the Lady Keystone Open, during the week, incidentally, that her winning streak was ended. As the year came to a close, she could say with typical modesty, "I am happy about my career, my marriage, my life."

Lopez played in six fewer tournaments in 1979, yet matched her nine-victory total and won nearly $10,000 more, leading the official money list with a record $197,488 and topping $200,000 overall. Even her worst finish, a tie for 13th place, was darn good. She was in the top 10 for 16 of 19 tournaments. She won the Vare Trophy with a 71.20 stroke average, considerably lower than her record 71.76 of the previous year, and nearly a full stroke better than the second-best average (Jane Blalock's 72.15). Considering those statistics alone, one might conclude that it was a one-woman show, which it certainly was not. Amy Alcott and Pat Bradley, for instance, had more top-10 finishes than did Lopez, with 17 each. Blalock won three tournaments by six strokes, wire-to-wire. Seven other players had $100,000-plus seasons, and Sandra Post's $178,750 for the runner-up position was less than $20,000 off Lopez's total, whereas Nancy had a margin of over $70,000 in 1978.

There were 17 tournament winners, with Blalock and Alcott having four victories each, and Sally Little, JoAnne Carner and Post having three each. Post repeated as champion in the prestigious Colgate-Dinah Shore Winner's Circle in a duel to the wire against Lopez. Carner opened the season by winning the Colgate Triple Crown and had three victories in eight weeks; then a motorcycle accident kept her from a truly sensational year. Donna Caponi Young and Jerilyn Britz were among the 10 players with one triumph each, but their wins were of the highest caliber, in the LPGA Championship and United States Open, respectively. And Beth Daniel won the Patty Berg Classic, as well as $97,206 in her first year, providing further evidence that the "L" in LPGA doesn't always mean Lopez.

Nancy Lopez and her father, Domingo, celebrate her ninth victory of the year in the Colgate European Open.

Three-time winners in 1979
—JoAnne Carner (above
left), *Sally Little* (above)
and Sandra Post (left).

Jane Blalock (above left) *and Amy Alcott* (above right) *each won four tournaments.*

Colgate Triple Crown—$100,000
Winner: JoAnne Carner

JoAnne Carner has a definite advantage in match play. She may not be better than the rest, but everyone believes she is. Pat Bradley called her "the master of match play" after losing, 4 and 3, in the final of the Colgate Triple Crown Championship. Carner successfully defended her title, dominating her opponents at Mission Hills Country Club in all four rounds of the LPGA's only match play tournament. She also beat Debbie Massey, 5 and 4; Sandra Post, 3 and 2; and Silvia Bertolaccini, 5 and 4.

Her reputation stems from her amateur career—she won the U.S. Amateur five times—and JoAnne clearly relishes it. "The more people talk about it, the better I like it," she said. "It's like starting one-up." Carner, 39 years old, was 30 before she joined the professional tour and settled into the routine of medal tournaments. She won not only those National Amateur titles but also the Women's Western, Trans-Miss, Northwest, Eastern, Pacific Northwest, Southwest and Doherty Challenge Cup events. She concluded her amateur play after winning an LPGA tournament, the 1969 Burdines Invitational. As an LPGA rookie, she won again in the Wendell West Open, then in 1971 she stopped Donna Caponi Young's bid for three consecutive U.S. Open victories. She was winless for the next two years, but produced six victories in 1974 and has been among the LPGA's most consistent players ever since.

She had no real challenger in the Colgate Triple Crown. Her semifinal against Bertolaccini was over just as the television coverage was starting. For the final, PBS put the match on video tape for a delayed telecast. Carner birdied three of the first five holes against Bertolaccini and was four-up after nine. She also crushed Bradley from the start, scoring an eagle on the second hole. Bradley bogeyed the third and fourth holes, while Carner birdied the fourth and was three up. She kept that margin through nine holes and halted Bradley's comeback by winning the 11th hole.

While the result was almost predictable, the tournament at Mission Hills Country Club began with a couple of surprises: snow in Palm Springs, California, and a first-round loss by Nancy Lopez. The two inches of snow, a record for Palm Springs, forced a cancellation of the pro-am. Then Lopez, although shooting under par, was beaten on the second extra hole in the opening round by Bertolaccini. Other gallery favorites, Jan Stephenson and Sally Little, were also knocked into the consolation bracket. Lopez and Little won all three of their consolation matches, frequently with galleries as large as those following Carner's steady march to the championship.

Elizabeth Arden Classic—$100,000
Winner: Amy Alcott

Amy Alcott was ready to step forward and accept the winner's check when Sandra Post drilled a four-wood to the flag, scored an eagle, and forced a play-off in the Elizabeth Arden Classic. Before Alcott could take her $15,000 prize, she had to play three extra holes, finally holing a 20-foot birdie putt from the edge of that fateful 18th green.

"Sure, I thought I had it in the bag," said Alcott, who finished in the group ahead of Post. "No one hits the 18th green in two. An eagle? Maybe, if you chip it in."

Post's daring play and her unwillingness to take a comfortable par for second place produced a dramatic conclusion to the LPGA's first official event of 1979. "I knew my only chance was an eagle," she said. "So I didn't hesitate about using my driver off the tee. It was either a three or I didn't care what."

The 18th hole of the Country Club of Adventura's South Course in Miami covers 485 yards, and the green is protected by water on the right. The pin was set toward the front, improving Post's chances. She explained, "I had enough confidence in my ability to reach the green in two and make the putt, even though I hadn't done it all week. I had been laying up with a nine-iron and then taking a wedge to the green. Of course, I had never birdied the hole before, either."

Post covered the flag with that four-wood, her shot stopping two feet beyond. Then Alcott, watching from the scorer's tent, said to her caddy, "It looks like we've got a play-off." She described her feelings in a subsequent column for *Golf World* magazine: "Sandra told me, 'I knew exactly what you were thinking when I made that eagle. Your throat had fallen to your feet.' And she certainly was right."

U.S. Open Champion Hollis Stacy shot 69 in the first round and led Alcott and Sandra Palmer by one stroke. Alcott shot another 70 in the second round and was two strokes ahead of Post. They were tied after three rounds, with Alcott shooting 72 and Post 70. Both had 73s in the fourth round for 285 totals, three strokes better than Pat Bradley and Jan Stephenson, while Palmer and Stacy tied for 12th place.

Player of the Year Nancy Lopez, starting the season with inflammation in her arms, tied for ninth place. And Judy Rankin, who led the LPGA for two years before Lopez arrived, failed to qualify for the last round. It was the first cut Rankin had ever missed.

Her tendonitis aside, Lopez was at ease, having recently married Tim Melton, a television sportscaster whom she met in 1978 in Hershey, Pennsylvania. She told reporters in Miami, "I always worried before if something should happen to me and I couldn't play golf any more. A lot of girls don't have any place to go. That's why they stay on the tour. Now I have a place to go and I have someone to fall back on. I feel a lot stronger mentally."

Melton was to be joining her on the tour on his days off. "Tim tries not to say to me, 'I wish you weren't going,' because he knows it would put a lot of pressure on me," Nancy said. "But I'm more lonely now than I was when I wasn't married, because I'm away from him. At night I'm very lonely. You get used to being with somebody and you get spoiled. I guess that's the only thing that bothers me."

Orange Blossom Classic—$75,000
Winner: Jane Blalock

A few golfers seem to thrive under the worst conditions. It can be said that Jane Blalock had the wind in her favor, with gusts to 25 and 30 miles an hour, when she won the Orange Blossom Classic for a second time. "I don't fear the wind," said Blalock, who held an impressive six-stroke margin. "I attack courses more when it's windy."

Sandra Post was second, conceding the victory, which she refused to do the previous week before losing a play-off to JoAnne Carner. "As good as Jane is in the wind and as good as she was playing, I had to be realistic," Post said. "I knew I was playing for second place." Silvia Bertolaccini held second at the start of the last round, then fell behind Post, Carner and Pat Bradley.

There was not a trace of wind at St. Petersburg, Florida, during the first round when Blalock shot 66, six under par and the best score of her career, for a two-stroke lead over Connie Chillemi at Pasadena Golf Club. Jan Stephenson caused an uproar that day over a warning for slow play, claiming she was harassed by LPGA officials. "It bothered me, but I let it bother me," she said. "I was in tears out there. It cost me five shots and totally broke my concentration." Her score was 72.

Bertolaccini had a miraculous first nine in the second round, despite the high winds, but Blalock didn't even notice the challenge. The Argentine holed a six-iron shot for eagle on the first hole, made birdies on five of the next six holes, and was seven under par after seven. She missed a putt from less than three feet on the ninth, but still tied an LPGA record with her 29. Blalock said she saw those scores, "but I just figured it was a mistake."

Blalock continued to shoot 69 while Bertolaccini struggled to finish with 67 and was three strokes behind. Bertolaccini thought she could still win, saying, "I have a chance." But Dale Lundquist disagreed, having been paired with Blalock for two rounds. "No one is going to beat Jane the way she's playing," Lundquist said. Two days later, after a postponement because of rain, Lundquist was proven correct.

Finishing with 70 and 205, 11 under par, Blalock said her ambition for the year was "to be No. 1, and if that means I have to beat Nancy Lopez, then that's what I want to do. [Lopez was not entered.] I don't mind that she wasn't here," Blalock said. "I opened up a magazine and she's all I saw. It was like it was her personal scrapbook. There are a lot of good players out here being ignored. I'm not saying I'm one of them. It's just that I'm out here to be No. 1. If it takes beating her week in and week out, I'll do my best."

Bent Tree Classic—$100,000

Winner: Sally Little

The understatement of the year came from Sally Little at the conclusion of the Bent Tree Classic in Sarasota, Florida. "I never used to be able to handle the pressure," she said. "I guess I did okay today."

Tied with Nancy Lopez after 10 holes, Little scored four consecutive birdies to spring clear with four holes remaining. Lopez then could not catch her, even with two birdies, and Little was secure with her third professional victory. "I've been on the tour for seven years," said Little, a 27-year-old South African, "and finally I'm demonstrating some maturity."

Surprising Dale Lundquist was also a contender, sharing the lead with Little and Lopez with nine holes remaining. All had pars on the 10th and birdies on the 11th. Little continued her string of birdies through the 14th, building a solid margin of four strokes on Lopez and two strokes on Lundquist. Lopez took second place with a two-shot deficit and Lundquist, who had problems in finishing, made a clutch birdie at the 18th hole to tie JoAnn Washam for third. Little's final round was 67, five under par, for a 278 total. Lopez finished with 68 for 280, two strokes ahead of Washam and Lundquist.

Little is best known for her dramatic victory in the 1976 Women's International, when she holed a bunker shot on the 18th to defeat Jan Stephenson by one stroke. She was 13th on the money list that year, then climbed to 10th place in 1977, then to eighth place in 1978 with $84,895 and a victory in the Kathryn Crosby/Honda Civic Classic. There, she also beat Lopez, winning the title in a play-off. "My goal was to be ready for California," Sally said. "I wanted to be prepared for the defense of my Honda Civic title. I guess I peaked a little early."

The Bent Tree Classic was Nancy Lopez's first as a defending champion, marking the anniversary of the start of that incredible 1978 season in which she won nine tournaments, including five in a row, and set an LPGA record with earnings of $189,813. "It's kind of weird," she said. "I've never defended a title before as a pro. It feels funny."

Lopez had left Miami two weeks earlier, having problems with her arms, and didn't play golf while she was away from the tour, finding 14 inches of snow at her home in Pennsylvania. Surprisingly, Lopez was free of pain and was able to play well. She may have been buoyed by the exceptionally warm weather. She posted 71 in the first round, then came back with 67 to tie Donna Horton White and rookie Lori Garbacz for the lead after 36 holes. Little then was one stroke behind, having scored an eagle on the 18th for her 67 in the second round.

Garbacz fell to 79 in the third round, but Lundquist played steadily and tied for the lead before eventually sharing third place. "That's the biggest gallery that has ever followed me," Lundquist exclaimed. "When I would hear the applause, I would almost laugh. They were clapping for me. It seemed funny. But I did love it."

A final note regarding Mickey Wright, who has heard as many cheers as any LPGA golfer. Her hole-in-one on the 136-yard seventh hole was her first since 1963. She said, "I guess 16 years is long enough to wait."

Sunstar Classic—$100,000

Winner: Nancy Lopez

Before Nancy Lopez won the Sunstar Classic, some people were asking her, "What's wrong with your game?"

Well, there was nothing wrong, other than that trouble with tendonitis to start the year, and even then Nancy tied for ninth place in the Elizabeth Arden Classic. She was under par for all four rounds of the Sunstar in Los Angeles and beat Hollis Stacy by one stroke with a 10-foot birdie putt on the 72nd hole. Without question, she was relieved to have won so early in the year.

It was 1978 all over again, for Lopez was the defending champion. (She also was defending in the Bent Tree Classic. Someone pointed out that, for instance, JoAnne Carner took eight years to repeat a victory, while Lopez needed just 53 weeks.)

She had no tendonitis to worry about and she was in a superb frame of mind. "I played my heart out on the back nine and really concentrated," Nancy said. "I think my game has improved 90 percent since I first started as a pro. I felt like I was just a little kid out there last year. I was nervous and actually never quite knew what was happening."

The crowds had tripled because of Lopez's emergence over the past year. The tour was much healthier because of her, yet some LPGA players were increasingly irritable about the tremendous attention that Lopez received from the spectators and the media. Even while Stacy was in the lead, and she began the last day with a two-stroke margin, Lopez had the larger gallery following. In an interview, Stacy remarked, "What am I supposed to say? That Nancy is better than I am? No way. I'm as good as Lopez."

Stacy, the U.S. Open champion for two years, felt she lost the tournament on the first nine. The eighth and ninth holes at Rancho Park were par-fives. Stacy played both holes conservatively for pars, while Lopez went for the greens and scored birdies. "I wasn't aggressive enough," Stacy said. "This was the same as match play. When you play head-to-head with Nancy, you had better play damned good."

Lopez drew even with Stacy with those birdies and kept plugging along for pars until the final hole. Twice Stacy went ahead with birdies, then dropped back with bogeys. Lopez's eight-under-par 280 total consisted of rounds of 70, 71, 70 and 69, while Stacy finished with 72 for her 281 total.

Despite greens that were somewhat bumpy, other outstanding scores included opening-round 68s by Sandra Spuzich, Jerilyn Britz and young Vicki Fergon. Stacy recorded seven birdies and shot 66 in the second round for the best score of the tournament. Hollis led after the second and third rounds, followed by Dale Lundquist, then by Lopez and Sue Berning. Kathy Whitworth and Marlene Floyd also posed threats but fell away.

Peggy Conley finished well, posting 69 to match Lopez's final round, and tied Sue Berning for third place in the highest finish of her brief career. Pat Bradley and Laura Baugh were tied for fifth. Still seeking her first victory after six years, Baugh disclosed her goals for 1979: To be among the top 10 money winners and to lower her stoke average to the 72 range. "If I do that," she said, "I will win."

Honda Civic Classic—$150,000
Winner: JoAnne Carner

The Honda Civic Classic was typical of the early tournaments. The first three finishers were also the first three on the money list for the year—JoAnne Carner, followed closely by Sandra Post and Pat Bradley. Carner won by three strokes, but it was more of a contest than that margin would indicate. Bradley led after three rounds, then Carner and Post were tied with nine holes remaining.

Although they were one hole apart, Carner and Post felt as if they were in a match. Perhaps that was an advantage for Carner, who earlier won the Colgate Triple Crown in match play. Post went ahead briefly with a birdie on the 11th, then Carner hit a seven-iron to four feet on the par-three 13th. The next moment, Post had her "first bad swing of the day," made bogey, and was one stroke behind. "I knew I was playing Sandra in match play," Carner said. "I knew after the 13th that she had to make a birdie to tie me, so I played conservatively so she could make the mistakes."

That most costly error came on the 17th tee. Post hit a drive that literally was buried in the rough. "I was three feet from the ball and had to ask the marshals where it was," Post said. "That's how deeply buried it was." She could hardly move an iron through the six-inch rough and her second shot was far short of the green. She took double bogey with a chip and three putts from 12 feet. Post then tied Bradley for second place, that being her third runner-up finish of the year. "I'm not upset with being second," Post said. "It pays awfully well and with the competition we have on the tour now, you have to play well just to finish second. And it's the next best thing to winning." Post and Bradley each received $12,600 while Carner earned $22,500, taking first place in the standings with $31,800. Post was second with $31,146 and Bradley third with $31,050.

Nayoko Yoshikawa, a 30-year-old Japanese pro who plays few tournaments in the United States, tied Vivian Brownlee for the first round lead with 68, four under par at Rancho Bernardo Inn in San Diego. Neither Brownlee nor Yoshikawa, who was second in Miami a year ago in her first American tournament, broke par again and they finished more than 10 strokes off Carner's 281 total, seven under par. Bradley went in front with 67 in the second round for a 138 total, while Post was at 141 and Carner 143. Bradley finished with two 73s, Carner with two 69s, and Post with 72 and 71.

The course was softened by three overnight rains, including a downpour that flooded the first and second holes before the third round. Play began that day on the third hole, allowing time for the water to drain off. Bradley might have secured the victory then, but instead she dropped three strokes on the last five holes.

National Pro-Am

Winner: Nancy Lopez

From the stage of Caesar's Palace, Frank Sinatra said, "Nancy, you're already a legend." And so Nancy Lopez was, breaking two records while winning the National Pro-Am. Over 20,000 people were out to see Lopez's second consecutive victory and her 11th in 37 tournaments as a professional.

This was the first LPGA tournament in Las Vegas since the Sealy Desert Inn Classic in 1974 (and the first professional tournament since 1976, the final year of the men's Sahara Invitational). Winter rules were in effect, with rain and temperatures in the 50s early in the week. The sunshine returned for the opening two rounds, which involved 216 amateurs and 72 professionals over two courses—Sahara Country Club and Las Vegas Country Club.

Lopez, who did not play in the Honda Civic Classic, started with a one-over-par 72 at Sahara, while JoAnne Carner set a course record with 64. "I'm tired, but I guess I play better when I'm tired," said Carner, the Honda Civic champion. Donna Caponi Young was second with 66, then shot 69 on the Las Vegas CC course and took the lead from Carner, who had 73. That day Lopez climbed within four strokes of first place with her course-record 67, six under par, including four birdies and an eagle. Husband Tim Melton had something to do with it, advising Nancy, "If you want to stay in this game, you had better start getting aggressive." She then birdied three holes in a row.

After 36 holes the amateurs departed, leaving the pros to decide the championship at Sahara. Behind Young at 135 were Carner at 137, Penny Pulz at 138, and Lopez, Judy Rankin, Chako Higuchi and Amy Alcott at 139. Young maintained her lead in the third round with 68, but Lopez again drew the galleries with her record 31 on the first nine and her 66 for the day. She was only two strokes behind Young and three ahead of the third-place golfer, Higuchi, who shot 69. After that round, Young wouldn't say Lopez was putting pressure on her. "I just have to play my own game, that's all," Young said. "She [Lopez] has no fears. She's so strong she can execute every shot. I'm going to have to shoot 68 to win the tournament."

Young did not need 68. She could have won with 70, but shot 73 while Lopez won by two strokes with 69 and a 274 total, including a birdie on the final hole. "I gave it to her on the front side," said Young, recounting three bogeys and a double bogey. While Young was playing the seventh hole, Lopez was finishing the ninth and glanced at the scoreboard, seeing that she was only one stroke behind. "I knew I had to be patient," Lopez said, "so I slowed my swing down." Nancy promptly bogeyed the 10th. Young was finding more trouble behind, so that didn't matter. All Lopez needed were pars on the remaining holes and she got one birdie for good measure.

Women's Kemper Open—$150,000
Winner: JoAnne Carner

For the first time in her career, Nancy Lopez could not hold a lead and, as a result, JoAnne Carner won the Women's Kemper Open in a five-way play-off. Carner's third victory of the year seemed unlikely until Lopez bogeyed four of the last eight holes, including the 16th and 17th. Nancy still might have won, having a 12-foot putt for birdie on the last hole. That one lipped the cup but wouldn't fall in. "I felt like crying," Lopez said. Instead she went to the first tee in an international play-off with Carner, Donna Caponi Young, Japan's Chako Higuchi and Australia's Jan Stephenson.

"I thought all week I had a chance to win," Carner said. "I was always within four shots of the lead. When we got in the play-off, then I really liked my chances, because it was match play time again." Only Carner and Higuchi were left after the first extra hole. Lopez and Young missed four-foot putts and Stephenson chipped poorly, all taking bogeys.

On the 165-yard second hole, Higuchi was putting from 40 feet and Carner from 18 feet. Higuchi was eight feet short on her first try, easing the pressure on Carner, who putted close enough for a safe par. The Japanese pro then missed again and Carner increased her bankroll by $22,500, bringing her total to $84,300 for the year, including her unofficial Colgate Triple Crown victory.

Carner's rounds were 72, 71, 72 and 71 for a 286 total, two over par on the Mesa Verde Country Club course in Costa Mesa, California. The course in rolling terrain, more like an Eastern course than those typical of Southern California, earned the golfers' respect. As Carner said, "This course, with the pins cut in tough positions and the very long rough, beat everybody this week." Lopez also was impressed, saying, "I would love to play this course every day."

The pro-am was canceled and the opening round was delayed because of rain, which softened the greens so that the scores were low in the first two rounds. Higuchi was in the second group and shot 69 with four birdies and two bogeys. Sandra Post almost caught her, but missed a two-foot putt on the last hole and was in the second-place group at 70. Lopez and Young were among those with 71s and Carner was another stroke behind. After two rounds Higuchi was joined in first place at 139 by Lopez and Sally Little, both having 68s. Carner, Young and Stephenson were all four strokes behind at that stage.

The third round was most notable in the play of Beth Daniel, in her first year on the tour, advancing from the Furman University *men's* team, for whom she played several matches during her last year. Daniel was the leader of the LPGA qualifying school and, of all the young players, seems the most likely challenger to Lopez in future years. For the first time, she was a threat to Nancy, shooting 71 for a 213 total. Lopez was two strokes ahead after a disappointing 72. "I played poorly," she said. "I had to scramble a lot and made some stupid mistakes. I wasn't satisfied with my putting at all. I'm just happy to be where I am because I like the pressure. And if I don't win, I'll just thank God I was able to win those two tournaments early this year."

Tied with Daniel were Young and Higuchi, one stroke ahead of Carner. Daniel birdied the first two holes in the final round but couldn't sustain her play and took eight bogeys while shooting 77. That left the other three to contend with Lopez, who had to collapse before they could catch her. At least it was a memorable tournament for Lopez's roommate of the week, JoAnn Washam. She had never scored a hole-in-one in seven years on the tour, but made *two* for the week while placing sixth, two strokes out of the play-off.

Colgate-Dinah Shore Winner's Circle—$250,000
Winner: Sandra Post

"How strange this game is," Sandra Post remarked during the Colgate-Dinah Shore Winner's Circle tournament. The comment was particularly appropriate because this week some players' resentment of Nancy Lopez's success finally boiled over. To Sandra's and Nancy's credit, they had the restraint to avoid contributing to this ridiculous situation.

The jealousy began simmering in the late spring and summer of 1978, when Lopez won five tournaments in a row and created an unprecedented interest in women's golf. The press was interested in Nancy, and Nancy alone, as were the vast majority of spectators. She had the attention of people who had never before been interested in the LPGA or even golf. Perhaps there was over-reaction, but that surely would pass. Meanwhile, Lopez was providing the tour with undreamed-of exposure. The entire LPGA would benefit as, a generation earlier, the men's tour did in clinging to Arnold Palmer's coattails.

Some LPGA golfers were impatient with even this temporary obsession with Nancy Lopez. Others had very good seasons, but Nancy's was a great one, the one that mattered. This was true on into 1979. The way they reacted, you had to wonder if they would prefer the old days, when nearly all players were equal—equally obscure.

A Los Angeles newspaper reported that there were cheers among the players when Lopez lost in a play-off the previous week. JoAnne Carner, for one, refused to add to the controversy. "You don't need to go out and win." How right JoAnne was! As Nancy said, "All they have to do is go out and beat me."

Still, Post was reminded that, as defending champion, she should have been on the program cover and in the pro-am pairing with Dinah Shore. Instead, Lopez was. Post was not entitled to be featured because these were marketing decisions, not courtesies that automatically were extended to a defending champion. Post had an appropriate response, "I don't have time to dwell on such things. Nancy can't control it and I can't control it." Sandra then went out and won the golf tournament. She beat Lopez, as a matter of fact.

She became the first to successfully defend the prestigious Colgate-Dinah Shore title by shooting 276, 12 strokes under par and the lowest score in the tournament's seven-year history. It was quite different from her 1978 victory, painless by comparison, you might say. Post then was suffering from severely injured tendons in her left hand. "I was really hurting," she recalled. "My friends saw me in practice rounds and thought I should go home. . . . I was aggravating the problem with a block-out action, thinking I was easing up on impact. It was just the opposite." Her cure was lessons from her pro, Elmer Priestorn, over the winter. "I didn't have a proper swing plane at all," she said. "And with a proper swing plane, I discovered the tensions were reduced in my hand. It didn't hurt to swing, to swing properly."

Post was confident upon returning to Mission Hills, having had two second-place finishes to start the year. She and Lopez shot the same scores for the first three rounds, 68, 70 and 68. "I knew what I had to do all week, beat Nancy, and I knew this course better and I knew I was going to get some birdies and she was going to make a mistake," Post said. That was exactly what happened. She made birdies on the 11th, 12th and 16th holes in the final round. When Lopez made bogey on the 17th, Post was two strokes ahead. Lopez got a birdie to finish, but Sandra needed only a par to win with 70 to Nancy's 71.

Florida Lady Citrus Open—$100,000
Winner: Jane Blalock

The Florida Lady Citrus Open appeared on the 1979 schedule in a change of venues which was beneficial to both the women's and men's tours. I must say it was a pleasant surprise, one I did not anticipate when I was involved in the transfer of the men's Florida Citrus Open across Orlando to Arnold Palmer's Bay Hill Club. That inaugural Bay Hill Citrus Classic was hailed by *Sports Illustrated* as possibly "one of the brightest pre-Masters fixtures." Orlando is one of America's best golfing areas and the members of Rio Pinar Country Club demonstrated that in their new Florida Lady Citrus, which replaced the LPGA tournament in Raleigh, North Carolina. Estimates placed the final-round attendance at 17,000 people, a marvelous turnout.

The champion was as familiar to Central Florida's golf followers as were the tournament name and venue. "I feel this is coming home," said Jane Blalock, who played on the golf team at nearby Rollins College and won two of the three Lady Errol Classics held in Orlando from 1972 to 1974. The victory was Blalock's second of the year and the 24th of her career. It could hardly have come at a better time for Blalock who, exactly one month earlier, found her career jeopardized by a back injury.

She awoke before the last round of the National Pro-Am and found that her left arm was numb. "I couldn't make my fingers close. I couldn't pick up a Kleenex," she said. "At first I thought it was just a bad dream. I knew it would be better if I could just get some sleep and get out to the course the next morning." She discovered she could not even hold a club. She withdrew and checked into an orthopedic clinic. Blalock, who has a history of back trouble, was told that a slipped disc was rubbing against her spinal cord.

Blalock was five strokes behind JoAnne Carner and Debbie Meisterlin at the start of the last round in Orlando. She shot 70, three under par, then defeated Carner on the second play-off hole. Carner's final round was 75 and Meisterlin, who has yet to win on the tour, shot 77. Other contenders in the hectic chase included Donna Horton White and Beth Daniel. Daniel birdied the last hole, also for 70, and was the clubhouse leader until Blalock and Carner also birdied the 18th. Carner made two bogeys in the play-off and Blalock won with a two-putt par on the short 16th hole.

Otey Crisman Classic—$100,000
Winner: Jane Blalock

In the Otey Crisman Classic, Jane Blalock was confronted with a rather different problem from that which she had only a few weeks earlier. Blalock went from wondering "whether I would be able to play at all this year" to worrying about maintaining a huge lead in the final round. She did, winning by six strokes for her third victory in seven tournaments. She missed three of the LPGA's first ten tournaments because of a back ailment, then returned to win the Florida Lady Citrus Open. That victory relieved any doubts about her fitness, but it was a struggle, with Blalock coming from five strokes behind on the last day. There were seldom any questions about the outcome of this event.

Since the tournament was in Birmingham, Alabama, Blalock took advantage of her proximity to Pell City for a visit to Jimmy Ballard, the noted doctor of professional swings at Pine Harbor Country Club. "I had to work really hard to win in Orlando," Jane said. "Jimmy got me to do a couple of things I had been lazy about. We looked at some films and talked a lot about what I needed to do. It restored my confidence. I hit the ball extremely well throughout the tournament."

Her 68 was the only score below 70 in the opening round. She then posted a masterful 65, equaling the course record at Green Valley Country Club despite two bogeys. "There are not many days in this game that go for you like this," she said. "The round started out to be mediocre. I was only one under at the turn. But then the fun started. I made just about every putt I looked at. It was really exciting." An eagle and seven birdies later, Blalock commanded an eight-stroke margin. That was only one stroke off the 36-hole record, which Blalock set in 1976 in Dallas. "I was absolutely petrified in Dallas," she recalled. "I thought, 'What could be more embarrassing than blowing a nine-stroke lead?' I wound up playing well then, and the way I'm playing now, I expect to again."

Try as Blalock might, she could not help but be affected by her margin. Though no one came closer than five strokes, Blalock was apprehensive while shooting her 72 for a 205 total, six strokes better than Pat Bradley. "I was scared to death," Jane admitted afterward. "Sometimes with that big a lead, you think you can't lose. But you can. It's hard to let fly with a big lead. You want to make birdies, but the spark is just not there."

Women's International—$80,000

Winner: Nancy Lopez

Three in a row for Jane Blalock? That question was being asked at the start and the halfway mark of the Women's International. Blalock, gunning for her fourth win of the year, shared the lead until taking 75 in the third round. Then, on the final day, Nancy Lopez came along to reclaim from Blalock the No. 1 position on the LPGA circuit. The victory was Lopez's third of the season, the same total as Blalock, and the $12,000 prize enabled Nancy to take first on the money list.

The Women's International, intended by the sponsors to be the ladies' equivalent to the Masters, was again an outstanding showpiece at Moss Creek Plantation on Hilton Head Island. South Carolinian Beth Daniel, who grew up in nearby Charleston, started things off by making birdies on the last two holes for a two-under-par 70, the best score of the first round. Daniel stumbled to 77 in the second round and was out of it, although she recovered nicely with a closing 68 and shared fifth place, five strokes behind Lopez. The second-round leaders with rounds of 72 and 69 were Blalock, Donna Young and Donna White. After three rounds, White held first place with 72 and a 213 total, following Blalock's 75 and Young's 73. Lopez's early rounds were 72, 71 and 71. Then she posted a four-under-par 68 for a 282 total and beat White by three strokes.

Lopez overtook White at the fourth green, where Donna had a double bogey. White got in trouble again at the ninth hole, losing another stroke to par. "That was the turnaround," Nancy said. "Donna three-putted and I birdied it from 10 feet." Lopez said she kept pushing herself, however, because she remembered a couple of earlier tournaments in which she finished second because she waited too long to make a charge. "I didn't want to do that again," she said. Her five-footer to save par at the 15th hole virtually shut the door on White. The possibility of a play-off was eliminated two holes later, when White made bogey from a bunker.

Lady Michelob—$100,000

Winner: Sandra Post

It took Sandra Post only a dozen tournaments to match her accomplishments of 1978, which had been her best season ever. When Post won the Lady Michelob, she had two victories and over $96,000 for the year. For a time, at least, she also had first place on the money list. More importantly, Sandra was becoming recognized as an LPGA star after 11 years on the tour. She had shown that potential since 1968, her first year, when she won the LPGA Championship.

She won only one tournament, the unofficial 1974 Colgate Far East Open, over the next nine years while having an unhappy marriage and a divorce. In 1978, she won twice and was seventh on the money list. She altered her swing plane over the winter because of a hand injury and now was in the group with Nancy Lopez, JoAnne Carner, Jane Blalock and Pat Bradley—five golfers who virtually dominated the first three months of the 1979 tour.

Neither Lopez nor Carner was entered in the Lady Michelob. Lopez was resting before a strenuous summer schedule and Carner was recovering from a trail-bike accident. Bradley and Blalock offered the expected competition, while an unexpected threat came from Amelia Rorer.

The Atlanta-area tournament was previously known as the Lady Tara Classic and, although Michelob beer became the sponsor, the organization was unchanged. The event was held at Brookfield West in the suburb of Roswell, Georgia, and reportedly had an advance sale of 100,000 tickets. While one may be skeptical of that figure, we can hope they were prepared for the worst, because that is what the weather offered. There were lengthy delays during the last two rounds of the 54-hole tournament.

Pam Higgins, who was receiving cortisone shots to relieve her tendonitis, went ahead in the first round with 67, six under par and two strokes clear of Bradley. Post shot 72 and those ahead of her also included, with 70s, Rorer, Blalock, Beth Daniel and Clifford Ann Creed. Higgins kept the lead with 73 in the second round. Post and Rorer were tied for second place, one stroke behind, after Post's 69 and Rorer's 71. Rorer was challenging for the first time in her four years on the tour. "I was so nervous for the first seven holes," she admitted, "that my hands were numb."

Rorer took a share of sixth place with 75. Higgins also shot 75 and was tied for third. Post had 69, taking first by two strokes over Bradley. The duel between Post and Higgins lasted into the last nine. Higgins kept pace until making bogeys on the 10th and 11th holes and double bogey on the 13th. When Post got a birdie on the 13th, she had the comfort of a three-shot margin and could afford a bogey at the 18th.

Coca-Cola Classic—$100,000
Winner: Nancy Lopez

It is far too early to place Nancy Lopez on the pedestal as the best golfer in LPGA history. She is only 22 years old and has been on the tour for but two seasons. Years from now, there will be a time for serious debate, and I imagine that Mickey Wright's admirers will take delight in mentioning the 1979 Coca-Cola Classic. Mickey, twice Nancy's age, had not competed regularly for 10 years. Her battle with Lopez and three others was beyond anyone's dreams. Her shots in the two-hole play-off were closer to the flags than those of Lopez and Nancy won with simply sensational putting.

Injuries forced Wright to curtail her schedule after the 1969 season. "That," she said, "and the fact I was tired of playing." She must now wear tennis shoes instead of golf spikes because of chronic trouble with her left metatarsal arch. She was playing in the sixth of her eight tournaments for the year and said she had no desire to return as a fulltime competitor. She explained, "I am content to study the stock market and to cook." Wright was leaving golf just as the purses began to soar. The last of her 82 victories, an LPGA record, came in the first of the big-money tournaments, the Colgate-Dinah Shore Winner's Circle. Her career earnings after the Coca-Cola Classic were $368,215. Lopez would pass that figure before the year was over. This was her 13th career victory and her fourth of the season.

More than 20,000 spectators came for the final round at the Upper Montclair Country Club in Clifton, New Jersey. Even with Lopez defending her championship, the total attendance did not surpass last year's record turnout of 47,500. The reason was plain. There was a steady downpour in the first round and the weather for the second day was even worse, with occasional torrents. The last day was the best. The sky was merely dark and overcast.

Wright shared the first-round lead with Kathy Ahern, both having 70s, while Lopez was three strokes behind. Nancy birdied the first three holes in the second round, shot 70 and took a one-stroke margin over the previous leaders, who again posted the same score, 74. Also within four strokes of first place were JoAnn Washam, Beth Daniel, Hollis Stacy, Amy Alcott, Sandra Palmer, Judy Rankin and Laura Baugh. Tournament director Betsy Rawls noted, "I haven't seen that much quality up there on top ready to go into one of our final rounds in a long, long time. We should have a bang-up finish tomorrow."

How accurate that was. The play-off included Bonnie Bryant, Stacy, Washam, Wright and Lopez, who needed a 20-foot putt for par on the 17th hole to qualify. Their scores ranged from Bryant's 68 to Lopez's 73, all finishing with 216, three under par. The play-off started on the par-three 15th hole. Wright placed her five-iron shot merely 18 *inches* from the hole, while none of the others got within fifteen *feet*. Washam missed from 25 feet. Bryant missed from 20 feet. Stacy missed from 18 feet. Lopez holed her putt from 17 feet and was off to the 16th tee after Wright tapped her putt in. There, Nancy's approach shot with a wedge was eight feet from the flag and Mickey's seven feet. The fact that Wright's putt did not go in hardly tarnished a great performance.

Corning Classic—$100,000

Winner: Penny Pulz

Any nervousness which Penny Pulz felt over her first professional victory was not reflected in her putting. The 26-year-old Australian took only 21 putts in the final round while shooting 68, the lowest score of the tournament, and winning the Corning Classic by two strokes over Judy Rankin. "They were not short putts, either," Rankin said. "Penny probably had the finest putting round I have ever witnessed." Pulz made birdies on four of seven holes, starting on the last nine. "Each time I got over the putts I felt stronger and stronger," she said. "It was unbelievable."

Pulz's score was 284, four over par on the 6,203-yard Corning Country Club course in upstate New York. Several of the par-four holes were unreachable in two strokes and a steady rain made the course play even longer than was intended. Nevertheless, there was plenty of excitement in this LPGA tournament sponsored by Corning Glassworks, whose championship trophy was made of Steuben glass with a value of $40,000.

The leaders in the early rounds were Rankin, Susan O'Connor and Lynn Adams. O'Connor shot 69 in the first round. Rankin joined her in the lead with 142 after 36 holes. A first-year professional, Adams posted 69 in the third round and was alone in the lead at 214 when it was discovered that Rankin had signed an incorrect scorecard. Rankin signed for a bogey on the 16th hole rather than for the par she made and was credited with 74 instead of her actual 73. Pulz was two strokes behind.

The final round developed as Pulz expected. "I really thought it would be between Judy and myself," she said, "because Lynn hadn't been there before." Adams shot 72 while Pulz won with her 68. Rankin finished in 70 for second place, two behind Pulz and one ahead of Adams. She obviously was disturbed by that incorrect scorecard which cost her a better chance of victory. "I just couldn't settle down or sleep last night," Judy said. "It's the first time I have ever signed an incorrect card."

Golden Lights Championship—$100,000

Winner: Nancy Lopez

There were two persistent themes on the LPGA tour in late spring and early summer: rain and Nancy Lopez. The Golden Lights Championship was the sixth successive week for rain and the third successive victory for Nancy. "We're getting used to this [rain], after all these weeks of it," said Lopez, following her four-stroke triumph with 280, eight under par.

"I hope my winning so often is not bad for the tour," said Lopez, who won the same tournaments during her five-victory string in 1978. "I think everyone is working harder out here as a result of my success and there are a lot of strong players who could win each week." For one, there was Pat Bradley, who again was second. To that point in 1979, Bradley had had five second-place finishes and two thirds. "My day will come," she said.

Bradley equaled an LPGA record for nine holes with her 29 in the first round, which was played in unfamiliar sunshine on the Wykagyl Country Club course in New Rochelle, New York. Bradley, who led with 66, eagled the 495-yard fifth hole and made five consecutive birdies after that. "I was in a trance," she said. "No matter where I was, I hit it close. I had an invisible line to the hole." Lopez was second with 67 and Judy Rankin third with 69.

Stronger winds made club selection more difficult in the second round. Lopez took command with a three-stroke margin, shooting 70 while Bradley posted 74. Lopez was still three ahead after her 73 in the overcast third round. Nancy had a 210 total, followed at 213 by Donna Young and Gail Toushin, an infrequent tour player. Bradley fell to fourth at 214 with another 74. Bradley was Lopez's only close challenger in the rain of the final day, although in the end Bradley had gained no ground, as both shot 70s.

Bradley was only one stroke behind after she birdied the 13th hole, standing five under par to Lopez's six-under figure. Lopez was playing in the group one hole behind. When she also birdied the 13th, and Bradley bogeyed the 14th, the margin began to widen.

LPGA Championship—$150,000
Winner: Donna Young

Some golfers appear to thrive on the toughest courses and in the most important tournaments. Donna Young is of this breed, having twice won the United States Open, in addition to the Peter Jackson Classic and the Colgate European Open. She achieved her 14th career victory in the LPGA Championship, truly a major event, and set a record in the process by going 50 consecutive holes without making a bogey.

This was the 25th LPGA Championship and huge crowds were there to mark the anniversary at the Jack Nicklaus Golf Center in Kings Island, Ohio. The attendance figures were 25,592 for the last day and 101,592 for the week, the most people ever to see an LPGA tournament. The crowds were far larger than those attending the men's pro tournament on the same course several years before. The best attendance for the Ohio Kings Island Open was 62,288 in 1977, the final year for that tournament.

Donna Young won the LPGA Championship.

The event had all the flavor of a major championship: tradition, crowds and a tough golf course with high rough and hard, slick greens. But Jerilyn Britz had the audacity to shoot 64, a record at eight under par, in the first round. "You know," she said later, "maybe I didn't know any better." She learned much about herself during the week, and never really yielded to the pressure or the golf course. Her second-place finish, three strokes behind Young, was her best showing in six years on the tour. Britz said, "I have had to dig deep down and I have discovered that I enjoy the pressure. I guess this is what it is all about. It is fun."

Nancy Lopez was never really in the groove for this tournament. She tied for 10th place. It was just the second time that Lopez had not either won or been runner-up in 1979. She had victories in her last three tournaments but "this was a horrible week. I had no confidence at all." While Lopez shot 73 in the first round, Britz was breaking the record which Nancy set with 65 last year. She congratulated Britz in the press interview, saying, "I wish I could have seen that round." Penny Pulz was second with 68 and Young was in the third-place group with 69.

Britz shot 72 in the second round and kept the lead by three strokes over Young and JoAnne Carner, who both posted 70s. Carner was regularly taking aspirin because of inflamed tendons in her right wrist, the result of a trail-bike accident a few weeks earlier. She could not cope with the problem for four rounds, finishing with 72, then 77. Young shot two more 70s, while Britz had two 73s. Donna caught her on the third day and passed her on the fourth.

Lopez, Pulz, Amy Alcott, JoAnn Prentice, Jan Stephenson, Judy Rankin and Bonnie Bryant were among those with chances to win until they finished poorly, and Lopez equaled her worst round of the year with 76. That left Young and Britz to decide the championship. They were tied until Britz bogeyed the 12th hole and Young birdied the 13th for a two-stroke margin. After a rain delay (the seventh week in a row) Young bogeyed the 16th hole, her first since the first hole of the second round. She immediately made a birdie at the 17th and was clear for the three-stroke victory.

Britz was not upset about the result. "I don't feel I lost it as much as Donna won it," said the 36-year-old Minnesotan. "I tried to play aggressively and I think I did. I'll be a little more confident in the future. I needed a good tournament to give me a boost because I haven't been playing that well up to now." At age 34, Young was pleased to prove "I'm not over the hill and can still win the big ones. . . . I don't even think I have reached my potential yet." She was reminded of a newspaper article that her husband had given her to read the night before. It was about the three C's to success: confidence, concentration and composure. In the LPGA Championship, Young added a fourth C—consistency.

The Sarah Coventry—$100,000
Winner: Jane Blalock

For whatever reason, Jane Blalock produced three of the most impressive victories of the LPGA season. The Sarah Coventry marked the third time she won by six strokes and the third time she won wire-to-wire. This time, the reason may have been her previous frustrations on the Locust Hill course in Rochester. She lost in 1977 because of a poor final round and faltered again in 1978 as Nancy Lopez streaked to her record-breaking fifth consecutive victory in the tournament which then was known as the Bankers Trust Classic.

"When I drove by the course on the way from the airport," Blalock said, "I started to remember the way I had lost the title last year to Nancy on this course. And I also was thinking of that double bogey on the last hole of the LPGA Championship [the week before] and how upset I got at myself for doing that. I sort of felt I might win this week. When I thought of this golf course, all I thought about was that it was time to redeem my previous efforts here. I told myself I was going to make up for everything by winning. When you win, all of your mistakes are rectified."

For the first time in more than two months, it didn't rain during the week of an LPGA tournament. The weather was windy and warm with temperatures in the 80s as Blalock started with 69, surging with birdies on the 11th, 12th and 13th holes. She shared the lead with Sally Little, who finished with an eagle on the 17th. Stronger, swirling winds took their toll in the second round, but Blalock returned with five birdies, two bogeys and a 70, placing one stroke ahead of Pat Bradley, 139 to 140. Bradley set course and tournament records with 31 on the first nine and 67 for the day. But Bradley was knocked from contention with a 79 in the third round, while Blalock built a five-stroke margin at 208 with another 69. Dot Germain was second, followed by Alice Ritzman, Vicki Fergon and Pat Meyers, all five strokes behind.

No one seriously challenged Blalock on the last day. She finished with a 72 for 280, her margin ranging from four to eight strokes during the round. Second place went to Ritzman after the rookie from Kalispell, Montana, birdied the 16th and eagled the 17th for her 72 and 286.

Lady Keystone Open—$100,000
Winner: Nancy Lopez

The only way to leave town is as a winner. No golfer knows that better than Nancy Lopez-Melton. One year ago, she came to Hershey, Pennsylvania, and found victory in defeat at the Lady Keystone Open. She lost the tournament, ending her victory streak as a rookie at five straight, but found a husband and a home.

This year she still had the husband but was giving up the home. Tim Melton, her radio sportscaster husband, had taken a job in Cincinnati, so the Meltons were giving up their seldom-visited Hershey residence. They were moving immediately after the Keystone and Nancy was determined to give the citizens of Hershey something to remember her by. What she left on the record books was a four-under-par 212 victory over the tricky, tree-lined Hershey Country Club course. She took $15,000 in "moving expenses" for her sixth victory in 11 attempts. With half the year left, she had earnings of $136,775 (more than $31,000 ahead of Sandra Post). In less than two full years as a professional, the young queen of golf had earned $349,827.

Lopez learned something about herself during her last weekend in Hershey. She discovered there is no time to scream but plenty of time to cry in the competitive world of sports. In the first round, Lopez made five birdies but only produced an even par 72. Her crisis came at No. 11, when her tee shot wound up in a pine tree. She gritted her teeth and took an unplayable lie. But then she missed an 18-inch putt, taking a double bogey. "If I could have screamed out loud, I would have felt better," admitted Lopez. "I lost my temper and that's not like me." Her husband was the first to agree. "Tim told me I wasn't the same girl he met here a year ago," she said. "He told me he loved me no matter how badly I played. My dad was like that. That makes me feel good."

A 68 on Saturday put Lopez into a tie with the game's matriarch, Kathy Whitworth. Lopez reverted to a 72 Sunday, but it was enough as Whitworth shot 74 and was tied for second at 214 by Sally Little, while Amy Alcott and Betsy King tied for fourth at 215. Lopez really won the tournament on the par-five 16th. Shooting birdie-eagle-birdie, that's where she earned her four-under-par total. It was a good thing, because she bogeyed the 18th hole all three days. By Sunday, it didn't matter. With a crowd of 20,000 cheering and saying good-bye on her approach to the final green, she did a poor job of fighting back tears.

Lady Stroh's Open—$150,000
Winner: Vicki Fergon

Rain reigned at the $150,000 Lady Stroh's Open on water-logged Dearborn Country Club instead of Nancy Lopez, who withdrew to find a home in Cincinnati. Amidst a sea of confusion, including mistaken identity of the champion, Vicki Fergon fought her way upstream to fulfill her promise.

Back in July 1977, Lopez qualified for the LPGA Tour. But one of the tour's great trivia questions in future years will be to name the girl who beat Lopez by *nine* strokes in that qualifying school. Vicki Fergon was the girl. The 24-year-old Californian failed to capitalize on her booming drives until Dearborn, where it took exceptional strength to hit the ball in and out of water for four days.

Strength didn't last for veteran Judy Rankin. Ignoring her back problems, Rankin shot a course-record 65 on the third round, taking a five-stroke lead into the final day. Fergon, starting seven strokes behind Rankin, shot a 69 to Rankin's weakening 75 for a one-stroke victory. Shooting a four-under-par 284, Fergon suddenly was $22,500 richer, jumping her from 25th to 12th on the money list at $42,356. The real winner may have been the tournament, which drew more than 40,000 spectators despite myriad problems. Besides Lopez, Jan Stephenson withdrew, JoAnne Carner had to drop out because of chronic hand problems, and Laura Baugh and Donna Caponi Young had to be disqualified for misunderstanding the rules on a water hazzard.

Scoreboard confusion denied Fergon the recognition she deserved on the second rainy day. After an opening 73, she shot a 69. It was the best round of the day and she was in second place, two strokes behind Debbie Austin. But the scoring system mixed her up with Sylvia Ferdon during the triple-delayed round and she was never paged to the interview room. With a third-round 73, Fergon went unnoticed on Saturday, too. All the attention was focused on Rankin and her remarkable round of 65.

Because of Rankin's five-stroke lead on the field, Sunday seemed like a formality. Only once before in her career had she lost a tournament she led going into the final round. This was to be the second time. While Rankin faded to a five-over-par 77, Fergon picked and chose her way to another three-under 69. Playing ahead of Rankin, Fergon birdied the 16th to tie for the lead. The blonde, blue-eyed sophomore bogeyed No. 17, but Rankin suffered a double bogey as she couldn't reach the par-four green with two woods. A tap-in par on the last hole clinched the win as Rankin had no hopes of reaching the green to shoot for a tying bird. "I just played very steady, very consistent," said Fergon, "and everything went my way." They know her name in Detroit now.

Mayflower Classic—$100,000
Winner: Hollis Stacy

As a July warmup for the United States Open, the Mayflower Classic in Noblesville, Indiana, was dramatically deceptive. Double-defending Open champion Hollis Stacy was enthused by her Mayflower win, while winless Jerilyn Britz was encouraged by her nearness to victory. Judy Rankin was enraged and Laura Baugh was entrapped in another brush with triumph.

Stacy, Rankin and Baugh were forced into playing off in the rain after tying at three-under-par on the Harbour Trees Golf Course. Britz missed a two-foot putt on the 72nd hole to miss the play-off by a stroke. Rankin fell on the first play-off hole when her approach shot took a bad bounce over the green, resulting in a bogey. It was the second straight frustrating finish for Rankin; she had lost a five-shot lead in the final round of the Lady Stroh's Open the week before. This time she blamed the course instead of herself. Baugh shot a last-round 67 to get as near victory as she has ever been in seven years of professional golf. It was her first play-off. She lasted until the second extra hole when her approach was too strong, leaving a difficult chip that failed to reach the green and resulted in bogey. Meanwhile, Stacy sailed the Mayflower toward the U.S. Open by taking routine pars on the two play-off holes, earning $15,000.

There was more talk about the upcoming U.S. Open than the Mayflower. Could Stacy write LPGA history by becoming the first to win that title three times? Was the Mayflower victory a sign of events to come? Stacy didn't know. "I really don't have a game plan," she said when asked about pre-Open strategy. "Before my first Open win in 1977, I didn't pick up a club for one week; before Indianapolis last year I was 48th at Columbus." This time she was entering the Open under a full sail aboard the Mayflower. However, while press and fans congratulated Stacy and consoled Rankin and Baugh, little was said to Britz. But she was smiling to herself. "I have confidence now in what I'm doing," she said quietly, "and I find myself in contention more as a result."

U.S. Open Championship—$125,000
Winner: Jerilyn Britz

When victory can come for the first time to a 36-year-old former schoolteacher who did not swing a golf club until age 17 and did not turn professional until age 31, we must be talking about the United States Open and Jerilyn Britz. We are. By its very precept, the Open is meant to be the most prestigious tournament for all women golfers and not just LPGA superstars. You do not have to have double last names like Lopez-Melton, Gunderson Carner, or Caponi Young to win the Open, even if it helps. All the Open asks is you mix consummate skill with considerable luck. And, in Britz's case, complete faith.

Britz stood on the 72nd tee at sedate Brooklawn Country Club, which lies between Fairfield and Bridgeport, Connecticut. She was waiting for playing partner and co-leader Debbie Massey to hit. Massey had birdied the last three holes. Calling herself a "USGA brat" because of her familiarity with the organization and its events, Massey seemed to be riding a crest of credentials and momentum. Britz knew all of this. She was all too aware she had never won any tournament. "If I could have won the Podunk Open, I would have been pleased," she admitted. Nobody would have blamed her, while facing the final hole, if she had quietly folded her tent and retired to wherever former physical education instructors go. Nobody would have blamed her—except herself.

So standing on the last tee, Britz turned to her caddy and whispered: "We have nothing to worry about." Her caddy tried to smile and failed miserably. But he was all grin 15 minutes later. Massey's drive rolled into a slashed divot on the left side of the fairway. Worried about an ailing wrist, she exploded

Jerilyn Britz came home a winner in the U.S. Open.

a four-iron into the ground and willed the ball within 20 feet of the green. "It looked like a hole made by a burrowing elephant—tusks and all—when I got through with it."

Meanwhile, Britz cooly placed her second shot 20 feet from the pin and safely on the green. Massey chipped eight feet past the pin, leaving her an icy-slick downhill putt to save par. Before the first round, Nancy Lopez had predicted: "What this tournament is going to come down to is who can stand over the eight-footer, downhill, and make it." Massey could stand over it—but she couldn't make it. Concentration shattered along with hopes, Massey missed again and settled for a double bogey, falling into a second-place tie at 286 with Sandra Palmer. Britz lagged to the cup and sank her par putt routinely for a most unroutine first victory. "I had an amazing amount of peace," said Britz, who had flubbed a two-foot putt the week before to miss the deciding play-off in the Mayflower.

Hollis Stacy entered the tournament with an amazing amount of confidence. She had just won the Mayflower and seemed fully capable of setting LPGA history by winning her third straight Open. Previewing what was to come, Massey and Britz led on the first day with one-under-par 71s—but Stacy was just a stroke behind. But a second round 75 left her six strokes behind at the halfway mark and there was no charge left in her as she finished 74–73.

Well, if not Stacy, what about Nancy Lopez? The Open is the one jewel still missing from her crown. Frankly, USGA courses with their treacherous greens are not suited for someone who charges every putt. And Lopez charges. She was never really in it as she opened with a two-over 73 and kept on shooting 73s for four days.

For the moment, the superstars were forgotten in the drama of the Britz-Massey duel to the end. Massey shot a horrid 41 on the front side in the final round but clawed her way back into it with a 33 on the back. Britz, however, was not to be denied. "This is what I've been working for for a long time. I have faith in the Lord, and I leave all the worries and frustrations to Him."

Greater Baltimore Golf Classic—$75,000
Winner: Pat Meyers

It was a Sunday morning in late July and the final round of the Greater Baltimore Golf Classic was only minutes away. Pat Meyers sat in her room and toyed with the intricate pieces of a jigsaw puzzle. The symbolism of the puzzle was not lost on Meyers. At age 25, she was in her third year on the LPGA tour. She had earned the respect of her peers. With good fundamentals and a solid swing, she was a model of consistency.

A consistent runner-up. Five times she had finished second. No times had she finished first. But on this Sunday—she was entering the final round as the tournament leader for the first time. Maybe that was the missing piece. Apparently so. By one-putting the first six greens for two birdies and four pars, she pulled away and then held off the attack of a half-dozen golfers for a one-stroke victory and $11,250. "I was in a good frame of mind before the round started," said the 5'4" resident of Ormond Beach, Florida, "and I was not going to back off any putts."

Life in sunny Florida with its lazy Bermuda greens was an aid to Meyers. The greens at the humid Pine Ridge County Club were as slow as most Florida greens, a disturbing change from the previous week's U.S. Open greens to many of the competitors. "I had some trouble adjusting to the greens," said Sally Little, speaking for many. "I'm just not a great putter on slow greens." Meyers was in her element. "I think the key was that I made some good putts early in the round when I had to. And when you're putting well, well, you don't put pressure on other parts of your game."

Her competitors did their best to pressure the leader. Nancy Lopez made her presence felt. After an opening 73, a second-round 69 put her into the hunt. But a double bogey on No. 13 Sunday led to a 72 and 214 total, four strokes behind Meyers' nine-under 210, shot on rounds of 70–69–71. Pat Bradley charged early and Jan Stephenson charged late, but both had to settle for 70s and 212 totals, two strokes behind. Dot Germain, a 32-year-old nonwinner, came within inches of an eagle on the final hole but had to settle for a birdie, a 69 and a 211 total. Despite her lack of confidence in her putter, Little also finished at 211 with a closing 70. All Meyers needed was a 71, as she really won the tournament with a 15-foot birdie putt on No. 16.

Meyers' triumph was the continuation of a mid-season surge by previous nonwinners. Penny Pulz started it two months earlier by winning the Corning Classic. Then, in the previous two weeks, Vicki Fergon won at Detroit and Jerilyn Britz became the oldest first-time winner in LPGA history by taking the U.S. Open at age 36. These new winners were proof the LPGA was not totally dominated by a few champions as some suspected.

Peter Jackson Classic—$150,000
Winner: Amy Alcott

Amy Alcott had to speak softly but carried a very big stick as she eagled her way past Nancy Lopez for a three-stroke victory in the Peter Jackson Classic, listed as the third of the LPGA's three major tournaments for the year. Suffering from laryngitis, Alcott was eating a penicillin derivative like candy and fighting off the final-round charge of six others who were within three strokes of her with five holes to play.

The last to go was Lopez. As Alcott was sinking a 30-foot birdie putt on No. 17, Lopez was bogeying No. 16 to fall two strokes behind. Still, both had the 72nd and final hole to play, and Mrs. Alcott didn't raise any foolish daughters. Amy knew all too well that you never count out Nancy Lopez until after you've accepted the winner's check. So, even though she was unable to even whisper "charge," Alcott did just that. She stroked a 35-foot, downhill, twisting putt that disappeared into the last cup for an eagle and what turned into a three-stroke win over Lopez.

Alcott shot rounds of 75–70–70–70 for a seven-under-par total of 285 on the Club de Golf de la Vallee de Richelieu course just outside Montreal. Lopez had rounds of 76-70-71-71 for 288, one shot ahead of Silvia Bertolaccini and two shots ahead of rookie Judy Clark. *"Merci bien, merci bien,"* croaked Alcott as she accepted the winner's share of $22,500. "If this hadn't been a major championship, I would have stayed home. But I've been playing well lately. I loved the name of the golf course even before I got here and it means a lot to win a major championship outside your country. At age 23, it is a tremendous thrill for me."

The Californian, who had already won the Elizabeth Arden Classic in February, was hardly thrilled with her opening 75. It left her six strokes behind rookie Cathy Sherk of Port Colborne, Ontario, who shot a course-record 69 for a three-stroke lead over the entire field. The Montreal press was ecstatic about the 1978 Canadian, U.S. and World Amateur champion. She even got equal billing with the return of Rusty Staub, Le Grand Orange, to the Montreal Expos baseball team. Sherk went to the Expos' game that night and watched Staub get a standing ovation—only to pop out. It was an omen as she went into a steady fade with rounds of 74, 75 and 76.

Next to take the spotlight was New Yorker Mary Dwyer, who got progressively better on rounds of 72, 71 and 70 to lead going into the final day. "I'm going to need all the leprechauns I can get," laughed the red-headed, Irish lass. "I'm kind of in a coma, and there's a fine line between winning and losing." For Dwyer, the fine line turned into a brick wall on Sunday. Paired last with Lopez, she fell to a tie for 16th by shooting an unfortunate 81. That left the door open for Alcott, who had neither the voice nor the French to ask to come in. But she had the stick.

Colgate European Open—$150,000
Winner: Nancy Lopez

Golfers and spectators alike departed from Sunningdale with mixed emotions. The Colgate European Open had been a splendid tournament, but they knew it was destined to be the final one sponsored by Colgate and might possibly be the last LPGA event on that side of the Atlantic. Colgate's announcement to that effect a few weeks later was met with sadness, for in merely six years the tournament had become a treasured part of British sport.

Sentiments were certainly magnified by Nancy Lopez's memorable play and by the thought that they might not see her again. After three rounds Nancy was 15 under par and she birdied two of the first three holes in the fourth round. Seventeen under par and nine strokes ahead! Her lead was nigh insurmountable, yet Joyce Kazmierski made a game of it until Lopez sealed the four-stroke victory with an eagle on the 16th hole. No wonder the great reception they had on the last green.

Aside from Nancy Lopez and Colgate's sponsorship, a third topic of general discussion that week was the BBC's complaint about advertisements on the golfers' sun visors, for Lily of France, in particular. The BBC, government-owned, does not permit advertising. It is unavoidable that commercials do appear on their screens regularly, in every fashion from billboards along-side football grounds to panther and penguin motifs on golfers' clothing. They object most strenuously when the advertisements cannot be ignored or quickly passed by the cameras. Slogans are deemed more offensive than simple motifs, however readily identifying a manufacturer. Confused though the logic may be, Lily of France was made the focal point of the BBC's protest to the tournament sponsor. Colgate relayed the complaint to the LPGA which, in turn, asked the girls not to wear the visors, at least not on the televised holes. Sally Little, for one, was taken aback because she had been wearing the Lily of France visor every year at Sunningdale. Placing little stock in the response, "We've only just noticed," Little plastered the letters BBC over Lily of France and on her Ram golf bag, as well. As you can imagine, that resulted in more than a few chuckles among the spectators.

Lopez's victory was wire-to-wire, with scores of 68, 70 and 75 for a 282 total, 14 under par. Other outstanding scores included Mardell Wilkins' eight-hole stretch in the first round, holes nine through 16, when she went eight under par with two pars, four birdies, and two eagles. She posted a 70 and was then in third place behind Lopez (68) and Kazmierski (60). In the second round, Alice Ritzman set an LPGA record with three eagles, following her initial 80 with a 68, while Lopez went three strokes ahead of Kazmierski and four in front of Wilkins. Kazmierski was still second, although eight strokes off Nancy's pace, when the third round ended. An astrology student, Joyce felt the moon was in her favor and, as the final round progressed, she may have been gaining some converts as she trimmed Lopez's formidable margin with a mere round of 72. Lopez had collected five bogeys by the 12th hole. "I kept telling myself it couldn't get worse and I had to keep going," Nancy said. "I felt that sooner or later I would get a birdie. It turned out to be an eagle." Lopez's lead had slipped to two strokes until that eagle with a 20-foot putt on the 409-yard 16th. Then came the rousing cheers at the home green and Nancy's sincere wish to the crowds that she and the LPGA would be back again.

WUI Classic—$100,000

Winner: Judy Rankin

It was the classic confrontation. In this corner, carrying the experience of 25 LPGA tour victories acquired over more than a decade, was Judy Rankin, who had not won in a year and a day. And in the other corner, with no official wins yet but a world of promise in front of her, was Beth Daniel, a sure bet for Rookie of the Year. Rankin, age 36, had won six tournaments in 1976, five tournaments in 1977 but only one—this one, the WUI Classic—in 1978. Returning from a back injury, she was trying to prove to herself and the world that her days in the winner's circle were not lost in the past. Daniel, age 22, was still playing with dolls when Rankin won her first tournament. As a pro she had already won an unofficial tournament in Japan but was driven to prove her credentials as two-time U.S. Amateur champion were more than statistics on her biography. A young lady with a passionate dream of becoming No. 1.

This time the veteran won. "I can't really be disappointed," said Daniel as she lost the battle to hold back a few tears, too. "My goal was to make $50,000 my rookie year and now I'm over that—but money is no consolation." The money didn't matter all that much to Rankin, either. "It's just awfully nice after such a long time," sighed the defending champion. "Maybe there comes a point when you wonder if you are the same player you once were . . ."

Rankin's back problems had forced her to skip five tournaments early in the season. But that period of rest seemed to have taken care of the problem. Now the problem and the challenge were to prove to herself she still had the intangible quality that separates champions from also-rans. Twice already in 1979 she had been an also-ran when she thought she should have been a winner. In the Lady Stroh's, she had a five-stroke lead with one round to play. But her closing 76 allowed Vicki Fergon to take the title. The next week, she lost the Mayflower Classic to Hollis Stacy and vehemently blamed course conditions for her defeat. "Looking back on them now," said a composed Rankin, "those losses look like a failure to concentrate."

Rankin received an extra day to build her concentration on the demanding Meadow Brook Country Club as the final round was rained out Sunday and played Monday. It was a tough break for Daniel, who birdied three of five holes played Sunday and had jumped to a four-shot lead only to see it washed out. On Monday morning, Rankin, Daniel and Donna Caponi Young were tied at one-under-par 219. Young, the LPGA champion, dropped out of contention with a bogey on the second hole and double bogey on No. 11. She shot 74 to finish two shots out of second but still three shots ahead of fourth. That left Rankin and Daniel in the center ring. "I had an edge with experience," said Rankin, "but Beth has a real advantage off the tee." They stayed side-by-side until No. 11. Daniel hit a four iron over the green, chipped back eight feet from the hole and missed. Then Rankin delivered the winning punch with a 16-foot birdie putt on No. 17 as Daniel simply could not produce any kind of charge. Rankin closed with a three-under 70 for a four-under-par 288 total to earn $15,000. Daniel shot 72 and 290 for $9,800 in consolation money.

Barth Classic—$100,000

Winner: Sally Little

Neither rain delay nor bee sting could keep Sally Little from her appointed rounds and victory in the Barth Classic, which began the final quarter of the LPGA tour year on the Plymouth (Indiana) Country Club course. Because of rain, Little had to wait an extra day before she could complete her eight-under-par total of 208 with a closing 71. And victory had a little sting to it when she was attacked by a bee on the 17th fairway during the final round. "At least he [the bee] waited until I hit my drive," said Little, the comely 27-year-old star who was stung on the chin. "You should have heard what I said after it happened. But at least he gave me a little adrenalin."

Little earned her second win of the season by holding off the charge of the defending champion, Pat Bradley, who had to settle for her sixth runner-up finish of the season. Bradley shot a closing 69 to finish one shot behind Little despite some physical soreness of her own. Bradley, age 28, decided to go roller skating Saturday night. "They cleared the whole place for me" she said, "and I was going around pretty good. But then I got too confident, a little too cocky, and fell on my bottom."

Being in the right place at the right time is important in all sports. Little has learned that. In her previous 10 events, she had been in the top 10 finishers each time and second twice. But she hadn't won. "In order to win, you've got to be in position, in the top 10," said the soft-spoken South African who would soon be a U.S. citizen. "That's why I feel I'm maturing, coming of age as a golfer. Every week now I set goals for myself. In the past, I'd just try to tee it up and win."

Only Little and Bradley were in real contention during the final round Monday, although Marlene Floyd shot a closing 69 for third place at 210. Amy Alcott could have been a contender but a 73 forced her to settle for fourth at 212. Bradley charged with birdies on the 12th and 13th. When Little bogeyed the 14th, they were tied. But a three-putt bogey by Bradley on the 16th was the difference as both parred in. "Sally's been playing really well for three months—she was due," said Bradley, graciously not pointing out her own half-dozen second-place finishes. "One of these weeks will be my week."

Patty Berg Classic—$100,000
Winner: Beth Daniel

It was not the stuff dreams are made of. Beth Daniel sat in an overloaded, stuffy locker room, making idle conversationn with other golfers. She was getting a headache and beginning to feel apprehensive about defending her four-stroke lead—if the rain ever stopped outside. Then a tournament official came in. "We've had to call off the last round for good and shorten the tournament from 72 to 54 holes . . . Congratulations, Beth, you're a winner." At that second, Daniel didn't feel like a winner. "It feels so strange," she said. "Almost like I

The LPGA found another outstanding rookie in Beth Daniel, winner of the Patty Berg Classic.

really haven't won. Winning this way, I never did get to jump into anybody's arms.''

Still, it seemed as if Daniel's abbreviated win at the Patty Berg Classic in St. Paul, Minnesota, was fate's way of evening the ledger. Two weeks previously at the WUI Classic, she had taken a four-shot lead after five holes of the final round, only to have rain cancel the round. The next day, she finished second to Judy Rankin. ''I guess those things have a way of evening out,'' said Daniel, the 22-year-old tour rookie and two-time U.S. Amateur champion.

Daniel's play was brilliant. She shot rounds of 68, 69, and 71 despite cold winds, constant rains and an unfortunate accident on what proved to be her last hole. Her second shot on the 18th hole, out of the right rough, went farther right and struck a gallery marshal in the forehead. ''I felt I should go over and see if she was all right,'' said Daniel. ''But when I looked at her, I really got shook up. There was blood all over her face.'' Despite the blood, the marshal was not seriously hurt. And, despite the resulting bogey, neither was Daniel. She still had a four-shot lead on Hollis Stacy that never had to be defended.

''You know, since I was 15, I've had this dream about winning my first professional tournament,'' said Daniel. ''The 18th green is surrounded by a huge gallery and I have to sink this curling putt to win. I sink it, and everybody cheers, and there's lots of excitement.'' She was denied the cheers and the excitement—but not the victory or the $15,000 that went with it. ''This isn't the way I dreamed I would get my first professional victory,'' she said, sighing, ''but I don't feel any less a champion.''

Rail Charity Golf Classic—$100,000
Winner: JoAnn Washam

In the Rail Charity Classic at Springfield, Illinois, JoAnn Washam discovered it's a lot easier to finish a round by not getting anywhere near the final green. In Saturday's third round, Washam was fighting to stay near the lead going into the Sunday finale. Standing 120 yards from the 18th green, she drilled a wedge and watched the ball disappear into the cup on the fly. Suddenly, as the news of her closing eagle sailed around the Rail Golf Club course, Washam was only a stroke out the lead.

A day later she was standing on the 18th green and sharing the lead with Silvia Bertolaccini. One putt would give her victory, two putts would mean a play-off, and three putts would be *sayonara*. ''I was so nervous,'' said Washam, who had not won in four years, ''that it looked like about 14,000 feet to the cup.'' Not quite. More like 18. Whatever the distance, Washam dropped the putt.

''This already was my best year for money,'' said the 29-year-old Washam. ''What was lacking was a championship. Confidence is a building process and I badly needed to win. I'm really playing well and I felt this win coming. But after going four years without a win, you get a little depressed and wonder what's going on.''

Bertolaccini was only a little depressed despite losing. ''This isn't a great disappointment because JoAnn went out and won it. I didn't lose it,'' she said.

"This is my best finish this year, and I feel like I'm close to winning." A flock of professionals were close to winning. Going into the final round, Bertolaccini and Carole Jo Skala were tied for the lead at 207. Washam and Betsy King were a stroke back, while eight more competitors were within five strokes of the lead. However, it developed into a race between the two leaders with Shelley Hamlin staying close by shooting the best final round of 68. But Hamlin and Bertolaccini both could point to the moment they eliminated themselves. "I blew it on No. 8," said Hamlin, "when I three-putted from inside 10 feet."

"My only bad mistake was on No. 9," said Bertolaccini. "I knocked a 15-foot putt six feet past the hole and wound up with a three-putt for bogey. Other than that, it was a good tournament." For JoAnn Washam, it was a great tournament, as her 72-hole total of 275 was 13-under-par and just four strokes short of the LPGA record.

Columbia Savings Classic—$100,000
Winner: Sally Little

"It has given me a high," said Sally Little as she sat atop the world after a wire-to-wire victory in the $100,000 Columbia Savings Classic in suburban Denver for her third triumph of the season. In eight years on the tour, this was her first season to win more than one tournament. Always appreciated for her comely appearance and demeanor, Little seems to have blossomed into one of the top half-dozen woman golfers in the world. "I feel like I'm getting there," declared the South African girl who has applied for U.S. citizenship. "You have the supers like Nancy [Lopez] and the established world players like [Judy] Rankin. I feel I have to prove myself to be close to them. I've made a big jump in winnings and I feel I'm maturing. I'm also getting older. I'm like 27, you know, and with all the rookies coming along, I'd better do it quick and then get off."

Little was quick and deadly on the 6,400-yard, par-72 Green Gables Country Club layout. She blasted into a three-stroke lead over Amy Alcott with an opening 66, then followed with rounds of 71 and 72 for a seven-under-par 209, two shots ahead of Rankin and hard-charging rookie Beth Daniel. Alcott tied for fourth at 212 with frustrated Jane Blalock. The first-place prize of $15,000 elevated Little's winnings to $115,442 for the year, fourth best on the tour behind Lopez, Pat Bradley and Sandra Post. Her good fortune began back in March when a blistering 67 on the final day gave her a two-shot win over Lopez in the Bent Tree Classic in Sarasota, Florida. And just three weeks before Denver, she beat Bradley by a shot in the Barth Classic.

Even though Lopez wasn't competing in Denver, Little credited her influence for at least part of her success. "Beating Nancy in Sarasota . . . that started my feeling I could play. Nancy and JoAnn [Carner] both out-hit me at Bent Tree and I felt I had to be so much better. I shot 67—played out of my mind. Every hole, every shot was tough. I finally broke through on the backside with four birdies. . . . Yes, beating Nancy convinced me I may have arrived."

Little could have beaten anyone with her first round of 66 at Denver but downplayed the effort that was based on needing just 26 putts. "It's easy to shoot lights out the first round," she said. "But then you go out and play under pressure. And I survived." Indeed. She actually played better on Saturday but missed five birdie putts inside of 10 feet and had to settle for a one-under 71. Meanwhile, Rankin chipped in three times and shot a 67 to move within a stroke of Little despite a strange allergy problem. "It would be my luck to be allergic to grass," quipped the veteran star. Blalock was only two shots back despite using a brand-new driver. Her favorite one had been buckled in airline transit. "It was a quick change after five years," said Blalock. "The other one died—and I cried." Although four shots back, Daniel was all smiles. In the previous three weeks she had had a win, a second and a ninth.

Nobody really smiled on Sunday. Little won with an even-par 72 that was momentarily spoiled by a bogey on the last hole. But she didn't need to worry as none of the others could make a charge. "I can't believe I've won a third," said Sally. "You know I haven't been the most positive under pressure. I've choked a few." That's something that only winners admit.

Ping Team Classic—$100,000
Winners: Nancy Lopez and JoAnn Washam

"Vibes." There was a time when all that meant was a musical instrument that Lionel Hampton could play sweeter than anyone in heaven or on earth. But, in this post-age of Aquarius, "good vibes" are something all competitors seek.

Before the Ping Team Championship ever began at the Portland (Oregon) Golf Course, JoAnn Washam was awash in good vibes. "I love it here," she said, remembering she had won the 1975 Portland Classic on the same course. "I get good vibes on this course. And the vibes are especially good when I have Nancy Lopez as a partner."

Understandable. Lopez, already a seven-time winner for the year and the tour's leading money winner, probably would have been favored with anyone. Teaming her with Washam, who loved the course and had won the Rail Classic just two weeks earlier, seemed like an unbeatable combination. And they were unbeatable—but just barely. It took a birdie on the final hole by Washam to edge "the golfing mothers," Susie Berning and Carole Jo Skala, by one stroke and take $20,000 in unofficial prize money for winning the annual team event.

Perfect playing conditions made everyone look brilliant. Lopez and Washam shot consistently super rounds of 66–65–67 for a 21-under-par finish of 198, a tournament record by five strokes. And it still almost wasn't enough as Berning and Skala were at 199, while youngsters Beth Daniel and Lori Garbacz tied Janet Coles and Lauren Howe at even 200. Berning and Skala, kidding as they went, birdied the 16th and 17th holes on the final day to move one stroke ahead of the favorites, who were playing farther back. But Skala's 15-foot birdie putt on the par-five final hole died on the cup's edge, leaving the door open. "We're just two old mothers who can't play anymore," said the 38-year-old Berning, who won the first of her three U.S. Open titles when Lopez was 11 years old. "We're just out for a walk in the park," said the 41-year-old Skala, whose son was caddying for her.

Lopez and Washam felt the pressure and responded to it by getting birdies on three of the last four holes. Washam applied the *coup de grace* when she chipped to within 12 inches on the last hole and tapped in a birdie putt to win. The vibes never felt better.

ERA Kansas City Classic—$100,000
Winner: Sandra Post

When exhausted Sandra Post took an impulsive vacation from competitive golf in August, she seriously considered sitting out the rest of the year. But when she came back in September at the ERA Kansas City Classic, it turned out to be perfect timing. "I was a little nervous when I first came back," said Post. "But you know, it quickly comes back to you." Very quickly in the case of the 31-year-old Canadian who shot steady rounds of 71–73–70–70 for an eight-under-par total of 284 on the ragged Brookridge Golf Course to pass Donna Caponi Young by two strokes for her third victory of the year. The $15,000 first-place prize pushed Post past Pat Bradley into second place behind Nancy Lopez with winnings of $138,344. Post would go on to win another $40,000 in the year's final five events to hold onto the No. 2 spot and come within $19,000 of catching Lopez. That kind of play is more fun than even the best of vacations.

But back in August, after early-season wins in the Colgate-Dinah Shore Winners Circle and the Lady Michelob, Post was tired and uncertain about her game. She finished 45th in the Patty Berg Classic and then took off. "I didn't know if I would stay off three weeks or the rest of the year," she said. "I went home [to Boynton Beach, Florida] and sat through Hurricane David, boarded up in my house for two days. I went to Toronto [her childhood home] and couldn't get much accomplished there. Finally, I went to Vancouver and just played. I just went out and didn't care where I hit it. I had never done that before."

Post regained the Tour in Kansas City because she felt mentally and physically refreshed. But did she feel competitive? She wasn't sure after opening rounds of 71 and 73 that left her three strokes behind Young, rookie Cathy Sherk and sophomore Barbara Moxness. Post fired a 70 in the third round to pass Moxness and Sherk but remained three shots behind Young, who seemed to be in the form that had carried her to the LPGA Championship earlier in the year.

"I have felt this year I have played as well as some other years when I have won three or four tournaments," said Young. "But someone else always plays better and I have one mediocre round." On Sunday, the "someone else" was Post, who shot her second straight 70, and the mediocre round was a 75 for Young. They were still tied with six holes to play, but Young bogeyed No. 13 while Post parred the last seven holes to steadily pull away. Even so, Young had the consolation of becoming the eighth woman in 1979 to go over $100,000 in winnings after cashing her runners-up check of $9,800.

Mary Kay Classic—$130,000
Winner: Nancy Lopez

Nobody realized it at the time but the $130,000 Mary Kay Classic in Dallas was the definitive tournament of the LPGA season in 1979. It was a four-day summary of the year as Nancy Lopez won, reflecting her supremacy; Sandra Post placed second, reflecting her role as the year's No. 2 competitor; and Beth Daniel was third, demonstrating the skill that made her rookie of the year and the future's most promising star.

It was the eighth win of the season for Lopez, pushing her official winnings to $193,752—breaking her own single-season record of the year before ($189,813). Dallas was vital for many reasons to Lopez, not the least of which was its effect on her surprisingly low morale. "Mentally, I was falling apart," said Lopez, talking about feelings just before the Mary Kay started at Bent Tree Country Club (far removed from the Bent Tree Classic played earlier in Sarasota, Florida). "I knew I needed help, somebody to look at me before I was mentally destroyed."

So, for the first time in her life, Lopez took a lesson from another pro. She called Buddy Phillips, a pro and friend living in Broken Arrow, Oklahoma, and begged him to take a look at her game. Phillips flew to Dallas and, the day before the first round, told Lopez to shift her feet slightly so she wouldn't be prone to the duck hooks that were beginning to haunt her game.

The results were inconclusive after an opening 71 that left her five shots behind Australian Jan Stephenson, who would like to be something more than "just" the reigning sex symbol on the Tour. But Friday's second round, especially its beginning, was Lopez at her finest. She birdied seven of the first eight holes and totaled 10 birdies, an LPGA single-round record. However, a bogey and double bogey held the round to a seven-under-par 66 to tie Stephenson, who shot 71. Lopez was humming now. She shot 67 on Saturday, taking a five-shot lead on Post. Stephenson stumbled in with a 77 and said: "Nancy knows she's a star and she plays like a star. Me? Well, I played like a star for a couple of days but now I'm embarrassed." Stephenson closed with a 71 to finish fourth—but 11 shots behind Lopez.

Post and Daniel played like stars on the final day. Post shot 67 for a 276, while Daniel shot 66 for a 278. But Lopez shot a 70 for an incredible total of 14-under-par 274—despite an emotional outburst that cost her two straight bogeys. It happened on the 11th green. "On my first putt, just as I took the putter back, I heard this camera snap and I jerked it. I really got mad. I felt like my temperature went to 150." She three-putted for a bogey. "I couldn't get my concentration back . . . and I made another bogey." That had cut her lead to one stroke over Post. But Lopez reached deep for her royal reserve and birdied the next two holes to regain a three-stroke lead. She not only coasted into eighth win but also into another year as the undisputed leading lady of golf.

Wheeling Classic—$100,000
Winner: Debbie Massey

For six months, the memory haunted her. True, Debbie Massey had finished second before. In 1978, she was second three times. But this time it was different. It was the U.S. Open—and Massey had thrown it away, finishing second to Jerilyn Britz. The only thing that could exorcise that memory was victory—something Massey had never done in her own country as a professional. She had won in Japan in 1977 but could she win in America? She could—and she did, although it was far from easy in miserable playing conditions at the Wheeling Classic in West Virginia. Massey not only had to overcome the cold, the wind and the rain but also had to do something about Betsy King's two-shot lead with two holes to play. What Massey did was make up the two shots and then earn her first pro win in the United States on the first hole of sudden-death.

"I feel awful good about winning this," said Massey. "I blew the U.S. Open and mentally it took me a long time to get over it. But I'm over it now, even though I have never played three worse days in a row before." Massey and King tied at three-over-par 219 at Speidel Country Club, which wasn't that bad considering low-40 temperatures, whipping winds and a demoralizing, drizzling rain. "When the sun's not out and the wind blows, you can feel it right down to the marrow," said Massey. "I don't mind the wind and the cold, but when it starts raining, that's a little bit too much."

Massey was a little too much for King, too, at the end. Playing head-to-head, Massey made a crucial six-foot par on the 17th while King bogeyed to cut the young blond's lead to a stroke. Then Massey birdied the par-five final hole and King missed a five-foot birdie putt that would have won the tournament for her. The play-off didn't take long. Massey two-putted for a regulation par and King missed a 12-foot par putt. The difference was $15,000 and peace for Massey, while King settled for $10,000 and a haunting memory of her own.

However, the happiest competitor may have been one who tied for 15th and won just $1,407.14 on rounds of 75–76–75 for a 10-over-par 226. It was JoAnne Carner's return to the tour after three months of recuperation from a wrist injury suffered in a motorcycle accident. Her game was rusty, but her wrists felt fine. Despite playing in just 15 events, Carner would just miss earning more than $100,000 for the fourth straight year by totaling $98,218 in 1979.

United Virginia Bank Classic—$100,000
Winner: Amy Alcott

Amy Alcott's elation over winning was tempered by her sympathy for playing partner Susie McAllister in the United Virginia Bank Classic. "I guess I managed a smile, but normally I would have screamed with joy," said Alcott, recording her third victory of the year. "I felt sorry for Susie. She played so well and she has worked so hard to make a comeback."

McAllister, whose best previous finish was a 15th-place tie in the Otey Crisman Classic, shared the lead with Alcott as they played the final hole. Both hit well off the tee on the par-five, 460-yard 18th. Three-woods were needed for their second shots. Unfortunately for Susie, that club was not in her bag. She didn't even own a three-wood. "I've been looking for a three-wood but I haven't found one I like," she said. So McAllister hit a four-wood and was left with a full nine-iron to the green. Alcott sailed her shot more than 30 yards past McAllister's and had but 80 yards left. Susie's third was pin-high, 30 feet away, while Alcott came within 10 feet of the hole. Amy took a two-putt birdie and won after McAllister three-putted, missing from five feet. Her winning total was 286, two under par, with a 73 in the fourth round. McAllister finished with 72 for 287.

"I just misread the putt," said McAllister, who has not won since the 1975 Wheeling Classic. She earned just $4,498 in 1978, but her $9,800 share in Portsmouth raised her 1979 total to $23,147. Alcott received $15,000 for a total of $124,251.

Tour leader Nancy Lopez, like McAllister, had a disappointing week. She arrived after a week's layoff with the intention of using the pro-am as her only practice round. The pro-am was cancelled by rain, Nancy played with hardly a warmup swing and double-bogeyed three of the last five holes for 79. She tied for 10th place at 292, earning $1,898, far short of the $6,300 she needed to become the first woman golfer to win over $200,000 in a season. Shelly Hamlin and Jan Stephenson were the first-round leaders with 69s, a stroke ahead of Alcott and JoAnne Carner. Alcott shot another 70 in the second round to take the lead and remained in front by a stroke with her 73 in the third round. Carner, who was making only her second tournament appearance since July, took third place behind Alcott and McAllister. Carner's winnings of $7,000 left her less than $2,000 shy of the $100,000 mark.

Colgate Far East Open—$110,000
Winner: Silvia Bertolaccini

No one was sadder than Silvia Bertolaccini to witness the demise of the Colgate Far East Open in the trimming of Colgate-Palmolive's sports budget. Two of Silvia's three career victories had been in that tournament. She won in Singapore in 1977 and in Manila in 1979. The Argentine star won in the Philippines despite an injured right heel, which made it necessary for her to wear sneakers on the course. But she left the others in her tracks, scoring six birdies on the first nine on her way to an opening-round 69 and a wire-to-wire victory.

Bertolaccini was two strokes ahead of Beverly Klass and three in front of Sandra Post after the first round. She shot 72 in the second round, holding a two-stroke margin over Post while Klass slipped to 77. Other contenders entering the final round were Marlene Floyd, Donna Young, JoAnn Washam and Pat Bradley. Floyd and Post challenged to the last, then Silvia sank birdie putts on the 16th and 17th holes to secure the two-stroke victory with another 72 and a 213 total. "I took pressure off myself by not thinking about winning, but just playing as well as I could," she said. "I did not want to blow it after building the lead the first two days. My only focus was on the shot confronting me. If someone else could do it better, so be it." No one could. Post was second, also with 72, for a 215 total and Floyd was third with 73 and 217.

Victory in the $110,000 tournament was worth $16,500 to Bertolaccini, who went over the $70,000 mark for her best season financially in five years on the LPGA circuit. Nancy Lopez entered the event needing to win only $4,349 to become the first LPGA player to surpass the $200,000 mark in one year. She won just $1,837 with rounds of 77, 75 and 73, finishing the year with $197,488.

Mizuno-Japan Classic—$125,000
Winner: Amy Alcott
Unlike their tours into some other countries, whenever the LPGA visits Japan the American pros have come to expect strong opposition from the home golfers. Japanese pros had won two of the previous six Mizuno-Japan Classic titles, with Chako Higuchi's victory in 1974 and Michiko Okada's win in 1978. This year was no different. Four Japanese golfers placed in the first 10, and eight in the first 20. Only a sensational 67, seven under par, by Amy Alcott in the final round enabled the Americans to leave with the first-place trophy.

Alcott began the round three strokes behind Higuchi, then proceeded to record her fourth and most impressive victory in the final event of the season. While Higuchi was finishing with 73, Sandra Post and Lori Garbacz also advanced with 70 and 71, respectively. One stroke separated each of the first four places, as Alcott was followed by Post, Garbacz and then Higuchi. The victory put Alcott in third place in the final standings with $144,383. The runner-up berth for the second successive week left Post second for the year with $178,750 to Nancy Lopez's $197,488.

Janet Coles went through the first round without a bogey, shooting 69, and led Higuchi, Yuko Moriguchi, Sally Little and Beverly Klass by one stroke. In the second round Coles slipped to 76 while Higuchi, with four birdies and one bogey, took command with her 71 and 141 total. Holding second place at that stage were Little, Beth Daniel, Masako Sasaki and Tatsuko Ohsako.

JCPenney Classic—$400,000
Winners: Dave Eichelberger and Murle Breer
The decision to revive a mixed team championship was met with some skepticism four years ago, the thought being that a majority of players and spectators would not support such a tournament. The logic was that the PGA Tour team event was struggling and the headaches would only be doubled under a mixed team format. Since then, the PGA Tour's team championship has had its troubles and the LPGA has introduced a team event, again with only modest success.

And what's become of the mixed team championship? Certainly to the surprise of the diehards, the JCPenney Classic has been more successful than either of its counterparts. By all appearances, it's fun for the golfers and the large galleries, an event that no one takes too seriously and almost everyone enjoys. The JCPenney Classic, played at Bardmoor Country Club near St. Petersburg, fits in perfectly as a casual season-ending tournament and, with each playing, grows stronger. It could well become the one event that will break the autumn stranglehold which football has over golf on the American television networks. So far, let's simply say that the championship has far exceeded expectations with its special and much-needed flair.

The LPGA has had better representation than the PGA Tour in the JCPenney Classic for a fundamental reason. The $400,000 purse with $72,000 for the winning team represents a tremendous payday for the women, while the men at that time of year find greater lures in foreign tournaments. The 1979 winners, Dave Eichelberger and Murle Breer, provide a case-in-point. With his $36,000 share, Eichelberger nearly doubled his PGA Tour earnings while Breer exceeded her LPGA winnings by almost $10,000. There were many, many stellar teams, nevertheless, including Andy Bean and Sally Little, Jerry Pate and Hollis Stacy, Tom Kite and Beth Daniel, Lanny Wadkins and Marlene Floyd, Curtis Strange and Nancy Lopez, Ben Crenshaw and Judy Rankin, Lee Trevino and JoAnne Carner.

Winning by one stroke over Jim Colbert and Silvia Bertolaccini, Eichelberger and Breer skipped a few of the formalities, such as consulting with one another about putts. As Eichelberger said, "She's been playing golf longer than I have. She ought to know how they go by now . . . The worst thing you can have on a putt is a second opinion." There surely was no doubt about Murle's 12-footer for birdie on the 18th green to clinch their victory. Breer and Eichelberger had a closing 69 for a 268 total.

They began with 73 in high winds. Just 13 teams broke par on the first day and Colbert and Bertolaccini led with 68. Gil Morgan and Marlene Hagge were at 69, along with Wadkins and Floyd, and Gardner Dickinson and Sandra Spuzich. A sterling 62 in the second round, one stroke off the tournament record, sent Eichelberger and Breer on their way to victory. They made nine birdies and one eagle, in addition to one bogey. Dave understated, "I thought it was a fairly good round of golf considering the bogey." Colbert and Bertolaccini had 67 and were tied for the lead. In the third round, as the weather turned for the better, Eichelberger and Breer went ahead with 64, including birdies on five of the last seven holes, capped by Dave's chip-in from 50 feet at the 18th green. Colbert and Bertolaccini were one stroke behind after their 65, and the head-to-head match continued into the final day. Both teams were one under par after in nine holes. Attention at that point shifted briefly to Dave Stockton and Donna Young, who turned in 31. They cooled off on the last nine and, again, the focus was on two teams, on to the 18th hole for Breer's birdie, the final stroke of the year.

APPENDIXES

WORLD MONEY LIST

This listing of the 200 leading money winners in the world of professional golf in 1979 was compiled from the results of all tournaments carried in the Appendix of this edition of the *Dunhill Golf Yearbook,* along with such other non-tour or international events for which accurate figures could be obtained and in which the players competed for prize money provided by somebody other than the competitors themselves. In the 14 years during which World Money Lists have been compiled, the earnings of the person in 200th position have risen from a total of $3,326 in 1966 to $28,455 in 1979. Tom Watson's $506,912 in 1979 was a new high. The top 200 players in 1966 earned a total of $4,680,287. In 1979, the comparable total was $17,790,763.

Because of the unsettled state of money throughout the world in 1979, it was necessary to determine an average value of British pounds, Japanese yen, South African rand and Australian and New Zealand dollars to U.S. dollars to prepare this listing. The conversion rates, also indicated on the first summary of each tour section, are: $2.10 to a pound, $1.20 to a rand, $1.09 to an Australian dollar, $1.03 to a New Zealand dollar and 220 yen to a U.S. dollar.

POS.	PLAYER	TOTAL MONEY
1	Tom Watson, *U.S.A.*	$506,912
2	Bill Rogers, *U.S.A.*	337,086
3	Ben Crenshaw, *U.S.A.*	294,550
4	Larry Nelson, *U.S.A.*	288,870
5	Lee Trevino, *U.S.A.*	287,030
6	Isao Aoki, *Japan*	275,616
7	Lon Hinkle, *U.S.A.*	273,286
8	Lanny Wadkins, *U.S.A.*	256,418
9	David Graham, *Australia*	251,567
10	Fuzzy Zoeller, *U.S.A.*	231,444
11	Andy Bean, *U.S.A.*	221,730
12	Bruce Lietzke, *U.S.A.*	209,285
13	Jerry Pate, *U.S.A.*	208,623
14	Hubert Green, *U.S.A.*	205,192
15	Lou Graham, *U.S.A.*	194,615
16	Hale Irwin, *U.S.A.*	188,061
17	Howard Twitty, *U.S.A.*	185,855
18	Jack Renner, *U.S.A.*	183,333
19	Tom Kite, *U.S.A.*	183,167
20	Gary Player, *South Africa*	180,125
21	Bobby Wadkins, *U.S.A.*	178,521
22	Jerry McGee, *U.S.A.*	175,834
23	Toru Nakamura, *Japan*	170,907
24	Graham Marsh, *Australia*	155,026
25	Tom Purtzer, *U.S.A.*	152,353
26	Curtis Strange, *U.S.A.*	151,415
27	Ed Sneed, *U.S.A.*	149,722
28	Raymond Floyd, *U.S.A.*	147,445
29	Wayne Levi, *U.S.A.*	146,297
30	Masaji Kusakabe, *Japan*	145,639
31	Kuo Chi Hsiung, *Taiwan*	143,931
32	Mark Hayes, *U.S.A.*	142,510
33	Bob Gilder, *U.S.A.*	140,695
34	George Burns, *U.S.A.*	135,295
35	Gil Morgan, *U.S.A.*	134,316
36	Calvin Peete, *U.S.A.*	133,354
37	Norio Suzuki, *Japan*	132,996
38	Rod Curl, *U.S.A.*	132,471
39	J.C. Snead, *U.S.A.*	131,598
40	Severiano Ballesteros, *Spain*	124,484
41	Bob Byman, *U.S.A.*	121,099
42	John Fought, *U.S.A.*	118,579
43	Sandy Lyle, *Great Britain*	118,411
44	Hsieh Min Nan, *Taiwan*	117,390
45	Grier Jones, *U.S.A.*	116,551
46	Jim Colbert, *U.S.A.*	116,464
47	Lu Liang Huan, *Taiwan*	110,120
48	Peter Jacobsen, *U.S.A.*	109,195
49	Bill Kratzert, *U.S.A.*	106,955
50	Masashi Ozaki, *Japan*	105,040
51	Jay Haas, *U.S.A.*	104,734

52	Teruo Sugihara, *Japan*	104,493
53	Rex Caldwell, *U.S.A.*	103,850
54	Al Geiberger, *U.S.A.*	101,512
55	Don January, *U.S.A.*	101,504
56	Alan Tapie, *U.S.A.*	101,176
57	Fujio Kobayashi, *Japan*	99,191
58	Keith Fergus, *U.S.A.*	98,965
59	Greg Norman, *Australia*	97,968
60	Jack Newton, *Australia*	97,839
61	Yoshitaka Yamamoto, *Japan*	96,135
62	John Mahaffey, *U.S.A.*	95,019
63	Victor Regalado, *Mexico*	94,318
64	Leonard Thompson, *U.S.A.*	93,280
65	Mike Brannan, *U.S.A.*	92,767
66	Haruo Yasuda, *Japan*	92,608
67	Hiroshi Ishii, *Japan*	92,114
68	Kikuo Arai, *Japan*	90,015
69	Tom Weiskopf, *U.S.A.*	88,969
70	Doug Tewell, *U.S.A.*	87,300
71	D.A. Weibring, *U.S.A.*	85,343
72	Jim Simons, *U.S.A.*	84,412
73	Joe Inman, *U.S.A.*	84,085
74	Mark James, *Great Britain*	83,502
75	Jack Nicklaus, *U.S.A.*	83,059
76	Craig Stadler, *U.S.A.*	82,992
77	Gibby Gilbert, *U.S.A.*	82,572
78	Andy North, *U.S.A.*	81,721
79	John Schroeder, *U.S.A.*	81,668
80	Yasuhiro Miyamoto, *Japan*	81,044
81	Bob Murphy, *U.S.A.*	80,441
82	Mark McCumber, *U.S.A.*	80,390
83	Miller Barber, *U.S.A.*	80,243
84	Lu Hsi Chuen, *Taiwan*	80,007
85	Dave Eichelberger, *U.S.A.*	79,187
86	Ed Fiori, *U.S.A.*	76,153
87	Johnny Miller, *U.S.A.*	74,865
88	Buddy Gardner, *U.S.A.*	73,820
89	Dale Hayes, *South Africa*	73,724
90	Gene Littler, *U.S.A.*	72,067
91	Lee Elder, *U.S.A.*	71,457
92	Kenji Mori, *Japan*	71,035
93	Chi Chi Rodriguez, *U.S.A.*	70,725
94	Tommy Aaron, *U.S.A.*	70,619
95	Brad Bryant, *U.S.A.*	69,413
96	Kosaku Shimada, *Japan*	68,338
97	Tsuneyuki Nakajima, *Japan*	67,927
98	Brian Barnes, *Great Britain*	67,375
99	Namio Takasu, *Japan*	67,354
100	Scott Simpson, *U.S.A.*	66,660
101	Kermit Zarley, *U.S.A.*	66,414
102	Mike Reid, *U.S.A.*	66,171
103	Morris Hatalsky, *U.S.A.*	65,162
104	Koichi Uehara, *Japan*	64,511
105	Bob Charles, *New Zealand*	64,482
106	Bruce Devlin, *Australia*	63,519
107	Bob Shearer, *Australia*	63,308
108	Rodger Davis, *Australia*	62,663
109	Tsutomu Irie, *Japan*	62,062
110	Mark Lye, *U.S.A.*	61,834
111	Michael King, *Great Britain*	61,181
112	Lindy Miller, *U.S.A.*	60,814
113	Tony Jacklin, *Great Britain*	60,312
114	Dave Stockton, *U.S.A.*	59,840
115	Akira Yabe, *Japan*	59,761
116	Charles Coody, *U.S.A.*	59,453
117	Barry Jaeckel, *U.S.A.*	58,192
118	Stewart Ginn, *Australia*	57,715
119	Ben Arda, *Philippines*	57,450
120	Wally Armstrong, *U.S.A.*	57,249
121	Maurice Bembridge, *Great Britain*	57,196
122	Orville Moody, *U.S.A.*	55,480
123	Mya Aye, *Burma*	54,993
124	Yoshikazu Yokoshima, *Japan*	54,645
125	Shigeru Uchida, *Japan*	54,443
126	Ken Brown, *Great Britain*	54,236
127	Jim Nelford, *Canada*	53,332
128	Jim Thorpe, *U.S.A.*	53,007
129	Antonio Garrido, *Spain*	52,333
130	Bobby Walzel, *U.S.A.*	52,208
131	Simon Hobday, *Rhodesia*	50,641
132	Gary Koch, *U.S.A.*	50,534
133	Seiichi Kanai, *Japan*	49,822
134	Larry Ziegler, *U.S.A.*	49,671
135	Hugh Baiocchi, *South Africa*	49,356

136	Vicente Fernandez, *Argentina*	48,958
137	Mike Morley, *U.S.A.*	48,860
138	Julius Boros, *U.S.A.*	48,810
139	Mike Sullivan, *U.S.A.*	48,321
140	Artie McNickle, *U.S.A.*	47,271
141	Tim Simpson, *U.S.A.*	47,173
142	Frank Conner, *U.S.A.*	46,970
143	Des Smyth, *Ireland*	46,967
144	Dave Edwards, *U.S.A.*	46,522
145	Gary McCord, *U.S.A.*	45,918
146	Peter Townsend, *Great Britain*	45,566
147	Koichi Inoue, *Japan*	45,105
148	Bernard Gallacher, *Great Britain*	45,043
149	Nick Faldo, *Great Britain*	44,548
150	Terry Diehl, *U.S.A.*	44,496
151	Eddie Pearce, *U.S.A.*	44,050
152	Mike McCullough, *U.S.A.*	43,664
153	Peter Oosterhuis, *Great Britain*	43,338
154	Sam Torrance, *Great Britain*	43,286
155	Dan Pohl, *U.S.A.*	42,393
156	Hsieh Yung Yo, *Taiwan*	42,371
157	Shinsaku Maeda, *Japan*	42,364
158	Shoichi Sato, *Japan*	42,194
159	Chen Tze Ming, *Taiwan*	42,127
160	Hsu Sheng San, *Taiwan*	41,962
161	Mike Hill, *U.S.A.*	41,450
162	Kazuo Yoshikawa, *Japan*	41,214
163	Nicky Price, *South Africa*	41,085
164	Simon Owen, *New Zealand*	40,534
165	Phil Hancock, *U.S.A.*	40,340
166	Masaru Amano, *Japan*	40,320
167	Neil Coles, *Great Britain*	40,290
168	Pat McGowan, *U.S.A.*	40,253
169	Ron Streck, *U.S.A.*	39,734
170	Roberto de Vicenzo, *Argentina*	39,410
171	Jeff Mitchell, *U.S.A.*	38,032
172	Dan Halldorson, *Canada*	37,959
173	Rod Funseth, *U.S.A.*	36,767
174	Brian Waites, *Great Britain*	36,747
175	John Morgan, *Great Britain*	36,598
176	Manuel Pinero, *Spain*	36,508
177	Terry Gale, *Australia*	35,408
178	Terry Kendall, *New Zealand*	35,059
179	Ikuhiro Funatogawa, *Japan*	34,447
180	Jose-Maria Canizares, *Spain*	34,427
181	Yoshihisa Iwashita, *Japan*	34,253
182	Danny Edwards, *U.S.A.*	34,245
183	Norio Mikami, *Japan*	33,267
184	Jim Dent, *U.S.A.*	32,909
185	Toshiharu Kawada, *Japan*	32,334
186	Mark McNulty, *South Africa*	32,003
187	Takahiro Takeyasu, *Japan*	31,890
188	Hsu Chi San, *Taiwan*	31,873
189	Bobby Verwey, *South Africa*	31,773
190	Steve Melnyk, *U.S.A.*	30,876
191	Art Wall, *U.S.A.*	30,353
192	Howard Clark, *Great Britain*	30,174
193	Tommy Horton, *Great Britain*	29,859
194	Bob Eastwood, *U.S.A.*	29,630
195	Kazunari Takahashi, *Japan*	29,486
196	Bernhard Langer, *West Germany*	28,958
197	Malcolm Gregson, *Great Britain*	28,790
198	John O'Leary, *Ireland*	28,744
199	George Cadle, *U.S.A.*	28,708
200	Baldovino Dassu, *Italy*	28,455

WORLD STROKE AVERAGES

If not done by comparison of money winnings, the relative performances of tournament players are best measured by the average strokes per round taken during a prescribed period, usually a full season. Stroke averages can be misleading though, because, among other things, they do not allow for the degree of difficulty of the many courses involved in a year of play. The World Stroke Averages which follow were compiled from the results of all tournaments carried in this Appendix for the year 1979, excluding, of course, the match play and team events. The list contains only those players who competed in at least 60 rounds during the year.

POS.	PLAYER	ROUNDS	STROKES	AVERAGE
1	Tom Watson, *U.S.A.*	98	6,920	70.61
2	Grier Jones, *U.S.A.*	73	5,165	70.75
3	Bill Rogers, *U.S.A.*	120	8,497	70.81
4	Lee Trevino, *U.S.A.*	117	8,317	71.09
5	Ben Crenshaw, *U.S.A.*	101	7,195	71.24
6	J.C. Snead, *U.S.A.*	113	8,055	71.28
7	Tom Purtzer, *U.S.A.*	117	8,346	71.33
8	Rod Curl, *U.S.A.*	103	7,349	71.35
9	Bruce Lietzke, *U.S.A.*	108	7,709	71.38
10	Curtis Strange, *U.S.A.*	120	8,567	71.39
11	Calvin Peete, *U.S.A.*	88	6,285	71.42
12	Hale Irwin, *U.S.A.*	89	6,362	71.48
13	Tom Kite, *U.S.A.*	113	8,080	71.50
14	John Mahaffey, *U.S.A.*	84	6,007	71.51
T15	Lanny Wadkins, *U.S.A.*	103	7,368	71.53
	Jerry Pate, *U.S.A.*	109	7,797	71.53
	Doug Tewell, *U.S.A.*	92	6,581	71.53
T18	Isao Aoki, *Japan*	113.5	8,122	71.56
	Larry Nelson, *U.S.A.*	112	8,015	71.56
20	Mike Morley, *U.S.A.*	71	5,082	71.58
T21	Jack Renner, *U.S.A.*	102	7,302	71.59
	Andy Bean, *U.S.A.*	108	7,732	71.59
T23	Bob Gilder, *U.S.A.*	119	8,524	71.63
	Chi Chi Rodriguez, *U.S.A.*	80	5,730	71.63
25	Gary Player, *South Africa*	81	5,803	71.64
T26	Howard Twitty, *U.S.A.*	116	8,311	71.65
	Gene Littler, *U.S.A.*	92	6,592	71.65
28	Mark Lye, *U.S.A.*	98	7,025	71.68
29	Leonard Thompson, *U.S.A.*	104	7,456	71.69
30	Sandy Lyle, *Great Britain*	98	7,028	71.71
31	Jim Colbert, *U.S.A.*	105	7,533	71.74
32	Gibby Gilbert, *U.S.A.*	103	7,391	71.76
T33	Don January, *U.S.A.*	96	6,890	71.77
	Rex Caldwell, *U.S.A.*	112	8,038	71.77
35	Jay Haas, *U.S.A.*	100	7,179	71.79
36	Jerry McGee, *U.S.A.*	99	7,108	71.80
37	Bobby Wadkins, *U.S.A.*	120	8,621	71.84
38	Mike Reid, *U.S.A.*	113	8,122	71.88
T39	Mike Hill, *U.S.A.*	92	6,614	71.89
	Alan Tapie, *U.S.A.*	107	7,692	71.89
T41	Hubert Green, *U.S.A.*	112	8,053	71.90
	Lu Liang Huan, *Taiwan*	81.5	5,860	71.90
T43	Fuzzy Zoeller, *U.S.A.*	104	7,479	71.91
	Bob E. Smith, *U.S.A.*	64	4,602	71.91
45	Dave Edwards, *U.S.A.*	89	6,403	71.94
46	Brad Bryant, *U.S.A.*	100	7,197	71.97
47	Hsieh Min Nan, *Taiwan*	101.5	7,306	71.98
48	Masashi Ozaki, *Japan*	105.5	7,596	72.00
T49	Peter Jacobsen, *U.S.A.*	120	8,644	72.03
	Bobby Walzel, *U.S.A.*	76	5,474	72.03

America's John Fought (above),
Curtis Strange (right) *and*
Peter Jacobsen (opposite).

U.S. TOUR

Bob Hope Desert Classic

Bermuda Dunes Country Club, Bermuda Dunes, California
Par 36–36—72; 6,778 yards

January 10–14
purse, $275,500

Indian Wells Country Club
Palm Desert, California
Par 36–36—72; 6,532 yards

LaQuinta Country Club
LaQuinta, California
Par 36–36—72; 6,911 yards

Tamarisk Country Club
Palm Springs, California
Par 36–36—72; 6,869 yards

	SCORES					TOTAL	MONEY
John Mahaffey	66	66	71	71	69	343	$50,000.00
Lee Trevino	71	68	66	70	69	344	29,700.00
Mark Hayes	70	72	68	69	66	345	18,700.00
Grier Jones	70	68	71	69	68	346	13,200.00
Lanny Wadkins	71	66	74	69	68	348	10,450.00
Keith Fergus	69	67	68	75	69	348	10,450.00
Bobby Wadkins	69	70	72	71	67	349	8,275.00
Tom Purtzer	69	68	70	74	68	349	8,275.00
Leonard Thompson	69	66	69	75	70	349	8,275.00
Allan Tapie	71	71	68	68	71	349	8,275.00
Jerry Pate	71	72	70	69	68	350	6,325.00
Jack Nicklaus	71	69	69	72	69	350	6,325.00
Lon Hinkle	72	67	73	69	69	350	6,325.00
Don Bies	73	68	69	72	69	351	4,675.00
Mark McCumber	70	73	70	70	68	351	4,675.00
Butch Baird	72	72	71	67	69	351	4,675.00
Andy Bean	72	68	74	68	69	351	4,675.00
Orville Moody	71	70	68	73	69	351	4,675.00
Kermit Zarley	71	68	72	73	68	352	3,451.25
Jim Colbert	72	72	70	69	69	352	3,451.25
Wayne Levi	74	68	69	71	70	352	3,451.25
Wally Armstrong	69	72	69	68	74	352	3,451.25
J.C. Snead	68	69	74	75	67	353	2,640.00
Dave Hill	71	76	67	70	69	353	2,640.00
Joe Inman	72	73	70	69	69	353	2,640.00
Curtis Strange	72	69	73	71	69	354	1,884.45
D. A. Weibring	74	71	68	72	69	354	1,884.45
Mike Hill	73	68	76	69	68	354	1,884.45
Tom Kite	70	69	74	73	68	354	1,884.45
Gene Littler	72	74	69	68	71	354	1,884.44
Rex Caldwell	75	74	72	64	69	354	1,884.44
Raymond Floyd	74	71	72	70	67	354	1,884.44
Ben Crenshaw	70	72	69	71	72	354	1,884.44
Charles Coody	65	73	73	69	74	354	1,884.44
Ed Sneed	73	72	69	71	70	355	1,390.00
Gay Brewer	72	74	68	72	69	355	1,390.00
Mike McCullough	70	72	73	72	68	355	1,390.00
Andy North	71	74	69	73	68	355	1,390.00
Larry Nelson	71	69	72	73	71	356	1,180.00
Bill Rogers	70	73	68	72	73	356	1,180.00
Art Wall	67	67	73	75	74	356	1,180.00
Bob Murphy	65	74	72	75	72	358	926.67
Mike Morley	73	72	73	69	71	358	926.67
Jay Haas	72	77	67	72	70	358	926.67
Bobby Nichols	73	70	73	73	69	358	926.67
Dave Eichelberger	73	68	73	76	68	358	926.66
Bob Zender	72	75	72	71	68	358	926.66
Tim Simpson	74	72	73	69	71	359	702.00
Gil Morgan	71	71	75	72	70	359	702.00
Mike Reid	77	70	72	70	70	359	702.00

Phoenix Open

Phoenix Country Club, Phoenix, Arizona
Par 36–35—71; 6,726 yards

January 18–22
purse, $187,500

(Tournament shortened to 54 holes because of weather postponements)

	SCORES			TOTAL	MONEY
Ben Crenshaw	67	61	71	199	$33,750.00
Jay Haas	65	67	68	200	20,250.00
Tom Kite	73	66	63	202	12,750.00
Pat McGowan	71	66	66	203	7,382.82
Lon Hinkle	66	69	68	203	7,382.81

Jerry Pate	66	66	71	203	7,382.81
Andy Bean	66	66	71	203	7,382.81
Wayne Levi	71	68	66	205	5,250.00
Joe Inman	69	68	68	205	5,250.00
Phil Hancock	68	68	69	205	5,250.00
Rod Funseth	70	66	69	205	5,250.00
Mike Reid	71	68	67	206	3,250.00
Bob Gilder	69	70	67	206	3,250.00
Mark Hayes	73	66	67	206	3,250.00
Dave Stockton	71	66	69	206	3,250.00
Bob Zender	71	66	69	206	3,250.00
Dave Eichelberger	69	67	70	206	3,250.00
George Burns	69	66	71	206	3,250.00
Jim Nelford	70	65	71	206	3,250.00
Bruce Lietzke	66	69	71	206	3,250.00
Mark McCumber	68	70	69	207	1,875.00
Grier Jones	68	71	68	207	1,875.00
Tom Purtzer	70	68	69	207	1,875.00
Charles Coody	69	69	69	207	1,875.00
Jim Colbert	66	70	71	207	1,875.00
Keith Fergus	67	70	70	207	1,875.00
Bobby Walzel	73	66	69	208	1,221.92
Mike Bodney	68	69	71	208	1,221.92
Gene Littler	69	68	71	208	1,221.92
John Mahaffey	68	69	71	208	1,221.92
Bill Kratzert	71	65	72	208	1,221.92
Andy North	66	70	72	208	1,221.92
Bobby Nichols	70	71	67	208	1,221.91
Jerry McGee	72	64	72	208	1,221.91
Howard Twitty	68	66	74	208	1,221.91
Dave Barr	71	68	70	209	902.25
Mike Hill	70	68	71	209	902.25
Jeff Hewes	69	67	73	209	902.25
Rex Caldwell	74	67	68	209	902.25
Tom Weiskopf	69	70	71	210	693.75
Mark Pfeil	69	69	72	210	693.75
Fuzzy Zoeller	70	69	71	210	693.75
Bill Sander	68	70	72	210	693.75
Leonard Thompson	70	67	73	210	693.75
Curtis Strange	68	68	74	210	693.75
Bill Rogers	70	65	75	210	693.75
Orville Moody	70	70	71	211	495.75
Lanny Wadkins	67	70	74	211	495.75
Bob Byman	71	69	71	211	495.75
Gibby Gilbert	71	70	70	211	495.75
Roger Maltbie	71	70	70	211	495.75

Andy Williams San Diego Open

Torrey Pines, San Diego, California
North Course (Thursday, Friday only)
Par 36-36—72; 6,667 yards

January 25–28
purse, $250,000

South Course (all four days)
Par 36-36—72; 7,047 yards

	SCORES				TOTAL	MONEY
Fuzzy Zoeller	76	67	67	72	282	$45,000.00
Wayne Levi	79	68	72	68	287	16,500.00
Tom Watson	74	70	72	71	287	16,500.00
Artie McNickle	73	71	71	72	287	16,500.00
Bill Kratzert	73	68	72	74	287	16,500.00
Victor Regalado	71	73	70	74	288	8,093.75
Lee Trevino	75	69	70	74	288	8,093.75
Jerry Pate	72	70	72	74	288	8,093.75
Jerry McGee	71	67	74	76	288	8,093.75
Keith Fergus	74	73	72	70	289	6,000.00
Howard Twitty	74	70	73	72	289	6,000.00
Scott Simpson	73	73	71	72	289	6,000.00
Larry Nelson	77	68	70	74	289	6,000.00
John Fought	78	70	69	73	290	4,000.00
Randy Erskine	73	74	70	73	290	4,000.00
Tom Weiskopf	74	70	73	73	290	4,000.00
J.C. Snead	79	67	70	74	290	4,000.00
Mark Hayes	77	69	70	74	290	4,000.00
Tommy Aaron	69	70	75	76	290	4,000.00
Tom Purtzer	78	66	70	76	290	4,000.00
Bob Gilder	74	71	70	76	291	2,700.00
Jim Colbert	75	67	73	76	291	2,700.00
Leonard Thompson	73	70	71	77	291	2,700.00
Grier Jones	71	71	72	77	291	2,700.00
Danny Edwards	75	71	72	74	292	1,828.13
Mike McCullough	77	71	70	74	292	1,828.13
Curtis Strange	78	68	73	73	292	1,828.13
Craig Stadler	78	69	71	74	292	1,828.13
Miller Barber	79	67	70	76	292	1,828.12
Al Geiberger	75	72	74	71	292	1,828.12

Gil Morgan	74	67	72	79	292	1,828.12
Billy Casper	71	73	69	79	292	1,828.12
Bobby Walzel	76	71	71	75	293	1,212.50
Gary Koch	73	76	69	75	293	1,212.50
Tommy Valentine	78	69	71	75	293	1,212.50
Chi Chi Rodriguez	73	72	73	75	293	1,212.50
Lon Hinkle	77	69	73	74	293	1,212.50
Jim Thorpe	76	70	73	74	293	1,212.50
Jack Renner	76	71	72	74	293	1,212.50
Alan Tapie	74	73	72	74	293	1,212.50
Lanny Wadkins	78	67	75	73	293	1,212.50
Andy Bean	79	68	70	76	293	1,212.50
Jack Spradlin	72	72	73	77	294	825.00
Mac McLendon	77	69	73	75	294	825.00
Bill Rogers	79	69	72	74	294	825.00
David Graham	78	71	71	74	294	825.00
Cesar Sanudo	76	71	76	71	294	825.00
Steve Spray	76	70	73	76	295	615.63
Rod Funseth	79	68	70	78	295	615.63
Dale Douglass	78	67	72	78	295	615.63
Don January	75	68	73	79	295	615.63

Bing Crosby National Pro-Amateur

Pebble Beach, California
Pebble Beach Golf Links
Par 36–36—72; 6,815 yards

February 1–4
purse, $300,000

Cypress Point Golf Club
Par 37–35—72; 6,464 yards

Spyglass Hill Golf Club
Par 36–36—72; 6,810 yards

	SCORES				TOTAL	MONEY
Lon Hinkle	70	68	69	77	284	$54,000.00
Mark Hayes	73	73	66	72	284	26,400.00
Andy Bean	72	73	70	69	284	26,400.00

(Hinkle defeated Bean and Hayes in sudden-death play-off: Bean on second extra hole, Hayes on third)

Leonard Thompson	71	69	76	70	286	13,200.00
Brad Bryant	71	70	73	72	286	13,200.00
Jim Nelford	72	74	70	71	287	10,425.00
Jay Haas	68	77	74	68	287	10,425.00
Curtis Strange	70	70	74	74	288	8,700.00
J.C. Snead	74	72	69	73	288	8,700.00
Gibby Gilbert	72	73	70	73	288	8,700.00
Mark Pfeil	71	75	71	72	289	6,900.00
Bobby Wadkins	75	70	73	71	289	6,900.00
Lee Elder	73	70	75	71	289	6,900.00
Gil Morgan	69	73	72	76	290	5,550.00
John Schroeder	70	71	75	74	290	5,550.00
Fuzzy Zoeller	72	72	73	74	291	4,350.00
Grier Jones	75	70	69	77	291	4,350.00
Jerry Heard	71	72	72	76	291	4,350.00
Orville Moody	71	72	75	73	291	4,350.00
Tommy Aaron	74	72	73	72	291	4,350.00
Bruce Lietzke	73	75	72	71	291	4,350.00
Tom Watson	72	76	73	71	292	2,785.00
Kermit Zarley	75	73	71	73	292	2,785.00
Gene Littler	73	71	74	74	292	2,785.00
Vance Heafner	72	77	73	72	292	2,785.00
Mike Morley	71	76	73	72	292	2,785.00
Tommy Valentine	71	71	78	72	292	2,785.00
Andy North	73	76	74	70	293	2,040.00
Jim Thorpe	72	71	74	76	293	2,040.00
Craig Stadler	70	73	74	76	293	2,040.00
Tom Weiskopf	74	74	67	78	293	2,040.00
Bob Gilder	73	76	70	74	293	2,040.00
George Knudson	71	76	73	74	294	1,518.75
Lou Graham	75	70	78	71	294	1,518.75
Bruce Fleisher	71	75	76	72	294	1,518.75
George Burns	75	71	75	73	294	1,518.75
Lanny Wadkins	71	74	76	73	294	1,518.75
Graham Marsh	68	77	76	73	294	1,518.75
Cesar Sanudo	70	73	78	73	294	1,518.75
Mike McCullough	67	75	77	74	294	1,518.75
Ed Sneed	75	76	68	76	295	1,080.00
Forrest Fezler	73	71	74	77	295	1,080.00
Jerry McGee	73	73	73	76	295	1,080.00
Scott Simpson	74	72	76	73	295	1,080.00
Jim Colbert	71	75	74	75	295	1,080.00
Frank Conner	76	76	68	75	295	1,080.00
Johnny Miller	73	74	72	77	296	770.58
Steve Melnyk	76	74	73	73	296	770.57
Victor Regalado	71	74	78	73	296	770.57
Pat McGowan	75	67	81	73	296	770.57
Danny Edwards	74	76	72	74	296	770.57

Hawaiian Open

Waialae Country Club, Honolulu, Hawaii
par 36–36—72; 6,881 yards

February 8–11
purse, $300,000

	SCORES				TOTAL	MONEY
Hubert Green	68	67	63	69	267	$54,000.00
Fuzzy Zoeller	66	68	71	65	270	32,400.00
Larry Nelson	66	69	70	67	272	20,400.00
Charles Coody	66	72	66	69	273	12,400.00
Miller Barber	71	68	65	69	273	12,400.00
Lindy Miller	65	70	68	70	273	12,400.00
Don January	68	70	66	70	274	9,675.00
Dan Halldorson	68	66	69	71	274	9,675.00
Hale Irwin	67	70	67	71	275	8,400.00
George Burns	71	63	68	73	275	8,400.00
John Schroeder	68	73	70	65	276	7,200.00
Tom Storey	68	70	66	72	276	7,200.00
Leonard Thompson	67	70	73	67	277	5,460.00
Wayne Levi	66	73	71	67	277	5,460.00
Jeff Mitchell	71	68	72	66	277	5,460.00
Wally Armstrong	66	71	69	71	277	5,460.00
Frank Conner	68	68	69	72	277	5,460.00
Bill Calfee	71	71	68	68	278	4,200.00
Bill Rogers	70	72	68	68	278	4,200.00
Andy Bean	66	71	72	69	278	4,200.00
Joe Hager	69	70	71	69	279	3,000.00
Isao Aoki	72	68	70	69	279	3,000.00
Bruce Lietzke	67	74	68	70	279	3,000.00
Tom Chain	67	72	69	71	279	3,000.00
Ed Sneed	71	71	69	68	279	3,000.00
Lanny Wadkins	65	72	70	72	279	3,000.00
Jim Thorpe	69	67	74	70	280	2,130.00
Danny Edwards	70	69	69	72	280	2,130.00
Brad Bryant	72	67	69	72	280	2,130.00
Bob Murphy	68	74	69	69	280	2,130.00
Howard Twitty	71	69	67	73	280	2,130.00
Pat McGowan	67	75	68	71	281	1,590.00
Rod Curl	71	71	68	71	281	1,590.00
Grier Jones	69	72	68	72	281	1,590.00
Tom Watson	68	71	70	72	281	1,590.00
Tom Purtzer	70	69	73	69	281	1,590.00
Jack Renner	69	66	72	74	281	1,590.00
Gil Morgan	66	74	73	68	281	1,590.00
Jay Haas	65	70	68	78	281	1,590.00
Lee Trevino	72	69	69	72	282	1,170.00
Graham Marsh	69	69	72	72	282	1,170.00
Dave Stockton	69	68	72	73	282	1,170.00
Peter Jacobsen	69	70	69	74	282	1,170.00
Lee Elder	70	71	71	70	282	1,170.00
Bob Gilder	66	72	72	73	283	801.00
Mark Lye	66	76	67	74	283	801.00
George Knudson	70	70	71	72	283	801.00
Gene Littler	68	71	72	72	283	801.00
Dana Quigley	70	69	72	72	283	801.00
J.C. Snead	66	75	71	71	283	801.00

Joe Garagiola Tucson Open

Randolph North Golf Club, Tucson, Arizona
Par 35–35—70; 6,708 yards

February 15–18
purse, $250,000

	SCORES				TOTAL	MONEY
Bruce Lietzke	63	66	68	68	265	$45,000.00
Tom Watson	67	66	66	68	267	18,666.67
Jim Thorpe	67	65	67	68	267	18,666.67
Buddy Gardner	69	66	67	65	267	18,666.66
Marty Fleckman	66	67	66	69	268	8,781.25
Victor Regalado	66	68	67	67	268	8,781.25
Curtis Strange	64	71	67	66	268	8,781.25
Howard Twitty	69	68	66	65	268	8,781.25
Lee Trevino	67	68	66	68	269	7,000.00
Dave Barr	69	67	66	67	269	7,000.00
Tommy Aaron	64	72	67	67	270	5,750.00
Mark Hayes	69	65	66	70	270	5,750.00
Chi Chi Rodriguez	70	67	67	66	270	5,750.00
J.C. Snead	70	68	64	69	271	4,625.00
Tom Purtzer	70	68	68	65	271	4,625.00
Mike Morley	70	69	66	67	272	3,750.00
Jim Nelford	64	70	70	68	272	3,750.00
Rod Funseth	71	67	66	68	272	3,750.00
Jim Colbert	67	71	66	68	272	3,750.00
Jeff Mitchell	69	70	66	67	272	3,750.00
Frank Beard	65	70	71	67	273	2,600.00
Wayne Levi	67	68	69	69	273	2,600.00
Bill Sander	70	64	69	70	273	2,600.00
Tom Kite	68	69	68	68	273	2,600.00
Bob Byman	72	67	67	67	273	2,600.00
Frank Conner	65	70	67	72	274	1,701.44
Wren Lum	67	69	68	70	274	1,701.44

Johnny Miller	70	66	67	71	274	1,701.44
Ed Dougherty	69	68	68	69	274	1,701.45
David Edwards	66	72	67	69	274	1,701.44
John Lister	69	69	67	69	274	1,701.45
Larry Nelson	66	68	70	70	274	1,701.45
Jim Simons	67	69	68	70	274	1,701.44
Peter Jacobsen	70	68	69	67	274	1,701.45
Fred Marti	69	70	68	68	275	1,232.40
Dan Halldorson	68	68	68	71	275	1,232.40
Don Bies	66	70	69	70	275	1,232.40
John Schroeder	65	69	72	69	275	1,232.40
Rod Curl	70	67	69	69	275	1,232.40
Barry Jaeckel	68	66	69	73	276	876.12
Mike Sullivan	67	71	70	68	276	876.11
Cesar Sanudo	69	70	69	68	276	876.11
Jack Renner	68	70	69	69	276	876.11
Keith Fergus	71	69	69	67	276	876.11
Gibby Gilbert	68	71	68	69	276	876.11
Artie McNickle	68	67	68	73	276	876.11
Gary McCord	69	67	71	69	276	876.11
Jack Ewing	68	67	70	71	276	876.11
Bob Eastwood	66	69	73	69	277	601.25
Mike Reid	71	69	67	70	277	601.25

Glen Campbell Los Angeles Open

Riviera Country Club, Palisades, California
Par 36–36—71; 7,029 yards

February 22–25
purse, $250,000

	SCORES				TOTAL	MONEY
Lanny Wadkins	66	72	69	69	276	$45,000.00
Lon Hinkle	67	69	71	70	277	27,000.00
Andy Bean	71	69	68	70	278	14,500.00
Kermit Zarley	68	71	68	71	278	14,500.00
Ed Sneed	69	72	69	69	279	9,500.00
Fuzzy Zoeller	70	67	72	70	279	9,500.00
Rod Curl	73	73	68	66	280	7,791.67
Tommy Aaron	73	70	68	69	280	7,791.67
Jim Colbert	73	67	71	69	280	7,791.66
Artie McNickle	71	69	72	69	281	6,750.00
Mike Reid	69	72	72	69	282	5,500.00
Gary McCord	74	71	68	69	282	5,500.00
Hale Irwin	68	73	70	71	282	5,500.00
Tom Purtzer	73	69	70	70	282	5,500.00
Masashi Ozaki	76	68	73	66	283	4,500.00
Mark Lye	71	73	72	68	284	4,125.00
Mike McCullough	73	72	68	71	284	4,125.00
Grier Jones	72	72	73	68	285	3,260.00
Frank Conner	76	70	71	68	285	3,260.00
Rik Massengale	74	72	69	70	285	3,260.00
Charles Coody	69	77	66	73	285	3,260.00
Dale Douglass	72	72	69	72	285	3,260.00
Bill Calfee	72	75	69	70	286	2,300.00
Antonio Cerda	74	72	69	71	286	2,300.00
Allen Miller	70	75	70	71	286	2,300.00
Dave Eichelberger	71	73	68	74	286	2,300.00
Jay Haas	74	72	71	70	287	1,700.00
Tom Watson	74	69	73	71	287	1,700.00
Ben Crenshaw	73	71	72	71	287	1,700.00
Jack Renner	75	71	71	70	287	1,700.00
J.C. Snead	72	69	74	72	287	1,700.00
Craig Stadler	69	74	75	69	287	1,700.00
Rex Caldwell	69	73	72	73	287	1,700.00
Greg Powers	73	72	72	71	288	1,318.75
Keith Fergus	77	68	70	73	288	1,318.75
Phil Hancock	70	71	73	74	288	1,318.75
Pat McGowan	71	76	71	70	288	1,318.75
Don January	74	73	69	73	289	1,050.00
Cesar Sanudo	72	72	72	73	289	1,050.00
Dan Halldorson	75	71	71	72	289	1,050.00
Tom Weiskopf	72	72	72	73	289	1,050.00
Bob Gilder	70	75	69	75	289	1,050.00
Joe Inman	71	74	74	70	289	1,050.00
Marty Fleckman	73	71	73	73	290	825.00
Mac McLendon	75	71	74	70	290	825.00
Al Geiberger	76	67	69	78	290	825.00
Tom Storey	73	72	72	74	291	627.78
Andy North	73	71	74	73	291	627.78
Jack Newton	72	74	72	73	291	627.78
Dave Barr	73	72	73	73	291	627.78

Bay Hill Citrus Classic

Bay Hill Club, Orlando, Florida
Par 36–35—71; 7,102 yards

March 1–4
purse, $250,000

	SCORES				TOTAL	MONEY
Bob Byman	67	70	70	71	278	$45,000.00

John Schroeder	68	68	72	70	278	27,000.00

(Byman defeated Schroeder on second hole of sudden-death play-off)

Bill Rogers	67	69	74	69	279	13,000.00
Hale Irwin	69	70	72	68	279	13,000.00
Andy Bean	64	69	76	70	279	13,000.00
Jerry Pate	68	68	77	70	283	7,562.50
Alan Tapie	70	71	72	70	283	7,562.50
Jay Haas	69	70	74	70	283	7,562.50
Grier Jones	69	69	73	72	283	7,562.50
Tom Watson	72	68	71	72	283	7,562.50
David Edwards	68	70	71	74	283	7,562.50
Larry Ziegler	73	72	70	69	284	5,250.00
Rik Massengale	71	67	72	74	284	5,250.00
Rex Caldwell	70	70	68	76	284	5,250.00
Joe Hager	70	66	81	68	285	3,750.00
Charles Coody	71	71	72	71	285	3,750.00
Jim Colbert	65	73	75	72	285	3,750.00
Andy North	71	70	72	72	285	3,750.00
Joe Inman	73	67	73	72	285	3,750.00
Tom Purtzer	73	70	69	73	285	3,750.00
Fuzzy Zoeller	71	70	69	75	285	3,750.00
Wally Armstrong	72	71	72	71	286	2,700.00
George Burns	70	73	71	72	286	2,700.00
John Fought	72	67	78	70	287	2,025.00
Craig Stadler	71	71	74	71	287	2,025.00
Don January	70	71	72	74	287	2,025.00
Larry Nelson	72	66	75	74	287	2,025.00
Ben Crenshaw	74	71	67	75	287	2,025.00
Ed Sneed	66	69	73	79	287	2,025.00
Bobby Wadkins	71	69	76	72	288	1,485.72
Mike Hill	72	71	74	71	288	1,485.72
Mark Hayes	75	70	71	72	288	1,485.72
Hubert Green	69	70	76	73	288	1,485.71
Lanny Wadkins	71	74	70	73	288	1,485.71
David Graham	71	74	70	73	288	1,485.71
Jack Nicklaus	68	70	72	78	288	1,485.71
Phil Hancock	68	69	80	72	289	1,125.00
Mike Reid	71	69	77	72	289	1,125.00
Sammy Rachels	70	73	73	73	289	1,125.00
Frank Beard	69	69	74	77	289	1,125.00
J.C. Snead	69	70	72	78	289	1,125.00
Mac McLendon	68	77	72	73	290	900.00
Gary McCord	68	74	73	75	290	900.00
Tommy McGinnis	69	73	72	76	290	900.00
Leonard Thompson	67	71	73	79	290	900.00
Howard Twitty	72	73	77	69	291	708.75
Jim Nelford	71	74	74	72	291	708.75
D.A. Weibring	68	73	76	74	291	708.75
Curtis Strange	71	74	70	76	291	708.75
Miller Barber	74	71	76	71	292	598.34

Jackie Gleason Inverrary Classic

Inverrary Country Club, Lauderhill, Florida
Par 36–36—72; 7,127 yards

March 8–11
purse, $300,000

	SCORES				TOTAL	MONEY
Larry Nelson	67	69	67	71	274	$54,000.00
Grier Jones	71	67	69	70	277	32,400.00
Hale Irwin	73	62	72	73	280	20,400.00
Lee Elder	72	71	68	70	281	13,200.00
Tommy Aaron	66	69	74	72	281	13,200.00
Ray Floyd	69	72	67	74	282	10,800.00
Andy North	69	71	71	72	283	10,500.00
Pat McGowan	72	74	67	71	284	8,700.00
Bob Gilder	76	69	68	71	284	8,700.00
Charles Coody	68	69	74	73	284	8,700.00
Kermit Zarley	75	71	70	69	285	5,775.00
Ben Crenshaw	72	72	69	72	285	5,775.00
Lou Graham	72	70	71	72	285	5,775.00
Jim King	72	73	68	72	285	5,775.00
Howard Twitty	75	70	67	73	285	5,775.00
Wayne Levi	66	73	72	74	285	5,775.00
Mike McCullough	70	74	67	74	285	5,775.00
Rod Curl	71	71	69	74	285	5,775.00
Wally Armstrong	73	70	72	71	286	3,765.00
Frank Conner	72	73	70	71	286	3,765.00
J.C. Snead	72	74	68	72	286	3,765.00
Bill Rogers	72	67	73	74	286	3,765.00
Mike Hill	71	72	71	73	287	2,670.00
Curtis Strange	71	69	71	76	287	2,670.00
Don January	70	75	67	75	287	2,670.00
Mark Lye	72	71	69	75	287	2,670.00
DeWitt Weaver	71	71	69	76	287	2,670.00
Keith Fergus	72	73	73	70	288	1,910.63
Mark Hayes	69	72	75	72	288	1,910.63
D.A. Weibring	73	71	72	72	288	1,910.63
Sam Snead	74	71	70	73	288	1,910.63
Jim Simons	69	74	71	74	288	1,910.62
Gary McCord	71	72	70	75	288	1,910.62
Scott Simpson	72	72	68	76	288	1,910.62

Mark James	68	71	70	79	288	1,910.62
Lindy Miller	70	72	77	70	289	1,352.15
David Graham	70	74	73	72	289	1,352.15
Joe Kunes	72	71	73	73	289	1,352.14
Orville Moody	71	75	70	73	289	1,352.14
Peter Oosterhuis	70	73	71	75	289	1,352.14
Chi Chi Rodriguez	71	71	72	75	289	1,352.14
Bruce Lietzke	72	71	70	76	289	1,352.14
George Burns	76	70	72	72	290	936.00
Marty Fleckman	70	71	75	74	290	936.00
Bob E. Smith	73	71	73	73	290	936.00
Julius Boros	73	72	71	74	290	936.00
Joe Hager	73	70	72	75	290	936.00
Larry Ziegler	75	69	71	75	290	936.00
Bob Byman	72	73	68	77	290	936.00
Bobby Wadkins	72	72	72	75	291	730.00

Doral-Eastern Open

Doral Country Club, Miami Florida
Blue Monster Course: Par 36–36—72; 7,065 yards

March 15–18
purse, $250,000

	SCORES				TOTAL	MONEY
Mark McCumber	67	71	69	72	279	$45,000.00
Bill Rogers	70	68	70	72	280	27,000.00
Rod Curl	67	76	70	68	281	17,000.00
Mike McCullough	70	71	74	67	282	9,843.75
Gibby Gilbert	67	77	70	68	282	9,843.75
Kermit Zarley	73	72	66	71	282	9,843.75
Alan Tapie	66	71	69	76	282	9,843.75
Bill Kratzert	67	69	75	72	283	7,750.00
Tom Kite	73	72	70	69	284	6,750.00
Bobby Wadkins	73	70	71	70	284	6,750.00
David Graham	69	72	73	70	284	6,750.00
Michael Brannan	74	71	72	68	285	5,500.00
Andy Bean	69	71	73	72	285	5,500.00
Tommy Aaron	70	73	74	69	286	4,375.00
J.C. Snead	73	73	72	68	286	4,375.00
Wayne Levi	68	76	71	71	286	4,375.00
Jim Dent	68	71	73	74	286	4,375.00
Jim Colbert	69	74	76	68	287	3,375.00
Dick Mast	70	74	72	71	287	3,375.00
Eddie Pearce	72	72	72	71	287	3,375.00
Lou Graham	71	72	72	72	287	3,375.00
Lindy Miller	71	73	75	69	288	2,600.00
Gil Morgan	75	69	73	71	288	2,600.00
Wally Kuchar	70	73	73	72	288	2,600.00
Mike Reid	70	75	75	69	289	1,950.00
Bruce Devlin	71	75	73	70	289	1,950.00
Brad Bryant	69	72	75	73	289	1,950.00
Scott Simpson	69	76	71	73	289	1,950.00
Ed Sneed	71	73	71	74	289	1,950.00
Keith Fergus	69	74	77	70	290	1,392.50
Dana Quigley	74	71	75	70	290	1,392.50
Jeff Mitchell	71	71	77	71	290	1,392.50
Jack Newton	71	75	73	71	290	1,392.50
Joe Hager	74	72	72	72	290	1,392.50
Mike Morley	73	72	72	73	290	1,392.50
Howard Clark	70	70	77	73	290	1,392.50
Calvin Peete	68	77	73	72	290	1,392.50
Bruce Fleisher	72	75	69	74	290	1,392.50
Wally Armstrong	69	71	74	76	290	1,392.50
Jim Chancey	71	76	73	71	291	1,000.00
Mark Lye	70	73	76	72	291	1,000.00
George Burns	70	75	71	75	291	1,000.00
Jack Renner	67	71	76	77	291	1,000.00
Allen Miller	73	74	76	69	292	755.84
Mark Hayes	70	73	77	72	292	755.84
Larry Webb	68	72	79	73	292	755.83
Jack Sommers	72	73	74	73	292	755.83
Pat McGowan	71	76	72	73	292	755.83
Frank Conner	74	68	74	76	292	755.83
Grier Jones	73	74	76	70	293	615.00

Tournament Players Championship

Sawgrass Jacksonville, Florida
Par 36–36—72; 7,139 yards

March 22–25
purse, $437,292

	SCORES				TOTAL	MONEY
Lanny Wadkins	67	68	76	72	283	$72,000.00
Tom Watson	70	72	75	71	288	43,200.00
Jack Renner	73	70	71	75	289	27,200.00
Phil Hancock	69	73	75	74	291	19,200.00
Wayne Levi	69	72	77	75	293	14,600.00
Bill Kratzert	69	70	75	79	293	14,600.00
Lee Trevino	70	69	75	79	293	14,600.00
Andy Bean	72	73	74	75	294	12,400.00

Tom Kite	72	73	75	75	295	10,800.00
Jack Newton	69	74	77	75	295	10,800.00
Jay Haas	71	74	74	76	295	10,800.00
Mike McCullough	71	73	79	73	296	8,800.00
Gil Morgan	68	77	76	75	296	8,800.00
Ray Floyd	71	72	80	74	297	6,600.00
Peter Jacobsen	74	72	76	75	297	6,600.00
Graham Marsh	72	75	75	75	297	6,600.00
Ed Fiori	69	71	79	78	297	6,600.00
Victor Regalado	70	74	73	80	297	6,600.00
George Burns	72	66	76	83	297	6,600.00
Rex Caldwell	70	76	78	74	298	4,035.00
Hubert Green	73	72	78	75	298	4,035.00
Tim Simpson	69	73	80	76	298	4,035.00
Larry Nelson	72	75	74	77	298	4,035.00
Jerry Pate	69	73	77	79	298	4,035.00
Andy North	67	74	76	81	298	4,035.00
Howard Twitty	75	67	76	80	298	4,035.00
Gary Koch	70	72	74	82	298	4,035.00
John Schroeder	71	76	76	76	299	2,720.00
Jim Thorpe	72	73	77	77	299	2,720.00
Lindy Miller	69	76	77	77	299	2,720.00
Jim Colbert	73	72	76	78	299	2,720.00
Alan Tapie	71	72	75	81	299	2,720.00
Gibby Gilbert	71	75	78	76	300	2,310.00
Jack Nicklaus	67	73	82	78	300	2,310.00
Marty Fleckman	72	74	79	76	301	1,847.50
Charles Coody	71	76	77	77	301	1,847.50
Bruce Fleisher	73	72	78	78	301	1,847.50
Mike Reid	71	73	78	79	301	1,847.50
Jim Nelford	68	76	78	79	301	1,847.50
Mark McCumber	70	70	80	81	301	1,847.50
Dave Stockton	69	72	79	81	301	1,847.50
Bob Byman	70	74	75	82	301	1,847.50
Lee Elder	70	76	78	78	302	1,248.00
Bob Gilder	72	74	81	75	302	1,248.00
Ron Streck	68	77	78	79	302	1,248.00
Bobby Cole	71	75	77	79	302	1,248.00
Orville Moody	73	73	77	79	302	1,248.00
Miller Barber	70	75	77	80	302	1,248.00
Lou Graham	70	76	76	80	302	1,248.00
Randy Erskine	76	68	82	77	303	950.86
Arnold Palmer	72	75	79	77	303	950.86
Mark Lye	71	76	79	77	303	950.86
Cesar Sanudo	72	75	78	78	303	950.86
David Graham	73	70	80	80	303	950.86
Morris Hatalsky	71	73	78	81	303	950.85
Jim Simons	71	73	76	83	303	950.85
Don January	68	79	79	78	304	904.00
Allen Miller	72	75	80	78	305	892.00
Kermit Zarley	66	79	78	82	305	892.00
Gary McCord	72	74	81	79	306	864.00
Artie McNickle	73	73	85	75	306	864.00
Mark Hayes	72	75	79	80	306	864.00
Pat McGowan	73	74	79	80	306	864.00
Bob Eastwood	72	74	76	84	306	864.00
Barney Thompson	74	72	80	81	307	836.00
Buddy Gardner	71	75	78	83	307	836.00
Craig Stadler	72	73	81	82	330	820.00
Al Geiberger	71	75	80	82	308	820.00
Rik Messengale	71	76	78	84	309	804.00
Dan Halldorson	69	70	81	89	309	804.00
Bob Murphy	75	71	74	92	312	792.00

Out of final 36 holes

	SCORES		TOTAL
Don Bies	70	78	148
Danny Edwards	69	79	148
David Edwards	74	74	148
Dave Eichelberger	71	77	148
Hale Irwin	71	77	148
Bruce Lietzke	73	75	148
Jeff Mitchell	73	75	148
Florentino Molina	71	77	148
Peter Oosterhuis	74	74	148
Chi Chi Rodriguez	71	77	148
Curtis Strange	73	75	148
Leonard Thompson	72	76	148
Bobby Wadkins	74	74	148
Larry Ziegler	72	76	148
Wally Armstrong	72	77	149
Dave Barr	73	76	149
Billy Casper	78	71	149
Ben Crenshaw	74	75	149
Rod Curl	75	74	149
Jim Dent	75	74	149
Keith Fergus	73	76	149
Rod Funseth	77	72	149
Mike Hill	75	74	149
Don Iverson	72	77	149
Bob Lunn	73	76	149
Mike Morley	75	74	149
Eddie Pearce	73	76	149

Scott Simpson	74	75	149
J.C. Snead	71	78	149
Brad Bryant	69	81	150
Fred Marti	71	79	150
Johnny Miller	74	76	150
Mark Pfeil	75	75	150
Greg Powers	70	80	150
Carlton White	72	78	150
Fuzzy Zoeller	73	77	150
Bill Calfee	73	78	151
Joe Inman	73	78	151
John Lister	73	78	151
Tom Purtzer	75	76	151
Bill Rogers	73	78	151
Tom Storey	75	76	151
Terry Diehl	76	76	152
Mac McLendon	75	77	152
Steve Melnyk	77	75	152
Lee Mikles	78	74	152
Calvin Peete	74	78	152
Gary Player	73	79	152
Don Pooley	77	75	152
Ed Sneed	76	76	152
D.A. Weibring	73	79	152
Frank Conner	74	79	153
Bob Mann	76	77	153
Bobby Walzel	72	81	153
Tommy Aaron	76	78	154
Homero Blancas	75	79	154
George Cadle	77	77	154
Barry Jaeckel	75	79	154
Mike Sullivan	76	78	154
Lon Hinkle	75	80	155
Tom Weiskopf	73	82	155
Joe Hager	75	81	156
Jerry Heard	79	77	156
Ed Sabo	75	81	156
Severiano Ballesteros	76	81	157
Dale Douglass	79	78	157
Bob Shearer	75	82	157
Bob Zender	78	80	158
Jeff Hewes	78	81	159
Dave Hill	79	80	159
Frank Beard	82	77	159
Alan Pate	84	80	164
Bob Wynn	84	80	164

Each player who finished 36 holes received $500.00.

Sea Pines Heritage Golf Classic

Harbour Town Golf Links, Hilton Head Island, South Carolina   March 29–April 1
Par 36-35—71; 6,804 yards   purse, $300,000

	SCORES				TOTAL	MONEY
Tom Watson	65	65	69	71	270	$54,000.00
Ed Sneed	69	69	71	66	275	32,400.00
Mike Morley	69	68	72	70	279	17,400.00
Tom Kite	69	68	71	71	279	17,400.00
Bill Rogers	69	68	72	71	280	11,400.00
Ray Floyd	72	68	69	71	280	11,400.00
Bob Murphy	71	67	74	69	281	9,675.00
George Burns	67	72	72	70	281	9,675.00
Don January	72	70	69	71	282	8,400.00
Lanny Wadkins	66	67	74	75	282	8,400.00
Jerry Pate	67	72	76	69	284	6,900.00
Joe Inman	72	70	72	70	284	6,900.00
Hubert Green	71	71	67	75	284	6,900.00
Rod Curl	73	70	73	69	285	5,400.00
Bob Gilder	71	70	75	69	285	5,400.00
Craig Stadler	70	70	74	71	285	5,400.00
Larry Nelson	75	69	73	69	286	3,795.00
Bobby Walzel	72	67	75	72	286	3,795.00
Gene Littler	69	73	72	72	286	3,795.00
Miller Barber	68	73	73	72	286	3,795.00
Jack Newton	74	70	69	73	286	3,795.00
Allen Miller	72	71	70	73	286	3,795.00
Tom Purtzer	71	73	69	73	286	3,795.00
Lee Trevino	73	67	71	75	286	3,795.00
Mike Reid	74	67	74	72	287	2,392.50
Tim Simpson	68	73	74	72	287	2,392.50
Victor Regalado	74	69	69	75	287	2,392.50
Gary Koch	69	71	72	75	287	2,392.50
Howard Twitty	73	72	74	69	288	1,786.67
Mike Hill	69	72	77	70	288	1,786.67
Phil Hancock	68	72	78	70	288	1,786.67
Wayne Levi	74	72	72	70	288	1,786.67
Hale Irwin	74	72	69	73	288	1,786.67
Rex Caldwell	73	73	69	73	288	1,786.67
Ben Crenshaw	70	72	73	73	288	1,786.66
Jim Colbert	71	72	70	75	288	1,786.66

Charles Coody	72	70	68	78	288	1,786.66
Wally Armstrong	70	74	73	72	289	1,230.00
Eddie Pearce	72	72	72	73	289	1,230.00
Jim Simons	72	73	71	73	289	1,230.00
Bruce Lietzke	71	75	70	73	289	1,230.00
Kermit Zarley	73	69	73	74	289	1,230.00
Keith Fergus	69	74	72	74	289	1,230.00
Arnold Palmer	73	70	71	75	289	1,230.00
Ed Fiori	72	74	72	72	290	858.00
Julius Boros	75	70	73	72	290	858.00
John Fought	73	70	74	73	290	858.00
Leonard Thompson	74	69	73	74	290	858.00
Mike Sullivan	72	69	73	76	290	858.00
Doug Tewell	68	72	71	79	290	858.00

Greater Greensboro Open

Forest Oaks Country Club, Greensboro, North Carolina
Par 36–36—72; 6,984 yards

April 5–8
purse, $250,000

	SCORES				TOTAL	MONEY
Ray Floyd	73	71	71	67	282	$45,000.00
George Burns	73	71	69	70	283	22,000.00
Gary Player	70	71	71	71	283	22,000.00
Bobby Wadkins	70	73	67	74	284	12,000.00
Rex Caldwell	70	74	71	72	287	10,000.00
Doug Tewell	72	74	71	71	288	8,375.00
Lee Elder	73	73	69	73	288	8,375.00
Tom Purtzer	70	71	72	75	288	8,375.00
Bobby Walzel	68	75	74	72	289	6,750.00
Curtis Strange	71	75	71	72	289	6,750.00
Jack Renner	68	71	70	80	289	6,750.00
Severiano Ballesteros	72	74	74	70	290	4,750.00
Fuzzy Zoeller	70	74	74	72	290	4,750.00
Leonard Thompson	73	76	70	71	290	4,750.00
Bob Eastwood	69	77	72	72	290	4,750.00
Bob Gilder	71	74	71	74	290	4,750.00
Jim Thorpe	68	75	71	76	290	4,750.00
Jay Haas	76	70	76	69	291	2,937.50
Jim Chancey	73	71	76	71	291	2,937.50
Bobby Nichols	71	76	72	72	291	2,937.50
Marty Fleckman	73	70	75	73	291	2,937.50
Miller Barber	70	73	74	74	291	2,937.50
Craig Stadler	72	74	72	73	291	2,937.50
Joe Inman	71	72	74	74	291	2,937.50
Tommy Valentine	73	72	71	75	291	2,937.50
Peter Jacobsen	72	73	77	70	292	1,737.50
Jim Simons	74	73	73	72	292	1,737.50
Mike Morley	70	78	72	72	292	1,737.50
Gene Littler	76	72	72	72	292	1,737.50
Artie McNickle	74	73	72	73	292	1,737.50
Gary McCord	72	73	73	74	292	1,737.50
Dave Eichelberger	71	73	72	76	292	1,737.50
Howard Twitty	71	72	74	75	292	1,737.50
Morris Hatalsky	72	74	75	72	293	1,290.00
Florentino Molina	73	76	72	72	293	1,290.00
Bob Lunn	73	74	72	74	293	1,290.00
Jim Dent	71	73	74	75	293	1,290.00
Hale Irwin	70	76	72	75	293	1,290.00
Graham Marsh	74	74	74	72	294	1,025.00
Keith Fergus	68	79	75	72	294	1,025.00
Gibby Gilbert	75	73	74	72	294	1,025.00
Mike Sullivan	74	75	70	75	294	1,025.00
Barry Jaeckel	72	75	71	76	294	1,025.00
Mike Reid	72	74	76	73	295	737.86
Nick Faldo	75	74	74	72	295	737.86
Al Geiberger	71	76	75	73	295	737.86
Tom Weiskopf	71	76	75	73	295	737.86
Jack Newton	73	76	73	73	295	737.86

Masters Tournament

Augusta National Golf Club, Augusta Georgia
Par 36–36—72; 7,040 yards

April 12–15
purse, $299,625

	SCORES				TOTAL	MONEY
Fuzzy Zoeller	70	71	69	70	280	$50,000.00
Ed Sneed	68	67	69	76	280	30,000.00
Tom Watson	68	71	70	71	280	30,000.00
(Zoeller defeated Sneed and Watson on second hole of sudden-death play-off)						
Jack Nicklaus	69	71	72	69	281	15,000.00
Tom Kite	71	72	68	72	283	13,000.00
Bruce Lietzke	67	75	68	74	284	11,500.00
Lanny Wadkins	73	69	70	73	285	9,000.00
Leonard Thompson	68	70	73	74	285	9,000.00
Craig Stadler	69	66	74	76	285	9,000.00
Hubert Green	74	69	72	71	286	6,500.00
Gene Littler	74	71	69	72	286	6,500.00

*Hubert Green and his caddy, Smiley
Jenkins.*

Fuzzy Zoeller does a victory dance at the Masters.

Jack Newton	70	72	69	76	287	3,740.00
Severiano Ballesteros	72	68	73	74	287	3,740.00
Miller Barber	75	64	72	76	287	3,740.00
Lee Trevino	73	71	70	73	287	3,740.00
Andy North	72	72	74	69	287	3,740.00
Bill Kratzert	73	68	71	76	288	2,700.00
Ray Floyd	70	68	73	77	288	2,700.00
Gary Player	71	72	74	71	288	2,700.00
Lee Elder	73	70	74	71	288	2,700.00
Artie McNickle	71	72	74	71	288	2,700.00
J.C. Snead	73	71	72	73	289	2,400.00
Joe Inman	68	71	76	75	290	2,225.00
Lou Graham	69	71	76	74	290	2,225.00
Jim Simons	72	70	75	73	290	2,225.00
Hale Irwin	72	70	74	74	290	2,225.00
Bobby Clampett*	73	71	73	73	290	
Tommy Aaron	72	73	76	70	291	2,000.00
Andy Bean	69	74	74	74	291	2,000.00
Graham Marsh	71	72	73	75	291	2,000.00
Gil Morgan	72	69	71	80	292	1,975.00
Victor Regalado	71	74	75	72	292	1,975.00
Larry Nelson	70	75	70	77	292	1,975.00
Isao Aoki	71	72	72	78	293	1,950.00
Bob Byman	71	71	75	76	293	1,950.00
Scott Hoch*	72	73	74	74	293	
Charles Coody	71	72	74	76	293	1,950.00
Peter Oosterhuis	73	72	73	75	293	1,950.00
John Cook*	72	72	75	76	295	
Nick Faldo	73	71	79	73	296	1,875.00
Jerry Pate	72	70	75	80	297	1,850.00
Tom Weiskopf	73	72	71	81	297	1,850.00
Billy Casper	69	75	80	75	299	1,800.00
Rod Funseth	70	73	78	79	300	1,775.00
Lindy Miller	73	67	75	86	301	1,750.00

Out of final 36 holes

	SCORES		TOTAL	MONEY
Jerry McGee	77	69	146	$1,500.00
Arnold Palmer	74	72	146	1,500.00
Barry Jaeckel	75	71	146	1,500.00
Don January	73	73	146	1,500.00
Wally Armstrong	73	74	147	1,500.00
Jay Sigel*	72	75	147	
Johnny Miller	77	71	148	1,500.00
Jerry Heard	75	73	148	1,500.00
Sam Snead	74	74	148	1,500.00
Lon Hinkle	77	72	149	1,500.00
Dave Stockton	74	75	149	1,500.00
Simon Owen	74	75	149	1,500.00
Dave Hill	75	74	149	1,500.00
Art Wall	74	75	149	1,500.00
Mike McCullough	73	77	150	1,500.00
Gay Brewer	75	75	150	1,500.00
Nasashi Ozaki	76	75	151	1,500.00
Mac McLendon	74	77	151	1,500.00
Ben Crenshaw	73	80	153	1,500.00
Mark McCumber	75	78	153	1,500.00
Mike Peck*	78	75	153	
Ron Streck	78	76	154	1,500.00
Peter McEvoy*	79	79	158	
Bob Goalby	79	81	160	1,500.00
Bob Shearer	73	WD		1,500.00
David Graham	79	WD		1,500.00
Doug Ford	77	WD		1,500.00

*Amateur

Magnolia Classic

Hattiesburg Country Club, Hattiesburg, Mississippi
Par 35–35—70; 6,280 yards

April 12–15
purse, $50,000

	SCORES				TOTAL	MONEY
Bobby Walzel	72	68	67	65	272	$9,000.00
Buddy Gardner	66	71	66	69	272	5,400.00
(Walzel defeated Gardner on second hole of sudden-death play-off)						
Ed Fiori	66	69	72	66	273	2,691.67
Bruce Fleisher	72	68	66	67	273	2,691.67
Wren Lum	70	64	69	70	273	2,691.66
Greg Powers	67	70	67	70	274	1,670.00
Homero Blancas	70	67	67	70	274	1,670.00
Lee Mikles	69	69	65	71	274	1,670.00
Ed Byman	68	69	67	70	274	1,670.00
Scott Simpson	69	67	66	72	274	1,670.00
George Johnson	70	69	70	66	275	1,200.00
Marty Fleckman	72	66	69	68	275	1,200.00
Bill Calfee	67	68	69	71	275	1,200.00
Roger Calvin	69	70	70	67	276	860.00
Steve Veriato	69	71	68	68	276	860.00

Robert Donald	69	69	69	69	276	860.00
Fred Marti	68	72	66	70	276	860.00
Jack Ferenz	72	66	68	70	276	860.00
Bob Charles	71	67	72	67	277	587.50
Bob Heins	68	72	69	68	277	587.50
Dana Quigley	72	68	69	68	277	587.50
Lon Nielsen	69	68	70	70	277	587.50
Bob Lunn	70	65	69	73	277	587.50
Ron Mobley	70	70	64	63	277	587.50
Tom Storey	68	71	70	69	278	420.84
Joe Porter	71	68	70	69	278	420.84
Mark Lye	75	65	68	70	278	420.83
Bob Wynn	70	68	70	70	278	420.83
David Lundstrom	65	68	72	73	278	420.83
Rives McBee	72	69	64	73	278	420.83
Peter Chapin	73	68	71	67	279	317.15
Dan Pohl	74	66	70	69	279	317.15
Bill Garrett	71	68	71	69	279	317.14
Mike Morley	70	69	70	70	279	317.14
Joe Kunes	71	68	69	71	279	317.14
Elroy Marti	69	71	69	70	279	317.14
Jim Chancey	69	65	72	73	279	317.14
Barney Thompson	73	67	70	70	280	260.00
Tony Hollifield	68	72	67	73	280	260.00
Bob Mann	70	65	71	74	280	260.00
Chris Clark	75	66	72	68	281	240.00
Jack Sommers	71	70	70	70	281	240.00
Bobby Mitchell	71	69	65	76	281	240.00
Jack Spradlin	69	70	75	68	282	225.00
Michael Brannan	72	67	73	70	282	225.00
Kip Byrne	68	68	74	72	282	225.00
Sammy Rachels	71	70	72	70	283	210.00
Larry Ziegler	71	67	74	71	283	210.00
Antonio Cerda	72	67	72	72	283	210.00
Tab Hudson	72	69	71	72	284	200.00

Tournament of Champions

LaCosta Country Club, Carlsbad, California
Par 36-36—72; 6,889 yards

April 19–22
purse, $300,000

	SCORES				TOTAL	MONEY
Tom Watson	69	66	70	70	275	$54,000
Jerry Pate	72	71	65	73	281	29,500
Bruce Lietzke	72	66	70	73	281	29,500
Gary Player	71	69	74	68	282	18,000
Lee Trevino	72	68	72	72	284	15,000
Larry Nelson	74	69	69	72	284	15,000
Tom Kite	76	69	68	72	285	12,000
Ben Crenshaw	75	71	75	67	288	10,625
Lee Elder	72	73	68	75	288	10,625
Andy Bean	75	72	71	73	291	8,750
Lon Hinkle	75	70	73	73	291	8,750
Hubert Green	73	71	73	74	291	8,750
Lanny Wadkins	79	70	73	71	293	7,250
Jim Simons	73	72	75	73	293	7,250
Jack Nicklaus	72	72	77	73	294	6,250
Raymond Floyd	71	74	75	74	294	6,250
Gil Morgan	71	72	76	78	297	5,600
Ron Streck	70	78	75	75	298	5,150
Andy North	75	76	71	76	298	5,150
Fuzzy Zoeller	77	72	74	76	299	4,500
Bob Byman	80	71	75	73	299	4,500
Victor Reglado	71	76	75	77	299	4,500
Mac McLendon	73	76	74	76	299	4,500
Rod Funseth	77	74	73	76	300	4,000
Jack Newton	72	78	78	73	301	3,800
Barry Jaeckel	78	73	78	74	303	3,700
Mark McCumber	78	78	75	78	309	3,600
Jerry Heard	79	76	83	75	313	3,500

Tallahassee Open

Killearn Golf and Country Club, Tallahassee, Florida
Par 36-36—72; 7,124 yards

April 19–22
purse, $100,000

	SCORES				TOTAL	MONEY
Chi Chi Rodriguez	66	69	67	67	269	$18,000.00
Lindy Miller	65	72	67	68	272	10,800.00
Bobby Wadkins	68	69	65	72	274	6,800.00
Rex Caldwell	69	67	68	71	275	4,950.00
Billy Casper	68	71	70	67	276	3,660.00
Gary Koch	68	68	71	69	276	3,660.00
Bobby Walzel	70	68	68	70	276	3,660.00
Bob Eastwood	68	69	70	69	276	3,660.00
Bob Mann	64	71	70	71	276	3,660.00
Bob E. Smith	71	70	68	68	277	2,600.00

Jim Thorpe	68	69	69	71	277	2,600.00
Wayne Levi	67	69	68	73	277	2,600.00
John Lister	69	67	73	69	278	1,925.00
Tim Simpson	67	68	72	71	278	1,925.00
Bill Rogers	71	69	67	71	278	1,925.00
Allen Miller	70	69	67	72	278	1,925.00
Barney Thompson	74	67	72	66	279	1,550.00
Jim Chancey	70	69	70	70	279	1,550.00
Buddy Gardner	73	68	72	67	280	1,210.00
Mark Lye	68	72	71	69	280	1,210.00
Don Iverson	69	71	71	69	280	1,210.00
Doug Tewell	69	69	72	70	280	1,210.00
Bob Murphy	67	71	70	72	280	1,210.00
Frank Beard	71	70	69	71	281	950.00
Jay Haas	69	69	70	73	281	950.00
Carlton Wyite	71	69	67	74	281	950.00
Dana Quigley	69	72	71	70	282	816.67
Tom Shaw	70	70	71	71	282	816.67
Randy Erskine	69	72	69	72	282	816.66
Tony Hollifield	71	68	72	72	283	705.00
Michael Brannan	69	67	74	73	283	705.00
David Graham	70	71	68	74	283	705.00
Larry Webb	68	69	70	76	283	705.00
Ed Sneed	68	72	74	70	284	603.34
Dave Eichelberger	68	71	73	72	284	603.33
Ed Dougherty	72	67	72	74	284	603.33
Bob Charles	68	73	69	75	285	560.00
Curtis Strange	70	69	74	73	286	530.00
Jim Knoll	67	70	75	74	286	530.00
Ron Mobley	70	70	73	74	287	490.00
Forrest Fezler	70	70	72	75	287	490.00
Jerry McGee	69	70	71	77	287	490.00
Gary Wintz	70	71	73	74	288	455.00
Joe Porter	68	73	72	75	288	455.00
Lon Nielsen	71	70	72	75	288	455.00
Bill Murchison	70	71	71	76	288	455.00
Bob Lunn	68	70	80	71	289	415.00
John Fought	72	69	74	74	289	415.00
Larry Degenhart	71	69	75	74	289	415.00
Tom Chain	70	70	73	76	289	415.00

First NBC New Orleans Open

Lakewood Country Club, New Orleans, Louisiana   April 26–29
Par 36–36–72; 7,080 yards   purse, $250,000

	SCORES				TOTAL	MONEY
Hubert Green	69	67	69	68	273	$45,000.00
Bruce Lietzke	68	70	69	67	274	16,500.00
Steve Melnyk	68	68	70	68	274	16,500.00
Frank Conner	65	71	68	70	274	16,500.00
Lee Trevino	68	67	69	70	274	16,500.00
Calvin Peete	70	67	69	69	275	8,375.00
Curtis Strange	66	70	67	72	275	8,375.00
Bob Gilder	71	73	62	69	275	8,375.00
Jim Colbert	66	71	71	68	276	7,250.00
Leonard Thompson	72	68	69	68	277	6,500.00
Doug Tewell	66	72	68	71	277	6,500.00
Gary Koch	69	71	72	66	278	5,500.00
Bob Shearer	69	68	69	72	278	5,500.00
Lon Hinkle	69	72	73	65	279	4,500.00
Mike Morley	69	73	70	67	279	4,500.00
Mike Sullivan	71	70	67	71	279	4,500.00
Roger Calvin	71	70	73	66	280	3,750.00
Bob E. Smith	69	70	69	72	280	3,750.00
Jim Dent	69	72	68	71	280	3,750.00
Tom Watson	71	73	70	67	281	2,708.34
Homero Blancas	72	72	68	69	281	2,708.34
Billy Casper	71	72	68	70	281	2,708.33
Gibby Gilbert	69	69	72	71	281	2,708.33
Joe Inman	70	71	69	71	281	2,708.33
Allen Miller	67	75	66	73	281	2,708.33
David Edwards	73	71	69	69	282	1,812.50
Don January	71	71	70	70	282	1,812.50
Jack Ferenz	73	70	68	71	282	1,812.50
Larry Ziegler	73	71	67	71	282	1,812.50
Bob Charles	70	74	67	71	282	1,812.50
Orville Moody	74	70	66	72	282	1,812.50
Mark Lye	69	74	73	67	283	1,415.00
Antonio Cerda	72	71	70	70	283	1,415.00
Fred Marti	72	72	69	70	283	1,415.00
Jim Chancey	72	69	71	71	283	1,415.00
Tim Simpson	68	72	68	75	283	1,415.00
Howard Twitty	70	68	74	72	284	1,125.00
Wren Lum	69	73	70	72	284	1,125.00
Mark Pfeil	71	71	70	72	284	1,125.00
Phil Hancock	67	74	69	74	284	1,125.00
Mike Reid	71	68	71	74	284	1,125.00
Miller Barber	70	71	75	69	285	739.17
Chi Chi Rodriguez	71	72	72	70	285	739.17

Butch Baird	71	70	73	71	285	739.17
Jack Renner	71	73	71	70	285	739.17
Randy Erskine	69	72	73	71	285	739.17
Gene Littler	69	72	72	72	285	739.17
Joe Porter	73	71	70	71	285	739.17
Jerry McGee	69	71	72	73	285	739.17
Woody Blackburn	71	70	71	73	285	739.16

Houston Open

Woodlands Country Club, Houston, Texas
Par 36–35—71; 6,918 yards

May 3–6
purse, $300,000

		SCORES			TOTAL	MONEY
Wayne Levi	69	65	63	71	268	$54,000.00
Mike Brannan	68	66	66	70	270	32,400.00
Orville Moody	72	64	67	69	272	14,400.00
Hale Irwin	69	64	71	68	272	14,400.00
Bob Gilder	70	64	70	68	272	14,400.00
Sammy Rachels	68	65	68	71	272	14,400.00
Bill Rogers	67	69	69	68	273	9,675.00
Calvin Peete	70	70	68	65	273	9,675.00
John Schroeder	68	66	70	70	274	8,400.00
Dave Stockton	72	66	67	69	274	8,400.00
Rod Curl	69	70	66	70	275	6,360.00
Jim Colbert	66	70	69	70	275	6,360.00
Buddy Gardner	69	67	69	70	275	6,360.00
Leonard Thompson	66	68	70	71	275	6,360.00
David Edwards	68	70	68	69	275	6,360.00
Scott Simpson	69	67	70	70	276	4,500.00
Mike Reid	70	70	69	67	276	4,500.00
J.C. Snead	70	66	69	71	276	4,500.00
Barney Thompson	67	70	73	66	276	4,500.00
Grier Jones	71	67	68	70	276	4,500.00
Lon Hinkle	70	70	68	69	277	2,816.25
Tom Purtzer	70	66	72	69	277	2,816.25
Mike Sullivan	70	69	68	70	277	2,816.25
Lee Trevino	69	66	69	73	277	2,816.25
Doug Tewell	68	68	70	71	277	2,816.25
Jerry McGee	70	67	71	69	277	2,816.25
Mike Morley	70	68	70	69	277	2,816.25
Tom Kite	72	67	68	70	277	2,816.25
Curtis Strange	69	68	73	68	278	1,950.00
Mark Lye	72	69	68	69	278	1,950.00
Jim Dent	66	71	70	71	278	1,950.00
Lou Graham	71	70	67	70	278	1,950.00
Bobby Walzel	72	66	67	73	278	1,950.00
Dave Eichelberger	68	71	72	68	279	1,482.86
Bob Mann	69	67	73	70	279	1,482.86
George Burns	73	67	72	67	279	1,482.86
Joe Inman	68	68	70	73	279	1,482.86
Bob Murphy	68	73	71	67	279	1,482.86
Gary McCord	67	71	67	74	279	1,482.85
Bob Shearer	68	71	72	68	279	1,482.85
Keith Fergus	71	68	71	70	280	1,110.00
Charles Coody	69	71	72	68	280	1,110.00
Al Geiberger	67	70	73	70	280	1,110.00
Andy North	69	72	69	70	280	1,110.00
Alan Tapie	67	72	70	71	280	1,110.00
Phil Hancock	72	69	71	69	281	831.60
Jack Renner	74	67	73	67	281	831.60
Bruce Lietzke	66	72	74	69	281	831.60
Cesar Sanudo	71	67	73	70	281	831.60
Gary Player	71	68	71	71	281	831.60

Byron Nelson Golf Classic

Preston Trail Golf Club, Dallas, Texas
Par 35–35—70; 6,993 yards

May 10–13
purse, $300,000

		SCORES			TOTAL	MONEY
Tom Watson	64	72	69	70	275	$54,000.00
Bill Rogers	68	73	68	66	275	32,400.00
(Watson defeated Rogers on first hole of sudden-death play-off)						
Larry Nelson	65	68	74	69	276	20,400.00
Jerry Pate	69	70	67	72	278	14,400.00
Jerry McGee	71	72	69	67	279	10,537.50
Michael Brannan	69	73	69	68	279	10,537.50
Calvin Peete	68	70	73	68	279	10,537.50
Morris Hatalsky	67	71	72	69	279	10,537.50
Brad Bryant	67	73	73	67	280	8,400.00
Gene Littler	69	72	71	68	280	8,400.00
Gary Koch	70	72	70	69	281	6,900.00

Larry Ziegler	69	74	69	69	281	6,900.00
George Burns	66	68	76	71	281	6,900.00
Alan Tapie	71	70	71	70	282	5,250.00
Jay Haas	72	69	71	70	282	5,250.00
Lee Trevino	70	72	69	71	282	5,250.00
Ed Sneed	70	70	71	71	282	5,250.00
Curtis Strange	68	76	70	69	283	4,500.00
Grier Jones	70	73	73	68	284	3,636.00
Johnny Miller	70	71	72	71	284	3,636.00
Lanny Wadkins	67	67	78	72	284	3,636.00
Scott Simpson	70	71	72	71	284	3,636.00
Rod Curl	70	69	73	72	284	3,636.00
Homero Blancas	70	71	73	71	285	2,321.25
Hubert Green	71	70	75	69	285	2,321.25
Mark Hayes	69	75	70	71	285	2,321.25
Charles Coody	72	72	69	72	285	2,321.25
Ray Floyd	72	70	71	72	285	2,321.25
Barry Jaeckel	70	73	70	72	285	2,321.25
Tom Kite	71	74	74	66	285	2,321.25
Bruce Devlin	66	71	72	76	285	2,321.25
Greg Powers	70	74	72	70	286	1,698.00
Bob Mann	69	72	73	72	286	1,698.00
Doug Tewell	70	75	71	70	286	1,698.00
Mike Reid	70	73	70	73	286	1,698.00
John Mahaffey	69	71	77	69	286	1,698.00
Gibby Gilbert	72	71	72	72	287	1,410.00
Bill Calfee	73	69	73	72	287	1,410.00
Don January	71	71	75	70	287	1,410.00
Jim Simons	71	72	73	72	288	1,170.00
Ron Mobley	72	70	74	72	288	1,170.00
Ben Crenshaw	71	74	71	72	288	1,170.00
Phil Hancock	71	74	71	72	288	1,170.00
Dave Stockton	71	73	69	75	288	1,170.00
Ken Still	71	72	72	74	289	903.00
Arnold Palmer	68	72	76	73	289	903.00
Lindy Miller	73	72	71	73	289	903.00
Bob Gilder	67	78	74	70	289	903.00
Eddie Pearce	74	70	74	72	290	768.00
Jim Dent	70	74	76	70	290	768.00

Colonial National Invitational

Colonial Country Club, Fort Worth, Texas
Par 35–35–70; 7,151 yards

May 17–20
purse, $300,000

	SCORES				TOTAL	MONEY
Al Geiberger	68	69	64	73	274	$54,000.00
Don January	72	70	68	65	275	26,400.00
Gene Littler	70	70	67	68	275	26,400.00
Tom Watson	71	73	65	67	276	13,200.00
Jim Colbert	70	73	64	69	276	13,200.00
Fuzzy Zoeller	70	68	70	70	278	10,425.00
Leonard Thompson	65	68	73	72	278	10,425.00
Bruce Lietzke	66	73	74	66	279	8,100.00
Lindy Miller	68	74	70	67	279	8,100.00
Ed Sneed	69	74	69	67	279	8,100.00
Jack Renner	70	74	66	69	279	8,100.00
Wayne Levi	68	71	71	69	279	8,100.00
D.A. Weibring	70	69	69	72	280	6,000.00
Gil Morgan	69	67	71	73	280	6,000.00
Bob Shearer	73	71	69	68	281	4,800.00
Ben Crenshaw	70	70	70	71	281	4,800.00
Keith Fergus	71	69	70	71	281	4,800.00
Howard Twitty	72	68	69	72	281	4,800.00
Barry Jaeckel	70	67	68	76	281	4,800.00
Lee Elder	73	72	70	67	282	3,250.00
Buddy Gardner	71	72	71	68	282	3,250.00
Alan Tapie	74	70	69	69	282	3,250.00
Bob Clampett°	71	72	69	70	282	
Bruce Devlin	70	69	71	72	282	3,250.00
Hale Irwin	70	72	69	71	282	3,250.00
Grier Jones	67	69	72	74	282	3,250.00
Lee Trevino	66	73	74	70	283	2,041.67
Mark Hayes	73	68	72	70	283	2,041.67
Orville Moody	71	72	70	70	283	2,041.67
Hubert Green	72	70	70	71	283	2,041.67
Gibby Gilbert	68	73	71	71	283	2,041.67
Jerry Pate	68	71	72	72	283	2,041.67
Jim Nelford	69	71	71	72	283	2,041.66
Bobby Wadkins	72	66	73	72	283	2,041.66
Mike Sullivan	70	66	74	73	283	2,041.66
Kermit Zarley	69	74	77	64	284	1,447.50
Bill Rogers	73	72	71	68	284	1,447.50
Craig Stadler	72	72	69	71	284	1,447.50
Tom Purtzer	69	76	68	71	284	1,447.50
Jay Haas	68	73	80	73	284	1,447.50
Mark Lye	75	70	64	75	284	1,447.50
David Edwards	74	70	74	67	285	1,050.00
Bobby Walzel	74	71	71	69	285	1,050.00
J.C. Snead	70	72	72	71	285	1,050.00
David Graham	69	73	73	70	285	1,050.00

Tom Weiskopf	72	69	72	72	285	1,050.00	*APPENDIXES*
Charles Coody	71	73	68	73	285	1,050.00	
Jerry McGee	69	69	72	75	285	1,050.00	
Lanny Wadkins	71	72	73	70	286	754.00	
Mac McLendon	69	73	74	70	286	754.00	

*Amateur

Memorial Tournament

Muirfield Village Golf Club, Dublin, Ohio
Par 36–36—72; 7,101 yards

May 24–27
purse, $329,885

	SCORES				TOTAL	MONEY
Tom Watson	73	69	72	71	285	$54,000.00
Miller Barber	74	73	71	70	288	32,400.00
Bob Gilder	74	80	68	69	291	20,400.00
Lanny Wadkins	69	79	73	71	292	13,200.00
Tom Kite	74	72	74	72	292	13,200.00
Ed Sneed	71	78	75	69	293	10,800.00
Howard Twitty	75	76	74	69	294	9,350.00
Jim Colbert	73	78	73	70	294	9,350.00
Bill Rogers	77	75	71	71	294	9,350.00
George Burns	76	78	73	68	295	7,800.00
Jay Haas	73	78	73	71	295	7,800.00
Fuzzy Zoeller	79	74	71	72	296	6,075.00
Hubert Green	75	77	72	72	296	6,075.00
Hale Irwin	73	80	76	67	296	6,075.00
Bruce Lietzke	75	74	72	75	296	6,075.00
Terry Diehl	79	71	74	73	297	4,350.00
Alan Tapie	75	76	73	73	297	4,350.00
Tom Weiskopf	76	73	74	74	297	4,350.00
Barry Jaeckel	76	77	76	68	297	4,350.00
Lon Hinkle	75	73	72	77	297	4,350.00
Lee Elder	75	76	77	69	297	4,350.00
John Mahaffey	78	78	72	70	298	2,880.00
Jim Nelford	73	78	75	72	298	2,880.00
J.C. Snead	76	73	77	72	298	2,880.00
Bobby Walzel	73	78	75	72	298	2,880.00
Leonard Thompson	78	75	72	73	298	2,880.00
Craig Stadler	76	80	67	76	299	2,220.00
Wally Armstrong	76	75	71	77	299	2,220.00
Jack Nicklaus	73	73	74	79	299	2,220.00
Chi Chi Rodriguez	75	81	71	73	300	1,822.50
David Graham	73	76	76	75	300	1,822.50
Keith Fergus	76	79	71	74	300	1,822.50
Bob Mann	76	76	78	70	300	1,822.50
Peter Oosterhuis	73	76	74	77	300	1,822.50
Mike McCullough	70	82	76	72	300	1,822.50
Don Bies	72	76	76	77	301	1,491.67
Peter Jacobsen	72	74	76	77	301	1,491.67
Ron Streck	74	78	77	72	301	1,491.66
Victor Regalado	75	79	73	75	302	1,390.00
Orville Moody	75	79	76	72	302	1,390.00
Art Wall	74	81	73	74	302	1,390.00
Gibby Gilbert	82	75	74	72	303	1,270.00
Gil Morgan	80	76	75	72	303	1,270.00
Gary Koch	78	74	78	73	303	1,270.00
Arnold Palmer	75	81	74	73	303	1,270.00
Wayne Levi	72	84	73	74	303	1,270.00
Phil Hancock	78	79	75	72	304	1,151.43
Graham Marsh	75	78	80	71	304	1,151.43
Dave Hill	75	76	74	79	304	1,151.43
Raymond Floyd	75	80	78	71	304	1,151.43

Kemper Open

Quail Hollow Country Club, Charlotte, North Carolina
Par 36–36–72; 7,160 yards

May 31–June 3
purse, $350,000

	SCORES				TOTAL	MONEY
Jerry McGee	61	74	69	68	272	$63,000.00
Jerry Pate	71	70	64	68	273	37,800.00
Andy Bean	69	68	72	68	277	20,300.00
J.C. Snead	71	65	71	70	277	20,300.00
Raymond Floyd	70	68	68	72	278	14,000.00
Mark Hayes	69	71	68	71	279	12,600.00
Homero Blancas	71	68	72	69	280	10,185.00
Bill Rogers	69	71	70	70	280	10,185.00
Victor Regalado	71	66	72	71	280	10,185.00
Bobby Walzel	68	71	69	72	280	10,185.00
Craig Stadler	62	69	73	76	280	10,185.00
Mark Lye	71	69	71	70	281	6,450.00
Tom Purtzer	70	69	71	71	281	6,450.00

Fred Marti	68	72	70	71	281	6,450.00
Gary McCord	67	73	69	72	281	6,450.00
Jim Thorpe	69	72	68	72	281	6,450.00
Rod Funseth	70	68	71	72	281	6,450.00
John Schroeder	72	72	70	67	281	6,450.00
Mike Hill	71	71	71	69	282	3,950.00
Rex Caldwell	70	68	73	71	282	3,950.00
Bobby Wadkins	67	73	70	72	282	3,950.00
Lanny Wadkins	72	68	70	72	282	3,950.00
Chi Chi Rodriguez	72	69	69	72	282	3,950.00
Bob Gilder	69	69	70	74	282	3,950.00
Dennis Sullivan	70	72	72	68	282	3,950.00
Doug Tewell	70	72	71	70	283	2,382.00
Buddy Gardner	73	71	69	70	283	2,382.00
Jim Dent	73	70	70	70	283	2,382.00
Mike Morley	73	68	70	72	283	2,382.00
Joe Hager	67	71	72	73	283	2,382.00
Terry Diehl	71	71	68	73	283	2,382.00
Gibby Gilbert	68	72	70	73	283	2,382.00
Mark Pfeil	71	70	69	73	283	2,382.00
Joe Inman	73	70	71	69	283	2,382.00
Barry Jaeckel	70	73	73	68	284	1,763.00
Morris Hatalsky	71	73	68	72	284	1,763.00
Scott Simpson	76	68	73	67	284	1,763.00
Steve Veriato	73	69	72	70	284	1,763.00
Barney Thompson	71	71	71	72	285	1,330.00
Gene Littler	73	71	74	67	285	1,330.00
Alan Tapie	72	69	75	69	285	1,330.00
John Mahaffey	70	68	74	73	285	1,330.00
George Johnson	72	70	73	70	285	1,330.00
Charles Coody	69	74	72	70	285	1,330.00
George Cadle	72	70	72	71	285	1,330.00
Ed Sneed	72	72	70	71	285	1,330.00
Keith Fergus	70	72	71	73	286	899.00
Johnny Miller	71	71	71	73	286	899.00
Arnold Palmer	70	73	74	69	286	899.00

Atlanta Golf Classic

Atlanta Country Club, Marietta, Georgia
Par 36–36—72; 7,019 yards

June 7–10
purse, $300,000

	SCORES				TOTAL	MONEY
Andy Bean	70	67	61	67	265	$54,000.00
Joe Inman	71	64	68	70	273	32,400.00
David Graham	71	70	67	68	276	17,400.00
Grier Jones	68	68	70	70	276	17,400.00
Fuzzy Zoeller	68	71	64	74	277	12,000.00
Wally Armstrong	71	71	70	67	279	10,800.00
Doug Tewell	72	70	69	69	280	9,350.00
Hubert Green	69	71	70	70	280	9,350.00
Jack Renner	68	71	70	71	280	9,350.00
Bob Murphy	68	71	74	68	281	7,200.00
Curtis Strange	70	71	70	70	281	7,200.00
Ed Dougherty	71	73	65	72	281	7,200.00
Barry Jaeckel	67	72	68	74	281	7,200.00
Peter Oosterhuis	68	72	73	69	282	5,250.00
Ed Fiori	67	74	72	69	282	5,250.00
Larry Ziegler	70	74	66	72	282	5,250.00
Mark Lye	63	75	71	73	282	5,250.00
Bob Byman	69	74	70	70	283	3,651.43
Hale Irwin	71	69	71	72	283	3,651.43
Leonard Thompson	69	73	70	71	283	3,651.43
Mike Reid	70	71	69	73	283	3,651.43
Ben Crenshaw	71	69	70	73	283	3,651.43
Mike Hill	71	70	68	74	283	3,651.43
Morris Hatalsky	71	68	68	76	283	3,651.42
Gibby Gilbert	71	70	71	72	284	2,290.00
Bruce Devlin	71	67	74	72	284	2,290.00
Gene Littler	68	70	72	74	284	2,290.00
Homero Blancas	70	72	69	73	284	2,290.00
Keith Fergus	71	69	70	74	284	2,290.00
Larry Nelson	67	70	72	75	284	2,290.00
Dave Stockton	72	70	73	70	285	1,740.00
Antonio Cerda	70	72	73	70	285	1,740.00
Lanny Wadkins	71	71	72	71	285	1,740.00
Calvin Peete	71	74	69	71	285	1,740.00
George Johnson	75	66	72	72	285	1,740.00
Tim Simpson	68	74	69	74	285	1,740.00
Lindy Miller	75	67	74	70	286	1,320.00
Mac McLendon	76	69	70	71	286	1,320.00
Jerry McGee	71	71	72	72	286	1,320.00
Al Geiberger	72	70	71	73	286	1,320.00
Mike Morley	70	71	72	73	286	1,320.00
Charles Coody	68	72	70	76	286	1,320.00
Rik Massengale	70	75	71	71	287	1,050.00
Rod Funseth	69	72	73	73	287	1,050.00
Allen Miller	70	74	70	73	287	1,050.00
Jim Colbert	72	70	75	71	288	850.50
J.C. Snead	71	72	73	72	288	850.50

Craig Stadler	71	71	72	74	288	850.50
Rex Caldwell	73	70	68	77	288	850.50
Bill Calfee	68	76	74	71	289	723.60
George Cadle	73	72	72	72	289	723.60

U.S. Open Championship

Inverness Club, Toledo, Ohio
Par 35–36—71; 6,982 yards

June 14–17
purse, $315,400

	SCORES				TOTAL	MONEY
Hale Irwin	74	68	67	75	284	$50,000.00
Gary Player	73	73	72	68	286	22,250.00
Jerry Pate	71	74	69	72	286	22,250.00
Bill Rogers	71	72	73	72	288	13,733.33
Larry Nelson	71	68	76	73	288	13,733.33
Tom Weiskopf	71	74	67	76	288	13,733.33
David Graham	73	73	70	73	289	10,000.00
Tom Purtzer	70	69	75	76	290	9,000.00
Jack Nicklaus	74	77	72	68	291	7,500.00
Keith Fergus	70	77	72	72	291	7,500.00
Ed Sneed	72	73	75	73	293	4,340.00
Andy North	77	74	68	74	293	4,340.00
Ben Crenshaw	75	71	72	75	293	4,340.00
Calvin Peete	72	75	71	75	293	4,340.00
Lee Elder	74	72	69	78	293	4,340.00
Jim Simons	74	74	78	68	294	2,833.33
Graham Marsh	77	71	72	74	294	2,833.33
Bob Gilder	77	70	69	78	294	2,833.33
Lee Trevino	77	73	73	72	295	2,410.00
D.A. Weibring	74	76	71	74	295	2,410.00
Lanny Wadkins	73	74	71	77	295	2,410.00
Bobby Walzel	74	72	71	78	295	2,410.00
Al Geiberger	74	74	69	78	295	2,410.00
Hubert Green	74	77	73	72	296	2,200.00
Wayne Levi	77	73	75	72	297	2,000.00
Mike Reid	74	75	74	74	297	2,000.00
Lou Graham	70	75	77	75	297	2,000.00
Bobby Nichols	76	75	71	75	297	2,000.00
Bob Murphy	72	79	69	77	297	2,000.00
Andy Bean	70	76	71	80	297	2,000.00
Bob E. Smith	77	71	69	80	297	2,000.00
Lynn Janson	77	71	77	73	298	1,725.00
Dale Douglass	72	76	76	74	298	1,725.00
Howard Twitty	73	78	71	76	298	1,725.00
Chi Chi Rodriguez	73	76	71	78	298	1,725.00
Isao Aoki	73	77	76	73	299	1,560.00
Jim Dent	75	76	75	73	299	1,560.00
John Mahaffey	77	73	74	75	299	1,560.00
Dave Stockton	75	70	78	76	299	1,560.00
Bill Kratzert	77	73	73	76	299	1,560.00
Larry Ziegler	77	72	78	73	300	1,430.00
Jack Renner	76	75	75	74	300	1,430.00
Bruce Lietzke	74	77	73	76	300	1,430.00
Jim Nelford	75	76	73	76	300	1,430.00
Jim Colbert	71	74	78	77	300	1,430.00
Dana Quigley	71	78	74	77	300	1,430.00
Forrest Fezler	73	77	73	78	301	1,360.00
Fred Couples*	76	74	80	72	302	
George Burns	74	73	78	77	302	1,312.50
Greg Norman	76	74	74	78	302	1,312.50
Frank Conner	73	78	73	78	302	1,312.50
Rod Funseth	73	74	74	81	302	1,312.50
David Edwards	74	76	84	70	304	1,265.00
Eddie Pearce	75	75	76	78	304	1,265.00
Joe Inman	72	77	75	80	304	1,265.00
Lon Hinkle	70	77	76	81	304	1,265.00
John Cook*	71	80	77	76	304	
Joe Rassett*	75	75	77	77	304	
Eric Batten	74	76	77	78	305	1,235.00
Arnold Palmer	76	73	75	81	305	1,235.00
John Gentile	73	75	77	81	306	1,220.00
Mac McLendon	77	74	80	78	309	1,210.00
Tony Peterson	74	75	84	79	312	1,280.00

Out of final 36 holes

	SCORES		TOTAL
Scott Steger	77	75	152
Lindy Miller	79	73	152
Raymond Floyd	76	76	152
Johnny Miller	74	78	152
Tom Watson	75	77	152
Steve Melnyk	79	73	152
Mark Pfeil	73	79	152
Miller Barber	74	78	152
Ted Goin	80	73	153
Gene Littler	79	74	153
Bob Clampett*	74	79	153

Hale Irwin and his caddy, Joe Foy.

Bill Britton*	80	73	153
Dennis Sullivan	74	79	153
Wally Armstrong	76	77	153
Larry Gilbert	77	76	153
Rik Massengale	77	77	154
Tom Kite	75	79	154
Alan Tapie	78	76	154
John Fought	77	77	154
Leonard Thompson	78	76	154
J.C. Snead	76	78	154
Fuzzy Zoeller	77	78	155
Jon Feinberg	75	80	155
Richard Horgan	75	80	155
Jim Masserio	77	78	155
David Ogrin*	77	78	155
Gil Morgan	78	77	155
Bill Pelham	80	75	155
Vance Heafner	77	79	156
Rick Terrell	77	79	156
Jerry Heard	75	81	156
Charlie Gibson	77	79	156
David Zabell	83	74	157
Don Padgett	75	82	157
Craig Stadler	78	79	157
Mike Slipko	78	79	157
Bob Shearer	77	80	157
Austin Straub	77	80	157
Kenneth Leber	82	76	158
John McGough*	81	77	158
Steve Spray	85	73	158
Tom Valentine	80	78	158
Mark Hayes	80	78	158
Steve Veriato	77	81	158
Randy O'Linger	81	77	158
Douglas Brown	78	80	158
Tim Simpson	79	80	159
Jeff Jerrel	78	81	159
Larry Griffin	80	79	159
Kip Byrne	77	82	159
Rick Whitfield	79	80	159
Dick Grout	84	76	160
Don Iverson	80	80	160
Severiano Ballesteros	79	81	160
Frank Gusmus*	80	80	160
Mike McCullough	82	79	161
Michael Burke	79	82	161
Sale Omohundro	79	82	161
Ron Streck	80	81	161
Bob Byman	80	81	161
Tom Sieckmann	79	82	161
Dennis Coscina	82	80	162
Joe Kunes	78	84	162
John Schroeder	80	82	162
William Loeffler	84	79	163
Harcourt Kemp*	83	80	163
Lawrence Rentz*	76	87	163
Thomas Inskeep*	86	77	163
Terry Peddy*	78	85	163
Hsu Sheng Sau	79	84	163
Brad Sherfy	84	80	164
Lennie Clements*	84	80	164
Fred Haney	79	86	165
Stephen Groves	84	81	165
Dave Eichelberger	84	81	165
Mick Soli	83	82	165
Clifford Cook	84	81	165
Darrell Kestner	82	83	165
Lee Vandover	81	84	165
Herb Holzacheiter	80	85	165
Chris Nordling*	80	86	166
Mike Atkins	76	90	166
David Glenz	83	84	167
Shuford Dunaway	84	83	167
Stan Thirsk	86	82	168
mark Taylor*	82	86	168
monte Money	84	87	171
Buddy Gardner	82	WD	
Fran Marrello*	85	WD	
Hugh Baiocchi	87	WD	

All professional contestants who missed cut received $600.

*Amateur

Canadian Open

Glen Abbey Golf Club, Oakville, Ontario, Canada
Par 35–36—71; 7,059 yards

June 21–24
purse, $350,000

	SCORES				TOTAL	MONEY
Lee Trevino	67	71	72	71	281	$63,000.00

Ben Crenshaw	70	70	73	71	284	37,800.00
Tom Watson	66	69	72	78	285	23,800.00
Bob Gilder	70	70	76	70	286	16,800.00
Howard Twitty	69	76	73	69	287	12,775.00
Bruce Lietzke	71	74	72	70	287	12,775.00
David Graham	72	70	74	'71	287	12,775.00
Jim Nelford	71	72	73	72	288	10,850.00
Eddie Pearce	74	72	72	71	289	9,100.00
Keith Fergus	70	75	71	73	289	9,100.00
Johnny Miller	67	73	75	74	289	9,100.00
D.A. Weibring	68	70	75	76	289	9,100.00
Gil Morgan	69	72	77	72	290	6,562.50
Tommy Aaron	75	70	73	72	290	6,562.50
Barry Jaeckel	70	74	72	74	290	6,562.50
Jack Newton	64	74	73	79	290	6,562.50
Bobby Wadkins	71	75	72	73	291	5,075.00
Mike Reid	69	71	76	75	291	5,075.00
Morris Hatalsky	77	68	72	74	291	5,075.00
Hale Irwin	72	73	71	75	291	5,075.00
Curtis Strange	72	69	73	78	292	4,280.00
Bob Lunn	68	72	78	75	293	3,640.00
Bob Murphy	68	77	75	73	293	3,640.00
Jack Nicklaus	70	75	71	77	293	3,640.00
Wayne Levi	72	73	78	71	294	2,671.67
Victor Regalado	71	74	77	72	294	2,671.67
Bob Byman	73	73	75	73	294	2,671.67
Bruce Devlin	72	69	78	75	294	2,671.67
Dave Stockton	72	73	74	75	294	2,671.66
Bob Eastwood	71	75	71	77	294	2,671.66
George Burns	75	73	78	69	295	1,862.00
Forrest Fezler	73	71	79	72	295	1,862.00
Jay Haas	77	68	78	72	295	1,862.00
David Edwards	72	73	78	72	295	1,862.00
Tom Storey	76	68	78	73	295	1,862.00
Frank Conner	72	74	76	73	295	1,862.00
Charles Coody	71	70	80	74	295	1,862.00
John Schroeder	71	74	75	75	295	1,862.00
Leonard Thompson	71	74	75	75	295	1,862.00
Rod Funseth	72	75	71	77	295	1,862.00
Rex Caldwell	70	77	78	71	296	1,330.00
Don Bies	72	74	76	74	296	1,330.00
Wally Armstrong	77	71	74	74	296	1,330.00
Tom Kite	70	74	74	78	296	1,330.00
Terry Diehl	68	76	79	74	297	1,085.00
Kermit Zarley	72	71	79	75	297	1,085.00
Lee Elder	72	73	76	76	297	1,085.00
Jim Chancey	72	72	82	72	298	903.00
Jim Dent	72	75	80	71	298	903.00
Ed Fiori	71	75	77	75	298	903.00

Danny Thomas Memphis Classic

Colonial Country Club, Cordova, Tennessee
Par 36–36—72; 7,249 yards

June 28–July 1
purse, $300,000

	SCORES				TOTAL	MONEY
Gil Morgan	72	71	69	66	278	$54,000.00
Larry Nelson	72	71	70	65	278	32,400.00
(Morgan defeated Nelson on second hole of sudden-death play-off)						
Tom Kite	71	70	69	70	280	20,400.00
Bruce Lietzke	71	73	72	66	282	11,812.50
J.C. Snead	69	70	76	67	282	11,812.50
Mark Hayes	71	70	74	67	282	11,812.50
Graham Marsh	72	70	70	70	282	11,812.50
Tom Purtzer	74	72	70	67	283	8,100.00
Bob Byman	71	69	75	68	283	8,100.00
Andy Bean	71	74	68	70	283	8,100.00
Peter Jacobsen	71	71	69	72	283	8,100.00
Cesar Sanudo	72	68	71	72	283	8,100.00
Gary Player	69	75	70	70	284	5,800.00
Rod Curl	70	75	67	72	284	5,800.00
Wally Armstrong	69	73	69	73	284	5,800.00
George Burns	73	69	76	67	285	4,350.00
Morris Hatalsky	71	74	72	68	285	4,350.00
Stan Lee	75	70	72	68	285	4,350.00
Gibby Gilbert	73	70	71	71	285	4,350.00
Brad Bryant	69	72	68	76	285	4,350.00
Jim Simons	70	72	69	74	285	4,350.00
Rex Caldwell	75	69	73	69	286	2,880.00
Jack Newton	70	68	76	72	286	2,880.00
Gary Koch	68	76	71	71	286	2,880.00
George Johnson	70	70	74	72	286	2,880.00
Larry Ziegler	71	70	71	74	286	2,880.00
Hale Irwin	74	72	72	69	287	2,265.00
Jack Renner	74	69	71	73	287	2,265.00
Ron Streck	70	74	75	69	288	1,907.50
Bruce Devlin	71	75	72	70	288	1,907.50
Frank Conner	73	72	73	70	288	1,907.50
Scott Simpson	72	72	72	72	288	1,907.50
Don Pooley	72	75	69	72	288	1,907.50
Bill Kratzert	70	73	72	73	288	1,907.50

Orville Moody	73	74	72	70	289	1,447.50
D.A. Weibring	72	75	72	70	289	1,447.50
John Schroeder	72	72	73	72	289	1,447.50
Jeff Mitchell	76	71	70	72	289	1,447.50
Parker Moore	71	76	69	73	289	1,447.50
Mike Schroder	74	72	70	73	289	1,447.50
David Edwards	71	75	78	66	290	994.67
Tommy McGinnis	74	73	74	69	290	994.67
Dave Stockton	73	71	76	70	290	994.67
Bob Mann	71	74	74	71	290	994.67
Barry Jaeckel	71	73	74	72	290	994.67
Ed Fiori	74	70	72	74	290	994.67
Bobby Wadkins	74	71	71	74	290	994.66
Harlan "Buzz" Fly	73	73	70	74	290	994.66
Dave Hill	77	67	71	75	290	994.66
Miller Barber	72	72	76	71	291	738.00

Western Open

Butler National Golf Club, Oak Brook, Illinois   July 5–8
Par 36-36—72; 7,083 yards   purse, $300,000

	SCORES				TOTAL	MONEY
Larry Nelson	71	69	70	76	286	$54,000.00
Ben Crenshaw	75	69	71	71	286	32,400.00
(Nelson defeated Crenshaw on first hole of sudden-death play-off)						
Dan Pohl	71	72	71	73	287	17,400.00
Bruce Devlin	69	71	76	71	287	17,400.00
Bruce Lietzke	73	73	73	69	288	12,000.00
John Schroeder	75	73	74	67	289	9,712.50
Jim Simons	69	76	72	72	289	9,712.50
Mark Hayes	75	71	72	71	289	9,712.50
Tom Watson	70	73	68	78	289	9,712.50
Graham Marsh	72	74	75	69	290	7,500.00
Calvin Peete	70	75	74	71	290	7,500.00
Bobby Wadkins	75	72	70	73	290	7,500.00
Gibby Gilbert	73	74	75	69	291	5,625.00
Howard Twitty	74	74	72	71	291	5,625.00
John Fought	70	73	74	74	291	5,625.00
Jim Colbert	71	74	73	73	291	5,625.00
Curtis Strange	78	71	75	68	292	4,500.00
Tim Simpson	74	71	77	70	292	4,500.00
Tom Jenkins	72	70	76	74	292	4,500.00
Ed Sneed	75	74	73	71	293	3,750.00
Andy North	74	75	72	72	293	3,750.00
Peter Oosterhuis	74	76	74	70	294	2,880.00
Tom Weiskopf	71	78	73	72	294	2,880.00
George Burns	72	75	75	72	294	2,880.00
Mike Sullivan	73	76	73	72	294	2,880.00
Barney Thompson	74	76	70	74	294	2,880.00
David Graham	74	76	74	71	295	2,220.00
Eddie Pearce	73	70	78	74	295	2,220.00
Gary McCord	73	72	73	77	295	2,220.00
Dale Douglass	70	75	81	70	296	1,822.50
Mark Lye	75	73	75	73	296	1,822.50
Craig Stadler	79	72	72	73	296	1,822.50
Ed Byman	72	79	72	73	296	1,822.50
Bill Rogers	74	72	75	75	296	1,822.50
Andy Bean	73	73	74	76	296	1,822.50
Bob Clampett*	69	72	78	77	296	
Ron Terry	72	74	78	73	297	1,321.88
Peter Jacobsen	77	73	74	73	297	1,321.88
Tom Kite	73	76	75	73	297	1,321.88
Chip Beck	79	72	72	74	297	1,321.88
Mark Pfeil	74	75	73	75	297	1,321.87
Kermit Zarley	74	75	72	76	297	1,321.87
Bob Murphy	76	72	71	78	297	1,321.87
Mick Soli	73	69	75	80	297	1,321.87
Victor Regalado	76	72	76	74	298	990.00
Larry Ziegler	77	72	75	74	298	990.00
Jay Haas	78	72	72	76	298	990.00
Wally Armstrong	77	73	77	72	299	793.20
Ron Streck	71	77	78	73	299	793.20
Alan Tapie	79	71	75	74	299	793.20

*Amateur

Greater Milwaukee Open

Tuckaway Country Club, Franklin, Wisconsin   July 12–15
Par 36-36—72; 7,010 yards   purse, $200,000

	SCORES				TOTAL	MONEY
Calvin Peete	69	67	68	65	269	$36,000.00
Jim Simons	68	68	71	67	274	14,933.34
Victor Regalado	66	68	69	71	274	14,933.33
Lee Trevino	70	68	66	70	274	14,933.33

John Lister	67	69	71	68	275	7,600.00
Ed Dougherty	67	66	70	72	275	7,600.00
Brad Bryant	69	70	70	67	276	6,450.00
David Graham	68	67	71	70	276	6,450.00
Rex Caldwell	71	71	69	66	277	5,400.00
Grier Jones	69	67	71	70	277	5,400.00
Jim Dent	70	67	70	70	277	5,400.00
Chi Chi Rodriguez	70	68	75	65	278	3,685.72
Wayne Levi	70	70	71	67	278	3,685.72
Johnny Miller	68	68	73	69	278	3,685.72
Hubert Green	70	69	69	70	278	3,685.71
Kermit Zarley	68	67	72	71	278	3,685.71
Bill Kratzert	69	68	70	71	278	3,685.71
Andy North	66	70	69	73	278	3,685.71
Bob Mann	68	67	74	70	279	2,424.00
Jack Ferenz	72	68	70	69	279	2,424.00
Dave Eichelberger	68	69	71	71	279	2,424.00
Bobby Wadkins	69	70	70	70	279	2,424.00
Mike Reid	66	69	69	75	279	2,424.00
Ron Streck	73	70	70	67	280	1,513.34
Mike Morley	69	71	71	69	280	1,513.34
Don Pooley	73	70	68	69	280	1,513.34
Dave Eger	66	71	71	72	280	1,513.33
Lon Nielsen	70	69	70	71	280	1,513.33
D.A. Weibring	67	69	72	72	280	1,513.33
Keith Fergus	67	71	68	74	280	1,513.33
Mark Lye	67	68	70	75	280	1,513.33
Mike Nicolette	68	70	69	73	280	1,513.33
Dave Edwards	70	69	76	66	281	1,105.00
Sam Trahan	72	70	71	68	281	1,105.00
Joe Hager	67	68	72	74	281	1,105.00
Fred Marti	69	67	70	75	281	1,105.00
Dan Pohl	71	70	73	68	282	900.00
George Cadle	70	69	75	68	282	900.00
Gibby Gilbert	69	70	73	70	282	900.00
Allen Miller	70	71	71	70	282	900.00
Doug Tewell	72	70	68	72	282	900.00
Ed Byman	71	72	71	69	283	700.00
Mike Hill	70	70	73	70	283	700.00
Lindy Miller	72	68	73	70	283	700.00
Tim Simpson	71	67	72	73	283	700.00
Cesar Sanudo	67	73	70	73	283	700.00
Roger Calvin	73	68	73	70	284	538.00
Bobby Cole	71	72	71	70	284	538.00
George Burns	71	72	71	70	284	538.00
Morris Hatalsky	71	68	73	72	284	538.00

Ed McMahon Quad Cities Open

Oakwood Country Club, Coal Valley, Illinois
Par 35–35—70; 6,514 yards

July 19–22
purse, $200,000

	SCORES				TOTAL	MONEY
D.A. Weibring	67	65	69	65	266	$36,000.00
Calvin Peete	68	70	67	63	268	21,600.00
Ken Still	67	68	67	68	270	13,600.00
Craig Stadler	70	66	66	69	271	9,600.00
Victor Regalado	64	70	72	66	272	7,300.00
Ed Sabo	71	66	69	66	272	7,300.00
Lon Nielsen	66	69	68	69	272	7,300.00
Brad Bryant	70	70	69	64	273	5,000.00
Dan Pohl	68	70	70	65	273	5,000.00
Mike Morley	70	68	69	66	273	5,000.00
Curtis Strange	69	70	66	68	273	5,000.00
Morris Hatalsky	66	71	67	69	273	5,000.00
Rod Curl	67	65	70	71	273	5,000.00
Dan Halldorson	65	68	67	73	273	5,000.00
Dennis Sullivan	65	68	73	68	274	2,813.34
Jeff Mitchell	66	67	72	69	274	2,813.34
Roger Maltbie	69	68	69	68	274	2,813.34
George Cadle	63	74	68	69	274	2,813.33
Peter Jacobsen	66	72	67	69	274	2,813.33
Mike Reid	68	69	68	69	274	2,813.33
Bob Gilder	67	67	70	70	274	2,813.33
Keith Fergus	68	66	70	70	274	2,813.33
Lindy Miller	71	68	65	70	274	2,813.33
Jim Dent	69	70	70	66	275	1,620.00
Jim Thorpe	68	68	72	67	275	1,620.00
Mark Lye	70	69	69	67	275	1,620.00
John Fought	70	66	71	68	275	1,620.00
Bobby Cole	69	64	72	70	275	1,620.00
Bob Murphy	67	66	69	73	275	1,620.00
Skip Dunaway	69	69	70	68	276	1,215.00
Ray Arrino	68	67	73	68	276	1,215.00
Bobby Walzel	71	65	69	71	276	1,215.00
Jack Sommers	69	68	68	71	276	1,215.00
Jim VonLossow	68	68	67	73	276	1,215.00
John Mahaffey	68	69	65	74	276	1,215.00
Ed Sneed	70	67	74	66	277	942.00
Barry Jaeckel	69	71	69	68	277	942.00
Buddy Gardner	69	68	70	70	277	942.00

Joe Kunes	68	69	69	71	277	942.00
Bill Sander	67	70	69	71	277	942.00
Gene Littler	69	72	69	68	278	681.00
David Canipe	69	68	71	70	278	681.00
Ron Terry	70	70	68	70	278	681.00
Larry Webb	66	71	70	71	278	681.00
Don Pooley	69	69	69	71	278	681.00
Gary Koch	68	67	70	73	278	681.00
Mike Hill	70	67	68	73	278	681.00
John Lister	72	65	68	73	278	681.00
Bill Kratzert	70	71	70	68	279	499.00
Tommy Valentine	75	66	68	70	279	499.00

IVB Philadelphia Classic

Whitemarsh Valley Country Club, Whitemarsh Valley, Pennsylvania — July 26–29
Par 36-35—71; 6,687 yards — purse, $250,000

	SCORES				TOTAL	MONEY
Lou Graham	68	70	71	64	273	$45,000.00
Bobby Wadkins	67	69	67	70	273	27,000.00
(Graham defeated Wadkins on first hole of sudden-death play-off)						
Jack Nicklaus	72	70	67	65	274	13,000.00
J.C. Snead	68	64	73	69	274	13,000.00
Mark Hayes	68	70	67	69	274	13,000.00
Bill Kratzert	69	72	68	66	275	8,687.50
David Graham	65	69	70	71	275	8,687.50
Jerry Pate	69	71	70	66	276	7,250.00
Ray Floyd	71	68	70	67	276	7,250.00
Ben Crenshaw	69	66	72	69	276	7,250.00
Bob Byman	67	70	71	69	277	6,250.00
Dave Stockton	68	72	69	69	278	5,750.00
Morris Hatalsky	67	73	72	67	279	4,550.00
Barry Jaeckel	69	72	69	69	279	4,550.00
Jeff Mitchell	68	71	70	70	279	4,550.00
Andy Bean	68	68	72	71	279	4,550.00
Doug Tewell	71	71	65	72	279	4,550.00
Lanny Wadkins	70	71	72	67	280	3,500.00
Jay Sigel°	71	72	69	68	280	
Howard Twitty	71	69	69	71	280	3,500.00
Gene Littler	72	70	65	73	280	3,500.00
Wally Armstrong	71	71	70	69	281	2,346.88
Tom Purtzer	70	72	69	70	281	2,346.88
Kermit Zarley	70	70	70	71	281	2,346.88
Mike Reid	68	72	70	71	281	2,346.88
Tommy Valentine	67	69	72	73	281	2,346.87
Steve Veriato	68	73	68	72	281	2,346.87
Forrest Fezler	67	72	69	73	281	2,346.87
Calvin Peete	70	70	68	73	281	2,346.87
Jim Colbert	70	68	75	69	282	1,662.50
Victor Regalado	68	72	71	71	282	1,662.50
Bob Gilder	72	69	69	72	282	1,662.50
Bill Rogers	65	71	71	75	282	1,662.50
Tom Kite	72	68	74	69	283	1,265.63
George Cadle	67	75	71	70	283	1,265.63
Don January	70	72	70	71	283	1,265.63
Leonard Thompson	69	73	70	71	283	1,265.63
Scott Simpson	71	69	71	72	283	1,265.62
John Schroeder	68	69	74	72	283	1,265.62
David Thore	69	73	69	72	283	1,265.62
Mark McCumber	67	73	69	74	283	1,265.62
Ron Streck	73	68	73	70	284	950.00
Peter Jacobsen	68	72	73	71	284	950.00
Mike Sullivan	70	73	70	71	284	950.00
Jim Chancey	72	70	69	73	284	950.00
Jim Simons	69	71	74	71	285	700.72
Dan Halldorson	73	70	73	69	285	700.72
Jack Ferenz	71	72	71	71	285	700.72
Ed Fiori	74	69	71	71	285	700.71
Isao Aoki	68	75	69	73	285	700.71

° Amateur

PGA Championship

Oakland Hills Country Club, Birmingham, Michigan — August 2–5
Par 35-35—70; 7,014 yards — purse, $350,000

		SCORES			TOTAL	
	MONEY					
David Graham	69	68	70	65	272	$60,000.00
Ben Crenshaw	69	67	69	67	272	40,000.00
(Graham defeated Crenshaw on third hole of sudden-death play-off)						
Rex Caldwell	67	70	66	71	274	25,000.00
Ron Streck	68	71	69	69	276	20,000.00
Gibby Gilbert	69	72	68	69	278	14,500.00

Jerry Pate	69	69	69	71	278	14,500.00
Howard Twitty	70	73	69	67	279	9,200.00
Jay Haas	68	69	73	69	279	9,200.00
Don January	69	70	71	69	279	9,200.00
Gary Koch	71	71	71	67	280	6,750.00
Lou Graham	69	74	68	69	280	6,750.00
Jerry McGee	73	69	71	68	281	5,250.00
Andy Bean	76	69	68	68	281	5,250.00
Jack Renner	71	74	66	70	281	5,250.00
Tom Watson	66	72	69	74	281	5,250.00
Bob Gilder	73	71	68	70	282	3,780.00
Hubert Green	69	70	72	71	282	3,780.00
Graham Marsh	69	70	71	72	282	3,780.00
Gene Littler	71	71	67	73	282	3,780.00
Bruce Lietzke	69	69	71	73	282	3,780.00
John Schroeder	72	72	70	69	283	3,250.00
Bob Byman	73	72	69	69	283	3,250.00
Rod Funseth	70	69	76	69	284	2,900.00
Alan Tapie	73	65	76	70	284	2,900.00
Frank Conner	70	73	69	72	284	2,900.00
Gary Player	73	70	70	71	284	2,900.00
Peter Jacobsen	70	74	67	73	284	2,900.00
Gil Morgan	72	73	70	70	285	2,300.00
Larry Nelson	70	75	70	70	285	2,300.00
Miller Barber	73	72	69	71	285	2,300.00
Ed Sneed	77	67	70	71	285	2,300.00
Mark McCumber	75	68	70	72	285	2,300.00
Artie McNickle	69	70	72	74	285	2,300.00
George Burns	71	74	67	73	285	2,300.00
Dave Stockton	70	75	72	70	287	1,600.00
Lynn Janson	73	71	72	71	287	1,600.00
Lee Trevino	70	73	72	72	287	1,600.00
Bill Rogers	70	72	73	72	287	1,600.00
Lee Elder	70	71	73	73	287	1,600.00
Jim Masserio	69	73	71	74	287	1,600.00
Tom Kite	72	72	69	74	287	1,600.00
Calvin Peete	75	71	70	72	288	1,050.00
Sam Snead	73	71	71	73	288	1,050.00
Jimmy Wright	72	69	72	75	288	1,050.00
Kermit Zarley	73	69	71	75	288	1,050.00
Don Padgett	71	75	73	70	289	704.00
Jim Simons	76	68	73	72	289	704.00
Jim Colbert	73	73	72	71	289	704.00
Chi Chi Rodriguez	71	72	72	74	289	704.00
Tommy Aaron	73	73	69	74	289	704.00
Rod Curl	72	72	73	73	290	600.00
John Mahaffey	72	74	71	73	290	600.00
Bob Mann	71	73	71	75	290	600.00
Fuzzy Zoeller	70	75	75	71	291	567.50
Jim Dent	70	72	76	73	291	567.50
Leonard Thompson	72	67	78	74	291	567.50
Wally Armstrong	74	71	73	73	291	567.50
DeWitt Weaver	73	73	71	74	291	567.50
Dave Barber	74	69	71	77	291	567.50
Barry Jaeckel	71	73	75	73	292	547.50
Keith Fergus	73	70	73	76	292	547.50
Mark Hayes	71	73	77	72	293	535.00
Raymond Floyd	74	70	77	72	293	535.00
Rocky Thompson	72	72	73	76	293	535.00
Jack Nicklaus	73	72	78	71	294	515.00
Scott Bess	73	72	75	74	294	515.00
Allen Geiberger	76	70	73	75	294	515.00
Lon Hinkle	73	72	71	78	294	515.00
Austin Straub	73	70	72	79	294	515.00
Lanny Wadkins	71	75	73	76	295	500.00
Bobby Wadkins	77	68	75	76	296	500.00
Dean Refram	75	69	79	75	298	500.00
Ronald Smoak	72	74	78	79	303	500.00
Dennis Coscine	76	70	74	83	303	500.00

Out of final 36 holes

	SCORES		TOTAL
Tommy Aycock	75	72	147
Randy Erskine	72	75	147
Lindy Miller	76	71	147
Al Mengert	76	71	147
Jim Thorpe	71	76	147
Jim Nelford	74	73	147
Orville Moody	72	75	147
Billy Casper	75	72	147
Michael Brannan	73	74	147
Tim Collins	74	74	148
Ron Terry	74	74	148
Jim White	78	70	148
Bobby Walzel	75	73	148
Hale Irwin	73	75	148
J.C. Snead	72	76	148
Doug Tewell	75	73	148
Tom Purtzer	73	75	148
Victor Regalado	72	76	148
Grier Jones	73	75	148
Buddy Gardner	76	72	148
Craig Stadler	73	75	148
Woody Dame	75	73	148

Paul Purtzer	76	73		149
Michael Nilon	75	74		149
D.A. Weibring	76	73		149
Bob Murphy	71	78		149
John Gentile	75	74		149
Andy North	76	73		149
Michael Reid	75	74		149
Waddy Stokes	78	71		149
Curtis Strange	74	76		150
Jay Overton	74	76		150
Lloyd Monroe	74	76		150
Howell Fraser	73	77		150
Ralph Montoya	76	74		150
Billy Kratzert	74	76		150
Jim Ferree	75	75		150
George Shortridge	76	74		150
Phillip Hancock	79	71		150
Isao Aoki	78	72		150
Tom Weiskopf	79	71		150
Julius Boros	77	73		150
Jimmy Paschal	76	75		151
Dow Finsterwald	77	74		151
Charles Coody	79	72		151
Larry Startzel	77	75		152
Mac McLendon	78	74		152
Bruce Summerhays	78	74		152
David Jimenez	77	75		152
Larry Ringer	78	74		152
Bobby Phillips	78	75		153
Tony Kaloustian	74	79		153
Tom Joyce	74	79		153
Jack Sommers	74	79		153
Mike McCullough	82	71		153
Guy Cullins	74	79		153
Mark Alwin	77	77		154
Joe Inman	80	74		154
Steve Spray	77	77		154
Jim Logue	78	76		154
Babe Lichardus	78	76		154
Roger Ginsberg	76	78		154
Arnold Palmer	81	74		155
Roy Abrameit	80	76		156
Mike Davis	81	75		156
Bobby Nichols	74	82		156
Gary Clark	78	78		156
Bob Galloway	82	75		157
Mike Felker	77	80		157
Jerry Barber	83	75		158
Alan White	80	79		159
Craig Bunker	79	80		159
Emil Esposito	81	79		160
Rob Bragg	81	81		162
Doug Ford	81	82		163
Richard Martinez	82	WD		

Each player who finished 36 holes received $350.00

Sammy Davis, Jr., Greater Hartford Open

Wethersfield Country Club, Wethersfield, Connecticut
Par 35-36—71; 6,568 yards

August 9–14
purse, $300,000

		SCORES			TOTAL	MONEY
Jerry McGee	68	67	67	65	267	$54,000.00
Jack Renner	68	67	66	67	268	32,400.00
Curtis Strange	70	66	69	65	270	17,400.00
George Cadle	62	73	66	69	270	17,400.00
Mark Hayes	66	66	73	66	271	10,950.00
Lou Graham	69	69	67	66	271	10,950.00
J.C. Snead	65	66	71	69	271	10,950.00
Hubert Green	67	71	68	66	272	9,000.00
Michael Brannan	67	67	70	68	272	9,000.00
Dave Eichelberger	69	71	67	66	273	7,200.00
Victor Regalado	69	70	67	67	273	7,200.00
Raymond Floyd	70	69	67	67	273	7,200.00
Peter Oosterhuis	67	68	69	69	273	7,200.00
Bob Murphy	68	68	72	66	274	5,250.00
Keith Fergus	66	69	71	68	274	5,250.00
John Fought	68	67	69	70	274	5,250.00
Joe Inman	67	68	68	71	274	5,250.00
Don Bies	70	70	69	66	275	4,350.00
Morris Hatalsky	73	67	66	69	275	4,350.00
D.A. Weibring	68	73	70	65	276	3,026.25
Kermit Zarley	71	69	68	68	276	3,026.25
Alan Tapie	67	72	69	68	276	3,026.25
Lee Elder	69	71	68	68	276	3,026.25
Tom Purtzer	70	69	68	69	276	3,026.25
Craig Stadler	68	68	70	70	276	3,026.25
Pat McGowan	66	71	71	68	276	3,026.25
Rod Curl	67	69	69	71	276	3,026.25

Dave Barr	68	71	72	66	277	2,085.00
Ron Streck	70	70	70	67	277	2,085.00
Ed Fiori	69	71	68	69	277	2,085.00
Butch Baird	69	70	68	70	277	2,085.00
Leonard Thompson	69	69	71	69	278	1,775.00
Danny Edwards	68	71	70	69	278	1,775.00
Mike McCullough	70	70	67	71	278	1,775.00
Forrest Fezler	68	69	72	70	279	1,511.25
Jay Haas	65	71	73	70	279	1,511.25
George Archer	70	69	70	70	279	1,511.25
Jim Dent	68	70	65	76	279	1,511.25
Austin Straub	70	68	74	68	280	1,140.00
Jimmy Paschal	72	69	70	69	280	1,140.00
Tim Simpson	69	71	72	68	280	1,140.00
David Thore	70	71	70	69	280	1,140.00
Peter Jacobsen	71	69	71	69	280	1,140.00
Rod Funseth	69	70	72	69	280	1,140.00
Allen Miller	70	69	70	71	280	1,140.00
Tommy Aaron	68	68	72	72	280	1,140.00
Jim Simons	69	71	74	67	281	761.25
Bill Sander	73	68	73	67	281	761.25
Fuzzy Zoeller	70	66	76	69	281	761.25
Bobby Nichols	71	70	70	70	281	761.25

Manufacturers Hanover Westchester Classic

Westchester Country Club, Harrison, New York
Par 36–35—71; 6,603 yards

August 16–19
purse, $400,000

	SCORES				TOTAL	MONEY
Jack Renner	69	71	70	67	277	$72,000.00
Howard Twitty	70	70	71	67	278	35,200.00
David Graham	65	73	69	71	278	35,200.00
Peter Oosterhuis	70	75	71	63	279	17,600.00
Scott Simpson	70	68	70	71	279	17,600.00
Tom Kite	69	67	74	70	280	14,400.00
George Burns	69	70	72	70	281	12,466.67
J.C. Snead	73	68	71	69	281	12,466.67
Bob Murphy	73	68	69	71	281	12,466.66
Gil Morgan	71	68	76	67	282	10,000.00
Tom Watson	69	75	70	68	282	10,000.00
Lon Hinkle	70	69	72	71	282	10,000.00
Alan Tapie	73	69	72	69	283	7,500.00
Rex Caldwell	77	68	69	69	283	7,500.00
Mike Hill	74	71	68	70	283	7,500.00
Hubert Green	73	69	70	71	283	7,500.00
Andy North	73	71	73	67	284	5,413.34
Greg Powers	73	71	71	69	284	5,413.34
Chi Chi Rodriguez	73	71	71	69	284	5,413.33
Bob Eastwood	69	74	71	70	284	5,413.33
Jerry McGee	71	67	74	72	284	5,413.33
Leonard Thompson	72	70	70	72	284	5,413.33
Charles Coody	72	73	72	68	285	3,371.43
Bob Byman	69	71	75	70	285	3,371.43
Fred Marti	70	69	76	70	285	3,371.43
Bob Gilder	72	73	70	70	285	3,371.43
Ed Dougherty	76	68	71	70	285	3,371.43
Jim Simons	74	70	70	71	285	3,371.43
Bruce Lietzke	76	68	69	72	285	3,371.42
Kermit Zarley	73	70	73	70	286	2,484.00
Bill Rogers	73	73	69	71	286	2,484.00
Gene Littler	75	71	69	71	286	2,484.00
Phil Hancock	74	70	70	72	286	2,484.00
Jimmy Wright	71	69	73	73	286	2,484.00
John Mahaffey	72	72	75	68	287	1,930.00
Bill Kratzert	73	71	74	69	287	1,930.00
D.A. Weibring	73	70	75	69	287	1,930.00
Don January	70	74	73	70	287	1,930.00
Ed Sabo	72	74	71	70	287	1,930.00
Bob E. Smith	72	72	71	72	287	1,930.00
Jerry Pate	78	68	76	66	288	1,440.00
Artie McNickle	70	70	77	71	288	1,440.00
Lon Nielsen	74	71	72	71	288	1,440.00
Wayne Levi	75	70	71	72	288	1,440.00
Fuzzy Zoeller	74	72	70	72	288	1,440.00
Gibby Gilbert	72	71	70	75	288	1,440.00
Art Wall	75	71	72	71	289	1,098.67
Peter Jacobsen	72	72	72	73	289	1,098.67
Tommy Aaron	71	75	68	75	289	1,098.66
Bruce Devlin	74	68	75	73	290	950.86

Colgate Hall of Fame Classic

Pinehurst Country Club, Pinehurst, North Carolina
Course No. 2: Par 35–36—71; 7,020 yards

August 23–26
purse, $250,000

	SCORES				TOTAL	MONEY
Tom Watson	70	68	65	69	272	$45,000.00

Johnny Miller	69	63	70	70	272	27,000.00
(Watson defeated Miller on second hole of sudden-death play-off)						
Keith Fergus	68	68	67	71	274	17,000.00
Danny Edwards	67	68	69	71	275	12,000.00
Andy North	69	70	67	70	276	10,000.00
Bill Rogers	74	66	69	69	278	9,000.00
Bob Zender	73	71	69	66	279	8,062.50
Michael Brannan	67	68	74	70	279	8,062.50
Lyn Lott	72	70	72	66	280	6,750.00
Bruce Devlin	70	67	70	73	280	6,750.00
Kermit Zarley	68	70	70	72	280	6,750.00
Charles Coody	70	69	70	72	281	5,250.00
Larry Nelson	70	69	69	73	281	5,250.00
Tommy Aaron	69	66	71	75	281	5,250.00
Bob Eastwood	72	71	68	71	282	3,875.00
Lou Graham	67	74	71	70	282	3,875.00
Bobby Baker	71	68	71	72	282	3,875.00
Cesar Sanudo	68	72	70	72	282	3,875.00
Craig Stadler	67	73	69	73	282	3,875.00
Bob Murphy	71	70	68	73	282	3,875.00
Allen Miller	71	71	71	70	283	3,000.00
Hubert Green	72	71	72	69	284	2,500.00
Bob Mann	70	71	71	72	284	2,500.00
Curtis Strange	69	70	72	73	284	2,500.00
Dana Quigley	63	74	73	74	284	2,500.00
Roger Maltbie	68	74	74	69	285	1,850.00
Miller Barber	71	73	71	70	285	1,850.00
Jay Haas	71	70	72	72	285	1,850.00
Hale Irwin	68	71	74	72	285	1,850.00
Andy Bean	71	68	73	73	285	1,850.00
Terry Mauney	72	72	73	69	286	1,387.50
Bob Shearer	74	70	72	70	286	1,387.50
Lon Nielsen	72	71	72	71	286	1,387.50
Chip Beck	70	70	74	72	286	1,387.50
Mick Soli	71	72	71	72	286	1,387.50
David Eger	71	72	71	72	286	1,387.50
Joe Inman	72	70	71	73	286	1,387.50
Lanny Wadkins	69	75	66	76	286	1,387.50
Tim Simpson	71	73	71	72	287	1,050.00
Ed Sabo	71	71	72	73	287	1,050.00
John Lister	68	74	72	73	287	1,050.00
Chris Clark	77	67	70	73	287	1,050.00
Mike McCullough	69	72	75	72	288	780.00
Buddy Gardner	71	73	72	72	288	780.00
David Thore	73	71	72	72	288	780.00
Morris Hatalsky	70	74	71	73	288	780.00
J.C. Snead	70	74	71	73	288	780.00
Lon Hinkle	70	69	75	74	288	780.00
Fred Marti	74	70	71	73	288	780.00
Wally Armstrong	73	71	73	72	289	598.34

B.C. Open

En Joie Golf Club, Endicott, New York
Par 37-34—71; 6,915 yards

August 30–September 2
purse, $275,000

	SCORES				TOTAL	MONEY
Howard Twitty	69	70	64	67	270	$49,500.00
Tom Purtzer	70	67	68	66	271	29,700.00
Doug Tewell	67	69	66	70	272	18,700.00
Rod Curl	70	66	70	68	274	12,100.00
Tom Kite	72	68	67	67	274	12,100.00
Brad Bryant	67	67	68	73	275	9,900.00
Jay Haas	71	66	68	71	276	8,850.00
Curtis Strange	64	73	68	71	276	8,850.00
Peter Jacobsen	68	69	75	65	277	6,600.00
Grier Jones	71	68	70	68	277	6,600.00
Chi Chi Rodriguez	70	69	70	68	277	6,600.00
Craig Stadler	69	70	69	69	277	6,600.00
Jerry Pate	72	66	69	70	277	6,600.00
Parker Moore	69	72	66	70	277	6,600.00
Lindy Miller	71	72	70	65	278	4,125.00
Alan Tapie	65	67	76	70	278	4,125.00
Gary Koch	69	68	71	70	278	4,125.00
Bill Rogers	71	69	68	70	278	4,125.00
Dave Eichelberger	71	69	68	70	278	4,125.00
John Mazza	72	67	67	72	278	4,125.00
Mike Reid	70	69	66	73	278	4,125.00
Tommy Valentine	67	68	76	68	279	2,860.00
Buddy Gardner	70	70	67	72	279	2,860.00
Don Iverson	69	67	69	74	279	2,860.00
Bob Byman	70	70	73	67	280	1,938.00
Rex Caldwell	70	66	74	70	280	1,938.00
Beau Baugh	71	68	70	71	280	1,938.00
Bob Zender	71	71	68	70	280	1,938.00
Mike Hill	70	68	70	72	280	1,938.00
Frank Conner	67	74	68	71	280	1,938.00
Bill Kratzert	70	72	66	72	280	1,938.00
Bobby Wadkins	71	69	68	72	280	1,938.00
Barney Thompson	67	67	71	75	280	1,938.00
Gil Morgan	66	67	71	76	280	1,938.00

Cesar Sanudo	73	67	73	68	281	1,330.00
Tom Weiskopf	69	72	71	69	281	1,330.00
Dick Mast	76	67	68	70	281	1,330.00
Orville Moody	73	68	70	70	281	1,330.00
Barry Jaeckel	71	67	69	74	281	1,330.00
Morris Hatalsky	70	67	69	75	281	1,330.00
Bill Calfee	69	71	74	68	282	1,006.00
Dan Pohl	73	68	70	71	282	1,006.00
Roger Maltbie	69	71	70	72	282	1,006.00
Joe Kunes	72	71	67	72	282	1,006.00
Tommy Aaron	68	73	68	73	282	1,006.00
Dana Quigley	74	69	70	70	283	737.15
George Archer	71	72	69	71	283	737.15
Ed Dougherty	68	69	74	72	283	737.14
Jack Ferenz	72	69	70	72	283	737.14
Johnny Miller	70	69	71	73	283	737.14

American Optical Pleasant Valley Classic

Pleasant Valley Country Club, Sutton, Massachusetts
Par 36–35—71; 7,119 yards

September 6–9
purse, $250,000

	SCORES				TOTAL	MONEY
Lou Graham	68	67	71	69	275	$45,000.00
Ben Crenshaw	67	71	68	70	276	27,000.00
Terry Diehl	66	71	69	72	278	17,000.00
Jeff Mitchell	70	70	67	72	279	12,000.00
Rod Curl	74	68	69	70	281	8,475.00
Bruce Devlin	70	70	69	72	281	8,475.00
Rex Caldwell	69	71	72	69	281	8,475.00
Tim Simpson	70	70	69	72	281	8,475.00
David Eger	69	69	70	73	281	8,475.00
Jeff Thomsen	70	71	71	70	282	6,250.00
Larry Ziegler	71	73	71	67	282	6,250.00
David Edwards	72	67	66	77	282	6,250.00
John Lister	69	74	71	69	283	4,416.67
Bob Byman	71	72	69	71	283	4,416.67
Bruce Lietzke	70	75	70	68	283	4,416.67
George Archer	70	67	71	75	283	4,416.67
Al Geiberger	69	68	72	74	283	4,416.66
Ron Terry	68	70	72	73	283	4,416.66
Dana Quigley	73	70	70	71	284	3,250.00
Bob Zender	70	69	70	75	284	3,250.00
Tom Weiskopf	74	71	70	69	284	3,250.00
Jack Renner	72	70	73	70	285	2,320.84
Jim Thorpe	70	71	72	72	285	2,320.84
Leonard Thompson	70	75	70	70	285	2,320.83
Gibby Gilbert	68	71	75	71	285	2,320.83
Dave Stockton	74	71	67	73	285	2,320.83
Mark Lye	69	70	74	72	285	2,320.83
Bill Calfee	72	70	73	71	286	1,812.50
Don January	68	73	71	74	286	1,812.50
Craig Stadler	72	70	72	73	287	1,453.13
Mick Soli	71	71	72	73	287	1,453.13
Marty Fleckman	67	74	76	70	287	1,453.13
J.C. Snead	70	73	69	75	287	1,453.13
Morris Hatalsky	71	72	73	71	287	1,453.12
Jim Colbert	71	71	70	75	287	1,453.12
Bobby Baker	67	72	74	74	287	1,453.12
Mark Pfeil	69	70	72	76	287	1,453.12
Mike Reid	71	71	73	73	288	1,075.00
Jack Newton	68	74	72	74	288	1,075.00
Beau Baugh	74	67	75	72	288	1,075.00
Bill Sander	70	74	72	72	288	1,075.00
Brad Bryant	74	71	71	72	288	1,075.00
Tommy Aaron	72	70	75	72	289	780.00
Don Pooley	71	72	73	73	289	780.00
Jim Chancey	72	69	73	75	289	780.00
Lon Nielsen	70	72	75	72	289	780.00
Robert Donald	73	70	72	74	289	780.00
Roger Calvin	70	74	74	71	289	780.00
John Fought	72	72	75	70	289	780.00
Buddy Gardner	70	72	73	75	290	615.00

Buick-Goodwrench Open

Warwick Hills Country Club, Grand Blanc, Michigan
Par 36–36—72; 7,001 yards

September 13–16
purse, $150,000

	SCORES				TOTAL	MONEY
John Fought	71	72	68	69	280	$27,000.00
Jim Simons	72	71	70	67	280	16,200.00
(Fought defeated Simons on second hole of sudden-death play-off)						
Dave Eichelberger	68	70	72	71	281	10,200.00
Jim Colbert	69	72	72	69	282	7,425.00
Bob Eastwood	68	75	74	66	283	6,000.00

Lon Hinkle	73	69	73	68	283	6,000.00
Bill Kratzert	71	72	70	70	283	6,000.00
Lindy Miller	71	71	75	67	284	4,075.00
David Edwards	72	70	71	71	284	4,075.00
David Graham	68	74	70	72	284	4,075.00
George Burns	68	72	72	72	284	4,075.00
Tom Weiskopf	69	74	70	71	284	4,075.00
Dana Quigley	70	71	70	73	284	4,075.00
Tommy Valentine	73	72	72	68	285	2,421.43
Steve Melnyk	70	73	74	68	285	2,421.43
Terry Diehl	69	72	74	70	285	2,421.43
Bob Zender	70	71	74	70	285	2,421.43
Bob E. Smith	73	68	72	72	285	2,421.43
Jeff Mitchell	70	73	68	74	285	2,421.43
George Archer	68	72	71	74	285	2,421.42
Dan Halldorson	71	70	71	74	286	1,725.00
Mike Hill	69	73	69	75	286	1,725.00
Dan Pohl	70	73	73	71	287	1,500.00
Eddie Pearce	71	72	72	72	287	1,500.00
Cesar Sanudo	67	73	74	73	287	1,500.00
Morris Hatalsky	69	72	75	72	288	1,350.00
Brad Bryant	73	72	75	69	289	1,106.25
Jack Newton	73	71	75	70	289	1,106.25
Beau Baugh	72	73	73	71	289	1,106.25
Marty Fleckman	73	69	75	72	289	1,106.25
Danny Edwards	71	72	73	73	289	1,106.25
Rodney Morrow	71	72	73	73	289	1,106.25
Buddy Gardner	72	70	73	74	289	1,106.25
Scott Steger	69	72	71	77	289	1,106.25
Mike Reid	71	74	73	72	290	840.00
Tom Chain	72	73	73	72	290	840.00
Mark Lye	70	74	73	73	290	840.00
Gary McCord	73	70	73	74	290	840.00
Jim Masserio	72	72	72	74	290	840.00
David Lundstrom	76	69	73	74	292	735.00
Lynn Janson	73	72	73	74	292	735.00
Ed Dougherty	67	75	74	76	292	735.00
Bill Sander	74	71	74	74	293	675.00
Greg Powers	72	73	75	73	293	675.00
John Traub	73	71	75	74	293	675.00
D.A. Weibring	71	74	75	73	293	675.00
Tommy Aaron	73	72	71	77	293	675.00
Peter Jacobsen	72	73	78	71	294	622.50
Tim Simpson	72	73	73	76	294	622.50
Mark McCumber	71	72	80	73	296	600.00

Anheuser-Busch Golf Classic

Silverado Country Club, Napa, California
North Course: Par 36—36—72; 6,870 yards
South Course (first two rounds only): Par 35—37—72; 6,619 yards

September 20–23
purse, $300,000

	SCORES				TOTAL	MONEY
John Fought	69	68	71	69	277	$54,000.00
Alan Tapie	68	75	69	66	278	22,400.00
Bobby Wadkins	66	72	71	69	278	22,400.00
Buddy Gardner	68	72	68	70	278	22,400.00
Bill Rogers	68	71	72	68	279	12,000.00
Andy North	71	69	71	69	280	10,050.00
Mark Lye	66	72	67	75	280	10,050.00
Lon Hinkle	69	66	70	75	280	10,050.00
Rod Curl	73	69	73	66	281	7,800.00
Bruce Lietzke	71	68	71	71	281	7,800.00
Mike Sullivan	70	70	70	71	281	7,800.00
Bob Gilder	69	68	70	74	281	7,800.00
Tom Weiskopf	71	72	70	69	282	5,800.00
J.C. Snead	71	70	69	72	282	5,800.00
Lou Graham	68	66	72	76	282	5,800.00
Pat McGowan	73	69	72	69	283	4,950.00
Jerry McGee	69	74	72	68	283	4,950.00
Dave Eichelberger	72	72	70	70	284	3,651.43
Craig Stadler	70	73	72	69	284	3,651.43
Jack Renner	72	69	72	71	284	3,651.43
Tom Kite	70	72	74	68	284	3,651.43
Steve Melnyk	72	69	70	73	284	3,651.43
Rod Funseth	73	68	68	75	284	3,651.43
Tim Simpson	70	71	67	76	284	3,651.42
Gary McCord	70	74	70	71	285	2,340.00
Ed Fiori	71	70	71	73	285	2,340.00
Jay Haas	70	70	71	74	285	2,340.00
Skip Dunaway	71	68	72	74	285	2,340.00
Ben Crenshaw	71	72	74	68	285	2,340.00
Fuzzy Zoeller	71	72	71	72	286	1,782.86
Wally Armstrong	72	71	72	71	286	1,782.86
Mike Reid	69	75	69	73	286	1,782.86
Grier Jones	72	67	73	74	286	1,782.86
Victor Regalado	68	74	74	70	286	1,782.86
Don Bies	71	70	71	74	286	1,782.85
Larry Ziegler	73	71	72	70	286	1,782.85
Dan Halldorson	74	70	68	75	287	1,410.00

Charles Coody	68	74	74	71	287	1,410.00
George Knudson	72	72	73	70	287	1,410.00
Bob Byman	72	70	73	73	288	1,110.00
Andy Bean	70	72	72	74	288	1,110.00
Lee Elder	67	73	75	73	288	1,110.00
John Mahaffey	69	75	71	73	288	1,110.00
Mike Hill	71	72	73	72	288	1,110.00
Eddie Pearce	76	68	67	77	288	1,110.00
Mike Brannan	69	72	76	71	288	1,110.00
Phil Hancock	75	64	75	75	289	781.00
Bob Betley	73	67	74	75	289	781.00
Antonio Cerda	74	69	70	76	289	781.00
Joe Inman	74	69	72	74	289	781.00

World Series of Golf

Firestone Country Club, Akron, Ohio
South Course: Par 35–35—70; 7,173 yards

September 27–30
purse, $400,000

	SCORES				TOTAL	MONEY
Lon Hinkle	67	67	71	67	272	$100,000.00
Bill Rogers	69	67	68	69	273	37,266.67
Larry Nelson	68	67	68	70	273	37,266.67
Lee Trevino	67	68	72	66	273	37,266.66
Hale Irwin	69	70	70	65	274	15,000.00
Tom Watson	68	65	72	69	274	15,000.00
Tom Kite	67	68	70	70	275	12,800.00
Howard Twitty	69	67	71	69	276	11,600.00
Bob Gilder	74	67	67	70	278	10,400.00
Bruce Lietzke	71	68	71	69	279	9,400.00
Andy Bean	64	75	70	70	279	9,400.00
John Mahaffey	74	68	68	71	281	8,200.00
Jerry Pate	68	72	65	76	281	8,200.00
J.C. Snead	66	70	73	73	282	7,000.00
Fuzzy Zoeller	69	69	71	73	282	7,000.00
Tohru Nakamura	70	71	70	72	283	6,100.00
Ben Crenshaw	73	69	73	69	284	5,800.00
John Fought	73	68	76	68	285	5,200.00
David Graham	72	73	70	70	285	5,200.00
Lou Graham	73	70	70	72	285	5,200.00
Graham Marsh	66	74	71	75	286	4,450.00
Lanny Wadkins	72	71	70	73	286	4,450.00
Isao Aoki	71	70	77	69	287	3,850.00
Dale Hayes	72	74	72	69	287	3,850.00
Gil Morgan	71	71	72	74	288	3,350.00
Ed Sneed	70	72	76	70	288	3,350.00
Bobby Wadkins	74	74	70	71	289	3,060.00
Hubert Green	74	69	75	72	290	2,700.00
Raymond Floyd	82	71	68	69	290	2,700.00
Mark Hayes	70	73	75	72	290	2,700.00
Greg Norman	73	73	75	70	291	2,340.00
Mark O'Meara*	74	74	70	74	292	
Jerry McGee	71	75	75	71	292	2,160.00
Jay Sigel*	76	73	72	73	294	
Wayne Levi	77	78	74	68	297	2,025.00
Jack Renner	73	75	73	76	297	2,025.00
Lu Hsi Chuen	76	78	78	69	301	1,890.00
Hsu Chi San	78	72	77	80	307	1,800.00

*Amateur

San Antonio Texas Open

Oak Hills Country Club, San Antonio, Texas
Par 35–35—70; 6,525 yards

October 4–7
purse, $250,000

	SCORES				TOTAL	MONEY
Lou Graham	69	64	69	66	268	$45,000.00
Doug Tewell	66	68	63	72	269	18,666.67
Bill Rogers	72	68	62	67	269	18,666.67
Eddie Pearce	69	65	65	70	269	18,666.67
Gary McCord	70	69	67	65	271	8,781.25
Keith Fergus	69	65	69	68	271	8,781.25
Ben Crenshaw	70	65	68	68	271	8,781.25
Lee Trevino	68	65	69	69	271	8,781.25
Bob Gilder	72	68	67	65	272	7,000.00
Mike Sullivan	68	69	68	67	272	7,000.00
Rex Caldwell	69	72	68	64	273	5,500.00
Calvin Peete	71	67	68	67	273	5,500.00
Bob Murphy	69	69	67	68	273	5,500.00
John Mahaffey	71	64	67	71	273	5,500.00
Scott Simpson	72	69	66	67	274	4,375.00
Bill Kratzert	69	70	65	70	274	4,375.00
Orville Moody	69	69	70	67	275	3,750.00
Gibby Gilbert	66	71	68	70	275	3,750.00

Tom Weiskopf	71	67	67	70	275	3,750.00	
Dale Douglass	72	66	70	68	276	2,912.50	
Curtis Strange	69	69	69	69	276	2,912.50	
Mark McCumber	69	69	69	69	276	2,912.50	
Marty Fleckman	72	68	67	69	276	2,912.50	
Mark Pfeil	68	75	66	68	277	2,200.00	
Jim Colbert	71	68	69	69	277	2,200.00	
Ed Fiori	68	72	68	69	277	2,200.00	
Jay Haas	73	68	72	65	278	1,812.50	
George Cadle	69	70	70	69	278	1,812.50	
Terry Mauney	73	70	66	69	278	1,812.50	
Peter Jacobsen	71	70	68	69	278	1,812.50	
Greg Pitzer	75	67	69	68	279	1,417.86	
Lon Hinkle	69	73	68	69	279	1,417.86	
Grier Jones	71	70	69	69	279	1,417.86	
Buddy Gardner	67	71	70	71	279	1,417.86	
Brad Bryant	70	69	69	71	279	1,417.86	
Rik Massengale	69	66	70	74	279	1,417.85	
J.C. Snead	71	71	65	72	279	1,417.85	
Antonio Cerda	71	72	71	66	280	1,075.00	
David Edwards	72	68	70	70	280	1,075.00	
Bill Calfee	72	70	69	69	280	1,075.00	
Tom Purtzer	72	69	69	70	280	1,075.00	
Dennis Sullivan	69	73	65	73	280	1,075.00	
Bob Betley	76	66	74	65	281	825.00	
Charles Coody	69	71	71	70	281	825.00	
Don January	71	68	71	71	281	825.00	
David Lundstrom	71	67	71	72	281	825.00	
Beau Baugh	73	65	69	74	281	825.00	
Dave Stockton	75	67	72	68	282	628.34	
Tony Hollifield	68	72	73	69	282	638.34	
Tim Simpson	72	70	71	69	282	628.33	

Southern Open

Green Island Country Club, Columbus, Georgia
Par 35–35—70; 6,791 yards

October 11–14
purse, $200,000

	SCORES				TOTAL	MONEY
Ed Fiori	69	72	65	68	274	$36,000.00
Tom Weiskopf	69	67	68	70	274	21,600.00
(Fiori defeated Weiskopf on second hole of sudden-death play-off)						
Artie McNickle	70	68	68	69	275	10,400.00
Calvin Peete	69	67	67	72	275	10,400.00
Mike Reid	67	69	68	71	275	10,400.00
Barney Thompson	69	70	68	69	276	7,200.00
David Edwards	72	69	67	69	277	6,450.00
Gibby Gilbert	69	66	71	71	277	6,450.00
Michael Brennan	68	69	72	69	278	5,600.00
Jerry Pate	66	69	69	74	278	5,600.00
Hubert Green	70	70	73	66	279	4,600.00
Dan Pohl	69	67	73	70	279	4,600.00
George Burns	70	69	67	73	279	4,600.00
Eddie Pearce	66	74	72	68	280	3,300.00
Ben Crenshaw	67	70	71	72	280	3,300.00
Mike Nicolette	71	72	66	71	280	3,300.00
Doug Tewell	70	69	70	71	280	3,300.00
Dale Douglass	70	68	70	72	280	3,300.00
Mike Hill	69	72	68	71	280	3,300.00
Bill Kratzert	69	72	71	69	281	2,248.00
Butch Baird	70	70	71	70	281	2,248.00
Mike Sullivan	72	68	71	70	281	2,248.00
Brad Bryant	70	68	72	71	281	2,248.00
Mike McCullough	65	69	73	74	281	2,248.00
Arnold Palmer	74	69	68	71	282	1,633.34
Skip Dunaway	71	71	69	71	282	1,633.33
Gary Koch	68	70	69	75	282	1,633.33
Terry Diehl	74	69	73	67	283	1,273.75
Peter Osterhuis	68	73	73	69	283	1,273.75
Lee Carter	72	69	72	70	283	1,273.75
Barry Jaeckel	68	74	71	70	283	1,273.75
Miller Barber	73	69	71	70	283	1,273.75
Lyn Lott	75	65	71	72	283	1,273.75
David Thore	75	66	70	72	283	1,273.75
Bill Sander	71	67	72	73	283	1,273.75
Bill Calfee	71	69	76	68	284	921.67
Jim Simons	71	69	74	70	284	921.67
Bobby Heins	73	67	72	72	284	921.67
Bob Proben	70	71	71	72	284	921.67
Roger Maltbie	73	69	70	72	284	921.66
Charles Coody	70	72	70	72	284	921.66
Dave Eichelberger	68	71	74	72	285	643.50
Tim Simpson	72	70	71	72	285	643.50
Curtis Strange	72	69	71	73	285	643.50
Dan Halldorson	70	72	70	73	285	643.50
Peter Jacobsen	73	69	69	74	285	643.50
Scott Simpson	68	71	71	75	285	643.50
DeWitt Weaver	69	71	69	76	285	643.50
Frank Beard	68	69	71	77	285	643.50
Don Pooley	70	72	75	69	286	492.00

341

Pensacola Open

Perdido Bay Country Club, Pensacola, Florida
Par 36—36—72; 7,133 yards

October 18–21
Purse, $200,000

	SCORES				TOTAL	MONEY
Curtis Strange	69	71	62	69	271	$36,000.00
Bill Kratzert	64	70	70	68	272	21,600.00
Morris Hatalsky	64	69	72	69	274	11,600.00
John Mahaffey	67	67	70	70	274	11,600.00
Don January	70	67	68	70	275	7,025.00
Keith Fergus	69	69	68	69	275	7,025.00
Terry Diehl	67	71	69	68	275	7,025.00
Orville Moody	68	67	68	72	275	7,025.00
Bob Murphy	70	69	69	68	276	5,600.00
Dan Pohl	68	69	67	72	276	5,600.00
Juan Rodriguez	73	68	68	68	277	4,800.00
Peter Jacobsen	70	71	68	68	277	4,800.00
Mark Lye	69	72	70	67	278	3,533.34
Doug Tewell	69	70	70	69	278	3,533.34
Tom Purtzer	68	71	69	70	278	3,533.33
Mike Sullivan	71	68	69	70	278	3,533.33
Wally Armstrong	70	72	66	70	278	3,533.33
Mike Nicolette	67	73	64	74	278	3,533.33
Mike Hill	72	70	69	68	279	2,700.00
Tom Weiskopf	73	68	69	69	279	2,700.00
Rex Caldwell	73	69	71	67	280	2,080.00
Bob Wynn	71	67	73	69	280	2,080.00
Frank Beard	70	71	69	70	280	2,080.00
Robert Donald	71	71	68	70	280	2,080.00
Jeff Mitchell	68	71	69	72	280	2,080.00
Brad Bryant	69	70	74	68	281	1,420.00
Mike Reid	71	70	72	68	281	1,420.00
Roger Maltbie	71	71	72	67	281	1,420.00
Jerry McGee	70	71	72	68	281	1,420.00
Mark Hayes	66	71	74	70	281	1,420.00
Gary Koch	70	70	71	70	281	1,420.00
Buddy Allin	69	69	71	72	281	1,420.00
Ron Terry	70	72	74	66	282	1,034.29
Don Halldorson	67	69	77	69	282	1,034.29
Lee Trevino	71	71	71	69	282	1,034.29
Leonard Thompson	67	73	71	71	282	1,034.29
Andy North	69	71	70	72	282	1,034.28
Terry Mauney	66	71	72	73	282	1,034.28
Larry Ziegler	68	71	70	73	282	1,034.28
Steve Melnyk	71	70	73	69	283	760.00
Marty Fleckman	71	70	72	70	283	760.00
Craig Stadler	68	73	72	70	283	760.00
Bob Mann	73	69	70	71	283	760.00
Dave Barr	71	69	72	71	283	760.00
Bob Proben	67	71	68	77	283	760.00
Jim Nelford	74	68	72	70	284	620.00
Jim Simons	69	70	76	70	285	513.72
George Knudson	70	71	73	71	285	513.72
Sammy Rachels	71	67	76	71	285	513.72
Gary McCord	67	71	75	72	285	513.71

Walt Disney World National Team Championship

Walt Disney World, Lake Buena Vista, Florida
Palm Course: Par 36–36–72; 6,951 yards (2 rounds)
Magnolia Course: Par 36–36–72; 7,197 yards (4 rounds)

October 25–28
purse, $250,000

	SCORES				TOTAL	MONEY
George Burns—Ben Crenshaw	62	66	62	65	255	$22,500.00
Peter Jacobsen—D.A. Weibring	64	64	68	62	258	10,500.00
Scott Bess—Dan Halldorson	66	66	64	62	258	10,500.00
Jeff Hewes—Sammy Rachels	65	65	64	64	258	10,500.00
Forrest Fezler—Larry Ziegler	61	68	68	62	259	5,350.00
Brad Bryant—Joe Hager	67	65	65	62	259	5,350.00
Wayne Levi—Bob Mann	65	67	65	63	260	3,725.00
Jim Colbert—Mike Sullivan	62	65	69	64	260	3,725.00
Terry Diehl—Ken Venturi	66	67	64	63	260	3,725.00
Miller Barber—Don January	64	66	65	65	260	3,725.00
Gibby Gilbert—Grier Jones	64	68	62	66	260	3,725.00
Gary Koch—Curtis Strange	62	67	65	66	260	3,725.00
Mark Hayes—Gil Morgan	67	66	66	62	261	2,700.00
Bruce Fleisher—Tom Jenkins	64	64	66	67	261	2,700.00
Morris Hatalsky—Don Pooley	67	66	64	65	262	2,500.00
Mark Lye—Tommy Valentine	66	66	67	64	263	2,250.00
Dave Hill—Mike Hill	66	66	67	64	263	2,250.00
Tom Chain—Jack Ferenz	69	63	66	65	263	2,250.00
Barry Jaeckel—Gary McCord	66	65	66	66	263	2,250.00
Dave Barr—Ed Fiori	67	65	67	65	264	1,700.00
Joe Carr—Tom Shaw	67	66	66	65	264	1,700.00
Roger Maltbie—Lee Mikles	67	65	66	66	264	1,700.00
Tom Purtzer—Howard Twitty	63	64	70	67	264	1,700.00

Don Iverson—Bob Zender	65	67	66	66	264	1,700.00
Bruce Devlin—Jerry McGee	64	65	68	67	264	1,700.00
George Archer—Jim Simons	63	67	66	68	264	1,700.00
Mike Reid—Ron Streck	68	64	68	65	265	1,250.00
Tom Kite—John Mahaffey	67	65	68	65	265	1,250.00
Frank Conner—Orville Moody	66	67	68	65	266	950.00
John Fought—Lindy Miller	64	65	70	67	266	950.00
Mark McCumber—Dan Sikes	63	67	69	67	266	950.00
Lee Elder—Buddy Gardner	63	70	66	67	266	950.00
Calvin Peete—Carlton White	68	65	66	67	266	950.00
Chip Beck—Tim Simpson	66	65	67	68	266	950.00
Pat McGowan—Jim Nelford	65	68	65	68	266	950.00
Keith Fergus—Phil Hancock	67	65	69	66	267	725.00
Bob Goalby—Jay Haas	67	66	68	66	267	725.00
Bruce Lietzke—Bobby Wadkins	64	67	69	67	267	725.00
Jim Dent—George Johnson	64	68	68	67	267	725.00
Don Bies—Julius Boros	65	64	70	68	267	725.00
Bob Murphy—Bob E. Smith	66	66	70	66	268	625.00
Bob Duval—David Eger	66	65	70	67	268	625.00
Jim Jamieson—Jim Masserio	64	69	69	66	268	625.00
Danny Edwards—David Edwards	64	69	70	68	271	562.50
Gay Brewer—Bobby Nichols	68	65	69	69	271	562.50
Lon Nielsen—Cesar Sanudo	66	67	68	71	272	525.00

EUROPEAN TOUR

Portuguese Open Championship

Vilamoura Golf Club, Algarve, Portugal
Par 35—38—73; 6,963 yards

April 12–15
purse, £28,810.69

	SCORES				TOTAL	MONEY
Brian Barnes	69	75	71	72	287	£4,801.96
Francisco Abreu	71	70	73	75	289	3,196.09
Dale Hayes	73	77	69	72	291	1,807.34
Mark James	74	73	75	70	292	1,329.10
Eamonn Darcy	71	75	75	71	292	1,329.10
Antonio Garrido	73	72	76	72	293	1,017.11
Tommy Horton	76	75	71	73	295	743.28
Sandy Lyle	77	71	71	76	295	743.28
Tony Jacklin	74	73	72	76	295	743.28
Ken Brown	76	70	76	74	296	542.79
Simon Hobday	73	75	74	74	296	542.79
Baldovino Dassu	78	76	72	71	297	474.33
Des Smyth	67	71	79	80	297	474.33
Harold Henning	75	76	76	71	298	396.78
Manuel Pinero	76	71	77	74	298	396.78
John Morgan	76	74	73	75	298	396.78
Manuel Ballesteros	80	73	70	75	298	396.78
German Garrido	77	78	72	76	298	396.78
Jose Cabo	73	75	73	77	298	396.78
Noel Hunt	74	73	70	81	298	396.78
Angel Gallardo	76	72	76	75	299	342.30
Salvador Balbuena	76	75	72	76	299	342.30
Martin Poxon	72	77	71	79	299	342.30
Michael King	75	75	76	74	300	303.18
Tony Price	77	76	73	74	300	303.18
Jeff Hawkes	72	75	79	74	300	303.18
David Vaughan	75	74	74	77	300	303.18
Nick Job	75	74	73	78	300	303.18
Manuel Montes	76	75	74	76	301	264.06
Patricio Garrido	73	72	78	78	301	264.06
Charles Dernie	75	74	73	79	301	264.06
Sam Torrance	76	73	78	75	302	244.50
Steve Wildman	73	78	76	76	303	203.75
Malcolm Gregson	76	73	78	76	303	203.75
Howard Clark	79	74	74	76	303	203.75
Gordon Brand	77	76	74	76	303	203.75
Roberto Bernardini	79	71	76	77	303	203.75
David Chillas	74	76	74	79	303	203.75
Bill Lockie	78	74	72	79	303	203.75
Philip Elson	73	79	72	79	303	203.75
Vince Baker	76	76	71	80	303	203.75
Massimo Mannelli	72	80	77	74	304	171.15
Warren Humphreys	77	77	75	75	304	171.15
Bob Verwey	75	76	72	81	304	171.15
Jose-Maria Canizares	75	77	77	76	305	161.37
Ian Mosey	75	76	79	76	306	141.80
Guy Hunt	75	79	76	76	306	141.80
Peter Townsend	77	76	76	77	306	141.80
Garry Cullen	76	77	75	78	306	141.80
Gar Hamilton	75	75	77	79	306	141.80

Spanish Open Championship

Torrequebrada Golf Club, Nr. Torremolinos, Spain
Par 36–36—72; 6,465 yards

April 19–22
purse £34,750

	SCORES				TOTAL	MONEY
Dale Hayes	70	75	67	66	278	£6,788.65
Brian Barnes	69	73	66	72	280	3,802.41
Bernard Gallagher	74	70	69	68	281	1,956.03
Jose-Maria Canizares	67	70	73	71	281	1,956.03
Baldovino Dassu	71	71	68	72	282	1,474.47
John Morgan	74	71	70	68	283	1,042.55
Martin Poxon	67	70	76	70	283	1,042.55
Sandy Lyle	70	70	71	72	283	1,042.55
Antonio Garrido	74	71	70	69	284	737.23
Nick Price	74	68	70	72	284	737.23
David Jones	73	69	68	75	285	645.39
Ernesto Acosta	69	72	71	74	280	605.67
Michael King	70	72	75	70	287	546.10
Francisco Abreu	70	73	73	71	287	546.10
Mark James	69	70	75	73	287	546.10
Angel Gallardo	77	71	71	69	288	456.74
Gordon Brand	75	71	72	70	288	456.74
Tony Price	74	68	73	73	288	456.74

Manuel Ballesteros	77	68	69	74	288	456.74
Eddie Polland	73	73	73	70	289	397.16
Tony Jacklin	70	76	73	70	289	397.16
German Garrido	72	72	70	75	289	397.16
Trevor Johnson	71	71	71	76	289	397.16
Tommy Horton	68	75	74	72	289	397.16
Des Smyth	79	70	72	69	290	342.55
Brian Huggett	72	75	73	70	290	342.55
Philip Elson	73	70	76	71	290	342.55
Manuel Montes	73	76	70	71	290	342.55
John Bland	72	74	72	72	290	342.55
Hugh Baiocchi	67	72	72	79	290	342.55
Armando Saavedra	77	73	70	71	291	297.87
Peter Dawson	76	69	71	75	291	297.87
Salvador Balbuena	71	73	70	77	291	297.87
John O'Leary	75	73	76	68	292	253.19
Harold Henning	74	74	72	72	292	253.19
Bernhard Langer	76	72	72	72	292	253.19
Jeff Hawkes	69	78	69	76	292	253.19
Nick Job	72	73	72	75	292	253.19
Gavin Levenson	69	74	71	78	292	253.19
Gar Hamilton	73	72	74	74	293	210.17
Garry Cullen	73	75	73	72	293	210.17
Jaime Benito	73	74	74	72	293	210.17
Bob Wynn	71	77	75	71	294	186.17
Juan Jiminez	75	74	72	73	294	186.17
Jose Rivero	72	73	75	74	294	186.17
Manuel Pinero	73	73	74	74	294	186.17
Ian Mosey	76	67	75	76	294	186.17
Jose Mangas	74	74	69	77	294	186.17
Jose Cabo	73	77	73	72	295	153.90
Manuel Ramos	74	75	72	74	295	153.90

Madrid Open Championship

Real Club de la Puerta de Hierro, Madrid, Spain
Par 36–36—72; 6,888 yards

April 26–29
purse, £33,100

	SCORES				TOTAL	MONEY
Simon Hobday	67	73	71	74	285	£5,514.71
Gordon Brand	69	73	76	69	287	2,463.24
Tienie Britz	73	76	69	69	287	2,463.24
Francisco Abreu	70	70	74	73	287	2,463.24
Bernard Gallacher	67	76	73	72	288	1,404.41
Salvador Balbuena	75	77	70	67	289	992.65
Hugh Baiocchi	67	74	75	73	289	992.65
Michael King	70	72	71	76	289	992.65
Jose-Maria Canizares	74	74	71	71	290	661.76
Antonio Garrido	73	74	68	75	290	661.76
Severiano Ballesteros	73	74	68	75	290	661.76
Manuel Montes	71	69	81	70	291	513.24
Vince Baker	73	73	73	72	291	513.24
Nick Job	72	72	74	73	291	513.24
Manuel Calero	72	74	71	74	291	513.24
Vincente Fernandez	74	74	68	75	291	513.24
Ken Brown	69	75	74	74	292	448.53
Valentin Barrios	73	78	73	69	293	404.41
Maurice Bembridge	72	79	72	70	293	404.41
Gavin Levenson	74	75	70	74	293	404.41
Malcolm Gregson	74	75	68	76	293	404.41
Gunnar Mueller	72	75	77	70	294	351.73
Philip Elson	75	77	71	71	294	351.73
Sam Torrance	77	74	70	73	294	351.73
Dale Hayes	69	79	72	74	294	351.73
Peter Townsend	70	79	70	75	294	351.73
Jose Rivero	73	74	71	76	294	351.73
Bobby Verwey	75	74	73	73	295	305.15
Manuel Ramos	72	75	74	74	295	305.15
Gar Hamilton	75	77	69	74	295	305.15
Jeff Hall	74	77	70	74	295	305.15
Bernhard Langer	76	73	75	72	296	275.74
Nick Price	74	73	75	74	296	275.74
John Fourie	72	77	73	74	296	275.74
Peter Dawson	76	72	72	76	296	275.74
Garry Cullen	74	77	76	70	297	253.68
John Bland	77	74	71	75	297	253.68
Martin Poxon	74	72	74	78	298	242.65
Manuel Ballesteros	72	76	80	72	300	221.51
Garry Harvey	72	81	72	75	300	221.51
Bill Longmuir	72	80	75	73	300	221.51
Rafe Botts	73	74	75	78	300	221.51
Nigel Blenkarne	77	76	77	71	301	191.18
Jaime Benito	75	75	76	75	301	191.18
Howard Clark	75	77	72	77	301	191.18
Martin Foster	74	75	75	77	301	191.18
Armando Saavedra	76	77	74	74	301	191.18
Manuel Sanchez	77	76	76	73	302	153.82
Donald Armour	72	81	74	75	302	153.82
Keith Waters	76	75	76	75	302	153.82

Italian Open Championship

Monticello Golf Club, Como, Italy
Par 36–36—72; 6,800 yards

May 3–6
purse, £33,520

	SCORES				TOTAL	MONEY
Brian Barnes	73	70	71	67	281	£5,582.39
Dale Hayes	73	69	71	68	281	3,724.43
(Barnes defeated Hayes on fourth hole of sudden-death playoff)						
Sam Torrance	72	73	69	70	284	1,886.36
Vicente Fernandez	72	74	67	71	284	1,886.36
Severiano Ballesteros	73	72	72	68	285	1,109.52
Antonio Garrido	73	73	68	71	285	1,109.52
Tony Jacklin	79	67	68	71	285	1,109.52
Ben Crenshaw	74	70	68	73	285	1,109.52
Brian Waites	72	71	71	72	286	711.08
Michael King	70	71	71	74	286	711.08
Delio Lovato	71	72	71	73	287	622.16
Malcolm Gregson	75	70	75	69	289	555.30
Gar Hamilton	73	75	70	71	289	555.30
Sandy Lyle	71	76	70	72	289	555.30
Gordon Brand	73	74	74	69	290	483.52
Garry Cullen	72	74	74	70	290	483.52
Massimo Mannelli	70	77	73	71	291	445.46
Baldovino Dassu	75	72	75	70	292	410.51
Harold Henning	76	69	75	72	292	410.51
Silvano Locatelli	73	72	74	73	292	410.51
Roberto Bernardini	76	73	70	73	292	410.51
Eddie Polland	73	74	76	70	293	359.09
John O'Leary	76	73	73	71	293	359.09
Manuel Pinero	78	71	72	72	293	359.09
Nick Price	78	69	74	72	293	359.09
Noel Ratcliffe	77	72	71	73	293	359.09
Robbie Stewart	74	74	71	74	293	359.09
Simon Hobday	76	73	72	73	294	311.08
Juan Anglada	71	72	76	75	294	311.08
Salvador Balbuena	72	73	73	76	294	311.08
Denis Watson	73	73	72	76	294	311.08
Glenn Ralph	74	75	76	70	295	258.52
Dennis Durnian	77	74	72	72	295	258.52
Angel Gallardo	75	72	74	74	295	258.52
John Colwell	73	76	72	74	295	258.52
Bobby Verwey	75	74	71	75	295	258.52
John Bland	77	71	72	75	295	258.52
Bill Longmuir	72	73	72	78	295	258.52
E. Della Torre	77	73	75	71	296	203.98
James Edman	76	70	76	74	296	203.98
John Fourie	72	73	76	75	296	203.98
Geromalo Delfino	72	75	73	76	296	203.98
Hugh Baiocchi	77	73	69	77	296	203.98
Tommy Horton	74	77	74	72	297	182.01
Nick Faldo	73	76	75	73	297	182.01
David A. Russell	74	72	78	73	297	182.01
Keith Waters	75	72	79	72	298	165.06
Manuel Ramos	75	75	77	71	298	165.06
Nick Job	76	72	76	74	298	165.06
Manuel Calero	72	71	77	78	298	165.06

French Open Championship

Lyon Golf Club, Lyon, France
Par 36–37—73; 7,072 yards

May 10–13
purse, £37,500

	SCORES				TOTAL	MONEY
Bernard Gallacher	71	69	74	70	284	£5,945.37
Willie Milne	76	70	67	72	285	3,960.42
Severiano Ballesteros	73	74	71	68	286	2,008.08
Hugh Baiocchi	73	69	69	75	286	2,008.08
Bill Longmuir	71	69	78	70	288	1,278.33
Nick Faldo	72	72	73	71	288	1,278.33
David Chillas	76	72	68	72	288	1,278.33
Eamonn Darcy	74	69	71	75	289	891.86
Dale Hayes	73	74	73	70	290	673.35
Garry Cullen	74	70	75	71	290	673.35
Noel Ratcliffe	75	72	71	72	290	673.35
Tony Jacklin	70	70	77	73	290	673.35
Gary Player	75	68	73	74	290	673.35
Manuel Calero	73	74	72	72	291	503.45
Angel Gallardo	73	73	72	73	291	503.45
Tienie Britz	73	68	76	74	291	503.45
Bobby Verwey	74	74	68	75	291	503.45
Vicente Fernandez	70	69	75	77	291	503.45
Gordon Brand	78	71	74	69	292	415.27
Jeff Hall	77	70	74	71	292	415.27
John Fourie	73	73	74	72	292	415.27
Francisco Abreu	74	71	74	73	292	415.27
John Bland	73	70	75	74	292	415.27
Terry Kendall	74	70	74	74	292	415.27
Eddie Polland	74	72	71	75	292	415.27
Garry Harvey	74	72	76	71	293	350.33

Peter Townsend	75	71	75	72	293	350.33
Robbie Stewart	76	71	73	73	293	350.33
Noel Hunt	76	70	72	75	293	350.33
Bernard Pascassio	76	73	73	72	294	309.36
Greg Norman	71	71	77	75	294	309.36
Nicky Price	75	66	78	75	294	309.36
Wayne Grady	78	70	73	74	295	269.78
Jan Sonnevi	75	72	73	75	295	269.78
Philippe Toussaint	74	73	73	75	295	269.78
Joe Higgins	73	71	73	78	295	269.78
Ewen Murray	75	74	71	76	296	247.21
Keith Waters	72	74	72	78	296	247.21
Malcolm Gregson	72	76	76	73	297	217.18
Michael King	77	73	74	73	297	217.18
Sam Torrance	78	72	74	73	297	217.18
Mark James	72	72	79	74	297	217.18
Juan Anglada	73	75	75	74	297	217.18
Manuel Ballesteros	75	73	74	75	297	217.18
Michael Damiano	76	74	71	76	297	217.18
Gavin Levenson	75	73	72	77	297	217.18
Rafe Botts	76	70	77	75	298	180.74
Horacio Carbonetti	77	68	77	76	298	180.74
Ken Brown	73	75	74	76	298	180.74
Donald Armour	74	76	71	77	298	180.74

Colgate PGA Championship

Old Course, St. Andrews Golf Club, St. Andrews, Scotland
Par 36–36—72; 6,933 yards

May 17–20
purse, £50,000

	SCORES				TOTAL	MONEY
Vicente Fernandez	71	70	72	75	281	£ 8,330.00
Gary Player	73	73	72	71	289	4,340.00
Baldovino Dassu	71	70	74	74	289	4,340.00
Brian Barnes	71	71	72	76	290	2,310.00
Gordon Brand	68	74	70	78	290	2,310.00
Raymond Floyd	74	75	71	71	291	1,405.00
Philip Elson	70	71	76	74	291	1,405.00
Andy North	69	70	73	69	291	1,405.00
Des Smyth	70	70	72	79	291	1,405.00
Neil Coles	71	73	76	72	292	870.00
Severiano Ballesteros	70	72	75	75	292	870.00
Greg Norman	72	70	75	75	292	870.00
Eddie Polland	70	72	72	78	292	870.00
Nick Faldo	65	70	78	79	292	870.00
Brian Huggett	74	71	76	73	294	690.00
John Morgan	73	73	74	74	294	690.00
Garry Cullen	69	77	73	75	294	690.00
Howard Clark	72	74	70	78	294	690.00
Martin Poxon	73	72	76	74	295	586.00
Nick Job	68	78	75	74	295	586.00
Peter Oosterhuis	74	75	72	74	295	586.00
Vince Baker	73	75	70	77	295	586.00
John Fowler	71	75	71	78	295	586.00
Michael King	74	73	72	77	296	525.00
Sandy Walker	73	70	75	78	296	525.00
John Fourie	72	71	75	78	296	525.00
Doug McClelland	73	74	77	73	297	457.50
Willie Milne	74	71	77	75	297	457.50
Rodger Davis	71	73	78	75	297	457.50
Tienie Britz	72	74	74	77	297	457.50
Ken Brown	75	71	73	78	297	457.50
Ewen Murray	75	71	73	78	297	457.50
Hugh Baiocchi	72	74	78	74	298	395.00
David A. Russell	75	74	75	74	298	395.00
Donald Armour	71	76	76	75	298	395.00
Bob Charles	71	77	71	79	298	395.00
Dennis Durnian	74	74	76	75	299	335.00
Tommy Horton	74	75	75	75	299	335.00
John Bland	71	73	77	78	299	335.00
Bobby Verwey	74	74	73	78	299	335.00
Peter Townsend	74	75	72	78	299	335.00
Francisco Abreu	74	74	72	79	299	335.00
Peter Cowen	73	73	73	80	299	335.00
David Jagger	71	75	73	80	299	335.00
Angel Gallardo	74	75	78	73	300	275.00
Andrew Chandler	75	74	78	73	300	275.00
Noel Hunt	74	72	75	79	300	275.00
Bernhard Langer	74	73	73	80	300	275.00
Dale Hayes	72	74	79	76	301	220.00
Peter Senior	72	77	77	75	301	220.00

Martini International

Wentworth Golf Club, Virginia Water, Surrey, England
Par 35–37—72; 6,945 yards

May 25–28
purse, £42,000

	SCORES				TOTAL	MONEY
Greg Norman	75	67	72	74	288	£7,000.00

DUNHILL GOLF YEARBOOK 1980

Player					Total	Money
Antonio Garrido	73	71	72	73	289	3,645.00
John Morgan	69	72	74	74	289	3,645.00
Tienie Britz	75	71	76	69	291	1,783.33
Vicente Fernandez	73	71	74	73	291	1,783.33
Ken Brown	71	72	73	75	291	1,783.33
Severiano Ballesteros	75	75	70	72	292	1,155.00
Mark James	74	70	72	76	292	1,155.00
Michael King	73	76	72	72	293	940.00
Nick Job	75	73	73	73	294	786.66
Brian Barnes	75	69	79	71	294	786.66
Tommy Horton	74	70	75	75	294	786.66
Rodger Davis	78	72	72	73	295	622.00
Harold Henning	80	69	74	72	295	622.00
Nick Price	72	76	74	73	295	622.00
Garry Cullen	74	74	74	73	295	622.00
Gavin Levenson	75	70	74	76	295	622.00
Robbie Stewart	70	76	77	73	296	540.00
Warren Humphreys	72	72	76	76	296	540.00
Guy Hunt	73	73	74	75	297	490.00
Dale Hayes	75	72	74	76	297	490.00
David Jagger	76	69	78	74	297	490.00
John Fourie	78	72	73	75	298	431.00
Peter Tupling	76	74	75	73	298	431.00
David Good	73	71	76	78	298	431.00
Tony Jacklin	75	69	77	77	298	431.00
Andries Oosthuizen	73	71	75	79	298	431.00
Brian Waites	74	74	74	77	299	375.00
Neil Coles	74	74	76	75	299	375.00
Peter Butler	73	75	74	77	299	375.00
Manuel Ballesteros	74	73	76	76	299	375.00
Manuel Pinero	72	74	70	83	299	375.00
Peter Berry	75	70	78	76	299	375.00
Sam Torrance	78	70	76	76	300	340.00
Eamonn Darcy	77	72	75	77	301	320.00
Vaughan Somers	75	74	75	77	301	320.00
Malcolm Gregson	76	72	74	79	301	320.00
Hugh Baiocchi	75	73	76	78	302	300.00
Brian Huggett	76	73	79	75	303	285.00
Martin Foster	74	75	79	75	303	285.00
Maurice Bembridge	74	73	78	79	304	260.00
Peter Cowen	72	75	78	79	304	260.00
Ian Mosey	74	73	77	80	304	260.00
Robin Mann	75	72	79	79	305	240.00
Anthony Charnley	77	72	81	76	306	230.00
Juan Cabrera	77	72	80	78	307	220.00
Derrick Cooper	74	76	79	79	308	205.00
Bob Charles	73	76	83	76	308	205.00
Simon Owen	75	75	84	75	309	195.00
Philip Loxley	76	74	82	78	310	190.00

British Airways/Avis Open Championship

La Moye Golf Club, Jersey, England
Par 36–35—71; 6,372 yards

May 31–June 3
purse, £30,000

Player		SCORES			TOTAL	MONEY
Sandy Lyle	66	71	66	68	271	£5,000.00
Howard Clark	70	68	67	69	274	3,300.00
Sam Torrance	69	69	72	65	275	1,425.00
Tony Jacklin	64	75	68	68	275	1,425.00
Bernard Gallacher	64	69	69	73	275	1,425.00
Michael King	69	70	67	69	275	1,425.00
Hugh Baiocchi	68	71	71	66	276	773.33
Noel Ratcliffe	70	70	70	66	276	773.33
Bob Charles	72	68	69	67	276	773.33
Peter Cowen	70	72	71	64	277	600.00
Brian Huggett	69	69	72	68	278	535.00
Manuel Pinero	73	70	66	69	278	535.00
Jeff Hawkes	68	71	69	71	279	490.00
Peter Headland	72	72	68	68	280	409.28
Eddie Polland	67	73	71	69	280	409.28
James Edman	70	74	67	69	280	409.28
Baldovino Dassu	70	70	70	70	280	409.28
Gavin Levenson	66	71	72	71	280	409.28
Peter Townsend	69	71	69	70	280	409.28
Willie Milne	68	69	68	75	280	409.28
Robin Mann	73	71	72	65	281	345.00
Des Smyth	69	74	69	69	281	345.00
Rodger Davis	69	71	72	69	281	345.00
Peter Tupling	69	70	69	73	281	345.00
Eamonn Darcy	66	76	71	69	282	305.00
Mark McNulty	68	70	74	70	282	305.00
Dale Hayes	69	68	74	71	282	305.00
Christy O'Connor, Jr.	67	73	70	72	282	305.00
Greg Norman	72	71	70	70	283	280.00
John Hay	68	72	74	70	284	260.00
John Fourie	75	69	69	71	284	260.00
John Morgan	72	70	70	72	284	260.00
Malcolm Gregson	71	71	73	70	285	235.00
Jeff Hall	73	71	70	71	285	235.00
Nick Price	71	75	72	68	286	212.50

Ian Mosey	73	73	71	69	286	212.50
Glenn Ralph	70	72	75	69	286	212.50
Carl Mason	70	73	70	73	286	212.50
Guy Hunt	72	72	72	71	287	192.50
Keith Waters	71	74	72	70	287	192.50
David Good	70	75	71	71	287	192.50
Nick Job	72	68	74	73	287	192.50
Rafe Botts	69	77	72	70	288	165.00
Martin Foster	70	70	77	71	288	165.00
Stephen Rolley	73	71	73	71	288	165.00
Maurice Bembridge	73	72	71	72	288	165.00
Garry Harvey	71	72	72	73	288	165.00
Bobby Verwey	71	71	73	73	288	165.00
Bobby Lincoln	72	72	68	76	288	165.00
John Fowler	74	71	72	72	289	142.50

Belgian Open Championship

Royal Waterloo Golf Club, Brussels, Belgium
Par 36–37—73; 6,873 yards

June 7–10
purse, £32,300

	SCORES				TOTAL	MONEY
Gavin Levenson	68	71	68	72	279	£5,382.19
Michael King	70	73	71	68	282	2,411.35
Bobby Cole	71	71	71	69	282	2,411.35
Nick Faldo	69	72	70	71	282	2,411.35
Baldovino Dassu	73	66	71	73	283	1,252.96
Jeff Hall	69	74	73	67	283	1,252.96
Simon Owen	70	74	69	71	284	890.46
Mark James	71	68	73	72	284	890.46
Ken Brown	72	70	72	71	285	685.58
Tony Jacklin	68	72	71	74	285	685.58
Robin Fyfe	71	74	66	75	286	605.20
Don Levin*	73	72	71	71	287	
Peter Townsend	71	74	70	72	287	550.83
Eddie Polland	72	74	68	73	287	550.83
Bob Charles	71	76	73	68	288	468.09
Nick Job	75	69	74	70	288	468.09
Gordon Brand	69	74	74	71	288	468.09
Vaughn Somers	74	70	73	71	288	468.09
Peter Headland	73	73	73	70	289	408.98
Adam Sowa	69	73	74	73	289	408.98
Peter Cowen	69	72	78	71	290	373.52
Howard Clark	73	72	73	72	290	373.52
Mark McNulty	69	73	73	75	290	373.52
David Robertson	75	70	74	72	291	345.94
David Chillas	70	72	73	76	291	345.94
Donald Armour	72	75	75	70	292	307.33
Bill Longmuir	73	75	72	72	292	307.33
Carl Mason	74	71	74	73	292	307.33
Sandy Lyle	76	72	71	73	292	307.33
Ian Mosey	75	71	72	74	292	307.33
Bobby Lincoln	74	72	70	76	292	307.33
Steve Martin	71	75	74	73	293	263.99
Bernhard Langer	71	76	71	75	293	263.99
Armando Saavedra	76	75	67	75	293	263.99
Ewen Murray	71	73	73	76	293	263.99
Peter Senior	73	79	71	71	294	240.35
Noel Ratcliffe	73	79	69	73	294	240.35
Maurice Bembridge	76	70	76	73	295	223.80
Warren Humphreys	73	75	74	73	295	223.80
Robin Mann	75	73	71	76	295	223.80
Chris Moody	75	76	72	73	296	208.04
Martin Poxon	73	72	75	76	296	208.04
Nigel Blenkarne	72	77	76	72	297	186.29
Massimo Mannelli	71	77	76	73	297	186.29
Ross Drummond	74	74	77	72	297	186.29
Peter Barber	75	76	73	73	297	186.29
Richard Eyles	74	78	72	73	297	186.29
John Morgan	75	73	78	72	298	163.12
Philippe Toussaint	74	76	76	72	298	163.12
Mike Inglis	77	74	72	75	298	163.12
Andrew Chandler	77	73	73	75	298	163.12

*Amateur

The Welsh Classic

Wenvoe Castle Golf Club, Cardiff, Wales
Par 36–35—71; 6,367 yards

June 14–17
purse, £30,000

	SCORES				TOTAL	MONEY
Mark James	72	68	68	70	278	£5,000.00
Eddie Polland	66	73	72	67	278	2,605.00
Michael Miller	72	68	69	69	278	2,605.00
(James defeated Polland and Miller on third hole of sudden-death play-off)						
Sandy Lyle	69	72	72	66	279	1,385.00

Name					Total	Money
Bob Charles	73	69	69	68	279	1,385.00
Howard Clark	70	72	68	70	280	1,050.00
Philip Elson	64	74	75	68	281	773.33
Neil Coles	76	67	69	69	281	773.33
Ken Brown	69	72	70	70	281	773.33
Nick Faldo	74	70	73	65	282	600.00
Malcolm Gregson	71	73	71	68	283	550.00
Nick Job	69	75	69	71	284	520.00
Ewen Murray	72	71	71	71	285	490.00
Don Levin*	75	72	70	68	285	
Vaughan Somers	74	74	70	68	286	441.66
Des Smyth	70	72	75	69	286	441.66
Gary Birch	72	71	73	70	286	441.66
Christy O'Connor, Jr.	73	78	70	66	287	375.00
John Morgan	72	71	76	68	287	375.00
Brian Waites	72	75	72	68	287	375.00
Mike Krantz	77	72	69	69	287	375.00
Massimo Mannelli	77	70	68	72	287	375.00
Tony Jacklin	71	69	73	74	287	375.00
Vicente Fernandez	71	75	72	70	288	325.00
Bill Longmuir	70	74	74	70	288	325.00
Anthony Charnley	72	75	71	70	288	325.00
Simon Owen	76	72	70	70	288	325.00
Jeff Hawkes	69	75	75	70	289	295.00
Martin Poxon	73	74	71	71	289	295.00
Brian Barnes	75	75	73	67	290	255.00
Bobby Verwey	77	74	70	69	290	255.00
Bernard Gallacher	75	72	73	70	290	255.00
Gavin Levenson	73	69	77	71	290	255.00
Steve Martin	74	72	70	74	290	255.00
Robin Fyfe	75	73	70	72	290	255.00
Willie Milne	74	75	75	67	291	202.50
Peter Berry	75	74	74	68	291	202.50
Mike Inglis	75	73	73	70	291	202.50
Eamonn Darcy	74	77	70	70	291	202.50
Warren Humphreys	77	74	69	71	291	202.50
Guy Hunt	74	75	71	71	291	202.50
Ian Mosey	73	74	71	73	291	202.50
Michael King	71	76	71	73	291	202.50
Keith Benson	73	72	76	71	292	177.50
Gordon Brand	78	72	71	71	292	177.50
Richard Fish	72	75	75	71	293	167.50
Carl Mason	76	71	71	75	293	167.50
Noel Ratcliffe	73	77	73	71	294	150.00
Jeff Hall	79	69	73	73	294	150.00
Dennis Durnian	76	74	70	74	294	150.00
Tommy Horton	77	71	71	75	294	150.00

Greater Manchester Open Championship

Wilmslow Golf Club, Cheshire, England
Par 36–34—70; 6,457 yards

June 21–24
purse, £30,000

Name	SCORES				TOTAL	MONEY
Mark McNulty	64	66	71	66	267	£5,000.00
Manuel Pinero	69	69	66	68	272	3,330.00
Brian Waites	69	67	69	68	273	1,880.00
Des Smyth	70	69	66	69	274	1,385.00
Neil Coles	68	66	71	69	274	1,385.00
Ken Brown	70	69	70	66	275	1,050.00
Antonio Garrido	68	72	69	67	276	825.00
Sandy Lyle	66	72	67	71	276	825.00
David Jagger	71	71	68	67	277	635.00
Brian Barnes	70	71	67	69	277	635.00
Mike Ingham	70	71	69	68	278	480.83
Bill Lockie	68	70	71	69	278	480.83
Jeff Hall	73	68	68	69	278	480.83
Howard Clark	67	71	70	70	278	480.83
Vicente Fernandez	65	70	72	71	278	480.83
Robin Mann	68	69	70	71	278	480.83
Martin Poxon	70	72	71	66	279	365.00
Greg Norman	70	68	73	68	279	365.00
Vaughan Somers	72	69	69	69	279	365.00
Nick Job	69	71	69	70	279	365.00
Martin Foster	68	73	68	70	279	365.00
Doug McClelland	70	71	68	70	279	365.00
Michael Gallagher	72	67	68	72	279	365.00
Michael King	70	72	65	72	279	365.00
Jose-Marie Canizares	71	73	69	67	280	310.00
Terry Gale	72	68	71	69	280	310.00
Mike Slater	73	69	68	70	280	310.00
Peter Tupling	70	71	71	69	281	265.00
Bill Longmuir	67	73	71	70	281	265.00
Mark James	68	68	73	72	281	265.00
Ewen Murray	73	69	67	72	281	265.00
Bob Charles	72	70	67	72	281	265.00
David Vaughan	72	70	66	73	281	265.00
Steve Martin	75	62	74	71	282	221.66
Philip Elson	71	69	69	73	282	221.66
Christy O'Connor, Jr.	69	68	71	74	282	221.66

Craig Defoy	69	74	70	70	283	205.00	
Peter Cowen	72	70	69	72	283	205.00	
Gavin Levenson	72	69	69	73	283	205.00	
Juan-Carlos Martin	70	73	71	70	284	185.00	
Warren Humphreys	71	71	70	72	284	185.00	
Garry Cullen	70	68	72	74	284	185.00	
Sam Torrance	71	66	73	74	284	185.00	
Peter Senior	72	70	66	76	284	185.00	
Keith Waters	69	71	74	71	285	162.50	
Michael Miller	71	68	72	74	285	162.50	
Manuel Calero	69	69	71	76	285	162.50	
John O'Leary	70	72	67	76	285	162.50	
Ross Drummond	73	70	75	68	286	137.50	
Juan Cabrera	75	67	72	72	286	137.50	

Lada English Golf Classic

The Belfry, Barbazon Course, Sutton Coldfield, England
Par 36–36—72; 7,118 yards

June 28–July 1
purse, £ 50,000

	SCORES				TOTAL	MONEY
Severiano Ballesteros	73	71	71	71	286	£8,330.00
Neil Coles	73	77	72	70	292	4,340.00
Simon Hobday	73	71	73	75	292	4,340.00
Sandy Lyle	76	70	75	72	293	2,310.00
Nick Faldo	72	71	77	73	293	2,310.00
Greg Norman	74	74	73	73	294	1,500.00
Brian Huggett	71	77	72	74	294	1,500.00
Hugh Baiocchi	72	75	73	74	294	1,500.00
Eddie Polland	73	73	79	71	296	1,013.33
Tommy Horton	80	71	72	73	296	1,013.33
Manuel Pinero	71	76	75	74	296	1,013.33
Bobby Verwey	74	75	74	74	297	791.25
Hugh Boyle	76	74	74	73	297	791.25
Brian Barnes	79	73	71	74	297	791.25
Armando Saavedra	73	74	73	77	297	791.25
Peter Senior	74	74	80	70	298	690.00
Francisco Abreu	73	74	73	78	298	690.00
Vaughan Somers	72	77	79	71	299	604.00
Bob Charles	78	71	78	72	299	604.00
David Dunk	78	73	75	73	299	604.00
Graham Burroughs	71	72	77	79	299	604.00
Ken Brown	72	74	77	76	299	604.00
Martin Poxon	73	75	78	74	300	510.00
Rodger Davis	69	73	83	75	300	510.00
Steve Martin	74	77	75	74	300	510.00
Antonio Garrido	75	77	74	74	300	510.00
George Will	75	76	74	75	300	510.00
Carl Mason	71	78	72	79	300	510.00
Brian Waites	75	74	72	79	300	510.00
Dale Hayes	75	77	77	72	301	417.50
Jeff Hawkes	77	74	74	76	301	417.50
Howard Clark	79	73	75	74	301	417.50
Guy Hunt	74	76	76	75	301	417.50
Mike Krantz	73	74	77	77	301	417.50
Vin Baker	75	74	75	77	301	417.50
Anthony Charnley	74	77	76	75	302	360.00
Martin Foster	76	72	78	76	302	360.00
David Vaughan	76	75	74	77	302	360.00
Michael King	74	74	77	77	302	360.00
Bill Longmuir	76	74	73	79	302	360.00
David Good	76	76	76	75	303	320.00
Baldovino Dassu	73	74	76	80	303	320.00
David Jagger	75	74	70	84	303	320.00
Ewen Murray	73	77	78	76	304	290.00
Trevor Johnson	76	74	77	77	304	290.00
Peter Townsend	74	77	76	77	304	290.00
Mark McNulty	72	79	79	75	305	260.00
Noel Ratcliffe	76	75	76	78	305	260.00
David Jones	74	74	76	81	305	260.00
Bernhard Langer	77	73	79	77	306	220.00

Scandinavian Enterprise Open

Vasatorp Golf Club, Helsingborg, Sweden
Par 36–36—72; 6,780 yards

July 5–8
purse, £31,800

	SCORES				TOTAL	MONEY
Sandy Lyle	73	69	65	69	276	£5,300.82
Severiano Ballesteros	70	72	68	69	279	3,530.35
Mike Krantz	71	72	65	73	281	1,993.12
Ken Brown	71	70	72	71	284	1,468.33
Dale Hayes	70	72	71	72	284	1,468.33
Eamonn Darcy	70	73	74	68	285	1,033.66
Michael King	73	71	69	72	285	1,033.66
Terry Gale	72	72	74	70	288	681.15
Eddie Polland	71	73	71	73	288	681.15

Armando Saavedra	71	72	70	75	288	681.15
Peter Townsend	70	73	70	75	288	681.15
Mark McNulty	75	74	72	68	289	495.10
Peter Senior	72	76	69	72	289	495.10
Baldovino Dassu	74	74	68	73	289	495.10
Tommy Horton	71	75	70	73	289	495.10
Jose-Maria Canizares	70	73	71	75	289	495.10
Mike Ferguson	69	75	73	73	290	424.07
Hugh Baiocchi	71	76	74	70	291	408.16
Robbie Stewart	72	74	74	71	291	408.16
Nick Faldo	69	78	74	71	292	371.06
Peter Headland	73	72	76	71	292	371.06
Gordon Brand	73	72	75	72	292	371.06
Simon Hobday	77	68	75	72	292	371.06
Garry Cullen	72	74	74	72	292	371.06
Brian Jones	72	78	74	69	293	323.35
Guy Wolstenholme	75	74	71	73	293	323.35
Steve Martin	72	78	69	74	293	323.35
Simon Owen	72	74	73	74	293	323.35
Gavin Levenson	74	78	76	66	294	291.54
Garry Hallberg*	74	74	77	69	294	
Vin Baker	75	76	72	71	294	291.54
Carl Mason	74	72	79	70	295	270.34
Martin Foster	76	72	74	73	295	270.34
Mikael Sorling*	74	76	73	73	296	
Dennis Durnian	76	70	77	74	297	254.44
Denis Clark	77	75	75	71	298	235.04
Chris Tickner	73	78	73	74	298	235.04
Mark James	76	74	73	75	298	235.04
Jaime Gonzalez	78	75	77	69	299	212.03
Tohru Nakamura	78	76	75	70	299	212.03
Mike Inglis	80	74	71	74	299	212.03
Per Andersson*	78	75	71	75	299	
Rick Mallicoat	74	75	74	76	299	212.03
Jan Sonnevi	80	76	67	76	299	212.03
Bernhard Langer	76	76	76	72	300	180.23
Philip Morley	73	80	74	73	300	180.23
Gunnar Mueller	77	76	74	73	300	180.23
Gar Hamilton	78	77	73	72	300	180.23
Jeff Hawkes	78	75	71	76	300	180.23
Maurice Bembridge	73	74	76	77	300	180.23
John Benda	75	74	74	77	300	180.23
Olle Dahlgren*	71	77	74	78	300	
Dag Aurell*	74	74	76	77	301	
Peter Lindwall	80	73	74	75	302	153.72
Juan Cabrera	77	72	76	77	302	153.72

*Amateur

Dutch Open

Noordwijkse Golf Club, Noordwijk, Holland
Par 36–36–72; 6,963 yards

July 26–29
purse, £35,000

	SCORES				TOTAL	MONEY
Graham Marsh	71	70	74	70	285	£5,015.01
Malcolm Gregson	72	71	69	74	286	2,615.05
Antonio Garrido	73	71	70	72	286	2,615.05
Manuel Pinero	70	73	73	71	287	1,391.40
John Bland	72	66	72	77	287	1,391.40
Denis Watson	74	74	68	72	288	846.24
Rodger Davis	72	72	72	72	288	846.24
Michael King	70	72	74	72	288	846.24
Nick Job	71	71	72	74	288	846.24
Bobby Verwey	73	70	74	72	289	580.65
Geoffrey Parslow	74	73	66	76	289	580.65
Ken Brown	70	76	74	70	290	498.92
David Ingram	71	77	68	74	290	498.92
Jeff Hall	67	71	77	75	290	498.92
Noel Ratcliffe	71	76	72	72	291	434.41
Brian Barnes	74	71	72	74	291	434.41
Terry Gale	69	77	71	75	292	387.10
Maurice Bembridge	68	78	70	76	292	387.10
Eamonn Darcy	71	73	72	76	292	387.10
Sandy Lyle	72	71	80	70	293	339.78
Robbie Stewart	73	75	74	71	293	339.78
Eddie Polland	76	75	68	74	293	339.78
Vicente Fernandez	71	78	69	75	293	339.78
David Vaughan	76	70	71	76	293	339.78
Tommy Horton	71	72	70	80	293	339.78
Philip Elson	76	74	72	72	294	288.17
Gavin Levenson	75	73	73	73	294	288.17
Guy Wolstenholme	74	70	75	75	294	288.17
Christy O'Connor, Jr.	73	72	73	76	294	288.17
Gar Hamilton	75	67	76	76	294	288.17
Sam Torrance	73	67	78	76	294	288.17
Garry Cullen	74	74	73	74	295	245.16
Vaughan Somers	74	76	69	76	295	245.16
Doug McClelland	76	74	69	76	295	245.16

Gary Logan	75	74	68	78	295	245.16
Bill Loeffler	73	78	71	74	296	202.15
Noel Hunt	77	72	73	74	296	202.15
Martin Poxon	77	73	71	75	296	202.15
Mark McNulty	72	74	75	75	296	202.15
John O'Leary	74	72	70	80	296	202.15
Carl Mason	69	75	72	80	296	202.15
Armando Saavedra	72	72	78	75	297	169.89
Simon Hobday	73	75	72	77	297	169.89
Mike Inglis	74	76	68	79	297	169.89
Peter Cowen	73	73	72	79	297	169.89
Martin Foster	76	75	74	73	298	146.24
Willie Milne	75	75	72	76	298	146.24
Mitch Adcock	80	71	71	76	298	146.24
Bill Longmuir	76	72	74	76	298	146.24
Peter Senior	77	71	74	76	298	146.24

British Open Championship

Royal Lytham & St. Annes Golf Club, Blackpool, England
Par 35—36—72; 6,822 yards

July 18–21
purse, £155,000

	SCORES				TOTAL	MONEY
Severiano Ballesteros	73	65	75	70	283	£15,000.00
Jack Nicklaus	72	69	73	72	286	11,250.00
Ben Crenshaw	72	71	72	71	286	11,250.00
Mark James	76	69	69	73	287	7,500.00
Rodger Davis	75	70	70	73	288	6,500.00
Hale Irwin	68	68	75	78	289	6,000.00
Graham Marsh	74	68	75	74	291	5,000.00
Isao Aoki	70	74	72	75	291	5,000.00
Bob Byman	73	70	72	76	291	5,000.00
Bob Charles	78	72	70	72	292	4,000.00
Masashi Ozaki	75	69	75	73	292	4,000.00
Greg Norman	73	71	72	76	292	4,000.00
John O'Leary	73	73	74	73	293	3,125.00
Terry Gale	71	74	75	73	293	3,125.00
Wally Armstrong	74	74	73	72	293	3,125.00
Simon Owen	75	76	74	68	293	3,125.00
Lee Trevino	71	73	74	76	294	2,500.00
Peter McEvoy°	71	74	72	77	294	
Nick Faldo	74	74	78	69	295	1,810.00
Sandy Lyle	74	76	75	70	295	1,810.00
Orville Moody	71	74	76	74	295	1,810.00
Ken Brown	72	71	75	77	295	1,810.00
Gary Player	77	74	69	75	295	1,810.00
Tony Jacklin	73	74	76	73	296	1,150.00
Tohru Nakamura	77	75	67	77	296	1,150.00
Peter Thomson	76	75	72	74	297	887.50
Ed Sneed	76	75	70	76	297	887.50
Jerry Pate	69	74	76	78	297	887.50
Tom Watson	72	68	76	81	297	887.50
Mark Hayes	75	75	77	71	298	712.50
Bobby Verwey	75	77	74	72	298	712.50
Armando Saavedra	76	76	73	73	298	712.50
Tom Kite	73	74	77	74	298	712.50
Simon Hobday	75	77	71	75	298	712.50
Bill Longmuir	65	74	77	82	298	712.50
Lee Elder	75	72	76	76	299	575.00
Peter Cowen	79	72	72	76	299	575.00
Christy O'Connor, Sr.	79	73	71	76	299	575.00
Raymond Floyd	76	73	71	79	299	575.00
Michael King	75	70	73	81	299	575.00
Martin Foster	77	75	74	74	300	477.78
Philippe Toussaint	76	75	74	75	300	477.78
Noel Ratcliffe	79	73	72	76	300	477.78
Hugh Baiocchi	72	73	78	77	300	477.78
Peter Oosterhuis	75	74	73	78	300	477.78
Denis Watson	75	70	76	79	300	477.78
Hubert Green	77	71	73	79	300	477.78
John Schroeder	74	75	72	79	300	477.78
Dennis Clark	72	69	76	83	300	477.78
Brian Barnes	78	71	77	75	301	462.50
Carl Mason	77	72	76	76	301	462.50
DeWitt Weaver	73	71	80	77	301	462.50
Garry Cullen	72	74	77	78	301	462.50
Geoffrey Parslow	75	75	76	76	302	450.00
Ian Richardson	75	73	77	77	302	450.00
Kosaku Shimada	75	74	75	78	302	450.00
Jack Newton	76	73	78	76	303	450.00
Yoshitaka Yamamoto	76	74	77	76	303	450.00
Johnny Miller	77	73	77	76	303	450.00
Guy Wolstenholme	77	75	71	80	303	450.00
Robin Fyfe	74	73	79	81	307	450.00
Out of Final 18 holes						
Gordon Brand	75	77	76		228	300.00
Peter Dawson	76	74	78		228	300.00
John May	75	77	76		228	300.00
Ewen Murray	77	75	76		228	300.00
Peter Senior	75	76	77		228	300.00

John Bland	77	75	77	229	300.00
Guy Hunt	74	78	77	229	300.00
Kim Dabson	78	73	78	229	300.00
Brian Jones	76	74	79	229	300.00
Gil Morgan	76	76	77	299	300.00
Fuzzy Zoeller	78	72	79	229	300.00
Manuel Ballesteros	74	76	80	230	300.00
Joe Higgins	77	75	78	230	300.00
Tommy Horton	76	75	79	230	300.00
David Ingram	74	77	79	230	300.00
Juan Anglada	73	76	82	231	300.00
Peter Butler	74	78	79	231	300.00
Wayne Player*	75	75	82	232	
David Thorpe	74	74	84	232	300.00
Mike Cahill	73	75	85	233	300.00
David Feherty	76	75	82	233	300.00
Out of Final 36 holes					
Sam Torrance	75	78		153	200.00
Ian Mosey	75	78		153	200.00
Dale Hayes	76	77		153	200.00
Lon Hinkle	75	78		153	200.00
Willie Milne	81	72		153	200.00
Robin Mann	79	75		154	200.00
David Jones	78	76		154	200.00
Vicente Fernandez	75	79		154	200.00
Anthony Charnley	76	78		154	200.00
Tsuneyuki Nakajima	79	75		154	200.00
Malcolm Gregson	76	78		154	200.00
Warren Humphreys	80	74		154	200.00
Bob Shearer	80	74		154	200.00
Tom Weiskopf	79	75		154	200.00
Jim Rhodes	78	77		155	200.00
Bernard Gallacher	77	78		155	200.00
Brian Huggett	79	76		155	200.00
Eamonn Darcy	83	72		155	200.00
David Watkinson	79	76		155	200.00
Manuel Pinero	77	79		156	200.00
Gary Hallberg*	78	78		156	
David Jagger	78	78		156	200.00
Gavin Levenson	80	76		156	200.00
Wayne Grady	75	81		156	200.00
Marc Farry	77	79		156	200.00
Antonio Garrido	80	76		156	200.00
Jimmy Martin	78	78		156	200.00
Andy North	82	74		156	200.00
Peter Tupling	79	78		157	200.00
Adam Sowa	80	77		157	200.00
John Morgan	77	80		157	200.00
Paul Hoad*	77	80		157	
Tom Melville	78	79		157	200.00
Dennis Durnian	76	81		157	200.00
John Fowler	80	77		157	200.00
Hsi Chuen Lu	78	79		157	200.00
Terry Healey	82	76		158	200.00
Maurice Bembridge	83	75		158	200.00
Mike Ferguson	78	80		158	200.00
Peter Barber	78	80		158	200.00
Osamu Hatano	79	79		158	200.00
Brian Waites	76	82		158	200.00
David Regan	81	77		158	200.00
Jyoji Yokoi	76	82		158	200.00
Alan Mew	77	81		158	200.00
Nick Job	82	77		159	200.00
Howard Clark	83	76		159	200.00
Tony Minshall	79	80		159	200.00
Jeremy G. Bennett*	80	79		159	
Peter Mitchell	83	77		160	200.00
Roger Fidler	80	80		160	200.00
Scott Myers*	85	75		160	
Stephen Rolley	80	80		160	200.00
Mike Krantz	83	78		161	200.00
Peter Highmoor	85	76		161	200.00
Roberto DeVicenzo	79	82		161	200.00
Philip Harrison	82	80		162	200.00
Bill Murray	80	82		162	200.00
Garry Harvey	82	80		162	200.00
Steven Laws	82	80		162	200.00
James Edman	80	82		162	200.00
R. W. Guy*	80	82		162	
John Benda	82	80		162	200.00
David J. Russell	81	82		163	200.00
Andrew Bownes	82	81		163	200.00
Philip Morley	83	82		165	200.00
David Whelan*	86	79		165	
Ron Wood	83	84		167	200.00
B. Maestroni	87	90		177	200.00
Neil Coles	WD–Inj.				200.00

(Professionals playing 54 holes received £300, other professionals starting but not playing more than 36 holes received £200.)

* Amateur

Sun Alliance European Match Play

Fulford Golf Club, York, England
Par 35–36—71; 6,579 yards

August 2–5
purse, 40,000

First Round

Peter Cowen defeated Derek Small, 1 up.
Tony Price defeated Malcolm Gregson, 1 up.
Peter Highmoor defeated Armando Saavedra, 4 and 3.
Brian Waites defeated Liam Higgins, 1 up.
Doug McClelland defeated Nick Brunyard, 3 and 2.
Hugh Baiocchi defeated Alan Mew, 1 up.
Tommy Horton defeated Nigel Blenkarne, 5 and 4.
David Jagger defeated Robert Webster, 2 and 1.
Bernard Gallacher defeated David Robertson, 5 and 4.
Jeff Hawkes defeated Noel Hunt, 2 and 1.
Geoff Tickell defeated Michael King, 2 and 1.
Alex Caygill defeated Peter Dawson, 3 and 2.
Peter Berry defeated Robin Mann, 1 up.
Ian Mosey defeated Patrick Lemaire, 3 and 2.
Nick Price defeated Vicente Fernandez, 2 and 1.
Antonio Garrido defeated David Lythgoe, 7 and 5.
James Airth defeated Vince Baker, 1 up.
Stephen Rolley defeated Tony Jacklin, 5 and 4.
Steve Martin defeated Christy O'Connor Jr., 1 up.
Mark James defeated Pip Elson, 4 and 3.
Harold Henning defeated Trevor Powell, 1 up.
David Regan defeated Gordon Brand, 1 up.
Peter Townsend defeated Gar Hamilton, 4 and 3.
David Vaughan defeated Monty Moseley, 7 and 5.
Ken Brown defeated Jeff Hall, 4 and 3.
Bernhard Langer defeated Jaime Gonzalez, 1 up.
Howard Clark defeated Brian Hessay, 1 up, 20 holes.
Warren Humphreys defeated Peter Senior 1 up, 19 holes.
Gavin Levenson defeated Gary Harvey, 2 and 1.
Simon Hobday defeated Robbie Stewart, 3 and 2.
Sam Torrance defeated Stuart Brown, 1 up.
Anan Sowa defeated Bob Risch, 3 and 2.
Hedley Muscroft defeated Gordon Manson, 5 and 4.
Guy Hunt defeated Bill Longmuir, 5 and 3.
Alex Bickerdike defeated Mohamed Moussa, 1 up, 20 holes.
Mitch Adcock defeated Brain Huggett, 1 up.
Ian Woosnam defeated Ron Wood, 2 and 1.
Garry Cullen defeated Ray Peters, 2 and 1.
Jose-Maria Canizares defeated Mike Ingham, 1 up.
Greg Norman defeated Keith Waters, 1 up.
Sandy Lyle defeated Wayne Grady, 3 and 1.
John Bland defeated Guy Wolstenholme, 3 and 2.
Carl Mason defeated Robert Kelland, 6 and 5.
Eamonn Darcy defeated John Hay, 1 up.
John O'Leary defeated Mike Inglis, 1 up.
Martin Foster defeated Anthony Charnley, 2 and 1.
Ewan Murray defeated David Huish, 6 and 5.
Vaughan Somers defeated John Morgan, 2 up.
Simon Owen defeated Nick Job, 2 up.
Michael Steadman defeated Nick Faldo, 1 up.
Bob Verwey defeated Martin Ross, 6 and 5.
Rodger Davis defeated Peter Wilcock, 4 and 3.
Des Smyth defeated Norman Wood, 1 up, 19 holes.
Martin Green defeated David Russell, 2 and 1.
Willie Milne defeated James Edman, 3 and 2.
Manuel Pinero defeated David Ingram, 1 up.
Mark McNulty defeated Dennis Durnian, 5 and 4.
Brian Barnes defeated Martin Poxon, 5 and 4.
Denis Watson defeated Mike Nutter, 1 up, 19 holes.
John Wraith defeated Peter Tupling, 1 up.
Noel Ratcliffe defeated Stephen Evans, 3 and 2.
Richard Fish defeated Baldovino Dassu, 2 and 1.
Eddie Polland defeated Roger Holland, 5 and 4.
David Webster defeated Trevor Johnson, 3 and 2.

Second Round

Townsend defeated Regan, 3 and 2.
Brown defeated Vaughan, 5 and 4.
Woosnam defeated Cullen, 4 and 3.
Canizares defeated Norman, 1 up.
Bland defeated Lyle, 2 and 1.
Mason defeated Darcy, 2 and 1.
Foster defeated O'Leary, 4 and 3.
Owen defeated Somers, 1 up.
Steadman defeated Murray, 1 up.
Verwey defeated Davis, 1 up.
Smyth defeated Green, 7 and 6.
Pinero defeated Milne, 4 and 3.
Watson defeated McNulty, 7 and 6.
Ratcliffe defeated Wraith, 5 and 4.
Barnes defeated Fish, 2 up.
Polland defeated Webster, 2 and 1.
Cowen defeated Tony Price, 4 and 2.
Waites defeated Highmoor, 4 and 3.
McClelland defeated Baiocchi, 1 up.

Horton defeated Jagger, 2 and 1.
Gallacher defeated Hawkes, 4 and 2.
Caygill defeated Tickell, 4 and 3.
Mosey defeated Berry, 2 and 1.
Nick Price defeated Langer, 1 up.
Garrido defeated Clar, 3 and 2.
Humphreys defeated Levenson, 2 and 1.
Hobday defeated Torrance, 1 up, 19 holes.
Sowa defeated Muscroft, 2 and 1.
G. Hunt defeated Airth, 4 and 3.
Rolley defeated Martin, 2 and 1.
Bickerdike defeated James, 2 and 1.
Henning defeated Adcock, 2 and 1.
Each defeated player received £ 200.

Third Round

Brown defeated Townsend, 1 up.
Canizares defeated Woosnam, 2 and 1.
Foster defeated Owen, 5 and 4.
Mason defeated Brand, 3 and 1.
Verwey defeated Steadman, 3 and 2.
Smyth defeated Pinero, 1 up.
Watson defeated Ratcliffe, 3 and 2.
Barnes defeated Polland, 4 and 3.
Waites defeated Owen, 1 up, 21 holes.
Horton defeated McClelland, 1 up.
Gallacher defeated Caygill, 2 up.
Price defeated Mosey, 5 and 4.
Garrido defeated Humphreys, 5 and 4.
Sowa defeated Hobday, 1 up.
Henning defeated Bickerdike, 4 and 3.
Rolley defeated Hunt, 1 up, 19 holes.
Each defeated player received £400.

Fourth Round

Garrido defeated Sowa, 5 and 4.
Waites defeated Horton, 1 up, 20 holes.
Henning defeated Rolley, 2 up.
Mason defeated Foster, 1 up.
Smyth defeated Verwey, 3 and 2.
Barnes defeated Watson, 4 and 3.
Canizares defeated Brown, 1 up, 25 holes.
Price defeated Gallacher, 1 up, 20 holes.
Each defeated player received   700.

Quarter-Finals

Price defeated Waites, 4 and 3.
Garrido defeated Henning, 6 and 5.
Smyth defeated Barnes, 3 and 2.
Mason defeated Canizares, 1 up.

Consolation Semifinals

Waites defeated Henning, 5 and 4.
Canizares defeated Barnes, 1 up.

Consolation Finals

Garrido defeated Mason, 1 up, 20 holes.
Waites defeated Canizares, 1 up.
Barnes defeated Henning, 1 up.

Semifinals

Price defeated Garrido, 2 and 1.
Smyth defeated Mason, 1 up.

Finals

Smyth defeated Price, 1 up.

Prize money: Smyth £6,600; Price £4,450; Garrido £2,500; Mason £2,100; Waites £1,800; Canizares £1,500; Barnes £1,340; Henning £1,200.

Benson & Hedges International Open

St. Mellion Golf & Country Club, Plymouth, England   August 9–12
Par 35–36—71; 6,614 yards   purse, £60,000

	SCORES				TOTAL	MONEY
Maurice Bembridge	67	67	69	69	272	£10,000.00
Ken Brown	71	65	70	68	274	6,660.00
Sam Torrance	73	68	69	66	276	3,380.00
Jaime Gonzalez	72	71	67	66	276	3,380.00
Tony Jacklin	76	67	67	67	277	2,540.00
Jose-Maria Canizares	74	71	67	66	278	1,800.00
Michael King	72	73	65	68	278	1,800.00

Harold Henning	74	65	70	69	278	1,800.00
David Ingram	72	69	71	67	279	1,213.33
Brian Huggett	71	67	70	71	279	1,213.33
David J. Russell	76	69	64	70	279	1,213.33
Nick Faldo	75	71	68	66	280	934.00
Jeff Hall	68	72	71	69	280	934.00
Baldovino Dassu	74	68	68	70	280	934.00
Hugh Baiocchi	73	67	69	71	280	934.00
Nick Job	73	68	67	72	280	934.00
Manuel Ballesteros	76	68	70	67	281	790.00
Brian Barnes	69	73	70	69	281	790.00
Christy O'Connor, Jr.	73	72	70	67	282	700.00
Gavin Levenson	73	70	71	68	282	700.00
Ian Mosey	77	68	69	68	282	700.00
Dale Hayes	73	72	69	68	282	700.00
Mark James	73	68	72	69	282	700.00
Lee Trevino	76	68	67	71	282	700.00
Peter Berry	75	68	66	73	282	700.00
Ross Drummond	76	69	71	67	283	580.00
Bernard Gallacher	73	69	71	70	283	580.00
Simon Hobday	74	69	70	70	283	580.00
Peter Townsend	72	69	71	71	283	580.00
Vin Baker	73	68	70	72	283	580.00
Garry Cullen	73	70	75	66	284	451.11
John O'Leary	75	71	72	66	284	451.11
Sandy Lyle	71	73	72	68	284	451.11
Manuel Pinero	73	71	70	70	284	451.11
Des Smyth	72	68	73	71	284	451.11
Doug McClelland	71	75	68	70	284	451.11
Simon Owen	74	69	70	71	284	451.11
Carl Mason	70	75	68	71	284	451.11
Brian Waites	74	70	69	71	284	451.11
Philip Elson	76	68	72	69	285	385.00
George Will	75	69	71	70	285	385.00
Jamie Edman	74	70	72	70	286	345.00
Howard Clark	72	72	72	70	286	345.00
Malcolm Gregson	74	71	71	70	286	345.00
Richard Fish	76	67	72	71	286	345.00
Massimo Mannelli	73	72	70	71	286	345.00
Bernhard Langer	74	71	68	73	286	345.00
Peter Butler	73	73	74	67	287	295.00
Tommy Horton	74	69	73	71	287	295.00
David Jagger	72	71	73	71	287	295.00

German Open

Frankfurt Golf Club, Frankfurt, Germany
Par 35-36—71; 6,175

August 16–19
purse, £33,990

	SCORES				TOTAL	MONEY
Tony Jacklin	68	68	70	71	277	£5,665.02
Antonio Garrido	70	71	71	67	279	2,961.82
Lanny Wadkins	71	71	71	66	279	2,961.82
Simon Hobday	71	74	69	68	282	1,699.51
Howard Clark	69	71	70	73	283	1,428.57
James Edman	68	76	72	68	284	857.96
Hugh Baiocchi	69	74	73	68	284	857.96
David Ingram	75	73	68	68	284	857.96
John Bland	73	69	72	70	284	857.96
Maurice Bembridge	70	72	71	71	284	857.96
Jose-Maria Canizares	69	73	69	73	284	857.96
Jeff Hall	75	73	70	67	285	543.41
Bob Charles	72	74	70	69	285	543.41
Martin Foster	69	74	70	69	285	543.41
Mark McNulty	72	72	70	71	285	543.41
Severiano Ballesteros	70	74	71	71	286	467.98
Nick Price	76	69	73	69	287	437.19
Dale Hayes	71	70	75	71	287	437.19
John Fourie	69	73	73	72	287	437.19
Vance Haefner	72	75	73	68	288	397.78
Sam Torrance	74	70	73	71	288	397.78
Gordan Brand	74	69	73	72	288	397.78
Baldovino Dassu	74	73	71	71	289	378.08
Vicente Fernandez	77	70	74	69	290	344.83
Pip Elson	75	72	73	70	290	344.83
Alan Mew	72	75	72	71	290	344.83
Nick Job	74	73	72	71	290	344.83
Bernard Gallacher	76	69	73	72	290	344.83
Steve Martin	76	72	68	74	290	344.83
Bernhard Langer	70	76	73	72	291	296.80
Wayne Grady	71	75	73	72	291	296.80
Simon Owen	74	74	75	68	291	296.80
Nick Faldo	72	75	73	71	291	296.80
Eamonn Darcy	73	70	71	78	292	245.69
Gary Cullen	73	75	68	76	292	245.69
Karl-Heinz Gogele	71	75	75	71	292	245.69
Mitch Adcock	76	72	73	71	292	245.69
Francisco Abreu	72	73	75	72	292	245.69
Gavin Levenson	72	75	73	72	292	245.69
Arnold Palmer	75	73	73	72	292	245.69
Vaughan Somers	70	73	76	73	292	245.69

Vin Baker	74	73	76	70	293	200.74
Eddie Polland	71	72	78	72	293	200.74
Richard Eyles	78	68	75	72	293	200.74
Peter Dawson	72	70	78	73	293	200.74
Michael King	76	72	75	71	294	182.27
Massimo Mannelli	72	76	77	71	296	174.88
Denis Watson	71	79	74	73	297	163.79
Robbie Stewart	74	74	74	75	297	163.79
Wolfgang Jersombeck	77	73	70	78	298	155.17

Carrolls Irish Open

Portmarnock Golf Club, Dublin, Ireland
Par 36–36—72; 7,097 yards

August 23–26
purse, £60,000

	SCORES				TOTAL	MONEY
Mark James	73	75	69	65	282	£10,000.00
Ed Sneed	75	72	71	65	283	6,660.00
Mark McCumber	75	71	70	69	285	3,760.00
Jose-Maria Canizares	73	73	73	68	287	2,546.66
Brian Barnes	81	69	67	70	287	2,546.66
Simon Hobday	73	74	67	73	287	2,546.66
Howard Clark	71	69	73	75	288	1,650.00
Tony Jacklin	73	69	72	74	288	1,650.00
Michael King	73	71	75	70	289	1,213.33
Guy Hunt	73	72	73	71	289	1,213.33
Philip Elson	76	70	71	72	289	1,213.33
Al Geiberger	75	70	75	70	290	934.00
John O'Leary	78	72	70	70	290	934.00
Doug McClelland	78	67	74	71	290	934.00
John Bland	69	75	74	72	290	934.00
David Jones	71	73	72	74	290	934.00
Christy O'Connor, Jr.	76	74	71	70	291	760.00
Severiano Ballesteros	77	74	70	70	291	760.00
Bill Longmuir	74	71	73	73	291	760.00
Rodger Davis	78	67	72	74	291	760.00
Bernard Gallacher	76	69	71	75	291	760.00
Dale Hayes	78	73	72	69	292	670.00
David Ingram	76	74	72	70	292	670.00
John Morgan	77	70	72	73	292	670.00
Sandy Lyle	76	72	69	75	292	670.00
Maurice Bembridge	80	71	73	69	293	570.00
Garry Cullen	77	71	74	71	293	570.00
Manuel Pinero	79	72	69	73	293	570.00
John Mahaffey	74	75	70	74	293	570.00
Robbie Stewart	77	71	70	75	293	570.00
Nick Faldo	78	71	69	75	293	570.00
Mike Miller	73	74	76	71	294	480.00
Bob Charles	75	75	72	72	294	480.00
Tommy Halpin	76	71	71	76	294	480.00
Nick Price	76	74	73	72	295	430.00
Christy O'Connor	76	73	73	73	295	430.00
Eddie Polland	75	74	73	73	295	430.00
Antonio Garrido	73	77	75	71	296	395.00
Des Smyth	77	73	74	72	296	395.00
Tienie Britz	79	71	74	72	296	395.00
Jaime Gonzalez	77	72	74	73	296	395.00
Tommy Horton	77	74	77	69	297	350.00
Sam Torrance	75	74	75	73	297	350.00
Ken Brown	75	76	73	73	297	350.00
Noel Ratcliffe	73	76	72	76	297	350.00
Harold Henning	75	71	74	77	297	350.00
Jimmy Heggarty	82	69	77	70	298	305.00
Neil Coles	77	74	73	74	298	305.00
Steve Martin	75	73	74	76	298	305.00
Alan Mew	78	70	73	77	298	305.00

Swiss Open

Crans-Sur-Sierre, Valais, Switzerland
Par 36–36—72; 6,811 yards

August 30–September 2
purse, £48,400

	SCORES				TOTAL	MONEY
Hugh Baiocchi	68	67	73	67	275	£8,064.52
Antonio Garrido	69	71	72	68	280	3,607.53
Dale Hayes	68	71	68	73	280	3,607.53
Delio Lovato	67	70	68	75	280	3,607.53
Ken Brown	72	70	71	68	281	1,731.18
Bernhard Langer	72	69	70	70	281	1,731.18
Mitch Adcock	66	72	72	71	281	1,731.18
Ewen Murray	73	67	68	74	282	1,209.68
Tienie Britz	72	70	73	68	283	943.55
Manuel Pinero	73	68	71	71	283	943.55
Rafe Botts	68	67	75	73	283	943.55
Al Geiberger	69	68	72	74	283	943.55
Vicente Fernandez	70	72	73	69	284	731.85
Jean Garaialde	70	70	74	70	284	731.85
Robbie Stewart	75	68	71	70	284	731.85
Manuel Ballesteros	71	71	69	73	284	731.85

Angel Gallardo	73	73	70	69	285	629.03
Mark James	75	71	69	70	285	629.03
Bernard Pascassio	68	74	72	71	285	629.03
Luciano Grapposonni	72	73	72	69	286	540.32
James Edman	73	70	73	70	286	540.32
Juan Anglada	71	72	73	70	286	540.32
Gavin Levenson	74	70	72	70	286	540.32
Nick Job	73	68	74	71	286	540.32
David Ingram	72	70	73	71	286	540.32
Garry Cullen	70	72	73	71	286	540.32
R. Adham*	72	72	71	71	286	
Jeff Hawkes	72	73	69	72	286	540.32
Vin Baker	67	71	77	72	287	411.29
Trevor Johnson	70	75	72	70	287	411.29
Tommy Horton	72	69	74	72	287	411.29
Maurice Bembridge	72	71	72	72	287	411.29
Manual Garcia	72	73	70	72	287	411.29
Alberto Croce	69	76	70	72	287	411.29
P. Hessemer	71	73	70	73	287	411.29
Massimo Mannelli	70	71	72	74	287	411.29
Gordon Brand	72	71	74	71	288	326.61
Geromalo Delfino	71	72	74	71	288	326.61
Evan Williams	71	73	73	71	288	326.61
Silvano Locatelli	74	71	71	72	288	326.61
Peter Cowen	73	69	73	73	288	326.61
Harold Henning	67	75	71	75	288	326.61
Warren Humphreys	70	73	74	72	289	282.26
John Benda	72	72	72	73	289	282.26
Manuel Calero	72	74	70	73	289	282.26
Vaughan Somers	69	72	73	75	289	282.26
Roberto Campagnoli	72	70	70	77	289	282.26
Pietro Molteni	74	70	78	69	291	237.90
Rodger Davis	69	71	78	73	291	237.90
Peter Dawson	72	69	77	73	291	237.90
Bobby Verwey	71	72	74	74	291	237.90

* Amateur

European Open

Ailsa Course, Turnberry Hotel, Ayrshire, England
Par 35–35—70; 6,875 yards

September 6–9
purse, £105,000

	SCORES				TOTAL	MONEY
Sandy Lyle	71	67	72	65	275	£17,500.00
Dale Hayes	72	72	70	68	282	9,025.00
Peter Townsend	72	68	70	72	282	9,025.00
Tommy Horton	74	72	71	66	283	4,227.50
Neil Coles	73	70	66	74	283	4,227.50
Sam Torrance	71	72	71	70	284	2,233.33
Severiano Ballesteros	69	69	75	71	284	2,233.33
Mark James	73	72	64	75	284	2,233.33
Howard Clark	74	71	67	73	285	1,675.00
Jose-Maria Canizares	70	70	72	73	285	1,675.00
Ken Brown	70	68	74	75	287	1,500.00
Bill Longmuir	73	73	72	70	288	1,400.00
Des Smyth	73	68	76	71	288	1,400.00
Gordon Brand	75	66	74	73	288	1,400.00
Larry Nelson	77	70	74	68	289	1,143.75
Noel Ratcliffe	75	68	77	69	289	1,143.75
Robin Fyfe	75	70	75	69	289	1,143.75
Robbie Stewart	77	70	72	70	289	1,143.75
Bobby Wadkins	75	71	71	72	289	1,143.75
Brian Waites	72	72	73	72	289	1,143.75
John Morgan	75	70	70	74	289	1,143.75
Manuel Pinero	74	72	70	73	289	1,143.75
Trevor Johnson	71	77	72	70	290	945.00
Tienie Britz	77	69	70	74	290	945.00
David Jagger	75	73	74	69	291	862.50
David Huish	73	73	73	72	291	862.50
Peter Cowen	76	71	70	74	291	862.50
James Farmer	75	69	73	74	291	862.50
Michael King	74	71	74	73	292	763.75
Bob Charles	70	70	77	75	292	763.75
Nick Faldo	73	74	70	75	292	763.75
Garry Cullen	70	74	69	79	292	763.75
Brian Barnes	75	67	80	71	293	660.00
Ewen Murray	74	73	73	73	293	660.00
Tony Jacklin	73	73	73	74	293	660.00
Bill Murray	73	74	72	74	293	660.00
Christy O'Connor, Jr.	75	71	72	75	293	660.00
Jeff Hall	71	73	74	75	293	660.00
Nick Price	73	74	74	73	294	556.00
Malcolm Gregson	73	71	75	75	294	556.00
Vin Baker	69	74	75	76	294	556.00
Rodger Davis	73	74	71	76	294	556.00
Tony Charnley	68	76	75	76	294	556.00
Doug McClelland	74	74	76	71	295	470.00
Martin Foster	74	72	76	73	295	470.00
Bernard Gallacher	73	75	73	74	295	470.00

John Bland	74	70	76	75	295	470.00
Carl Mason	75	73	71	76	295	470.00
Baldovino Dassu	74	67	78	76	295	470.00
Graham Burroughs	74	71	74	76	295	470.00

S.O.S. Talisman Tournament Players Championship

Moor Park Golf Club, Richmansworth, England
Par 37—35—72; 6,893 yards

September 20–23
purse, £50,000

	SCORES				TOTAL	MONEY
Michael King	71	67	72	71	281	£8,330.00
Brian Waites	75	69	70	68	282	5,550.00
Ewen Murray	68	68	74	74	284	3,130.00
Gary Player	72	68	72	74	286	2,500.00
Bernard Gallacher	74	71	73	69	287	2,120.00
Neil Coles	74	70	75	69	288	1,500.00
Peter Townsend	70	73	72	73	288	1,500.00
Des Smyth	74	68	72	74	288	1,500.00
Sam Torrance	75	69	75	71	290	1,060.00
Peter Dawson	73	73	69	75	290	1,060.00
Christy O'Connor, Jr.	75	74	73	69	291	837.50
Greg Norman	75	70	75	71	291	837.50
Mark James	71	74	70	76	291	837.50
Bill Longmuir	71	74	70	76	291	837.50
David Graham	75	71	76	70	292	663.33
John O'Leary	71	77	73	71	292	663.33
Brian Marchbank	75	71	72	74	292	663.33
Bob Charles	75	69	74	74	292	663.33
Nick Price	73	73	72	74	292	663.33
John Bland	74	68	71	79	292	663.33
Howard Clark	72	75	72	74	293	577.50
Sandy Lyle	74	72	72	75	293	577.50
Nick Faldo	72	72	78	72	294	555.00
Rafe Botts	76	75	74	70	295	502.50
Simon Hobday	75	72	76	72	295	502.50
Andrew Chandler	78	74	72	71	295	502.50
Stephen Rolley	72	73	77	73	295	502.50
Nick Job	73	73	75	74	295	502.50
Mark McNulty	71	73	73	78	295	502.50
Manuel Caleró	77	74	75	70	296	435.00
Warren Humphreys	74	74	72	76	296	435.00
Garry Cullen	74	74	71	77	296	435.00
Geoff Tickell	73	76	76	72	297	395.00
Derrick Cooper	75	74	74	74	297	395.00
Michael Miller	72	77	74	74	297	395.00
Denis Watson	75	71	76	75	297	395.00
Charles Dernie	77	72	76	73	298	365.00
Graham Burroughs	74	71	75	78	298	365.00
Malcolm Gregson	74	75	81	69	299	330.00
Philip Loxley	74	78	74	73	299	330.00
Brian Barnes	77	70	77	75	299	330.00
Bernhard Langer	79	71	73	76	299	330.00
Ken Brown	69	76	76	78	299	330.00
Brian Evans	75	73	76	76	300	295.00
Carl Mason	77	71	76	76	300	295.00
Peter Tupling	80	70	76	75	301	265.00
David Ingram	77	72	77	75	301	265.00
Norman Wood	79	72	74	76	301	265.00
Peter Cowen	77	73	72	79	301	265.00
Richard Eyles	76	74	79	73	302	210.00

Dunlop Masters

Woburn Golf and Country Club, Bedfordshire, England
Par 34—38—72; 6,839 yards

October 3–6
purse, £60,000

	SCORES				TOTAL	MONEY
Graham Marsh	70	68	72	73	283	£10,000.00
Isao Aoki	73	73	68	70	284	5,210.00
Neil Coles	72	68	71	73	284	5,210.00
Tony Jacklin	69	69	74	74	286	3,000.00
Michael King	69	77	73	68	287	2,540.00
Roger Maltbie	73	71	75	69	288	2,020.00
Malcolm Gregson	74	70	72	72	288	2,020.00
Ken Brown	75	75	69	70	289	1,416.66
Fuzzy Zoeller	71	74	71	73	289	1,416.66
Nick Price	71	73	71	74	289	1,416.66
Jose-Maria Canizares	74	71	73	72	290	1,170.00
Bob Shearer	74	73	72	72	291	1,080.00
Sam Torrance	72	71	72	76	291	1,080.00
Philip Elson	69	76	75	72	292	953.33
Bob Charles	72	71	76	73	292	953.33
Eddie Polland	71	74	74	73	292	953.33
Mark McNulty	73	74	73	73	293	860.00
Tienie Britz	69	67	77	80	293	860.00
Sandy Lyle	71	76	80	67	294	790.00

Nick Faldo	71	76	75	72	294	790.00
Bernard Gallacher	76	71	75	72	294	790.00
Peter Townsend	72	72	74	76	294	790.00
Brian Waites	71	79	66	78	294	790.00
Simon Owen	71	78	75	71	295	730.00
Severiano Ballesteros	73	75	78	70	296	690.00
Toru Nakamura	70	78	75	73	296	690.00
Tommy Horton	77	71	75	73	296	690.00
Brian Barnes	74	77	73	73	297	630.00
Bill Longmuir	80	74	68	75	297	630.00
Brian Huggett	74	71	73	79	297	630.00
Antonio Garrido	70	78	76	74	298	570.00
Simon Hobday	75	75	71	77	298	570.00
David Jones	73	74	73	78	298	570.00
Gordon Brand	72	76	78	73	299	520.00
Baldovino Dassu	78	74	73	74	299	520.00
Gavin Levenson	78	78	70	74	300	495.00
Maurice Bembridge	73	73	78	76	300	495.00
John Morgan	79	74	74	74	301	470.00
Nick Job	77	74	72	78	301	470.00
John O'Leary	70	73	76	82	301	470.00
Garry Cullen	73	76	75	80	304	450.00
Manuel Pinero	72	77	77	79	305	435.00
Howard Clark	76	77	74	78	305	435.00
Hubert Green	74	77	80	76	307	415.00
Des Smyth	70	77	82	78	307	415.00
Ian Woosnam	74	78	80	76	308	400.00
Mark James	70	80	77	84	311	390.00
Guy Hunt	80	76	78	78	312	380.00
Willie Milne	84	76	77	80	317	365.00
Gaylord Burrows	81	77	78	81	317	365.00

Suntory World Match Play Championship

Wentworth Golf Club, West Course, Virginia Water, Surrey, England   October 11–14
Par 434 534 444–35
345 434 455–37
6,945 yards   purse, £110,000

First Round

David Graham defeated Mark James, 3 and 2.

Graham	c34	434	c54–x	344	43w	55–x . . . x
James	335	445	346–37	245	436	444–36. . . 73

James 1 up.

Graham	534	334	544–35	233	334 4	
James	434	344	445–35	244	c34 5	

Lanny Wadkins defeated Vicente Fernandez, 3 and 1.

Wadkins	434	43w	434–x	445	424	464–37. . . x
Fernandez	435	43c	434–x	345	434	354–35. . . x

Match even.

Wadkins	444	554	445–39	245	434	35
Fernandez	544	434	446–38	344	435 4c	

Bill Rogers defeated Sandy Lyle, 4 and 2.

Lyle	446	334	444–36	443	433	364–34. . . 70
Rogers	534	344	344–34	344	434	444–34. . . 68

Match even.

Lyle	535	534	534–37	445	434 c
Rogers	524	434	444–34	435	435 w

Gary Player defeated Toru Nakamura, 2 up.

Player	434	c4c	444–x	335	424	4c5–x. . . x
Nakamura	444	543	544–37	344	434	455–36. . . 73

Match even.

Player	43c	4c4	544–x	344	434	44w–x. . . x
Nakamura	43w	4w3	454–x	345	444	55c–x. . . x

Second Round

Isao Aoki defeated Graham, 3 and 1.

Aoki	514	433	444–32	344	53c	455–x . . . x
Graham	324	434	444–32	344	44w	445–x . . . x

Graham 1 up.

Aoki	434	534	444–35	334	434	44
Graham	535	533	443–35	445	434	45

Severiano Ballesteros defeated Wadkins, 3 and 1.

Ballesteros	435	434	444–35	345	324	454–34. . . 69
Wadkins	434	435	444–35	445	324	355–35. . . 70

Ballesteros 1 up.

Ballesteros	524	434	444–34	344	434	44
Wadkins	534	344	443–34	444	434	45

361

Rogers defeated Hale Irwin, 3 and 2.

| Irwin | 445 | 434 | 434–35 | 344 | 434 | 455–36. . . 71 |
| Rogers | 435 | 433 | 434–33 | 445 | 434 | 455–38. . . 71 |

Match even.

| Irwin | 43c | 434 | 444–x | 344 | 434 4 | |
| Rogers | 434 | 424 | 444–33 | 334 | 434 4 | |

Fuzzy Zoeller defeated Player, 1 up.

| Player | 435 | 434 | 444–35 | 344 | 444 | 455–38. . . 71 |
| Zoeller | 444 | 334 | 434–35 | 445 | 435˙ | 364–37. . . 72 |

Zoeller 1 up.

| Player | 444 | 434 | 435–35 | 344 | 434 | 445–35. . . 70 |
| Zoeller | 434 | 544 | 345–36 | 344 | 335 | 444–34. . . 70 |

Semifinals

Aoki defeated Ballesteros, 1 up, 40 holes.

| Aoki | 435 | 434 | 454–36 | 444 | 534 | 444–36. . . 72 |
| Ballesteros | 434 | 624 | 444–35 | 344 | 534 | 444–35. . . 70 |

Ballesteros 3 up.

| Aoki | 434 | 434 | 434–33 | 244 | 434 | 445–34. . . 67 |
| Ballesteros | 425 | 424 | 445–34 | 334 | 436 | 455–37. . . 71 |

Match even.

| Aoki | 444 4 | | | | | |
| Ballesteros | 444 5 | | | | | |

Rogers defeated Zoeller, 2 up.

| Rogers | 424 | 434 | 544–34 | 344 | 334 | 354–33. . . 67 |
| Zoeller | 435 | 523 | 443–33 | 255 | 434 | 353–34. . . 67 |

Match even.

| Rogers | 525 | 333 | 534–33 | 245 | 434 | 444–34. . . 67 |
| Zoeller | 535 | 434 | 434–35 | 334 | 424 | 545–34. . . 69 |

Consolation Finals

Zoeller defeated Ballesteros, 1 up.

| Ballesteros | 524 | 424 | 444–33 | 346 | 534 | 444–37. . . 70 |
| Zoeller | 435 | 434 | 344–34 | 334 | 334 | 544–33. . . 67 |

Finals

Rogers defeated Aoki, 1 up.

| Aoki | 433 | 434 | 644–35 | 344 | 433 | 454–34. . . 69 |
| Rogers | 424 | 534 | 445–35 | 344 | 424 | 344–32. . . 67 |

Rogers 1 up.

| Aoki | 424 | 533 | 444–33 | 444 | 433 | 455–36. . . 69 |
| Rogers | 434 | 434 | 444–34 | 344 | 434 | 454–35. . . 69 |

Prize money: Rogers £30,000; Aoki £18,000; Zoeller £12,500; Ballesteros £9,500; Graham, Wadkins, Irwin, Player £6,000; James, Fernandez, Lyle, Nakamura £4,000.

Legend: c—conceded hole to opponent; w—won hole by concession without holing out; x—no total score.

Lancome Trophy

Golf de St. Nom la Bretesche, Paris, France
Par 36–36—72; 6,800 yards

October 25–28
purse, £23,670

	SCORES				TOTAL	MONEY
Johnny Miller	70	71	69	71	281	£9,478.67
Sandy Lyle	71	71	72	70	284	3,317.54
Lee Trevino	74	72	68	70	284	3,317.54
Ray Floyd	72	65	74	74	285	1,658.77
Mark James	69	75	73	70	287	1,303.32
Bill Rogers	72	71	73	71	287	1,303.32
Tony Jacklin	72	67	74	75	288	947.87
Arnold Palmer	72	75	73	72	292	758.29
Brian Barnes	75	76	72	71	294	568.72
Dale Hayes	77	71	70	76	294	568.72
Jean Garaialde	74	74	71	78	297	473.93
Bobby Clampett*	74	75	79	70	298	

*Amateur

Moroccan Grand Prix

Dar-es-Salam Royal Golf Club, Rabat, Morocco
Par 73; 7,478 yards

November 15–18
purse, U.S. $71,500

	SCORES				TOTAL	MONEY
Mike Brannan	72	70	69	77	288	$15,000

Ed Fiori	72	78	70	70	290	8,500
Alan Tapie	75	72	73	70	290	8,500
Antonio Garrido	74	72	74	72	292	5,000
Victor Regalado	75	75	71	71	293	4,000
Jose-Maria Canizares	77	72	69	75	293	4,000
Barry Vivian	67	75	75	77	295	3,200
Vivian Cook	73	74	76	73	296	2,800
Michael King	78	76	74	71	299	2,250
Baldovino Dassu	75	75	72	77	299	2,250
Orville Moody	76	76	75	74	301	1,700
Pat McGowan	79	71	77	74	301	1,700
Greg Owen	73	84	74	71	302	1,300
Bernard Pascassio	77	75	78	72	302	1,300
Colin Bishop	77	75	76	77	303	900
Bob Murphy	79	76	76	72	303	900
Eddie Polland	72	81	74	76	303	900
Doug Tewell	75	75	76	78	304	800
Sukree Onsham	83	76	72	74	305	700
Morris Hatalsky	78	73	82	72	305	700
Mohammed Fatmi	79	76	77	74	306	600
Dave Stockton	79	78	73	78	308	480
Bill Casper	79	77	76	76	308	480
John Harmon, Jr.	78	85	72	73	308	480
Oswald Gartenmaier	79	77	78	74	308	480
Jean Garaialde	80	74	78	76	308	480
Bob Zender	80	77	77	75	309	300
Dave Hill	81	81	76	71	309	300
Jerry Heard	80	78	79	74	311	300
Ali Bennaceur	77	77	75	82	311	300
Archie Sopon	80	77	80	75	312	300
Ahmed Bouazza	76	78	81	81	316	300
Omar Belghitio	79	87	86	87	339	300

SOUTH AFRICAN TOUR

Nigerian Open

Ikoyi Club, Lagos, Nigeria
Par 35–36—71; 6,024 yards

February 22–25
purse, £25,740.00*

	SCORES				TOTAL	MONEY
John Morgan	67	67	68	67	269	£4,290.00
Philip Elson	68	64	72	70	274	2,223.00
Tommy Horton	68	69	65	72	274	2,223.00
Ewen Murray	68	65	70	73	276	1,287.00
Malcolm Gregson	66	75	69	67	277	998.40
Steve Martin	70	65	69	73	277	998.40
Sandy Lyle	69	68	69	72	278	772.20
Mike Miller	67	72	70	72	279	647.40
Andrew Brooks	69	70	70	71	280	546.00
Bill Longmuir	70	70	68	72	280	546.00
Carl Mason	71	73	71	67	282	460.20
Bob Wynn	72	67	69	74	282	460.20
Gary Smith	75	72	71	65	283	421.20
Mohammed Moussa	74	70	69	71	284	386.10
James Lebbie	68	71	73	72	284	386.10
Mike Inglis	73	67	73	72	285	336.96
Martin Poxon	73	72	69	71	285	336.96
Jimmy Heggarty	70	71	73	71	285	336.96
Peter Akakasiaka	73	69	71	72	285	336.96
David Chillas	68	71	70	76	285	336.96
Tony Charnley	73	71	69	73	286	312.00
David Vaughan	71	72	72	72	287	304.20
Martin Hattam	74	73	69	72	288	280.80
Stuart Brown	71	74	71	72	288	280.80
Simon Cox	70	75	70	73	288	280.80
Claytus Iriaka	73	74	72	70	289	249.60
Usman Yesuf	76	73	68	72	289	249.60
John Whitehead	70	69	77	73	289	249.60
Abdul Hanafi	70	71	76	72	289	249.60
Raphel Ohai	69	72	77	77	289	249.60
Paul Osanebi	74	74	70	72	290	222.30
Andrew Bownes	69	73	73	75	290	222.30
Gary Potter	74	71	75	71	291	195.00
Peter Berry	76	68	74	73	291	195.00
Joe Higgins	75	73	68	75	291	195.00
Jacob Omoruah	72	73	76	71	292	181.35
Bachary Samateh	73	72	72	75	292	181.35
Mike Gallagher	76	73	70	74	293	169.65
Phil Morley	74	72	72	75	293	169.65
Ian Woosnam	71	70	74	78	293	169.65
Patrick Okpomu	70	69	73	81	293	169.65
Festus Makalemi	73	76	75	71	295	154.70
David A. Russell	76	71	76	72	295	154.70
Harry Bannerman	74	75	70	76	295	154.70
Chris Okwu	74	74	73	75	296	140.40
Bello Seibidor	70	73	75	78	296	140.40
Paul Tetteh	69	72	78	77	296	140.40
David Owoyemi	71	69	77	80	297	132.60
James McCallum	76	73	74	77	300	128.70
Jones Esioyibo	79	73	79	70	301	124.80

*One Pound = U.S. $2.10

Kenyan Open

Muthaiga Golf Club, Nairobi, Kenya
Par 36–35—71; 6,765 yards

March 15–18
purse, £40,000

	SCORES				TOTAL	MONEY
Maurice Bembridge	67	65	69	70	271	£6,666.67
Bernard Gallacher	69	69	68	65	271	4,166.67
(Bembridge defeated Gallacher on first hole of sudden-death play-off)						
Peter Townsend	71	67	71	65	274	2,083.33
Brian Waites	71	69	70	67	277	1,416.67
Brian Hugget	69	70	69	69	277	1,416.67
Manuel Ballesteros	68	68	71	70	277	1,416.67
Sandy Lyle	70	69	70	69	278	812.50
Simon Owen	66	68	71	73	278	812.50
Garry Cullen	66	71	68	73	278	812.50
Malcolm Gregson	72	72	64	70	278	812.50
Bob Charles	66	72	73	68	279	543.75
Billy Casper	70	69	70	70	279	543.75
Nick Faldo	68	73	68	70	279	543.75
Bob Wynn	67	73	68	71	279	543.75
Garry Harvey	72	69	68	72	281	475.00
Bill Longmuir	72	69	67	73	281	475.00

Peter Cowen	69	75	69	69	282	437.50
Al Geiberger	70	69	72	71	282	437.50
David Jones	69	72	69	72	282	437.50
Paul Tembo	74	68	68	72	282	437.50
Trevor Powell	71	72	75	65	283	416.67
John Morgan	74	68	68	74	284	404.17
Tony Jacklin	69	73	66	76	284	404.17
David Vaughan	68	72	76	69	285	383.33
David Chillas	70	71	71	73	285	383.33
Simon Cox	70	67	74	74	285	383.33
John Fowler	72	71	73	70	286	350.56
Ian Woosnam	73	73	67	73	286	350.56
Mike Ingham	68	74	69	75	286	350.56
Steve Martin	70	76	74	67	287	290.00
Peter Berry	73	73	70	71	287	290.00
Carl Mason	74	71	72	71	288	270.84
Tommy Horton	73	68	73	74	288	270.84
Peter Highmoor	70	73	73	73	289	254.17
Gar Hamilton	74	70	72	73	289	254.17
Joe Higgins	69	76	69	76	290	241.67
Mike Inglis	74	75	72	70	291	214.72
Stuart Brown	72	75	73	71	291	214.72
John Whitehead	75	71	73	72	291	214.72
Doug Sanders	73	72	73	73	291	214.72
Andrew Payne	73	70	72	76	291	214.72
Dennis Durnian	73	69	73	76	291	214.72
Eddie Polland	77	70	74	71	292	193.50
John Hay	76	71	70	75	292	193.50
Christy O'Connor, Jr.	74	74	72	73	293	186.67
Mike Miller	73	74	73	74	294	181.00
Gordon Brand	70	74	74	76	294	181.00
Nick Job	73	73	73	76	295	175.00
Charles Dernie	69	76	76	76	297	114.64
Philip Morley	70	73	76	78	297	114.64

Lusaka Open

Lusaka Golf Club, Zambia
Par 35–38–73; 6,599 yards

March 22–25
purse, £18,696.10

	SCORES				TOTAL	MONEY
John Morgan	71	70	68	73	282	£3,100.00
Trevor Powell	72	74	69	70	285	2,064.60
Sandy Lyle	74	70	74	68	286	1,047.80
Eamonn Darcy	75	70	73	68	286	1,047.80
Gary Harvey	73	76	69	71	289	787.40
Brian Waites	78	73	71	69	291	589.00
Gary Cullen	73	76	70	72	291	589.00
Malcolm Gregson	71	74	69	77	291	589.00
Peter Berry	73	74	73	72	292	465.00
Peter Cowen	74	74	73	72	293	370.45
Gar Hamilton	69	76	76	72	293	370.45
David Jones	72	78	70	73	293	370.45
Mike Ingham	70	77	71	75	293	370.45
Maurice Bembridge	76	71	75	73	295	300.70
Gordon Brand	70	75	74	76	295	300.70
Martin Poxon	70	73	75	77	295	300.70
Stewart Brown	76	75	74	73	298	272.80
Christy O'Connor, Jr.	74	76	74	75	299	260.40
David Vaughan	76	73	74	76	299	260.40
Dennis Durnian	76	77	72	77	299	260.40
John Fowler	79	77	73	71	300	248.00
Mike Steadman	74	74	78	75	301	238.70
Steve Martin	75	80	68	78	301	238.70
Michael Miller	80	77	72	73	302	229.40
John Whitehead	77	71	79	76	303	217.00
Paul Tembo	74	75	73	76	303	217.00
Mike Inglis	75	80	70	78	303	217.00
Robert Wynn	78	80	77	69	304	204.60
Peter Sinyama*	70	79	78	78	305	
Ewen Murray	76	74	76	79	305	198.40
Peter Highmoor	82	75	75	74	306	182.90
John Hay	77	76	76	77	306	182.90
Philip Morley	77	75	75	79	306	182.90
John Hammond	74	80	73	79	306	182.90
Peter Armstrong*	76	77	81	73	307	
Ian Woosnam	72	76	83	76	307	161.20
Tim Giles	79	78	74	76	307	161.20
Andrew Brooks	79	74	75	79	307	161.20
Peter Dawson	76	74	82	77	309	142.60
Charles Dernie	74	79	79	77	309	142.60
Jan Sonnevi	77	72	78	82	309	142.60
Simon Cox	79	75	77	79	310	130.20
Andrew Bownes	80	82	75	74	311	124.00
Tony Price	80	77	80	77	314	117.80
Joe Higgins	78	82	76	78	314	117.80
Martin Hattam	78	74	82	80	314	117.80
Bernhard Langer	81	80	73	81	315	111.60
Francis Boillat	76	80	79	83	318	108.50
Tommy McGuirk*	79	80	75	85	319	

Barry Myers*	78	78	82	81	319	
Richard Fish	85	79	81	78	323	105.40
Gary Potter	78	89	83	78	328	102.30

*Amateur

Zambian Open

Ndola Golf Club, Zambia
Par 37–36—73; 7,080 yards

March 29–April 1
purse, £26,474

	SCORES				TOTAL	MONEY
Brian Barnes	71	64	72	73	280	£4,340.00
Sandy Lyle	69	69	76	69	283	2,892.30
Brian Waites	71	71	69	73	284	1,565.50
David Jones	69	72	69	74	284	1,565.50
Gordon Brand	73	69	72	71	285	1,162.50
Bernhard Langer	69	71	75	71	286	992.00
Gary Cullen	74	72	71	71	288	868.00
Dennis Durnian	71	69	75	74	289	759.50
Christy O'Connor, Jr.	72	75	72	71	290	663.40
Ewen Murray	72	75	73	71	291	507.78
Maurice Bembridge	71	73	74	73	291	507.78
Bob Wynn	69	72	77	73	291	507.78
Mike Ingham	71	74	71	75	291	507.78
David Vaughan	70	72	73	76	291	507.78
Joe Higgins	71	74	75	72	292	390.60
John Hay	75	71	74	72	292	390.60
Eamonn Darcy	75	70	75	72	292	390.60
Malcolm Gregson	71	74	73	74	292	390.60
Steve Martin	70	74	74	74	292	390.60
Gar Hamilton	72	75	74	73	294	341.00
Peter Cowen	73	73	75	73	294	341.00
Garry Harvey	74	73	70	71	294	341.00
Ian Woosnam	73	75	77	70	295	310.00
Martin Poxon	69	73	78	75	295	310.00
John Morgan	75	72	77	72	296	285.20
Michael Miller	80	72	72	72	296	285.20
Richard Fish	73	73	76	76	298	272.80
Mike Steadman	77	74	75	74	300	257.30
Mike Inglis	76	72	77	75	300	257.30
John Hammond	75	75	73	77	300	257.30
Stewart Brown	71	76	76	77	300	257.30
John Fowler	77	70	75	79	301	241.80
Peter Armstrong*	74	74	78	75	301	
Paul Tembo	76	75	75	76	302	235.60
Philip Morley	77	75	80	71	303	223.20
Trevor Powell	76	71	78	78	303	223.20
Jan Sonnevi	70	76	77	80	303	223.20
Tony Price	75	76	79	75	305	204.60
Peter Berry	75	75	79	76	305	204.60
Andrew Brooks	71	78	79	77	305	204.60
John Whitehead	75	76	77	78	306	192.20
Colin Van der Merwe*	74	77	74	81	306	
Charles Dernie	73	75	85	74	307	182.90
Martin Hattan	75	75	76	81	307	182.90
Peter Highmoor	77	77	79	75	308	· 173.60
Lyson Mbayole*	81	73	78	76	308	
Andrew Bownes	81	76	77	76	310	167.40
Dave Rigby*	80	74	82	74	310	
Tim Giles	78	75	81	77	311	161.20
Tony McGuirk*	73	77	83	78	311	

*Amateur

Zimbabwe Rhodesian Open

Henry Chapman Golf Club, Salesbury, Zimbabwe
Par 36–36—72; 7,131 yards

November 8–11
purse, R30,000*

	SCORES				TOTAL	MONEY
Simon Hobday	69	71	65	70	275	R4,500.00
Denis Watson	66	68	71	70	275	2,750.00
(Hobday defeated Watson on second hole of sudden-death play-off)						
Mark McNulty	69	68	73	67	277	2,185.00
Allan Henning	74	69	70	66	279	1,700.00
John Bland	71	71	67	71	280	1,400.00
Nicky Price	73	68	68	73	282	1,200.00
Cobie Legrange	66	73	72	72	283	1,100.00
Tienie Britz	74	73	69	68	284	883.34
Gavin Levenson	71	70	73	70	284	883.33
Bob Verwey	66	73	69	76	284	833.33
Bill Longmuir	73	72	68	72	285	750.00
Harold Henning	69	72	68	76	285	750.00
Jeff Hawkes	71	74	72	69	286	637.50
John Fourie	70	71	71	74	286	637.50
Fred Beaver	70	72	74	71	287	562.50
Vin Baker	69	72	73	73	287	562.50
Noel Hunt	72	75	73	68	288	500.00

George Harvey	74	73	73	68	288	500.00
Brian Jacobs	75	70	74	69	288	500.00
Anthony Johnstone	75	72	72	70	289	409.00
Bobby Lincoln	76	71	71	71	289	409.00
Fulton Allem	72	75	69	73	289	409.00
Ian Mosey	70	74	72	73	289	409.00
Hugh Inggs	73	72	71	73	289	409.00
Andrew Chandler	74	76	70	71	291	360.00
Denis Bruyns	77	69	71	74	291	360.00
Jannie Legrange	72	76	70	73	291	360.00
Nick Job	74	74	73	71	292	335.00
D. Stratton	78	73	69	72	292	335.00
Robbie Stewart	72	74	73	74	293	236.67
Donald Gammon	72	73	73	75	293	236.67
Tertius Claassens	74	72	71	76	293	236.66
Graham Henning	70	75	77	73	295	180.00
Warren Humphreys	72	75	75	74	296	160.00
Phil Simmons	73	75	71	77	296	160.00
Teddie Webber	72	74	72	78	296	160.00
Gary Baleson	74	76	73	74	297	135.00
G. Brown	80	68	72	77	297	135.00
Paul vanZyl	76	78	68	76	298	95.66
M. Bright	74	78	76	70	298	95.66
Andries Oosthuizen	70	76	80	72	298	95.66
Jimmy Falconer	75	72	73	78	298	95.66
Dennis Hutchinson	75	74	72	79	300	76.32
Donald Armour	79	75	72	74	300	76.32
C. Pope	76	75	75	74	300	76.32
Terry Westbrook	74	75	77	75	301	76.32
Reggie Mamashela	74	79	72	77	302	76.32
C. Williams	81	74	72	76	303	76.32
Mike Worroll	75	81	75	76	307	76.32
P. Mhlongo	76	75	77	80	308	76.32

*One Rand = U.S. $1.20

ICL International

Kensington Golf Club, Johannesburg
Par 36–35–71; 6,774 yards

November 14–17
purse, R40,000

	SCORES				TOTAL	MONEY
Nick Faldo	68	66	69	65	268	R6,000.00
Allan Henning	69	69	66	67	271	4,000.00
Harold Henning	67	69	69	68	273	1,937.50
George Harvey	70	66	67	70	273	1,937.50
Denis Watson	67	65	65	76	273	1,937.50
John Fourie	66	68	67	72	273	1,937.50
Nicky Price	68	69	66	71	274	1,250.00
Nick Job	66	69	68	72	275	1,100.00
Tertius Claassens	72	67	69	69	277	1,000.00
Mark McNulty	73	66	68	71	278	925.00
Bobby Cole	66	71	70	71	278	925.00
Vin Baker	69	74	70	66	279	850.00
Tienie Britz	74	70	67	69	280	775.00
Jeff Hawkes	68	73	67	72	280	775.00
Phil Simmons	73	69	65	73	280	775.00
Gavin Levenson	73	70	66	72	281	712.50
Dale Hayes	72	72	66	71	281	712.50
Noel Hunt	72	72	71	67	282	637.50
Denis Bruyns	71	72	68	71	282	637.50
Cobie Legrange	69	71	68	74	282	637.50
Simon Hobday	69	69	69	75	282	637.50
John Bland	72	70	72	69	283	562.50
Bill Longmuir	71	74	68	70	283	562.50
Andries Oosthuizen	71	72	68	73	284	525.00
G. Brown	70	72	71	72	285	460.00
Donald Gammon	74	72	67	72	285	460.00
Bob Verwey	70	74	69	72	285	460.00
John O'Leary	69	72	70	74	285	460.00
Teddie Webber	70	72	69	74	285	460.00
Hugh Baiocchi	75	74	67	71	287	400.00
Graham Henning	72	72	74	70	288	340.00
Robbie Stewart	67	71	73	77	288	340.00
Ross Drummond	70	73	75	70	288	340.00
Jannie Legrange	73	74	69	72	288	340.00
Bobby Lincoln	75	73	67	73	288	340.00
Ian Mosey	72	73	72	73	290	290.00
D. Whitfield	72	76	72	71	291	270.00
M. Wilson	72	76	69	74	291	270.00
Terry Halpin	73	73	68	77	291	270.00
Dennis Hutchinson	73	73	77	69	292	170.00
Dennis Durnian	73	74	71	74	292	170.00
Paul vanZyl	72	74	70	76	292	170.00
Roddy Carr	74	71	71	76	292	170.00
Warren Humphreys	74	71	70	77	292	170.00
Reggie Mamashala	76	71	75	71	293	150.00
D. Griffin	73	73	76	72	294	150.00
R. Vosloo	73	75	74	72	294	150.00
Paul Curry	73	74	74	73	294	150.00
Ian Martin	74	72	74	74	294	150.00
Andrew Chandler	72	74	71	77	294	150.00

Lexington PGA Championship

Wanderers Golf Club, Johannesburg
Par 36–34–70; 6,906 yards

November 21–23
purse, R83,000

	SCORES			TOTAL	MONEY
Gary Player	71	66	66	203	R12,450.00
Harold Henning	69	70	65	204	5,363.87
Denis Watson	66	71	67	204	5,363.87
Bobby Cole	67	69	68	204	5,363.87
Nicky Price	68	68	68	204	5,363.87
Nick Job	68	68	69	205	3,154.00
Dale Hayes	64	70	71	205	3,154.00
Mark McNulty	69	68	69	206	2,573.00
Allan Henning	71	66	69	206	2,573.00
Hugh Baiocchi	68	69	70	207	2,199.50
Jimmy Johnson	67	68	72	207	2,199.50
Ian Mosey	70	69	69	208	1,763.75
Noel Hunt	70	67	71	208	1,763.75
John Bland	71	70	68	209	1,294.80
John Fourie	71	68	70	209	1,294.80
Calvin Peete	67	72	70	209	1,294.80
Jannie Legrange	69	69	71	209	1,294.80
Bill Longmuir	69	68	72	209	1,294.80
Donald Gammon	71	70	69	210	1,058.25
Tienie Britz	69	71	70	210	1,058.25
Rod Funseth	70	75	66	211	933.85
Bobby Lincoln	70	72	69	211	933.85
Ken Brown	71	70	70	211	933.85
Gavin Levenson	71	68	72	211	933.85
Ross Drummond	71	71	70	212	809.25
Hugh Inggs	68	73	71	212	809.25
Tertius Claassens	69	72	71	212	809.25
Anthony Johnstone	71	74	68	213	736.62
John Mahaffey	71	73	69	213	736.62
Robbie Stewart	68	74	71	213	736.62
Martin Poxon	71	69	73	213	736.62
Jeff Hawkes	71	72	71	214	653.62
Solly Sepeng	70	71	73	214	653.62
Denis Bruyns	70	68	76	214	653.62
Bob Verwey	70	68	76	214	653.62
Vin Baker	73	72	70	215	539.50
Carl Mason	69	75	71	215	539.50
Graham Henning	72	72	71	215	539.50
John O'Leary	71	73	71	215	539.50
Nick Faldo	70	73	72	215	539.50
Algy Kietzman	72	71	72	215	539.50
Teddie Webber	75	67	73	215	539.50
Andy North	76	69	71	216	417.49
A. Jones	66	78	72	216	417.49
Des Smyth	70	73	73	216	417.49
Mike Worroll	71	72	73	216	417.49
Paul Curry	69	74	73	216	417.49
Cobie Legrange	74	71	72	217	348.60
James Edman	72	72	73	217	348.60
Andries Oosthuizen	74	70	73	217	348.60

Kronenbrau "1308"

Milnerton Golf Club, Cape Town
Par 36–36–72

November 28–December 1
purse, R83,000

	SCORES				TOTAL	MONEY
Gary Player	67	65	70	68	270	R12,450.00
John O'Leary	68	66	68	74	276	8,300.00
Des Smyth	68	65	70	74	277	5,395.00
Calvin Peete	64	68	74	72	278	4,150.00
Bob Verwey	72	68	69	70	279	3,610.50
John Bland	66	71	69	74	280	2,988.00
John Mahaffey	66	67	75	72	280	2,988.00
Hugh Baiocchi	68	69	68	75	280	2,988.00
Nick Faldo	65	70	70	76	281	2,490.00
Ken Brown	68	69	76	69	282	2,199.50
Michael King	65	70	71	76	282	2,199.50
Harold Henning	70	69	70	74	283	1,673.83
Mark McNulty	70	68	70	75	283	1,673.83
Don Bies	68	68	72	75	283	1,673.83
Cobie Legrange	70	71	72	71	284	1,245.00
Denis Watson	70	68	74	72	284	1,245.00
Vin Baker	70	69	72	73	284	1,245.00
Jay Haas	71	68	68	77	284	1,245.00
Stephen Bennett	74	68	75	68	285	996.00
Tertius Claassens	70	73	72	70	285	996.00
Brian Marchbank	69	71	68	77	285	996.00
Bill Longmuir	65	70	73	77	285	996.00
Keith Fergus	72	66	68	79	285	996.00
Bobby Cole	72	71	71	72	286	836.92
Simon Hobday	72	67	74	73	286	836.92
Anthony Johnstone	70	68	75	73	286	836.92
Tienie Britz	70	73	74	70	287	778.12
Noel Hunt	72	72	72	71	287	778.12

Ian Mosey	76	69	73	70	288	715.87
Michael Steadman	69	69	73	77	288	715.87
Ian Woosnam	71	70	71	76	288	715.87
Gavin Levenson	68	71	72	77	288	715.87
Richard Mogoerane	68	70	78	73	289	612.12
L. vanNiekerk	73	70	68	78	289	612.12
Andries Oosthuizen	71	70	74	74	289	612.12
Joe Higgins	72	73	71	73	289	612.12
David Russell	65	74	75	75	289	612.12
James Edman	71	71	71	76	289	612.12
Pietro Molteni	72	70	77	71	290	477.25
Carl Mason	69	72	71	78	290	477.25
D. Stratton	76	69	74	71	290	477.25
Phil Simmons	68	69	71	82	290	477.25
Simon Cox	71	73	73	73	290	477.25
Ross Drummond	74	70	73	73	290	477.25
Robbie Stewart	68	75	70	77	290	477.25
Allan Henning	72	73	74	72	291	302.70
Paul Curry	73	72	69	77	291	302.70
Stephen Rolley	71	71	72	77	291	302.70
Jeff Hawkes	70	69	73	79	291	302.70
Chris Moody	70	69	75	77	291	302.70
Dennis Durnian	69	71	73	78	291	302.70
Philip Morley	73	67	73	78	291	302.70

Yellow Pages–British Airways South African Open

Houghton Golf Culb, Johannesburg
Par 37–35—72; 7,320 yards

December 5–8
purse, R65,000

	SCORES				TOTAL	MONEY
Gary Player	67	75	71	66	279	R9,780.00
Ian Mosey	68	70	69	73	280	6,390.00
Jeff Hawkes	69	73	70	70	282	3,636.67
Allan Henning	71	68	72	71	282	3,636.67
Simon Hobday	71	69	69	73	282	3,636.67
Bobby Cole	71	71	71	70	283	2,710.00
Hugh Baiocchi	70	73	71	70	284	2,110.00
Des Smyth	72	73	69	70	284	2,110.00
Mark McNulty	70	70	71	73	284	2,110.00
John Bland	72	70	72	71	285	1,485.00
Robbie Stewart	68	77	70	70	285	1,485.00
Nicky Price	71	75	68	71	285	1,485.00
James Edman	74	72	71	69	286	1,096.67
Bob Verwey	70	73	72	71	286	1,096.67
Ken Brown	74	75	67	70	286	1,096.67
Gavin Levenson	72	75	70	71	288	925.00
Tienie Britz	69	78	73	69	289	890.00
Bill Longmuir	72	75	72	71	290	831.66
Phil Simmons	74	75	68	73	290	831.66
Cobie Legrange	74	71	71	74	290	831.66
Carl Mason	76	74	73	68	291	780.00
Nick Faldo	72	73	71	75	291	780.00
Bob Bruno	74	74	74	70	292	740.00
Martin Poxon	73	72	70	77	292	740.00
John O'Leary	74	74	77	68	293	670.00
Michael King	75	73	75	70	293	670.00
Jannie Legrange	74	75	72	72	293	670.00
Chris Moody	75	73	73	72	293	670.00
Teddie Webber	75	74	71	73	293	670.00
Denis Watson	72	78	72	72	294	610.00
Dennis Durnian	76	72	75	72	295	535.00
Trevor Powell	71	72	74	78	295	535.00
John Fourie	72	76	74	73	295	535.00
Michael Steadman	76	72	74	73	295	535.00
Anthony Johnstone	71	72	78	74	295	535.00
Jimmy Johnson	76	74	71	74	295	535.00
Tertius Claassens	77	73	75	71	296	465.00
Pietro Molteni	74	74	78	71	297	445.00
Reggie Mamashala	78	72	74	74	298	415.00
Warren Humphreys	74	74	75	75	298	415.00
Nigel Burch	72	75	75	77	299	390.00
Andries Oosthuizen	71	77	74	77	299	390.00
Donald Gammon	74	70	80	76	300	375.00
Andrew Chandler	73	76	78	74	301	360.00
George Harvey	77	72	73	79	301	360.00
Tony Finlayson	75	74	75	78	302	345.00
Gary Baleson	77	72	75	78	302	345.00
Denis Bruyns	73	72	75	82	302	345.00
Bobby Lincoln	75	75	75	78	303	335.00
A. Jones	77	72	78	79	306	295.00
Comrie du Toit	76	74	77	79	306	295.00

Sun City Classic

Gary Player Country Club, Baputhatsana
Par 36–36—72; 7,693 yards

December 12–15
purse, R100,000

	SCORES				TOTAL	MONEY
Gary Player	70	71	67	70	278	R15,000.00

Bob Verwey	68	71	71	72	282	9,900.00
Nicky Price	73	73	70	68	284	6,400.00
Des Smyth	73	73	73	67	286	4,416.67
Denis Watson	72	70	75	69	286	4,416.67
Tertius Claassens	73	70	70	73	286	4,416.66
Bobby Cole	70	73	70	74	287	3,350.00
Jim Thorpe	74	73	67	73	287	3,350.00
Mark Hayes	72	75	71	70	288	2,850.00
Noel Hunt	68	72	75	73	288	2,850.00
Arnold Palmer	69	76	73	71	289	2,450.00
John Bland	73	74	73	71	291	1,875.00
Teddie Webber	71	75	71	74	291	1,875.00
Hugh Baiocchi	75	70	73	73	291	1,875.00
Martin Poxon	71	70	75	75	291	1,875.00
James Edman	74	77	70	72	293	1,450.00
Phil Simmons	72	74	72	75	293	1,450.00
Mark McNulty	75	76	73	70	294	1,275.00
Cobie Legrange	75	75	73	71	294	1,275.00
Selwyn Bennett	73	76	74	72	295	1,175.00
John O'Leary	67	79	72	77	295	1,175.00
Jannie Legrange	71	76	76	73	296	1,075.00
Dennis Durnian	73	75	74	74	296	1,075.00
Andrew Chandler	71	75	78	73	297	975.00
Vincent Tshabalala	77	76	71	73	297	975.00
Joe Higgins	73	74	77	74	298	900.00
D. Stratton	76	69	77	76	298	900.00
Trevor Powell	72	78	71	77	298	900.00
Vince Baker	77	76	74	72	299	812.50
Nick Faldo	73	73	80	73	299	812.50
Dale Hayes	73	76	73	77	299	812.50
Allan Henning	69	73	77	80	299	812.50
Steve Martin	77	77	72	74	300	700.00
Hugh Inggs	76	72	76	76	300	700.00
John Fourie	75	75	74	76	300	700.00
Fulton Allem	78	73	71	78	300	700.00
Tienie Britz	72	77	79	72	300	700.00
Anthony Johnstone	73	78	73	77	301	587.50
Robbie Stewart	75	74	75	77	301	587.50
Martin Green	74	75	74	78	301	587.50
Chris Moody	76	79	74	72	301	587.50
Brian Marchbank	75	76	74	77	302	500.00
Bobby Lincoln	74	77	72	79	302	500.00
Ian Mosey	74	74	72	82	302	500.00
Donald Gammon	79	75	73	76	303	430.00
David Russell	78	69	78	78	303	430.00
D. Williams	76	77	76	74	303	430.00
Harold Henning	72	78	77	77	304	244.29
Michael King	76	73	78	77	304	244.29
Gavin Levenson	77	76	73	78	304	244.29
Carl Mason	74	75	75	80	304	244.29
Robbie Chapman	71	71	78	84	304	244.28
Reggie Mamashala	78	78	74	74	304	244.28
Philip Morley	74	74	80	76	304	244.28

Philippine Open

Wack Wack Golf and Country Club, East Course, Manila
Par 36—36—72; 7,134 yards

February 15–18
purse, U.S. $100,000

	SCORES				TOTAL	MONEY
Ben Arda	69	71	71	75	286	$25,000
Hung Fa	72	74	70	73	289	11,250
Hsu Sheng San	72	70	74	73	289	11,250
Mya Aye	77	73	68	72	290	5,100
Yoshikasu Yokoshima	71	71	78	70	290	5,100
Kuo Chi Hsiung	74	67	77	72	290	5,100
Hsu Chi San	73	73	69	76	291	4,100
Hsieh Yung Yo	71	73	75	73	292	3,600
Tsutomu Irie	69	74	72	78	293	3,100
Paterno Braza	71	75	73	75	294	2,425
Ireneo Legaspi	73	73	75	73	294	2,425
Lu Liang Huan	72	73	79	71	295	1,650
Lim Kian Tiong	76	76	71	72	295	1,650
Rudy Lavares	75	72	73	75	295	1,650
Lu Hsi Chuen	72	74	69	80	295	1,650
akashi Kurihara	73	76	71	75	295	1,650
Wu Chin Fa	71	73	77	75	296	1,025
Chen Tze Ming	72	74	74	76	296	1,025
Chang Chung Fa	78	73	75	71	297	950
Hideyo Sugimoto	74	76	76	72	298	750
Mike Soli	72	75	76	75	298	750
Chen Chien Chung	74	75	75	74	298	750
Hsieh Min Nan	79	73	72	74	298	750
Rick Mallicoat	74	75	74	75	298	750
Gaylord Burrows	71	73	78	76	298	750
Sukree Onsham	72	74	74	78	298	750
James Booros	74	75	72	78	299	525
Dennis Saunders	77	72	77	74	300	390
Curt Worley	76	74	73	77	300	390
Cho Ho Sang	72	77	73	78	300	390
Don Klenk	76	74	72	78	300	390
Fritz Gambetta	74	74	78	75	301	335
Ho Ming Chung	71	73	80	77	301	335
Takahiro Takeyasu	75	74	76	77	302	300
Masaru Sasaki	74	76	75	77	302	300
Eleuterio Nival	82	70	74	76	302	300
Kim Seung Hak	75	75	74	78	302	300
Kazunari Takahashi	76	75	72	79	302	300
Lee I1 Ahn	77	73	76	77	303	54
Tomomi Suzuki	74	77	75	77	303	54
Hahn Chang Sang	75	77	73	78	303	54
Hisashi Suzumura	78	73	74	78	303	54
Tom Ducey	76	76	71	80	303	54

Cathay Pacific Hong Kong Open

Royal Hong Kong Golf Club, Fanling, Hong Kong

February 22–25
purse, U.S. $100,000

Eden Course: Par 35–34—69; 6,165 yards (First two rounds only)
New Course: Par 34–36—70; 6,503 yards (First two rounds only)
Composite Course: Par 34–36—70; 6,691 yards (Last two rounds only)

	SCORES				TOTAL	MONEY
Greg Norman	70	66	69	68	273	$20,000.00
Lu Hsi Chuen	68	65	69	74	276	8,500.00
Hsu Chi San	66	67	69	74	276	8,500.00
Chen Tze Ming	69	67	70	70	276	8,500.00
Hisashi Suzumura	67	68	73	71	279	3,500.00
Yoshikazu Yokoshima	69	68	69	73	279	3,500.00
Chen Chien Chin	73	68	72	68	281	3,000.00
Kosaku Shimada	67	71	69	74	281	3,000.00
Graham Marsh	66	65	74	76	281	3,000.00
Minoru Nakamura	69	74	71	68	282	2,300.00
Ireneo Legaspi	69	68	70	75	282	2,300.00
Hsu Sheng San	67	69	71	75	282	2,300.00
Kurt Cox	70	67	73	72	282	2,300.00
Don Klenk	71	70	70	72	283	1,700.00
Mya Aye	70	66	74	73	283	1,700.00
Jaime Gonzalez	71	70	73	70	284	1,300.00
Kuo Chi Hsiung	71	71	70	72	284	1,300.00
Yasuhiro Miyamoto	69	72	70	74	285	1,016.66
Hsieh Yung Yo	69	71	70	75	285	1,016.66
Ben Arda	72	68	74	71	285	1,016.66
Norio Mikami	70	72	70	74	286	808.00
Kikuo Arai	75	71	70	70	286	808.00

Terry Gale	70	72	68	76	286	808.00
Choi Sang Ho	73	68	74	71	286	808.00
Chen Chien Chung	73	73	70	70	286	808.00
Paterno Braza	69	72	73	73	287	720.00
Gar Hamilton	73	72	70	72	287	720.00
Sukree Onsham	71	74	68	74	287	720.00
Dennis Saunders	71	70	72	75	288	675.00
Ho Ming Chung	69	72	70	77	288	675.00
Eleuterio Nival	71	71	70	76	288	675.00
Tom Sieckmann	70	73	73	72	288	675.00
Shozo Miyamoto	73	70	70	75	288	675.00
Lu Liang Huan	71	73	72	72	288	675.00
Shen Chung Shyan	70	72	72	75	289	620.00
Mark Thomas	71	72	68	78	289	620.00
Tony Jacklin	74	71	68	76	289	620.00
Hideyo Sugimoto	75	70	71	73	289	620.00
Kim Seung Hak	70	75	68	76	289	620.00
Wo Ching Fa	67	71	73	79	290	580.00
Ken Riley	73	72	71	74	290	580.00
George Serhan	73	72	71	74	290	580.00
Masayuki Imai	71	73	71	76	291	555.00
Dean Lind	71	71	74	75	291	555.00
Takashi Kurihara	72	69	75	76	292	540.00
Mamoru Kondo	74	68	73	77	292	540.00

Singapore Open

Singapore Island Country Club, Bukit Course, Singapore
Par 35–36—71; 6,645 yards

March 1–4
purse, U.S. $50,000

	SCORES				TOTAL	MONEY
Lu Hsi Chuen	71	70	70	69	280	$10,000.00
Hsu Sheng San	72	71	68	69	280	6,000.00
(Lu defeated Hsu on second hole of sudden-death play-off)						
Kazunari Takahashi	75	68	68	70	281	3,666.60
Hsieh Min Nan	69	70	72	70	281	3,666.60
Walter Godfrey	69	74	68	70	281	3,666.60
George Serhan	72	69	71	70	282	2,500.00
Kuo Chi Hsiung	71	71	73	69	284	2,250.00
Mike Soli	74	69	71	71	285	1,875.00
Kevin Jones	70	71	72	72	285	1,875.00
Masakichi Toda	72	70	75	69	286	1,375.00
Ho Ming Chung	74	69	74	69	286	1,375.00
James Booros	70	74	74	69	287	993.50
Marty Bohen	74	69	73	71	287	993.50
Yurio Akitomi	71	73	71	72	287	993.50
Lim Swee Chew	72	70	71	74	287	993.50
Kikuo Arai	71	72	75	70	288	675.00
Chen Chien Chin	78	67	72	71	288	675.00
Abdul Latiff	73	72	71	72	288	675.00
Maurice Bembridge	70	71	74	73	288	675.00
Peter Thomson	75	70	70	73	288	675.00
Mike Krantz	75	71	69	73	288	675.00
Sukree Onsham	70	71	71	76	288	675.00
Fritz Gambetta	70	74	65	79	288	675.00
Chang Chung Fa	73	70	75	71	289	462.50
Takeshi Shibata	72	66	72	74	289	462.50
Ben Arda	79	69	73	69	290	337.50
Toshiki Matsui	72	74	73	71	290	337.50
Lim Swee Wah	71	72	75	72	290	337.50
Poh Eng Chong	70	73	74	73	290	337.50
Tom Ducey	77	68	70	75	290	337.50
Wu Chin Fa	72	69	74	75	290	337.50
Hsu Chi San	73	70	72	75	290	337.50
Mya Aye	70	72	70	78	290	337,50
Norio Mikami	74	73	71	73	291	220.00
Ireneo Legaspi	74	68	74	75	291	220.00
Lim Kian Tiong	75	70	70	76	291	220.00
Mike Sholdar	70	73	77	72	292	47.50
Hung Fa	76	72	72	72	292	47.50
Lance Ten Broeck	74	72	74	72	292	47.50
David Milne	75	72	73	72	292	47.50
Sam Torrance	74	70	75	73	292	47.50
Kurt Cox	74	74	72	72	292	47.50
Mayalayan Ramayah	75	73	72	72	292	47.50
Blair Douglas	72	75	73	72	292	47.50
Keizo Yamada	77	69	73	73	292	47.50
Chen Tze Ming	74	74	71	73	292	47.50
Masayuki Imai	75	69	73	75	292	47.50
Lee Il Ahn	74	74	69	75	292	47.50
Choi Tae Woon	70	76	71	75	292	47.50
Tadaaki Uehara	71	72	74	75	292	47.50
Tatso Fujima	74	73	69	76	292	47.50

Malaysian Open

Royal Selangor Golf Club, Kuala Lumpur, Malaysia

March 8–11
purse, U.S $60,000

East Course: Par 36–36—72; 6,697 yards (First two rounds only)
West Course: Par 36–36—72; 6,621 yards (First two rounds only)
Old Course: Par 36–36—72; 6,888 yards (Last two rounds only)

	SCORES				TOTAL	MONEY
Lu Hsi Chuen	69	71	67	70	277	$10,000.00
Ron Milanovich	68	75	71	70	284	5,000.00
Tsutomu Irie	73	67	73	71	284	5,000.00
Chen Chien Chin	70	71	72	71	284	5,000.00
Kuo Chi Hsiung	75	67	74	69	285	3,250.00
Hal Underwood	69	77	70	69	285	3,250.00
Kurt Cox	73	72	73	68	286	1,741.50
Hsieh Min Nan	73	70	74	69	286	1,741.50
Bruce Douglas	70	72	74	70	286	1,741.50
George Serhan	70	72	72	72	286	1,741.50
Mayalayan Ramayah	69	74	71	72	286	1,741.50
Mike Soli	71	68	74	73	286	1,741.50
Sukree Onsham	73	73	71	70	287	1,150.00
Gar Hamilton	74	69	73	71	287	1,150.00
Chang Chung Fa	74	70	70	73	287	1,150.00
Mike Sholdar	74	70	75	69	288	875.00
Ho Ming Chung	77	70	72	69	288	875.00
Shen Chung Shyan	72	69	76	71	288	875.00
Ben Arda	69	74	72	73	288	875.00
Maurice Bembridge	74	73	69	72	288	875.00
Gaylord Burrows	73	72	70	73	288	875.00
Walter Godfrey	70	73	69	76	288	875.00
Mya Aye	72	73	68	75	288	875.00
Don Klenk	73	74	70	72	289	650.00
Nazamuddin Yusof	75	72	71	72	290	525.00
Kazunari Takahashi	78	69	71	72	290	525.00
Tsao Chien Teng	74	71	73	72	290	525.00
Chen Tze Ming	77	68	72	73	290	525.00
Norio Mikami	74	70	73	73	290	525.00
Rudy Lavares	68	71	75	76	290	525.00
Yurio Akitomi	72	69	73	76	290	525.00
Mike Hillsinger	71	75	72	73	291	390.50
Tatsuo Fujima	74	73	71	73	291	390.50
Mike Krantz	71	72	75	73	291	390.50
Hsu Sheng San	74	73	69	75	291	390.50
Kim Hak Seh	72	73	74	73	292	345.50
Choi Sang Ho	74	71	73	74	292	345.50
Tom Ducey	76	70	71	75	292	345.50
Choi Youn Soo	75	71	73	74	293	168.50
Jerry Minor	72	70	77	74	293	168.50
Marty Bohen	72	73	73	75	293	168.50
Hahn Chang Sang	71	73	73	76	293	168.50

Thailand Open

Royal Thai AFB Golf Course,, Don Muang, Bangkok, Thailand
Par 36–35—71; 6,817 yards

March 15–18
purse, U.S. $40,000

	SCORES				TOTAL	MONEY
Mike Krantz	71	70	74	67	282	$6,400
Jaime Gonzalez	74	69	68	71	282	3,600
(Krantz defeated Gonzalez on first hole of sudden-death play-off)						
Kurt Cox	69	73	72	69	283	2,350
Hahn Chang Sang	74	69	70	70	283	2,350
Lim Kian Tiong	71	72	70	71	284	1,733
Norio Mikami	76	71	67	70	284	1,733
Ron Milanovich	70	74	68	72	284	1,733
Hsu Chi San	67	74	74	70	285	1,450
George Serhan	72	71	68	74	285	1,450
Chen Tze Ming	73	78	67	68	286	1,150
Bruce Douglass	72	73	66	75	286	1,150
Pradhana Ngarmprom	73	70	70	73	286	1,150
Ireneo Legaspi	70	70	70	76	286	1,150
Mya Aye	70	78	69	70	287	925
Ho Ming Chung	73	75	69	70	287	925
Hsu Sheng San	72	74	71	71	288	800
Shen Chung Shyan	72	70	75	71	288	800
Takahiro Takeyasu	71	74	70	73	288	800
Kuo Chi Hsiung	71	75	74	69	289	650
Jeff Thomas	73	72	75	69	289	650
Matt Ellison	71	73	72	73	289	650
Tsutomu Irie	78	72	70	70	290	530
Chen Jung Chun	72	71	75	72	290	530
Martin Bohen	76	73	71	71	291	425
Brian Jones	76	69	74	72	291	425
Kazunari Takahashi	75	72	72	72	291	425
Rudy Lavares	73	72	73	73	291	425
Don Klenk	71	77	70	73	291	425

Preung Toyai	73	75	71	73	292	350
Cho Tae Woon	75	74	70	74	293	320
Tomomi Suzuki	74	73	73	74	294	200
Ben Arda	74	73	73	74	294	200
Chang Teh Kwei	72	75	74	73	294	200
Lu Hsi Chuen	71	75	77	71	294	200
Brian Evans	80	71	70	73	294	200
Doug Talley	75	78	70	71	294	200
Sukree Onsham	71	74	76	73	294	200
Tom Ducey	78	73	69	74	294	200
Prasarn Reuyruen	74	78	68	74	294	200
Adul Dhabpavibul	73	74	75	73	295	120
Boonta Srisakdi	74	73	75	73	295	120
Mamoru Kondo	74	76	73	73	296	100
Gaylord Burrows	73	78	71	74	296	100
Somsakdi Srisanga	72	76	74	74	296	100
Cho Tae Ho	73	73	73	77	296	100
Bob Henderson	75	75	71	76	297	
John Benda	73	78	72	76	299	
Barry Fleming	76	75	71	77	299	
Samruey Krutkaew	76	72	75	78	301	

Indian Open

Delhi Golf Club, New Delhi, India   March 22–25
Par 36–36—72; 6,925 yards   purse, U.S. $30,000

	SCORES				TOTAL	MONEY
Gaylord Burrows	73	70	70	71	284	$5,225
Hsu Chi San	75	68	67	75	285	3,325
Mike Krantz	67	69	76	75	287	2,280
Kazunari Takahashi	71	72	71	74	288	1,757
Peter Thomson	73	68	74	73	288	1,757
Brian Jones	69	79	70	71	289	1,520
Minoru Kumabe	73	75	72	70	290	1,377
Mya Aye	75	71	72	72	290	1,377
Lu Hsi Chuen	76	73	74	70	293	1,187
Jaime Gonzalez	73	74	71	75	293	1,187
Mike Sholdar	73	76	74	74	297	1,045
Noni	72	77	72	77	298	950
Ashok Malik°	72	79	72	75	298	
Lance Ten Broeck	76	75	77	71	299	855
Shen Chung Shyan	69	75	82	73	299	855
Marty Bohen	72	73	74	80	299	855
Okiji Yanagisawa	74	77	76	73	300	722
Hiroshi Wakita	73	72	77	78	300	722
Tom Ducey	69	80	73	78	300	722
John Benda	75	76	77	73	301	589
Barry Fleming	73	73	81	74	301	589
Sale Omohundro	74	75	76	76	301	589
Inder Pal	75	73	76	77	301	589
Rohtas	76	76	78	73	303	475
Om Prakash	79	75	73	76	303	475
Mike Soli	76	72	77	78	303	475
Archie Sopon	73	72	77	81	303	475
P. Pilling	71	77	77	79	304	418
Tomomi Suzuki	79	74	73	79	305	360
George Serhan	74	79	71	81	305	360
Michiyuki Kawanami	81	73	71	81	306	304
Yoshio Ichikawa	78	79	74	76	307	261
Ramesh Chand	79	76	81	71	307	261
Bob Henderson	76	81	75	76	308	218
Vikramjit Singh°	77	74	78	79	308	
Bruce Douglass	79	75	78	77	309	167
Mitsuo Kaneko	75	75	78	81	309	167
Toshihiko Kikuichi	81	75	72	81	309	167
Hisao Inoue	77	73	72	87	309	167
Jerry Minor	77	79	76	77	309	167
Alan Singh°	79	72	77	81	309	
Sandy Galbraith	74	79	78	80	311	128
Rick Mallicoat	75	71	78	87	311	128
Ryuzo Yamaguchi	78	74	83	77	312	104
Manmohan Singh°	80	74	77	82	313	
Peter Oakley	81	77	79	77	314	76
Rick Arguello	78	79	76	81	314	76
Koichi Hirabashi	77	79	78	80	314	76
Doug Talley	78	76	79	81	314	76
Simran Singh	78	81	74	81	314	76
Takayoshi Nishikawa	77	77	81	80	315	
Motomasa Aoki	76	76	78	85	315	
Mike Hillsinger	80	81	78	78	317	
Likhi Chand	79	79	79	80	317	
Ram Dayal	78	74	85	80	317	
Koichi Moriguchi	81	78	79	81	319	
Bob Burton	84	79	77	80	320	

°Amateur

Indonesian Open

Jakarta Golf Club, Rawamangun Course, Jakarta, Indonesia
Par 35—35—70; 6,400 yards

March 29–April 1
purse, U.S. $45,000

	SCORES				TOTAL	MONEY
Lu Hsi Chuen	67	67	70	68	272	$6,800.00
Mya Aye	63	70	69	71	273	3,900.00
Sukree Onsham	71	71	67	70	279	2,550.00
Don Klenk	70	71	70	68	279	2,550.00
Mike Hillsinger	74	67	68	71	280	2,000.00
Shen Chung Shyan	65	73	71	72	281	1,750.00
Hsu Chi San	71	68	70	72	281	1,750.00
Gaylord Burrows	69	73	71	69	282	1,550.00
Lance Ten Broeck	70	73	69	70	282	1,550.00
Bob Henderson	70	67	69	77	283	1,200.00
Brian Jones	74	74	67	68	283	1,200.00
Mayalayan Ramayah	68	71	71	73	283	1,200.00
Sandy Galbraith	74	68	70	71	283	1,200.00
Ryuzo Yamaguchi	72	69	70	72	283	1,200.00
Hal Underwood	68	69	72	75	284	937.50
Poh Eing Chong	74	69	68	73	284	937.50
Ireneo Legaspi	69	73	67	76	285	775.00
Kurt Cox	70	70	70	75	285	775.00
Kazunari Takahashi	66	70	74	75	285	775.00
Lim Swee Chew	70	71	71	73	285	775.00
Tom Ducey	69	73	71	73	286	565.00
Mike Krantz	69	69	78	70	286	565.00
Barry Fleming	69	72	71	74	286	565.00
Koichi Hirabayashi	71	72	69	74	286	565.00
Jaime Gonzalez	67	71	72	76	286	565.00
Bruce Douglass	74	72	70	70	286	565.00
Michiyuki Kawanami	70	73	72	72	287	407.00
Mike Soli	72	69	74	72	287	407.00
Hisao Inoue	69	73	73	72	287	407.00
Peter Thomson	71	71	74	71	287	407.00
Mitsuru Kojima	73	73	72	70	288	300.00
George Serhan	69	69	72	78	288	300.00
John Benda	72	73	75	68	288	300.00
Mike Sholdar	71	71	74	73	289	300.00
Toshihiko Kikuichi	73	75	70	72	290	300.00
Richard Mallicoat	71	74	70	75	290	300.00
Nazamudin Yusof	75	73	70	72	290	300.00
Lim Kian Tiong	71	77	71	71	290	300.00
Okiji Yanagisawa	73	74	75	69	291	300.00
Bob Burton	68	77	72	74	291	300.00
Sale Omohundro	71	75	69	76	291	300.00
Lim Swee Wah	73	77	71	71	292	300.00
Frank Conallin	70	73	76	73	292	300.00
Minoru Kumabe	69	75	74	75	293	300.00
Matt Ellison	73	74	74	72	293	300.00
Kishio Murata	77	73	72	72	294	
Kiyoshi Nakagawa	74	75	74	71	294	
Blair Douglas	72	73	73	76	294	
Takayoshi Nishikawa	75	76	72	72	295	
Tom Sieckmann	75	72	73	75	295	
Yoshio Ishikawa	71	76	72	76	295	

China Open

Peitou Kuo Hua Golf and Country Club, Taipei
Par 36—36—72; 6,866 yards

April 5–8
purse, U.S. $50,000

	SCORES				TOTAL	MONEY
Lu Liang Huan	70	72	71	74	287	$10,000.00
Chen Tze Ming	77	68	74	70	289	5,250.00
Hsu Chi San	72	72	71	75	290	3,250.00
Hsieh Min Nan	75	72	73	71	291	2,500.00
Hsu Sheng San	72	74	73	74	293	2,250.00
Kuo Chi Hsiung	71	76	74	73	294	2,000.00
Tsuneyuki Nakajima	72	75	72	77	296	1,625.00
Hsieh Yung Yo	75	73	73	75	296	1,625.00
Lu Hsi Chuen	76	75	75	70	296	1,625.00
Chen Tze Chung°	74	74	75	73	296	
Mike Krantz	76	75	76	71	298	1,375.00
Ho Ming Chung	78	75	75	71	299	1,111.00
Chen Chien Chin	76	72	75	76	299	1,111.00
Hasakichi Toda	74	73	76	76	299	1,111.00
Shen Chung Shyan	74	78	76	71	299	1,111.00
Hal Underwood	73	76	77	73	299	1,111.00
George Serhan	75	73	75	77	300	795.00
Bob Henderson	74	74	80	72	300	795.00
Chen Ching Po	75	81	74	70	300	795.00
Hung Fa	74	77	75	75	301	553.33
Chen Chien Yi	77	76	76	72	301	553.33
Chen Chin Chi	77	75	76	73	301	553.33
Chen K. C.	75	80	74	72	301	553.33
Sukree Onsham	72	82	73	74	301	553.33

Tsao Chien Teng	74	76	80	71	301	553.33
Jaime Gonazalez	77	78	73	74	302	440.00
Mitsuo Kaneko	78	78	73	74	303	427.50
Ryuko Yamaguchi	80	71	74	78	303	427.50
Lu Chun I	77	77	75	75	304	377.50
Hiroshi Wakita	81	73	77	73	304	377.50
Lai T. H.	76	76	74	79	305	286.43
Motomasa Aoki	78	76	77	74	305	286.43
Chang Ming Hsiung	76	80	73	76	305	286.43
Tom Sieckmann	76	76	77	76	305	286.43
Lim Kian Tiong	75	74	78	78	305	286.43
Lu Liang Wong	80	76	73	76	305	286.43
Mitsuru Kojima	75	76	76	78	305	286.43
Yoshio Ichikawa	78	74	77	77	306	210.00
Chen P. T.	78	78	74	76	306	210.00
Lance Ten Broeck	78	76	74	78	306	210.00
Wu Chin Fa	77	76	72	82	307	173.33
John Benda	76	74	80	77	307	173.33
Huang Ming Sheng	77	77	74	79	307	173.33
Chang Tong Liang°	79	77	80	71	307	
Eleuterio Nival	78	76	77	77	308	170.00
Chen Jung Chun	77	79	75	77	308	170.00
Chuang Cheng Hsiung	74	80	77	77	308	170.00
Lu C. S.°	79	76	79	74	308	
Tom Ducey	78	74	76	81	309	
Barry Fleming	78	76	77	79	310	

°Amateur

Korea Open

Seoul Country Club, Seoul, Korea
Par 36–36—72; 7,100 yards

April12–15
purse, U.S. $60,000

	SCORES				TOTAL	MONEY
Shen Chung Shyan	70	72	71	76	289	$11,000
Chen Tze Ming	69	71	73	78	291	5,700
Kuo Chi Hsiung	68	75	78	72	293	3,166
Lu Hsi Chuen	70	73	78	72	293	3,166
Hsu Sheng San	69	76	75	73	293	3,166
Kim Suk Bong	70	80	75	70	295	2,300
Bruce Douglass	73	78	76	69	296	2,000
Hsu Chi San	71	74	79	72	296	2,000
Ho Ming Chung	72	76	76	72	296	2,000
Jerry Minor	72	77	75	74	298	1,700
Cho Tae Woon	72	75	79	73	299	1,550
Son Heung Soo	75	80	75	70	300	1,375
Tatsuo Fugima	75	79	74	72	300	1,375
Chin S.H.	73	76	76	75	300	1,375
Chang Teh Kwei	72	78	74	76	300	1,375
Kurt Cox	75	77	77	72	301	1,025
Barry Fleming	71	84	74	72	301	1,025
Cho Tae Ho	74	75	78	74	301	1,025
Hahn Chang Sang	75	75	77	74	301	1,025
Kim Duck Joo	73	74	79	75	301	1,025
Mamoru Kondo	72	76	75	78	301	1,025
Choi Yoon III	74	74	83	71	302	675
Tsao Ching Teng	71	78	80	73	302	675
Park Jung Woong	72	76	80	74	302	675
Chen Chien Chi	73	77	75	77	302	675
Cho Am Gill	72	76	77	77	302	675
Norio Mikami	72	77	75	78	302	675
Chen Jung Chun	75	77	78	73	303	482
Kim Duk Choon	72	83	75	73	303	482
Takuo Terajima	7$	77	79	75	303	482
Lee II Ahn	74	71	80	78	303	482
Choi Sang Ho	70	78	77	78	303	482
Kiyoshi Nakagawa	77	77	75	75	304	390
Kang Young II	73	80	74	77	304	390
Choi Keum Cheon	73	77	77	81	304	390
Akira Yabe	74	77	80	74	305	340
Kim Seung Hak	72	78	77	78	305	340
Takayoshi Nishikawa	74	77	78	77	306	290
Kim Hack Seh	70	75	83	78	306	290
Toshihiko Kikuichi	73	79	75	79	306	290
Masahiko Yamamoto	74	80	76	77	307	200
Yeom Se Weon	73	81	77	77	308	200
Lim Kian Tiong	68	84	77	79	308	200
Moon Hong Sik	72	80	77	81	310	200
Park Kyong Chool°	74	80	77	77	312	
Mike Soli	69	79	83	83	314	200
Kim Joo Heun°	75	86	81	73	315	

°Amateur

Shizuoka Open

Shizuoka Country Club, Hamaoka Course, Shizuoka, Japan
Par 72; 6,917 yards

March 29–April 1
purse, ¥24,214,994[†]

	SCORES			TOTAL	MONEY
Akira Yabe	71	75	71	217	¥5,000,000
Kikuo Arai	71	79	69	219	1,900,000
Shigeru Noguchi	71	73	75	219	1,900,000
Yoshitaka Yamamoto	76	77	67	220	1,000,000
Masashi Ozaki	71	78	71	220	1,000,000
Koichi Uehara	66	77	77	220	1,000,000
Haruo Yasuda	74	76	71	221	800,000
Yoshihisa Iwashita	73	80	70	223	650,000
Katsuji Hasegawa	72	80	71	223	650,000
Seiichi Kanai	73	77	73	223	650,000
Masaji Kusakabe	73	81	70	224	475,000
Hsieh Yung Yo	75	77	72	224	475,000
Kazuo Yoshikawa	73	78	74	225	400,000
Akio Kanamoto	77	76	73	226	304,444
Namio Takasu	79	76	71	226	304,444
Masayuki Naito[*]	74	79	73	226	
Norio Suzuki	75	78	73	226	304,444
Toru Nakamura	74	78	74	226	304,444
Kosaku Shimada	74	78	74	226	304,444
Hideyo Sugimoto	72	79	75	226	304,444
Yuichi Yokoshima	74	77	75	226	304,444
Shinsaku Maeda	74	77	75	226	304,444
Tsuneyuki Nakajima	72	76	78	226	304,444
Ichiroh Togawa	74	82	71	227	215,000
Kenji Ueda	75	80	72	227	215,000
Sadao Sakashita	75	75	77	227	215,000
Yasuhiro Miyamoto	74	76	77	227	215,000
Toshiaki Sekimizu	72	84	72	228	170,000
Atsuo Takahashi	74	82	72	228	170,000
Masayuki Imai	76	79	73	228	170,000
Hiroshi Ishii	72	83	73	228	170,000
Isao Ohba	74	80	74	228	170,000
Mitsuhiko Masuda	74	80	75	229	145,000
Ichiro Teramoto	73	81	75	229	145,000
Shigeru Uchida	75	78	76	229	145,000
Chen Chien Chin	75	78	76	229	145,000
Isao Aoki	75	78	76	229	145,000
Kentaro Yamamoto	73	79	77	229	145,000
Kyoji Asai	73	77	79	229	145,000
Hsieh Min Nan	73	78	78	229	145,000
Osamu Hatano	76	80	74	230	126,666
Yoshimi Watanabe	73	80	77	230	126,666
Takashi Murakami	68	85	77	230	126,666
Masaru Amano	78	78	75	231	115,000
Kenji Mori	77	79	74	231	115,000
Tadami Ueno	76	79	76	231	115,000
Fujio Kobayashi	76	77	78	231	115,000
Hisashi Suzumura	72	78	81	231	115,000
Kazushige Kawano	78	78	76	232	100,000
Tomishige Ikeda	74	82	76	232	100,000

[*]Amateur
[†]220 yen = $1.00

Aso National Park Open

Aso Country Club, Kumamoto, Japan
Par 72; 7,012 yards

April 7–8
purse, ¥10,250,000

	SCORES		TOTAL	MONEY
Takashi Kurihara	73	76	149	¥1,500,00
Shinsaku Maeda	73	76	149	650,00
Haruo Yasuda	74	75	149	650,00
(Kurihara defeated Maeda and Yasuda on third hole of sudden-death play-off)				
Shigeru Noguchi	73	77	150	485,000
Isao Ohba	72	78	150	485,000
Fujio Kobayashi	76	75	151	433,334
Tadami Ueno	75	76	151	433,333
Shigeru Uchida	72	79	151	433,333
Masamitsu Oguri	73	79	152	304,000
Masaru Sasaki	73	79	152	304,000
Takashi Murakami	72	80	152	304,000
Hideo Ishii	75	77	152	304,000
Masaji Kusakabe	71	81	152	304,000
Katsuji Kikuchi	76	77	153	168,334
Kazunari Takahashi	74	79	153	168,334
Shichiro Enomoto	73	80	153	168,333
Seiji Katayama	73	80	153	168,333
Koichi Uehara	72	81	153	168,333
Minoru Nakamura	71	82	153	168,333
Yoshiteru Aranoh	75	79	154	108,334

Toshiki Matsui	75	79	154	108,334
Toshihiro Matsuda	74	80	154	108,333
Toshiaki Sekimitzu	74	80	154	108,333
Satsuki Takahashi	73	81	154	108,333
Kazushige Kawano	73	81	154	108,333
Seiichi Kanai	74	81	155	100,000
Namio Takasu	76	79	155	100,000
Minoru Nakamura	76	79	155	100,000
Toshiyuki Tsuchiyama	72	83	155	100,000
Seiji Ebihara	74	82	156	80,000
Koichi Inoue	76	80	156	80,000
Kazuo Hashimoto	76	80	156	80,000
Yuichi Yokoshima	74	83	157	70,000
Osamu Hatano	74	83	157	70,000
Masahiko Yamamoto	76	81	157	70,000
Mitsuhiro Kitta	76	81	157	70,000
Fumio Tanaka	73	84	157	70,000
Ichiro Teramoto	75	82	157	70,000
Kazuo Yoshikawa	75	82	157	70,00
Toshikazu Torisawa	72	85	157	70,000
Kenji Ueda	74	84	158	60,000
Hisashi Suzumura	73	85	158	60,000
Hideyo Sugimoto	75	83	158	60,000
Shimon Takamatsu	75	84	159	56,667
Saburo Fujiki	76	83	159	56,667
Minoru Hiyoshi	75	84	159	56,666
Takemitsu Uranishi	75	85	160	50,000
Nobuhiro Sakata	74	86	160	50,000
Shoichi Sato	76	84	160	50,000
Takahiro Takeyasu	76	85	161	30,000

Kuzuha International

*Kuzuha Public Golf Course,*Osaka, Japan   April 14–15
Par 70; 6,238 yards   purse, ¥11,928,000

	SCORES		TOTAL	MONEY
Hsieh Min Nan	68	66	134	¥2,500.000
Fujio Kobayashi	72	64	136	1,000,000
Kikuo Arai	72	66	138	458,000
Teruo Sugihara	70	68	138	458,000
Takashi Kurihara	70	68	138	458,000
Koichi Inoue	70	68	138	458,000
Koichi Uehara	69	69	138	458,000
Tadashi Kitta	69	70	139	290,000
Akio Kanamoto	68	71	139	290,000
Masaji Kusakabe	72	68	140	202,000
Namio Takasu	71	69	140	202,000
Yoshihisa Iwashita	71	69	140	202,000
Greg Norman	69	71	140	202,000
Masayuki Imai	69	71	140	202.000
Toru Nakamura	69	71	140	202,000
Mitsuhiro Kitta	69	71	140	202,000
Hiroshi Ishii	67	73	140	202,000
Michael Krantz	71	70	141	145,000
Kosaku Shimada	70	71	141	145,000
Yoshitaka Yamamoto	72	70	142	120,000
Lu Liang Huan	72	70	142	120,000
Tadami Ueno	72	70	142	120,000
Katsuji Hasegawa	72	70	142	120,000
Yoshikazu Yokoshima	71	71	142	120,000
Norio Suzuki	71	71	142	120,000
Shinsaku Maeda	70	72	142	120,000
Akira Yabe	70	72	142	120,000
Toshiharu Kawada	74	69	143	108,000
Fritz Gambetta	73	70	143	108,000
Kesahiko Uchida	71	72	143	108,000
Ichiro Teramoto	71	72	143	108,000
Shozo Miyamoto	69	74	143	108,000
Hisashi Suzumura	68	75	143	108,000
Takao Hara	67	76	143	108,000
Sukree Onsham	74	70	144	100,000
Haruo Yasuda	73	71	144	100,000
Hsieh Yung Yo	73	71	144	100,000
Brian Jones	73	71	144	100,000
Masaru Yano	71	73	144	100,000
Takaaki Kawano	70	74	144	100,000
Kenji Mori	73	72	145	80,000
Kazuo Yoshikawa	73	72	145	80,000
Chen Chien Chin	73	72	145	80,000
Eleuterio Nival	72	73	145	80,000
Kenichi Yamada	72	73	145	80,000
Seiichi Kanai	71	74	145	80,000
Hideo Ishii	72	73	145	80,000
Shigeru Uchida	70	75	145	80,000
Takahiro Takeyasu	74	72	146	66,000
Ben Arda	73	73	146	66,000

Dunlop International

Ibaraki Country Club, Tokyo, Japan
Par 36-36—72; 7,003 yards

April 19–22
purse, U.S. $100,000

	SCORES				TOTAL	MONEY
Hiroshi Ishii	70	68	70	70	278	$20,000.00
Seiji Ebihara	70	74	73	64	281	8,500.00
Tateo Ozaki	70	71	72	68	281	8,500.00
Kazunari Takahashi	72	70	68	71	281	8,500.00
Isao Aoki	70	73	72	67	282	3,666.67
Mya Aye	71	69	72	70	282	3,666.67
Lu Liang Huan	71	69	69	73	282	3,666.67
Taichi Nakagawa	72	72	73	67	284	2,250.00
Mike Soli	71	68	72	73	284	2,250.00
Tadami Ueno	73	73	66	73	285	1,450.00
Kurt Cox	72	69	70	74	285	1,450.00
Yoshitaka Yamamoto	72	69	76	69	286	1,200.00
Kazuo Yoshikawa	71	71	73	71	286	1,200.00
Masashi Ozaki	69	67	74	76	286	1,200.00
Greg Norman	73	71	73	70	287	980.00
Haruo Yasuda	73	71	72	71	287	980.00
Namio Takasu	73	70	70	74	287	980.00
Kosaku Shimada	72	73	73	70	288	785.00
Yasuhiro Funatogawa	73	69	72	74	288	785.00
Fujio Kobayashi	68	72	74	74	288	785.00
Hsieh Yung Yo	73	71	68	76	288	785.00
Kenji Mori	70	76	74	69	289	715.00
Ho Ming Chung	73	74	70	74	289	715.00
Yoshihisa Iwashita	75	70	71	73	289	715.00
Masaji Kusakabe	71	72	70	76	289	715.00
Seiichi Kanai	74	73	72	71	290	680.00
Kuo Chi Hsiung	73	69	75	73	290	680.00
Mike Krantz	73	73	71	73	290	680.00
Yasuhiro Miyamoto	71	76	72	72	291	650.00
Johji Yokoi	70	74	74	73	291	650.00
Bob Henderson	72	70	74	75	291	650.00
Koichi Inoue	72	76	72	72	292	610.00
Noel Ratcliffe	71	74	74	73	292	610.00
Mario Siodina	70	76	73	73	292	610.00
Yoshikazu Yokoshima	70	73	75	74	292	610.00
Katsuji Hasegawa	72	72	73	75	292	610.00
Bruce Douglass	74	74	76	69	293	570.00
Akira Yabe	73	75	74	71	293	570.00
Mitsuhito Sekiya	74	73	73	73	293	570.00
Lu Hsi Chuen	76	72	75	71	294	542.00
Chen Chien Chun	74	73	74	73	294	542.00
Norio Suzuki	75	71	73	75	294	542.00
Kesahiko Uchida	73	73	72	76	294	542.00
Tatsuo Fujima	70	72	73	79	294	542.00
Minoru Nakamura	75	73	76	71	295	537.50
Tomomi Suzuki	75	71	76	73	295	537.50
Tsuneyuki Nakajima	76	72	74	73	295	537.50
Yurio Akitomi	73	75	73	74	295	537.50
Shigeru Uchida	73	73	74	75	295	537.50
Shen Chung Shyan	74	74	72	75	295	537.50
Chen Chien Chin	76	71	72	76	295	537.50
Kikuo Arai	74	72	72	77	295	537.50

Chunichi Crowns

Nagoya Golf Club, Aichi, Japan
Par 70; 6,578 yards

April 26–29
purse, ¥60,000,000

	SCORES				TOTAL	MONEY
Isao Aoki	67	73	69	70	279	¥12,000,000
Toru Nakamura	71	77	65	67	280	5,250,000
Haruo Yasuda	69	71	70	70	280	5,250,000
Lu Hsi Chuen	69	73	71	70	283	2,700,000
Namio Takasu	73	73	69	69	284	2,150,000
Kenji Mori	67	74	69	74	284	2,150,000
Lu Liang Huan	68	72	69	76	285	1,700,000
Graham Mash	69	71	71	74	285	1,700,000
Yoshikazu Yokoshima	68	74	75	69	286	1,450,000
Hsu Sheng San	71	76	70	69	286	1,450,000
Cho Tae Un	74	74	70	69	287	1,110,000
Koichi Inoue	70	76	70	71	287	1,110,000
Kurt Cox	70	77	66	74	287	1,110,000
Ben Arda	69	76	70	72	287	1,110,000
Masashi Ozaki	70	73	70	75	287	1,110,000
Kosaku Shimada	68	77	73	70	288	900,000
Chen Chien Chung	77	72	73	67	289	825,000
Peter Thomson	70	76	70	73	289	825,000
Chi Tze Ming	73	71	75	71	290	682,500
Hideo Noguchi	71	76	71	72	290	682,500
Chen Chien Chin	73	73	70	74	290	682,500

Shigeru Uchida	70	74	73	73	290	682,500
Masaji Kusakabe	69	75	77	70	291	560,000
Kuo Chi Hsiung	70	75	75	71	291	560,000
Hsieh Min Nan	72	74	74	71	291	560,000
Koichi Uehara	71	76	71	73	291	560,000
Seiichi Kanai	72	75	71	73	291	560,000
Yoshitaka Yamamoto	72	75	68	76	291	560,000
Tsuneyuki Nakajima	74	76	73	69	292	480,000
Greg Norman	75	75	69	73	292	480,000
Teruo Suzuki	73	75	70	75	293	410,000
Hsieh Yung Yo	74	75	67	77	293	410,000
Isao Ohba	70	76	77	70	293	410,000
Tadashi Kitta	76	73	75	69	293	410,000
Taichiro Kanaya°	73	73	74	73	293	
Masayuki Imai	75	74	71	73	293	410,000
Hisashi Suzumura	75	74	71	73	293	410,000
Michael Krantz	74	73	72	74	293	410,000
Hideyo Sugimoto	72	79	69	73	293	410,000
Katsuji Hasegawa	73	75	76	70	294	335,000
Takahiro Takeyasu	73	76	74	71	294	335,000
Osamu Hatano	75	76	72	71	294	335,000
Fujio Kobayashi	71	76	74	73	294	335,000
Bob Byman	73	77	71	73	294	335,000
Masahiko Yamamoto	72	74	74	74	294	335,000
Kazuo Yoshikawa	70	77	77	72	296	290,000
Akio Kanamoto	74	75	75	73	296	290,000
Yasuhiro Miyamoto	77	74	70	75	296	290,000
Toshiki Matsui	73	76	74	74	297	265,000
Akira Yabe	70	74	76	77	297	265,000

° Amateur

Kanagawa Open

Yokohama Country Club, Yokohama, Japan
Par 72; 6,925 yards

May 1–2
purse, ¥11,387,000

	SCORES		TOTAL	MONEY
Kenji Mori	75	68	143	¥2,000,000
Takashi Murakami	74	70	144	1,000,000
Yoshihisa Iwashita	72	72	144	1,000,000
Yutaka Hanekawa°	71	73	144	
Seiichi Kanai	72	74	146	456,000
Shichiroh Enomoto	72	74	146	456,000
Keiji Yoshitake	73	73	146	456,000
Haruo Yasuda	70	77	147	300,000
Isao Aoki	75	72	147	300,000
Akira Yabe	77	70	147	300,000
Takaaki Kawano	73	74	147	300,000
Sho Murakami	75	73	148	240,000
Fumio Tanaka	73	75	148	240,000
Yoshio Kusayanagi	75	74	149	190,000
Masaru Sasaki	76	73	149	190,000
Mitsuo Kaneko	75	74	149	190,000
Tamotsu Kiyota	74	75	149	190,000
Shun Nakamura	74	75	149	190,000
Hiroshi Tomizuka	77	72	149	190,000
Mitsutaka Kawano	76	74	150	155,000
Shuichi Yamaguchi	73	77	150	155,000
Tomonori Uchida	77	73	150	150,000
Akira Yatabe	76	75	151	113,000
Tsutomu Ogino	74	77	151	113,000
Yoshio Sotoyama	74	77	151	113,000
Masayuki Naito°	77	74	151	
Shigeo Moriyama°	76	75	151	
Munehiro Yamauchi°	75	76	151	
Kikuo Arai	77	75	152	100,000
Masami Hashimoto	76	76	152	100,000
Kuniaki Sato	75	77	152	100,000
Ryoichi Tomomitsu	76	77	153	80,000
Kinshiroh Tsukimoto	75	78	153	80,000
Eiji Komatsuzaki	75	78	153	80,000
Takao Tsuchida	75	78	153	80,000
Mitsuo Uehara	76	78	154	70,000
Masayuki Asahi	77	77	154	70,000
Yukio Ito	73	81	154	30,000
Toru Kawaguchi	74	81	155	60,000
Isao Someya	75	80	155	60,000
Shigeru Kanaumi	76	80	156	60,000
Torakichi Nakamura	77	80	157	52,500
Koichi Ono	77	80	157	52,500
Minoru Nakamura	77	80	157	52,500
Yoshio Kakizawa	74	83	157	52,500
Futoshi Irino	77	80	157	20,000
Teruo Maruyama	77	81	158	50,000
Hideo Jindoh	77	84	161	50,000

° Amateur

Fuji Sankei Classic

Higashi Matsuyama Country Club
Par 72; 7,112 yards

May 10–13
purse, ¥29,210,000

		SCORES			TOTAL	MONEY
Shoichi Sato	68	71	75	69	283	¥6,000,000
Isao Aoki	69	70	71	74	284	3,000,000
Toru Nakamura	73	71	74	68	286	2,000,000
Toshiharu Kawada	75	70	73	69	287	1,500,000
Hiroshi Ishii	72	71	73	72	288	950,000
Masashi Ozaki	70	74	69	75	288	950,000
Hsieh Min Nan	73	71	73	72	289	750,000
Akira Yabe	71	72	73	73	289	750,000
Kosaku Shimada	71	71	74	73	289	750,000
Toshiaki Sekimizu	77	70	74	69	290	600,000
Lu Hsi Chuen	75	72	72	71	290	600,000
Kikuo Arai	72	69	76	73	290	600,000
Osamu Hatano	76	71	74	70	291	432,500
Mya Aye	75	72	73	71	291	432,500
Seiichi Kanai	73	73	74	71	291	432,500
Chi Tze Ming	74	70	74	73	291	432,500
Kenichi Yamada	76	70	76	70	292	315,000
Katsuji Hasegawa	74	73	75	70	292	315,000
Hsieh Yung Yo	73	76	72	71	292	315,000
Takashi Kurihara	77	69	73	73	292	315,000
Tsuneyuki Nakajima	75	69	73	75	292	315,000
Takashi Murakami	71	72	73	76	292	315,000
Kazuo Yoshikawa	73	76	72	72	293	255,000
Yoshikazu Yokoshima	71	76	74	72	293	255,000
Haruo Yasuda	71	75	74	73	293	255,000
Norio Suzuki	72	74	73	74	293	255,000
Tsutomu Irie	68	72	75	79	294	177,500
Nobuo Takahashi	74	70	72	78	294	177,500
Tateo Ozaki	70	73	78	73	294	177,500
Namio Takasu	74	74	73	73	294	177,500
Lu Liang Huan	70	72	78	74	294	177,500
Tatsuo Fujima	73	74	73	74	294	177,500
Shen Chung Shyan	72	70	75	77	294	177,500
Tadashi Kitta	75	69	73	77	294	177,500
Shichiro Enomoto	75	74	73	73	295	132,000
Mitsuo Watanabe	78	81	82	74	295	132,000
Fujio Kobayashi	74	75	76	70	295	132,000
Koichi Uehara	76	72	77	70	295	132,000
Shiroh Matsuda	68	81	70	76	295	132,000
Masahiko Yamamoto	72	76	74	74	296	122,500
Seiji Ogawa	77	71	73	75	296	122,500
Yasuhiro Miyamoto	73	76	72	75	296	122,500
Brian Jones	73	71	79	73	296	122,500
Masayuki Imai	72	76	74	75	297	116,666
Yoshimasa Fujii	75	72	79	71	297	116,666
Takahiro Takeyasu	73	76	75	73	297	166,666
Kuo Chi Hsiung	73	73	76	76	298	110,000
Masaru Amano	72	77	72	77	298	110,000
Akio Toyoda	70	75	75	78	298	110,000
Fumio Tanaka	75	74	74	76	299	105,000

Yomiuri Open

Yomiuri Country Club, Osaka, Japan
Par 73; 7,047 yards

May 24–27
purse, ¥30,000,000

		SCORES			TOTAL	MONEY
Teruo Sugihara	72	71	71	73	287	¥6,000,000
Masashi Ozaki	72	71	72	72	287	3,300,000
(Sugihara defeated Ozaki on second hole of sudden-death play-off)						
Lu Liang Huan	76	71	69	72	288	2,000,000
Hsieh Yung Yo	74	72	72	71	289	1,500,000
Akira Yabe	73	76	70	72	291	1,000,000
Kikuo Arai	72	73	73	73	291	1,000,000
Seiichi Kanai	71	79	71	70	291	1,000,000
Kenji Mori	73	73	74	71	291	1,000,000
Yoshio Kaku	76	73	70	72	291	1,000,000
Lu Hsi Chuen	72	73	74	72	291	1,000,000
Tsuneyuki Nakajima	72	69	80	71	292	725,000
Yasuhiro Miyamoto	70	75	75	72	292	725,000
Hsieh Min Nan	75	72	73	72	292	725,000
Ben Arda	72	74	73	73	292	725,000
Kosaku Shimada	71	70	79	73	293	575,000
Fujio Kobayashi	73	75	71	74	293	575,000
Shinsaku Maeda	73	74	72	76	295	480,000
Masaji Kusakabe	77	69	71	78	295	480,000
Koichi Inoue	77	74	74	71	296	403,000
Isao Aoki	74	73	74	75	296	403,000
Kohichi Uehara	74	73	74	75	296	403,000
Hiroshi Ishii	70	77	77	73	297	350,000
Kenichi Yamad	79	72	69	77	297	350,000
Akio Kanamoto	72	77	73	76	298	310,000
Toru Nakamura	69	79	72	78	298	310,000

Norio Suzuki	77	76	74	72	299	285,000
Haruo Yasuda	77	77	70	75	299	285,000.
Takashi Murakami	79	78	70	73	300	270,000
Tademi Ueno	76	73	79	73	301	260,000
Takahisa Ohtsuka*	77	78	74	72	301	
Kesahiko Uchida	77	75	75	75	302	250,000
Namio Takasu	76	76	77	74	303	240,000
Yoshikazu Yokoshima	79	71	82	72	304	230,000
Shigeru Uchida	75	81	79	71	306	220,000
Seiji Katayama	78	73	77	79	307	210,000
Fuminori Sano*	81	75	73	78	307	
Peter Thomson	73	85	75	76	309	200,000
Noriaki Kimura*	76	79	79	75	309	
Masao Shioda*	81	75	78	76	310	
Shinsuke Maeda*	84	80	75	77	316	
Tomo Ichinose*	83	73	82	81	319	
Katsuyuki Miura*	81	82	79	82	324	

*Amateur

Mitsubishi Gallant

Oharai Golf Club
Par 72; 7,190 yards

May 31–'une 3
purse, ¥29,939,944

	SCORES				TOTAL	MONEY
Toru Nakamura	74	72	71	68	285	¥6,000,000
Yoshio Kusayanagi	72	69	75	70	286	3,100,000
Masashi Ozaki	70	72	77	68	287	1,533,333
Masaji Kusakabe	71	73	73	70	287	1,533,333
Miller Barber	75	67	73	72	287	1,533,333
Isao Aoki	71	72	77	68	288	1,000,000
Lu Hsi Chuen	75	70	72	72	289	900,000
Fujio Kobayashi	75	73	73	69	290	750,000
Yasuhiro Miyamoto	68	73	72	77	290	750,000
Kikuo Arai	75	69	72	74	290	750,000
Tateo Ozaki	72	77	70	72	291	625,000
Hsu Sheng San	72	73	72	74	291	625,000
Seiichi Kanai	76	70	74	72	292	530,000
Hsieh Min Nan	73	71	74	74	292	530,000
Kazuo Hashimoto	70	70	78	74	292	530,000
Tsuneyuki Nakajima	75	73	72	73	293	425,000
Toshiki Matsui	75	72	72	74	293	425,000
Koichi Inoue	71	75	78	69	293	425,000
Tsutomu Irie	79	70	75	69	293	425,000
Yoshikazu Yokoshima	76	69	76	73	294	310,000
Hsieh Yung Yo	73	72	74	75	294	310,000
Hiroshi Ishii	76	72	72	74	294	310,000
Akira Yabe	73	73	78	70	294	310,000
Kazuo Yoshikawa	71	73	74	76	294	310,000
Kesahiko Uchida	76	73	73	73	295	230,000
Seiji Ebihara	72	75	75	73	295	230,000
Naomichi Ozaki	73	72	75	75	295	230,000
Sukree Onsham	71	72	77	75	295	230,000
Fujio Ishii	72	74	73	76	295	230,000
Chen Chien Chung	75	73	73	75	296	190,000
Ben Arda	71	71	78	76	296	190,000
Shoichi Sato	73	74	71	78	296	190,000
Teruo Sugihara	76	74	73	74	297	155,000
Norio Suzuki	77	73	75	72	297	155,000
Isao Ohba	75	74	76	72	297	155,000
Minoru Kawakami	73	75	75	74	297	155,000
Ikuhiro Funatogawa	74	74	74	76	298	138,000
Fumio Tanaka	73	72	76	77	298	138,000
Kuo Chi Hsiung	73	74	74	77	298	138,000
Tomomi Suzuki	77	69	74	78	298	138,000
Yoshihisa Iwashita	76	71	80	71	298	138,000
Saburoh Fujiki	71	75	76	77	299	125,714
Osamu Hatano	75	73	74	77	299	125,714
Chohji Noguchi	74	74	74	77	299	125,714
Masahiko Yamamoto	73	75	76	75	299	125,714
Shiroh Kubo	73	72	78	76	299	125,714
Hsu Chi San	76	73	74	76	299	125,714
Shinsaku Maeda	75	73	75	76	299	125,714
Nobuo Takahashi	78	70	75	77	300	113,333
Hideo Noguchi	78	71	72	79	300	113,333

Tohoku Classic

Nishi Sendai Country Club, Miyagi, Japan
Par 72; 6,996 yards

June 7–10
purse, ¥24,579,997

	SCORES				TOTAL	MONEY
Toru Nakamure	73	67	69	69	278	¥5,000,000
Hsieh Min Nan	69	71	66	72	278	2,700,000

(Nakamura defeated Min Nan on second hole of sudden-death play-off)

Hiroshi Ishii	69	67	69	74	279	1,500,000
Yoshitaka Yamamoto	68	71	71	71	281	1,000,000
Chi Tze Ming	67	72	73	71	283	800,000
Haruo Yasuda	71	71	71	70	283	800,000
Yoshihisa Iwashita	69	69	74	71	283	800,000
Shoichi Sato	73	70	68	73	284	600,000
Kikuo Arai	76	71	70	68	285	500,000
Teruo Sugihara	71	74	71	69	285	500,000
Akio Kanamoto	67	70	73	75	285	500,000
Kuo Chi Hsiung	69	77	70	70	286	350,000
Chen Chien Chin	71	72	72	71	286	350,000
Tsuneyuki Nakajima	67	70	76	73	286	350,000
Yasuhiro Miyamoto	72	71	71	72	286	350,000
Lu Liang Huan	69	70	74	73	286	350,000
Masashi Ozaki	69	70	72	75	286	350,000
Hsu Chi San	72	74	71	70	287	240,000
Norihiko Matsumoto	69	75	73	70	287	240,000
Ichiro Teramoto	70	73	73	71	287	240,000
Kosaku Shimada	74	66	74	73	287	240,000
Hsieh Yung Yo	70	73	70	74	287	240,000
Kenji Mori	68	71	72	76	287	240,000
Seiichi Kanai	71	72	75	70	288	213,333
Toshiki Matsui	69	74	71	74	288	213,333
Takashi Murakami	73	67	73	75	288	213,333
Norio Suzuki	71	76	72	70	289	196,000
Tsutomu Irie	71	76	72	70	289	196,000
Satsuki Takahashi	72	71	75	71	289	196,000
Hisashi Suzumura	70	70	74	75	289	196,000
Lu Hsi Chuen	70	71	72	76	289	196,000
Yoshikazu Yokoshima	75	72	72	71	290	180,000
Wataru Murakami	70	71	77	72	290	180,000
Sadao Sakashita	75	68	74	73	290	180,000
Kazuo Yoshikawa	69	75	77	70	291	164,000
Shinsaku Maeda	74	72	72	73	291	164,000
Ichiro Togawa	72	72	73	74	291	164,000
Koichi Uehara	71	75	70	75	291	164,000
Minoru Hiyoshi	72	72	72	75	291	164,000
Toshiaki Sekimizu	75	69	76	72	292	152,500
Isao Ohba	70	73	75	74	292	152,500
Brian Jones	73	74	75	70	292	152,500
Ben Arda	74	72	75	71	292	152,500
Shiro Kubo	73	71	77	72	293	146,666
Hisao Inoue	71	73	74	75	293	146,666
Shigeru Uchida	75	72	75	71	293	146,666
Masaji Kusakabe	74	70	77	73	294	138,000
Jinya Taniguchi	70	76	73	75	294	138,000
Koji Nakajima	71	71	77	75	294	138,000
Harunobu Fujii	71	73	73	77	294	138,000

Sapporo Tokyu Open

Sapporo Kokusai Country Club, Sapporo, Japan
Par 72; 6,949 yards

June 14–17
purse, ¥24,930,000

	SCORES				TOTAL	MONEY
Yasuhiro Miyamoto	69	67	71	73	280	¥5,000,000
Teruo Sugihara	68	73	71	70	282	2,800,000
Hisashi Suzumura	70	70	73	70	283	1,425,000
Masaji Kusakabe	72	69	70	72	283	1,425,000
Norio Suzuki	71	69	75	69	284	1,000,000
Kenji Mori	71	74	71	69	285	800,000
Kazuo Yoshikawa	71	75	69	70	285	800,000
Lu Liang Huan	69	72	70	74	285	800,000
Haruo Yasuda	70	73	73	70	286	600,000
Satsuki Takahashi	70	71	71	74	286	600,000
Tsuneyuki Nakajima	77	70	71	69	287	490,000
Hsieh Min Nan	72	74	71	70	287	490,000
Teruo Suzumura	73	73	70	71	287	490,000
Peter Thomson	69	75	72	72	288	400,000
Hiroshi Ishii	68	73	73	74	288	400,000
Namio Takasu	70	72	73	73	288	400,000
Hsieh Yung Yo	73	72	76	68	289	320,000
Akio Kanamoto	77	69	74	69	289	320,000
Chen Chien Chin	75	68	72	74	289	320,000
Ichiroh Togawa	70	72	73	74	289	320,000
Akira Yabe	71	74	76	69	290	255,000
Wataru Horiguchi	71	74	74	71	290	255,000
Isao Ohba	74	72	71	73	290	255,000
Mya Aye	71	70	75	74	290	255,000
Brian Jones	76	72	72	71	291	225,000

Yoshikazu Yokoshima	71	70	76	74	291	225,000
Yoshitaka Yamamoto	75	69	75	73	292	205,000
Tsutomu Irie	76	71	74	71	292	205,000
Kanae Nobechi	74	74	72	73	293	180,000
Shiroh Kubo	72	71	74	76	293	180,000
Chen Chien Chung	72	74	76	71	293	180,000
Takashi Kurihara	71	73	78	71	293	180,000
Shinsaku Maeda	72	71	79	72	294	160,000
Mitsuhiko Masuda	72	75	72	76	295	155,000
Toru Nakamura	74	73	75	73	295	155,000
Fujio Kobayashi	72	75	69	79	295	155,000
Renkyoku Sugiyama	72	76	71	77	296	130,000
Tadami Ueno	71	73	75	77	296	130,000
Koichi Inoue	73	75	76	72	296	130,000
Saburoh Fujimoto	75	72	76	73	296	130,000
Shigeru Uchida	72	73	73	78	296	130,000
Tadashi Kitta	75	72	76	73	296	130,000
Nobuo Takahashi	72	76	74	74	296	130,000
Chen Ching Po	69	78	77	73	297	115,000
Hideyo Noguchi	75	72	77	73	297	115,000
Akio Toyoda	70	76	76	75	297	115,000
Kikuo Arai	70	77	76	73	298	110,000
Kuo Chi Hsiung	74	72	76	76	298	110,000
Osamu Watanabe	75	70	76	78	299	110,000
Ichiro Teramoto	74	72	80	83	299	110,000

Pepsi-Wilson

Hachinohe Country Club
Par 71; 6,702 yards

June 21–24
purse, ¥25,000,000

	SCORES				TOTAL	MONEY
Mya Aye	64	70	67	73	274	¥5,000,000
Hiroshi Ishii	70	68	68	71	277	2,500,000
Ben Arda	70	64	74	70	278	1,500,000
Isao Aoki	66	70	69	74	279	933,400
Koichi Inoue	71	68	67	73	279	933,400
Lu Liang Huan	67	68	71	73	279	933,400
Teruo Sugihara	71	68	66	75	280	650,000
Shinsaku Maeda	72	64	73	71	280	650,000
Fujio Kobayashi	69	71	71	70	281	550,000
Toru Nakamura	70	68	67	77	282	480,000
Namio Takasu	72	66	70	74	282	480,000
Kuo Chie Hsiung	67	70	69	76	282	480,000
Haruo Yasuda	70	71	71	71	283	430,000
Hsieh Min Nan	69	71	69	74	283	430,000
Peter Thomson	66	73	73	73	285	390,000
Hsieh Yung Yo	70	69	73	73	285	390,000
Toshiyuki Tsuchiyama	70	70	75	71	286	315,000
Masahiko Yamamoto	69	73	69	75	286	315,000
Takashi Murakami	68	69	72	77	286	315,000
Kim Seck Hack	73	66	72	75	286	315,000
Yasuhiro Miyamoto	71	73	70	72	286	315,000
Mitsuo Watanabe	71	71	73	71	286	315,000
Masashi Ozaki	74	69	75	69	287	250,000
Seiji Ebihara	65	72	76	74	287	250,000
Yoshio Kusayanagi	70	71	74	72	287	250,000
Hisashi Suzumura	71	70	74	72	287	250,000
Norio Suzuki	71	71	75	70	287	250,000
Yurio Akitomi	72	65	68	83	288	203,000
Gen Tahara	70	70	69	79	288	203,000
Kazuo Yoshikawa	70	71	70	77	288	203,000
Tadao Nakamura	70	72	70	76	288	203,000
Hsu Chi San	71	73	74	70	288	203,000
George Yokoi	76	66	69	78	289	160,000
Masaji Kusakabe	68	73	70	78	289	160,000
Ichiro Togawa	70	69	72	78	289	160,000
Brian Jones	71	73	72	73	289	160,000
Tsuneyuki Nakajima	71	72	69	77	289	160,000
Minoru Kawakami	68	75	70	76	289	160,000
Ikuhiro Funatogawa	70	72	71	76	289	160,000
Shigeru Uchida	72	68	73	76	289	160,000
Kenichi Yamada	69	71	77	72	289	160,000
Minoru Nakamura	69	73	74	73	289	160,000
Naomichi Ozaki	72	70	78	69	289	160,000
Yuichi Yokoshima	70	73	71	76	290	125,000
Kenji Mori	72	69	71	78	290	125,000
Toshiki Matsui	71	71	71	77	290	125,000
Hideyo Sugimoto	73	67	77	74	291	115,000
Yoshihisa Iwashita	70	68	71	83	292	103,800
Masao Kanaya	69	75	75	73	292	103,800
Tadayoshi Ueno	74	70	70	78	292	103,800

Tokinodai Country Club
Par 72;

June 28–July 1
purse, ¥12,480,000

	SCORES				TOTAL	MONEY
Toru Nakamura	69	66	68	70	273	¥2,000,000
Yasuhiro Miyamoto	69	67	70	71	277	1,100,000
Shigeru Uchida	65	72	72	68	277	1,100,000
Norio Suzuki	70	68	69	72	279	700,000
Yoshitaka Yamamoto	68	71	70	71	280	550,000
Koichi Inoue	71	71	70	68	280	550,000
Hiroshi Ishii	65	76	69	71	281	375,000
Kazuo Yoshikawa	69	72	70	70	281	375,000
Isao Ohba	72	71	67	72	282	250,000
Tsutomu Irie	68	72	69	73	282	250,000
Eitaro Deguchi	69	69	73	71	282	250,000
Akio Kanamoto	73	70	69	71	283	175,000
Hisashi Suzumura	72	72	70	69	283	175,000
Norio Mikami	72	72	71	69	284	146,670
Kazuo Kanayama	71	72	70	71	284	146,670
Takuo Terashima	72	71	72	69	284	146,660
Toshiki Matsui	71	70	71	73	285	124,000
Ichiro Teramoto	70	72	72	71	285	124,000
Shinsaku Maeda	72	71	69	73	285	124,000
Norihiko Matsumoto	68	70	72	75	285	124,000
Hideo Ishii	67	71	73	74	285	124,000
Nobuhiro Sakata	72	71	74	69	286	100,000
Shunji Morimoto	68	72	73	73	286	100,000
Kunikazu Kishimoto	69	73	71	73	286	100,000
Tadami Ueno	68	74	73	71	286	100,000
Kosaku Shimada	71	72	75	69	287	90,000
Yutaka Suzuki	69	71	72	75	287	90,000
Yurio Akitomi	68	75	73	71	287	90,000
Teruo Suzumura	69	72	77	70	288	90,000
Hisashi Morioka	70	74	71	73	288	90,000
Shunji Kanazawa	70	73	71	75	289	80,000
Kenji Togame	70	71	76	72	289	80,000
Akira Azuma	72	74	69	74	289	80,000
Noboru Honjo	74	71	70	74	289	80,000
Hisao Inoue	73	72	70	75	290	80,000
Reiji Banto	71	75	72	72	290	80,000
Toshiyuki Itoh	70	75	68	77	290	80,000
Shiro Matsuda	68	72	76	74	290	80,000
Tetsuhiro Ueda	73	73	72	73	291	74,000
Yoshiji Miura	69	74	74	74	291	74,000
Teruo Sugihara	70	76	73	72	291	74,000
Akinori Tamura	72	74	75	70	291	74,000
Mitsuhiko Masuda	73	72	70	76	291	74,000
Noribumi Mizuno	71	71	72	78	292	70,000
Akio Toyoda	74	72	70	76	292	70,000
Kiyoshi Nakagawa	72	74	73	74	293	70,000
Kazuhiro Tamura	72	74	72	75	293	70,000
Shigemi Nakazono	69	76	73	75	293	70,000
Yoshio Matsumoto	72	70	76	75	293	70,000
Hiroshi Oku	73	71	72	77	293	70,000

Kanto PGA Championship

Higashi Tsukuba Country Club
Par 72; 7,164 yards

June 28–July1
purse, ¥19,830,000

	SCORES				TOTAL	MONEY
Isao Aoki	68	66	72	73	279	¥3,000,000
Seiichi Kanai	72	70	71	71	284	1,350,000
Toshiharu Kawada	73	68	71	72	284	1,350,000
Katsuji Hasegawa	74	71	71	72	288	850,000
Masashi Ozaki	67	75	71	75	288	850,000
Kenichi Yamada	70	71	72	75	288	850,000
Fumio Hitachi	71	74	68	75	288	850,000
Masayuki Imai	75	74	72	68	289	476,000
Hsieh Min Nan	73	74	70	72	289	476,000
Hsieh Yung Yo	73	69	74	73	289	476,000
Katsuji Kikuchi	68	73	75	73	289	476,000
Tsuneyuki Nakajima	70	77	70	72	289	476,000
Wataru Horiguchi	69	73	73	74	289	476,000
Yoshimi Watanabe	75	74	73	68	290	330,000
Haruo Yasuda	69	69	76	76	290	330,000
Kikuo Arai	71	72	76	72	291	280,000
Jinya Taniguchi	71	73	75	72	291	280,000
Takahiro Takeyasu	73	73	73	72	291	280,000
Minoru Nakamura	67	77	74	73	291	280,000
Fujio Kobayashi	71	74	74	73	291	280,000
Seiichi Sato	73	77	71	71	292	245,000
Makoto Ioka	71	74	78	69	292	245,000

385

Takashi Murakami	76	73	73	71	293	215,000
Peat Izumikawa	76	70	75	72	293	215,000
Koichi Uehara	72	72	73	76	293	215,000
Shichiroh Enomoto	76	69	73	75	293	215,000
Minoru Hiyoshi	70	75	76	73	294	180,000
Nobuyoshi Hisamori	71	74	73	76	294	180,000
Shigeru Takeuchi	73	75	76	70	294	180,000
Kusuo Uchida	72	76	75	72	295	130,000
Akira Yabe	76	73	73	73	295	130,000
Kanae Nobechi	75	75	72	73	295	130,000
Osamu Hatano	70	78	81	66	295	130,000
Sadao Sakashita	71	78	70	76	295	130,000
Masaji Kusakabe	70	78	71	76	295	130,000
Kyoji Asai	78	71	74	72	295	130,000
Tomomi Suzuki	74	74	75	73	296	98,000
Toshikazu Torisawa	71	73	75	77	296	98,000
Hiromi Sugitani	74	73	76	73	296	98,000
Kenji Mori	71	77	75	73	296	98,000
Namio Takasu	75	76	72	73	296	98,000
Takashi Kurihara	71	74	77	75	297	90,000
Tokio Kaneko	75	76	74	72	297	90,000
Shoichi Sato	74	76	74	73	297	90,000
Shinobu Sotooka	74	76	73	74	297	90,000
Shuichi Yamaguchi	74	76	72	76	298	90,000
Tateo Ozaki	71	75	76	76	298	90,000
Hideyo Sugimoto	76	74	75	73	298	90,000
Chen Ching Po	71	77	77	73	298	90,000
Choji Noguchi	74	75	74	75	298	90,000

Nagano Open

Suwako Country Club
Par 72; 6,642 yards

July 3–4
purse, ¥13,915,000

	SCORES		TOTAL	MONEY
Fujio Kobayashi	74	66	140	¥2,000,000
Shichiro Enomoto	73	68	141	975,000
Yoshio Ichikawa	71	70	141	975,000
Kikuo Arai	71	70	141	975,000
Toshiharu Kawada	71	70	141	975,000
Ben Arda	73	69	142	450,000
Hsieh Min Nan	70	72	142	450,000
Mitsuo Watanabe	74	70	144	300,000
Masaji Kusakabe	73	71	144	300,000
Takeshi Teranuma	72	72	144	300,000
Kenji Mori	78	68	146	195,000
Tsutomu Irie	73	73	146	195,000
Yoshio Kusayanagi	74	73	147	170,000
Renkyoku Sugiyama	73	74	147	170,000
Masahiko Yamamoto	72	75	147	170,000
Takeo Abe	74	74	148	142,900
Takashi Murakami	78	70	148	142,850
Chen Chien Chin	77	71	148	142,850
Katsuji Kikuchi	80	68	148	142,850
Katsuyuki Hirano	76	72	148	142,850
Koichi Inoue	76	72	148	142,850
Tsuneyuki Nakajima	74	74	148	142,850
Isao Matsui	77	72	149	132,500
Minoru Hatsumi	76	73	149	132,500
Hideo Noguchi	76	73	149	132,500
George Yokoi	74	75	149	132,500
Toshiaki Kansui	73	76	149	132,500
Hiroshi Ishii	72	77	149	132,500
Seiichi Kanai	74	76	150	126,700
Koichi Uehara	76	74	150	126,700
Takaaki Fukuzawa	77	73	150	126,600
Isao Isozaki	76	75	151	120,000
Norihiko Matsumoto	75	76	151	120,000
Shigeru Uchida	74	77	151	120,000
Yasuhiro Miyamoto	74	77	151	120,000
Tadao Nakamura	77	75	152	120,000
Kesahiko Uchida	81	71	152	120,000
Hideyo Sugimoto	75	77	152	120,000
Toshiyuki Tsuchiyama	74	78	152	120,000
Hsieh Yung Yo	77	76	153	120,000
Yasunori Uehara	76	77	153	120,000
Shoichi Sato	75	78	153	120,000
Takao Hara	79	75	154	120,000
Akira Yabe	75	79	154	120,000
Satsuki Takahashi	79	76	155	120,000
Nobuyuki Horigome	73	82	155	120,000
Masaru Ariga	79	77	156	80,000
Hideo Kanakubo	79	77	156	80,000

Wakayama Open

Kunigihara Golf Club
Par 72; 6,594 yards

July 6–7
purse, ¥4,985,100

	SCORES		TOTAL	MONEY
Takemitsu Uranishi	69	71	140	¥1,000,000
Kisho Nishikawa	69	72	141	500,000
Toshimitsu Kai	74	68	142	300,000
Toshiharu Kusaka	71	71	142	300,000
Masaharu Ohshima	68	74	142	300,000
Saburo Kubo	71	72	143	160,000
Hsu Chi San	69	74	143	160,000
Natsuo Itoh	68	75	143	160,000
Shinsaku Maeda	74	70	144	110,000
Seizo Yamamoto	74	71	145	95,000
Takeshi Matsukawa	71	74	145	95,000
Kuniichi Kishimoto	74	71	145	95,000
Seiji Noda	75	71	146	85,000
Masabumi Shimasaka	76	71	147	80,000
Hiromi Watanabe	74	74	148	70,000
Kokuchi Ryo	73	75	148	70,000
Minoru Kawakami	73	75	148	70,000
Kiyoyuki Maeda	75	74	149	49,300
Masuo Sawagi	75	74	149	49,300
Yoshiji Miura	74	75	149	49,300
Akira Azuma	74	75	149	49,300
Yasuo Tanabe	77	72	149	49,300
Tsutai Shimojo	70	79	149	49,300
Toshiyuki Yoshida	76	73	149	49,300
Atsuo Sugihara	73	77	150	45,000
Keizo Yamada	76	74	150	45,000
Kinji Naito	75	76	151	45,000
Sechio Tamaoki	75	76	151	45,000
Kazuhiko Kimoto	73	78	151	45,000
Tetsuya Fukuzaki	76	75	151	45,000
Noboru Tachikawa	75	77	152	30,000
Yoichi Yokoyama	75	77	152	30,000
Yoshinosuke Kyoda	74	78	152	30,000
Sadao Hikosaka	74	78	152	30,000
Masato Itoh	77	75	152	30,000
Masanori Hamada	74	79	153	30,000
Kazuo Yoshikawa	70	83	153	30,000
Masayomi Miura	77	76	153	30,000
Atsushi Nakano	74	80	154	30,000
Kunihiko Kimoto	73	81	154	30,000
Osami Kitano	77	77	154	30,000
Kenji Tokuyama	77	77	154	30,000
Kazuyuki Ohnishi	77	78	155	30,000
Kiyoshi Yamaura	72	83	155	30,000
Ryosuke Ohta	77	78	155	30,000
Hideo Hashimoto	71	84	155	30,000
Satsuki Nishii	77	78	155	30,000
Yoshimitsu Kitayoshi	77	78	155	30,000
Noriaki Kabashima	76	80	156	30,000
Michiaki Matsuoka	74	83	157	30,000

Toyama Prefecture Open

Kureha Country Club, Nihonkai Course
Par 72; 6,821 yards

July 6–8
purse, ¥7,830,000

	SCORES			TOTAL	MONEY
Akio Toyoda	67	75	69	211	¥1,500,000
Koichi Inoue	69	72	70	211	800,000
Naomichi Ozaki	69	73	70	212	525,000
Norihiko Matsumoto	73	68	71	212	525,000
Seiichi Kanai	71	73	69	213	350,000
Yasuhiro Miyamoto	71	71	71	213	350,000
Kikuo Arai	68	73	72	213	350,000
Toshiaki Kansui	73	71	70	214	270,000
Isao Ohba	70	73	72	215	215,000
Shoichi Sato	68	73	74	215	215,000
Tadao Nakamura	76	74	66	216	180,000
Isao Kobayashi	76	69	72	217	150,000
Kazunari Takahashi	71	71	75	217	150,000
Shigeru Uchida	73	73	72	218	105,000
Hideo Ishii	73	72	73	218	105,000
Hisashi Suzumura	73	71	74	218	105,000
Shigeo Kanami	73	70	75	218	105,000
Noboru Sugai	72	75	72	219	92,500
Yasukazu Nakagawa	73	74	72	219	92,500
Kazuo Hashimoto	69	75	75	219	92,500
Shizume Izuhara	71	73	75	219	92,500
Norihiko Maei	70	75	75	220	70,000
Noboru Honjo	74	72	74	220	70,000
Yasunori Uehara	74	71	75	220	70,000
Hideyo Sugimoto	73	72	75	220	70,000

Fujio Kobayashi	72	79	70	221	70,000
Teruo Suzumura	75	76	70	221	70,000
Manohiro Saitoh	77	73	71	221	70,000
Hideo Noguchi	73	76	72	221	70,000
Masaji Kikuchi	69	72	80	221	70,000
Masayoshi Kajio	73	78	71	222	50,000
Mitsutaka Kono	73	76	73	222	50,000
Koichi Uehara	74	75	73	222	50,000
Hiroshi Yorikawa	71	75	76	222	50,000
Masahiko Yamamoto	71	75	76	222	50,000
Yoshizo Ogino	73	73	76	222	50,000
Shunji Morimoto	74	77	72	223	50,000
Kenji Hirota	76	74	73	223	50,000
Koji Nakajima	74	76	73	223	50,000
Toshikazu Shimazawa	72	72	79	223	50,000
Teruo Furusawa	75	74	75	224	30,000
Masataka Yagi	77	72	75	224	30,000
Seiichi Numazawa	72	74	79	225	30,000
Masamitsu Oguri	75	71	79	225	30,000
Nobuo Takahashi	75	71	79	225	30,000
Namio Takasu	75	74	77	226	30,000
Chisato Yamashita	72	75	79	226	30,000
Hiroshi Ishii	77	74	76	227	30,000
Toru Hayami	76	72	79	227	30,000
Katsuyuki Hirano	74	74	80	228	30,000

Hyogo Prefecture Open

Akashi Shin-Nihon Golf Club
Par 72;

July 18–20
purse, ¥5,000,000

	SCORES			TOTAL	MONEY
Mitsuhiro Kitta	72	69	70	211	¥1,000,000
Ichiro Teramoto	70	73	68	211	500,000
Tsutomu Irie	71	72	68	211	500,000
Hisashi Morioka	73	67	72	212	300,000
Terumasa Higuchi	74	72	70	216	200,000
Tsuneo Uchida	73	74	70	217	140,000
Hisao Inoue	71	72	74	217	140,000
Akihiro Teramoto	70	74	73	217	140,000
Seichi Kashiwagi	71	73	74	218	120,000
Kazuo Kanayama	71	74	74	219	110,000
Susumu Wakita	72	77	71	220	90,000
Shiro Matsuda	74	74	72	220	90,000
Tetsuo Ishii	73	74	73	220	90,000
Tadashi Kitta	74	75	72	221	60,000
Hiromi Ogino	76	71	74	221	60,000
Hiroshi Oku	75	72	74	221	60,000
Osamu Watanabe	76	73	74	223	60,000
Keiichi Kobayashi	74	72	77	223	50,000
Kiyomasa Sugimoto	74	76	74	224	46,700
Akihide Koyama	74	77	73	224	46,700
Koh Hatanaka	74	76	74	224	46,600
Naohiro Okamura	73	82	70	225	40,000
Yoshihiro Takada	74	75	76	225	40,000
Yuji Kashiwagi	73	76	76	225	40,000
Michio Fujita	73	81	73	227	40,000
Junji Bantoh	79	74	74	227	40,000
Yoshio Ichikawa	76	76	75	227	40,000
Mikio Yamaguchi	76	75	76	227	40,000
Tsutomu Matsuzawa	76	78	74	228	40,000
Kiyoshi Sakamoto	75	79	74	228	40,000
Masayoshi Toda	76	78	76	230	30,000
Kazumi Nakao	78	74	78	230	30,000
Masahiro Nishikawa	82	74	74	230	30,000
Michio Ishii	76	78	76	230	30,000
Naruo Osada	79	75	76	230	30,000
Hiroshi Wakita	73	79	78	230	30,000
Satoshi Terada	75	75	80	230	30,000
Yoshinori Sasayama	79	77	75	231	30,000
Toshitsugu Kita	79	72	80	231	30,000
Takashi Nakama	79	75	78	232	30,000
Norio Morimoto	81	78	74	233	20,000
Hiroyuki Amano	81	76	76	233	20,000
Kunio Yamashita	79	77	78	234	20,000
Ineji Nohara	80	75	79	234	20,000
Shimon Takamatsu	69	82	83	234	20,000
Isao Akutagawa	83	75	76	234	20,000
Toshio Ohta	80	77	77	234	20,000
Toyohiro Kawai	80	79	76	235	20,000
Yoshiaki Inada	76	79	81	236	20,000
Takahisa Okuyama	78	80	78	236	20,000

Chiba Prefecture Open

Sodegaura Country Club, Sodegaura Course
Par 72; 7,151 yards

July 19–20
purse ¥5,200,000

	SCORES		TOTAL	MONEY
Katsuji Hasegawa	69	66	135	¥1,500,000
Sadao Hiyoshi	72	71	143	650,000
Masaji Kusakabe	71	72	143	650,000
Fujio Kobayashi	73	71	144	400,000
Shigeru Kubota	72	73	145	350,000
Takahiro Takeyasu	75	71	146	275,000
Tomoaki Masuda	74	72	146	275,000
Fumio Hitachi	75	72	147	125,000
Shohei Nishida	75	72	147	125,000
Shigeru Takeuchi	72	75	147	125,000
Seiji Ogawa	70	77	147	125,000
Yoshihiko Kudo	77	71	148	45,714
Ryoichi Hotchi	75	73	148	45,714
Kenji Takayama	75	73	148	45,714
Toru Nakayama	74	74	148	45,714
Inenori Yoshikawa	72	76	148	45,714
Mamoru Kondo	77	71	148	45,714
Okiji Yanagisawa	75	73	148	45,714
Namio Takasu	76	73	149	35,000
Yoshio Iizuka	74	75	149	35,000
Kyoji Asai	75	74	149	35,000
Asao Ishii	73	76	149	35,000
Chen Junt Chun	77	73	150	30,000
Kazuaki Yamamoto	76	74	150	30,000
Takumi Horiuchi	74	76	150	30,000
Yoshihiro Hayashi	76	74	150	30,000
Setsuo Jibiki	75	75	150	30,000
Kiyoshi Harigaya	77	74	151	30,000
Makoto Iioka	74	77	151	30,000
Naomichi Ozaki	75	76	151	30,000
Akira Nakada	77	75	152	30,000
Katsunori Abe	74	78	152	30,000
Sumio Hino	77	75	152	30,000
Seiji Ebihara	77	76	153	30,000
Teruaki Watabe	77	76	153	30,000
Takanobu Yamataka	77	76	153	30,000
Tohru Harai	76	77	153	30,000
Takashi Kubota	77	77	154	30,000
Shinichi Katoh	74	80	154	30,000
Hiroshi Gunji	77	78	155	30,000
Katsutoshi Miura	76	79	155	30,000
Yuichi Yokoshima	77	78	155	30,000
Masayuski Miyazaki	77	79	156	30,000

Kokudo Keikaku Summers

Shirasagi Country Club, Tochigi
Par 72; 6,764 yards

August 2–5
purse, ¥30,000,000

	SCORES				TOTAL	MONEY
Norio Mikami	73	70	66	70	279	¥6,000,000
Kenji Mori	71	71	69	71	282	3,000,000
Kazuo Yoshikawa	73	71	68	70	282	3,000,000
Minoru Hiyoshi	69	72	68	74	283	1,500,000
Hsieh Min Nan	70	72	74	68	284	670,000
Kikuo Arai	73	68	73	70	284	670,000
Yoshitaka Yamamoto	71	71	71	71	284	670,000
Shigeru Noguchi	71	69	73	71	284	670,000
Lu Liang Huan	68	71	72	73	284	670,000
Toru Nakamura	69	76	70	70	285	400,000
Satsuki Takahashi	71	74	72	69	286	310,000
Yoshiteru Arayoshi	73	71	70	72	286	310,000
Minoru Nakamura	69	75	70	72	286	310,000
Koichi Inoue	71	74	71	71	287	243,333
Masaru Amano	70	75	70	72	287	243,333
Takahiro Takeyasu	72	72	71	72	287	243,334
Kazuo Hashimoto	71	75	69	73	288	215,000
Masashi Kikuchi	71	75	69	73	288	215,000
Hiroshi Ishii	73	70	74	72	289	185,000
Koichi Uehara	74	71	72	72	289	185,000
Kenichi Yamada	73	67	75	74	289	185,000
Masaji Kusakabe	69	73	73	74	289	185,000
Kazushige Kono	73	71	71	74	289	185,000
Takeshi Shibata	72	70	72	75	289	185,000
Kyoji Asai	74	71	72	73	290	172,500
Yoshiharu Takai	76	70	76	68	290	172,500
Tadayoshi Ueno	73	70	73	74	290	172,500
Akio Kanamoto	74	73	73	70	290	172,500
Tadashi Kitta	73	70	77	71	291	170,000
Hisashi Suzumura	71	70	72	78	291	170,000
Yoshihisa Iwashita	72	72	74	74	292	160,000
Haruo Yasuda	71	73	73	75	292	160,000
Ichio Sato	75	71	73	73	292	160,000
Ichiro Teramoto	71	75	73	73	292	160,000

389

Shigeru Uchida	74	71	73	75	293	147,777
Namio Takasu	74	72	72	75	293	147,777
Takemitsu Uranishi	71	73	74	75	293	147,778
Osamu Hatano	73	74	71	75	293	147,778
Mitsuhiro Kitta	72	70	79	72	293	147,778
Fujio Kobayashi	77	69	75	72	293	147,778
Yurio Akitomi	73	72	75	73	293	147,778
Seiichi Kanai	71	72	76	74	293	147,778
Taiichi Nakagawa	73	73	73	74	293	147,778
Akira Yabe	69	77	74	74	294	136,666
Isao Matsui	73	73	74	74	294	136,667
Hsieh Yung Yo	74	73	73	74	294	136,667
Saburo Fujiki	75	71	79	70	295	130,000
Masami Kawamura	75	72	76	72	295	130,000
Kunio Iwase	73	74	76	72	295	130,000
Yoshitaka Ogawa	73	74	80	69	296	121,666

Mizuno

Tokinodai Country Club, Ishikawa Pref.
Par 71; 6,707 yards

August 9–12
purse, ¥20,000,000

	SCORES				TOTAL	MONEY
Mitsuhiro Kitta	67	70	68	67	272	¥4,000,000
Ichiro Teramoto	70	65	67	72	274	1,750,000
Teruo Sugihara	66	67	71	70	274	1,750,000
Kazuo Yoshikawa	71	67	66	72	276	1,000,000
Kosaku Shimada	72	69	71	65	277	650,000
Kikuo Arai	67	71	72	67	277	650,000
Shinsaku Maeda	74	64	70	69	277	650,000
Norio Suzuki	69	67	70	71	277	650,000
Yoshitaka Yamamoto	69	71	67	71	278	360,000
Masahiko Yamamoto	72	69	66	71	278	360,000
Kenji Mori	69	67	70	72	278	360,000
Yasuhiro Miyamoto	70	67	69	72	278	360,000
Shigeru Uchida	70	69	67	72	278	360,000
Norihiko Matsumoto	71	69	71	68	279	260,000
Minoru Kawakami	71	70	70	68	279	260,000
Masaji Kusakabe	71	70	69	69	279	260,000
Takemitsu Uranishi	68	74	68	69	279	260,000
Akira Yabe	69	66	72	72	279	260,000
Fujio Kobayashi	71	69	72	68	280	180,000
Masuaki Nakamura	71	67	70	72	280	180,000
Yuichi Yokoshima	71	69	68	72	280	180,000
Hiroshi Ishii	67	68	75	71	281	160,000
Hsieh Min Nan	71	68	71	71	281	160,000
Kazushige Kono	69	70	70	72	281	160,000
Yoshio Matsumoto	69	69	68	75	281	160,000
Kazumasa Tamura	69	71	73	69	282	145,000
Haruhiko Banto	72	68	72	70	282	145,000
Saburo Fujiki	69	71	72	70	282	145,000
Shinichi Hayashi	68	74	70	70	282	145,000
Shozo Miyamoto	71	70	70	71	282	145,000
Tadayoshi Ueno	69	73	69	71	282	145,000
Kyoji Asai	69	69	71	73	282	145,000
Mitsuhiko Masuda	70	69	70	73	282	145,000
Isao Matsui	72	69	68	73	282	145,000
Toshihiro Matsuda	67	70	69	76	282	145,000
Chen Chien Chung	70	69	72	72	283	130,000
Kesahiko Uchida	69	73	70	72	284	130,000
Rikizo Katoh	68	73	70	73	284	130,000
Hsieh Yung Yo	73	69	68	74	284	130,000
Seiichi Kanai	69	73	70	73	285	123,333
Toshiyuko Tsuchiyama	70	70	70	75	285	123,333
Yoshimi Watanabe	72	70	67	76	285	123,333
Sadao Sakashita	69	71	74	72	286	117,500
Kiyoshi Yamaura	73	69	72	72	286	117,500
Kazunori Mizuno	68	73	72	73	286	117,500
Tadao Nakamura	67	75	67	77	286	117,500
Kenji Ueda	72	70	76	69	287	108,000
Atsuo Takahashi	71	69	74	73	287	108,000
Kenjiro Iwama	70	70	74	73	287	108,000
Noribumi Mizuno	73	67	73	74	287	108,000
Natsuo Itoh	71	71	70	75	287	108,000

Gunma Open

Minohara Country Club, Gunma Pref.
Par 72; 7,155 yards

August 11–12
purse, ¥9,550,000

	SCORES		TOTAL	MONEY
Kazunari Takahashi	68	72	140	¥2,000,000
Takashi Kurihara	70	70	140	1,000,000
(Takahashi defeated Kurihara on second hole of sudden-death play-off)				
Kiyoharu Ebihara	70	72	142	800,000
Satsuki Takahashi	74	69	143	462,500
Toshikazu Torisawa	71	72	143	462,500
Takaaki Kono	71	72	143	462,500
Eisei Sugimoto	68	75	143	462,500
Isao Aoki	73	71	144	224,000
Mitsuo Uehara	72	72	144	224,000
Tateo Ozaki	72	72	144	224,000
Akio Toyoda	71	73	144	224,000
Johji Yokoi	71	73	144	224,000
Takahiro Takeyasu	74	71	145	160,000
Hiroshi Tahara	72	73	145	160,000
Nobuyuki Ikenotani	70	75	145	160,000
Katsuji Hasegawa	75	71	146	130,000
Minoru Nakamura	68	78	146	130,000
Masayuki Imai	73	73	146	130,000
Kiyoshi Hiuga	75	72	147	71,250
Yoshihisa Iwashita	75	72	147	71,250
Shigeru Noguchi	75	72	147	71,250
Mitsutaka Kono	74	73	147	71,250
Haruyoshi Kobari	73	74	147	71,250
Isao Isozaki	72	75	147	71,250
Ikuhiro Funatogawa	72	75	147	71,250
Fujio Ishii	72	75	147	71,250
Sadao Hiyoshi	75	73	148	60,000
Shoji Kikuchi	75	73	148	60,000
Haruji Inamura	73	75	148	60,000
Yoshio Kusayangi	73	75	148	60,000
Toshiki Matsui	76	74	150	50,000
Shinobu Uehara	76	74	150	50,000
Tsutomu Irie	76	74	150	50,000
Wataru Horiguchi	75	75	150	50,000
Kazuo Hashimoto	75	75	150	50,000
Hisashi Iwamoto	75	76	151	50,000
Minoru Hiyoshi	75	76	151	50,000
Seiichi Sato	75	76	151	50,000
Keiichi Hoshino	74	77	151	50,000
Taiichi Nakagawa	76	76	152	50,000
Fumio Tanaka	76	76	152	50,000
Toshimi Ebisawa	75	77	152	50,000
Masayuki Suzuki	76	77	153	50,000
Inetoshi Yoshikawa	76	77	153	50,000
Tsugio Igarashi	74	79	153	50,000
Hideo Ishii	73	80	153	50,000
Jinya Taniguchi	76	78	154	50,000
Kazuhiro Niina	75	79	154	50,000
Isao Katsumata	76	79	155	50,000
Naomichi Ozaki	76	79	155	50,000

KBC Augusta

Fukuoka Country Club, Kyushu, Japan
Par 72; 6,668 yards

August 23–26
purse, ¥32,000,000

	SCORES				TOTAL	MONEY
Masaji Kusakabe	67	71	68	34	240	¥6,000,000
Kuo Chi Hsiung	67	66	71	39	243	3,000,000
Shigeru Uchida	69	68	71	36	244	2,000,000
Kenji Mori	72	69	71	33	245	1,100,000
Norio Suzuki	71	68	71	36	245	1,100,000
Fujio Kobayashi	69	67	70	39	245	1,100,000
Shinsaku Maeda	68	72	71	35	246	750,000
Hsieh Yung Yo	71	70	69	36	246	750,000
Teruo Sugihara	71	67	69	39	246	750,000
Takahiro Takeyasu	71	68	73	35	247	530,000
Graham Marsh	73	68	70	36	247	530,000
Akio Kanamoto	73	68	69	37	247	530,000
George Yokoi	69	72	67	39	247	530,000
Chen Tze Ming	68	72	73	35	248	405,000
Masashi Ozaki	73	70	70	35	248	405,000
Lu Hsi Chuen	71	69	70	38	248	405,000
Saburo Fujiki	71	69	68	40	248	405,000
Isao Aoki	73	71	70	35	249	330,000
Kikuo Arai	72	71	71	35	249	330,000
Kosaku Shimada	70	74	68	37	249	330,000
Seiichi Kanai	69	70	73	38	250	295,000
Hideo Ishii	71	69	71	39	250	295,000
Masayuki Imai	71	73	69	38	251	275,000
Kesahiko Uchida	71	68	71	41	251	275,000
Yuichi Yokoshima	69	75	74	34	252	225,625

Brian Jones	74	70	72	36	252	225,625
Akio Toyoda	72	72	71	37	252	225,625
Yoshimasa Fujii	70	74	71	37	252	225,625
Masaru Amano	70	71	72	39	252	225,625
Hisao Inoue	73	68	72	39	252	225,625
Kyoji Asai	68	74	70	40	252	225,625
Koichi Inoue	70	70	71	41	252	225,625
Minoru Hiyoshi	73	71	75	34	253	185,000
Lu Liang Huan	72	70	73	38	253	185,000
Noboru Shibata	73	71	69	40	253	185,000
Naomichi Ozaki	72	72	74	36	254	160,000
Akira Yabe	72	72	74	36	254	160,000
Nariyuki Wakisaka	74	70	73	37	254	160,000
Bill Kratzert	77	67	72	38	254	160,000
Tetsuhiro Ueda	76	68	72	38	254	160,000
Hiroshi Ishii	67	77	72	38	254	160,000
Kazuo Yoshikawa	69	71	76	38	254	160,000
Masao Kikuchi	74	70	75	36	255	137,500
Reiji Banto	70	72	71	42	255	137,500
Yoshitaka Yamamoto	75	69	74	38	256	122,500
Toru Nakamura	72	72	72	40	256	122,500
Nobuo Takahashi	70	70	74	42	256	122,500
Masahiko Yamamoto	71	73	73	39	256	122,500
Ichiro Togawa	73	70	76	38	257	105,000
Tadao Nakamura	72	72	75	38	257	105,000
Yoshihisa Iwashita	71	73	73	40	257	105,000

Hokkaido Open

Mitsui Kanko Tomakomai Country Club, South Course, Hokkaido, Japan   August 24–26
Par 72; 7,063 yards   purse, ¥4,100,000

	SCORES				TOTAL	MONEY
Masaichi Sato	71	72	69	67	279	¥1,300,000
Hiroshi Yamada	71	68	72	73	284	600,000
Toshiaki Nakamura	74	71	71	71	287	500,000
Koichi Uehara	68	75	74	72	289	400,000
Shinji Kubota	73	73	77	68	291	300,000
Yasuo Kuninaka	74	70	71	77	292	200,000
Harunobu Fujii	72	71	75	75	293	100,000
Kanae Nobeji	74	72	75	73	294	75,000
Fumio Hatanaka	72	76	72	74	294	75,000
Kazunair Takahashi	72	77	71	75	295	60,000
Akio Watanabe	73	74	71	78	296	45,000
Masaaki Fujii	74	72	75	75	296	45,000
Mitsuyoshi Goto	74	74	77	72	297	33,333
Ei Onodera	76	73	70	78	297	33,333
Kenji Takeda	78	75	71	73	297	33,333
Masaaki Yamamoto	73	77	72	76	298	20,000
Noritaka Shiraishi	77	72	76	75	300	20,000
Nobukatsu Yasuda	70	83	72	75	300	20,000
Toshikazu Takagi	77	74	76	74	301	20,000
Yoshitaka Ikawa	75	73	75	79	302	15,000
Kazumi Takai	77	76	76	73	302	15,000
Jun Nobeji	75	76	80	72	303	10,000
Toshimi Ebisawa	76	80	75	72	303	10,000
Seiji Takahashi°	75	78	77	73	303	
Akira Nakahara°	74	78	77	74	303	
Takahiro Kuroda	78	75	77	74	304	10,000
Akihiko Kojima	73	76	75	81	305	10,000
Masanori Yoshimizu°	74	79	79	73	305	
Hiromichi Kida	77	77	77	74	305	10,000
Nobuhiko Ikeda°	76	77	76	77	306	
Kazutaka Yamahiro°	75	79	75	77	306	
Seiichi Arai°	77	75	81	74	307	

°Amateur

ANA Sapporo Open

Sapporo Golf Club, Hokkaido, Japan   August 30–September 2
Par 72; 7,098 yards   purse, ¥29,300,000

	SCORES				TOTAL	MONEY
Graham Marsh	71	73	68	72	284	6,000,000
Kikuo Arai	73	71	71	71	286	3,000,000
Isao Aoki	69	72	77	69	287	1,750,000
Lu Liang Huan	68	70	73	76	287	1,750,000
Masashi Ozaki	68	74	74	72	288	1,200,000
Teruo Sugihara	71	70	72	76	289	1,100,000
Tsuneyki Nakajima	71	72	75	73	291	900,000
Norio Suzuki	72	72	71	76	291	900,000
Yasuhiro Miyamoto	68	71	74	78	291	900,000
Fujio Kobayashi	70	76	70	76	292	700,000
Shinsaku Maeda	70	76	70	77	293	660,000
Yoshitaka Yamamoto	76	70	71	77	294	610,000
Kenji Mori	73	69	73	79	294	610,000

Kuo Chi Hsiung	72	73	74	76	295	540,000
Saburo Fujiki	70	77	73	76	296	495,000
Takashi Murakami	74	69	76	77	296	495,000
Koichi Uehara	70	78	75	74	297	450,000
Fumio Tanaka	72	74	77	75	298	390,000
Chen Chien Chung	71	74	74	79	298	390,000
Namio Takasu	72	73	74	79	298	390,000
Nobumitsu Yuhara*	75	75	75	74	299	
Ichiro Togawa	73	74	77	75	299	294,000
Nobuo Takahashi	70	76	74	79	299	294,000
Koichi Inoue	73	73	73	80	299	294,000
Masaji Kusakabe	72	72	74	81	299	294,000
Mya Aye	75	70	72	82	299	294,000
Shoichi Sato	72	73	81	74	300	240,000
Yasukazu Nakagawa	74	74	78	74	300	240,000
Shigeru Uchida	73	73	78	76	300	240,000
Kosaku Shimada	71	76	75	78	300	240,000
Naomichi Ozaki	71	76	72	81	300	240,000
Shohei Nishida	74	74	74	79	301	200,000
Sadao Sakashita	74	72	72	83	301	200,000
Norihito Shimada*	74	75	71	81	301	
Hsieh Yung Yo	73	74	76	79	302	200,000
Akira Yabe	74	73	74	81	302	200,000
Yoshihisa Iwashita	71	74	78	80	303	185,000
Toshiyuki Tsuchiyama	71	76	76	80	303	185,000
Mitsuhiro Kitta	73	75	71	84	303	185,000
Haruo Yasuda	72	76	72	83	303	185,000
Hiroshi Ishii	74	74	77	79	304	180,000
Minoru Kawakami	76	72	79	78	305	180,000
Masayuki Imai	73	73	80	80	306	160,000
Isao Matsui	73	75	76	82	306	160,000
Takeshi Teranuma	73	75	77	82	307	160,000
Akio Kanamoto	74	72	79	82	307	160,000
Tadayoshi Ueno	76	71	73	87	307	160,000
Shichiro Enomoto	74	74	79	81	308	140,000
Masayoshi Sugimoto	70	74	82	82	308	140,000
Takashi Kurihara	71	77	77	83	308	140,000

*Amateur

Suntory Open

Narashino Country Club, Chiba, Japan
Par 72; 7,102 yards

September 6–9
purse, ¥40,000,000

	SCORES				TOTAL	MONEY
Masaji Kusakabe	66	73	69	69	277	¥8,000,000
Lu Liang Huan	71	69	69	69	278	4,250,000
Yoshihisa Iwashita	66	76	66	71	279	2,700,000
Tateo Ozaki	69	76	70	65	280	1,440,000
Isao Aoki	68	72	73	67	280	1,440,000
Katsuji Hasegawa	70	70	71	69	280	1,440,000
Hubert Green	65	75	70	70	280	1,440,000
Haruo Yasuda	71	72	67	70	280	1,440,000
Kosaku Shimada	69	71	71	70	281	900,000
Ho Ming Chung	73	70	68	70	281	900,000
Graham Marsh	69	70	75	68	282	725,000
Ikuhiro Funatogawa	73	71	69	69	282	725,000
Koichi Uehara	73	71	71	68	283	582,500
Tomomi Suzuki	72	73	68	70	283	582,500
Toshiki Matsui	70	74	67	72	283	582,500
Hiroshi Ishii	70	69	72	72	283	582,500
Toshiyuki Tsuchiyama	71	77	70	66	284	480,000
Teruo Sugihara	71	70	74	69	284	480,000
Takahiro Takeyasu	70	70	74	70	284	480,000
Fumio Tanaka	68	72	69	75	284	480,000
Brian Jones	73	72	73	69	286	420,000
Yuichi Yokoshima	70	73	72	71	286	420,000
Yasuhiro Miyamoto	69	68	76	73	286	420,000
Kikuo Arai	70	73	70	73	286	420,000
Hideyo Sugimoto	72	70	69	75	286	420,000
Tsuneyuki Nakajima	69	74	71	73	287	380,000
Seiji Ebihara	73	75	72	67	287	380,000
Ben Arda	70	72	71	74	287	380,000
Kenji Mori	73	73	74	68	288	355,000
Yurio Akitomi	75	73	72	68	288	355,000
Makoto Iioka	76	71	72	70	289	330,000
Tadashi Kitta	71	73	73	72	289	330,000
Kazuo Yoshikawa	69	72	72	76	289	330,000
Toru Nakamura	71	72	76	71	290	290,000
Ichiro Teramoto	73	73	73	71	290	290,000
Wataru Horiguchi	68	73	76	73	290	290,000
Yoshimi Watanabe	74	74	70	72	290	290,000
Masamitsu Oguri	72	73	69	76	290	290,000
Kazunari Takahashi	72	72	75	72	291	245,000
Akio Kanamoto	73	73	73	72	291	245,000

Namio Takasu	71	72	73	75	291	245,000
Hsieh Yung Yo	70	73	77	71	291	245,000
Koichi Hirabayashi	75	71	73	73	292	215,000
Takashi Murakami	69	75	75	73	292	215,000
Isao Matsui	73	73	73	74	293	175,000
Masashi Ozaki	73	71	75	74	293	175,000
Masuaki Nakamura	70	76	74	73	293	175,000
Shinsaku Maeda	69	78	76	70	293	175,000
Mitsuhiko Masuda	72	73	71	77	293	175,000
Lu Hsi Chuen	71	70	73	79	293	175,000

Japan PGA Championship

Asami Country Club, Ibaraki, Japan
Par 72; 6,913 yards

September 13–16
purse, ¥24,700,000

	SCORES				TOTAL	MONEY
Hsieh Min Nan	67	68	66	71	272	¥4,000,000
Teruo Sugihara	69	67	70	67	273	2,000,000
Masaji Kusakabe	71	68	69	66	274	1,500,000
Tsuneyuki Nakajima	70	68	69	68	275	1,300,000
Toru Nakamura	69	72	67	68	276	1,050,000
Toshiharu Kawada	70	69	68	69	276	1,050,000
Hiroshi Ishii	69	73	68	69	279	850,000
Masami Kawamura	73	68	67	71	279	850,000
Fujio Kobayashi	70	70	71	70	281	675,000
Yoshitaka Yamamoto	69	69	72	71	281	675,000
Isao Aoki	71	70	71	70	282	575,000
Mitsuhiro Kitta	71	70	71	70	282	575,000
Fumio Hitachi	69	69	70	75	283	500,000
Masashi Ozaki	68	73	75	68	284	450,000
Kosaku Shimada	73	71	69	71	284	450,000
Ichiro Teramoto	66	75	71	72	284	450,000
Hsieh Yung Yo	70	73	69	72	284	450,000
Kyoji Asai	74	71	70	70	285	390,000
Saburo Fujiki	72	71	69	73	285	390,000
Koichi Uehara	73	72	71	70	286	300,000
Harunobu Fujii	71	73	71	71	286	300,000
Toshiyuki Tsuchiyama	70	74	71	71	286	300,000
Minoru Nakamura	74	69	71	72	286	300,000
Seiji Ebihara	70	74	69	73	286	300,000
Akira Yabe	70	72	71	73	286	300,000
Akio Toyoda	71	74	72	69	286	300,000
Yoshihisa Iwashita	70	73	71	73	287	210,000
Chen Chien Chung	73	72	69	73	287	210,000
Shinsaku Maeda	72	69	75	72	288	170,000
Takashi Murakami	70	72	74	72	288	170,000
Yurio Akitomi	70	74	76	68	288	170,000
Shiro Kubo	68	74	75	71	288	170,000
Tadashi Kitta	72	72	72	73	289	132,000
Kazushige Kawano	73	71	75	70	289	132,000
Akira Azuma	69	69	80	71	289	132,000
Namio Takasu	69	72	73	75	289	132,000
Tsukasa Hirakawa	74	70	69	76	289	132,000
Shigeru Uchida	67	76	73	74	290	117,500
Ichiro Togawa	74	69	71	76	290	117,500
Koichi Inoue	73	70	75	72	290	117,500
Fujio Ishii	71	73	73	73	290	117,500
Kenji Ueda	70	74	74	73	291	110,000
Shozo Miyamoto	68	75	71	77	291	110,000
Mitsuo Watanabe	69	76	72	75	292	110,000
Isao Oba	72	71	76	73	292	110,000
Masataka Yagi	71	71	74	77	293	110,000
Chen Chien Chin	73	72	73	75	293	110,000
Shinichi Hayashi	68	73	76	76	293	110,000
Teruo Suzumura	69	73	71	80	293	110,000
Shunji Morimoto	69	74	74	77	294	103,334
Kunio Iwase	69	74	77	74	294	103,333
Takao Kamo	74	71	73	76	294	103,333

Kanto Open

Ikaho Country Club, Gunma, Japan
Par 72; 6,781 yards

September 20–23
purse, ¥19,760,000

	SCORES				TOTAL	MONEY
Masaru Amano	68	76	69	65	278	¥4,000,000
Kenji Mori	74	73	66	67	280	1,566,667
Kikuo Arai	71	68	72	69	280	1,566,667
Masashi Ozaki	70	70	68	72	280	1,566,666
Haruo Yasuda	70	74	67	70 28		1,000,000
Isao Aoki	71	68	72	71	282	750,000
Masaji Kusakabe	72	68	69	73	282	750,000
Yuichi Yokoshima	69	70	75	70	284	600,000
Fujio Kobayashi	66	73	71	74	285	500,000
Satsuki Takahashi	71	71	71	73	286	400,000
Seiichi Kanai	73	71	70	73	287	330,000

Toshiharu Kawada	71	67	74	75	287	330,000
Takashi Murakami	70	72	76	70	288	312,500
Minoru Hiyoshi	72	76	70	70	288	312,500
Akira Yabe	75	68	72	73	288	312,500
Sadao Sakashita	74	72	68	74	288	312,500
Takaaki Kawano	71	72	74	72	289	260,000
Minoru Nakamura	70	75	72	72	289	260,000
Hsieh Min Nan	71	73	71	74	289	260,000
Wataru Horiguchi	70	73	72	74	289	260,000
Katsutoshi Abe	71	75	72	72	290	200,000
Ikuhiro Funatogawa	74	71	72	73	290	200,000
Hsieh Yung Yo	75	72	70	73	290	200,000
Yoshio Kusayanagi	73	72	71	74	290	200,000
Hiroshi Yamada	73	72	70	75	290	200,000
Seiji Ebihara	72	71	73	75	291	150,000
Namio Takasu	70	75	76	71	292	150,000
Isao Isozaki	70	74	74	74	292	150,000
Fumio Tanaka	70	75	72	75	292	150,000
Yoshihisa Iwashita	70	76	74	73	293	125,000
Yoshiharu Takai	73	75	72	73	293	125,000
Takahiro Takeyasu	71	72	74	76	293	125,000
Kazushige Kono	72	69	76	76	293	125,000
Nobumitsu Yuhara	72	71	74	76	293	125,000
Masayuki Naito	70	76	71	76	293	125,000
Tsuguo Igarashi	73	72	71	77	293	125,000
Koichi Uehara	73	68	72	80	293	125,000
Takao Hara	75	72	76	71	294	100,000
Chen Ching Po	73	76	73	72	294	100,000
Norio Adachi	72	75	72	75	294	100,000
Takao Kamo	73	73	75	74	295	100,000
Shigeru Noguchi	74	72	74	75	295	100,000
Tetsuo Sakata*	76	72	72	75	295	
Mamoru Kondo	74	72	76	74	296	90,000
Kenji Uchiyama*	75	75	73	73	296	
Mtisuo Watanabe	70	74	75	77	296	90,000
Nobuo Takahashi	70	74	75	77	296	90,000
Yasutomo Ishii	70	77	71	78	296	90,000
Osamu Hatano	73	75	74	75	297	85,000
Koji Takahashi	78	71	72	76	297	85,000

*Amateur

Kansai Open

Rokko Kokosai Golf Club, Kobe, Japan
Par 72; 7,070 yards

September 20–23
purse, ¥14,700,000

		SCORES			TOTAL	MONEY
Yasuhiro Miyamoto	70	74	72	67	283	4,000,000
Toru Nakamura	70	72	72	70	284	2,000,000
Masanori Miura	70	73	71	72	286	1,000,000
Fuminori Sano*	67	73	71	75	286	
Teruo Sugihara	74	71	70	72	287	750,000
Hisashi Morioka	73	74	67	73	287	750,000
Shinichi Hayashi	72	71	74	71	288	500,000
Kosaku Sjimada	70	73	73	72	288	500,000
Shinsaku Maeda	73	73	71	71	288	500,000
Yoshitaka Yamamoto	74	71	71	72	288	500,000
Tsutomu Irie	70	72	73	73	288	500,000
Kazuo Kanayama	75	70	73	71	289	350,000
Kazuo Yoshikawa	72	77	72	70	291	300,000
Shiro Matsuda	74	71	77	70	292	168,000
Tadashi Kitta	75	73	71	73	292	168,000
Shozo Miyamoto	74	71	74	73	292	168,000
Ichiro Teramoto	70	73	75	74	292	168,000
Yoshio Ichikawa	72	70	72	78	292	168,000
Terumasa Higuchi	72	75	72	74	293	120,000
Osamu Watanabe	69	74	76	75	294	110,000
Yoshitsugi Nakamura	73	67	79	75	284	110,000
Tsuneo Uchida	73	72	73	76	294	110,000
Seizo Yamamoto	76	72	67	79	294	110,000
Risaku Kikiji*	73	71	77	75	296	
Ataeru Kimoto	74	73	74	75	296	100,000
Shiji Suwa	75	74	72	75	296	100,000
Masao Shioda*	75	74	76	72	297	
Seiji Noda	75	73	78	71	297	84,000
Keizo Yamada	72	77	73	75	297	84,000
Akira Azuma	77	70	74	76	297	84,000
Takemitsu Uranisih	74	73	73	77	297	84,000
Toshimitsu Kai	72	76	71	78	297	84,000
Mitsuhiro Kitta	74	75	75	74	298	73,333
Ichiro Togawa	73	75	76	74	298	73,333
Kunihiko Kimoto	73	73	79	73	298	73,333
Hiroshi Ueda*	78	71	72	77	298	
Zenzaburo Isoda*	78	71	71	78	298	
Haruki Oda	74	75	76	74	299	70,000
Junji Ohshima*	73	74	77	75	299	
Minoru Kawakami	77	71	74	77	299	70,000
Hisashi Terada	72	73	76	78	299	70,000
Takeshi Matsukawa	74	75	77	74	300	60,000

Yoshiaki Inada	72	74	71	83	300	60,000
Keiichi Kobayashi	75	74	75	77	301	60,000
Takashi Nakauma	75	74	74	78	301	60,000
Saburo Kubo	73	74	76	78	301	60,000
Munehiro Aida	76	73	81	73	303	50,000
Hiroyuki Amano	76	72	80	75	303	50,000
Hideo Nakamura	76	72	72	83	303	50,000
Akihiro Teramoto	72	72	76	83	303	50,000

*Amateur

Chubu Open

Gifuseki Country Club, Gifu, Japan
Par 72; 7,231 yards

September 20–23
purse, ¥2,000,000

	SCORES				TOTAL	MONEY
Kinichi Matsuoka	73	74	74	69	290	¥2,500,000
Takeshi Shibata	74	69	73	74	290	1,500,000
(Matsuoka won sudden-death play-off)						
Haruhiko Bando	70	68	75	78	291	800,000
Akio Toyoda	70	71	76	74	291	800,000
Mitsuo Hirukawa	72	72	75	72	291	800,000
Koichi Inoue	75	72	74	71	292	500,000
Masahiko Yamamoto	76	74	69	75	294	325,000
Yutaka Suzuki	75	73	73	73	294	325,000
Teruo Suzumura	76	74	71	73	294	325,000
Yoshio Matsumoto	69	77	71	77	294	325,000
Hideo Noguchi	77	76	70	72	295	250,000
Toshihiro Matsuda	74	71	76	76	297	180,000
Hideo Ishii	68	76	73	80	297	180,000
Hiroshi Ishii	78	74	70	75	297	180,000
Yuzo Noda	76	75	75	72	298	160,000
Chen Chien Chin	74	78	71	76	299	140,000
Shigeru Uchida	73	71	75	80	299	140,000
Hisashi Suzumura	73	74	75	77	299	140,000
Makoto Ueda	72	71	81	76	300	105,000
Toshihiko Kikuichi	73	75	77	75	300	105,000
Kazumasa Tamura	74	76	74	76	300	105,000
Kiyoshi Nakagawa	77	73	72	78	300	105,000
Masamitsu Oguri	74	76	73	77	300	105,000
Norihiko Matsumoto	76	74	77	73	300	105,000
Masashi Terajima	73	71	77	80	301	95,000
Katsuyuki Hirano	76	76	77	72	301	95,000
Kiyotoshi Takahashi	76	75	74	77	302	90,000
Isao Ohba	78	74	74	76	302	90,000
Seiji Mitsuki	70	78	75	80	303	86,667
Ikuhiro Niina	79	74	75	75	303	86,667
Masataka Yagi	75	71	80	77	303	86,667
Toshiki Matsui	76	76	74	78	304	86,667
Toshiharu Morimoto	81	71	75	77	304	80,000
Hiroshi Kondo	78	75	73	78	304	80,000
Toshiharu Kanazawa	73	79	77	75	304	80,000
Tsukasa Yasui	76	73	74	82	305	70,000
Hatsutoshi Sakai	76	75	79	75	305	70,000
Eitaro Deguchi	72	77	74	82	305	70,000
Tetsuo Yamura	72	74	82	77	305	70,000
Nobuyoshi Tsukuba	76	76	76	77	305	70,000
Shimesu Tajima	77	76	78	77	308	60,000
Isao Kobayashi	74	72	77	75	308	60,000
Kazuo Hanamura	69	73	84	82	308	60,000
Toshiaki Yokoi	79	74	78	78	309	60,000
Yoichi Enomoto	77	75	75	74	309	60,000
Migiri Kato	77	75	80	80	312	50,000
Toshiyuki Itoh	77	76	79	81	312	50,000
Tainen Terashita	73	79	81	79	312	50,000

Hiroshima Open

Hiroshima Country Club, Happonmatsu Course
Par 72; 6,884 yards

September 27–30
purse, ¥20,000,000

	SCORES				TOTAL	MONEY
Yoshitaka Yamamoto	67	70	67	66	270	¥4,000,000
Yoshikazu Yokoshima	65	73	69	71	278	1,750,000
Haruo Yasuda	70	66	71	71	278	1,750,000
Chen Tze Ming	70	70	65	74	279	1,100,000
Mya Aye	69	66	70	74	279	1,100,000
Tadami Ueno	71	73	71	65	280	800,000
Tsutomu Irie	66	73	74	68	281	600,000
Ho Ming Chung	66	72	72	71	281	600,000
Koichi Inoue	75	67	67	72	281	600,000
Yoshiharu Takai	69	75	72	66	282	370,000
Tsuneyuki Nakajima	71	72	69	70	282	370,000
Fumio Hitachi	70	72	70	70	282	370,000
Seiichi Kanai	70	73	69	70	282	370,000

Yoshihisa Iwashita	70	72	70	71	283	300,000
Keiichi Hoshino	67	72	70	74	283	300,000
Hsieh Min Nan	71	71	68	73	283	300,000
Yoshio Kusayanagi	70	70	74	70	284	215,000
Hideo Ishii	70	73	71	70	284	215,000
Akira Yabe	68	70	75	71	284	215,000
Shinsaku Maeda	67	72	73	72	284	215,000
Norio Suzuki	72	70	69	73	284	215,000
Kikuo Arai	70	69	72	73	284	215,000
Shigeru Uchida	71	70	74	70	285	155,000
Yasutomo Ishii	70	72	73	70	285	155,000
Koichi Uehara	73	72	68	72	285	155,000
Yutaka Hanekawa°	71	72	68	74	285	
Fumio Tanaka	69	69	70	77	285	155,000
Brian Jones	73	68	72	73	286	140,000
Kazuo Yoshikawa	70	69	72	75	286	140,000
Keiji Mori	71	74	71	72	288	140,000
Kazunari Takahashi	73	70	71	74	288	140,000
Kosaku Shimada	68	76	72	73	289	130,000
Ichiro Teramoto	68	75	70	76	289	130,000
Masaru Amano	72	68	78	72	290	127,500
Masashi Ozaki	70	66	81	73	290	127,500
Ichiro Togawa	70	75	71	74	290	127,500
Hideyo Sugimoto	71	71	72	76	290	127,500
Tateo Ozaki	71	71	74	75	291	120,000
Shinichi Hayashi	70	70	77	74	291	120,000
Yuji Ishii	71	74	73	73	291	120,000
Minoru Nakamura	69	71	74	77	291	120,000
Teruo Sugihara	69	74	76	73	292	110,000
Takemitsu Uranishi	72	73	74	73	292	110,000
Toshiki Matsui	70	73	72	77	292	110,000
Hideto Shigenobu	71	71	72	78	292	110,000
Mitsuhiko Masuda	74	69	71	78	292	110,000
Namio Takasu	74	70	72	77	293	100,000
Saburo Fujii	69	74	78	74	295	100,000
Toshihiko Kikuichi	72	68	79	77	296	100,000

Gene Sarazen Jun Classic

Jun Classic Golf Course, Tochigi, Japan
Par 72; 7,090 yards

October 4–7
purse, ¥35,000,000

	SCORES				TOTAL	MONEY
Kuo Chi Hsiung	68	73	69	38	248	¥7,000,000
Ikuhiro Funatogawa	70	69	74	35	248	3,500,000
(Kuo defeated Funatogawa on fifth hole of sudden-death play-off)						
Hiroshi Ishii	71	71	70	37	249	2,500,000
Haruo Yasuda	71	68	73	38	250	1,533,333
Fujio Kobayashi	69	71	70	40	250	1,533,333
Tsuneyuki Nakajima	69	72	69	40	250	1,533,333
Seiji Ebihara	72	74	69	36	251	900,000
Naomichi Ozaki	72	73	68	38	251	900,000
Yoshitaka Yamamoto	68	72	71	40	251	900,000
Hsieh Min Nan	71	70	75	37	253	700,000
Satsuki Takahashi	68	73	73	40	254	625,000
Norio Suzuki	71	72	71	40	254	625,000
Mitsuhiko Masuda	71	75	73	36	255	510,000
Brian Jones	72	71	75	37	255	510,000
Teruo Suzumura	71	74	73	37	255	510,000
Hideyo Sugimoto	73	69	77	37	256	420,000
Shichiro Enomoto	73	70	75	38	256	420,000
Ben Arda	70	74	72	40	256	420,000
Koichi Uehara	71	72	73	40	256	420,000
Akira Yabe	71	72	71	42	256	420,000
Chen Tze Ming	72	71	76	38	257	350,000
Toshiyuki Tsuchiyama	74	71	72	40	257	350,000
Hisashi Suzumura	73	72	71	41	257	350,000
Nobuo Takahashi	72	70	73	42	257	350,000
Hiroshi Tahara	72	70	74	41	257	350,000
Yoshio Kusayanagi	73	71	76	38	258	295,000
Kenji Mori	73	73	73	39	258	295,000
Takaaki Kono	71	72	75	40	258	295,000
Yasuhiro Miyamoto	69	71	76	42	258	295,000
Masami Kawamura	68	72	76	42	258	295,000
Mitsuhiro Kitta	73	73	71	41	258	295,000
Akio Kanamoto	73	71	75	40	259	250,000
Hsieh Yung Yo	73	71	74	41	259	250,000
Hideo Ishii	68	75	73	43	259	250,000
George Knudson	72	74	78	36	260	210,714
Masayuki Imai	74	73	74	39	260	210,714
Masaji Kusakabe	73	74	73	40	260	210,714
Kuniaki Sato	73	74	73	40	260	210,714
Namio Takasu	71	72	75	42	260	210,714
Shigeru Noguchi	75	71	72	42	260	210,714
Tadami Ueno	69	75	73	43	260	210,714
Shinichi Hayashi	75	72	74	40	261	172,500
Shigeru Uchida	73	74	75	39	261	172,500
Kosaku Shimada	73	74	75	39	261	172,500

Kazunari Takahashi	73	73	77	38	261	172,500
Toshiharu Kawada	74	72	77	38	261	172,500
Mya Aye	74	72	78	37	261	172,500
Peter Thomson	72	71	77	41	261	172,500
Minoru Hiyoshi	72	72	75	42	261	172,500
Hiroshi Yamada	71	72	78	41	262	140,000
Katsuji Hasegawa	73	73	74	42	262	140,000
Seiichi Kanai	71	75	74	42	262	140,000
Teruo Sugihara	72	73	74	43	262	140,000

Tokai Classic

Miyoshi Country Club, Negoya, Japan
Par 72; 7,065 yards

October 11–14
purse, ¥32,025,000

	SCORES				TOTAL	MONEY
Tsutomu Irie	70	69	68	68	275	¥7,000,000
Hsieh Min Nan	67	72	71	70	280	2,900,000
Masaji Kusakabe	69	71	68	72	280	2,900,000
Ben Arda	70	70	67	74	281	1,500,000
Toshiharu Kawada	72	69	71	70	282	1,150,000
Tadashi Kitta	70	70	70	72	282	1,150,000
Andy Bean	69	69	72	72	282	1,150,000
Lu Liang Huan	73	70	71	69	283	800,000
Tsuneyuki Nakajima	71	71	71	70	283	800,000
Norio Suzuki	71	72	68	72	283	800,000
Teruo Sugihara	71	70	71	72	284	550,000
Yutaka Suzuki	71	68	73	72	284	550,000
Shigeru Uchida	70	71	70	73	284	550,000
Hsu Sheng San	74	69	70	73	286	450,000
Yoshitaka Yamamoto	72	71	72	72	287	350,000
Koichi Inoue	73	69	72	73	287	350,000
Kikuo Arai	72	70	71	74	287	350,000
Masashi Ozaki	69	72	73	73	287	350,000
Hiroshi Ishii	72	71	73	71	287	350,000
Kenji Mori	72	71	73	71	287	350,000
Kazuo Yoshikawa	69	70	70	79	288	255,000
Akio Toyoda	71	72	74	71	288	255,000
Kesahiko Uchida	69	72	76	71	288	255,000
Haruhiko Bando	74	70	71	73	288	255,000
Seiichi Kanai	71	69	75	73	288	255,000
Haruo Yasuda	71	74	71	72	288	255,000
Saburo Fujiki	73	73	70	72	288	255,000
Fujio Kobayashi	70	71	70	77	288	255,000
Hideto Shigenobu	74	70	73	72	289	193,333
Kuo Chi Hsiung	71	71	71	76	289	193,333
Masaru Amano	73	72	73	71	289	193,333
Masahiko Yamamoto	69	74	76	70	289	193,333
Tadami Ueno	69	72	74	74	289	193,333
Toshiki Matsui	70	72	73	74	289	193,000
Johji Yokoi	69	71	76	75	291	172,500
Mya Aye	74	68	75	74	291	172,500
Akinori Tamura	69	75	72	77	293	156,000
Shoichi Sato	71	73	75	74	293	156,000
Katsuji Kikuchi	74	72	72	75	293	156,000
Yurio Akitomi	74	72	77	70	293	156,000
Hideo Noguchi	73	70	77	73	293	156,000
Yoshio Matsumoto	71	73	74	77	295	150,000
Namio Takasu	74	72	74	75	295	150,000
Teruo Suzumura	74	72	74	75	296	150,000
Shinsaku Maeda	69	76	78	73	296	150,000
Masaharu Ohshima	73	73	72	78	296	150,000
Satsuki Takahashi	72	74	78	73	296	150,000

Golf Digest

Tomei Country Club, Shizuoka, Japan
Par 72; 6,857 yards

October 18–21
purse, ¥25,000,000

	SCORES			TOTAL	MONEY
Kuo Chi Hsiung	69	68	69	206	¥5,000,000
Fujio Kobayashi	64	70	75	209	2,500,000
Namio Takasu	68	72	70	210	1,500,000
Lu Hsi Chuen	72	71	68	211	1,100,000
Tsuneyuki Nakajima	71	68	72	211	1,100,000
Saburo Fujiki	70	72	70	212	900,000
Hsieh Min Nan	72	71	70	213	750,000
Masaji Kusakabe	72	67	74	213	750,000
Tsutomu Irie	72	74	68	214	523,330
Takaaki Kono	77	65	72	214	523,330
Ho Ming Chung	72	70	72	214	523,330
Hahn Chang Sang	74	70	71	215	380,000
Takahiro Takeyasu	69	75	71	215	380,000
Masayuki Imai	73	70	72	215	380,000
Akira Yabe	72	70	73	215	380,000
Hideo Ishii	69	69	77	215	380,000

Hiroshi Ishii	72	71	73	216	280,000
Haruo Yasuda	72	69	75	216	280,000
Koichi Inoue	70	70	76	216	280,000
Johji Yokoi	74	70	73	217	205,000
Satsuki Takahashi	72	71	74	217	205,000
Chen Chien Chung	72	71	74	217	205,000
Ichiro Teramoto	69	71	77	217	205,000
Koichi Uehara	78	70	70	218	188,000
Isao Isozaki	71	74	73	218	188,000
Teruo Suzumura	71	73	74	218	188,000
Toru Nakamura	69	74	75	218	188,000
Mya Aye	69	71	78	218	188,000
Shoichi Sato	77	71	71	219	166,660
Teruo Sugihara	76	71	72	219	166,660
Hsu Sheng San	74	71	74	219	166,660
Norio Suzuki	73	71	75	219	166,660
Masashi Ozaki	75	70	74	219	166,660
Mitsuhiro Kitta	72	71	76	219	166,660
Tatsuo Fujima	75	71	74	220	145,000
Chi Tze Ming	72	73	75	220	145,000
Masami Kawamura	74	72	74	220	145,000
Shinsaku Maeda	72	71	77	220	145,000
Kenichi Yamada	1	75	75	221	133,330
Kikuo Arai	73	72	76	221	133,330
Seiichi Kanai	75	69	77	221	133,330
Masahiko Yamamoto	75	73	74	222	120,000
Chen Ching Po	72	76	74	222	120,000
Chen Chien Chin	74	71	77	222	120,000
Kenji Mori	76	72	75	223	120,000
Shinobu Tonooka	75	72	76	223	120,000
Minoru Hiyoshi	72	74	77	223	120,000
Sadao Sakashita	74	74	76	224	120,000
Masaru Amano	68	79	77	224	120,000
Yoshikazu Yokoshima	71	76	77	224	120,000

Bridgestone

Sodegaura Country Club, Chiba, Japan
Par 72; 7,151 yards

October 25–28
purse, ¥30,000,000

		SCORES			TOTAL	MONEY
Lanny Wadkins	66	71	69	71	277	¥6,000,000
Yoshikazu Yokoshima	67	68	71	72	278	3,000,000
Seiichi Kanai	72	70	71	68	281	1,566,666
Norio Suzuki	70	72	68	71	281	1,566,666
Ikuhiro Funatogawa	72	69	68	72	281	1,566,666
Fujio Kobayashi	72	73	70	67	282	940,000
Kenichi Yamada	73	71	67	71	282	940,000
Kuo Chi Hsiung	72	70	72	68	282	940,000
Shinsaku Maeda	74	71	69	69	283	725,000
Masaji Kusakabe	69	72	71	71	283	725,000
Masashi Ozaki	72	71	72	69	284	620,000
Shigeru Uchida	70	68	73	74	285	590,000
Koichi Uehara	74	72	75	65	286	455,000
Hsu Sheng San	69	75	72	70	286	455,000
Isao Aoki	70	73	72	71	286	455,000
Tsuneyuki Nakajima	70	72	71	73	286	455,000
Hale Irwin	73	70	70	73	286	455,000
Kikuo Arai	71	74	67	74	286	455,000
Fumio Tanaka	71	69	69	77	286	455,000
Tateo Ozaki	72	71	68	75	286	455,000
Masuaki Nakamura	73	72	71	71	287	295,000
Tsutomu Irie	71	70	74	72	287	295,000
Tadami Ueno	73	72	75	68	288	270,000
Shigeru Noguchi	72	74	70	72	288	270,000
Kuzuo Hashimoto	74	70	69	75	288	270,000
Haruo Yasuda	71	75	70	73	289	237,142
Toshimitsu Kai	71	70	74	74	289	237,142
Katsuji Hasegawa	73	70	76	70	289	237,142
Yoshitaka Yamamoto	73	72	73	71	289	237,142
Naomichi Ozaki	71	71	76	71	289	237,142
Shinichi Hayashi	72	71	71	75	289	237,142
Masahiko Yamamoto	69	73	75	72	289	237,142
Hiroshi Ishii	71	70	74	75	290	205,000
Isao Ohba	74	68	75	73	290	205,000
Tadashi Kitta	75	71	70	74	290	205,000
Harunobu Fujii	71	71	74	75	291	190,000
Lyao Kuo Chih	71	73	76	71	291	190,000
Kazuo Yoshikawa	68	75	75	73	291	190,000
Seiji Ogawa	72	73	75	72	292	155,000
Minoru Hiyoshi	70	76	73	73	292	155,000
Hsieh Yung Yo	74	72	73	73	292	155,000
Lu Liang Huan	71	75	73	73	292	155,000
Kenji Mori	71	74	73	74	292	155,000

Yoshiteru Arano	72	70	76	74	292	155,000
Toshiaki Sekimizu	72	72	73	75	292	155,000
Wataru Murakami	70	73	74	75	292	155,000
Takaaki Kono	69	73	73	78	293	125,000
Sadao Sakashita	73	70	76	74	293	125,000
Hisao Inoue	70	74	74	75	293	125,000
Takashi Murakami	72	73	77	72	294	110,000
Kenji Ueda	73	73	74	74	294	110,000

Japan Open

Hino Golf Club, King Course, Shiga, Japan
Par 72; 7,043 yards

November 1–4
purse, ¥48,633,000

	SCORES				TOTAL	MONEY
Kuo Chi Hsiung	71	70	70	74	285	¥8,000,000
Yoshitaka Yamamoto	73	71	67	74	285	3,433,334
Isao Aoki	75	73	66	71	285	3,433,333
Koichi Uehara	74	72	74	65	285	3,433,333

(Kuo defeated Yamamoto, Aoki and Uehara in sudden-death play-off, Aoki and Uehara on first extra hole, Yamamoto on fourth)

Lon Hinkle	71	74	68	73	286	1,650,000
Shigeru Uchida	71	74	69	72	286	1,650,000
Severiano Ballesteros	74	71	73	69	287	1,200,000
Haruo Yasuda	71	74	71	71	287	1,200,000
Teruo Sugihara	73	69	72	73	287	1,200,000
Yoshikazu Yokoshima	76	71	72	69	288	950,000
Masaji Kusakabe	73	74	71	70	288	950,000
Norio Suzuki	74	72	70	72	288	950,000
Toru Nakamura	71	75	73	70	289	700,000
Tadashi Kitta	71	72	75	71	289	700,000
Lu Liang Huan	72	75	70	72	289	700,000
Kosaku Shimada	74	74	69	72	289	700,000
Teruo Suzumura	77	72	68	72	289	700,000
Tadami Ueno	70	69	75	75	289	700,000
Shigeru Kubota	70	69	71	79	289	700,000
Tsuneyuki Nakajima	73	76	71	70	290	480,000
Toshiharu Kawada	71	73	75	71	290	480,000
Chi Tze Ming	76	72	70	72	290	480,000
Hideyo Sugimoto	71	73	76	72	292	430,000
Kenichi Yamada	72	69	75	76	292	430,000
Fujio Kobayashi	75	72	77	69	293	277,500
Namio Takasu	71	71	79	72	293	377,500
Ikuhiro Funatogawa	75	73	72	73	293	377,500
Chen Chien Chung	71	74	73	75	293	377,500
Koichi Inoue	74	75	75	70	294	310,000
Toshiharu Morimoto	73	72	75	74	294	310,000
Nikuo Arai	73	73	74	74	294	310,000
Hahn Chang Sang	74	74	72	74	294	310,000
Chen Chien Chung	72	72	75	75	294	310,000
Masami Kawamura	70	75	72	77	294	310,000
Lu Hsi Chuen	73	71	73	77	294	310,000
Shichiro Enomoto	75	74	75	71	295	265,000
Masuaki Nakamura	74	73	73	75	295	265,000
Takahiro Takeyasu	72	75	71	77	295	265,000
Hiroshi Ishii	75	74	74	73	296	245,834
Akio Kanamoto	75	72	75	74	296	245,834
Shinsaku Maeda	75	73	74	74	296	245,833
Toshiharu Kanazawa	75	74	73	74	296	245,833
Mitsuhiko Masuda	75	72	73	76	296	245,833
Chen Ching Po	73	74	73	76	296	245,833
Hsieh Min Nan	75	74	75	73	297	230,500
Seiichi Kanai	72	77	72	76	297	230,500
Hsieh Yung Yo	77	71	73	76	297	230,500
Shinichi Hayashi	74	72	70	81	297	230,500
Graham Marsh	75	71	77	75	298	223,000

United States vs Japan

Sports Shinko Country Club, Hyogo, Japan
Par 72; 6,958 yards

November 8–11
purse, ¥30,000,000

	SCORES				TOTAL	MONEY
Tom Purtzer	69	67	68	72	276	¥6,000,000
Bill Rogers	73	73	69	71	286	3,000,000
Isao Aoki	71	72	72	72	287	1,067,000
Fujio Kobayashi	73	71	72	71	287	1,067,000
Yoshitaka Yamamoto	71	70	74	72	287	1,067,000
Masashi Ozaki	71	76	70	72	289	575,000
Ray Floyd	66	74	73	76	289	575,000
Tsuneyuki Nakajima	73	70	73	74	290	475,000

Andy North	76	71	72	71	290	475,000
Kosaku Shimada	75	72	74	70	291	375,000
Toru Nakamura	71	73	74	73	291	375,000
Ed Sneed	70	72	77	74	293	317,000
Lee Trevino	73	74	74	72	293	317,000
Dave Stockton	71	75	73	74	293	317,000
Teruo Sugihara	72	72	80	70	294	250,000
Haruo Yasuda	75	72	75	73	295	250,000
Bruce Lietzke	75	74	75	72	296	250,000
Bob Byman	73	73	77	76	299	250,000

Final Team Results: Japan, 2,306; United States, 2,311. Each member of winning team received ¥1,000,000; each member of losing team ¥400,000. Best eight of nine scores for each counted each round.

Omote Zao International Tohoku Open

Omote Zao International Golf Club, Yamagata, Japan
Par 72; 6,819 yards

November 9–11
purse, ¥11,000,000

	SCORES			TOTAL	MONEY
Hideo Ishii	69	73	73	215	¥2,000,000
Koichi Uehara	73	70	73	216	766,666
Kyoji Asai	68	72	76	216	766,666
Toshitsugu Ebara	71	71	74	216	766,666
Fumio Tanaka	71	72	74	217	416,666
Hisashi Suzumura	71	70	76	217	416,666
Lyao Kuo Chih	71	72	74	217	416,666
Takashi Kurihara	72	73	73	218	275,000
Hiroshi Tahara	73	74	71	218	275,000
Shigeru Kubota	70	73	76	219	200,000
Shinsaku Maeda	78	69	72	219	170,000
Kukuo Arai	74	71	74	219	170,000
Toshiyuki Amano	73	71	75	219	170,000
Motomasa Aoki	76	72	72	220	170,000
Namio Takasu	74	73	73	220	170,000
Yoshio Kusayanagi	71	74	76	221	150,000
Toshiaki Sekimizu	75	73	73	221	150,000
Isao Matsui	74	73	74	221	150,000
Fumio Hitachi	72	73	76	221	150,000
Mikio Ichikawa	74	73	75	222	140,000
Seiji Kobayashi	74	72	76	222	140,000
Naomichi Ozaki	76	75	72	223	130,000
Takaaki Kono	76	74	73	223	130,000
Hsu Chi San	73	75	75	223	130,000
Yoshiteru Arano	73	72	78	223	130,000
Masahiko Yamamoto	77	74	73	224	110,000
Takahiro Takeyasu	74	75	75	224	110,000
Shigehiko Tonooka	76	74	75	225	103,750
Satsuki Takahashi	71	78	76	225	103,750
Chen Chien Chin	72	76	77	225	103,750
Akira Masuda	70	76	79	225	103,750
Masamitsu Oguri	72	75	79	226	85,000
Harunobu Fujii	73	76	77	226	85,000
Toshiyuki Tsuchiyama	77	75	74	226	85,000
Tomio Ishii	78	73	75	226	85,000
Kiyokuni Kimoto	75	73	79	227	75,000
Yoshimu Niizeki	72	77	78	227	75,000
Masaru Sasaki	76	75	77	228	75,000
Koji Nakajima	80	73	75	228	75,000
Tateo Ozaki	79	72	78	229	67,500
Ichio Sato	76	75	78	229	67,500
Kenji Mori	75	75	79	229	67,500
Ikuhiro Funatogawa	79	73	77	229	67,500
Takashi Iwai	77	75	78	230	60,000
Taiichi Nakagawa	75	75	80	230	60,000
Kesahiko Uchida	74	75	81	230	60,000
Takao Kage	77	76	77	230	60,000
Toshiki Matsui	75	76	80	231	55,000
Makoto Ioka	81	72	78	231	55,000
Hisao Inoue	71	81	79	231	55,000

Taiheiyo Club Masters

Taiheiyo Club, Gotemba Course, Shizuoka, Japan
Par 72; 7,100 yards

November 15–18
purse, ¥68,034,159

	SCORES				TOTAL	MONEY
Norio Suzuki	73	69	67	71	280	¥16,139,500
Bill Rogers	69	71	69	73	282	5,586,750
Tom Watson	73	69	68	72	282	5,586,750
Rod Curl	71	72	67	72	282	5,586,750
Masaru Amano	66	72	73	72	283	2,731,300
Fujio Kobayashi	73	72	70	69	284	1,986,400

Naomichi Ozaki	79	68	68	70	285	1,576,705
Bruce Lietzke	70	77	67	71	285	1,576,705
Masashi Ozaki	75	71	70	70	286	1,117,350
Shigeru Uchida	72	71	72	71	286	1,117,350
Lu Liang Huan	68	71	72	75	286	1,117,350
Hiroshi Ishii	71	73	71	71	286	1,117,350
Gil Morgan	72	71	68	75	286	1,117,350
John Fought	72	69	73	72	286	1,117,350
Lon Hinkle	70	71	72	73	286	1,117,350
Shinsaku Maeda	71	73	73	70	287	780,369
Kosaku Shimada	68	73	72	74	287	780,369
Jim Simons	75	70	70	72	287	780,369
Danny Edwards	77	70	66	74	287	780,369
Bobby Wadkins	73	72	71	71	287	780,369
Jerry Pate	68	74	69	76	287	780,369
Lee Trevino	73	69	73	72	287	780,369
Isao Aoki	70	77	68	73	288	636,268
Toru Nakamura	75	69	70	74	288	636,268
Tom Purtzer	71	72	72	73	288	636,268
Larry Nelson	69	77	69	73	288	636,268
George Archer	73	74	70	72	289	583,505
Lee Elder	71	76	69	73	289	583,505
Mark Hayes	72	72	69	76	289	583,505
Koichi Inoue	73	71	70	76	290	546,260
Kuo Chi Hsiung	72	73	73	72	290	546,260
Mark McCumber	73	72	71	74	290	546,260
Tsuneyuki Nakajima	75	69	70	77	291	521,430
Takahiro Takeyasu	73	72	74	73	292	477,977
Yoshitaka Yamamoto	73	70	74	75	292	477,977
Yoshikazu Yokoshima	77	70	71	74	292	477,977
Hideyo Sugimoto	71	74	71	76	292	477,977
Hsieh Min Nan	75	72	71	74	292	477,977
Toshiharu Kawada	73	74	70	75	292	477,977
Bob Gilder	72	75	73	73	293	428,317
Don January	76	71	70	76	293	428,317
Saburo Fujiki	74	73	70	77	294	383,089
Tadami Ueno	75	70	72	77	294	383,089
Minoru Nakamura	75	72	74	73	294	383,089
Kikuo Arai	73	72	75	74	294	383,089
Takashi Murakami	71	73	75	75	294	383,089
Aki Kanamoto	73	74	74	73	294	383,089
Peter Jacobsen	72	70	81	71	294	383,089
Namio Takasu	72	74	73	76	295	372,450
Seiichi Kanai	73	72	75	76	296	372,450
Hsieh Yung Yo	72	73	75	76	296	372,450

Dunlop Phoenix

Phoenix Country Country Club, Miyazaki, Japan
Par 72; 6,989 yards

November 22–25
purse, ¥60,000,000

	SCORES				TOTAL	MONEY
Bobby Wadkins	73	67	71	73	284	¥10,000,000
Lu Liang Huan	72	72	74	69	287	5,000,000
Namio Takasu	69	70	73	75	287	5,000,000
Takahiro Takeyasu	68	75	70	75	288	7,750,000
Sandy Lyle	70	72	70	76	288	2,750,000
Bob Byman	73	73	72	71	289	2,050,000
Tom Watson	73	75	67	74	289	2,050,000
Masashi Ozaki	75	72	74	69	290	1,516,666
Toru Nakamura	71	72	73	74	290	1,516,666
Lon Hinkle	76	71	72	71	290	1,516,666
Hubert Green	73	72	74	72	291	1,300,000
Masaji Kusakabe	75	71	75	71	292	1,200,000
Koichi Uehara	74	74	74	71	293	1,060,000
Akio Kanamoto	71	73	71	78	293	1,060,000
Lou Graham	71	72	78	73	294	833,333
Fuzzy Zoeller	74	75	73	72	294	883,333
Ed Sneed	74	75	71	74	294	883,333
Johnny Miller	75	76	72	72	295	745,000
Howard Twitty	73	72	75	75	295	745,000
Kenichi Yamada	70	72	77	77	296	660,000
Isao Aoki	70	73	76	77	296	660,000
Yasuhiro Miyamoto	76	73	75	73	297	544,000
Takaaki Kono	73	72	77	75	297	544,000
John Fought	69	76	78	74	297	544,000
Danny Edwards	72	78	78	69	297	544,000
Saburo Fujiki	70	74	81	72	297	544,000
Katsuji Hasegawa	79	73	77	69	298	424,285
Tadami Ueno	76	73	76	73	298	424,285
Larry Nelson	76	72	75	75	298	424,285
Fujio Kobayashi	75	74	73	76	298	424,285
Shigeru Kubota	72	74	75	77	298	424,285
Akira Yabe	75	73	72	78	298	424,285
Seiichi Kanai	71	76	72	79	298	424,285
Yoshikazu Yokoshima	73	76	74	76	299	370,000
Teruo Sugihara	78	73	77	72	300	345,000
Teruo Suzumura	80	72	74	74	300	345,000

Ikuhiro Funatogawa	70	79	74	77	300	345,000
Shigeru Uchida	69	79	75	77	300	345,000
Mya Aye	73	78	74	76	301	315,000
Kazuo Yoshikawa	73	72	78	78	301	315,000
Takashi Murakami	74	72	76	80	302	300,000
Takashi Kurihara	74	72	80	76	302	300,000
Bob Gilder	73	69	84	76	302	300,000
Chen Chien Chin	73	75	78	76	302	300,000
Mark Hayes	74	75	75	78	302	300,000
Tsutomu Irie	75	74	74	79	302	300,000
Norio Suzuki	71	80	74	77	302	300,000
Seiji Ebihara	76	74	78	75	303	300,000
Kenji Mori	74	75	76	78	303	300,000
Koichi Inoue	75	77	78	74	304	258,333
Kikuo Arai	70	77	82	75	304	258,333
Masaru Amano	76	73	79	76	304	258,333
Tadashi Kitta	75	75	78	76	304	258,333
Jerry McGee	77	74	74	79	304	258,333
Shinsaku Maeda	74	74	75	81	304	258,333

Japan Series

Yomiuri Country Clubs, Tokyo and Osaka, Japan
Osaka: Par 73; 7,183 yards (First two rounds)
Tokyo: Par 72; 7,017 yards (Last two rounds)

November 28–December 1
purse, ¥16,000,000

	SCORES				TOTAL	MONEY
Isao Aoki	68	71	66	71	276	¥5,000,000
Toru Nakamura	71	75	73	70	289	1,900,000
Kikuo Arai	73	71	71	74	289	1,900,000
Fujio Kobayashi	71	76	68	75	290	900,000
Norio Suzuki	71	71	73	77	292	800,000
Masashi Ozaki	81	69	70	73	293	650,000
Kuo Chi Hsiung	73	72	72	76	293	650,000
Teruo Sugihara	76	71	67	80	294	500,000
Yasuhiro Miyamoto	77	72	74	72	295	466,666
Haruo Yasuda	75	74	73	73	295	466,666
Hsieh Min Nan	71	73	73	78	295	466,666
Masaru Amano	74	72	75	76	297	375,000
Namio Takasu	74	74	75	74	297	375,000
Masaji Kusakabe	69	78	78	75	300	325,000
Hiroshi Ishii	75	76	73	76	300	325,000
Tsuneyuki Nakajima	80	73	73	75	301	300,000
Yoshitaka Yamamoto	77	79	79	78	313	300,000
Hideo Shigenobu	78	80	80	79	317	300,000

AUSTRALIAN TOUR

Traralgon Loy Yang Classic

Traralgon Golf Club, Traralgon, Victoria
Par 37–35—72; 6,342 yards

January 26–29
purse, A.$15,000[†]

	SCORES				TOTAL	MONEY
Greg Norman	69	65	71	72	277	A.$3,000.00
Ian Stanley	73	71	68	68	280	1,462.50
Glenn McCully	69	68	69	74	280	1,462.50
David Good	66	70	74	71	281	765.00
Rodger Davis	69	73	73	67	282	540.00
Trevor McDonald	67	72	71	72	282	540.00
Brian Jones	71	65	73	73	282	540.00
Guy Wolstenholme	74	71	68	70	283	405.00
Stewart Ginn	71	67	73	72	283	405.00
Deray Simon	70	71	73	70	284	309.60
Bill Britten	72	70	72	70	284	309.60
Paul Firmstone	71	71	72	70	284	309.60
Mike Ferguson	72	68	72	72	284	309.60
Richard Coombes	72	73	67	72	284	309.60
Bob Beauchemin	71	72	72	70	285	247.50
Mike Cahill	69	73	71	72	285	247.50
Ron Wood	70	72	73	71	285	187.50
Peter Senior	72	70	74	70	286	187.50
Geoff Parslow	68	72	73	73	286	187.50
Rick Barker	71	71	71	73	286	187.50
Terry Kendall	70	73	71	72	286	187.50
Ted Ball	70	70	72	74	286	187.50
Col Bishop	73	77	69	68	287	127.50
Gary Merrick	72	70	74	71	287	127.50
Richard Lee	73	71	73	71	288	105.00
Marty Bohen	73	72	70	73	288	105.00
John Downs	71	71	73	73	288	105.00
Peter Headland	72	69	72	75	288	105.00
Gerry Goss	72	69	76	72	289	88.50
Gary Doolan	72	69	73	75	289	88.50
Duncan Moodie	74	75	74	67	290	82.50
Tim Ward	74	71	74	71	290	82.50
Colin Stott	73	71	74	73	291	73.50
Bob Shaw	65	76	76	74	291	73.50
Ian Cross	73	74	70	74	291	73.50
Terry Gilmore	70	73	70	78	291	73.50
Vaughan Somers	74	73	74	71	292	63.00
George Serhan	73	72	73	74	292	63.00
Harry Berwick	67	80	72	73	292	63.00
Ramon Kesur	73	75	71	74	293	57.00
Rob McNaughton	76	74	72	72	294	54.00
Graeme Bugden	75	71	76	73	295	51.00
Peter Davidson	69	77	75	75	296	48.00
Tim Ireland	76	74	77	70	297	39.00
David Leary	74	76	76	71	297	39.00
Mark Griffin	74	72	75	76	297	39.00
Greg Hohnen	70	74	75	78	297	39.00
Keith Testro	73	76	72	76	297	39.00
Alex Bonnington	75	75	75	73	298	28.50
Rod Mills	71	73	77	77	298	28.50

[†]One Australian dollar = U.S. $1.09

Tattersall's Tasmanian Open

Devonport Golf Club, Woodrising, Tasmania
Par 35–35—70; 6,480 yards

February 1–4
purse, A.$20,000

	SCORES				TOTAL	MONEY
Marty Bohen	66	68	67	70	271	A.$4,000.00
Terry Kendall	66	72	65	72	275	2,400.00
Col Bishop	69	70	69	71	279	936.00
Billy Dunk	68	71	70	70	279	936.00
Rob McNaughton	73	63	72	71	279	936.00
Greg Norman	66	69	72	72	279	936.00
Ian Stanley	71	67	68	73	279	936.00
Rodger Davis	68	68	75	69	280	560.00
Bob Beauchemin	75	71	65	70	281	480.00
Stewart Ginn	72	70	66	73	281	480.00
Trevor McDonald	70	66	71	74	281	480.00
Gary Doolan	71	73	67	71	282	400.00
Ted Ball	71	73	68	71	283	351.00
Terry Gale	70	71	69	73	283	351.00
David Good	71	70	71	71	283	351.00
Stuart Reese	69	70	71	73	283	351.00
Barry Burgess	75	66	71	72	284	250.00

Paul Firmstone	69	70	72	73	284	250.00
Brian Jones	72	71	69	72	284	250.00
Deray Simon	70	74	69	71	284	250.00
Chris Tickner	69	70	73	72	284	250.00
Guy Wolstenholme	74	70	70	70	284	250.00
Bill Wellington°	70	72	71	72	285	
Greg Alexander°	74	68	70	73	285	
Greg Hohnen	72	70	71	73	286	159.00
Craig Owen	74	70	70	72	286	159.00
Bob Shaw	70	68	73	75	286	159.00
Colin Stott	66	71	76	73	286	159.00
Peter Senior	76	68	74	69	287	132.00
Harry Berwick	71	70	75	71	287	132.00
Rick Barker	74	72	70	72	288	118.00
Richard Lee	72	74	70	72	288	118.00
Alex Bonnington	73	72	70	74	289	112.00
Vaughan Somers	73	71	70	76	290	106.00
Robert Werrell	76	70	71	73	290	106.00
Gerry Goss	71	72	71	77	291	94.00
Ramon Kesur	71	72	74	74	291	94.00
Glenn McCully	76	70	74	71	291	94.00
Peter Pearce	72	72	70	77	291	94.00
Richard Coombes	76	72	72	72	292	78.00
Mike Ferguson	71	73	75	73	292	78.00
Paul Foley	72	72	75	73	292	78.00
Steve Slater	71	75	73	73	292	78.00
Terry Gilmore	73	72	71	77	293	68.00
Chris Witcher	75	72	74	74	295	64.00
John Downs	76	70	73	77	296	52.00
Peter Headland	75	72	76	73	296	52.00
David Leary	71	77	78	70	296	52.00
John Mellish	73	73	77	73	296	52.00
Gary Merrick	76	70	75	75	296	52.00
Bruce Hodson	73	71	74	79	297	38.00
Geoff Moore	72	75	74	76	297	38.00

° Amateur

Victorian Open Championship

Kingston Heath Golf Club, Melbourne, Victoria
Par 36–36—72; 6,808 yards

February 15–18
purse, A.$60,000

	SCORES				TOTAL	MONEY
Rodger Davis	75	73	70	73	291	A.$12,000.00
Gary Player	72	76	70	73	291	5,905.00
Geoff Parslow	72	71	75	73	291	5,905.00
(Davis defeated Player and Parslow on second hole of sudden-death play-off)						
Tony Gresham°	79	73	72	68	292	
Ian Stanley	69	77	74	72	292	2,730.00
Trevor McDonald	76	70	72	74	292	2,730.00
Greg Norman	73	81	71	68	293	2,160.00
Terry Gilmore	73	75	76	70	294	1,720.00
Billy Dunk	73	76	69	76	294	1,720.00
Guy Wolstenholme	74	72	71	77	294	1,720.00
Ted Ball	73	73	76	73	295	1,320.00
Stewart Ginn	71	73	76	75	295	1,320.00
Terry Gale	74	69	77	75	295	1,320.00
Geoff Smart	75	71	76	74	296	1,115.00
Greg Hohnen	73	76	74	73	296	1,115.00
Ray Jenner°	73	72	77	75	297	
David Good	72	76	73	76	297	1,020.00
Peter Sweeney°	80	68	76	74	298	
Glenn McCully	79	74	72	73	298	930.00
Art Russell	73	78	73	74	298	930.00
Phil Wood°	75	80	70	74	299	
Peter Senior	74	75	75	75	299	810.00
John Kelly°	76	71	71	81	299	
Rob McNaughton	75	75	74	75	299	810.00
Bob Beauchemin	75	75	75	75	300	690.00
Bill Britten	73	72	79	76	300	690.00
Wayne Grady	75	79	75	72	301	517.50
Graham Marsh	73	77	76	75	301	517.50
Peter Pearce	76	74	76	75	301	517.50
Terry Kendall	78	74	73	76	301	517.50
Clyde Boyer°	73	80	77	72	302	
Vaughan Somers	78	77	75	72	302	403.34
Mike Clayton°	78	73	76	75	302	
Alex Bonnington	77	76	74	75	302	403.33
Warren Young	78	77	74	73	302	403.33
John Lindsay°	74	78	75	76	303	
Noel Ratcliffe	79	76	75	73	303	337.50
Richard Coombes	77	78	71	77	303	337.50
Bob Shaw	74	79	73	77	303	337.50
Rick Barker	75	74	77	77	303	337.50
David Leary	76	75	76	77	304	310.00
Colin Stott	74	80	78	73	305	300.00
Tim Ireland	76	74	81	75	306	275.00
Paul Firmstone	78	75	77	76	306	275.00
Gary Doolan	75	78	79	75	307	255.00
Ray Hore	77	77	76	77	307	255.00

Trevor Henley*	80	71	77	80	308	
John Davis	76	79	77	76	308	
Richard Lee	72	76	80	80	308	230.00
Alan Lehner*	75	80	77	77	309	230.00
Howard McHutchison	73	71	81	78	309	
Perry See Hoe	73	79	78	79	309	195.00
Peter Headland	73	81	77	78	309	195.00
Peter Beames	76	79	74	80	309	195.00
						195.00

*Amateur

Dunhill South Australian Open Championship

Glenelg Golf Club, Adelaide, South Australia
Par 36–36—72; 6,622 yards

February 22–25
purse, A.$25,000

	SCORES				TOTAL	MONEY
Peter Senior	70	72	70	70	282	A.$5,000.00
Graham Stevens*	70	69	70	73	282	
(Senior defeated Stevens on first hole of sudden-death play-off)						
Bob Shaw	71	67	72	75	285	$3,000.00
Tony Gresham*	71	70	74	71	286	
Rodger Davis	72	74	68	72	286	1,875.00
Ray Hore	72	72	73	70	287	1,137.50
Peter Pearce	70	73	71	73	287	1,137.50
Bob Beauchemin	71	73	73	71	288	900.00
Glenn McCully	73	69	77	70	289	687.50
Dennis Ingram	68	76	73	72	289	687.50
George Bell	67	75	71	76	289	687.50
Terry Kendall	71	74	69	75	289	687.50
Chris Whitford	71	74	75	70	290	
Rob McNaughton	73	73	69	76	291	550.00
Deray Simon	70	75	77	70	292	425.70
Ian Stanley	77	77	68	70	292	425.70
Richard Lee	76	73	71	72	292	425.70
Col Bishop	74	71	75	72	292	425.70
Randall Vines	74	71	74	73	292	425.70
Trevor McDonald	72	74	72	74	292	425.70
Wayne Grady	70	72	73	77	292	425.70
Bill Britten	74	76	74	69	293	275.00
Peter Headland	75	71	74	73	293	275.00
Colin Stott	74	68	76	75	293	275.00
Art Russell	76	75	67	75	293	275.00
Alex Bonnington	72	77	67	77	293	275.00
Greg Alexander*	74	75	73	72	294	
Perry See Hoe	69	77	77	71	294	190.00
Bob Wallace	74	75	73	72	294	190.00
Stewart Ginn	75	74	71	74	294	190.00
David Cherry*	73	73	75	74	295	
Billy Dunk	70	82	72	71	295	153.00
Elliot Booth*	75	72	73	75	295	
Greg Hohnen	73	77	70	75	295	153.00
Phil Tierney	71	80	69	75	295	153.00
Roger Stephens	71	73	73	78	295	153.00
Gary Doolan	73	75	70	77	295	153.00
Mike Clayton*	75	75	73	73	296	
Stuart Reese	75	76	74	72	297	130.00
Peter Croker	72	75	74	76	297	130.00
David Galloway	69	75	75	78	297	130.00
Gerry Goss	75	74	75	74	298	120.00
Eban Dennis	74	77	72	76	299	115.00
Terry Gilmore	77	77	74	72	300	110.00
Gary Thompson	75	76	73	77	301	
Ramon Kesur	72	77	72	81	302	105.00
Kel Nagle	72	76	77	78	303	90.00
Rick Barker	73	81	72	77	303	90.00
Gary Campbell	80	74	73	76	303	90.00
Ron Wood	76	75	73	79	303	90.00
Lyndsay Stephen	73	73	75	82	303	90.00

*Amateur

Australian Masters

Huntington Golf Club, Melbourne, Victoria
Par 37–36—73; 6,955 yards

March 1–4
purse, A.$30,000

	SCORES				TOTAL	MONEY
Barry Vivian	67	69	73	80	289	A.$6,000.00
Bob Shearer	70	69	73	78	290	3,600.00
Terry Kendall	71	71	75	75	292	2,250.00
Rodger Davis	70	72	75	76	293	1,192.50
Ian Stanley	76	72	69	76	293	1,192.50
Bill Britten	70	73	77	73	293	1,192.50
Jack Newton	73	71	75	74	293	1,192.50
Richard Coombes	74	73	72	76	295	810.00
Mike Cahill	78	69	71	77	295	810.00
Glenn McCully	73	76	74	73	296	690.00
Rob McNaughton	75	72	72	77	296	690.00

Noel Ratcliffe	69	78	77	73	297	556.50
Geoff Parslow	76	71	75	75	297	556.50
Bob Shaw	72	76	74	75	297	556.50
Randall Vines	76	70	76	75	297	556.50
David Good	70	72	80	76	298	465.00
Kel Nagle	73	73	75	77	298	465.00
Deray Simon	74	76	74	75	299	420.00
Billy Dunk	72	76	78	74	300	375.00
Art Russell	74	72	75	79	300	375.00
Wayne Grady	72	76	79	74	301	315.00
Bruce Green	76	75	75	75	301	315.00
Greg Norman	73	79	73	77	302	270.00
Peter Headland	72	77	82	72	303	228.00
Trevor McDonald	77	76	74	76	303	228.00
Robert Werrell	75	71	78	79	303	228.00
Alan Heil	76	76	76	76	304	183.60
Perry See Hoe	75	78	73	78	304	183.60
Col Bishop	73	75	78	78	304	183.60
Peter Senior	71	77	77	79	304	183.60
Harry Berwick	77	74	76	77	304	183.60
Greg Hohnen	77	76	77	75	305	150.00
Peter Fowler	75	80	76	74	305	150.00
John Davis	74	78	75	78	305	150.00
David Galloway	78	69	79	79	305	150.00
Stewart Ginn	73	72	77	83	305	150.00
Guy Wolstenholme	76	79	75	76	306	126.00
Paul Foley	70	73	82	81	306	126.00
Colin Stott	77	76	73	80	306	126.00
Paul Firmstone	73	77	75	82	307	114.00
Peter Pearce	78	76	78	77	309	102.00
Stuart Reese	76	79	76	78	309	102.00
Eban Dennis	79	72	78	80	309	102.00
Peter Croker	76	77	76	81	310	87.00
Craig Jewell	76	77	80	77	310	87.00
Tim Moore	74	81	73	83	311	69.00
Chris Mellish	76	79	78	78	311	69.00
Bob Beauchemin	78	74	81	78	311	69.00
Terry Hulls	74	74	80	83	311	69.00
Rick Barker	78	77	76	81	312	54.00

Western Australian PGA Championship

Melville Glades Golf Club, Perth, Western Australia
Par 36–36—72; 6,983 yards

March 15–18
purse, A.$15,000

	SCORES				TOTAL	MONEY
Richard Coombes	72	71	70	72	285	A.$3,000.00
Rodger Davis	74	71	68	74	287	1,800.00
Mike Ferguson	72	69	76	71	288	1,125.00
Stuart Reese	72	72	74	72	290	765.00
Terry Kendall	74	76	68	73	291	570.00
Col Bishop	74	72	71	74	291	570.00
David Good	78	72	73	69	292	480.00
Wayne Grady	70	76	74	73	293	420.00
Bob Beauchemin	72	75	75	72	294	345.00
Mike Cahill	75	72	76	71	294	345.00
Lyndsay Stephen	73	73	74	74	294	345.00
John Clifford	75	74	70	75	294	345.00
Allan Cooper	71	76	74	74	295	279.00
Ted Ball	74	76	71	74	295	279.00
Rob McNaughton	74	73	75	74	296	240.00
Ross Metherell	75	72	73	76	296	240.00
Terry Gale	69	75	76	76	296	240.00
Graham Johnson	73	72	78	74	297	195.00
Peter Fowler	74	73	75	75	297	195.00
Ian Stanley	74	76	72	75	297	195.00
Peter Headland	73	75	75	75	298	157.50
Rick Barker	75	74	72	77	298	157.50
Deray Simon	79	75	73	72	299	123.00
Vaughan Somers	74	78	76	71	299	123.00
Peter Croker	77	72	74	76	299	123.00
John Victorsen	78	76	71	75	300	108.00
Terry Gilmore	78	77	72	74	301	93.75
Geoff Moore	77	78	72	74	301	93.75
Peter Randall	74	77	73	77	301	93.75
Eban Dennis	71	76	76	78	301	93.75
Trevor Downing	76	73	78	75	302	81.00
Alan Heil	81	73	74	74	302	81.00
Barry Vivian	77	76	73	76	302	81.00
Jim Mercer	76	79	71	77	303	75.00
Ray Hore	78	75	75	76	304	70.50
Graeme Warwick	79	73	75	77	304	70.50
Harry Berwick	77	80	76	72	305	60.00
Chris Witcher	76	76	79	74	305	60.00
Kel Nagle	78	74	78	75	305	60.00
Leith Payne	80	74	75	76	305	60.00
Roy Draddy	76	76	73	80	305	60.00
Philip Bidwell	75	79	77	75	306	51.00
Paul Firmstone	78	76	75	78	307	48.00
Dennis Bell	81	78	76	74	309	43.50
David Leary	74	80	76	79	309	43.50

Bob Mesnil	76	76	78	80	310	39.00
David Botten	80	75	77	79	311	33.00
George Bell	79	75	77	80	311	33.00
Richard Lee	74	80	75	82	311	33.00
Colin Stott	79	77	79	77	312	9.00
Alex Bonnington	79	80	76	77	312	9.00
Frank Conallin	78	71	85	78	312	9.00

Royal Fremantle Open

Royal Fremantle Golf Club, Perth, Western Australia
Par 36–36–72; 6,599 yards

March 22–25
purse, A.$15,000

	SCORES				TOTAL	MONEY
Terry Gale	69	73	67	71	280	A.$3,000.00
Ray Hore	71	69	72	69	281	1,800.00
Terry Kendall	72	70	71	69	282	1,125.00
Ian Stanley	72	72	70	70	284	765.00
Mike Ferguson	70	70	71	74	285	570.00
Lyndsay Stephen	69	72	74	70	285	570.00
Paul Foley	72	71	72	71	286	450.00
Allan Cooper	73	70	72	71	286	450.00
Harry Berwick	71	78	70	69	288	333.60
David Good	72	73	74	69	288	333.60
Kel Nagle	70	71	70	77	288	333.60
Rodger Davis	72	73	68	75	288	333.60
Col Bishop	76	68	69	75	288	333.60
Ron Wood	69	77	72	71	289	240.00
Rob McNaughton	71	72	77	69	289	240.00
John Clifford	72	72	71	74	289	240.00
Wayne Grady	74	70	71	74	289	240.00
Chris Tickner	68	75	72	74	289	240.00
Ross Metherell	70	71	77	72	290	165.00
Noel Ratcliffe	76	72	72	70	290	165.00
Peter Randall	75	70	75	70	290	165.00
Stuart Reese	67	78	71	74	290	165.00
Gary Doolan	74	72	72	72	290	165.00
Barry Vivian	73	72	74	72	291	111.00
Peter Croker	76	72	71	72	291	111.00
Ted Ball	69	73	74	75	291	111.00
John Victorsen	71	76	71	73	291	111.00
Dennis Bell	75	72	72	73	292	93.00
Bob Beauchemin	75	71	70	76	292	93.00
Roy Draddy	74	73	74	72	293	82.50
Vaughan Somers	72	73	78	70	293	82.50
Colin Stott	69	78	73	73	293	82.50
Deray Simon	70	72	72	79	293	82.50
Trevor Downing	74	77	69	74	294	75.00
Don Leary°	70	72	76	76	294	
Pat Harness°	78	68	75	74	295	
Mike Cahill	71	74	72	79	296	72.00
Frank Conallin	73	78	75	71	297	67.50
Terry Gilmore	74	74	75	74	297	67.50
Paul Firmstone	73	75	76	74	298	61.50
Pat Tobin	74	79	71	74	298	61.50
Richard Coombes	72	80	73	74	299	55.50
Chris Witcher	72	72	74	81	299	55.50
David Galloway	78	74	74	74	300	51.00
Richard Lee	76	76	73	76	301	48.00
Alan Heil	76	74	74	78	302	43.50
Bob Tuohy	74	77	75	76	302	43.50
Terry Purser	76	73	77	77	303	39.00
David Botten	76	76	77	75	304	36.00
John Davis	77	76	73	79	305	33.00
Leith Payne	77	76	79	74	306	30.00
Allen Topham	81	72	81	73	307	27.00

°Amateur

The W.A.Y. Celebration Open

Mount Lawley Golf Club, Perth, Western Australia
Par 36–36—72; 6,750 yards

March 29–April 1
purse, A.$20,000

	SCORES				TOTAL	MONEY
Terry Kendall	70	69	70	71	280	A.$4,000.00
Terry Gale	70	74	70	71	285	1,950.00
Col Bishop	71	71	73	70	285	1,950.00
Noel Ratcliffe	78	70	68	70	286	1,020.00
Bob Beauchemin	72	70	73	72	287	800.00
Richard Coombes	74	70	72	72	288	680.00
Rodger Davis	73	73	69	73	288	680.00
Billy Dunk	71	75	70	73	289	540.00
Barry Vivian	76	69	71	73	289	540.00
Harry Berwick	77	72	72	69	290	480.00
John Victorsen	69	73	80	69	291	420.00
Ross Metherell	76	76	69	70	291	420.00
Glenn McCully	72	70	78	72	292	330.67

Colin Stott	71	72	76	73	292	330.67
Peter Fowler	72	72	75	73	292	330.67
Ray Hore	71	71	76	74	292	330.67
David Good	72	73	72	75	292	330.66
Allan Cooper	74	69	73	76	292	330.66
Mike Ferguson	74	69	73	77	293	250.00
Deray Simon	76	71	73	73	293	250.00
George Bell	77	72	72	73	294	190.00
Terry Gilmore	77	71	71	75	294	190.00
Ted Ball	75	73	70	76	294	190.00
Vaughan Somers	72	73	72	77	294	190.00
Lyndsay Stephen	75	72	76	72	295	144.00
Ron Wood	73	76	73	73	295	144.00
Graham Johnson	72	75	71	77	295	144.00
Stuart Reese	79	73	72	72	296	124.00
Chris Tickner	77	75	72	72	296	124.00
Peter Headland	77	70	73	77	297	114.00
Peter Randall	76	73	71	77	297	114.00
Rob McNaughton	75	75	74	74	298	102.00
Mike Cahill	75	77	72	74	298	102.00
Richard Beer	71	76	74	77	298	102.00
Chris Witcher	75	73	72	78	298	102.00
Dennis Bell	76	75	76	72	299	88.00
Peter Croker	74	77	75	73	299	88.00
Paul Foley	72	72	74	81	299	88.00
Dennis Ingram	75	73	77	75	300	74.00
Allen Topham	76	75	72	77	300	74.00
Paul Firmstone	73	74	73	80	300	74.00
David Botten	71	76	71	82	300	74.00
Gary Campbell	75	74	78	74	301	62.00
Jim Barden	79	73	72	77	301	62.00
Trevor Downing	80	74	70	78	302	52.00
Graeme Warwick	74	75	72	81	302	52.00
David Galloway	77	74	70	81	302	52.00
Kerry Ellis	79	75	77	74	305	44.00
David Fox	76	77	77	76	306	19.00
John Davis	74	80	74	78	306	19.00
Geoff Moore	75	75	75	81	306	19.00
Bob Mesnil	73	78	71	84	306	19.00

Nedlands Masters

Nedlands Golf Club, Perth, Western Australia
Par 36–36—72; 6,351 yards

August 2–5
purse, A.\$15,000

	SCORES				TOTAL	MONEY
Terry Gale	69	68	71	71	279	A.\$3,004.00
Ross Metherell	70	70	74	70	284	1,804.00
Stewart Ginn	71	74	74	68	287	1,129.00
Ian Stanley	70	73	72	73	288	686.50
Mike Ferguson	72	70	71	75	288	686.50
Graham Johnson	73	70	74	75	292	514.00
Allan Cooper	73	72	74	73	292	514.00
John Clifford	69	74	75	75	293	424.00
Col Bishop	70	74	76	74	294	364.00
Greg Hohnen	71	73	74	76	294	364.00
David Galloway	75	70	74	75	294	364.00
Peter Kohlsdorf	72	77	74	72	295	298.00
Roy Draddy	75	76	71	73	295	298.00
Lyndsay Stephen	70	74	77	75	296	274.00
Trevor Downing	75	72	72	78	297	259.00
Rob Culbert	69	73	75	82	299	236.50
Richard Coombes	76	70	77	76	299	236.50
Mike Cahill	73	72	77	80	302	214.00
Richard Lee	76	75	77	75	303	199.00
Leith Payne	75	75	77	77	304	184.00
John Hadley	76	81	76	72	305	161.50
Peter Randall	80	79	75	71	305	161.50
George Bell	76	79	76	76	307	139.00
Barry Fry	76	75	77	81	309	121.00
Barry Podmore	81	76	77	75	309	121.00
Richard Mercer	78	76	78	79	311	109.00
John Roberts	77	81	78	75	311	109.00
Trevor Bristow-Stagg	79	78	84	73	314	100.00
Frank Brooks	81	78	75	82	316	94.00
Peter Hopkins	77	85	78	78	318	91.00
John Downing	79	74	86	80	319	86.50
Graeme Warwick	78	80	81	80	319	86.50
Jock Borthwick	80	83	76	84	323	80.50
Pat Tobin	79	84	80	80	323	80.50
John Mackie	81	80	79	84	324	76.00
David Breen	84	77	82	84	327	73.00
Dave Waterman	79	82	87	81	329	70.00
Hilary Lawler		80	83		163	67.00
Colin Douglas		84	81		165	64.00
Garry Duncan		84	83		167	58.00
Tim Messenger		83	84		167	58.00
Gary Metcalf		84	83		167	58.00
Craig Duncan		81	87		168	52.00
Graeme Warburton		80	89		169	49.00

Joe Jansen New South Wales PGA Championship

Penrith Golf Club, Penrith
Par 36—36—72; 6,941 yards

September 6–9
purse, A.$15,000

	SCORES				TOTAL	MONEY
Stewart Ginn	68	71	69	67	275	A.$3,000.00
Richard Coombes	71	69	73	70	283	1,800.00
Rob McNaughton	71	71	75	67	284	945.00
Col Bishop	72	72	71	69	284	945.00
Kel Nagle	70	75	72	69	286	570.00
George Serhan	70	73	70	73	286	570.00
Bryan Smith	76	68	70	73	287	480.00
Tom Linskey	74	73	68	73	288	405.00
Bob Shaw	73	74	66	75	288	405.00
Richard Lee	72	74	72	71	289	330.00
David Merriman	72	70	73	74	289	330.00
Ted Ball	72	71	70	76	289	330.00
Ian Stanley	73	71	72	74	290	288.00
Allen Topham	73	73	73	72	291	255.00
Gary Doolan	77	71	70	73	291	255.00
Billy Dunk	73	75	71	72	291	255.00
Ray Hore	78	72	72	70	292	217.50
Terry Kendall	74	74	70	74	292	217.50
Richard Beer	75	75	73	70	293	151.30
Bruce Smith	75	74	72	72	293	151.30
John Clifford	73	79	68	73	293	151.30
Chris Witcher	73	75	72	73	293	151.30
Peter Croker	74	74	72	73	293	151.30
Bob Wallace	70	71	75	77	293	151.30
Chris Tickner	75	75	71	72	293	151.30
Michael Harwood	77	72	74	71	294	99.00
Greg Hohnen	75	71	76	72	294	99.00
Mike Cahill	74	71	74	75	294	99.00
Geoff Andrew	76	74	71	73	294	99.00
Art Russell	76	76	72	71	295	84.00
Charles Henderson	79	72	71	73	295	84.00
Chris Mellish	73	75	73	74	295	84.00
Barry Coxon	75	76	71	74	296	76.50
Peter Fowler	77	73	71	75	296	76.50
Robert Werrell	74	75	74	74	297	72.00
John Ballard	74	76	77	71	298	63.00
Bryan Wearne	75	73	77	73	298	63.00
Bill Britten	77	75	71	75	298	63.00
David Leary	78	70	74	76	298	63.00
Ian Alexander	75	72	75	76	298	63.00
Dan Cullen	76	76	72	75	299	52.50
Peter Jackson	76	72	75	76	299	52.50
Doug Murray	74	75	78	73	300	43.50
Len Woodward	77	75	76	72	300	43.50
Craig Jewell	79	72	76	73	300	43.50
Lyndsay Stephen	77	70	75	78	300	43.50
Garry Overy	74	76	77	74	301	33.00
Colin Arnold	74	75	73	79	301	33.00
Phil Dolby	76	73	73	79	301	33.00
Rick Baker	79	71	75	77	302	9.00
Geoff Moore	76	71	77	78	302	9.00
Peter Headland	75	76	73	78	302	9.00

WIN-TV Illawarra Open

The Grange Golf Club, Woolongong, New South Wales
Par 37—35—72; 6,965 yards

September 20–23
purse, A.$20,000

	SCORES				TOTAL	MONEY
Mike Ferguson	70	69	76	73	288	A.$4,000.00
Chris Tickner	69	73	73	74	289	1,950.00
Tom Linskey	68	71	73	77	289	1,950.00
Randall Vines	73	72	72	73	290	795.00
Stewart Ginn	72	69	72	77	290	795.00
George Serhan	74	72	69	75	290	795.00
Billy Dunk	74	66	73	77	290	795.00
Ted Ball	73	72	73	74	292	560.00
Terry Kendall	71	73	73	77	294	520.00
Peter Fowler	74	72	76	73	295	480.00
Ray Hore	71	73	79	73	296	408.00
Chris Mellish	77	74	72	73	296	408.00
George Bell	76	77	69	74	296	408.00
Richard Lee	73	72	76	76	297	360.00
Wayne Grady	72	76	73	77	298	320.00
Vaughan Somers	74	73	73	78	298	320.00
John Clifford	71	72	76	79	298	320.00
Steven Rippon°	75	73	73	79	300	
Rob McNaughton	73	74	78	75	300	280.00
Rob McKay	79	73	75	74	301	240.00
Peter Jackson	72	71	79	79	301	240.00
Peter Headland	73	73	75	80	301	240.00
Dick Flood	74	77	77	74	302	153.50
Bob Shaw	76	72	·78	76	302	153.50
Paul Connell	74	76	77	75	302	153.50

Phil Dolby	75	78	72	77	302	153.50
Lyndsay Stephen	72	74	77	79	302	153.50
Tony Attwill	76	75	74	77	302	153.50
Mike Cahill	71	76	74	81	302	153.50
Col Bishop	71	72	75	84	302	153.50
Terry Gilmore	74	75	78	76	303	112.00
Garry Overy	72	78	75	78	303	112.00
Peter Pearce	72	74	74	83	303	112.00
Matt Ellison	76	76	77	75	304	98.00
Ian Stanley	73	75	78	78	304	98.00
Harvey Graham	74	74	74	82	304	98.00
Jeff Short	76	71	75	82	304	98.00
Ian Brander	76	73	77	79	305	86.00
Kel Nagle	73	77	73	82	305	86.00
Edwin Rechters	79	73	78	76	306	80.00
Glen Sullivan	73	75	77	82	307	72.00
Vic Bennetts	77	74	77	79	307	72.00
Paul Murray	77	73	76	81	307	72.00
Bill Jordan°	72	75	79	82	308	
Graeme Bugden	75	74	83	76	308	60.00
Bob Wallace	77	76	76	79	308	60.00
Bruce Hodson	73	76	77	82	308	60.00
Colin Stott	71	77	80	81	309	45.00
Richard Beer	75	74	75	85	309	45.00
Keith Pepper°	74	77	78	81	310	
Darryl Johnston	77	75	74	85	311	40.00
Bruce Smith	76	77	79	79	311	40.00
Harry Berwick	79	74	78	80	311	40.00

° Amateur

Tooth's Gold Coast-Tweed Classic

Coolangatta-Tweed Heads Golf Club, Coolangatta, Queensland
Par 36–36—72; 6,663 yards

September 27–30
purse, A.\$20,000

	SCORES				TOTAL	MONEY
Mike Ferguson	71	67	71	72	281	A.\$4,000.00
Stewart Ginn	69	65	78	69	281	2,400.00
(Ferguson defeated Ginn on third hole of sudden-death play-off)						
Randall Vines	72	68	76	68	284	1,260.00
Bob Shaw	73	66	73	72	284	1,260.00
Terry Gale	71	71	71	72	285	800.00
Ray Hore	69	73	75	69	286	680.00
Wayne Grady	70	74	72	70	286	680.00
Barry Vivian	71	72	74	71	288	560.00
Sam Snead	69	74	72	74	289	500.00
Billy Dunk	71	69	73	76	289	500.00
Col Bishop	73	76	71	70	290	408.00
Allan Cooper	73	71	75	71	290	408.00
Vaughan Somers	76	72	70	72	290	408.00
Ian Stanley	72	74	77	68	291	340.00
Art Russell	73	72	73	73	291	340.00
Ted Ball	69	72	76	74	291	340.00
Trevor Russell	70	76	72	74	292	300.00
Rob McNaughton	69	76	74	74	293	280.00
Michael Harwood	78	69	76	71	294	230.00
Tommy Bolt	74	72	76	72	294	230.00
Matt Ellison	78	69	75	72	294	230.00
George Serhan	69	73	77	75	294	230.00
Chris Witcher	71	76	76	72	295	170.00
George Bayer	70	76	74	75	295	170.00
Richard Lee	75	74	77	70	296	144.00
Jeff Woodland	74	68	81	73	296	144.00
Barry Burgess	77	74	73	72	296	144.00
Stuart Reese	74	75	72	76	297	121.34
Colin Stott	71	72	77	77	297	121.33
Peter Senior	72	71	77	77	297	121.33
Chris Mellish	77	72	77	72	298	108.00
Paul Foley	72	77	76	73	298	108.00
Mike Cahill	72	77	75	74	298	108.00
Glen Vines	72	71	83	73	299	96.00
Doug Murray	71	73	78	77	299	96.00
Peter Pearce	70	80	73	76	299	96.00
Paul King	74	74	77	75	300	82.00
Stan Peach	75	76	75	74	300	82.00
Trevor McDonald	73	78	73	76	300	82.00
David Good	74	73	76	77	300	82.00
Geoff Moore	75	75	78	73	301	68.00
Rob Culbert	78	72	78	73	301	68.00
Peter Croker	78	73	76	74	301	68.00
Peter Headland	73	74	83	72	302	54.00
Bruce Smith	75	75	78	74	302	54.00
Ian Davis	77	74	76	75	302	54.00
Brandon Coleman	76	75	72	79	302	54.00
Rick Baker	75	75	78	75	303	40.00
Greg Hohnen	76	71	80	76	303	40.00
Terry Kendall	73	77	77	76	303	40.00

Dunhill Queensland Open

Indooroopilly Golf Club, Brisbane, Queensland
Par 37–35—72; 6,439 yards

October 4–7
purse, A.$30,000

	SCORES				TOTAL	MONEY
Jeff Senior°	68	71	73	67	279	
Jack Newton	66	68	75	72	281	A.$6,000.00
Vaughan Somers	73	69	70	71	283	3,600.00
Billy Dunk	68	72	68	76	284	2,250.00
Stuart Reese	72	68	70	75	285	1,365.00
Terry Gale	69	67	75	74	285	1,365.00
Glenn Cogill°	74	64	75	73	286	
David Good	70	71	72	73	286	960.00
Ian Stanley	67	73	74	72	286	960.00
Art Russell	69	70	74	73	286	960.00
Brandon Coleman	72	72	70	73	287	690.00
Ted Ball	73	74	69	71	287	690.00
Greg Norman	71	71	72	73	287	690.00
Randall Vines	75	71	69	72	287	690.00
Rob McNaughton	73	72	71	72	288	511.20
Paul Foley	73	71	73	71	288	511.20
George Serhan	73	71	71	73	288	511.20
Ron Wood	71	72	69	76	288	511.20
Wayne Grady	73	73	70	72	288	511.20
Bob Shaw	72	70	74	73	289	405.00
Terry Kendall	74	67	71	77	289	405.00
Craig Owen	73	70	73	74	290	315.00
Barry Vivian	73	74	69	74	290	315.00
Lyndsay Stephen	70	76	74	70	290	315.00
Peter Beames	70	69	75	76	290	315.00
Stewart Ginn	72	72	74	73	291	234.00
Peter Pearce	71	74	73	73	291	234.00
Tony Gresham°	73	70	75	75	293	
Guy Wolstenholme	75	71	71	76	293	198.00
Errol Hartvigsen	69	79	69	76	293	198.00
Ray Hore	69	74	75	75	293	198.00
Mike Cahill	69	78	75	71	293	198.00
Pat Mateer	74	74	72	74	294	162.00
Glenn McCully	72	71	74	77	294	162.00
Mike Ferguson	71	68	75	80	294	162.00
Allan Cooper	77	71	75	71	294	162.00
Rob Culbert	73	68	79	74	294	162.00
Gerry Taylor	74	74	75	72	295	141.00
Ian Davis	74	73	74	74	295	141.00
Mark Nash°	73	74	74	75	296	
Peter Headland	69	71	77	79	296	129.00
Peter Croker	72	74	75	75	296	129.00
Deray Simon	71	73	77	76	297	114.00
Peter Senior	69	78	77	73	297	114.00
Larry Canning	74	71	77	75	297	114.00
Matt Ellison	71	73	77	77	298	102.00
Peter McWhinney	72	75	76	76	299	96.00
Ian Baker-Finch	76	67	76	81	300	81.00
Paul Smith	75	74	73	78	300	81.00
Peter Barry	71	77	77	75	300	81.00
Doug Murray	73	73	74	80	300	81.00

°Amateur

Citizen Watches Australian Seniors' Open Championship

Manly Golf Club, Sydney, New South Wales
Par 37–35—72; 6,656 yards

October 5–7
purse, A.$25,000

	SCORES			TOTAL	MONEY
Tommy Bolt	68	72	74	214	A. $5,000.00
Jack Fleck	72	71	72	215	3,000.00
Jimmy Martin	71	72	74	217	2,090.00
George Bayer	71	77	70	218	1,305.00
Dow Finsterwald	68	77	73	218	1,305.00
Kel Nagle	70	75	74	219	1,030.00
Tomoo Ishii	76	67	78	221	842.50
Art Wall	76	73	72	221	842.50
Christy O'Connor	74	71	78	223	730.00
Sam Snead	73	78	73	224	675.00
Jack Harris	79	69	77	225	615.00
Don Sharp°	78	74	74	225	
Harry Berwick	71	77	78	226	565.00
Keith Pepper°	75	74	78	227	
Dan Cullen	72	78	78	228	545.00
Ron Brown	79	70	80	229	495.00
Yoshi Fujii	77	75	77	229	495.00
Bobby Locke	75	77	78	230	450.00
John Kelly	75	74	82	231	391.67
John Kalinka	78	78	75	231	391.67
Peter Nakamura	76	78	77	231	391.66
Jim McInnes	76	77	79	232	340.00
Reg Want	75	81	78	234	310.00
Tom McNaughton	77	77	81	235	290.00
Ivan Cross	78	76	82	236	265.00

Chris Porter	78	76	83	237	230.00
Terry Brady	75	83	82	240	220.00
Dennis Denehy	78	80	84	242	210.00
Graham Belle	84	77	82	243	195.00
Keith Foxton	85	78	83	246	185.00
Sid Cowling	85	79	86	250	175.00
Colin de Groot	89	80		169	85.00
Colin Newman	87	87		174	85.00

*Amateur

Victorian Garden State PGA Championship

Woodlands Golf Club, Melbourne, Victoria
Par 36–36—72; 6,617 yards

October 11–14
purse, A.$50,000

	SCORES				TOTAL	MONEY
Ian Stanley	71	70	73	72	286	A.$10,000.00
Stewart Ginn	72	73	69	72	286	6,000.00
(Stanley defeated Ginn on second hole of sudden-death play-off)						
Bob Shearer	69	74	74	72	289	3,750.00
Greg Norman	69	78	71	72	290	2,275.00
Terry Kendall	70	73	73	74	290	2,275.00
Mike Ferguson	73	72	70	77	292	1,800.00
Bobby Wadkins	71	73	79	70	293	1,600.00
Terry Gale	71	76	74	73	294	1,160.00
Rob McNaughton	76	73	72	73	294	1,160.00
Bob Beauchemin	70	77	72	75	294	1,160.00
Stuart Reese	73	74	73	74	294	1,160.00
Mike Cahill	72	72	76	74	294	1,160.00
Billy Dunk	74	72	74	74	294	1,160.00
Bill Britten	74	75	74	72	295	875.00
Vaughan Somers	73	75	70	77	295	875.00
Lyndsay Stephen	5	74	74	73	296	775.00
Bruce Milgate	72	77	73	74	296	775.00
Bob Shaw	76	73	74	74	297	650.00
Ted Ball	72	75	76	74	297	650.00
Paul Foley	72	74	73	78	297	650.00
Trevor McDonald	72	75	76	75	298	500.00
George Serhan	75	72	76	75	298	500.00
David Galloway	74	75	73	76	298	500.00
Chris Tickner	79	70	79	71	299	390.00
Kel Nagle	72	74	75	78	299	390,00
Brian Jones	74	77	77	72	300	360.00
Geoff Parslow	77	76	75	73	301	306.00
John Benda	76	77	74	74	301	306.00
Glenn McCully	75	78	73	75	301	306.00
Gerry Taylor	69	76	77	79	301	306.00
Noel Ratcliffe	72	74	75	80	301	306.00
Barry Vivian	78	74	77	73	302	245.00
Peter Headland	76	78	75	73	302	245.00
Colin Stott	73	75	79	75	302	245.00
Craig Owen	70	77	79	75	302	245.00
Wayne Grady	74	76	75	77	302	245.00
Rodger Davis	79	75	72	76	302	245.00
Mike Bodney	77	76	76	74	303	205.00
Bryan Smith	70	78	78	77	303	205.00
Christy O'Connor	73	77	78	76	304	185.00
Bill Britton	76	74	77	77	304	185.00
Randall Vines	76	78	74	77	305	155.00
Deray Simon	75	77	75	78	305	155.00
Richard Coombes	78	73	75	79	305	155.00
Barry Burgess	75	77	72	81	305	155.00
Peter Fowler	78	76	78	74	306	125.00
David Armstrong	72	70	86	78	306	125.00
Art Russell	80	73	76	79	308	110.00
Duncan Moodie	79	72	78	80	309	63.34
Terry Gilmore	79	74	76	80	309	63.33
Marty Bohen	76	74	77	82	309	63.33

CBA Westlakes Classic

Grange Golf Club, Adelaide, South Australia
Par 38–34—72; 6,865 yards

October 25–28
purse, A.$65,000

	SCORES				TOTAL	MONEY
David Graham	72	70	72	71	285	A.$13,000.00
Gary Vanier	71	74	75	67	287	6,337.50
Bob Shearer	69	72	73	73	287	6,337.50
Guy Wolstenholme	71	72	77	68	288	2,583.75
Greg Norman	73	74	69	72	288	2,583.75
Mike Ferguson	70	72	71	75	288	2,583.75
Christy O'Connor	70	76	69	73	288	2,583.75
Terry Kendall	69	74	75	71	289	1,755.00
Randall Vines	72	76	66	75	289	1,755.00

Bob Charles	74	75	71	72	292	1,430.00
Stewart Ginn	74	73	72	73	292	1,430.00
Barry Vivian	75	70	72	75	292	1,430.00
Walter Godfrey	77	73	72	71	293	1,209.00
Geoff Parslow	72	78	68	75	293	1,209.00
Bill Britton	75	74	75	70	294	910.00
Maurice Bembridge	75	75	74	70	294	910.00
Simon Owen	74	70	76	74	294	910.00
Vaughan Somers	73	73	74	74	294	910.00
Bob Shaw	75	73	72	74	294	910.00
Graham Marsh	72	76	71	75	294	910.00
Glenn McCully	70	66	76	82	294	910.00
Jack Newton	75	75	77	68	295	585.00
Paul Foley	76	73	71	75	295	585.00
Charles Henderson	70	72	75	78	295	585.00
Peter Beames	73	73	76	74	296	468.00
Kel Nagle	73	76	72	75	296	468.00
Billy Dunk	72	76	70	78	296	468.00
Col Bishop	74	75	78	70	297	352.45
Phil Tierney	71	75	77	74	297	352.45
Terry Gilmore	74	75	74	74	297	352.45
George Serhan	74	71	76	76	297	352.45
John Kalinka	74	75	73	75	297	352.45
Trevor Johnson	74	76	71	76	297	352.44
Bryan Smith	80	70	71	76	297	352.44
Peter Senior	68	76	74	79	297	352.44
Deray Simon	73	72	72	80	297	352.44
Marty Bohen	74	70	75	79	298	286.00
Stuart Reese	76	74	78	71	299	247.00
Rob McNaughton	74	73	79	73	299	247.00
Allan Cooper	75	71	79	74	299	247.00
Trevor McDonald	78	71	75	75	299	247.00
Leith Payne	76	72	73	78	299	247.00
Brian Jones	73	73	80	74	300	188.50
Terry Gale	75	71	77	77	300	188.50
Wayne Grady	75	75	74	76	300	188.50
Ross Metherell	71	72	76	81	300	188.50
Ted Ball	76	73	72	80	301	156.00
Chris Tickner	73	75	80	74	302	130.00
Richard Coombes	75	75	75	77	302	130.00
Gerry Taylor	74	74	76	78	302	130.00

New South Wales Open Championship

The Lakes Golf Club, Sydney, New South Wales — November 1–4
Par 36–37–73; 6,830 yards — purse, A.\$60,000

	SCORES				TOTAL	MONEY
Jack Newton	69	70	70	72	281	A.\$12,000.00
Wayne Grady	74	68	70	78	290	4,956.67
Gary Vanier	69	72	72	77	290	4,956.67
Jeff Hall	72	72	71	75	290	4,956.66
Scott Simpson	74	76	71	70	291	2,400.00
Martin Foster	71	74	76	71	292	1,830.00
Mike Ferguson	73	77	70	72	292	1,830.00
Chris Tickner	72	75	72	73	292	1,830.00
Maurice Bembridge	72	72	75	73	292	1,830.00
Tony Gresham*	75	71	75	72	293	
Barry Vivian	75	75	72	71	293	1,277.50
Greg Norman	73	70	76	74	293	1,277.50
Richard Coombes	74	71	72	76	293	1,277.50
Chris Witcher	72	74	72	75	293	1,277.50
Simon Owen	71	76	73	74	294	1,020.00
Bob Shaw	73	71	73	77	294	1,020.00
Gerry Taylor	76	70	71	77	294	1,020.00
Craig Owen	78	70	77	70	295	870.00
Bob Charles	70	72	75	78	295	870.00
Paul Foley	73	76	74	73	296	690.00
Christy O'Connor	75	71	73	77	296	690.00
Stewart Ginn	71	75	72	78	296	690.00
Vaughan Somers	71	76	72	77	296	690.00
Peter Fowler	70	76	78	73	297	475.00
Deray Simon	75	72	77	73	297	475.00
Trevor McDonald	74	77	73	73	297	475.00
David Graham	73	75	72	77	297	475.00
Ian Stanley	78	71	73	76	298	390.00
Stuart Reese	75	76	70	77	298	390.00
Ted Ball	75	76	76	72	299	320.00
Peter Headland	75	76	73	75	299	320.00
Glenn McCully	71	77	74	77	299	320.00
Richard Lee	74	71	77	77	299	320.00
Ray Hore	74	75	72	78	299	320.00
Terry Kendall	71	80	71	77	299	320.00
Kel Nagle	72	74	73	80	299	320.00
Mike Cahill	74	72	79	75	300	248.00
Guy Wolstenholme	75	76	74	75	300	248.00
John Clifford	74	74	76	76	300	248.00
Mike Bodney	73	75	75	77	300	248.00
Bryan Smith	73	75	75	77	300	248.00
Allan Cooper	75	74	76	76	301	175.72
George Bullock	74	73	77	77	301	175.72

Paul Firmstone	69	77	77	78	301	175.72
Allen Topham	78	72	73	78	301	175.71
Tony Corrin	77	71	75	78	301	175.71
Marty Bohen	75	76	72	78	301	175.71
Terry Gale	73	72	74	82	301	175.71
John Sheargold	74	77	76	75	302	130.00
Rob McNaughton	75	70	76	82	303	110.00
Trevor Johnson	76	75	70	82	303	110.00

*Amateur

Mayne Nickless PGA Championship of Australia

Royal Melbourne Golf Club, Melbourne, Victoria
Composite Course: Par 35–36—71; 6,961 yards

November 8–11
purse, A.\$125,000

	SCORES				TOTAL	MONEY
Stewart Ginn	71	72	69	72	284	A.\$25,000.00
Bob Shearer	70	70	77	70	287	12,185.00
Bob Charles	75	71	71	70	287	12,185.00
Scott Simpson	71	73	76	69	289	5,690.00
Simon Owen	74	69	73	73	289	5,690.00
Hubert Green	68	79	77	69	293	3,812.00
Bruce Devlin	73	72	77	71	293	3,812.00
Bob Shaw	73	72	77	71	293	3,812.00
Terry Kendall	70	76	73	74	293	3,812.00
Greg Norman	73	75	76	70	294	2,750.00
Peter Cowen	70	75	74	75	294	2,750.00
Bruce Green	72	72	74	76	294	2,750.00
Mike Cahill	78	72	74	71	295	2,325.00
Terry Gale	74	73	73	75	295	2,325.00
Jack Newton	74	74	77	71	296	2,000.00
Gary Player	75	69	75	77	296	2,000.00
Walter Godfrey	73	73	74	76	296	2,000.00
David Graham	74	74	76	73	297	1,690.00
John Lister	73	75	75	74	297	1,690.00
Mike Bodney	75	72	78	73	298	1,250.00
Johnny Miller	77	72	74	75	298	1,250.00
Billy Dunk	77	72	73	76	298	1,250.00
Richard Coombes	73	74	74	77	298	1,250.00
Rob McNaughton	76	71	76	75	298	1,250.00
Graham Marsh	75	73	78	73	299	828.34
Martin Foster	74	75	76	74	299	828.34
Maurice Bembridge	76	75	73	75	299	828.33
Chris Tickner	69	78	76	76	299	828.33
David Murray	78	71	74	76	299	828.33
Bill Britton	73	75	74	77	299	828.33
Allan Cooper	72	77	78	73	300	638.34
Peter Fowler	75	74	78	73	300	638.34
George Bullock	77	72	77	74	300	638.33
Steve Long	73	75	76	76	300	638.33
Barry Burgess	79	72	73	76	300	638.33
Bill Britten	75	71	75	79	300	638.33
Randall Vines	75	75	78	74	302	512.50
Marty Bohen	78	70	79	75	302	512.50
Guy Wolstenholme	77	75	76	74	302	512.50
Peter Beames	76	76	74	76	302	512.50
Trevor McDonald	71	80	77	75	303	435.00
Rodger Davis	75	73	77	78	303	435.00
Geoff Parslow	74	74	80	76	304	376.67
Vaughan Somers	73	76	76	79	304	376.67
Peter Pearce	71	74	78	81	304	376.66
Mike Ferguson	75	72	79	79	305	300.00
George Serhan	71	77	78	79	305	300.00
John Clifford	75	77	75	78	305	300.00
Chris Mellish	73	77	79	77	306	235.00
Art Russell	75	76	77	78	306	235.00

Dunhill Australian Open Championship

Metropolitan Golf Club, Melbourne, Victoria
Par 37–35—72; 7,000 yards

November 15–18
purse, A.\$150,000

	SCORES				TOTAL	MONEY
Jack Newton	74	72	70	72	288	A.\$30,000.00
Graham Marsh	76	68	73	72	289	14,625.00
Greg Norman	73	69	73	74	289	14,625.00
Bob Shearer	73	76	69	72	290	7,650.00
Bill Britton	74	72	74	71	291	5,700.00
Scott Tuttle	73	72	71	75	291	5,700.00
Gary Player	74	72	72	74	292	4,800.00
Severiano Ballesteros	79	73	70	71	293	4,200.00
David Graham	74	74	73	73	294	3,750.00
Bob Shaw	74	75	71	74	294	3,750.00
Hubert Green	76	75	70	74	295	3,300.00
Terry Kendall	71	77	75	73	296	2,940.00
Rob McNaughton	78	72	74	72	296	2,940.00
Bruce Devlin	76	71	78	72	297	2,400.00

Mike Cahill	77	73	76	71	297	2,400.00
Terry Gale	71	77	76	73	297	2,400.00
Jim Nelford	72	74	76	75	297	2,400.00
John Lister	74	73	73	77	297	2,400.00
Stuart Reese	71	76	75	76	298	1,650.00
Chris Tickner	78	73	70	77	298	1,650.00
Trevor McDonald	75	74	73	76	298	1,650.00
Trevor Johnson	70	81	68	79	298	1,650.00
Deray Simon	70	74	75	79	298	1,650.00
Barry Jaeckel	73	77	77	72	299	1,050.00
Matt Ellison	73	76	76	74	299	1,050.00
Mike Ferguson	76	72	75	76	299	1,050.00
Peter Cowen	75	74	73	77	299	1,050.00
Brian Jones	76	75	72	76	299	1,050.00
Mark James	72	73	77	77	299	1,050.00
Stewart Ginn	74	77	76	73	300	780.00
Rodger Davis	74	71	80	75	300	780.00
Paul Hart	70	79	75	76	300	780.00
Bob Byman	74	73	76	77	300	780.00
Ted Ball	75	74	74	77	300	780.00
Fuzzy Zoeller	75	74	73	78	300	780.00
Glenn McCully	71	77	71	81	300	780.00
Tony Gresham°	74	75	71	80	300	
Ed Sneed	80	72	74	75	301	660.00
Simon Owen	75	75	78	74	302	585.00
Maurice Bembridge	74	74	81	73	302	585.00
Geoff Parslow	75	73	76	78	302	585.00
Peter Senior	76	74	75	77	302	585.00
Rick Mallicoat	72	76	82	74	304	450.00
Wayne Player°	78	71	80	75	304	
Scott Simpson	72	75	80	77	304	450.00
Kel Nagle	74	78	74	78	304	450.00
Noel Ratcliffe	76	73	75	80	304	450.00
David Galloway	72	78	74	80	304	450.00
Sandy Galbraith	75	74	81	75	305	345.00
Billy Dunk	73	79	73	80	305	345.00
Tom Linskey	78	74	79	76	307	285.00
Walter Godfrey	71	78	81	77	307	285.00

Western Australian 150th Anniversary Open

Lake Karrinyup Country Club, Perth, Western Australia
Par 36–36—72; 6,720 yards

November 22–25
purse, A.$150,000

	SCORES				TOTAL	MONEY
Peter Jacobsen	71	70	70	68	279	A.$30,000.00
David Graham	70	74	70	70	284	18,000.00
Bob Charles	73	73	69	70	285	7,575.00
Graham Marsh	72	71	72	70	285	7,575.00
Barry Jaeckel	74	69	70	72	285	7,575.00
Severiano Ballesteros	70	71	72	72	285	7,575.00
Jerry Pate	69	73	70	74	286	4,500.00
Bob Shearer	70	74	67	75	286	4,500.00
Peter Thomson	74	70	73	70	287	3,750.00
Greg Norman	77	71	66	73	287	3,750.00
Curtis Strange	73	73	72	70	288	3,300.00
John Cook	74	70	74	71	289	2,860.00
Chris Tickner	71	70	76	72	289	2,860.00
Terry Kendall	72	72	70	75	289	2,860.00
Vaughan Somers	71	68	77	74	290	2,400.00
John Lister	70	69	74	77	290	2,400.00
Mike Cahill	72	70	73	75	290	2,400.00
Barry Vivian	74	71	73	73	291	1,875.00
Bill Britten	74	70	72	75	291	1,875.00
Rodger Davis	76	71	70	74	291	1,875.00
Bruce Devlin	73	73	71	74	291	1,875.00
Jack Newton	70	75	76	71	292	1,425.00
Simon Owen	71	71	75	75	292	1,425.00
Walter Godfrey	73	72	76	72	293	1,170.00
Ted Ball	71	77	72	73	293	1,170.00
Martin Foster	74	73	75	72	294	990.00
Stuart Reese	74	73	75	72	294	990.00
Michael Clayton°	79	70	70	75	294	
Terry Gale	69	75	73	77	294	990.00
George Serhan	74	76	71	73	294	990.00
Victor Regalado	74	74	76	71	295	855.00
Bob Shaw	75	70	73	77	295	855.00
Jim Nelford	76	72	75	73	296	765.00
Stewart Ginn	75	76	71	74	296	765.00
Bill Britton	73	73	75	75	296	765.00
John Schroeder	71	75	73	77	296	765.00
Trevor Downing	73	73	75	76	297	690.00
Ross Metherell	73	75	79	71	298	570.00
Elroy Marti	75	76	72	75	298	570.00
Rick Mallicoat	77	73	78	70	298	570.00
Sandy Galbraith	75	74	74	75	298	570.00
Maurice Bembridge	75	70	74	79	298	570.00
Graham Johnson	79	69	72	78	298	570.00
Wayne Grady	73	72	71	82	298	570.00
John Godwin	74	71	76	78	299	405.00
John Benda	71	78	78	72	299	405.00
Brian Jones	74	78	73	74	299	405.00

Rob McNaughton	75	76	74	74	299	405.00
Billy Casper	77	75	76	72	300	300.00
Art Russell	74	76	79	71	300	300.00
Ian Stanley	74	74	78	74	300	300.00

South Seas Classic

Pacific Harbour Golf Club, Fiji
Par 36–36—72; 6,908 yards

December 13–16
purse, F.$40,000[+]

	SCORES				TOTAL	MONEY
Rick Mallicoat	71	73	73	68	285	F.$8,000.00
Wayne Grady	66	75	70	75	286	3,900.00
Mike Ferguson	71	71	71	73	286	3,900.00
Maurice Bembridge	70	75	70	72	287	2,040.00
Greg Norman	68	74	70	76	288	1,600.00
Bob Shearer	74	71	73	72	290	1,360.00
Terry Kendall	70	76	72	72	290	1,360.00
Ted Ball	66	74	76	75	291	1,120.00
Simon Owen	71	74	74	73	292	1,040.00
Guy Wolstenholme	76	76	70	71	293	880.00
Vaughan Somers	70	79	73	71	293	880.00
Rodger Davis	76	71	73	73	293	880.00
Richard Coombes	74	73	73	74	294	768.00
Deray Simon	73	73	72	77	295	720.00
Barry Vivian	76	74	75	71	296	680.00
Gunnar Mueller	69	79	75	75	298	620.00
Ron Wood	71	75	76	76	298	620.00
Glenn McCully	75	76	72	76	299	480.00
Scott Stegner	74	77	72	76	299	480.00
John Godwin	76	74	80	69	299	480.00
John Clifford	70	81	76	72	299	480.00
Art Russell	73	75	77	74	299	480.00
Don Klenk	75	76	72	77	300	340.00
Stewart Ginn	71	78	73	78	300	340.00
Bill Britton	71	80	75	75	301	296.00
Arun Kumar	79	75	73	74	301	296.00
George Serhan	78	75	76	73	302	256.00
Ken Dukes	73	75	78	76	302	256.00
George Bullock	73	74	77	78	302	256.00
Fred Voelkel	78	74	76	75	303	228.00
Marty Bohen	78	74	76	75	303	228.00
John Lister	83	71	79	71	304	208.00
Bob Beauchemin	79	68	80	77	304	208.00
Greg Hohnen	74	72	75	83	304	208.00
Robert Werrell	76	73	78	78	305	188.00
Sandy Galbraith	73	77	77	78	305	188.00
John Benda	82	75	74	75	306	172.00
Scott Tuttle	79	77	75	75	306	172.00
Bose Lutunatabua	76	75	83	73	307	148.00
Veramu Rokotavaga	78	76	76	77	307	148.00
Gary Brookman	75	76	76	80	307	148.00
Elroy Marti	79	71	74	83	307	148.00
Mark Mathews	71	76	84	77	308	124.00
Cec Ferguson	75	77	76	80	308	124.00
Peter Headland	81	79	73	77	310	112.00
Paul Murray	78	79	78	76	311	104.00
Peter Jackson	78	82	72	81	313	96.00
Richard Lee	79	75	77	83	314	88.00
David Williams	77	81	80	78	316	80.00
Steve Long	80	80	81	78	319	72.00

[+] One Fiji dollar = Australian $1.08

NEW ZEALAND TOUR

New Zealand PGA Championship

Mount Maunganui Golf Club, Tauranga
Par 35–36—71; 6,656 yards

December 30–January 2, 1979
purse, N.Z.$30,000*

	SCORES				TOTAL	MONEY
Bob Charles	72	67	67	71	277	N.Z.$6,000.00
Guy Wolstenholme	70	68	70	72	280	3,600.00
Simon Owen	71	66	69	75	281	2,250.00
Bob Beauchemin	73	67	69	73	282	1,530.00
Barry Vivian	68	73	71	72	284	1,200.00
Bill Dunk	68	74	73	70	285	960.00
Stewart Reese	69	71	74	71	285	960.00
Art Russell	73	72	67	73	285	960.00
Bob Shaw	71	70	71	74	286	780.00
Murray Young	72	74	73	68	287	619.20
Paul Firmstone	68	71	76	72	287	619.20
David Good	71	67	76	73	287	619.20
Richard Coombes	68	74	73	72	287	619.20
Terry Kendall	69	70	69	79	287	619.20
Harry Berwick	72	77	73	68	290	435.00
Marty Bohen	73	70	75	72	290	435.00
Dave Leary	72	72	73	73	290	435.00
John Lister	70	66	80	74	290	435.00
Rodger Davis	73	72	72	74	291	375.00
Allan Snape	72	73	73	74	291	375.00
John Carter	75	69	73	75	292	315.00
Kim Southerden	71	74	72	75	292	315.00
Gerry Goss	75	71	73	74	293	270.00
Mike Moynihan	69	76	75	74	294	234.00
Mike Nicholson*	71	72	76	75	294	
Noel Hayden	71	75	72	76	294	234.00
Dennis Clark	76	74	72	73	295	210.00
Tim Ireland	72	74	72	77	295	210.00
Ross Morpeth	79	74	74	69	296	182.00
Erie Fisher*	76	75	74	71	296	
Dan Cullen	76	74	74	72	296	182.00
Richard Lee	75	72	75	74	296	182.00
Stephen Partridge*	75	75	69	77	296	
Brendan Perry	77	76	71	73	297	168.00
Bill Sipson*	73	75	74	75	297	
Kevin Billington*	77	74	75	72	298	
Craig Owen	70	76	75	77	298	159.00
Alex Bonnington	71	71	76	80	298	159.00
Wayne Macintosh	76	74	76	73	299	138.00
Murray Thompson	75	74	74	76	299	138.00
Peter Hamblett	75	76	72	76	299	138.00
Ian Peters*	77	74	70	78	299	
Geoff Smart	79	72	69	79	299	138.00
Peter Crocker	73	79	70	77	299	138.00
Greg Holst	72	76	72	80	300	111.00
Noel Johnson*	70	79	74	77	300	
Steve Charles	74	77	73	76	300	111.00
Doug Machray	75	76	75	74	300	111.00
John Evans	75	78	74	73	300	111.00
Frank Nobilo*	72	77	73	79	301	
Brian Doyle	77	77	70	77	301	93.00
Paul Mahoney	73	81	74	73	301	93.00

*Amateur

*One New Zealand dollar = U.S. $1.03

Air New Zealand-Shell Open

Wellington Golf Club, Heretaunga
Par 71; 6,717 yards

November 28–December 2
purse, N.Z.$75,000

	SCORES				TOTAL	MONEY
David Graham	70	67	69	73	279	N.Z.$12,500.00
Rodger Davis	69	70	72	76	287	8,300.00
Bob Charles	72	73	72	71	288	4,220.00
Victor Regalado	72	75	68	73	288	4,220.00
Simon Owen	71	71	72	76	290	2,905.00
Barry Vivian	69	73	73	75	290	2,905.00
Tom Kite	67	72	76	76	291	2,250.00
Bob Gilder	70	72	72	78	292	1,875.00
Terry Kendall	78	73	71	71	293	1,685.00
Gene Littler	76	75	71	72	294	1,500.00
Rick Barker	69	73	73	80	295	1,280.00
John Schroeder	72	72	79	73	295	1,280.00
John Godwin	72	67	84	72	295	1,280.00
Brian Jones	69	77	75	74	295	1,280.00
Maurice Bembridge	74	71	74	77	296	1,027.00

Bob Shearer	73	73	73	77	296	1,027.00
Bruce Devlin	71	73	78	74	296	1,027.00
Guy Wolstenholme	73	70	76	77	296	1,027.00
John Lister	71	73	81	71	296	1,027.00
Ted Ball	70	72	75	81	298	882.50
Don Klenk	73	73	76	76	298	882.50
Richard Coombes	72	73	76	78	299	830.00
Rick Mallicoat	76	75	76	72	299	830.00
Stewart Ginn	73	75	76	76	300	770.00
Deray Simon	73	72	76	79	300	770.00
Terry Gale	80	73	72	75	300	770.00
Greg Hohnen	73	76	76	75	300	770.00
Craig Owen	71	76	75	79	301	700.00
Brian Barnes	73	75	73	80	301	700.00
John Benda	74	73	80	74	301	700.00
Martin Foster	72	74	74	82	302	640.00
Elroy Marti	75	71	75	81	302	640.00
Bill Dunk	75	73	75	79	302	640.00
Kel Nagle	73	77	77	76	303	590.00
Pat Cowan	74	78	79	72	303	590.00
Paul Murray	70	80	78	76	304	540.00
Bill Britton	73	75	77	79	304	540.00
Don Williams	74	77	75	78	304	540.00
Tony Johnson	73	72	83	77	305	455.00
Stuart Reese	77	70	80	78	305	455.00
George Serhan	78	75	74	78	305	455.00
Scott Stegner	79	72	76	78	305	455.00
Peter Thomson	76	74	79	76	305	455.00
Bill Casper	77	74	79	75	305	455.00
Colin Ferguson	76	73	79	79	306	385.00
Sandy Galbraith	71	72	83	80	306	385.00
Marty Bohen	75	74	77	80	306	385.00
Rob McNaughton	72	74	80	80	306	385.00
Pat Mateer	74	78	76	79	307	350.00
Bob Beauchemin	75	76	80	76	307	350.00
Peter Hamblett	74	76	79	78	307	350.00
Vaughan Somers	72	69	82	85	308	330.00

New Zealand Open

St. Clair Golf Club, Dunedin
Par 35–36—71; 6,579 yards

December 6–9
purse, N.Z.$50,000

	SCORES				TOTAL	MONEY
Stewart Ginn	70	68	71	69	278	N.Z.$7,500.00
Simon Owen	65	71	71	74	281	5,600.00
Rodger Davis	67	73	73	70	283	4,250.00
Terry Gale	71	74	72	67	284	3,250.00
Ted Ball	63	78	72	72	285	2,475.00
Brian Jones	72	72	78	64	286	1,660.00
Jeff Short	70	72	72	72	286	1,660.00
Barry Vivian	71	73	73	70	287	1,250.00
Brian Barnes	69	71	71	76	287	1,250.00
George Bullock	75	73	71	69	288	1,100.00
Guy Wolstenholme	69	74	74	72	289	857.50
Frank Nobilo	71	70	74	74	289	857.50
Rick Mallicoat	76	70	69	74	289	857.50
Richard Coombes	69	73	70	77	289	857.50
Greg Hohnen	69	78	73	70	290	643.33
Peter Cowen	69	77	73	71	290	643.33
John Clifford	71	70	76	73	290	643.33
Marty Bohen	70	77	73	71	291	555.00
Craig Owen	70	72	77	72	291	555.00
Peter Headland	72	75	72	72	291	555.00
Art Russell	72	74	72	73	291	555.00
Terry Kendall	77	70	71	73	291	555.00
Dennis Clark	70	72	75	74	291	555.00
Bob Charles	67	71	75	78	291	555.00
Wayne Grady	74	75	70	73	292	495.00
George Serhan	76	73	74	70	293	453.00
Scott Stegner	75	74	74	70	293	453.00
Elroy Marti	77	76	67	73	293	453.00
Richard Lee	74	74	70	75	293	453.00
Martin Foster	67	79	70	77	293	453.00
Philip Atkinson°	71	79	74	70	294	
Peter Hamblett	76	77	69	72	294	410.00
John Godwin	74	71	73	76	294	410.00
Phillip Aickin°	69	77	75	73	294	
John Roche	71	76	73	74	294	410.00
Bill Britten	72	72	78	73	295	365.00
Paul Murray	73	75	74	73	295	365.00
Mark Harper°	72	73	76	74	295	
Vaughan Somers	73	79	74	73	295	365.00
Maurice Bembridge	74	74	72	75	295	365.00
Rob McNaughton	72	75	72	76	295	365.00
Geoff Clarke°	70	76	77	73	296	
Kel Nagle	74	73	73	76	296	330.00
Stuart Reese	69	75	76	88	297	320.00
Kim Southerden	74	76	77	71	298	300.00
Fred Voelkel	77	76	72	73	298	300.00
Don Klenk	73	74	74	77	298	300.00
Frank Muller	70	77	77	75	299	275.00

| Richard Ellis | 73 | 81 | 70 | 75 | 299 | 275.00 |
| Scott Tuttle | 76 | 73 | 74 | 77 | 300 | 260.00 |

*Amateur

LPGA MONEY LIST

POS.	PLAYER	TOTAL MONEY
1	Nancy Lopez	$215,988.61
2	Sandra Post	187,350.68
3	Donna Caponi Young	160,693.67
4	Amy Alcott	152,900.27
5	Pat Bradley	151,328.64
6	Sally Little	134,811.01
7	JoAnne Carner	122,543.64
8	Jane Blalock	120,557.97
9	Judy Rankin	109,836.62
10	Silvia Bertolaccini	108,904.31
11	Beth Daniel	106,871.89
12	Jo Ann Washam	89,378.71
13	Hollis Stacy	85,865.98
14	Jerilyn Britz	78,576.78
15	Donna H. White	77,041.94
16	Jan Stephenson	73,729.91
17	Debbie Massey	65,653.74
18	Murle Breer	64,092.07
19	Vicki Fergon	58,145.01
20	Dot Germain	56,857.09
21	Betsy King	55,610.00
22	Penny Pulz	54,854.75
23	Sandra Palmer	54,202.91
24	Joyce Kazmierski	52,270.09
25	Laura Baugh	47,176.75
26	Marlene Floyd	46,791.48
27	Shelley Hamlin	43,217.14
28	Pat Meyers	41,309.66
29	Lori Garbacz	40,657.54
30	Mary Dwyer	40,391.85
31	Sandra Spuzich	40,018.90
32	Kathy Whitworth	39,959.13
33	Debbie Austin	36,907.33
34	Marlene Hagge	36,643.90
35	Janet Coles	36,528.84
36	Peggy Conley	35,727.54
37	Kathy McMullen	34,320.34
38	Sue Berning	33,009.26
39	Kathy Postlewait	32,704.88
40	Lynn Adams	29,050.48
41	Cathy Thompson	28,987.24
42	Barbara Moxness	28,873.18
43	Jo Ann Prentice	27,855.84
44	Kathy Ahern	27,590.00
45	Susie McAllister	27,575.10
46	Judy Clark	26,961.55
47	Cathy Sherk	26,924.30
48	Bonnie Bryant	26,487.66
49	Chako Higuchi	25,675.00
50	Beverly Klass	24,923.16
51	Alice Ritzman	24,647.70
52	Bonnie Lauer	24,150.19
53	Barbara Barrow	23,833.30
54	Vivian Brownlee	23,713.32
55	Gloria Ehret	22,852.42
56	Dale Lundquist	22,293.34
57	Cathy Morse	21,274.66
58	Pam Higgins	20,429.16
59	Gail Toushin	18,864.04
60	Alexandra Reinhardt	18,428.75
61	Betty Burfeindt	18,303.84
62	Beth Solomon	18,267.86
63	Amelia Rorer	17,917.03
64	Mardell Wilkins	16,141.25
65	Mary Mills	16,087.33
66	Kathy Martin	15,054.60
67	Clifford Ann Creed	13,889.01
68	Sue Roberts	13,799.96
69	Julie Stanger	12,944.17
70	Debbie Meisterlin	12,833.95
71	Carole Jo Skala	12,508.33
72	M.J. Smith	12,023.49
73	Kathy Young	11,675.65
74	Janet Alex	11,398.02
75	Patty Hayes	10,896.83
76	Susan O'Connor	10,825.50
77	Louise Bruce	10,790.42
78	Carol Mann	10,438.50

79	Mickey Wright	9,894.17
80	Connie Chillemi	9,849.86
81	Alice Miller	9,563.32
82	Eva Chang	8,893.00
83	Cindy Chamberlin	8,882.44
84	Maria Combs	8,855.27
85	Susan Grams	8,465.79
86	Sandra Haynie	7,672.75
87	Jane Renner	7,538.69
88	Kathy Cornelius	7,393.32
89	Kathy Hite	7,244.44
90	Lauren Howe	7,120.00
91	Shirley Englehorn	6,897.75
92	Cindy Hill	6,738.66
93	Barbara Mizrahie	6,726.67
94	Tu Ai Yu	6,447.00
95	Karolyn Kertzman	6,154.50
96	Michelle Walker	6,121.28
97	Jan Ferraris	6,042.75
98	Cathy Mant	5,647.83
99	Mary Lou Crocker	5,544.50
100	Sylvia Ferdon	5,220.36

LPGA STROKE AVERAGES
(Only Players with 60 or more rounds)

POS.	PLAYER	ROUNDS	STROKES	AVERAGE
1	Nancy Lopez	71	5055	71.20
2	Jane Blalock	89	6421	72.15
3	Chako Higuchi	23	1660	72.17
4	Sandra Post	97	7013	72.30
5	Patricia Bradley	100	7231	72.31
6	JoAnne Carner	53	3837	72.40
7	Amy Alcott	93	6736	72.43
8	Donna Caponi Young	104	7546	72.56
9	Beth Daniel	88	6393	72.65
10	Sally Little	99	7193	72.66
11	Judy Rankin	87	6323	72.68
12	Donna Horton White	86	6270	72.91
13	Jo Ann Washam	95	6951	73.17
14	Hollis Stacy	97	7098	73.18
15	Jan Stephenson	100	7325	73.25
16	Sandra Palmer	94	6907	73.48
17	Penny Pulz	82	6033	73.57
18	Silvia Bertolaccini	104	7652	73.58
19	Debbie Massey	69	5079	73.61
20	Dorothy Germain	82	6045	73.72
21	Laura Baugh	80	5898	73.73
22	Kathy McMullen	95	7016	73.85
23	Jerilyn Britz	104	7682	73.87
24	Sandra Spuzich	92	6796	73.87
25	Pat Meyers	83	6138	73.95

LPGA TOUR

Colgate Triple Crown Match Play Championship

Mission Hills Country Club, Palm Springs, California
Par 36—36—72; 6,272 yards

February 1–4
purse, $100,000

First Round

Silvia Bertolaccini defeated Nancy Lopez, 1 up, 20 holes.
Amy Alcott defeated Mary Dwyer, 2 and 1.
JoAnne Carner defeated Debbie Massey, 5 and 4.
Sandra Post defeated Kathy Postlewait, 5 and 3.
Mary Mills defeated Jerilyn Britz, 1 up.
Pat Bradley defeated Jan Stephenson, 1 up.
Donna Caponi Young defeated Penny Pulz, 4 and 3.
Dot Germain defeated Sally Little, 3 and 1.

Second Round

Bertolaccini defeated Alcott, 2 and 1.
Carner defeated Post, 3 and 2.
Bradley defeated Mills, 3 and 2.
Young defeated Germain, 3 and 2.

Semifinals

Carner defeated Bertolaccini, 5 and 4.
Bradley defeated Young, 4 and 2.

Finals

Carner defeated Bradley, 4 and 3.

Prize Money: Carner, $23,000; Bradley, $15,000; Young, $11,000; Bertolaccini, $9,000; Alcott, Germain, Lopez and Little, $5,000 each; Post and Mills, $4,000 each; Massey and Britz, $3,000 each; Dwyer, Postlewait, Pulz and Stephenson, $2,500 each.

Elizabeth Arden Classic

Country Club Aventura, Miami, Florida
Par 36–36—72; 6,211 yards

February 15–18
purse, $100,000

	SCORES				TOTAL	MONEY
Amy Alcott	70	70	72	73	285	$15,000.00
Sandra Post	71	71	70	73	285	9,800.00
(Alcott defeated Post on third hole of sudden-death play-off)						
Pat Bradley	74	73	73	68	288	6,000.00
Jan Stephenson	72	74	71	71	288	6,000.00
Jane Blalock	74	72	72	71	289	3,750.00
Donna H. White	72	74	73	70	289	3,750.00
Beth Solomon	76	71	74	71	292	3,050.00
Beth Daniel	74	73	74	71	292	3,050.00
Nancy Lopez	76	72	75	70	293	2,500.00
Mary Dwyer	74	74	71	74	293	2,500.00
JoAnne Carner	75	71	78	69	293	2,500.00
Vivian Brownlee	73	78	72	71	294	1,852.50
Alexandra Reinhardt	77	71	77	69	294	1,852.50
Sandra Palmer	70	77	73	74	294	1,852.50
Hollis Stacy	69	74	74	77	294	1,852.00
Donna C. Young	77	71	72	75	295	1,540.00
Debbie Austin	75	74	73	75	297	1,390.00
Betty Burfeindt	73	74	74	76	297	1,390.00
Louise Bruce	77	76	70	75	298	1,142.50
Martha Nause	77	74	69	78	298	1,142.50
Karolyn Kertzman	74	76	75	73	298	1,142.50
Pat Meyers	73	73	77	75	298	1,142.50
Mary Mills	77	74	76	72	299	920.00
Judy Clark	74	76	77	72	299	920.00
Lori Garbacz	76	74	75	74	299	920.00
Penny Pulz	74	75	77	73	299	920.00
Murle Breer	72	76	76	75	299	920.00
Jerilyn Britz	73	74	76	76	299	920.00
Sandra Spuzich	77	75	77	71	300	706.00
Cathy Sherk	74	76	77	73	300	706.00
Silvia Bertolaccini	74	75	77	74	300	706.00
Roberta Speer	74	74	75	77	300	706.00
Betsy King	74	71	79	76	300	706.00
Dale Lundquist	79	75	75	72	301	517.50
Laura Baugh	75	79	74	73	301	517.50
Alice Miller	77	75	81	68	301	517.50
Kathy Whitworth	77	75	76	73	301	517.50
Cathy Morse	73	77	75	76	301	517.50
Susan O'Connor	71	78	79	73	301	517.50
Barbara Barrow	74	76	78	73	301	517.50
Sally Little	73	73	80	75	301	517.50
Janet Coles	75	78	79	70	302	390.00
Beverly Klass	77	74	73	78	302	390.00
Debbie Meisterlin	79	72	74	77	302	390.00
Marlene Floyd	72	75	74	81	302	390.00
Tatsuko Ohsako	74	74	77	78	303	330.00
Bonnie Bryant	77	71	75	80	303	330.00
Lynn Adams	72	74	79	78	303	330.00
Kathy Young	76	78	72	78	304	295.00
Barbara Mizrahie	75	77	76	76	304	295.00

Orange Blossom Classic

Pasadena Country Club, St. Petersburg, Florida
Par 36–36—72; 6,109 yards

February 23–25
purse, $75,000

	SCORES			TOTAL	MONEY
Jane Blalock	66	69	70	205	$11,250.00
Sandra Post	70	71	70	211	7,500.00
JoAnne Carner	71	74	68	213	4,700.00
Pat Bradley	71	72	70	213	4,700.00
Alice Miller	72	72	70	214	2,653.75
Judy T. Rankin	71	72	71	214	2,653.75
Laura Baugh	71	72	71	214	2,653.75
Silvia Bertolaccini	71	67	76	214	2,653.75
Peggy Conley	71	74	70	215	2,025.00

Julie Stanger	69	74	72	215	2,025.00
Kathy McMullen	69	79	68	216	1,725.00
Sally Little	72	74	70	216	1,725.00
Penny Pulz	75	70	72	217	1,333.75
Donna H. White	73	71	73	217	1,333.75
Amy Alcott	74	70	73	217	1,333.75
Kathy Whitworth	71	70	76	217	1,333.75
Gloria Ehret	73	74	71	218	1,013.75
Sandra Palmer	73	72	73	218	1,013.75
Alexandra Reinhardt	72	71	75	218	1,013.75
Connie Chillemi	68	74	76	218	1,013.75
Cathy Thompson	72	75	72	219	836.67
Kathy Ahern	72	74	73	219	836.67
Dale Lundquist	69	73	77	219	836.66
Bonnie Lauer	71	77	72	220	710.00
Jan Stephenson	72	75	73	220	710.00
Jo Ann Prentice	72	70	78	220	710.00
Nayoko Yoshikawa	73	76	72	221	585.00
Louise Bruce	75	72	74	221	585.00
Barbara Moxness	74	73	74	221	585.00
Kathy Postlewait	75	71	75	221	585.00
Beth Daniel	71	74	76	221	585.00
Pat Meyers	73	76	73	222	463.00
Tatsuko Ohsako	74	74	74	222	463.00
Judy Clark	73	74	75	222	463.00
Cathy Sherk	74	72	76	222	463.00
Jerilyn Britz	69	76	77	222	463.00
Karolyn Kertzman	73	76	74	223	390.00
Janet Alex	71	78	74	223	390.00
Hollis Stacy	75	76	73	224	335.00
Jo Ann Washam	73	77	74	224	335.00
Cathy Morse	74	76	74	224	335.00
Donna C. Young	70	79	75	224	335.00
Clifford A. Creed	71	78	75	224	335.00
Sandra Spuzich	72	79	74	225	261.00
Martha Nause	73	77	75	225	261.00
Mary Bea Porter	74	75	76	225	261.00
Maria Combs	73	75	77	225	261.00
Shelley Hamlin	76	73	76	225	261.00
Mary Dwyer	73	78	75	226	113.75
Debbie Meisterlin	75	76	75	226	113.75

Bent Tree Classic

Bent Tree Golf & Racquet Club, Sarasota, Florida
Par 36–36—72; 6,106 yards

March 1–4
purse, $100,000

	SCORES				TOTAL	MONEY
Sally Little	72	67	72	67	278	$15,000.00
Nancy Lopez	71	67	74	68	280	9,800.00
Jo Ann Washam	71	73	69	69	282	6,000.00
Dale Lundquist	71	68	72	71	282	6,000.00
Pat Bradley	70	70	73	72	285	4,000.00
Murle Breer	72	60	74	72	286	3,350.00
Hollis Stacy	67	73	72	74	286	3,350.00
Laura Baugh	72	71	74	70	287	2,700.00
Lynn Adams	75	69	72	71	287	2,700.00
Beth Daniel	74	71	69	73	287	2,700.00
Barbara Moxness	72	73	73	70	288	2,100.00
JoAnne Carner	72	72	72	72	288	2,100.00
Donna H. White	66	72	74	76	288	2,100.00
Judy T. Rankin	68	71	74	76	289	1,760.00
Shelley Hamlin	76	72	74	68	290	1,543.34
Lori Garbacz	71	67	79	73	290	1,543.33
Sandra Palmer	70	71	74	75	290	1,543.33
Sandra Spuzich	72	72	75	72	291	1,246.67
Sandra Post	74	73	72	72	291	1,246.67
Peggy Conley	69	73	73	76	291	1,246.66
Mary Dwyer	72	74	74	72	292	1,022.00
Vicki Fergon	74	73	71	74	292	1,022.00
Kathy McMullen	72	71	75	74	292	1,022.80
Cathy Thompson	77	69	71	75	292	1,022.00
Jo Ann Prentice	70	70	75	77	292	1,022.00
Karolyn Kertzman	74	71	75	73	293	880.00
Dot Germain	74	70	75	74	293	880.00
Kathy Ahern	76	75	74	69	294	742.00
Betty Burfeindt	70	75	76	73	294	742.00
Gloria Ehret	73	73	73	75	294	742.00
Barbara Barrow	74	70	73	77	294	742.00
Vivian Brownlee	70	72	74	78	294	742.00
Tatsuko Ohsako	77	71	76	71	295	566.67
Jerilyn Britz	76	70	75	74	295	566.67
Louise Bruce	72	70	79	74	295	566.67
Susan Grams	72	71	77	75	295	566.67
Lori Nelson	74	73	73	75	295	566.66
Marlene Floyd	73	76	71	75	295	566.66
Cathy Sherk	75	75	74	72	296	430.00
Marga Stubblefield	79	71	73	73	296	430.00
Debbie Austin	73	75	75	73	296	430.00
Pat Meyers	73	71	78	74	296	430.00
Mary Mills	72	77	73	74	296	430.00

Betsy King	74	71	75	76	296	430.00
Judy Clark	74	72	76	75	297	337.50
Joan Joyce	74	75	73	75	297	337.50
Alice Miller	73	74	74	76	297	337.50
Mickey Wright	72	72	73	80	297	337.50
Connie Chillemi	74	73	80	71	298	295.00
Eva Chang	75	73	78	72	298	295.00

Sunstar Classic

Rancho Park Golf Course, Los Angeles, California
Par 37–35–72; 6,268 yards

March 8–11
purse, $100,000

		SCORES			TOTAL	MONEY
Nancy Lopez	70	71	70	69	280	$15,000.00
Hollis Stacy	72	66	71	72	281	9,800.00
Peggy Conley	73	68	73	69	283	6,000.00
Sue Berning	72	69	71	71	283	6,000.00
Pat Bradley	71	69	73	71	284	3,750.00
Laura Baugh	74	70	69	71	284	3,750.00
Sandra Spuzich	68	79	70	69	286	3,200.00
Vicki Fergon	68	73	74	72	287	2,700.00
Kathy Whitworth	74	67	75	71	287	2,700.00
Jane Blalock	74	72	69	72	287	2,700.00
Barbara Barrow	71	75	71	71	288	2,300.00
Mardell Wilkins	73	69	74	73	289	2,000.00
Betty Burfeindt	73	73	69	74	289	2,000.00
Penny Pulz	73	73	73	71	290	1,705.00
Judy T. Rankin	73	74	72	71	290	1,705.00
Chako Higuchi	72	71	76	72	291	1,390.00
Gloria Ehret	75	72	71	73	291	1,390.00
Kathy Postlewait	74	74	70	73	291	1,390.00
Amy Alcott	72	74	67	78	291	1,3 0 0.00
Cathy Morse	74	73	75	70	292	1,066.00
Betsy King	74	72	75	71	292	1,066.00
Donna C. Young	74	71	76	71	292	1,066.00
Gail Toushin	73	71	74	74	292	1,066.00
Marlene Floyd	77	68	72	75	292	1,066.00
Jan Stephenson	73	70	77	73	293	900.00
Sharron Moran	75	74	71	73	293	900.00
Jerilyn Britz	68	72	78	75	293	900.00
Kathy McMullen	75	69	76	74	294	780.00
Alice Ritzman	75	74	71	74	294	780.00
Marlene Hagge	75	71	73	75	294	780.00
Kathy Ahern	73	77	72	73	295	625.00
Connie Chillemi	77	74	71	73	295	625.00
Jo Ann Prentice	76	74	72	73	295	625.00
Bonnie Bryant	74	76	71	74	295	625.00
Kathy Hite	74	71	74	76	295	625.00
Cathy Sherk	70	71	76	78	295	625.00
Julie Stanger	74	74	75	73	296	480.00
Kathy Cornelius	75	74	74	73	296	480.00
Nayoko Yoshikawa	73	75	74	74	296	480.00
Bonnie Lauer	75	72	74	75	296	480.00
Debbie Meisterlin	78	73	67	78	296	480.00
Lynn Adams	72	72	81	72	297	380.00
Joyce Kazmierski	75	73	76	73	297	380.00
Joyce Benson	74	76	73	74	297	380.00
Janet Coles	76	74	71	76	297	380.00
Lily Wu	71	74	73	79	297	380.00
Ai-Yu Tu	78	73	74	73	298	305.00
Cathy Thompson	78	71	75	74	298	305.00
Eva Chang	74	72	78	74	298	305.00
Lauren Howe	76	74	73	75	298	305.00

Honda Civic Golf Classic

Rancho Bernardo Inn, San Diego, California
Par 36–36—72; 6,212 yards

March 15–18
purse, $150,000

		SCORES			TOTAL	MONEY
JoAnne Carner	72	71	69	69	281	$22,500.00
Pat Bradley	71	67	73	73	284	12,600.00
Sandra Post	70	71	72	71	284	12,600.00
Betty Burfeindt	73	71	71	70	285	7,500.00
Sandra Palmer	71	71	72	72	286	6,000.00
Pam Higgins	74	72	73	70	289	5,250.00
Hollis Stacy	74	73	72	71	290	4,080.00
Mary Dwyer	71	73	74	72	290	4,080.00
Beth Solomon	72	71	73	74	290	4,080.00
Sally Little	71	70	75	74	290	4,080.00
Amy Alcott	69	75	71	75	290	4,080.00
Kathy Whitworth	75	71	75	70	291	2,880.00

Donna C. Young	77	72	70	72	291	2,880.00
Lori Garbacz	72	73	73	73	291	2,880.00
Penny Pulz	73	73	75	71	292	2,092.50
Jo Ann Washam	71	77	73	71	292	2,092.50
Gloria Ehret	74	72	74	72	292	2,092.50
Janet Coles	74	75	70	73	292	2,092.50
Gail Toushin	71	74	72	75	292	2,092.50
Jane Blalock	71	73	73	75	292	2,092.50
Mardell Wilkins	76	73	73	71	293	1,563.75
Kathy McMullen	73	69	80	71	293	1,563.75
Bonnie Lauer	75	73	73	72	293	1,563.75
Vivian Brownlee	68	72	74	79	293	1,563.75
Joyce Kazmierski	76	72	75	71	294	1,320.00
Marlene Floyd	71	75	75	73	294	1,320.00
Alexandra Reinhardt	71	75	71	77	294	1,320.00
Maria Combs	77	70	70	77	294	1,320.00
Barbara Moxness	69	72	78	76	295	1,110.00
Ai-Yu Tu	74	72	73	76	295	1,110.00
Chako Higuchi	72	70	73	80	295	1,110.00
Cathy Morse	73	74	76	73	296	937.50
Louise Bruce	70	76	77	73	296	937.50
Sylvia Ferdon	76	71	76	73	296	937.50
Sue Berning	74	73	74	75	296	937.50
Mary Bea Porter	71	74	79	73	297	785.00
Shirley Englehorn	74	75	74	74	297	785.00
Nayoko Yoshikawa	68	74	79	76	297	785.00
Peggy Conley	71	78	73	76	298	705.00
Sandra Spuzich	70	74	75	79	298	705.00
Kathy Postlewait	75	74	77	73	299	630.00
Connie Chillemi	72	75	76	76	299	630.00
Margie Masters	76	73	74	76	299	630.00
Clifford Ann Creed	74	74	79	73	300	519.00
Vicki Fergon	74	75	78	73	300	519.00
Kathy Ahern	73	72	80	75	300	519.00
Susie McAllister	70	76	77	77	300	519.00
Jan Stephenson	73	75	75	77	300	519.00
Jan Ferraris	77	72	78	74	301	435.00
Beth Stone	76	73	77	75	301	435.00

Sahara National Pro-Am

Par: Sahara CC 35–36—71; 6,108 yards
   Las Vegas CC 36–36—73; 6,087 yards

March 22–25
purse $100,000

	SCORES				TOTAL	MONEY
Nancy Lopez	72	67	66	69	274	$15,000.00
Donna Young	66	69	68	73	276	9,800.00
JoAnne Carner	64	73	74	67	278	7,000.00
Penny Pulz	69	69	72	71	281	4,500.00
Chako Higuchi	69	70	69	73	281	4,500.00
Amy Alcott	67	72	73	70	282	3,500.00
Judy Rankin	73	66	72	74	285	3,200.00
Jo Ann Washam	70	73	73	70	286	2,700.00
Sandra Palmer	70	73	73	70	286	2,700.00
Sandra Post	73	74	69	70	286	2,700.00
Mary Dwyer	68	78	72	69	287	2,015.00
Laura Baugh	72	72	72	71	287	2,015.00
Gloria Ehret	71	73	71	72	287	2,015.00
Kathy Postlewait	69	74	71	73	287	2,015.00
Dot Germain	72	69	74	73	288	1,650.00
Kathy Ahern	75	73	74	67	289	1,440.00
M.J. Smith	76	69	71	73	289	1,440.00
Jan Stephenson	73	72	70	74	289	1,440.00
Kathy McMullen	76	73	70	72	291	1,142.50
Alexandra Reinhardt	71	75	72	73	291	1,142.50
Donna White	73	71	74	73	291	1,142.50
Silvia Bertolaccini	73	72	69	77	291	1,142.50
Louise Bruce	72	73	75	72	292	960.00
Dale Lundquist	72	78	70	72	292	960.00
Beth Solomon	74	71	74	73	292	960.00
Karolyn Kertzman	71	73	75	73	292	960.00
Gail Toushin	71	76	76	70	293	820.00
Jo Ann Prentice	74	72	72	75	293	820.00
Mardell Wilkins	73	70	72	78	293	820.00
Cathy Morse	76	71	77	70	294	672.00
Betsy King	74	72	75	73	294	672.00
Roberta Speer	72	72	76	74	294	672.00
Kathy Whitworth	75	72	73	74	294	672.00
Susan O'Connor	73	73	74	74	294	672.00
Clifford Ann Creed	79	73	73	70	295	537.50
Peggy Conley	73	76	73	73	295	537.50
Murle Breer	74	71	76	74	295	537.50
Kathy Cornelius	69	74	75	77	295	537.50
Shirley Englehorn	75	76	74	71	296	470.00
Pam Higgins	73	75	75	73	296	470.00
Sally Little	73	75	78	71	297	381.43
Barbara Barrow	76	71	78	72	297	381.43
Janet Alex	72	71	82	72	297	381.43

Maria Combs	77	69	76	75	297	381.43
Bonnie Lauer	72	78	73	74	297	381.43
Jerilyn Britz	71	77	74	75	297	381.43
Susan Grams	71	74	75	77	297	381.42
Beth Stone	74	78	75	71	298	320.00
Marlene Floyd	71	81	72	75	299	305.00
Lily Wu	69	77	75	78	299	305.00

Women's Kemper Open

Mesa Verde Country Club, Costa Mesa, California — March 29–April 1
Par 36-35—71; 6,134 yards — purse, $150,000

	SCORES				TOTAL	MONEY
JoAnne Carner	72	71	72	71	286	$22,500.00
Donna C. Young	71	72	70	73	286	9,675.00
Jan Stephenson	70	73	72	71	286	9,675.00
Nancy Lopez	71	68	72	75	286	9,675.00
Chako Higuchi	69	70	74	73	286	9,675.00

(Carner won sudden-death play-off, defeating Young, Stephenson and Lopez on first extra hole and Higuchi on second extra hole)

Jo Ann Washam	73	68	74	73	288	5,025.00
Judy Rankin	72	70	72	74	288	5,025.00
Kathy McMullen	72	79	70	68	289	4,350.00
Sally Little	71	68	80	71	290	3,600.00
Pat Bradley	76	72	70	72	290	3,600.00
Amy Alcott	75	71	70	74	290	3,600.00
Beth Daniel	72	70	71	77	290	3,600.00
Maria Combs	75	73	76	67	291	2,487.00
Sandra Post	70	77	76	68	291	2,487.00
Beverly Klass	78	75	70	68	291	2,487.00
Peggy Conley	72	75	74	70	291	2,487.00
Laura Baugh	74	71	73	73	291	2,487.00
Debbie Austin	79	73	71	69	292	1,935.00
Dot Germain	72	71	76	73	292	1,935.00
Vivian Brownlee	75	73	72	73	293	1,665.00
Sandra Spuzich	71	75	73	74	293	1,665.00
Bonnie Bryant	70	75	73	75	293	1,665.00
Betsy King	73	76	74	71	294	1,410.00
Alice Ritzman	70	74	77	73	294	1,410.00
Sandra Palmer	73	78	69	74	294	1,410.00
Mary Dwyer	76	66	77	75	294	1,410.00
Silvia Bertolaccini	72	71	75	76	294	1,410.00
Mardell Wilkins	75	72	77	71	295	1,087.50
Joyce Kazmierski	73	75	75	72	295	1,087.50
Donna White	74	75	73	73	295	1,087.50
Mary Mills	74	77	71	73	295	1,087.50
Kathy Postlewait	75	73	73	74	295	1,087.50
Cathy Morse	73	70	76	76	295	1,087.50
Penny Pulz	76	70	78	72	296	847.50
Shelley Hamlin	74	74	76	72	296	847.50
Kathy Whitworth	76	73	72	75	296	847.50
Lynn Adams	72	75	73	76	296	847.50
Kathy Ahern	73	74	76	74	297	720.00
Hollis Stacy	79	74	71	73	297	720.00
Jerilyn Britz	71	79	72	75	297	720.00
Barbara Moxness	77	73	77	71	298	645.00
Betty Burfeindt	73	79	70	76	298	645.00
Pam Higgins	75	75	78	71	299	555.00
Janet Coles	75	73	77	74	299	555.00
Judy Kimball	76	75	75	73	299	555.00
Gail Toushin	71	79	75	74	299	555.00
Debbie Massey	74	75	80	71	300	450.00
Kathy Cornelius	73	75	79	73	300	450.00
Vicki Fergon	78	73	76	73	300	450.00
Gloria Ehret	76	74	75	75	300	450.00

Colgate-Dinah Shore Winners Circle

Mission Hills Country Club, Rancho Mirage, California — April 5–8
Par 36-36—72; 6,272 yards — purse, $250,000

	SCORES				TOTAL	MONEY
Sandra Post	68	70	68	70	276	$37,500.00
Nancy Lopez	68	70	68	71	277	24,500.00
Pat Bradley	72	73	67	69	281	15,000.00
Donna H. White	73	69	69	70	281	15,000.00
Judy Rankin	67	74	69	73	283	10,000.00
JoAnne Carner	69	70	70	75	284	8,750.00
Jo Ann Washam	74	67	75	70	286	7,625.00
Donna C. Young	69	72	72	73	286	7,625.00
Joyce Kazmierski	72	72	72	71	287	6,750.00
Penny Pulz	73	75	70	70	288	6,250.00
Jane Blalock	71	77	73	68	289	5,500.00
Amy Alcott	74	69	71	75	28'	5,500.00
Silvia Bertolaccini	75	74	69	72	290	4,281.25
Dot Germain	70	77	71	72	290	4,281.25
Betsy King	73	74	71	72	290	4,281.25

Shirley Englehorn	73	72	72	73	290	4,281.25
Kathy Ahern	72	74	74	71	291	3,237.50
Sandra Palmer	77	71	71	72	291	3,237.50
Debbie Austin	69	73	74	75	291	3,237.50
Laura Baugh	69	76	71	75	291	3,237.50
Jan Stephenson	76	71	75	70	292	2,712.50
Murle Breer	72	75	72	73	292	2,712.50
Bonnie Bryant	73	73	73	74	293	2,400.00
Shelley Hamlin	73	70	76	74	293	2,400.00
Hollis Stacy	72	74	73	74	293	2,400.00
Chako Higuchi	69	69	79	76	293	2,400.00
Roberta Speer	74	78	73	69	294	2,100.00
Janet Coles	75	72	72	75	294	2,100.00
Debbie Massey	72	76	74	73	295	1,765.00
Pat Meyers	72	73	77	73	295	1,765.00
Peggy Conley	71	74	75	75	295	1,765.00
Sally Little	72	72	74	77	295	1,765.00
Dale Lundquist	76	74	69	76	295	1,765.00
Marlene Floyd	76	72	77	71	296	1,487.50
Clifford Ann Creed	72	74	75	75	296	1,487.50
Bonnie Lauer	73	73	76	75	297	1,375.00
Mary Lou Crocker	70	76	77	75	298	1,150.00
Susie Berning	76	78	70	74	298	1,150.00
Marlene Hagge	72	73	79	74	298	1,150.00
Betty Burfeindt	74	72	75	77	298	1,150.00
Maria Combs	73	74	74	77	298	1,150.00
Alexandra Reinhardt	75	72	73	78	298	1,150.00
Carole Jo Skala	75	74	71	78	298	1,150.00
KJerilyn Britz	74	74	74	77	29'	881.25
Gloria Ehret	73	76	73	77	299	881.25
Sandra Haynie	75	75	72	77	299	881.25
Beth Solomon	71	77	73	78	299	881.25
Kathy McMullen	71	78	73	78	300	737.50
Sandra Spuzich	77	73	72	78	300	737.50
Vicki Fergon	74	76	72	78	300	737.50

Florida Lady Citrus

Rio Pinar Country Club, Orlando, Florida — April 18–22
Par 36-37—73; 6,209 yards — purse, $100,000

	SCORES				TOTAL	MONEY
Jane Blalock	74	68	74	70	286	$15,000.00
JoAnne Carner	73	71	67	75	286	9,800.00
(Blalock defeated Carner on second hole of sudden-death play-off)						
Beth Daniel	72	76	69	70	287	6,000.00
Donna White	74	71	69	73	287	6,000.00
Debbie Meisterlin	67	74	70	77	288	3,566.67
Joyce Kazmierski	72	69	73	74	288	3,566.67
Cathy Sherk	77	69	70	72	288	3,566.66
Jo Ann Prentice	72	73	70	74	289	2,800.00
Hollis Stacy	72	71	73	73	289	2,800.00
Dot Germain	73	71	73	73	290	2,500.00
Debbie Austin	74	73	76	68	291	2,200.00
Sandra Post	73	70	72	76	291	2,200.00
Jerilyn Britz	77	74	70	71	292	1,830.00
Sandra Spuzich	74	72	71	75	292	1,830.00
Pat Bradley	78	71	76	68	293	1,395.00
Martha Nause	74	76	71	72	293	1,395.00
Janet Coles	72	73	75	73	293	1,395.00
Kathy Cornelius	73	72	73	75	293	1,395.00
Connie Chillemi	71	70	76	76	293	1,395.00
Sally Little	72	75	70	76	293	1,395.00
Betty Burfeindt	75	75	72	72	294	1,063.34
Kathy Postlewait	76	76	70	72	294	1,063.33
Debbie Massey	71	73	76	74	294	1,063.33
Lynn Adams	75	74	72	74	295	940.00
Jan Ferraris	74	71	75	75	295	940.00
Sandra Palmer	72	71	75	77	295	940.00
Bonnie Bryant	74	77	74	71	296	800.00
Barbara Moxness	75	75	75	71	296	800.00
Jenny Lee Smith	74	76	73	73	296	800.00
Mickey Wright	76	71	72	77	296	800.00
Jo Ann Washam	74	70	79	74	297	625.00
Marlene Floyd	75	71	77	74	297	625.00
Dale Lundquist	72	74	76	75	297	625.00
Mary Lou Crocker	76	74	73	74	297	625.00
Patty Hayes	72	73	74	78	297	625.00
M.J. Smith	75	73	72	77	297	625.00
Mary Mills	76	75	74	73	298	480.00
Marlene Hagge	73	76	75	74	298	480.00
Pat Meyers	74	75	73	76	298	480.00
Kathy McMullen	75	73	73	77	298	480.00
Kathy Young	75	73	72	78	298	480.00
Beverly Klass	77	74	75	73	299	390.00
Julie Stanger	76	72	75	76	299	390.00
Lori Garbacz	79	71	72	77	299	390.00
Cathy Mant	72	74	71	82	299	390.00

Vivian Brownlee	75	69	83	73	300	330.00
Alice Ritzman	74	77	73	76	300	330.00
Susan Grams	72	76	74	78	300	330.00
Beth Stone	76	76	76	73	301	305.00
Leslie Shannon*	79	72	74	76	301	

*Amateur

Women's International

Moss Creek Plantation, Devil's Elbow Course, May 3–6
Hilton Head Island, South Carolina
Par 36–36—72; 6,290 yards purse, $80,000

	SCORES				TOTAL	MONEY
Nancy Lopez	72	71	71	68	282	$12,000.00
Donna H. White	72	69	72	72	285	7,600.00
Donna C. Young	72	69	73	72	286	4,725.00
Bonnie Lauer	73	71	71	71	286	4,725.00
Beth Daniel	70	77	72	68	287	2,980.00
Jane Blalock	72	69	75	71	287	2,980.00
Amy Alcott	76	72	70	73	291	2,480.00
Pat Bradley	77	74	72	69	292	2,100.00
Hollis Stacy	74	76	72	70	292	2,100.00
Jo Ann Prentice	75	71	71	75	292	2,100.00
Sharon Miller	73	70	73	77	293	1,780.00
Cathy Sherk	73	77	74	70	294	1,493.34
Jan Stephenson	73	72	77	72	294	1,493.33
Laura Baugh	73	75	71	75	294	1,493.33
Silvia Bertolaccini	77	74	70	74	295	1,206.67
Gloria Ehret	71	75	75	74	295	1,206.67
Pat Meyers	71	75	75	74	295	1,206.66
Judy Kimball	76	75	73	72	296	966.25
Peggy Conley	79	73	71	73	296	966.25
Mickey Wright	76	75	69	76	296	966.25
Sally Little	74	72	74	76	296	966.25
Kathy Whitworth	76	72	77	72	297	805.00
Jerilyn Britz	75	72	78	72	297	805.00
Debbie Meisterlin	79	73	72	73	297	805.00
Marlene Streit*	77	79	72	70	298	
Barbara Moxness	73	76	77	72	298	696.67
Kathy Martin	80	71	71	76	298	696.67
Debbie Massey	74	74	74	76	298	696.66
Penny Pulz	78	76	72	73	299	605.00
Kathy Postlewait	73	74	76	76	299	605.00
Clifford Ann Creed	76	69	77	77	299	605.00
Marlene Hagge	75	73	79	73	300	525.00
Barbara Barrow	76	73	77	74	300	525.00
M.J. Smith	74	73	77	76	300	525.00
Debbie Austin	76	73	75	77	301	475.00
Dot Germain	76	74	76	76	302	435.00
Mary Mills	78	73	75	76	302	435.00
Pam Higgins	75	74	74	79	302	435.00
Janet Alex	79	75	75	74	303	355.00
Kathy Baker*	78	75	76	74	303	
Kathy Hite	77	76	75	75	303	355.00
Maria Combs	73	77	78	75	303	355.00
Betsy King	75	72	80	76	303	355.00
Betty Burfeindt	75	76	72	80	303	355.00
Kathy Ahern	80	78	72	74	304	290.00
Murle Breer	73	75	80	76	304	290.00
Marilynn Smith	79	76	80	71	306	270.00
Mary Dwyer	77	77	72	80	306	270.00
Alexandra Reinhardt	72	80	78	77	307	255.00
Marlene Floyd	74	79	82	73	308	240.00

*Amateur

Lady Michelob

Brookfield West Golf and Country Club, Roswell, Georgia May 11–13
Par 36–37—73; 6,353 yards purse, $100,000

	SCORES			TOTAL	MONEY
Sandra Post	72	69	69	210	$15,000.00
Pat Bradley	69	73	70	212	10,000.00
Clifford Ann Creed	70	72	73	215	5,566.67
Dot Germain	72	70	73	215	5,566.67
Pam Higgins	67	73	75	215	5,566.66
Amelia Rorer	70	71	75	216	3,333.34
Jan Stephenson	72	70	74	216	3,333.33
Jane Blalock	70	72	74	216	3,333.33
Pat Meyers	73	72	72	217	2,700.00
Susie Berning	73	71	73	217	2,700.00
Sally Little	72	71	75	218	2,300.00
Silvia Bertolaccini	73	70	75	218	2,300.00
Beth Daniel	70	76	73	219	1,840.00
M.J. Smith	74	71	74	219	1,840.00
Alexandra Reinhardt	71	72	76	219	1,840.00

Connie Chillemi	75	74	71	220	1,450.00
Vicki Fergon	77	71	72	220	1,450.00
Laura Baugh	74	73	73	220	1,450.00
Joyce Kazmierski	75	70	75	220	1,450.00
Kathy Whitworth	72	75	74	221	1,150.00
Beverly Klass	74	73	74	221	1,150.00
Betsy King	72	72	77	221	1,150.00
Debbie Austin	76	77	69	222	925.00
Sharon Miller	73	76	73	222	925.00
Susan Grams	73	75	74	222	925.00
Gloria Ehret	75	73	74	222	925.00
Louise Bruce	74	73	75	222	925.00
Alice Miller	71	73	78	222	925.00
Eva Chang	77	76	70	223	695.00
Dale Lundquist	76	76	71	223	695.00
Kathy Martin	73	77	73	223	695.00
Mary Mills	72	77	74	223	695.00
Donna White	78	71	74	223	695.00
Penny Pulz	73	75	75	223	695.00
Janet Alex	76	77	71	224	547.50
Murle Breer	74	77	73	224	547.50
Janet Coles	71	78	75	224	547.50
Hollis Stacy	74	72	78	224	547.50
Mary Lou Crocker	76	77	72	225	470.00
Kathy Ahern	72	80	73	225	470.00
Mary Dwyer	75	74	76	225	470.00
Margie Masters	75	76	75	226	380.00
Amy Alcott	75	75	76	226	380.00
Barbara Mizrahie	75	74	77	226	380.00
Peggy Conley	76	73	77	226	380.00
Bonnie Bryant	74	74	78	226	380.00
Cathy Thompson	79	69	78	226	380.00
Betsy Cullen	74	78	75	227	310.00
Alice Ritzman	71	78	78	227	310.00
Cathy Mant	75	73	79	227	310.00

The Coca-Cola Classic

Upper Montclair Country Club, Clifton, New Jersey
Par 37-36—73; 6,327 yards

May 18–20
purse, $100,000

	SCORES			TOTAL	MONEY
Nancy Lopez	73	70	73	216	$15,000.00
Bonnie Bryant	74	74	68	216	6,675.00
Hollis Stacy	74	72	70	216	6,675.00
Mickey Wright	70	74	72	216	6,675.00
Jo Ann Washam	73	72	71	216	6,675.00
(Lopez won sudden-death play-off, defeating Bryant, Stacy and Washam on first extra hole and Wright on second extra hole)					
Beth Daniel	73	72	73	218	3,700.00
Sandra Post	74	76	69	219	3,150.00
Jane Blalock	73	73	73	219	3,150.00
Betsy King	73	76	71	220	2,600.00
Judy Rankin	75	72	73	220	2,600.00
Amy Alcott	73	74	73	220	2,600.00
Donna Young	76	75	71	222	1,864.00
Peggy Conley	77	73	72	222	1,864.00
Janet Coles	73	75	74	222	1,864.00
Laura Baugh	77	70	75	222	1,864.00
Sandra Palmer	75	72	75	222	1,864.00
Mardell Wilkins	81	72	70	223	1,400.00
Marga Stubblefield	74	76	73	223	1,400.00
Vicki Fergon	73	75	75	223	1,400.00
Vivian Brownlee	76	76	72	224	1,100.00
Louise Bruce	77	77	70	224	1,100.00
Lynn Adams	78	74	72	224	1,100.00
Kathy Whitworth	73	76	75	224	1,100.00
Kathy Ahern	70	74	80	224	1,100.00
Pat Bradley	78	75	72	225	835.00
Debby Rhodes	72	79	74	225	835.00
Kathy McMullen	77	75	73	225	835.00
Lori Garbacz	72	79	74	225	835.00
Julie Stanger	77	73	75	225	835.00
Karolyn Kertzman	77	73	75	225	835.00
Marlene Hagge	77	75	74	226	665.00
Kathy Young	76	76	74	226	665.00
Silvia Bertolaccini	78	75	73	226	665.00
Jerilyn Britz	75	74	77	226	665.00
Debbie Meisterlin	77	78	72	227	503.75
Lauren Howe	77	75	75	227	503.75
Barbara Barrow	76	76	75	227	503.75
Joyce Kazmierski	79	74	74	227	503.75
Susan O'Connor	73	80	74	227	503.75
Donna Davis	77	77	73	227	503.75
Penny Pulz	75	76	76	227	503.75
Jan Ferraris	75	74	78	227	503,75
Eva Chang	77	77	74	228	390.00
Sylvia Ferdon	80	75	73	228	390.00
Beth Stone	75	76	77	228	390.00
Mary Dwyer	79	75	75	229	340.00

Amelia Rorer	80	75	74	229	340.00
Cathy Sherk	79	76	75	230	155.00
Gloria Ehret	79	76	75	230	155.00
Bonnie Lauer	81	72	77	230	155.00

Corning Classic

Corning Country Club, Corning, New York
Par 34–36—70; 6,203 yards

May 24–27
purse, $100,000

	SCORES				TOTAL	MONEY
Penny Pulz	75	71	70	68	284	$15,000.00
Judy Rankin	72	70	74	70	286	9,800.00
Lynn Adams	71	75	69	72	287	7,000.00
Donna H. White	73	73	74	69	289	4,500.00
Donna C. Young	76	69	71	73	289	4,500.00
Debbie Austin	75	74	71	70	290	3,200.00
Amy Alcott	72	73	72	73	290	3,200.00
Alice Ritzman	73	73	70	74	290	3,200.00
Bonnie Bryant	76	71	70	74	291	2,700.80
Sally Little	73	74	70	75	292	2,500.00
Ai-Yu Tu	71	75	76	71	293	1,942.00
Beth Daniel	75	72	75	71	293	1,942.00
Gloria Ehret	80	72	70	71	293	1,942.00
Alexandra Reinhardt	75	73	70	75	293	1,942.00
Peggy Conley	77	71	70	75	293	1,942.00
Kathy McMullen	72	76	74	72	294	1,390.00
Sandra Palmer	73	74	73	74	294	1,390.00
Sue Roberts	73	72	74	75	294	1,390.00
Dot Germain	72	72	74	76	294	1,390.00
Lori Garbacz	77	74	74	70	295	1,024.29
Silvia Bertolaccini	76	75	73	71	295	1,024.29
Jo Ann Washam	77	71	75	72	295	1,024.29
Kathy Young	74	74	75	72	295	1,024.29
Julie Stanger	73	73	76	73	295	1,024.28
Barbara Barrow	75	73	74	73	295	1,024.28
Sandra Spuzich	72	72	73	78	295	1,024.28
Susan L. Grams	79	75	71	71	296	800.00
Shelley Hamlin	77	74	71	74	296	800.00
Susan O'Connor	69	73	76	78	296	800.00
Cathy Sherk	70	75	74	77	296	800.00
Mary Mills	75	78	70	74	297	655.00
Jane Renner	76	74	73	74	297	655.00
Cathy Thompson	76	70	74	77	297	655.00
Marlene Hagge	76	72	73	76	297	655.00
M.J. Smith	80	74	73	71	298	550.00
Beverly Klass	78	74	71	75	298	550.00
Susie McAllister	78	76	69	75	298	550.00
Amelia Rorer	78	73	75	73	299	490.00
Karolyn Kertzman	71	75	75	78	299	490.00
Mary Dwyer	76	74	74	76	300	440.00
Marbo Sasaki	78	76	71	75	300	440.00
Patty Hayes	76	75	73	76	300	440.00
Louise Bruce	76	78	77	70	301	380.00
Debby Rhodes	77	74	78	72	301	380.00
Judy Kimball	76	75	76	74	301	380.00
Mary Lou Crocker	77	73	78	74	302	310.00
Lauren Howe	78	76	75	73	302	310.00
Vicki Tabor	77	73	77	75	302	310.00
Mardell Wilkins	79	73	76	74	302	310.00
Joyce Kazmierski	78	76	73	75	302	310.00

Golden Lights Championship

Wykagyl Country Club, New Rochelle, New York
Par 35–37—72; 6,410 yards

May 31–June 2
purse, $100,000

	SCORES				TOTAL	MONEY
Nancy Lopez	67	70	73	70	280	$15,000.00
Pat Bradley	66	74	74	70	284	9,800.00
Gail Toushin	74	69	70	72	285	7,000.00
Sandra Post	72	69	75	73	289	4,166.67
Laura Baugh	74	73	70	72	289	4,166.67
Judy Rankin	69	74	73	73	289	4,166.66
Peggy Conley	70	76	75	69	290	3,050.00
Donna C. Young	72	72	69	77	290	3,050.00
Jane Blalock	74	74	71	72	291	2,500.00
Marlene Hagge	74	72	71	74	291	2,500.00
Jan Stephenson	72	71	73	75	291	2,500.00
Ai-Yu Tu	74	71	73	75	293	2,100.00
Judy Clark	73	76	74	71	294	1,712.50
Jenny Lee Smith	73	74	73	74	294	1,712.50
Kathy McMullen	71	76	73	74	294	1,712.50
Debbie Massey	74	74	73	73	294	1,712.50
Cathy Mant	79	72	71	73	295	1,295.00
Jo Ann Washam	70	73	78	74	295	1,295.00
Eva Chang	76	75	71	73	295	1,295.00
Barbara Mizrahie	73	71	75	76	295	1,295.00

Lori Garbacz	75	80	72	69	296	1,110.00
Jo Ann Prentice	70	76	78	73	297	1,020.00
Susie McAllister	74	75	74	74	297	1,020.00
Murle Breer	75	76	71	75	297	1,020.00
Silvia Bertolaccini	76	75	75	72	298	880.00
Connie Chillemi	77	77	72	72	298	880.00
Beverly Klass	70	75	78	75	298	880.00
Angie Tsai	72	74	77	75	298	880.00
Susan O'Connor	78	72	78	71	299	780.00
Cindy Chamberlin	72	77	77	74	300	720.00
Cathy Thompson	73	73	76	78	300	720.00
Marbo Sasaki	74	76	79	72	301	670.00
Alice Ritzman	72	77	77	76	302	625.00
Betty Burfeindt	75	78	73	76	302	625.00
Vicki Tabor	76	73	79	75	303	537.50
Carole Jo Skala	78	75	76	74	303	537.50
Vicki Fergon	75	77	76	75	303	537.50
Mary Dwyer	74	78	74	77	303	537.50
Kathy Hite	73	78	75	78	304	470.00
Amelia Rorer	74	76	75	79	304	470.00
Mary Bea Porter	79	78	77	71	305	430.00
Muffin Spencer-Devlin	75	77	78	76	306	400.00
Debby Rhodes	81	76	76	74	307	380.00
Mary Mills	76	78	76	78	308	350.00
Marga Stubblefield	76	80	75	77	308	350.00
Shannon Johnson	79	78	76	76	309	325.00
Sylvia Ferdon	79	77	76	77	309	325.00
Martha Nause	78	77	80	75	310	300.00
Sue Roberts	77	76	80	77	310	300.00

LPGA Championship

Jack Nicklaus Golf Center, Kings Island, Ohio
Par 36–36—72; 6,313 yards

June 4–10
purse, $150,000

	SCORES				TOTAL	MONEY
Donna C. Young	69	70	70	70	279	$22,500.00
Jerilyn Britz	64	72	73	73	282	14,700.00
Amy Alcott	69	72	69	74	284	10,500.00
Sally Little	72	73	73	68	286	7,500.00
Jo Ann Prentice	73	70	70	74	287	6,000.00
Peggy Conley	71	76	71	70	288	4,612.50
Penny Pulz	68	74	69	77	288	4,612.50
Jan Stephenson	73	72	68	75	288	4,612.50
JoAnne Carner	69	70	72	77	288	4,612.50
Laura Baugh	75	73	69	72	289	3,300.00
Pat Bradley	77	67	72	73	289	3,300.00
Nancy Lopez	73	71	69	76	289	3,300.00
Judy Rankin	72	71	70	76	289	3,300.00
Sandra Post	72	70	77	71	290	2,396.25
Jo Ann Washam	72	72	74	72	290	2,396.25
Shelley Hamlin	69	77	72	72	290	2,396.25
Jane Blalock	73	75	68	74	290	2,396.25
Debbie Massey	76	71	70	74	291	1,870.00
Bonnie Bryant	69	72	72	78	291	1,870.00
Pat Meyers	73	70	72	76	291	1,870.00
Marlene Hagge	74	75	71	72	292	1,563.75
Dot Germain	77	71	71	73	292	1,563.75
Lori Garbacz	72	74	70	76	292	1,563.75
Sandra Spuzich	74	71	70	77	292	1,563.75
Kathy Ahern	78	74	69	72	293	1,350.00
Kathy Hite	73	71	76	73	293	1,350.00
Silvia Bertolaccini	73	72	72	76	293	1,350.00
Donna H. White	76	76	70	72	294	1,200.00
Judy Kimball	71	72	73	78	294	1,200.00
Bonnie Lauer	72	74	77	72	295	939.38
Alice Ritzman	76	71	76	72	295	939.38
Kathy Postlewait	75	72	75	73	295	939.38
Cathy Sherk	74	74	74	73	295	939.38
Joyce Kazmierski	73	69	79	74	295	939.37
Cathy Thompson	71	75	74	75	295	939.37
Amelia Rorer	69	78	73	75	295	939.37
Barbara Moxness	77	73	70	75	295	939.37
Vivian Brownlee	72	76	75	73	296	675.00
Shirley Englehorn	74	76	72	74	296	675.00
Beth Daniel	76	74	71	75	296	675.00
Sue Roberts	71	75	75	75	296	675.00
Gail Toushin	79	73	69	75	296	675.00
Debbie Austin	74	73	72	77	296	675.00
Lauren Howe	76	74	72	75	297	540.00
Kathy Martin	76	72	72	77	297	540.00
Muffin Spencer-Devlin	71	72	76	78	297	540.00
Donna Davis	75	74	75	74	298	472.50
Hollis Stacy	73	73	76	76	298	472.50
Beth Stone	73	74	73	78	298	472.50
Janet Coles	77	73	69	79	298	472.50

Lady Keystone Open

Hershey Country Club, Hershey, Pennsylvania
Par 36–36—72; 6,398 yards

June 21–24
purse, $100,000

	SCORES			TOTAL	MONEY
Nancy Lopez	72	68	72	212	$15,000.00
Sally Little	71	73	70	214	8,600.00
Kathy Whitworth	69	71	74	214	8,600.00
Amy Alcott	68	74	73	215	4,750.00
Betsy King	70	71	74	215	4,750.00
Vicki Fergon	70	75	71	216	3,333.34
Debbie Massey	72	72	72	216	3,333.33
Janet Coles	74	70	72	216	3,333.33
Carol Mann	71	75	71	217	2,700.00
Jerilyn Britz	68	77	72	217	2,700.00
Beth Solomon	74	71	73	218	2,400.00
Hollis Stacy	75	72	72	219	2,100.00
Jan Stephenson	74	72	73	219	2,100.00
JoAnne Carner	75	72	73	220	1,604.00
Sandra Palmer	75	72	73	220	1,604.00
Jane Renner	71	75	74	220	1,604.00
Debbie Austin	71	74	75	220	1,604.00
Patty Hayes	72	72	76	220	1,604.00
Marlene Hagge	75	76	70	221	1,107.15
Angie Tsai	74	76	71	221	1,107.15
Beth Daniel	70	79	72	221	1,107.14
Pat Bradley	72	77	72	221	1,107.14
Barbara Moxness	72	76	73	221	1,107.14
Lynn Adams	78	71	72	221	1,107.14
Lauren Howe	76	70	75	221	1,107.14
Laura Baugh	74	76	72	222	830.00
Kathy McMullen	78	72	72	222	830.00
Pat Meyers	71	75	76	222	830.00
Silvia Bertolaccini	72	73	77	222	830.00
Gloria Ehret	73	74	76	223	725.00
Shelley Hamlin	69	74	80	223	725.00
Cathy Sherk	74	76	74	224	620.00
Sandra Spuzich	74	75	75	224	620.00
Susan Grams	74	74	76	224	620.00
Dot Germain	70	77	77	224	620.00
Donna Davis	77	71	76	224	620.00
Margie Masters	77	76	72	225	490.00
Joyce Kazmierski	74	76	75	225	490.00
Alexandra Reinhardt	75	75	75	225	490.00
M.J. Smith	76	74	75	225	490.00
Mary Dwyer	72	77	76	225	490.00
Susan O'Connor	74	78	74	226	400.00
Amelia Rorer	77	75	74	226	400.00
Murle Breer	73	76	77	226	400.00
Debby Rhodes	72	76	78	226	400.00
Barbara Mizrehie	76	77	74	227	268.34
Lori Garbacz	76	74	77	227	268.34
Janet Alex	73	76	78	227	268.33
Noreen Uihlein°	75	74	78	227	
Betsy Cullen	72	76	79	227	268.33

Lady Stroh's Open

Dearborn Country Club, Dearborn, Michigan
Par 36–36—72; 6,411 yards

June 28–July 1
purse, $150,000

	SCORES				TOTAL	MONEY
Vicki Fergon	73	69	73	69	284	$22,500.00
Judy Rankin	72	71	65	77	285	14,700.00
Jane Blalock	76	72	69	69	286	7,312.50
Beth Daniel	71	72	71	72	286	7,312.50
Amy Alcott	75	71	68	72	286	7,312.50
Sandra Post	70	73	71	72	286	7,312.50
Sally Little	73	70	73	71	287	4,800.00
Debbie Massey	70	77	72	69	288	4,050.00
Barbara Barrow	69	76	71	72	288	4,050.00
Debbie Austin	69	71	73	75	288	4,050.00
Pat Meyers	71	73	74	71	289	3,450.00
Pat Bradley	72	74	71	74	291	2,880.00
Susan O'Connor	71	75	72	73	291	2,880.00
Sandra Palmer	71	75	70	75	291	2,880.00
Sandra Spuzich	74	76	70	72	292	2,163.00
Kathy Martin	77	70	72	73	292	2,163.00
Hollis Stacy	71	76	72	73	292	2,163.00
Donna H. White	71	76	70	75	292	2,163.00
Kathy McMullen	71	73	72	76	292	2,163.00
Silvia Bertolaccini	73	75	71	74	293	1,702.50
JoAnn Dost	74	71	73	75	293	1,702.50
Alexandra Reinhardt	76	76	70	72	294	1,530.00
Jo Ann Prentice	72	74	76	72	294	1,530.00
Jo Ann Washam	76	71	72	75	294	1,530.00
Marlene Floyd	73	75	75	72	295	1,320.00
Mardell Wilkins	75	76	71	73	295	1,320.00
JanetColes	71	73	76	75	295	1,320.00
Mary Dwyer	73	71	74	77	295	1,320.00

Janet Alex	75	74	75	72	296	1,083.75
Gail Toushin	70	79	74	73	296	1,083.75
Lori Garbacz	76	73	71	76	296	1,083.75
Susie Berning	70	74	74	78	296	1,083.75
Marlene Hagge	75	75	77	70	297	892.50
Murle Breer	73	75	77	72	297	892.50
Beth Solomon	70	76	74	77	297	892.50
Beverly Klass	77	71	72	77	297	892.50
Sue Roberts	75	73	79	71	298	705.00
Cathy Thompson	74	74	78	72	298	705.00
Penny Pulz	74	72	77	75	298	705.00
Lauren Howe	74	76	73	75	298	705.00
Barbara Moxness	73	70	75	80	298	705.00
Betsy King	77	72	70	79	298	705.00
Julie Stanger	75	74	74	76	299	570.00
Joyce Kazmierski	72	74	73	80	299	570.00
Jan Ferraris	71	75	72	81	299	570.00
Alice Miller	75	75	76	74	300	502.50
Kathy Whitworth	75	75	73	77	300	502.50
Vivian Brownlee	77	71	80	73	301	465.00
Judy Kimball	78	73	75	75	301	465.00
Carole Jo Skala	76	77	73	75	301	465.00

Mayflower Classic

Harbour Trees Golf Club, Noblesville, Indiana
Par 36-36—72; 6,044 yards

July 6–8
purse, $100,000

	SCORES			TOTAL	MONEY
Hollis Stacy	74	67	72	213	$15,000.00
Laura Baugh	73	73	67	213	8,600.00
Judy Rankin	74	66	73	213	8,600.00

(Stacy defeated Rankin and Baugh in sudden-death play-off, Rankin on first extra hole, Baugh on second.)

Jerliyn Britz	70	68	76	214	5,300.00
Sandra Spuzich	76	72	67	215	3,550.00
Amy Alcott	75	69	71	215	3,550.00
Barbara Moxness	70	72	73	215	3,550.00
Shelley Hamlin	68	73	74	215	3,550.00
Barbara Barrow	72	72	72	216	2,700.00
Jan Stephenson	68	75	73	216	2,700.00
Marlene Floyd	70	74	73	217	2,024.00
Donna H. White	70	74	73	217	2,024.00
Susie Berning	73	71	73	217	2,024.00
Debbie Massey	74	69	74	217	2,024.00
Jane Blalock	71	70	76	217	2,024.00
Jo Ann Washam	77	73	68	218	1,500.00
Betsy King	72	75	71	218	1,500.00
Sandra Post	69	72	77	218	1,500.00
Donna C. Young	71	74	74	219	1,300.00
Bonnie Bryant	77	71	72	220	1,150.00
Gloria Ehret	74	72	74	220	1,150.00
Janet Coles	74	72	74	220	1,150.00
Kathy Postlewait	73	78	70	221	1,000.00
Sue Roberts	75	71	75	221	1,000.00
Susie McAllister	71	72	78	221	1,000.00
Penny Pulz	73	77	72	222	778.58
Murle Breer	75	74	73	222	778.57
Alice Ritzman	78	71	73	222	778.57
Vivian Brownlee	75	74	73	222	778.57
Alice Miller	77	71	74	222	778.57
Beverly Klass	73	74	75	222	778.57
Mary Dwyer	72	74	76	222	778.57
Joyce Kazmierski	76	74	73	223	635.00
Susan O'Connor	71	77	75	223	635.00
Julie Stanger	79	73	72	224	525.00
Marga Stubblefield	77	74	73	224	525.00
Cathy Sherk	76	74	74	224	525.00
Marlene Hagge	74	74	76	224	525.00
Dale Lundquist	71	77	76	224	525.00
Kathy Ahern	74	74	76	224	525.00
Judy Clark	72	78	75	225	440.00
Kathy Young	74	73	78	225	440.00
Kathy Cornelius	79	74	73	226	400.00
Vicki Fergon	75	74	77	226	400.00
Kathy Hite	76	75	76	227	360.00
Sharon Miller	75	76	76	227	360.00
JoAnn Dost	75	78	75	228	180.00
Betty Burfeindt	76	77	75	228	180.00
Patty Hayes	76	77	75	228	180.00
Jo Ann Prentice	76	76	76	228	180.00

Colgate European Open

Sunningdale Country Club, Sunningdale, Berkshire
Par 36-38—74; 6,174 yards

August 2–5
purse, $110,000

	SCORES				TOTAL	MONEY
Nancy Lopez	68	69	70	75	282	$16,500.00
Joyce Kazmierski	69	71	74	72	286	10,780.00

Name					Total	Money
Pat Bradley	73	72	70	74	289	7,700.00
Shelley Hamlin	74	73	73	71	291	5,500.00
Donna C. Young	77	68	76	71	292	4,125.00
Sally Little	72	71	76	73	292	4,125.00
Dot Germain	77	72	72	72	293	3,520.00
Mary Dwyer	72	76	76	70	294	2,860.00
Gail Toushin	72	78	73	71	294	2,860.00
Judy Rankin	76	73	71	74	294	2,860.00
Mardell Wilkins	70	71	76	77	294	2,860.00
Alice Ritzman	80	68	73	74	295	2,200.00
Michelle Walker	72	70	77	76	295	2,200.00
Beth Daniel	73	73	73	78	297	1,875.50
Debbie Massey	72	74	78	73	297	1,875.50
Jerilyn Britz	71	79	75	73	298	1,694.00
Kathy Ahern	74	79	72	74	299	1,474.00
Bonnie Bryant	79	71	73	76	299	1,474.00
Vivian Brownlee	74	77	72	76	299	1,474.00
Marlene Hagge	75	76	72	77	300	1,221.00
Silvia Bertolaccini	77	73	72	78	300	1,221.00
Murle Breer	72	76	74	78	300	1,221.00
Donna H. White	77	72	79	73	301	1,078.00
Lynn Adams	76	75	76	74	301	1,078.00
Betsy King	76	75	73	77	301	1,078.00
Jane Panter	75	79	72	76	302	946.00
Susan O'Connor	74	78	74	76	302	946.00
Peggy Conley	75	74	75	78	302	946.00
Irene Koehler	73	79	77	74	303	794.75
Dale Lundquist	75	78	75	75	303	794.75
Sandra Post	77	75	75	76	303	794.75
Beverly Klass	72	79	72	80	303	794.75
Barbara Barrow	77	76	75	76	304	704.00
Kathy Whitworth	78	77	74	76	305	671.00
Susie McAllister	82	70	79	75	306	621.50
Christine Trew	77	75	78	76	306	621.50
Amelia Rorer	75	78	81	73	307	517.00
Jan Ferraris	76	77	79	75	307	517.00
Kathy Martin	77	75	78	77	307	517.00
Mary McKenna*	83	70	78	76	307	
Alison Sheard	71	81	79	76	307	517.00
Marlene Floyd	74	78	77	78	307	517.00
Barbara Helbig	76	72	77	82	307	517.00
Lori Garbacz	79	71	77	81	308	440.00
Wilma Aitken*	75	78	79	77	309	
Julie Stanger	80	75	75	79	309	407.00
Sandra Palmer	72	77	76	84	309	407.00
Jenny Lee Smith	78	75	81	76	310	363.00
Susan Grams	79	79	75	77	310	363.00
M.J. Smith	77	77	78	78	310	363.00

*Amateur

Rail Charity Golf Classic

Rail Golf Course, Springfield, Illinois
Par 36–36—72; 6,278 yards

August 31–September 3
purse, $100,000

Name	SCORES				TOTAL	MONEY
Jo Ann Washam	69	71	68	67	275	$15,000.00
Silvia Bertolaccini	70	66	71	69	276	9,800.00
Shelley Hamlin	67	71	71	68	277	7,000.00
Cathy Thompson	68	68	73	70	279	5,000.00
Jane Blalock	68	68	75	70	281	3,750.00
Betsy King	69	69	70	73	281	3,750.00
Sally Little	70	72	69	72	283	3,050.00
Carole Jo Skala	70	68	69	76	283	3,050.00
Lynn Adams	72	74	69	69	284	2,600.00
Beth Daniel	73	70	69	72	284	2,600.00
Kathy Young	69	74	71	71	285	1,942.00
Vivian Brownlee	73	74	66	72	285	1,942.00
Patty Hayes	75	71	68	71	285	1,942.00
Sandra Palmer	70	73	71	71	285	1,942.00
Pat Bradley	67	71	74	73	285	1,942.00
Bonnie Lauer	72	72	71	71	286	1,490.00
Amelia Rorer	73	69	68	76	286	1,490.00
Sue Roberts	71	74	74	68	287	1,340.00
Barbara Barrow	72	69	76	71	288	1,200.00
Lori Garbacz	69	72	71	76	288	1,200.00
Dale Lundquist	71	72	77	69	289	1,022.00
Marlene Floyd	76	73	71	69	289	1,022.00
Cindy Chamberlin	76	74	68	71	289	1,022.00
Judy Clark	70	71	74	74	289	1,022.00
Donna Caponi Young	75	75	67	72	289	1,022.00
Susie McAllister	73	74	72	71	290	900.00
Beth Solomon	69	76	76	70	291	761.67
Jan Stephenson	77	69	73	72	291	761.67
Vicki Fergon	71	73	74	73	291	761.67
Janet Alex	67	78	73	73	291	761.67
Eva Chang	77	69	71	74	291	761.66
Julie Stanger	76	69	71	75	291	761.66
Carol Mann	75	71	76	70	292	595.00
Laura Baugh	74	76	71	71	292	595.00

Hollis Stacy	74	75	71	72	292	595.00
Penny Pulz	72	75	70	75	292	595.00
Lori Nelson	74	71	76	72	293	480.00
Gloria Ehret	75	72	72	74	293	480.00
Pat Meyers	74	70	74	75	293	480.00
Donna Davis	75	73	71	74	293	480.00
Donna H. White	74	73	70	76	293	480.00
M.J. Smith	68	79	74	73	294	420.00
Mary Dwyer	73	73	74	75	295	370.00
Debbie Meisterlin	71	76	73	75	295	370.00
Cynthia Hill	71	73	75	76	295	370.00
Kathy McMullen	75	72	72	76	295	370.00
Jane Renner	74	74	75	73	296	325.00
H.B. Duntz	76	74	73	73	296	325.00
Kathy Corneluis	71	78	73	75	297	305.00
Gail Hirata	76	72	73	76	297	305.00

Columbia Savings Classic

Green Gables Country Club, Denver, Colorado
Par 36–36—72; 6,401 yards

September 7–9
purse, $100,000

	SCORES			TOTAL	MONEY
Sally Little	66	71	72	209	$15,000.00
Judy Rankin	71	67	73	211	8,600.00
Beth Daniel	73	68	70	211	8,600.00
Amy Alcott	69	72	71	212	4,750.00
Jane Blalock	70	69	73	212	4,750.00
Betsy King	72	69	72	213	3,700.00
Cathy Sherk	71	71	72	214	3,300.00
Judy Clark	75	69	71	215	2,800.00
Silvia Bertolaccini	71	72	72	215	2,800.00
Vivian Brownlee	70	72	73	215	2,800.00
Cathy Thompson	76	68	72	216	2,300.00
Murle Breer	71	70	75	216	2,300.00
Vicki Fergon	70	76	71	217	1,910.00
Marlene Floyd	72	74	71	217	1,910.00
Sylvia Ferdon	73	74	71	218	1,500.00
Hollis Stacy	71	73	74	218	1,500.00
Sandra Palmer	75	70	73	218	1,500.00
Barbara Moxness	72	72	74	218	1,500.00
Kathy Martin	71	72	75	218	1,500.00
Susie McAllister	75	75	69	219	1,150.00
Pat Bradley	75	71	73	219	1,150.00
Jane Renner	73	71	74	219	1,150.00
Jerilyn Britz	70	79	71	220	975.00
Jo Ann Washam	73	75	72	220	975.00
Sandra Spuzich	76	72	72	220	975.00
Susan Grams	72	73	75	220	975.00
Barbara Barrow	73	77	71	221	727.50
Susie Berning	75	74	72	221	727.50
Alexandra Reinhardt	79	70	72	221	727.50
Kathy Whitworth	71	77	73	221	727.50
Mary Dwyer	76	71	74	221	727.50
Kathy Young	71	75	75	221	727.50
Carol Mann	74	72	75	221	727.50
Susan O'Connor	71	74	76	221	727.50
Janet Alex	77	73	72	222	493.34
Anne-Marie Palli	74	74	74	222	493.34
Janet Coles	76	72	74	222	493.34
Carole Jo Skala	75	73	74	222	493.33
Kathy Hite	75	72	75	222	493.33
Betsy Cullen	77	70	75	222	493.33
Julie Stanger	72	74	76	222	493.33
Dale Lundquist	73	73	76	222	493.33
Kathy Ahern	76	70	76	222	493.33
Marlene Hagge	73	76	74	223	352.00
Karolyn Kertzman	81	68	74	223	352.00
Kathy Postlewait	74	74	75	223	352.00
Eva Chang	74	74	75	223	352.00
Kathy Cornelius	72	72	79	223	352.00
M.J. Smith	74	76	74	224	87.15
Bonnie Lauer	75	75	74	224	87.15

Patty Berg Classic

Keller Golf Club, Maplewood, Minnesota
Par 37–36—73; 6,023 yards

August 22–26
purse, $100,000

	SCORES			TOTAL	MONEY
Beth Daniel	68	69	71	208	$15,000.00
Hollis Stacy	69	71	72	212	9,800.00
Pat Bradley	74	70	70	214	7,000.00
Vicki Fergon	72	72	72	216	4,500.00
Jan Stephenson	74	70	72	216	4,500.00
Debbie Meisterlin	79	70	68	217	3,075.00

Donna C. Young	73	72	72	217	3,075.00
Cathy Morse	72	73	72	217	3,075.00
Pat Meyers	75	68	74	217	3,075.00
Joyce Kazmierski	73	72	73	218	2,300.00
Jo Ann Washam	71	73	74	218	2,300.00
Shelley Hamlin	72	72	74	218	2,300.00
Nancy Lopez	76	74	69	219	1,552.86
Jerilyn Britz	73	76	70	219	1,552.86
Amy Alcott	73	75	71	219	1,552.86
Donna H. White	76	72	71	219	1,552.86
Mary Dwyer	77	71	71	219	1,552.86
Silvia Bertolaccini	71	76	72	219	1,552.85
Cathy Thompson	74	70	75	219	1,552.85
Kathy Martin	78	73	69	220	1,024.29
Gail Toushin	75	75	70	220	1,024.29
Susan Grams	80	69	71	220	1,024.29
Betsy Cullen	73	75	72	220	1,024.29
Kathy McMullen	74	71	75	220	1,024.28
Sandra Spuzich	72	74	74	220	1,024.28
Michelle Walker	72	73	75	220	1,024.28
Marlene Hagge	77	72	72	221	800.00
Mary Mills	69	76	76	221	800.00
Sandra Palmer	75	73	73	221	800.00
Alice Ritzman	75	74	72	221	800.00
Sandra Haynie	72	74	76	222	670.00
Barbara Moxness	76	74	72	222	670.00
Jo Ann Prentice	76	71	75	222	670.00
Barbara Barrow	74	74	75	223	552.00
Bonnie Bryant	74	74	75	223	552.00
Mary Lou Crocker	74	73	76	223	552.00
Renee Powell	74	74	75	223	552.00
Alexandra Reinhardt	78	70	75	223	552.00
Kathy Whitworth	75	76	73	224	430.00
Gail Hirata	75	76	73	224	430.00
Carole Jo Skala	75	75	74	224	430.00
Dot Germain	75	75	74	224	430.00
Dianne Dailey	75	74	75	224	430.00
Judy Kimball	74	73	77	224	430.00
Elaine Hand	80	72	73	225	306.00
Jane Blalock	75	77	73	225	306.00
Carol Mann	78	74	73	225	306.00
Cathy Sherk	78	73	74	225	306.00
Gloria Ehret	75	75	75	225	306.00
Sandra Post	76	75	74	225	306.00

WUI Classic

Meadow Brook Country Club, Jericho, New York
Par 37–36–73; 6,460 yards

August 9–12
purse, $100,000

	SCORES				TOTAL	MONEY
Judy Rankin	76	71	71	70	288	$15,000.00
Beth Daniel	73	71	74	72	290	9,800.00
Donna Caponi Young	73	75	70	74	292	7,000.00
Jane Blalock	73	74	75	73	295	4,166.67
Kathy Ahern	71	76	73	75	295	4,166.67
Cathy Morse	74	74	73	74	295	4,166.66
Donna H. White	74	75	75	73	297	3,050.00
Sally Little	76	71	76	74	297	3,050.00
Beverly Klass	79	73	73	74	299	2,400.00
Peggy Conley	74	76	72	77	299	2,400.00
Kathy McMullen	79	69	74	77	299	2,400.00
Amy Alcott	75	74	72	78	299	2,400.00
Carol Mann	75	76	77	72	300	1,770.00
Beth Solomon	79	74	73	74	300	1,770.00
Bonnie Lauer	77	75	73	75	300	1,770.00
Murle Breer	75	71	80	75	301	1,490.00
Judy Clark	72	78	74	77	301	1,490.00
Barbara Moxness	74	76	78	74	302	1,290.00
Sandra Spuzich	74	78	71	79	302	1,290.00
Debbie Austin	78	78	74	73	303	1,110.00
Vivian Brownlee	75	76	76	76	303	1,110.00
Silvia Bertolaccini	74	77	73	79	303	1,110.00
Janet Alex	75	75	79	75	304	980.00
Jerilyn Britz	74	72	81	77	304	980.00
Vicki Fergon	77	72	76	79	304	980.00
Debbie Massey	80	73	79	73	305	880.00
Betsy King	77	75	74	79	305	880.00
Lori Garbacz	81	77	73	75	306	780.00
Alice Ritzman	75	74	79	78	306	780.00
Sandra Post	77	73	77	79	306	780.00
Betsy Cullen	76	79	80	72	307	655.00
Gloria Ehret	76	77	79	75	307	655.00
Lynn Adams	78	71	83	75	307	655.00
Hollis Stacy	79	74	75	79	307	655.00
Mary Dwyer	74	81	79	74	308	526.00
Jo Ann Prentice	78	78	75	77	308	526.00
Betty Burfeindt	78	75	75	80	308	526.00
Kathy Postlewait	74	76	77	81	308	526.00
Elaine Hand	74	74	79	81	308	526.00
Joyce Kazmierski	76	77	78	78	309	460.00
M.J. Smith	78	80	78	74	310	420.00

Patty Hayes	78	78	76	78	310	420.00
Carla Glasgow	78	76	77	79	310	420.00
Gail Hirata	81	78	77	75	311	370.00
Dale Shaw	82	76	77	76	311	370.00
Sylvia Ferdon	81	80	79	72	312	330.00
Susan Grams	78	78	81	75	312	330.00
Sandra Haynie	77	80	78	77	312	330.00
Debbie Meisterlin	75	75	78	85	313	310.00
Mary Lou Crocker	84	76	80	74	314	290.00

Barth Classic

Plymouth Country Club, Plymouth, Indiana
Par 36–36—72; 6,156 yards

August 17–19
purse, $100,000

	SCORES			TOTAL	MONEY
Sally Little	68	69	71	208	$15,000.00
Pat Bradley	73	67	69	209	10,000.00
Marlene Floyd	72	69	69	210	7,200.00
Amy Alcott	68	70	73	211	5,300.00
Cynthia HIll	72	69	71	212	3,950.00
Dot Germain	70	68	74	212	3,950.00
Eva Chang	71	74	68	213	3,033.34
Hollis Stacy	72	70	71	213	3,033.33
Debbie Austin	71	70	72	213	3,033.33
Judy Clark	71	77	66	214	2,045.72
Jane Blalock	72	72	70	214	2,045.72
Kathy McMullen	74	69	71	214	2,045.72
Kathy Cornelius	72	71	71	214	2,045.71
Kathy Whitworth	72	70	72	214	2,045.71
Sue Roberts	70	71	73	214	2,045.71
Judy Rankin	70	70	74	214	2,045.71
Lori Garbacz	70	74	71	215	1,400.00
Sandra Palmer	69	73	73	215	1,400.00
Cathy Mant	72	68	75	215	1,400.00
Martha Nause	73	73	70	216	1,150.00
Kathy Postlewait	73	72	71	216	1,150.00
Cindy Chamberlin	75	69	72	216	1,150.00
Sandra Haynie	75	74	68	217	1,000.00
Michelle Walker	73	74	70	217	1,000.00
Beverly Klass	74	72	71	217	1,000.00
Marlene Hagge	73	73	72	218	830.00
Kathy Ahern	71	73	74	218	830.00
Bonnie Lauer	72	71	75	218	830.00
Sandra Spuzich	68	75	75	218	830.00
Lori Nelson	75	75	69	219	665.00
Mardell Wilkins	72	76	71	219	665.00
Laura Baugh	75	72	72	219	665.00
Pat Meyers	74	73	72	219	665.00
Penny Pulz	76	71	72	219	665.00
Mary Lou Crocker	73	72	74	219	665.00
Alexandra Reinhardt	78	72	70	220	512.00
Cathy Morse	72	77	71	220	512.00
Lynn Adams	74	75	71	220	512.00
Vivian Brownlee	77	72	71	220	512.00
Jan Stephenson	77	71	72	220	512.00
Joyce Kazmierski	77	73	71	221	381.25
Alice Ritzman	75	74	72	221	381.25
Barbara Moxness	77	72	72	221	381.25
Gloria Ehret	76	73	72	221	381.25
Cathy Sherk	78	71	72	221	381.25
Jane Renner	75	72	74	221	381.25
Beth Stone	69	77	75	221	381.25
Shelley Hamlin	75	70	76	221	381.25
JoAnn Dost	71	73	78	222	203.34
Peggy Conley	75	70	77	222	203.33

Portland PING Team Championship

Portland Country Club, Portland, Oregon
Par 36–37—73; 6,133 yards

September 14–16
purse, $110,000

	SCORES			TOTAL	MONEY
Nancy Lopez—Jo Ann Washam	66	65	67	198	$20,000.00
Susie Berning—Carole Jo Skala	68	66	65	199	12,000.00
Beth Daniel—Lorie Garbacz	68	67	65	200	7,200.00
Janet Coles—Lauren Howe	65	67	68	200	7,200.00
Kathy Whitworth— Donna Caponi Young	69	66	66	201	5,200.00
Amy Alcott—Debbie Massey	70	66	67	203	4,120.00
Joyce Kazmierski—Sandra Spuzich	64	69	70	203	4,120.00
Silvia Bertolaccini—Sally Little	66	67	70	203	4,120.00
Murle Breer—Barbara Moxness	68	71	65	204	3,200.00
Debbie Austin—Pat Meyers	68	70	66	204	3,200.00
Pat Bradley—Sandra Palmer	61	71	72	204	3,200.00

437

Janet Alex—Judy Clark	67	70	68	205	2,700.00
Kathy Ahern—Bonnie Bryant	66	69	70	205	2,700.00
Jerilyn Britz—Kathy Postlewait	68	68	70	206	2,400.00
Alexandra Reinhardt—					
Michelle Walker	70	70	67	207	2,000.00
Muffin Spencer-Devlin—Kathy Young	69	69	69	207	2,000.00
Betty Burfeindt—Pam Higgins	69	67	71	207	2,000.00
Marlene Hagge—Cathy Thompson	68	71	71	210	1,460.00
Jane Blalock—Sandra Haynie	72	67	71	210	1,460.00
Kati Biszantz—Robin Walton	72	67	71	210	1,460.00
Alice Miller—Julie Stanger	68	69	73	210	1,460.00
Lynn Adams—Marie Combs	68	71	72	211	1,126.68
JoAnn Dost—Beverly Klass	70	69	72	211	1,126.66
Clifford Ann Creed—Kathy McMullen	69	70	72	211	1,126.66
Peggy Conley—Dot Germain	71	70	71	212	1,020.00
Betsy Cullen—Marga Stubblefield	71	71	71	213	960.00
Cathy Mant—Mary Bea Porter	70	71	72	213	960.00
Marianne Bretton—					
Sydney Cunningham	73	67	73	213	960.00
Jo Ann Prentice—Beth Stone	75	72	67	214	920.00
Karolyn Kertzman—Renee Powell	73	72	70	215	225.00
Vivian Brownlee—Mardell Wilkins	72	72	71	215	225.00
Elaine Hand—Gail Hirata	70	74	71	215	225.00
Jocelyne Bourassa—Shelley Hamlin	69	71	75	215	225.00

ERA Real Estate Classic

Brookridge Country Club, Overland Park, Kansas
Par 36—37—73; 6,273 yards

September 20–23
purse, $100,000

	SCORES				TOTAL	MONEY
Sandra Post	71	73	70	70	284	$15,000.00
Donna Caponi Young	72	69	70	75	286	9,800.00
Cathy Sherk	72	69	73	73	287	7,000.00
Jan Stephenson	73	72	73	70	288	5,000.00
Debbie Massey	73	73	72	71	289	3,566.67
Penny Pulz	71	73	73	72	289	3,566.67
Jerilyn Britz	72	70	74	73	289	3,566.66
Cathy Morse	73	70	78	70	291	2,600.00
Marlene Floyd	73	73	71	74	291	2,600.00
Marlene Hagge	73	71	72	75	291	2,600.00
Barbara Moxness	70	71	75	75	291	2,600.00
Pat Meyers	72	75	71	74	292	2,100.00
Kathy McMullen	71	74	77	71	293	1,830.00
Sandra Haynie	68	75	75	75	293	1,830.00
Carol Mann	75	75	75	69	294	1,595.00
Kathy Ahern	75	77	71	71	294	1,595.00
Amy Alcott	77	75	68	75	295	1,390.00
Vivian Brownlee	71	72	76	76	295	1,390.00
Jo Ann Prentice	71	75	75	75	296	1,240.00
Shelley Hamlin	76	72	76	73	297	1,045.00
M.J. Smith	72	77	75	73	297	1,045.00
Jane Blalock	74	74	75	74	297	1,045.00
Susie McAllister	71	72	80	74	297	1,045.00
Judy Rankin	72	76	73	76	297	1,045.00
Janet Coles	75	75	71	76	297	1,045.00
Bonnie Bryant	76	72	78	72	298	820.00
Sue Roberts	75	75	73	75	298	820.00
Peggy Conley	77	74	72	75	298	820.00
Debbie Austin	73	75	73	77	298	820.00
Barbara Mizrahie	70	74	74	80	298	820.00
Clifford Ann Creed	76	78	74	71	299	655.00
Gail Hirata	77	76	74	72	299	655.00
Kathy Martin	76	75	75	73	299	655.00
Karolyn Kertzman	72	76	77	74	299	655.00
Joan Joyce	74	83	72	71	300	526.00
Donna Davis	73	79	76	72	300	526.00
Susan Grams	73	77	77	73	300	526.00
Dale Lundquist	75	75	77	73	300	526.00
Betsy King	73	74	72	81	300	526.00
Barbara Barrow	77	77	74	73	301	420.00
Beth Solomon	77	75	75	74	301	420.00
Dot Germain	73	71	81	76	301	420.00
Cindy Ferro	76	76	73	76	301	420.00
Debby Rhodes	72	77	75	77	301	420.00
Dianne Dailey	78	77	73	74	302	337.50
Jane Renner	76	76	73	77	302	337.50
Kathy Whitworth	74	74	76	78	302	337.50
Cindy Hill	71	78	75	78	302	337.50
Cathy Thompson	76	77	77	73	303	305.00
Debbie Meisterlin	76	81	71	75	303	305.00

Mary Kay Golf Classic

Bent Tree Country Club, Dallas, Texas
Par 36—36—72; 6,316 yards

September 26–30
purse, $130,000

	SCORES				TOTAL	MONEY
Nancy Lopez	71	66	67	70	274	$19,500.00
Sandra Post	71	69	69	67	276	12,740.00

Beth Daniel	69	73	70	66	278	9,100.00
Jan Stephenson	66	71	77	71	285	5,850.00
Donna Caponi Young	72	68	70	75	285	5,850.00
Donna H. White	70	73	72	71	286	4,550.00
Silvia Bertolaccini	71	73	72	71	287	3,672.50
Patty Hayes	76	72	69	70	287	3,672.50
Janet Coles	73	71	71	72	287	3,672.50
Betsy King	76	66	71	74	287	3,672.50
Hollis Stacy	74	71	72	71	288	2,619.50
Vicki Fergon	68	73	74	73	288	2,619.50
Jo Ann Washam	72	72	71	73	288	2,619.50
Penny Pulz	72	74	69	73	288	2,619.50
Jo Ann Prentice	74	74	69	72	289	2,006.34
Sandra Palmer	70	75	71	73	289	2,006.33
Bonnie Lauer	72	71	72	74	289	2,006.33
Sandra Spuzich	75	71	75	69	290	1,620.67
Murle Breer	70	81	69	70	290	1,620.67
Marlene Floyd	73	73	72	72	290	1,620.66
Susie Berning	78	75	70	68	291	1,382.34
Sally Little	73	75	72	71	291	1,382.33
Mary Mills	75	74	71	71	291	1,382.33
Judy Clark	72	76	72	72	292	1,274.00
Sue Roberts	73	75	74	71	293	1,118.00
Debby Rhodes	76	74	72	71	293	1,118.00
Dale Lundquist	73	73	73	74	293	1,118.00
Sandra Haynie	71	74	72	76	293	1,118.00
Jerilyn Britz	69	74	73	77	293	1,118.00
Cathy Morse	77	76	69	72	294	936.00
Joyce Kazmierski	76	70	69	79	294	936.00
Bonnie Bryant	73	77	76	69	295	812.50
Kathy Young	78	71	73	73	295	812.50
Dot Germain	72	72	77	74	295	812.50
Pat Meyers	71	73	76	75	295	812.50
Lori Garbacz	77	74	72	73	296	652.60
Susie McAllister	76	75	73	72	296	652.60
Cindy Chamberlin	78	73	73	72	296	652.60
Jane Renner	72	74	74	76	296	652.60
Cathy Thompson	71	73	74	78	296	652.60
Marlene Hagge	74	76	76	71	297	572.00
Peggy Conley	72	75	76	75	298	473.58
Susan Grams	77	76	72	73	298	473.57
Julie Stanger	72	77	76	73	298	473.57
Dianne Dailey	78	70	77	73	298	473.57
Judy Kimball	78	75	73	72	298	473.57
Amelia Rorer	73	77	73	75	298	473.57
H.B. Duntz	73	73	76	76	298	473.57
Elaine Hand	75	75	75	74	299	383.50
Vivian Brownlee	73	76	76	74	299	383.50

Wheeling Classic

Speidel Golf Course, Oglebay Park, Wheeling, West Virginia   October 5–7
Par 36–36—72; 6,240 yards   purse, $100,000

	SCORES			TOTAL	MONEY
Debbie Massey	75	71	73	219	$15,000.00
Betsy King	72	72	75	219	10,000.00
(Massey defeated King on first hole of sudden-death play-off)					
Marlene Floyd	72	73	75	220	7,200.00
Susie Berning	77	75	69	221	4,750.00
Marlene Hagge	74	74	73	221	4,750.00
Cathy Thompson	75	73	74	222	3,500.00
Sandra Spuzich	74	73	75	222	3,500.00
Barbara Barrow	78	74	71	223	2,900.00
Janet Coles	72	75	76	223	2,900.00
Jane Blalock	75	74	75	224	2,400.00
Donna C. Young	72	74	78	224	2,400.00
Sandra Palmer	76	71	72	224	2,400.00
Julie Stanger	75	75	75	225	1,910.00
Mary Dwyer	74	74	77	225	1,910.00
Hollis Stacy	82	75	69	226	1,407.15
Bonnie Lauer	79	75	72	226	1,407.15
Kathy Martin	80	72	74	226	1,407.14
JoAnne Carner	75	76	75	226	1,407.14
Shelley Hamlin	74	75	77	226	1,407.14
Lori Garbacz	81	68	77	226	1,407.14
H.B. Duntz	73	74	79	226	1,407.14
Kathy McMullen	79	75	73	227	1,025.00
Kathy Young	76	77	74	227	1,025.00
Janet Alex	74	78	75	227	1,025.00
Dale Lundquist	75	75	77	227	1,025.00
Silvia Bertolaccini	81	74	73	228	762.50
Judy Clark	75	79	74	228	762.50
Dot Germain	80	73	75	228	762.50
Cathy Sherk	74	78	76	228	762.50
Debby Rhodes	80	71	77	228	762.50
Barbara Moxness	77	74	77	228	762.50
Debbie Austin	72	77	79	228	762.50

Kathy Ahern	76	73	79	228	762.50
Mary Mills	78	77	74	229	605.00
Amelia Rorer	75	76	78	229	605.00
Jan Stephenson	78	78	74	230	522.50
Pat Bradley	73	82	75	230	522.50
Peggy Conley	79	76	75	230	522.50
Cindy Hill	77	74	79	230	522.50
Kathy Postlewait	79	78	74	231	450.00
Eva Chang	77	75	79	231	450.00
Sue Roberts	75	74	82	231	450.00
Louise Bruce	76	80	77	233	390.00
Joyce Kazmierski	77	78	78	233	390.00
Joyce Benson	79	74	80	233	390.00
Connie Chillemi	79	78	77	234	340.00
Barbara Mizrahie	79	77	78	234	340.00
JoAnn Dost	76	77	82	235	315.00
Robin Walton	76	77	82	235	315.00
Cindy Chamberlin	75	83	78	236	150.00

United Virginia Bank Golf Classic

Elizabeth Manor Country Club, Portsmouth, Virginia
Par 36–36—72; 6,152 yards

Ocotber 10–14
purse, $100,000

	SCORES				TOTAL	MONEY
Amy Alcott	70	70	73	73	286	$15,000.00
Susie McAllister	72	69	74	72	287	9,800.00
JoAnne Carner	70	72	73	73	288	7,000.00
Sandra Post	72	76	71	71	290	4,166.67
Kathy Postlewait	74	72	68	76	290	4,166.67
Shelley Hamlin	69	74	73	74	290	4,166.66
Lori Garbacz	72	73	73	73	291	2,933.34
Donna Horton White	73	73	71	74	291	2,933.33
Jan Stephenson	69	73	73	76	291	2,933.33
Nancy Lopez	79	73	70	70	292	1,898.75
Dot Germain	72	74	74	72	292	1,898.75
Joyce Kazmierski	74	71	75	72	292	1,898.75
Debbie Massey	75	69	75	73	292	1,898.75
Jerilyn Britz	75	76	69	72	292	1,898.75
Kathy McMullen	73	72	74	73	292	1,898.75
Sandra Spuzich	71	73	73	75	292	1,898.75
Beth Daniel	73	73	72	74	292	1,898.75
Cathy Sherk	75	74	74	70	293	1,246.67
Donna Caponi Young	74	71	74	74	293	1,246.67
Cindy Hill	73	72	73	75	293	1,246.66
Pat Meyers	79	70	73	72	294	1,085.00
Jo Ann Washam	76	77	69	72	294	1,085.00
Dale Lundquist	73	77	70	75	295	1,020.00
Mary Dwyer	74	71	78	73	296	940.00
Julie Stanger	72	75	74	75	296	940.00
Marlene Floyd	73	71	75	77	296	940.00
Marlene Hagge	74	78	69	76	297	840.00
Peggy Conley	72	73	75	77	297	840.00
Susan Grams	79	73	75	71	298	740.00
Cindy Chamberlin	75	70	77	76	298	740.00
Sandra Palmer	74	75	72	77	298	740.00
Cathy Morse	72	72	78	77	299	655.00
Mary Mills	75	76	72	76	299	655.00
Kathy Whitworth	75	76	73	76	300	580.00
M.J. Smith	76	74	73	77	300	580.00
Lori Nelson	74	75	72	79	300	580.00
Gloria Ehret	80	73	74	74	301	490.00
Carol Mann	75	75	74	77	301	490.00
Mary Lou Crocker	73	77	75	76	301	490.00
Vicki Fergon	74	77	71	79	301	490.00
Louise Bruce	75	76	77	74	302	390.00
Debbie Austin	76	72	79	75	302	390.00
Kathy Martin	77	74	76	75	302	390.00
Lynn Adams	77	78	71	76	302	390.00
Donna Davis	75	76	73	78	302	390.00
Silvia Bertolaccini	72	75	76	79	302	390.00
Amelia Rorer	76	79	74	74	303	310.00
Barbara Mizrahie	82	74	72	75	303	310.00
Vivian Brownlee	73	78	75	77	303	310.00
Kathy Young	76	76	74	77	303	310.00

Colgate Far East Open

Manila Golf Club, Manila, The Philippines
Par 37–36—73; 6,178 yards

October 26–29
purse, $110,000

	SCORES			TOTAL	MONEY
Silvia Bertolaccini	69	72	72	213	$16,500.00
Sandra Post	72	71	72	215	11,000.00
Marlene Floyd	73	71	73	217	7,920.00
Beth Daniel	75	73	70	218	5,225.00
Donna C. Young	77	69	72	218	5,225.00
Jan Stephenson	76	72	71	219	4,070.00
Beverly Klass	71	77	75	223	3,465.00
Shelley Hamlin	75	74	74	223	3,465.00
Mary Dwyer	79	71	74	224	2,750.00

Susie McAllister	73	75	76	224	2,750.00
Judy Rankin	75	72	77	224	2,750.00
Pat Bradley	73	73	78	224	2,750.00
Nancy Lopez	77	75	73	225	1,837.00
Gloria Ehret	73	77	75	225	1,837.00
Amy Alcott	76	75	74	225	1,837.00
Vicki Fergon	75	74	76	225	1,837.00
Mary Mills	77	71	77	225	1,837.00
Jo Ann Washam	78	68	79	225	1,837.00
Sally Little	82	74	70	226	1,276.00
Dale Lundquist	78	76	72	226	1,276.00
Judy Clark	75	77	74	226	1,276.00
Lori Garbacz	73	75	78	226	1,276.00
Debbie Austin	74	77	75	226	1,276.00
Vivian Brownlee	81	72	74	227	1,045.00
Sandra Palmer	77	75	75	227	1,045.00
Amelia Rorer	75	75	77	227	1,045.00
Barbara Moxness	74	77	77	228	907.50
Lynn Adams	73	76	79	228	907.50
Bonnie Lauer	75	79	75	229	797.50
Cathy Morse	73	79	77	229	797.50
Janet Coles	80	73	76	229	797.50
Penny Pulz	76	74	79	229	797.50
Michelle Walker	76	74	80	230	682.00
Betsy King	73	76	81	230	682.00
Peggy Conley	73	76	81	230	682.00
Alice Ritzman	76	80	75	231	599.50
Marlene Hagge	77	75	79	231	599.50
Debbie Massey	78	77	77	232	550.00
Jerilyn Britz	75	78	79	232	550.00
Cathy Thompson	83	78	73	234	495.00
Joan Joyce	79	78	77	234	495.00
Kathy Whitworth	79	75	80	234	495.00
Kathy Postlewait	79	78	79	236	451.00
Marga Stubblefield	81	79	77	237	418.00
Barbara Barrow	76	80	81	237	418.00
Leonora Mateo	79	80	79	238	366.67
Cindy Chamberlin	84	76	78	238	366.67
Joyce Kazmierski	79	74	85	238	366.66
Murle Breer	81	76	82	239	341.00
Tomoko Takigawa	79	83	81	243	330.00

Mizuno-Japan Classic

Hanayashiki Golf Club, Osaka, Japan
Par 37-37—74; 6,149 yards

November 1–3
purse, $125,000

	SCORES			TOTAL	MONEY
Amy Alcott	71	73	67	211	$18,750.00
Sandra Post	71	71	70	212	12,500.00
Lori Garbacz	73	69	71	213	9,000.00
Chako Higuchi	70	71	73	214	6,600.00
Debbie Massey	74	73	68	215	4,930.00
Donna Caponi Young	73	71	71	215	4,930.00
Silvia Bertolaccini	71	74	71	216	3,526.00
Kazuyo Tamura	71	74	71	216	3,526.00
Yuko Moriguchi°	70	74	72	216	3,526.00
Masako Sasaki	71	72	73	216	3,526.00
Beth Daniel	72	71	73	216	3,526.00
Janet Coles	69	76	72	217	2,506.67
Ayako Okamoto°	73	72	72	217	2,506.67
Tatsuko Ohsako	72	71	74	217	2,506.66
Kathy Whitworth	75	73	70	218	2,065.00
Murle Breer	72	74	72	218	2,065.00
Takako Kiyomoto	75	73	72	220	1,687.50
Joyce Kazmierski	74	74	72	220	1,687.50
Pat Bradley	75	73	72	220	1,687.50
Nayoko Yoshikawa	76	69	75	220	1,687.50
Judy Rankin	73	73	76	222	1,400.00
Sally Little	70	73	79	222	1,400.00
Marlene Hagge	74	79	70	223	1,220.00
Beverly Klass	70	79	74	223	1,220.00
Kathy Postlewait	77	73	73	223	1,220.00
Mardell Wilkins	76	73	74	223	1,220.00
Mary Mills	77	75	72	224	990.00
Amelia Rorer	75	76	73	224	990.00
Hollis Stacy	74	76	74	224	990.00
Ai-Yu Tu	71	75	78	224	990.00
Debbie Austin	75	77	73	225	790.00
Mary Dwyer	76	74	75	225	790.00
Angie Tsai	75	74	76	225	790.00
Nariko Kobayashi°	75	74	76	225	790.00
Barbara Barrow	73	75	77	225	790.00
Jan Stephenson	74	73	78	225	790.00
Vivian Brownlee	77	75	74	226	635.00
Atsuko Hikage°	74	77	75	226	635.00
Betsy King	72	75	79	226	635.00
Cindy Chamberlin	71	74	81	226	635.00
Susie McAllister	76	77	74	227	502.50

Gloria Ehret	78	74	75	227	502.50
Bonnie Lauer	73	78	76	227	502.50
Jo Ann Washam	78	74	75	227	502.50
Keiko Matsuda*	75	75	77	227	502.50
Yuriko Arakawa*	77	73	77	227	502.50
Dale Lundquist	77	77	74	228	393.75
Cathy Thompson	76	76	76	228	393.75
Barbara Moxness	73	78	77	228	393.75
Peggy Conley	75	76	77	228	393.75

*Japanese LPGA

JC Penney Mixed Team Classic

Bardmoor Country Club, Largo, Florida
Par 36–36—72; 7,015 yards

December 6–9
purse, $400,000

		SCORES			TOTAL	MONEY
Dave Eichelberger—Murle Breer	73	62	64	69	268	$72,000.00
Jim Colbert—Silvia Bertolaccini	68	67	65	69	269	43,200.00
Dave Stockton—Donna Young	71	66	66	67	270	27,200.00
Gil Morgan—Marlene Hagge	69	67	69	67	272	19,200.00
Andy Bean—Sally Little	72	67	67	69	275	16,500.00
Joe Inman, Jr.—Dot Germain	72	66	69	69	276	15,000.00
Tom Kite—Beth Daniel	75	65	70	67	277	12,450.00
John Fought—Donna White	72	70	68	67	277	12,450.00
Rod Curl—Jerilyn Britz	71	70	67	69	277	12,450.00
Jerry McGee—Cathy Thompson	72	66	66	73	277	12,450.00
Jerry Pate—Hollis Stacy	72	68	72	66	278	9,200.00
Bill Kratzert—Sandra Post	75	68	67	68	278	9,200.00
Tom Purtzer—Jane Blalock	73	69	68	68	278	9,200.00
Craig Stadler—Lori Garbacz	71	69	69	69	278	9,200.00
Curtis Strange—Nancy Lopez	73	70	67	69	279	7,000.00
Chi Chi Rodriguez—Lynn Adams	73	68	67	71	279	7,000.00
Peter Jacobsen—Laura Baugh	70	72	72	66	280	5,630.00
Leonard Thompson— Joyce Kazmierski	73	69	71	67	280	5,630.00
Jim Simons—Debbie Massey	73	69	69	69	280	5,630.00
Lanny Wadkins—Marlene Floyd	69	70	71	70	280	5,630.00
Calvin Peete—Beverly Klass	71	69	68	72	280	5,630.00
Lon Hinkle—Pat Bradley	74	71	70	66	281	4,600.00
Victor Regalado—Bonnie Lauer	72	71	71	68	282	4,150.00
Bobby Wadkins—JoAnn Washam	71	70	70	71	282	4,150.00
John Mahaffey—Debbie Austin	72	70	72	70	284	3,420.00
Miller Barber—Sandra Palmer	75	69	70	70	284	3,420.00
Frank Beard—Betsy King	76	71	68	69	284	3,420.00
Bob Byman—Jamet Coles	72	70	75	67	284	3,420.00
Lindy Miller—Jan Stephenson	76	69	72	67	284	3,420.00
Jim Dent—Pat Meyers	75	70	71	69	285	2,950.00
Larry Ziegler—Sue Berning	74	71	71	69	285	2,950.00
Gardner Dickinson—Sandra Spuzich	69	72	73	72	286	2,650.00
Ben Crenshaw—Judy Rankim	71	71	73	71	286	2,650.00
Lee Trevino—JoAnne Carner	72	69	70	75	286	2,650.00
Grier Jones—Shelley Hamlin	75	73	73	65	286	2,650.00
Bobby Nichols—Mary Dwyer	74	68	72	73	287	2,425.00
J.C. Snead—penny Pulz	71	72	72	72	287	2,425.00
Mark McCumber—Susie McAllister	73	70	69	76	288	2,350.00
Mike Hill—Vivian Brownlee	72	69	73	75	289	2,225.00
Don January—Sandra Haynie	73	68	75	73	289	2,225.00
Mike Souchak—Kathy Whitworth	74	69	74	72	289	2,225.00
Alan Tapie—Sue Roberts	74	74	73	68	289	2,225.00
Brad Bryant—Judy Clark	71	70	76	73	290	2,100.00
Julius Boros—Mickey Wright	77	71	69	74	291	2,003.34
Al Beiberger—Amy Alcott	75	70	75	71	291	2,003.33
Buddy Gardner—Debbie Meisterlin	75	72	73	71	291	2,003.33
Wayne Lavi—Dale Lundquist	72	72	75	74	293	1,920.00
Gibby Gilbert—Vicki Fergon	77	72	69	76	294	1,880.00
Rex Caldwell—Kathy Ahern	78	71	75	73	297	1,840.00
Dow Finsterwald—Mary Porter	77	71	79	75	302	1,800.00

MISCELLANEOUS

Labatt's Canadian PGA Championship

National Golf Club, Woodbridge, Ontario
Par 71; 6,975 yards

August 30–September 2
purse, C.$1000,000

		SCORES			TOTAL	MONEY
Lee Trevino	67	76	72	70	285	C.$20,000
Lanny Wadkins	73	71	72	72	288	11,800
Tom Watson	72	73	76	69	290	7,700

Jim Nelford	69	76	78	68	291	5,800
Peter Townsend	69	71	75	77	292	4,500
George Knudson	79	71	72	73	295	3,650
Tony Jacklin	70	73	75	77	295	3,650
Dan Halldorson	80	71	68	77	296	2,900
Dave Barr	72	71	82	72	297	2,700
Ben Kern	74	74	76	74	298	2,500
Jose Canizares	77	73	74	75	299	2,300
Baldovino Dassu	74	74	79	73	300	2,100
John Bland	74	75	77	76	302	2,000
Jerry Anderson	73	76	76	78	303	1,750
Mike Veilleux	78	76	73	76	303	1,750
Scott Knapp	77	73	79	74	303	1,750
Gar Hamilton	77	76	76	74	303	1,750
Eleuterio Nival	76	74	81	73	304	1,300
Bob Panasiuk	79	78	75	72	304	1,300
Bob Charles	73	76	80	75	304	1,300
Jim Rutledge	76	75	75	78	304	1,300
Ramon Munoz	77	75	78	74	304	1,300
Francisco Cerda	72	81	77	75	305	950
Bob Rose	69	74	80	82	305	950
Mark Shushack	75	77	78	76	306	780
Cec Ferguson	76	76	76	78	306	780
Phil Giroux	77	76	74	80	307	680
Wilf Homenuik	77	78	76	76	307	680
Karl Heinz Mahl	75	74	85	74	308	600
Herb Holzscheiter	83	77	79	69	308	600
Simon Owen	77	78	76	78	309	560
Pat O'Donnell	74	81	78	77	310	530
Paul Kennedy	71	75	84	80	310	530
Luis Carlos Pinto	77	80	77	78	312	480
Tom Whittle	75	81	78	78	312	480
Phillipe Toussaint	75	74	85	78	312	480
Serge Thivierge	78	80	75	80	313	430
Alberto Rivandeneira	74	79	79	81	313	430
Roger Klatt	77	80	77	80	314	390
Ken Trowbridge	82	74	78	80	314	390
John Morgan	75	79	79	82	315	320
Bob Cox	79	77	83	76	315	320
Bob Breen	77	82	80	76	315	320
Michael Damiano	77	75	85	78	315	320
Al Jensen	80	79	78	78	315	320
Lars Melander	80	80	80	77	317	260
Al Balding	74	80	83	81	318	240
Doug Bruton	80	77	80	82	319	215
Ted Maude	79	80	79	81	319	215
Bill Bevington	82	77	79	81	320	190
Greg Pidlaski	79	78	81	82	320	190
Bob Desautels	78	76	82	84	320	190

Ryder Cup Matches

The Greenbrier, White Sulphur Springs, West Virginia   September 14–16
Par 36–36—72; 6,721 yards

Final Score: United States 17, Europe 11.
Friday—*Four Ball:*
    Lanny Wadkins—Larry Nelson (U.S.) defeated Severiano Balleateros–Antonio Garrido, 2 and 1.
        Lee Trevino—Fuzzy Zoeller (U.S.) defeated Ken Brown–Mark James, 3 and 2.
        Andy Bean—Lee Elder (U.S.) defeated Peter Oosterhuis–Nick Faldo, 2 and 1.
        Bernard Gallacher—Brian Barnes (Europe) defeated Hale Irwin—John Mahaffey, 2 and 1.
U.S. leads, 3–1.
Foursomes:
    Trevino—Gil Morgan (U.S.) halved with Sandy Lyle—Tony Jacklin.
    Ballesteros—Garrido (Europe) defeated Zoeller—Hubert Green, 3 and 2.
    Irwin—Tom Kite (U.S.) defeated Brown—Des Smith, 7 and 6.
    Wadkins—Nelson (U.S.) defeated Gallacher—Barnes, 4 and 3.
U.S. leads, 5½–2½.
Saturday—*Foursomes:*
    Jacklin—Lyle (Europe) defeated Elder—Mahaffey, 5 and 4.
    Faldo—Oosterhuis (Europe) defeated Bean—Kite, 6 and 5.
    Nelson—Wadkins (U.S.) defeated Ballesteros—Garrido, 3 and 2.
    Barnes—Gallacher (Europe) defeated Zoeller—Mark Hayes, 2 and 1.
U.S. leads, 6½–5½.

World Cup and International Trophy Championships

Glyfada Golf Club, Athens, Greece   November 8–11
Par 36–36—72; 6,900 yards

Team Competition

		SCORES			TOTAL
United States	141	141	152	141	575
Scotland	145	145	150	140	580
Spain	147	153	143	147	590

Brazil	148	144	153	149	594
Taiwan	144	149	146	156	595
Ireland	150	153	148	146	597
Japan	147	150	151	151	599
Canada	150	148	155	146	599
France	151	150	150	149	600
England	153	145	147	156	601
Germany	160	145	150	147	602
Malaysia	149	154	149	150	602
Mexico	150	150	153	151	604
Columbia	151	154	151	152	608
New Zealand	156	155	150	149	610
Venezuela	155	155	150	157	613
Belgium	154	154	154	153	615
Korea	152	154	151	161	618
Philippines	147	155	159	158	619
Wales	150	157	155	157	619
Chile	155	158	161	148	622
Argentina	160	158	148	156	622
Greece	159	160	154	153	626
Thailand	165	158	154	151	628
Sweden	158	162	154	160	634
Australia	160	163	153	158	634
Denmark	161	163	155	157	636
Austria	166	155	155	161	637
Holland	161	161	154	162	638
Egypt	162	157	159	160	638
Guatemala	162	162	154	162	640
Switzerland	162	158	160	160	640
Hong Kong	158	156	162	167	643
Singapore	162	168	161	152	643
Portugal	159	164	156	167	646
Dominican Republic	160	156	166	164	646
Indonesia	169	164	158	163	654
Lebanon	172	157	158	168	655
Norway	169	165	158	170	662
Fiji	166	178	169	153	666
Burma	167	168	170	163	668
Israel	165	172	169	177	683
Paraguay	170	174	183	175	702
Yugoslavia	188	186	177	184	735
Italy					no score

Team prize money: United States, $3,000 per team member; Scotland, $2,000 per team member; Spain, $1,500 per team member; Brazil, $1,000 per team member.

Brazilian Open

Gavea Golf And Country Club, Rio de Janeiro
Par 68; 6,000 yards

November 29–December 2
purse, U.S. $40,000

	SCORES				TOTAL	MONEY
Fidel de Luca	73	66	64	67	270	$8,000
Roberto de Vicenzo	70	66	67	67	270	5,000
(De Luca defeated de Vicenzo on first hole of sudden-death play off)						
Arnold Palmer	67	69	70	66	272	3,300
Tommy Aaron	66	65	72	69	272	3,300
Bernhard Langer	71	68	66	68	273	2,400
Jaime Gonzalez	72	67	65	69	273	2,400
Vicente Fernandez	72	67	67	68	274	1,600
Sam Torrance	68	67	67	72	274	1,600
Juan Carlos Cabrera	69	70	69	67	275	1,200
Ewen Murray	69	69	68	70	276	1,050
Ramon Munoz	73	65	70	69	277	825
Manuel Pinero	69	69	70	69	277	825
Jerry Anderson	69	69	68	71	277	825
Mark Weibe	72	68	65	72	277	825
Malcolm Gregson	67	71	72	68	278	675
Peter Townsend	69	69	66	74	278	675
Mike Krantz	70	73	71	65	279	600
Tony Jacklin	69	72	71	68	280	468
Manuel Comacho	70	71	69	70	280	468
John Morgan	65	72	72	71	280	468
Dave Hill	67	70	68	75	280	468
Armando Saavedra	70	65	68	77	280	468
Mike Miller	69	72	73	68	282	380
Rafael Navarro	68	70	70	74	282	380
Jan Sonnevi	66	72	73	72	283	340
Federico German	67	72	70	77	283	340
Juan Pinzon	70	74	70	70	284	224
Oscar Nari	68	76	70	70	284	224
Matt Runge	69	72	71	72	284	224
Antonio Ortiz	71	73	66	74	284	224
Priscillo Diniz	71	69	70	74	284	224

Venezuelan Open

La Bonita Country Club, Caracas

December 6–9
purse, U.S. $40,000

	SCORES				TOTAL	MONEY
Tony Jacklin	68	69	70	69	276	$8,000.00
Manuel Pinero	68	68	70	72	278	5,000.00
Bernhard Langer	67	73	70	71	281	3,600.00
Vicente Fernandez	71	70	70	71	282	3,000.00
Mike Miller	72	71	71	70	284	2,600.00
Sam Torrance	69	71	72	73	285	1,800.00
Alberto Rivadeneira	73	71	70	71	285	1,800.00
Phil Hancock	73	71	70	71	285	1,800.00
Noel Machado	70	74	68	75	287	1,125.00
Tom Weiskopf	73	71	72	71	287	1,125.00
Bernard Pascassio	71	73	72	72	288	900.00
Jerry Anderson	73	73	71	72	289	837.50
Peter Townsend	73	67	75	74	289	837.50
Mike Krantz	69	73	75	73	290	675.00
John Morgan	71	75	72	72	290	675.00
Mel Calendar	75	70	71	74	290	675.00
Priscillo Diniz	74	68	75	73	290	675.00
Ramon Munoz	72	72	74	73	291	525.00
Craig Andersen	73	76	72	70	291	525.00
Angel Gallardo	72	75	71	74	292	440.00
George Burns	73	72	75	72	292	440.00
Ray Carrasco	74	73	72	74	293	400.00
Mark Weibe	73	75	73	72	293	400.00
Jan Sonnevi	73	77	72	72	294	340.00
Eduardo Martinez	70	76	75	73	294	340.00
Jose Gomez	77	70	74	73	294	340.00
Mac Hunter	75	71	74	74	294	340.00
Manuel Comacho	72	76	73	74	295	290.00
Richard Fish	80	71	74	71	296	270.00
Dennis Murray	70	74	79	74	297	250.00
Antonio Evangelista	75	69	78	75	297	250.00
Ismair Acevedo	75	72	74	76	297	250.00

Colombian Open

Le Club Compestre de Cali, Cali
Par 71; 6,900 yards

December 13–16
purse, U.S. $40,000

	SCORES				TOTAL	MONEY
Sam Torrance	67	64	70	72	273	$8,000
Ray Carrasco	70	68	68	70	276	5,000
Lee Trevino	66	72	70	71	279	3,600
Bernhard Langer	70	69	73	68	280	3,000
Angel Gallardo	67	72	73	70	282	2,200
Eduardo Martinez	70	71	69	72	282	2,200
George Burns	68	69	75	70	282	2,200
Armando Saavedra	69	72	71	71	283	1,400
Peter Townsend	68	73	73	70	284	1,050
Vicente Fernandez	71	69	71	73	284	1,050
Antonio Evangelista	69	70	73	72	284	1,050
Craig Andersen	69	72	75	69	285	800
Antonio Arevelo	72	71	72	70	285	800
Mark Weibe	70	72	67	76	285	800
Ramon Munoz	72	76	69	72	289	650
Priscillo Diniz	73	72	68	76	289	650
Juan Pinzon	76	71	72	70	289	600
Allen Mew	68	74	76	72	290	525
Jerry Anderson	72	73	72	73	290	525
Manuel Pinero	72	72	73	73	290	525
Dionisio Rios	75	74	74	68	291	420
Mac Hunter	72	70	73	76	291	420
Richard Fish	74	76	73	69	292	390
Mike Miller	79	71	70	73	293	370
Jose Gomez	74	73	75	72	294	340
Eduardo Blanco	72	76	72	74	294	340
Arnold Salinas	73	73	73	78	297	140
Mike Ford	72	75	73	77	297	140
Travis Hudson	77	72	72	76	297	140
Refael Anello	71	71	78	77	297	140
John Morgan	76	71	75	75	297	140

Individual Competition

	Scores				Total
Hale Irwin, *U.S.A.*	74	70	72	69	285
Bernhard Langer, *Germany*	74	70	71	72	287
Sandy Lyle, *Scotland*	72	73	73	69	287
Jaime Gonzalez, *Brazil*	73	71	72	72	288
Antonio Garrido, *Spain*	74	76	66	73	289

Player	R1	R2	R3	R4	Total
John Mahaffey, *U.S.A.*	67	71	80	72	290
Ramon Munoz, *Venezuela*	72	78	70	72	292
Kazuo Yoshikawa, *Japan*	71	74	73	75	293
Lu Hsi Chuen, *Taiwan*	71	73	72	77	293
Ken Brown, *Scotland*	73	72	77	71	293
Jim Nelford, *Canada*	73	74	73	74	294
Michael King, *England*	72	73	72	79	296
Des Smyth, *Ireland*	74	79	74	71	298
Marimuthu Ramayah, *Malaysia*	75	75	74	74	298
Juan Pinzon, *Colombia*	70	74	79	76	299
Victor Regalado, *Mexico*	76	76	73	74	299
Eddie Polland, *Ireland*	76	74	74	75	299
Jean Garaialde, *France*	74	74	76	75	299
Barry Vivian, *New Zealand*	74	76	76	74	300
Manuel Pinero, *Spain*	73	77	77	74	301
Bernard Pascassio, *France*	77	76	74	74	301
Chen Tze Ming, *Taiwan*	73	76	74	79	302
Flory Von Donck, *Belgium*	75	76	75	76	302
Sukree Onsham, *Thailand*	78	76	78	72	304
Nazamuddin Yusoff, *Malaysia*	74	79	75	76	304
Enrique Serna, *Mexico*	74	74	80	77	305
Mark James, *England*	81	72	75	77	305
Dan Halldorson, *Canada*	77	74	82	72	305
Oswald Gartenmaier, *Austria*	79	77	73	77	306
Colin Bishop, *Australia*	79	80	72	75	306
Koichi Inoue, *Japan*	76	76	78	76	306
Rafael Navarro, *Brazil*	75	73	81	77	306
Delio Lovato, *Italy*	80	75	73	79	307
Mohammed Said Moussa, *Egypt*	75	74	79	80	308
Eleuterio Nival, *Philippines*	73	77	79	79	308
Choi Yoon Soo, *Korea*	79	78	76	75	308
Jorge Soto, *Argentina*	80	77	75	76	308
Ian Sonnevi, *Sweden*	75	78	76	80	309
Luis Arevalo, *Colombia*	81	80	72	76	309
David Vaughan, *Wales*	76	79	75	79	309
Patricio Valenzuela, *Chile*	73	79	85	73	310
Bassili Karatzas, *Greece*	80	74	78	78	310
Craig Owen, *New Zealand*	82	79	74	75	310
Engkun Tjahyana, *Indonesia°*	82	77	75	76	310
Brian Huggett, *Wales*	74	78	80	78	310
Cho Tae Ho, *Korea*	73	76	75	86	310
Rodolfo Lavares, *Philippines*	74	78	80	79	311
Francisco Cerda, *Chile*	82	79	76	75	312
Philippe Toussaint, *Belgium*	79	78	79	77	313
Jan Dorrestein, *Holland*	80	79	77	78	314
Adan Sowa, *Argentina*	80	81	73	80	314
Herluf Hansen, *Denmark*	81	80	77	77	315
Manfred Kessler, *Germany*	86	75	79	75	315
Peter Tang, *Hong Kong*	79	77	77	83	316
Bassili Anastassiou, *Greece*	79	86	76	75	316
Maung Pyone, *Burma°*	82	80	80	75	317
Guillermo Gomez, *Dominican Republic*	81	76	82	79	318
Hilario Polo, *Guatemala*	84	79	77	79	319
Patrick Bagnoud, *Switzerland*	81	81	77	80	319
Domingos Silva, *Portugal*	76	85	79	80	320
Lim Swee Wah, *Singapore*	80	85	80	75	320
Tirso Machado, *Venezuela*	79	77	80	85	321
Roberto Galindo, *Guatemala*	78	83	77	83	321
Jorgen Korfitsen, *Denmark*	80	83	78	80	321
Franco Salmina, *Switzerland*	81	77	83	80	321
Poh Eng Chong, *Singapore*	82	83	81	77	323
Bose Lutunatabua, *Fiji*	81	92	79	71	323
Simon Van Den Berg, *Holland*	81	82	77	84	324
Archin Sopon, *Thailand*	87	82	76	79	324
Sayed Cherif, *Sweden*	83	84	78	80	325
Sebastiao Gil, *Portugal*	83	79	77	87	326
Robert Prince, *Lebanon°*	83	78	81	84	326
Lai Wai Che, *Hong Kong*	79	79	85	84	327
Ross Metherell, *Australia*	81	83	81	83	328
Jack Corrie, *Dominican Republic°*	79	80	84	85	328
Ziki Mukdad, *Lebanon*	89	79	77	84	329
Farouk Badr, *Egypt*	87	83	80	80	330
Rudolf Hauser, *Austria*	87	78	82	84	331
Ole Chr Hammer, *Norway°*	82	83	80	86	331
Johan Horn, *Norway°*	87	82	78	84	331
Laurie Been, *Israel°*	84	85	86	86	341
Neil Shochet, *Israel°*	81	87	83	91	342
Arun Kumar, *Fiji*	85	86	90	82	343
Murat Satibi, *Indonesia°*	87	87	83	87	344
Randall Murdoch, *Paraguay°*	85	88	95	82	350
Capt. Ko Ko Lay, *Burma*	85	88	90	88	351
Luis Boschian, *Paraguay*	85	86	88	93	352
Rafael Jerman, *Yugoslavia*	89	89	87	89	354
Marko Vovk, *Yugoslavia°*	99	97	90	95	381
Baldovino Dassu, *Italy*	78	68	WD		(Signed for wrong score)

Individual prize money: Irwin, $3,000; Langer and Lyle, $1,750 each; Gonzalez, $1,000.

SOUTH AMERICAN TOUR

Argentine Open

Olivos Golf Club, Buenos Aires
Par 72; 6,800 yards

November 15–18
purse, U.S. $40,000

	SCORES				TOTAL	MONEY
Tom Weiskopf	71	72	76	70	289	U.S.$8,000
Alberto Rivadeneira	76	68	74	74	292	5,000
Federico German	72	72	75	74	293	3,300
Bernhard Langer	73	74	73	73	293	3,300
Manuel Pinero	75	73	73	74	295	2,600
Florentino Molina	70	72	76	79	297	1,530
Rafael Navarro	72	78	73	74	297	1,530
Tommy Aaron	73	77	71	76	297	1,530
Armando Saavedra	74	71	78	74	297	1,530
Francisco Marchichi	75	74	74	74	297	1,530
Greg Powers	83	71	73	71	298	850
Jorge Soto	72	70	76	80	298	850
Juan Quinteros	77	72	76	773	298	850
Ray Carrasco	75	74	73	77	299	700
Roberto de Vicenzo	75	72	72	80	299	700
Francisco Cerda	75	75	76	73	299	700
Craig Andersen	73	71	80	76	300	550
Juan Carlos Cabrera	73	77	75	75	300	550
Fidel de Luca	71	78	77	74	300	550
Peter Townsend	80	72	76	73	301	440
Horacio Carbonetti	74	72	77	78	301	440
Buddy Gardner	78	73	76	75	302	400
Brad Sherfy	73	76	77	76	302	400
Rueben Terrier	75	77	75	76	303	340
Juan Carlos Martin	73	76	76	78	303	340
Mike Krantz	76	73	80	74	303	340
Dennis Murray	77	74	76	76	303	340
Vicente Fernandez	81	72	74	77	304	280
Carlos Liberto	73	74	78	79	304	280
Larry Collins	76	76	75	79	306	250
Tony Jacklin	74	73	81	78	306	250
Luis Carlos Pinto	76	74	80	76	306	250

Chilean Open

Los Leonas Golf Club, Santiago
Par 72; 6,750 yards

November 22–25
purse, U.S. $40,000

	SCORES				TOTAL	MONEY
Ramon Munoz	70	71	66	74	281	$8,000
Malcolm Gregson	72	71	72	67	282	4,300
Raymond Floyd	70	69	69	74	282	4,300
Felipe Tanverne°	71	73	71	68	283	
Bernhard Langer	72	72	70	69	283	2,800
Vicente Fernandez	71	71	71	71	284	1,425
Tony Jacklin	72	68	69	75	284	1,425
Antonio Araya	72	68	69	75	284	1,425
Tommy Aaron	69	69	71	75	284	1,425
Sam Torrance	70	69	72	73	284	1,425
Manuel Pinero	72	66	70	76	284	1,425
Greg Powers	72	74	72	67	285	800
Alberto Rivadeneira	75	68	72	70	285	800
Mark Wiebe	73	65	73	74	285	800
Ray Carrasco	71	73	74	69	287	675
Paulo Pino	74	69	72	72	287	675
Armando Saavedra	71	76	72	70	289	525
Ewen Murray	74	71	73	71	289	525
Horacio Carbonetti	73	73	70	73	289	525
Francisco Cerda	70	72	73	74	289	525
Roberto de Vicenzo	72	74	74	70	290	410
Larry Collins	78	69	71	72	290	410
Juan Pinzon	73	73	71	73	290	410
Federico German	70	76	74	71	291	340
Peter Townsend	74	74	72	71	291	340
Jose Gomez	76	73	71	71	291	340
Antonio Urzua	75	69	74	73	291	340
Mike Krantz	74	72	76	70	292	270
Rafael Anello	73	72	75	72	292	270
Eduardo Flores	70	76	74	73	293	270

° Amateur